Realism – Relativism – Constructivism

Publications of the Austrian
Ludwig Wittgenstein Society
New Series

Volume 24

Realism –
Relativism –
Constructivism

―

Edited by
Christian Kanzian, Sebastian Kletzl, Josef Mitterer,
Katharina Neges

DE GRUYTER

ISBN 978-3-11-065336-6
e-ISBN (PDF) 978-3-11-052405-5
e-ISBN (EPUB) 978-3-11-052342-3
ISSN 2191-8449

Library of Congress Cataloging-in-Publication Data
A CIP catalog record for this book has been applied for at the Library of Congress.

Bibliographic information published by the Deutsche Nationalbibliothek
The Deutsche Nationalbibliothek lists this publication in the Deutsche Nationalbibliografie;
detailed bibliographic data are available in the Internet at http://dnb.dnb.de.

© 2019 Walter de Gruyter GmbH, Berlin/Boston
This volume is text- and page-identical with the hardback published in 2017.
Printing: CPI books GmbH, Leck

♾ Printed on acid-free paper
Printed in Germany

www.degruyter.com

Preface

Philosophical ideas can change the way we perceive and experience our world and lead our lives. This is not only correct for philosophers but in a more indirect way also for people far away from philosophical seminars. Opinions and arguments that originated in philosophy ooze into common sense and change its direction and our understanding of the world we live in. Three important, spacious and far-reaching clusters of philosophical ideas that influenced for a long time how we describe different aspects of our world were the topic of the International Ludwig Wittgenstein Symposium in Kirchberg 2015 – realism, relativism, and constructivism.

To be sure all three are diffuse and heavily loaded concepts and in such cases we – as Wittgenstein put it – "struggle with language". If one asks two philosophers what realism is, one ends up with (at least) a dozen definitions, and of course, the same can be said concerning relativism and constructivism. This confusing situation is the reason why the central concern of many of our contributions is to provide a clear and distinct definition of one or more of those concepts.

This seems to be of utmost importance concerning relativism since the "self-refutation argument" lurks in the background of almost every discussion. Simply put it says that a position which is seriously relativistic is either an absolutist view in disguise because it assumes its relativistic thesis to be universally true, or it is itself only true relative to something else which makes it powerless and irrelevant. Constructivism, it is often argued, falls prey to a very similar problem. Constructivists replace the realist concept of truth with that of viability or a similar concept. But why, one could asked, is a way of describing the world viable and another is not? It seems that in the end the world singles out some ways of coping as successful – but this is simply a form of realism. Realism on the other hand is often deemed to be useless by critics because we can never silence our doubts if we have already arrived at a correct description of the world, a doubt which is fuelled by a history of failed attempts to find out about the real "inventory of the world". Therefore many discussions in this volume try to provide a remedy to such fundamental problems, for example by showing that realism is a reasonable position to take or that relativism, correctly understood, is not in any meaningful sense self-refuting.

Other contributions are an attempt to apply fundamental convictions concerning realism, relativism and constructivism to concrete cases and examples. Especially in such discussions it is important to be clear about the extension of the concepts involved. Realism, relativism and constructivism can be explicitly found as designators of distinct positions in ethics, epistemology, philosophy of mind, ontology, and philosophy of science. Moreover the use of these concepts is not limited to philosophy but they are also employed and discussed in social and natural sciences, for example, geology, history, and literature. It is important to keep in mind that in different fields those concepts might (and they usually do) describe different positions and connections. The structure of this volume attempts to make explicit some basic distinctions and to provide at least a broad scheme in which different positions and fine grained nuances are located.

On a final note we can happily say that suitable for a conference in Kirchberg most contributions in this volume are written in what can be called a "Wittgensteinian spirit". Wittgenstein himself was a tireless and intellectually honest thinker. He took philosophical arguments serious and did not hastily abort discussion but examined them again and again from different perspectives. This is also the guiding spirit of the contributions of this to volume. All participants are concerned with a collective philosophical endeavour, with a respectful exchange of thoughts, ideas and arguments and, of course, their critical examination. Regardless of disagreements, at the end of the day everyone feels that it is important to get a clearer grip of realism, relativism or constructivism aiming at a better understanding of phrases like "constructing reality", "really existing", "matter of fact", or "relatively true".

The crucial outcome of the IWS 2015 is not that we finally know that there is a real world independent of us or that relativism in ethics is after all a rational position, but rather that the discussion between realists, relativists, and constructivists is an ongoing, interesting and philosophically significant enterprise. Wittgenstein's greeting "Take your time!" may well be good advice.

The editors want to thank the Government of Lower Austria and the board of the Austrian Ludwig Wittgenstein Society for the support of our conference, and De Gryuter for the friendly and professional cooperation.

The editors

Table of Contents

1 Constructivism and Beyond

Krzysztof Abriszewski
Are Philosophers' Actions Realist or Constructivist? —— 3

Marzenna Cyzman
On the Non-Dualizing Rhetoric. Some Preliminary Remarks —— 17

Volker Gadenne
Ist der Konstruktivismus selbstwidersprüchlich? —— 31

Olaf Hoffjann
Die Wahrheitsspieler. Strategische Kommunikation als Spiel —— 45

Sebastian Kletzl
Who Wants to Be a Non-Dualist and Why? —— 59

Albert Müller
Jean Piaget und die Erfindung von Radikalem Konstruktivismus und Kybernetik Zweiter Ordnung —— 73

Karl H. Müller
Two Ways of Exploring the World —— 83

2 Epistemology/Epistemological Relativism

Hans-Herbert Kögler
The Truth of Social Constructivism —— 103

Gerhard Schönrich
The Objectivity of Epistemic Values and the Argument from Immersion —— 117

Erwin Tegtmeier
Epistemological Realism, Representation, and Intentionality —— 129

Martin G. Weiss
Angelina's Truth: Genetic Knowledge, Preventive Medicine, and the Reality of the Possible —— 137

3 Realism versus Relativism

Heike Egner
Neither Realism nor Anti-Realism: How to approach the Anthropocene? —— 153

Hans Rudi Fischer
Ein Bild – ohne Betrachter – hielt uns gefangen. Wittgensteins ambivalenter Abschied vom Realismus —— 167

Michael Krausz
Relativisms and Their Opposites —— 187

Martin Kusch
When Paul Met Ludwig: Wittgensteinian Comments on Boghossian's Antirelativism —— 203

Danièle Moyal-Sharrock
Fighting Relativism: Wittgenstein and Kuhn —— 215

Franz Ofner
Wissenschaftstheoretische Überlegungen jenseits von Realismus, Relativismus und Konstruktivismus —— 233

Peter Strasser
Realism without Foundation —— 241

4 Ontology/Ontological Relativism

Ludger Jansen
Constructed Reality —— 255

Peter Kügler
Ontological Relativism as Transcendental Nominalism —— 269

Martine Nida-Rümelin
Realism about Identity and Individuality of Conscious Beings —— 279

Nikos Psarros
What is the Thing Whose Measure is Money? —— 293

5 Values and Value Relativism

Paul Boghossian
Relativism about Morality —— 301

Cora Diamond
Slavery and Justice: Williams and Wiggins —— 313

Marie-Luisa Frick
A Plurality of True Moralities? Tracing 'Truth' in Moral Relativism —— 327

Martina Herrmann
Zum Wert von Vertrauen —— 339

Hans Kraml
Die Erfindung der Sein-Sollen-Dichotomie —— 353

Peter Schaber
Wird die Moral von uns geschaffen? —— 365

6 Wittgenstein

David Bloor
The Sociology of the Supernatural: Wittgenstein's *Lecture on Ethics* —— 381

Rom Harré
Can We Piece Together a Coherent Account of the "Person" from the Writings of Wittgenstein? —— 397

Ingolf Max
Wittgensteins Philosophieren zwischen *Kodex* und *Strategie*: Logik, Schach und Farbausdrücke —— 409

Jonathan Rée
Wittgenstein, Kierkegaard and the Significance of Silence —— 425

Anja Weiberg
Zweifeln *können* und zweifeln *wollen*: *Über Gewissheit* § 217 – 231 —— 435

Nick Zangwill
Rules and Privacy: Remarks on *Philosophical Investigations* § 202 —— 449

Index of names —— 459

Index of subjects —— 465

1 Constructivism and Beyond

Krzysztof Abriszewski
Are Philosophers' Actions Realist or Constructivist?

Abstract: In my article, I propose to discuss constructivism and realism in terms of actions instead of doing that in a usual way, in terms of theories, philosophers or general positions. To enable this, I offer two conceptual tools. First, I use modified model of four types of knowledge introduced by Andrzej Zybertowicz. It approaches any knowledge-building process as a cultural game, and recognizes reproduction, discovery, redefinition, and design of a new game. Second, I use Stanisław Lem's model of three types of geniuses. I illustrate my approach briefly using examples from Plato, Spinoza and Berkeley.

Keywords: Constructivism, realism, cultural theory, actions, knowledge

1 Who Constructs What Nowadays?

This apparently innocent question seems to be out of place when asked in presence of philosophers. Almost surely they will not recognise it as addressed to them. And when that is determined, they will inevitably shake off any responsibility. In other words, it is always others (Others) who construct, and never 'we'. 'We' will never admit: "Yes, constructing X is what we excel at". At best, 'we' will offer constructing this or that reasoning on a particular topic. More likely, constructing will appear in the way of reproach: 'construct this or that' – that is what a realist may say to a constructivist in fervour of discussion.

While the introductive question is looming in the background, I would like to ponder what philosophers may actually construct or may have constructed in the past. However, in order to take up these considerations, I must make some adjustments to our – philosophical – ways of speaking about constructing and constructivism. That is, to a certain degree I am going to enter the undefined area of discussion about realism and constructivism, but I would also like to introduce a perspective different from the dominant ones.

For the purposes of this text, I would like to adopt a very simple and general way of attributing either stance to specific statements or theories. In the vein of the tradition of George Lakoff's and Mark Johnson's *Metaphors We Live By* I am going to identify them by the prevalent kind of metaphors on which they are based (see Lakoff/Johnson 2003).

The realist stance(s) most often employ(s) the metaphor of reflection, which was thoroughly and scrupulously revealed by Richard Rorty in his classic work *Philosophy and the Mirror of Nature* (Rorty 1981). Traditionally, this genre of thought includes all epistemological stances that seek some kind of correspondence between the world (states of affairs, beings etc.) and language (propositions, claims, or – more traditionally – ideas). The constructivist approach is in turn aptly characterised by industrial metaphors of fabricating, producing, manufacturing or the aforementioned constructing. A different question is what exactly, how and by what kind of agents it is done. Radically simplified as this approach is, it nevertheless seems to grasp a certain academic convention of writing papers, conducting discussions and polemics, formulating critique and building lines of defence.

But what do we usually talk about using those labels? I dare suppose that the scope is limited: we like labelling philosophers or, more generally, scholars, by saying e.g. "Ernst von Glasersfeld was a constructivist", "Aristotle was a realist", etc. We are not going to hesitate to describe theories as realist or constructivist ones. For example, the latter category is likely to contain all those that we deem structurally similar to Kantian epistemology with its phenomena and things-in-themselves. In turn, realist theories will be those arguing for bridging the two in the vein of the aforementioned reflection metaphor. At last we can define the two in more detail and speak of realist and constructivist positions. This is where the cases of attributing realist and constructivist labels finish. Hence we have people, theories and positions.

For the purposes of our considerations, I would like to extend that three-entry list and attempt to also describe actions as realist and constructivist. Do we sometimes happen to treat philosophers' work as actions of realist or constructivist nature? I claim that it is far less important what one claims to be doing, or how one describes herself – as a realist or a constructivist; it is far more important what one is doing. This kind of assessment needs a good measure, though, that is, a good theory that would allow to interpret philosophical actions with the use of the two categories in question. Let us then proceed to analytic tools.

2 Tool No. 1: the Model of the Four Kinds of Knowledge-Building Processes

The first of the proposed tools is the model of the four kinds of knowledge-building processes introduced in *Przemoc i poznanie (Violence and Knowledge)* by

Andrzej Zybertowicz, who recognises those processes as different types of cultural games (Zybertowicz 1995, 127 ff). The main advantage of this tool for us depends on embracing different epistemologies (realist, constructivist) by identifying them as elements of particular types of cultural games. If we overlook its certain flaws resulting from the author's attachment to seeing constructing processes in terms of language, this model offers quite clear a thinking scheme, letting us articulate various knowledge-building processes in categories of culture theory. What is more, it allows us to easily switch from epistemological questions (methods of acquiring knowledge, representation of the world) to ontological (reshaping parts of the world).

Let us scrutinise those four types then.

2.1 Reproduction

This is the first and simplest kind of knowledge-building process in Zybertowicz's model. (Zybertowicz 1995, 128 f). It includes all the practices in which individuals absorb ready-made knowledge, undergo socialisation within the framework of stabilised cultural reality, enter the area of games whose rules they internalise in order to join them. Zybertowicz describes this scope of learning as follows:

> An individual learns the culturally produced world, stratified into ready-to-use categories. This world contains, as its integral component, definitions of situations that are in force there: words and meaning attributed to them. An individual is learning categories firmly established in the social practice network and in culturally regulated perception. He or she absorbs certain content of culture. (Zybertowicz 1995, 128)

He also points at the fact that within this type of learning the individual experiences reaching the truth awaiting her, which, according to the model, is related uniquely to how stabilised the area of knowledge being reproduced is. Consequently, we can say that the individual is learning to reproduce particular practices, and as a result, the reproduced content keeps up to circulate. Zybertowicz also stresses the significance of 'contexts established and rendered objective by institutions' in which the individual operates (Zybertowicz 1995, 128). The individual experiences a 'collision' with reality: the degree of stabilisation makes reality very resistant to non-standard manipulation. In this context let us think about students who produce an incorrect solution of an equation at physics classes, wrongly locate the capital of Austria on the map or mistakenly quote the definition of Kant's categorical imperative. No doubt that these areas of culture owe their stability not only to lasting institutions and situation definitions, stressed by the author, but more than anything to perpetuation through things and practices (institutions may be construed as combinations of things and practices of sorts). Therefore learning by reproducing is taking part in re-presentation (of events, phenomena, things etc.) We might say that reproduction is a significant element in the circulation of various elements of culture and contributes to stabilising them, by minimising changes (distortion) in consecutive representations. Speaking in terms of Josef Mitterer's nondualistic philosophy, reproduction is exercise in repeating stabilised transitions from descriptions *so far* to descriptions *from now on* (Mitterer 1992, 2001).

Reproduction is the least interesting kind of knowledge-building process. Nothing new emerges here. The whole game is about repeating, as faithfully as possible, something that has already existed in culture. It is a trite observation that for philosophers knowledge reproduced this way is not an interesting subject, although it is what widespread examples refer to (the cat is on the mat, it is raining, snow is white etc.), which must be considered erroneous in view of what the following models are distinguished for. Reproduction is by no means a model process for other types of knowledge-building processes, or for knowledge in general. Zybertowicz, after Anna Pałubicka, puts forward a thesis that positivist epistemology is a philosophical theory of knowledge reduced to reproduction (Pałubicka 1977, Zybertowicz 1995, 129).

2.2 Discovering

The second type is discovering: Zybertowicz speaks about "discovering the content of pre-existing cultural games" (Zybertowicz 1995, 129 ff). We encounter discovering wherever we have to do with a relatively stable area of public life which still has not gained its epistemological representation. We already have an experience but we still do not have its description – we have a certain kind of practices but we are not able to speak about it yet, we have phenomena but we cannot formulate their theory etc. This is how Zybertowicz puts it:

> Knowledge-building processes of this kind depend on attributing concepts to states of affairs that have already been appointed (pre-formed) by the matrices of our culture / practice. In other words, discovering is reaching truths for which the space has already been established but which have not yet been articulated in a particular culture. (Zybertowicz 1995, 130)

In discovering it is important that we still have to do with a stabilised area of culture, although it has not yet created a sufficient reflection mechanism (to use Anthony Giddens's term, see Giddens 1990). Here is an example: books considered part of philosophical canon (works of Aristotle, Kant, Spinoza and others) have existed for many years (decades, centuries), but it takes feminists to stumble upon the idea of looking up what the classics say about women and putting it together instead of habitual omitting the topic as insignificant for the main course of thought (see for example Freeland 1998, Schott 1997, Gatens 2009).

It seems that learning by discovering is a very heterogeneous category. It is a function of former stabilisation and recognition of a given area of culture. Hence there may exist well stabilised and quite well known areas, which expect to be subjected to relatively standard research procedures. There may also be equally stabilised areas but so far little examined, whose exploration (discovering) is to prove greater a challenge and supposedly more fruitful. This type of knowledge-building processes may also be treated as realist, as its essence is mapping an area which is already there and whose boundaries are well defined.

2.3 Redefining Games

Whereas discovering gave us an image of the most frequent kind of knowledge-building practices that introduce new elements, redefining takes us to an utterly new level. To put it in the most general way, if a particular cultural game is played by a certain set of pre-defined rules (explicit or not), then the process of redefining infringes those rules, diverts the course of the whole game (Zybertowicz 1995, 141 ff).

If the former two types operated in a stabilised area, here we begin to take into account alternative images of a specified domain, it ceases to be a homogeneous, or relatively homogeneous, field, in which epistemological objectives are clear beforehand, one knows what is important and what is trivial, which is worth pursuing and what is uninteresting or even does not belong to the field of interest. Here knowledge-building activities not only add new elements simply by filling blank spaces, applying colours to white patches, but they shape a new discipline, prove that the game is about something else than it has been believed, there is a different prize at stake, or the rules are in fact different. Or all of the above. If we recall the familiar figure of Janus introduced by Latour in *Science in Action* redefining will stand on the side of Janus's young face, for example when the young face asks what 'efficiency' is, whereas the old face strives to build a possibly efficient machine (see Latour 1987).

Although the author of *Przemoc i poznanie* draws attention to institutional mechanisms and the role of authority and violence in knowledge-building, as well as that of different definitions of situation, here I would like to reshape and extend his model by practice and materiality. Let us note that if work in the redefining mode disturbs the environment (a complex assemblage of things and material practices), then this mode of knowledge production requires *different* forms of activity than reproducing or discovering, as it *destabilises* and *stabilises again*. Whereas a researcher-discoverer can focus on uncontroversial methodology to bring new results, a redefining researcher must struggle to legitimise dismantling the well-worn practices, and for recognition of the new practices. The former refers to knowledge hiding in the field, while the latter elaborates complex diplomatic strategies of diminishing the merit of those with a strong position in the field without them noticing. Alternatively, she might develop another skill: winning over an army of allies to topple the old authorities.

2.4 Designing New Areas of Experience

Unfortunately, Zybertowicz's description of the last two types is much scarcer and vaguer than that of reproduction and discovering. However, we can cope with that by applying the previously proposed criterion of stability and destabilising the environment where the knowledge-building processes occur.

Designing takes place not only in unstable situations (ontology). In this case even epistemologial categories used by researchers or other individuals are subject to change. Redefinition can only be applied to an established system of concepts or ideas, even though it is meant to change along with the order which they referred to. The field of research can be redefined but its name and, in many cases, also the general description (now reinterpreted) remains. In designing there are no fixed points of this kind: explorers can neither find support in stability of the environment where they operate, nor in stability of epistemological categories. Both are yet to be formed.

It may be expected that the greatest achievements of mind are related to designing as a model form of innovation. This is in stark contrast with standard examples used in epistemology, which refer to reproduction practices (white snow, cat on the mat and so on). We now see the yawning gap: two degrees of instability, ontological instability (of the environment) and cognitive instability (of notions or ideas).

The model of four types of knowledge-building processes supplemented with my amendment introduces a relatively simple scheme: reproduction and discovering, essentially based on mapping, have a realist character. Redefining and designing, as processes involving destabilising the environment, participate in constructing a new collective order. If we prove capable of analysing philosophers' actions in such categories, we will be able to determine whether their actions are realist or constructivist. Nevertheless, I would also like to introduce another, additional analytic tool.

3 Tool No.2: Lem's Geniuses, 3 Types

The other analytical tool is the typology of geniuses proposed by Stanisław Lem in one of his reviews of non-existent books (Lem 1974). I am going to link his remarks with cultural theory, more strongly than he does himself. While his distinction will not let us tell realist actions from constructivist ones, as does the model of the four types of knowledge, nevertheless it will allow us to do some specifications, important in our context.

Let us begin with a certain metaphor of culture that facilitates presenting Lem's approach. Imagine culture as a river flowing through time, while the riverbed and the water are made of cultural forms, or games. Some of them are long-lasting and therefore cover long distances (or periods of time) and some are short-lived. To make culture 'flow', none of those forms can 'stand still', they must be perpetually reproduced in its inhabitants' practices. Similarly, to a lesser or greater extent it is necessary to invent new forms. Introducing various forms of this kind may be illustrated as choosing one or another riverbed by the river.

This general image, quite accurately reflecting a certain group of cultural models (Smith 2001, 2f), is ready to host Lem's geniuses. The third category of those, 'simple and common geniuses' as he calls them (Lem 1974, 90), are those at the forefront of the river. New cultural games that they invent mark the time horizon. They lead the culture and it follows them. That is why Lem says that they often earn money and fame (Lem 1974, 90). However, their 'weakness' depends on not trespassing the horizon of time.

The second kind of geniuses, as it is easy to figure out, is similar except they walk several miles ahead of the river's front. They design cultural forms that do not fit in today's riverbed, but in that of ten, twenty or fifty years from now. Among others, because they are too difficult or unintelligible for their contemporaries. Those are usually bound to fail, Lem writes that they starve, live in shelters, are deported or stoned. Their later recognition is treated as their posthumous victory. They are eventually commemorated in monuments and streets are named after them (Lem 1974, 90).

What is curious, there are two possible interpretations of what they do: the realist one and the constructivist one, at least in a way. Following the first lead, these geniuses predict the future shape of culture, basing on its present state, but their imagination is too powerful for their contemporaries and no one is able to follow them. The other interpretation says that predicting is a wrong term. Geniuses of the second category design specific new forms of culture that are later swept by the river, but it takes time to happen. That is, the present culture cannot incorporate those forms yet, but when their designs come into being, the river course gravitates towards them.

Finally, there are also geniuses of the first category. They are not those further ahead of the river's front compared to the second category. A completely different thing is going on here. They design certain possible forms of culture, or cultural games, but they are never to be absorbed by its course. They dig a riverbed that the river is never going to flow through. Lem says that no one knows these geniuses and never will, neither living nor dead (Lem 1974, 90 f). Their truths are so unheard of that nobody is going to understand them, nobody will remember them. The further culture proceeds, the further away a first category genius departs from reality, as he or she has been out of it right from the beginning and the distance only grows with time.

Let us use our tools for three selected philosophers and their actions.

4 Example of Philosophers' Actions: Plato

As the first example I am going to use Plato. Let us remind, though, that we are supposed to categorise actions and not theories, or researchers, hence we have to ask "What did Plato do". Therefore the default approach, describing Plato as the author of particular theories, that should be analysed in their own right, will not suffice.

There is, though, a certain tradition of construing Plato, surfacing in communication research rather than in philosophical mainstream, that can help us. This tradition, namely the orality and literacy studies, especially Eric Havelock's groundbreaking work (Havelock 1963, 1986), sees Plato as a very important figure. However, this is not because of his philosophical theories' significance in the tradition of the discipline, but because Plato stands at the historic moment of Greek oral culture's transformation into (partially) written one (see Olson 1994). Numerous traits indicate it, a few of them extraordinarily characteristic: Plato's preceptor, Socrates, did not leave any written work after him, but he could read and is undoubtedly an example of literate mind. Plato, his student, wrote texts being records of spoken language, i.e. dialogues. What is more, Plato's seventh letter and research tradition related to the so-called unwritten science, enhance this image, arguing that from Plato's point of view key knowledge was transmitted orally; the philosopher remained distrustful to writing as a medium of knowledge.

The crucial element is Plato's resentment towards poets. Generations of researchers pondered what on earth poets did to deserve this peculiar loathing by the author of *Phaedrus*. Here is where we reach Havelock's answer. This scholar says that poets of ancient Greece were not intellectuals creating rhymed or unrhymed verses, which are subsequently published in volumes read at meetings attended mainly by other poets. According to Havelock, Plato's poets constituted a key element in the mechanism of cultural reproduction: in oral culture human body is the only vessel for the whole accumulated knowledge: its actions and habits, mind, muscle memory etc. (Havelock 1963). A relatively complex culture, like that of ancient Greece, had already produced complex and broad resources of knowledge, and the only way to store them was in the bodies of subsequent generations. For efficiency of such cultural reproduction it does not suffice to force youths to learn all important information by heart, as knowledge does not work like that in oral culture. It remains concrete and contextual (Ong 2002). Hence the actual mechanism of reproduction could rather have resembled a cross between a rock concert and a religious celebration: the participants were seduced, or almost hypnotised, experienced deep emotional involvement, their bodies moved rhythmically to the sung verses, amplifying the message and its memorisation, they identified with protagonists of the songs listened to. That is why Plato was so upset by poets confusing people's minds.

It was not poets' fault, though, not any particular flaw of their personalities. If any, it was a trait of oral culture. The war that Plato declared on poets in his *Republic* acquires a due meaning which explains what his protagonist, Socrates, describes there. As we all know, he envisages a state where a particular emphasis is going to be put on extensive education, designed up to the smallest detail and encompassing many spheres of life. In the perspective offered by Havelock, Plato designs cultural reproduction for literate minds, which is meant to overcome oral culture (Havelock 1963).

How does it situate Plato in our criteria? As we can see, the author of *Symposium* does not reproduce old cultural games, because they are what he fights against, and he does not discover their content. We can discuss whether he only redefines the pre-existing game of cultural reproduction or he designs an utterly new game along with its correspondent mode of cultural reproduction. I would opt for the latter version. However, it does not matter much in view of a more general question: whether Plato's actions are realist at this stage, or constructivist. The answer is clear: Plato acts in a constructivist way.

If we resort to Lem's typology of geniuses, in Plato we will effortlessly recognise a genius of the second category, who designs future culture forms. In other aspects the Greek thinker might have proceeded with the front of the river, but with his sketch of long-distance education, he clearly went ahead of his time.

To conclude: Plato's analysed actions are constructivist, and as a genius of the second kind he designs states of culture that are to be only fully brought about by his heirs in the form of many years' mass education based on school textbooks. We have the philosopher, we have the action and we also know what he is constructing. We are then able to determine who constructs what.

5 Example of Philosophers' Actions: Spinoza

Spinoza provides the second example of philosophical action I am going to discuss. More accurately, I am going to examine a certain strand of his philosophy that focuses on emotions. This time, though, let us reverse the order and ask first what kind of genius Spinoza was. This task will be helped by cognitive scientist António Damásio, who wrote in his *Looking for Spinoza:*

> Spinoza dealt with the subjects that preoccupy me most as a scientist – the nature of emotions and feelings and the relation of mind to body – and those same subjects have preoccupied many other thinkers of the past. To my eyes, however, he seemed to have prefigured solutions that researchers are now offering on a number of these issues. That was surprising.
> [...] Spinoza had described a functional arrangement that modern science is revealing as fact: Living organisms are designed with an ability to react emotionally to different objects and events. The reaction is followed by some pattern of feeling and a variation of pleasure or pain is necessary component of feeling. (Damásio 2003, 11)

Damásio hugely simplifies our task. His remarks obviously imply that Spinoza should be considered a genius of the second category, as it was with Plato. What is more, we can estimate his advantage over the main stream of culture to be more than three hundred years, as this is how many separate his work from the research Damásio refers to.

We are left with the question which of the four types of knowledge Spinoza's theory of emotions belongs to. In my opinion the matter is ambiguous. Less trouble seems to be presented by the realist interpretation of dealing with a discovery: Spinoza takes part in a cultural game of experiencing emotions, strives to grasp its rules in the categories of his philosophy and recognises them far better than other contemporaneous thinkers. An analogical investigation of this area will only be possible, as we know from Damásio, three hundred years later and with the use of different methods of research (of previously outlined areas of the world).

However, we could consider an alternative constructivist interpretation. What if we have to do with an attempt at redefining the emotion game (as part of everyday life), known to Spinoza's contemporaries, but using new concepts developed by the philosopher?

6 Example of Philosophers' Actions: Berkeley

Finally, I would like to recall a third example: George Berkeley. If I tried again to embrace the problem in one quotation that would be the following fragment of his *Treatise Concerning the Principles of Human Knowledge:*

> Those Men who frame general Rules from the Phenomena, and afterwards derive the Phenomena from those Rules, seem to consider Signs rather than Causes. (Berkeley 2002, §CVIII)

This sentence appears in both editions published during Berkeley's life (from 1710 and 1734), but the later version lacks a fragment where a natural scientist is called a grammarian, and investigating nature described as grammar. Berkeley also refers to 'reading the Nature's language'.

At the first glance, the fragment above could be treated as an insignificant remark expressed in a metaphoric way. I would like to propose a different interpretation, though: in this fragment, including the part later omitted, Berkeley draws consequences from his communicational ontology, whereby experience of all the world is based on ideas which God sends to people, like a matrix transmitting to human brains ordered electric impulses that create the image of late twentieth-century reality in the famous film. He tries to redefine the study of nature – more precisely, the emerging modern science – replacing causal categories with semiotic ones. The reason is obviously Berkeley's specific ontology, in which recognising the existence of matter entails skepticism, and consequently, atheism. Matter functioning according the logic of causes and effects does not need God. Hence, from Berkeley's point of view, a Cartesian interpretation of triumphant science is a recipe for, as he put it, 'Atheism and Irreligion'.

If we agree for this interpretation, placing Berkeley inside the previously proposed scheme will not pose any problem. We can at least see his efforts leading to redefine (the third kind of knowledge) the quotidian in the categories of religion and communication (as a constant exchange of ideas with God). This redefinition also encompasses scientific research. We might even dare to seek cases of designing new areas of experience, as in Berkeley's famous experiment, when he tried to almost hang himself to discover how the ideas we experience change at the moment of death. The experiment almost took a fatal turn.

We know, however, that Berkeley's efforts did not bring long-term effect. Thinking of science in causal categories proved victorious, and imagining the world in communication categories had to wait for philosophically more complex ideas of German transcendentalism or for contemporary science fiction. The proposed cultural games did not take root. Therefore Berkeley makes an interesting example of a first-category genius, in Lem's terms, that is, someone who intellectually departed so far from the course of the cultural river that the river does not have the chance to incorporate him and drifts still further apart. This is the case at least in the subject we consider, because not all of the Irishman's concepts were equally unheard of and a significant part of them found their way into the history of philosophy. Although, the forms that he introduced became far less absorbed by it than those of two other empiricists from the British Isles, Locke and Hume.

7 Summary: Philosophers as Significant Constructors

The review of the three above examples with the use of the proposed analytic tools brought interesting results. We obtained constructivist actions of a second-category genius (Plato), second-category genius's realist actions (Spinoza) and constructivist actions of a first-category genius (Berkeley). Most importantly, though, we managed to shift the focus from philosophers themselves or their self-description, to their actions. Seemingly removed from the world in the abstract game of creating philosophical theories, some of them prove to have largely influenced the shape of the world surrounding them. Their interventions were sometimes efficient and sometimes not. What matters, however, from the proposed perspective, philosophers' work may have played an important role in constructing significant parts of our culture.

English translation by Maciej Smoczyński

References

Berkeley, George (2002): *A Treatise Concerning the Principles of Human Knowledge*. Edited by David R. Wilkins. http://www.maths.tcd.ie/~dwilkins/Berkeley/HumanKnowledge /1734/ HumKno.pdf (visited on 28 February 2016).
Damásio, António (2003): *Looking for Spinoza: Joy, Sorrow, and the Feeling Brain*, Hacourt: Mariner Books.

Freeland, Cynthia A. (ed.) (1998): *Feminist Interpretations of Aristotle*. Pennsylvania: Pennsylvania State University Press.
Gatens, Moira (ed.) (2009): *Feminist Interpretations of Spinoza*. Pennsylvania: Pennsylvania State University Press.
Giddens, Antony (1990): *The Consequences of Modernity*. Cambridge: Polity.
Havelock, Eric (1963): *Preface to Plato*. Cambridge: Harvard University Press.
Havelock, Eric (1986): *The Muse Learns to Write: Reflections on Orality and Literacy from Antiquity to the Present*. New Haven: Yale University Press.
Lakoff, George; Jonson, Mark (2003): *Metaphors We Live By*. Chicago: University of Chicago Press.
Lem, Stanisław (1974): "Kuno Mlatje: 'Odys z Itaki'". In: Lem, Stanisław: *Doskonała próżnia. Wielkość urojona*. Krakow: Wydawnictwo Literackie, 89–96.
Latour, Bruno (1987): *Science in Action. How to Follow Scientists and Engineers through Society*. Cambridge Mass.: Harvard University Press.
Mitterer, Josef (1992): *Das Jenseits der Philosophie. Wider das dualistische Erkenntnisprinzip*. Vienna: Passagen.
Mitterer, Josef (2001): *Die Flucht aus der Beliebigkeit*. Frankfurt am Main: Fischer.
Olson, David R. (1994): *The World on Paper: The Conceptual and Cognitive Implications of Writing and Reading*. New York: Cambridge University Press.
Ong, Walter J. (2002): *Orality and Literacy. The Technologizing of the Word*. New York: Routledge.
Pałubicka, Anna (1977): *Orientacje epistemologiczne, a rozwój nauki*. Warsaw: Państwowe Wydawnictwo Naukowe.
Rorty, Richard (1981): *Philosophy and the Mirror of Nature*. Princeton NJ: Princeton University Press.
Smith, Philip (2001): *Cultural Theory. An Introduction*. Maldes MA, Oxford: Blackwell Publishers.
Schott, Robin May (ed.) (1997): *Feminist Interpretations of Kant*. Pennsylvania: Pennsylvania State University Press.
Zybertowicz, Andrzej (1995): *Przemoc i poznanie. Studium z nie-klasycznej socjologii wiedzy*. Torun: Wydawnictwo Uniwersytetu Mikołaja Kopernika.

Marzenna Cyzman
On the Non-Dualizing Rhetoric.
Some Preliminary Remarks

Abstract: In the reception of Josef Mitterer's writings up to now, there are two predominant types of motifs: the radical constructivist background of his philosophy and the ontological and epistemological foundations and consequences of non-dualism. The critics are focused rather on some problematic consequences of non-dualism, ranging from the problem of infinite regress up to the thesis assuming that Mitterer's philosophy presupposes a world reduced to descriptions. However, these two types of readings are founded on dualizing assumptions which are not coherent with non-dualism.

Thus, in the present paper I interpret non-dualism in the frame of non-dualism, based on non-dualizing assumptions. I argue that non-dualism is a rhetorical project resulting in far-reaching consequences in the field of academic and scientific debates, poetics and practice of negotiations and deliberations, as well as in ordinary discourse. Non-dualism fulfills Richard Rorty's dream of culture as a never-ending conversation in which the argument of power is successfully replaced by the power of argument. Mitterer makes transparent the rhetorical techniques performed in the dualizing discourse (not only in situations of conflict) in order to present an alternative – the non-dualizing mode of discourse. Mitterer's philosophy – reread in the context of Rorty's pragmatism, Foucault's conception of discourses, Perelman's new rhetoric – offers the new *vocabulary* (in Rorty's meaning) which may change the practice of speaking

Keywords: non-dualizing mode of speaking, description "so far" / "from now on", constructivism, rhetoric, discourse

In the reception of non-dualism so far the ontological and epistemological involvement seems to be the predominant issue. The will to know the appropriate place of Josef Mitterer's philosophy on the philosophical map leads scholars to investigate its connections with radical constructivism, Ludwig Wittgenstein's philosophy as well as Richard Rorty's neopragmastism. Thus, it is helpful to divide these investigations into three main groups:

> *1. Problematizations:* in which non-dualism is seen in the context of essential philosophical problems, such as: the relations between words and the world, the infinite regress; the problem of distinctions, and the semantics of the notions *object* and *description;*

2. Contextualizations: in which Mitterer's conception is placed on the map of philosophy and among philosophers, such as Alfred North Whitehead, Bruno Latour or Ernst von Glasersfeld;

3. Implications: in which the potential consequences of the non-dualism are estimated for/ in different fields of knowledge and human activities: history, media science, education, public relation, and art performances.

In spite of the large number of articles assuming the significant implications of non-dualism, the practical value of the non-dualizing mode of speaking is still less recognized or even ignored by Mitterer's interpreters and followers. In the present paper I will argue that the non-dualizing way of speaking is a practice oriented project which is able to replace the former mode of discourse.[1] My use of the word 'discourse' is very broad; it does not only mean the philosophical discourse which Mitterer takes as a point of departure. Furthermore, in my interpretation there is a pragmatic development of Mitterer's theses, especially those which are assumed about the non-dualizing alternative for the situations of conflict. I argue that non-dualism should be estimated and developed further as a rhetorical, not as an ontological project. Mitterer's view, intentionally non-ontologizing, provides nonetheless some ontological consequences – the new radical anti-essentialist conception of an object in which this traditional dualizing notion is replaced by *the process* (Schmidt 2011). However, non–dualism does not offer a new vision of world or reality. Mitterer does not raise traditional ontological or epistemological questions. Moreover, all of the possible ontological implications are coherent only on the condition that they are developed in the frame of the non-dualizing assumptions (Neges 2013). The problems with Mitterer's philosophy seem to be the results of interpretations carried out in the context of dualism and by the notions of dualism. This is *the ontologization* of the non-dualizing mode of speaking which results in the vision of non-dualism as strange conception of reality.

While the dualists *speak about the object*, non-dualists *speak from* the object. This assumption changes the direction of the discourse which is not aimed at the object. According to non-dualism the object is considered as the description *so far* which is transformed into a description *from now on*. It goes further in the direction of change. Therefore, we have no need for the well-known

---

[1] The first part of my monography of the non-dualizing philosophy is connected with the rhetorical context, see (Cyzman 2015). (the book is in Polish, the original title *Nieznośna płynność rzeczy. Dyskurs, retoryka, interpretacja w nie-dualizującym sposobie mówienia* translates into English as: *The Unbearable Fluidity of Things. Discourse, Rhetoric, Interpretation in the Non-dualizing Mode of Speaking*).

two-level structure of the discourse or any meta-language. The *towards-object-cognition* is replaced by the *from-object-cognition*. As I argue this is the basic assumption which may lead to coherent non-dualizing considerations.

1 On the Practical Value of the Non-Dualizing Way of Speaking

Only a positive answer to the fundamental question *"is non-dualism really practically useful?"* may provide a foundation for the following considerations. As non-dualism is a philosophical conception expressed mostly by abstract theses, rather weakly exemplified in Mitterer's works, one may come to the conclusion that the practical value of this project is at least difficult to imagine (see Dellwing 2011). However, doing philosophy does not mean to exclude practical considerations, on the contrary it presupposes performing discourse in practice. Mitterer starts from the abstract in order to arrive at the practice. The philosopher performs the non-dualizing mode of speaking on the edge where the old vocabulary meets a new vocabulary. What is also important, the area of application of non-dualism is not limited to philosophical investigations. Concerning the philosophical questions it reaches for different human practices, organized and created by the discourse, including the ordinary acts of speech. Therefore, non-dualism may be used in the research on the discourse in general.

Before I consider the relation between the non-dualizing philosophy and the traditional rhetoric, let me specify a few notions which I use as a basis for my analysis.

Vocabulary– a notion introduced by Richard Rorty; it means: the set of particular beliefs, assumptions, prejudices, which are discursively actualised and organised. Vocabularies are contingent, changeable, however, they are stabilised in the particular interpretative communities (Rorty 1989, 6 f).

I am going to refer the notion of *vocabulary* primarily to the particular linguistic manifestations in the discourse, assuming their strict correlation with the foundations of the discourse.

Discourse – a notion which in semantics is defined in many different ways. There is no need to apply any particular definition. However, I argue that the general assumption that the discourse embraces written and spoken communication is not precise enough for the interpretation of the non-dualizing mode of speaking.

I assume the notion of the discourse refers to public forms of communication which construct all of our social practices within all its modalities. I follow Michel Foucault's general vision of discourse as the specific relation between actors, objects and subjects and I apply this term in the large areas of knowledge and people's activities (Foucault 1971). The discourse finds itself in its dynamic and practical form, so that it is the process which is not limited to performed acts of speech. It is the set of coordinated and coordinating activities which are not discursive consequences, but run along with it. This dynamic approach to the discourse is founded also on some of the radical constructivist ideas, especially in the works of Humberto Maturana (Maturana 1980).

Mitterer himself does not define the notion of discourse, however, it is the key word in his conception. He refers to its semantics once, arguing that the discourses become *sensu stricto* discursive in situations of conflict. He takes into consideration the etymology of the word *discourse*, which in Latin means *running to and from*. Its strict literal sense points to the situations of conflict in which two descriptions contradict each other.

Interpretative community – This term was established by Stanley Fish (Fish 1976). In spite of the high frequency of this notion in Fish's works, a precise definition was never provided. Interpretative community refers to the set of beliefs, models for reality, interpretative strategies, and conventions which stimulate our practices. Therefore it provides particular ways of reading texts, perceiving things, values, etc. We belong simultaneously to different interpretive communities.

I will use this term in order to functionalize Mitterer's conception of philosophy. It may be helpful in getting an answer to the question how we establish and change descriptions *so far* and where they are coming from.

2 The New or the Old Rhetoric?

If it is assumed that non-dualism is a rhetorical project, sooner or later several questions arise. Are the argumentative techniques, described and developed in the field of the traditional rhetoric, comparable with Mitterer's description of how arguments work? Does the non-dualizing description of persuasive means of expression differ from those given in the course books of rhetoric? Is it the reformulation, the actualization or the deconstruction of traditional rhetoric?

In order to answer those questions let me refer to four rhetorical tricks frequently used in discourse. Mitterer describes them in the frame of the non-dualizing procedure in the *Flight from the Arbitrariness* (Mitterer 2011).

The notion in the non-dualizing procedure	In non-dualizing explication	Comparable explication in traditional rhetoric
Appeal to the other side of the discourse / the beyond of discourse	This function may be fulfilled by many different instances, for example: *reality, god, religion, text "itself", eternal values, nature, real Christians/Muslims,* – as all of them are "dumb and silent" (Mitterer 2011, 143 ff), there is a necessity to speak in the name of them; a function fulfilled by the group of authorised representatives or spokesmen; – this rhetorical trick is performed in order to establish the truth, *my own truth*, which shall be guaranteed by the unquestionable instances localised in the beyond of discourse; – as Mitterer claims, the instances given *beyond the discourse* take responsibility for us speaking, therefore this trick is used also to fly from responsibility.	None of the traditions in rhetoric makes use of the notion of *the beyond the discourse*, however there are some ways of expression in rhetoric which are similar to Mitterer's notion: *Appeal to Authority/Argument from Authority (in Latin: ad autoritatem);* – furthermore, there are many rhetorical notions which may be pointed by the name given above, for example: * *Argumentum ad verecundiam* (Perelman 1977); * *Argument 30 = Berufung auf Autoritäten* (Schopenhauer 1983); * *Authority of the One* and the *Authority of the Selected Few* (Engel 1986); * *Ipse Dixit*; – the place of the Authority may be fulfilled by personalized individuals (for example: *real Christians, scientists, ...*), cultural clichés, values or abstract notions (for example: *god, nature, science, ...*); – in the situations of conflict the *Argument from Authority* is not questioned as a stabilized rhetorical trick, only the particular type of its fulfilment may be doubted.

| Depersonalization of the proponent's standpoint and personalization of the opponent's standpoint | The use of the collective subject – *we* instead of *I*, for example: in English: *let us begin, we can assume, we are arguing;*
– *we* consists of *me* and *my followers*, the group of people sharing the same premises;
– it is used in order to support my position which is this way universalised;
– the contradict standpoint is personalized by the expressions such as *xy* (personal names) *assumes, xy argues, xy thinks* with adequate adjectives and adverbs, such as: *inncorectly, falsly, improperly;*
– the Truth and Adequateness are generalised, the false and the mistake are always particular, so that its discursive power is weakened, *we* has the monopoly for truth, *I* is weak and blunders;
– the proponent's standpoint is depersonalized also by the words such as: *indeed, in fact, really, obviously,* which signalize that the conception is true and valid even if no one assumes it (the impression of unquestionable value of the theory);
– it suggests also a kind of the direct access to *reality itself, objectivity itself.* | Instead of the lack of the exact correlate in the traditional rhetoric, there are some analogical persuasive tricks which may be described as:
to avoid the burden of proof (in Latin "onus probandi"):
– it can be realised *by Argumentum ad numerum* which is called as *Authority of the Many* by Morris Engel and in the books on rhetoric it takes different lexical shapes
– (appeal to the masses, appeal to belief), in Latin *Argument ad populum;*
– the linguistic indicator of this type of argument is described as *exlusive/inclusive "we"* (so called: *pluralis majestatis, pluralis homileticus*);
– the thesis is treated as obvious, thus there is no necessity to prove it which results with the use of the typical phrases, for example: *everybody knows it, it was proved long time ago,*
– it liberates the proponent from the necessity of the logical argumentation and responsibility for her claims. |

Discreditation of the proponent's ("my own") conception (acting as if I take myself to be mistaken)	It is realised in the frame of the proponent's conception and by the notions and/or assumptions included in it; – however, one cannot question the theory A in the frame of the theory A, in order to do that it is required to use the notions and/or assumptions of the different theory B, which means that the theory A is abandoned.	– the rule of the psychological trustworthiness, the persuasive strategy performed in order to gain the opponent's confidence and to dull opponent's vigilance.
The use of simple, uncomplicated examples	The use of the noncontroversial examples used in order to support the main thesis; – their accuracy is assumed before the description is performed and it is a *conditio sine qua non* of discourse directed towards truth; – the examples are based on the *circulus vitiosus* mechanism; – their cognitive or logical value is problematic, in spite of their persuasive value (most examples work well as means of persuasion).	– in Latin: *Argumentum ab exemplo;* – it is one of the most typical persuasive arguments used in the discourse and described in rhetorical course books; – the persuasive value of the examples is acclaimed to be even better than statistic collations.

3 Two Sceptical Conjectures

Because there are those important parallels between non-dualism and rhetoric severe worries may arise, the following being one of them. Since there are means of expression in rhetoric which are more or less analogous to Mitterer's notions, the answer to the question *what difference does it make: dualism or non-dualism*, becomes an issue of great importance. It points towards possible practical consequences of non-dualism which may be denied by those who claim that Mitterer's conception is nothing but the traditional dualizing rhetoric, dressed in constructivist vocabulary. In other words it may seem as if non-dualism is not a new thing at all but the rather dangerous old thing.

In addressing this worry, my point is that the non-dualizing mode of speaking makes a difference, although it is not easy to perceive at first sight Mitterer reconstructs the dualizing mode of speaking in non-dualizing language. The philosopher refers to the typical rhetorical means of expression used in situations of conflict but not in order to support them. His aim is to point to the mechanism which is the very foundation of all dualizing discourse. That is why he avoids traditional rhetorical notions in his conception. In traditional rhetoric ancient techniques of argumentation are used and adjusted to present notions and their practical application. The non-dualizing description is developed aside the frame of the traditional rhetoric. Thus, the practical aim is to weaken the dualizing rhetoric and expose its irrationalities. The *vade mecum of the non-dualizing rhetoric* is rather ironical than literal and serious (Mitterer 2011). Non-dualism does not provide us with rhetorical means in order for throwing conversational partners off their guard Mitterer is not the sophistic teacher of argumentative techniques. He is rather the debunker of the dualizing rhetoric and its involvement into the violence. Making the discursive tricks transparent, he strengthens our resistance to their persuasive powers. While the traditional rhetorical course books present the methods of dualizing, Mitterer focuses on the mechanism which are the basis for such dualizations. This basis is constituted by the *paradogma* of the distinction between an object, given beyond the discourse, and a description, given on the level of the discourse. The dualizing moves, traditionally classified as fallacies from the logical point of view and as breaches of the rule of cooperation from the pragmatic perspective, are the fruit of deeply rooted and oppressive dualizing thinking and speaking.

The second sceptical worry is this. Does the non-dualizing mode of speaking formulate a significant alternative to the usual discourse? Mitterer describes precisely the order of the dualizing mode of speaking, however an alternative seems to be less developed.

As a rejoinder let me consider the following idea: The non-dualizing mode of speaking predicts the negotiations, precisely – the continuation of the negotiations which are stopped in the dualizing stale mate situation (non-dualism predicts the negotiations to be open in the situation of conflicts).

The negotiations assume the change of these standpoints with which the two opposite sides accede to the discussion. They introduce a series of changes to the former proposals.

In negotiations in order to reach an agreement the proponent and the opponent should change their initial positions. Before the negotiations start, they have to accept the basic consensual descriptions which are also compatible with the non-dualizing mode of speaking. However, let me consider the most typical argumentative techniques used in negotiations: *appeal to universal principle, appeal to a theme, appeal to authority, appeal to "status quo", appeal to "minor standards", appeal to "prevailing practice", "appeal to precedents as counterexamples, appeal to self-interest, and threats and promises*. (Sycara 1990) At least two of those techniques make us of *the other side of the discourse*; and all of them have persuasion of the opponent as central goal. They are based on the same dualizing mechanism which is abandoned by Mitterer. If one emphasizes the role of persuasion in discussions in this way it already shows a dualist predicament. Non-dualists will not focus on persuasion in this way. The aim of the negotiations is the correlate of the non-dualizing mode of speaking while the way in which it is supposed to be achieved is different from it. Negotiation in its usual form is the fruit of dualizing thinking and as such it is not embraced in non-dualism because of its implications, this is, negotiation as discursive figure implies serious rhetorical and discursive violence.

The problem is not that there is something to say in the situation of a conflict. The problem is that there is a conflict. The conflict connected with the necessity of the *settlement of a dispute*.

4 The Settlement of a Dispute

What does exactly mean to *settle a dispute, to clinch the deal, to reach an accord?* A settlement assumes a prior disagreement between x and y. It leads to the classification in the categories of true and false. To clinch the dispute refers to a situation in which the dispute is settled decisively. Such a settlement means that the thesis x wins and thesis y loses. Thus, the situation in which the settlement should be achieved is the final effect of the process of the argumentation founded on dualizing premises. The idea of a settlement of a dispute between opponent and proponent assumes that there is one possible, potentially common, result when the two opposite sides use persuasion. This solution of finding the one *true* result is suspended by the non-dualizing procedure as it is not aimed at agreement between two contradict sides. The problem is Mitterer himself uses the term of *Entscheidung* which is involved in the dualizing connotations. However, almost every notion in the non-dualizing procedure is taken from the dualizing vocabulary. As Mitterer claims, it is very difficult to find appropriate words in order to introduce the new way of thinking. However, inventing the new ones may lead to the misunderstanding of the conception. Therefore, it is an issue of a great importance to accurately carve out the vocabulary used by Mitterer. In regard to their function in the non-dualizing procedure, words do not mean the same.

5 The Compromise

Is there any possibility of the working around the settlement of this type? In the deliberations and democratized communication the compromise agreement is assumed as the way in which an accord may be reached. Two opposite sides focus on those elements in their standpoints which may be accommodate to each other. Does non-dualism predict the compromise in the situation of conflicts? My answer is negative as I claim that the compromise does not resolve this matter in a satisfactory way. Mostly a compromise does not lead to a solution which is satisfying for both sides.

What is also important, a compromise is based on the universalization of the rule of rationality which is not the same for the particular interpretative communities. Here are essential output and input problems, such as: how to arrange the discussion, in which institutional frame, how to assess the losses and profits, how to use the practical consequences of the compromise. It is still based upon the dualizing premises and as such it cannot be functionalised in the non-dualizing mode of speaking.

6 To Fit, Not to Match, and Some of the Non-Dualizing Consequences

In the non-dualizing mode of speaking the procedure of fitting – not matching – descriptions to one another is taken seriously. The research done together by opponent and proponent are aimed at searching fitting descriptions which are acceptable for both of them. The description is evaluated on the basis of other descriptions, not on basis of the object which is taken as a description *so far* transformed into the description *from now on*. In such a procedure the difference between two English verbs, *to fit* and *to match*, seem to be crucial. As Ernst von Glasersfeld claims, *match* refers to "an equivalence of relations, sequence, or characteristic structure – something, in other words that he [the realist, M.C.] can consider *the same*, because only then could he say that his knowledge is *of* the world". In contrary, *fit* does not assume any kind of "homomorphism" of this type (see von Glasersfeld 1984).

We can successfully relocate the epistemological distinction between *to fit* and *to match* in order to allocate it to the field of the discourse. If one does not claim that our descriptions have to match the world as it really is, we will not expect the settlements in contradictory terms. One will not expect the agreement to be established or reached as the aim of the research of this type as well. The questions *how to reach an agreement, how to win against my rival,* or *how to reach a compromise,* are not only unnecessary, they do not arise at all.

Moreover, the process of fitting the descriptions in non-dualizing research may also lead to the conclusion that two descriptions do not fit to one another. It results with the – let me say – the *protocol of discrepancies.* It means that at present it may not be possible to find common descriptions, however as it is only the contemporary state of affairs, this may change during further research. The whole reason of using the non-dualizing procedure is to forestall the situation of a dispute to be settled. The settlement, although this is not the adequate word in the non-dualizing context, is achieved by conjoined research and mutual open minded exchange of descriptions. Of course, Mitterer prefers mutual agreement, not conflict; however there is no non-dualizing recipe of what to do in a case of disagreement, no algorithmic method of how to solve disputes. We should listen to each other, be ready to retreat our descriptions, be open and generous as listeners. The non-dualizing discourse is not a discourse of obviousness in which no argumentation is needed. Non-dualism is not the project of ideal transparent discourse which may be based on obvious intuitions, a constant and unchangeable foundation which is very far from the anti-essentialist thinking. The discourse then, also philosophical discourse, is the space of exchanging opinions, without the oppressive techniques performed in the dualizing mode of speaking, but argumentation is still in use. In the light of the non-dualizing procedure it is performed in order to convince the opponent to the proponent's strategy of interpretation.

Non-dualism underlines the necessity of never ending dialogs. This way it fulfils Rorty's dream about the culture as the never ending conversation in which the argument of power is replaced by the power of the argument. In the non-dualizing context I do not ask: *how to win the argument, how to judge who is right.* I would rather ask: *which descriptions we can find together.* I do not raise the question which description matches the object, rather I ask which descriptions fit to one other.

Therefore, the non-dualizing mode of speaking does not demand the aim of the discourse to be universal agreement. In dualist approaches it is often reached by means of the discursive violence, this is symbolic violence. We can stabilise the current states of affairs, although it still implies readiness to change. Do not fundamentalize your descriptions but instead search for the biggest possible agreement between them – this is the only non-dualizing advice.

To summarize, my final theses are as follows:

> 1. The non-dualizing mode of speaking does not assume the necessity of a settlement of disputes in a strict sense. Non-dualism forestalls the situation of the dispute to be settled, the contradicting descriptions to be eliminated, the description A to win against the description B.
>
> 2. Therefore, non-dualism does not provide us with any of the usual, dualist methods of achieving a settlement of agreement.
>
> 3. In the non-dualizing way of speaking the consensus, compromise, or agreement are not assumed as the aim of the process of exchanging and fitting the descriptions to one another.
>
> 4. It predicts the process of fitting the descriptions to one another which may lead (or not) to the acceptance of the common descriptional basis.

The final thesis is that the non-dualizing mode of speaking is nothing but a new vocabulary, an alternative for the socially stabilised practice of thinking and speaking. If one shares its premises, one automatically uses the different linguistic manifestations on the level of the discourse. If we move in the space determined by the horizon of the classical or less classical rhetoric, we find ourselves beyond non-dualism. It results with the dualizing interpretation of the non-dualism which leads to the contradictions and aberrations. In so far as we share dualizing premises of discourse, we are not able to perform non-dualizing discourse. So far it is difficult to estimate its consequences, however the vision of the politics as *the art of conversation* based on the non-dualizing procedure may be promising. Therefore, these general assumptions should be lead further in the field of the philosophy of politics.

At present we observe the crisis in the democratic communication as it does not fulfil the expected pragmatic function and becomes more or less oppressive. It can be argued that all dualizing types of deliberation have their weaknesses. Thus, it is even more urgent to try to perform a non-dualizing procedure. I am convinced that *so far* there is nothing to lose. And *from now on* there is much to achieve.

References

Cyzman, Marzenna (2015): *Nieznośna płynność rzeczy. Dyskurs, retoryka, interpretacja w nie-dualizującym sposobie mówienia*. Toruń: Wydawnictwo Naukowe Mikołaja Kopernika.

Dellwing, Michael (2013): *Josef Mitterer and the Philosopher's Stone (Around His Neck)*. In: *Constructivist Foundations* 8 (2), 253–258.

Engel, Morris S. (1986): *With Good Reason. An Introduction to Informal Fallacies.* New York: St. Martin's Press.
Fish, Stanley (1976): "Interpreting the 'Variorum'". In: *Critical Inquiry* 2 (3), 465–485.
Foucault, Michel (1971): *L'ordre du Discours.* Paris: Flammarion.
von Glasersfeld, Ernst (1984): "An Introduction to Radical Constructivism". In: Watzlawick, Paul (ed.): *The Invented Reality: How Do We Know What We Believe We Know?* New York: Norton, 17–40.
Maturana, Umberto; Varela, Francisco (1980): *Autopoiesis and Cognition: the Realization of the Living.* Dordrecht: Reidel.
Mitterer, Josef (2011): *Die Flucht aus der Beliebigkeit.* Weilerswist: Velbrück Wissenschaft.
Neges, Katharina (2013): "Non-dualism and World. Ontological Questions in the Non-dualizing Mode of Discourse". In: *Constructivist Foundations* 8 (2), 158–165.
Perelman, Chaim (1977): *L'Empire Rhétorique: Rhétorique et Argumentation.* Paris: Vrin.
Rorty, Richard (1989): *Contingency, Irony, and Solidarity.* Cambridge: Cambridge University Press.
Schmidt, Siegfried (2011): *From Objects to Processes. A Proposal to Rewrite Radical Constructivism.* In: *Constructivist Foundations* 7 (1), 1–9.
Schopenhauer, Arthur (1983): *Eristische Dialektik oder Die Kunst Recht zu behalten.* Zürich: Haffmans Verlag.
Sycara, Katia (1990): "Persuasive Argumentation in Negotiation". In: *Theory and Decision* 28, 203–242.

Volker Gadenne
Ist der Konstruktivismus selbstwidersprüchlich?

Abstract: According to constructivism, the world we can know is a construction and it is not possible to gain knowledge about the world as it is in itself. This thesis of constructivism has been criticized as being self-refuting. It is discussed whether this criticism is sound. Constructivists have tried three ways in order to avoid self-refutation. It is argued that the first two ways are unconvincing. The third solution is tenable. However, at a closer look the third solution turns out as a moderate kind of realism since it gives up the central claim of constructivism.

Keywords: Anti-realism, fallibilism, radical constructivism, self refutation, social/cultural constructivism

Gegenstand dieses Artikels ist ein spezielles Problem, das alle Auffassungen haben, die behaupten, dass die Wirklichkeit in einem bestimmten Sinne konstruiert sei. Das Problem ist seit langem bekannt und wird etwa so formuliert: Der Konstruktivismus baut eine Argumentation auf, deren Konklusion den Ausgangsannahmen widerspricht oder die zumindest mit den Ausgangsannahmen praktisch unvereinbar ist. Es wird also gegenüber dem Konstruktivismus der Vorwurf eines *Selbstwiderspruchs* erhoben. Im Folgenden möchte ich analysieren, ob der Vorwurf zu Recht besteht, und wenn ja, welche Bedeutung dies für die konstruktivistischen Auffassungen hat.

Das Argument, um das es geht, wurde gegen den *radikalen Konstruktivismus* zuerst von Hans Jürgen Wendel vorgebracht (Wendel 1990), und dann auch von einigen anderen Kritikern, in den letzten Jahren z. B. von Paul Boghossian (Boghossian 2013). Einige Konstruktivisten haben den Einwand diskutiert, am ausführlichsten hat dies Gerhard Roth getan (Roth 1994). Warum sollte man erneut auf diesen Kritikpunkt eingehen? Mein Grund dafür ist, dass mir vieles an diesem Einwand noch immer unklar erscheint, und ich meine, dass sich eine klärende Analyse lohnt.

Worin besteht das Problem dieses Selbstwiderspruchs genau? Und unter welchen Bedingungen entsteht es? Ich möchte zeigen, dass nicht jede konstruktivistische Auffassung dieses Problem aufwirft. Es entsteht nur dann, wenn zusammen mit der Idee der *Konstruktion* eine *antirealistische These* vertreten wird. Anders ausgedrückt, das Problem entsteht nur, wenn ein Konstruktivismus als

Gegenposition zum Realismus aufgefasst wird, und dies muss nicht der Fall sein. Eine antirealistische Position findet man allerdings bei den Spielarten des Konstruktivismus, die Formulierungen wie die folgenden gebrauchen: Die Welt ist eine Konstruktion. Die Welt ist eine soziale Konstruktion. Die Wirklichkeit ist eine Konstruktion des Gehirns. Nelson Goodman behauptete, die Sterne seien von uns „gemacht", zwar nicht mit Händen, jedoch mit Worten (vgl. Goodman 1980). Und er fügte hinzu, er meine dies wörtlich. Er sprach auch ganz allgemein von „worldmaking" (Goodman 1978). Auch Hilary Putnam vertrat in einer bestimmten Phase seines Denkens eine antirealistische Auffassung, die er einmal durch die Formulierung ausdrückte: „Der Geist und die Welt erschaffen zusammen den Geist und die Welt." (Putnam 1987, 1) Es empfiehlt sich an dieser Stelle zu präzisieren, was der Realismus behauptet. Ich verstehe unter dem Realismus eine *erkenntnistheoretische* Position, die sich in Form der beiden folgenden Annahmen zusammenfassen lässt:

> R_1: Die Existenz und die Beschaffenheit der Welt (Wirklichkeit, Realität) hängen nicht von menschlichen kognitiven Zuständen ab (und auch nicht von Sprache, Theorien und Werten).
> R_2: Es ist möglich, und es ist in einigen Bereichen gelungen, Erkenntnisse über diese objektive (unabhängige, an sich existierende) Welt zu gewinnen.

Beide Thesen können missverstanden werden. R_1 bestreitet natürlich nicht, dass Wahrnehmungen und Überzeugungen einen *kausalen* Einfluss auf die Welt haben. Gemeint ist vielmehr eine ontologische Unabhängigkeit: Steine, Bäume, Planeten und Moleküle existieren, auch wenn sie gerade nicht Inhalte unseres Wahrnehmens oder Vorstellens sind. Sein ist *nicht* Wahrgenommenwerden oder Gedachtwerden.

In Bezug auf R_2 ist davon auszugehen, dass Erkenntnis oder Wissen im Sinne *gerechtfertigter*, jedoch *fehlbarer* Annahmen gemeint ist. So gut wie jeder, der heute einen erkenntnistheoretischen Realismus vertritt, ist *Fallibilist*, verzichtet also auf den Anspruch unfehlbarer Erkenntnis. Nun ist auch ein Skeptiker Fallibilist. Ein Realist benötigt Erkenntnisprinzipien, die es gestatten, unter bestimmtem Bedingungen eine Annahme über die reale Welt als rational gerechtfertigt anzusehen. Man kann es z. B. als gerechtfertigt ansehen, eine Beobachtungsaussage zu akzeptieren, so lange es keine ihr widersprechenden Beobachtungen gibt. Wir können es als gerechtfertigt ansehen, eine Hypothese vorläufig zu akzeptieren, wenn sie sorgfältig geprüft wurde und diese Prüfungen bestanden hat.

Es gibt verschiedene Möglichkeiten, solche Prinzipien rationaler Erkenntnisgewinnung auszugestalten und zu präzisieren. Hier möchte ich zu dieser Frage nur zwei extreme Positionen erwähnen, die mit einem Realismus unvereinbar sind und zwischen denen ein Realismus angesiedelt sein muss. Das eine Extrem wäre eine Position, die als Kriterium für die Akzeptanz einer Aussage über die Realität verlangt, dass sie absolut sicher begründet werden muss. Ein Realismus, der dies verlangt, lässt sich gegen skeptische Einwände nicht verteidigen.

Das andere Extrem ist ein Fallibilismus, wie er von manchen kritischen Rationalisten vertreten wird, z. B. von David Miller (Miller 1994). Danach kann es niemals eine rationale Rechtfertigung dafür geben, eine Hypothese auch nur vorläufig als wahr zu akzeptieren. Auch gibt es danach niemals eine Rechtfertigung dafür, von zwei nicht widerlegten Hypothesen zu sagen, die eine sei glaubwürdiger als die andere.

Die Forderung nach absoluter Sicherheit ist zu stark, ein entsprechender Rechtfertigungsanspruch kann nicht eingelöst werden. Die völlige Ablehnung der Idee der Rechtfertigung von Aussagen über die reale Welt ist zu schwach für einen Realismus. Eine vertretbare realistische Position muss sich zwischen diesen Extremen bewegen.

Es ist nun fast immer R_2, und nicht R_1, das von konstruktivistischer Seite in Frage gestellt wird. Konstruktivisten verstehen ihre eigene Position als eine nicht metaphysische. R_1 ist eine metaphysische These, und die Negation von R_1 wäre ebenfalls eine metaphysische These. Vertreter eines Konstruktivismus behaupten daher nicht, dass es keine von unserem Wahrnehmen und Denken existierende Welt gäbe. Sie bestehen nur darauf, dass wir über eine solche unabhängige Welt nichts wissen könnten. Wir könnten nicht einmal mit Begriffen auf eine unabhängige Welt bzw. auf ihre Gegenstände referieren und daher nicht sinnvoll über sie sprechen. Damit wird R_2 die folgende antirealistische These gegenüber gestellt:

Antirealistische These: Es ist nicht möglich, Erkenntnisse über eine objektive (unabhängige, an sich existierende) Welt zu gewinnen.

Dies wird auch oft so ausgedrückt, dass wir *keinen kognitiven Zugang* haben könnten zu den Dingen, wie sie *an sich* sind.

Nun sprechen wir aber doch über die Welt, machen Erfahrungen und erforschen sie. Doch diese Welt, die unserer Erfahrung und unserem Denken allein zugänglich ist, dies sei eine Welt, die durch unsere Sprache sowie durch fundamentale Theorien erst *konstituiert* oder *konstruiert* werde. In diesem Sinne betont z. B. von Glasersfeld, Begründer des radikalen Konstruktivismus, „dass unser rationales Wissen sich immer und ausschließlich auf die von uns konstruierte Wirklichkeit bezieht" (von Glasersfeld 1995, 42).

Warum verbindet der Konstruktivismus die Idee des Konstruierens mit einer antirealistischen These? Hierzu ist zunächst festzustellen, dass die beiden Ideen durchaus nicht notwendig miteinander verbunden sind. Von Konstruktion und

Konstruktivismus kann auf eine Weise gesprochen werden, die erkenntnistheoretisch neutral oder jedenfalls nicht antirealistisch ist.

So wird z. B. der Begriff der Konstruktion oft nur verwendet, um auszudrücken, dass Kognition kein passives Aufnehmen von Sinnesreizen ist, wie es der ältere Empirismus annahm, sondern ein aktiver Prozess.

Das Ergebnis eines Wahrnehmungsvorgangs beispielsweise wird nicht nur durch die jeweiligen Sinnesreize bestimmt, sondern auch dadurch, was Personen wissen und erwarten. Und was Menschen nach einiger Zeit erinnern, entspricht oft nicht genau dem, was sie wahrgenommen haben, sondern ist nachweislich beeinflusst durch das, was sie für möglich und wahrscheinlich halten. Metaphorisch gesprochen scheinen im menschlichen Gedächtnis nicht ganze frühere Wahrnehmungsinhalte aufbewahrt zu werden, sondern nur Spuren davon, Informationsbruchstücke, aus denen dann unter Verwendung des vorhandenen Wissens die jeweilige Erinnerung *konstruiert* wird. Wer so von Konstruktion spricht, kann es offen lassen, ob mentale Repräsentationen einen Wahrheitsanspruch erheben können oder nicht. Wahrnehmungen und Überzeugungen könnten, auch wenn sie in diesem Sinne Konstruktionen sind, reale Sachverhalte so erfassen, wie sie an sich sind.

Eine andere Verwendung des Begriffs der Konstruktion, die ebenfalls nicht antirealistisch ist, betrifft die „Konstruktion" sozialer Tatsachen, so wie sie in Teilen der Sozialwissenschaften und von manchen Philosophen wie z. B. Searle beschrieben wird (vgl. Searle 1997). Nach dieser Auffassung gibt es Gegenstände bzw. Tatsachen, deren Existenz davon abhängig ist, dass Menschen bestimmte Überzeugungen haben und in bestimmter Weise handeln. Hierzu gehört z. B., dass ein bestimmtes Stück Metall den Wert von einem Euro hat oder dass ein bestimmter Stein eine Landesgrenze markiert. Das Metallstück und der Stein existieren objektiv, unabhängig von Überzeugungen und Vereinbarungen. Die Euromünze und die Landesgrenze existieren aber nicht unabhängig davon, was Menschen glauben, beschlossen haben oder bezeugen können. Dennoch sind die Euromünze und die Landesgrenze real in dem Sinne, dass sie Wirkungen haben. Und die Tatsache, dass aus einem Metallstück eine Münze *gemacht* wird, ist nicht mit einem antirealistischen Gedanken verbunden.

Ein antirealistischer Konstruktivismus entsteht, wenn man den Konstruktionsprozess auf eine Weise auffasst, die ein Erkennen der realen Welt als zweifelhaft oder unmöglich erscheinen lässt. Dies ist z. B. der Fall, wenn der Konstruktionsprozess als etwas aufgefasst wird, das, zumindest teilweise, ohne unsere bewusste Absicht geschieht, und das wir niemals zur Gänze ergründen können. Durch den Konstruktionsprozess wird ein Ding an sich zu einem Erscheinungsding, aus der unabhängig von uns existierenden Welt wird die phänomenale Welt oder konstruierte Welt. Wie die phänomenalen Dinge beschaffen sind, hängt von unserem Erkenntnisapparat ab: nach Kant von unseren Anschauungsformen und Verstandeskategorien; nach heutiger konstruktivistischer Auffassung z. B. von der Art und Weise, wie das Gehirn aus elektrochemischen Ereignissen bewusste Wahrnehmungen und Gedanken konstruiert; oder davon, wie soziale Akteure durch den Gebrauch ihrer Sprache eine bestimmte Sicht von der Welt errichten und aufrechterhalten. Entscheidend ist hierbei die Annahme, dass die eine Seite in diesem Prozess uns *prinzipiell unzugänglich* ist: nämlich die Welt, wie sie an sich ist, noch nicht geprägt durch Begriffskategorien, grundlegende Theorien und Werte. Auf diese, unabhängige Welt einen Blick werfen zu wollen, das hieße, den „Gottesstandpunkt" einnehmen zu wollen. Die phänomenale, konstruierte Welt aber sei uns zugänglich, sie könne erforscht und beschrieben werden.

Eine andere Form eines antirealistischen Konstruktivismus entsteht, wenn über den Konstruktionsprozess angenommen wird, dass er durch Faktoren bestimmt wird, die einer Erkenntnis der realen Welt entgegen wirken. So könnte es z. B. sein, dass die Art und Weise, wie wissenschaftliche Lehrmeinungen entstehen und sich durchsetzen, erheblich durch Interessen und Machtverhältnisse beeinflusst wird. Ein Konstruktivismus, der zum Ziel hat, diese Einflüsse aufzudecken, kann dies mit der Annahme verbinden, dass es eine Illusion sei zu glauben, es könne so etwas wie objektive Wahrheit oder Erkenntnis im Sinne des Realismus geben.

An dieser Stelle möchte ich betonen, dass es auch aus realistischer Sicht allen Grund gibt, neurobiologische, psychologische und soziologische Studien zur Kenntnis zu nehmen. Wenn man Realitätserkenntnis für möglich hält, ist es von großem Interesse zu wissen, welche psychologischen und sozioökonomischen Faktoren es gibt, die Erkenntnis fördern, oder aber behindern können. Nur wird man aus realistischer Sicht aus entsprechenden Studien nicht schließen, dass Realitätserkenntnis gänzlich unmöglich ist. Denn wenn man dies tun würde, dann würde daraus unmittelbar folgen, dass auch diese Studien keinerlei Erkenntniswert besitzen.

Damit sind wir bei dem besagten Selbstwiderspruchsproblem. Wenn man davon spricht, dass Wirklichkeit konstruiert würde, so setzt dies voraus, dass es Konstrukteure gibt. Als Konstrukteure werden meist Personen angesehen, die durch interaktives Handeln, insbesondere sprachliches Handeln, den Konstruktionsprozess vornehmen. Eine Ausnahme bilden in dieser Hinsicht diejenigen radikalen Konstruktivisten, nach deren Auffassung das Gehirn die Welt konstruiert. Hier sind also die konstruierenden Instanzen Gehirne, und der Konstruktionsprozess besteht aus neuronalen Vorgängen. Konstruktivistische Richtungen bemühen sich auch darum, ihre Annahmen über den Konstruktionsprozess zu belegen. Sie stützen sich unter anderem auf Resultate der Kultur- und Sprachwissenschaft, der Soziologie, der kognitiven Psychologie, der Neurowissenschaft und der Kybernetik.

Auf dieser Grundlage lässt sich nun der Vorwurf eines Widerspruchs folgendermaßen formulieren: Der Konstruktivismus macht eine Reihe von Aussagen über den Konstruktionsprozess, und er versucht auch, diese Aussagen zu belegen, er erhebt also den Anspruch, über den Konstruktionsprozess etwas zu wissen. Auf dem Weg über die Einsicht, wie Wirklichkeit konstruiert wird, gelangt der Konstruktivismus dann aber zu der antirealistischen These: Wir können über die reale (objektive, unabhängige) Welt kein Wissen erlangen. Den Konstruktionsprozess ist nun aber selbst Teil der Welt. Personen, ihr interaktives Handeln, Sprechakte, Gehirne, neuronale Prozesse sind ja Teil des Weltgeschehens. Unter diesen Umständen folgt aus der antirealistischen These, dass wir auch über den Konstruktionsprozess kein Wissen haben können. Genauer gesagt, wenn wir über die reale Welt nichts wissen können, dann können wir auch nicht wissen, dass Menschen durch ihre Sprache die Welt konstruieren; und wir können auch nicht wissen, dass das Gehirn die Welt konstruiert. Wir wissen dann ja nicht einmal, dass es Gehirne gibt, geschweige denn, wie diese funktionieren. Wenn aber der Konstruktivismus dabei bleibt, über den Konstruktionsprozess etwas zu wissen, dann verstrickt er sich in einen Widerspruch.

Aber vielleicht wird mit diesem Einwand dem Konstruktivismus aus realistischer Perspektive etwas unterstellt, das er gar nicht behauptet oder nicht notwendigerweise behaupten muss. Auf jeden Fall gibt es eine Reihe von Möglichkeiten, es nicht zu einem Widerspruch kommen zu lassen. Allerdings muss man dann diskutieren, ob diese widerspruchsfreien Interpretationen den Konstruktivismus noch als eine überzeugende Auffassung erscheinen lassen.

Drei Lösungsmöglichkeiten, die naheliegend erscheinen, sind diese: *Erstens* kann man zugestehen, auch über den realen Konstruktionsprozess nichts wissen zu können. *Zweitens* kann man die antirealistische These auf einen Teil der Welt beschränken und den Teil der Welt, der den Konstruktionsprozess betrifft, von der These ausnehmen. *Drittens* kann man die antirealistische These so abschwächen, dass ein gemäßigter Wissensanspruch zugestanden wird.

Die *erste* Lösungsmöglichkeit besteht darin, dass der Konstruktivismus auch für die Aussagen, die er über den Konstruktionsprozess macht, keinen Wissensanspruch erhebt. Ein Autor, der von dieser Lösung Gebrauch macht und dies ganz deutlich ausspricht, ist z. B. der Sozialpsychologe Kenneth Gergen (Gergen 1999). Er legt zunächst ausführlich dar, wie im Alltag und in der Wissenschaft Wirklichkeit konstruiert wird. Dabei beruft er sich auf die Spätphilosophie Wittgensteins. Nach Gergen konstruieren die Menschen ihre Wirklichkeiten, indem sie *Sprachspiele* und *Lebensformen* entwickeln. Aus dieser Sicht sind Aussagen weder wahr noch falsch im Sinne des Realismus. Die Aussage „Die Erde ist rund und nicht flach" sei weder wahr noch falsch im Sinne einer Übereinstimmung mit dem, was real existiert. Es sei nur eben praktischer, das Sprachspiel „runde Erde" zu spielen, wenn wir z. B. mit dem Flugzeug von Kansas nach Köln fliegen. Das Sprachspiel „flache Erde" sei dagegen nützlicher, wenn wir uns innerhalb von Kansas selbst bewegen. Weiterhin sei es nicht schlechthin wahr, dass die Welt aus Atomen besteht. Doch sei das Atom-Sprachspiel in der Physik außerordentlich nützlich. Wir könnten auch mit vollem Recht sagen, dass der Mensch tatsächlich eine Seele besitzt, sofern wir uns innerhalb des Sprachspiels befinden, das man „Religion" nennt. Und auch der Ausdruck „Dies ist wahr" selbst macht nur Sinn innerhalb bestimmter Sprachspiele. Menschliche Gemeinschaften konstruieren sich jeweils ihre Welten. In einer solchen kann es Atome, eine Seele, Götter usw. geben oder auch nicht.

Dies hat nun für den *Sozialkonstruktivismus* eine enorme politische Konsequenz. Wenn man eingesehen hat, dass unsere Auffassungen nicht schlechthin wahr oder falsch sind, wird mit einem Male klar, dass wir die Freiheit besitzen, die Welt so oder so zu konstruieren. Und wenn jemand darauf beharrt, dass die Welt aber objektiv so oder so beschaffen sei, dann sollte man stets die Frage aufwerfen: Wem dient diese angeblich objektive Auffassung? Welche Interessen stehen dahinter? Und was wird durch die Beschreibung, die einige durchsetzen wollen, ausgelassen? (Gergen 1999, 39f)

Im Schlusskapitel seines Buches stellt Gergen dann an die Leser die rhetorische Frage, ob er denn nun selber behaupten würde, dass all das wahr und gerechtfertigt sei, was er über soziale Konstruktion gesagt habe. Und er antwortet: nein; denn wenn er das behaupten würde, dann würde er ja genau den Fehler machen, den er den Realisten vorwerfe. Auch das, was er selbst über gesellschaftliche Konstruktionsprozesse ausgeführt habe, sei vorgebracht ohne Anspruch auf Wahrheit und Rechtfertigung. Begriffe wie „real", „wahr", „rational" und „gerechtfertigt" seien verzichtbar, und sie seien auch schädlich, denn sie würden dazu verwendet, Macht über andere auszuüben, den jeweils eigenen Standpunkt gegenüber anderen durchzusetzen, Dialoge abzubrechen und letztes Endes dazu, andere zu unterdrücken (Gergen 1999, 228ff).

Was den letzten Punkt betrifft, so hängt Gergen, wie mir scheint, einem verbreiteten Missverständnis an, das wohl schwer zu beseitigen ist. Zwei Dinge werden hier verwechselt: 1) einen Wahrheitsanspruch zu erheben, und 2) den Anspruch zu erheben, selbst im alleinigen Besitz der Wahrheit und somit unfehlbar zu sein. Nur Letzteres ist geeignet, Dialoge zu beenden und andere Meinungen zu unterdrücken. Sobald wir Anderen das gleiche Recht zugestehen, ihre Behauptungen mit Wissensanspruch vorzubringen und für sie zu argumentieren, tritt das von Gergen beschriebene Problem gar nicht auf (Gadenne 2004, 176).

Aber kommen wir zurück auf die These Gergens, er würde auch für die eigenen konstruktivistischen Thesen keinen Anspruch auf Wahrheit und Rechtfertigung erheben. Was ist dann sein Ziel als Autor seines Buches? Sein Ziel sei es, die Leser einzuladen, an der gemeinsamen Konstruktion der Welt teilzunehmen, ohne dabei die anderen zu bevormunden. Der Konstruktivismus sei nicht eine Lehre, die beansprucht, wahr oder gerechtfertigt zu sein, er ähnele eher einer Einladung zum Tanz, zum Spiel, zum Gespräch oder zu einer Lebensform.

Doch warum sollte man dann dieser Einladung folgen? Schließlich gibt es auch andere Einladungen, gemeinsam die Welt zu verändern, darunter diejenigen von religiösen Fundamentalisten. Ist es aus konstruktivistischer Sicht beliebig, welcher Einladung man folgt?

Hierauf würde Gergen vermutlich erwidern, dass die von ihm vorgeschlagene Lebensform, im Unterschied zu vielen anderen, dazu geeignet sei, die Welt gerechter zu machen und das Leben der Menschen zu verbessern. Wenn er allerdings so argumentieren würde, dann hätte sein Argument nur dann Gewicht, wenn er für seine Prämissen einen Anspruch auf Wahrheit und Rechtfertigung erheben würde, und dies wäre inkonsistent mit seiner Lehre.

Ich habe diese Version des Sozialkonstruktivismus als Beispiel dafür genannt, das Selbstwiderspruchsproblem dadurch zu umgehen, dass man auch für die eigenen Aussagen über den Konstruktionsprozess keinen Wissensanspruch erhebt. Diese Lösung hat den Preis, dass sich der Konstruktivismus dadurch selbst jegliche argumentative Überzeugungskraft nimmt. Wenn es keinen Grund zu der Annahme gibt, dass sich die gesellschaftliche Konstruktion tatsächlich so vollzieht, wie es dargelegt wird, dann gibt es auch keinen Grund, irgendwelche Folgerungen daraus zu akzeptieren. Insbesondere fällt dann der Grund für die antirealistische These gänzlich weg.

Freilich kann man die antirealistische These dennoch akzeptieren, aus anderen Gründen oder ohne Gründe. Der Konstruktivismus wäre dann aber eine merkwürdige Erkenntnistheorie, die zunächst eine Geschichte erzählt, aus dieser gewisse Folgerungen zieht, um am Ende zuzugestehen, dass die anfängliche Geschichte gar nichts dazu beitragen kann, die Folgerungen als glaubwürdig zu erweisen. Auch wäre bei dieser Interpretation überhaupt nicht zu verstehen, warum manche Richtungen des Konstruktivismus ihre Besonderheit und das Neue an ihrem Ansatz darin erblicken, dass sie sich, im Unterschied zur traditionellen Erkenntnistheorie, auf die Wissenschaften zu stützen suchen, z. B. auf die Neurobiologie. Denn diese Wissenschaften können ja keine Stützung leisten, sobald angenommen wird, dass ihre Resultate keinen Rechtfertigungsanspruch erheben können.

Der zweite Lösungsvorschlag besteht darin, den Konstruktionsprozess aus dem Bereich herauszunehmen, über den gesagt wird, dass wir über ihn nichts wissen könnten. Man behauptet hier also z. B.: Über die reale Welt können wir nichts wissen, mit einer Ausnahme; wir können immerhin dies wissen, dass Personen ihre jeweilige Wirklichkeit konstruieren, und wie sie dies tun.

Hierbei kann man daran anknüpfen, dass sich viele Debatten über den Realismus ohnehin nur auf einen Teilbereich der Welt beziehen. Es gibt die Realismusdebatte über die Universalien, über mathematische Gegenstände oder über theoretische Entitäten. Nehmen wir z. B. die Kontroverse zwischen dem *wissenschaftstheoretischen Realismus* und dem *Instrumentatlismus*. Es ist widerspruchsfrei möglich, eine Position zu vertreten, die etwa Folgendes besagt: Wissenschaftler konstruieren durch ihre Aussagen, Formeln und Modelle solche theoretischen Entitäten wie Elementarteilchen oder physikalische Kräfte. Von diesen theoretischen Entitäten kann nicht sinnvoll behauptet werden, dass sie existieren. Sie spielen nur die Rolle von Konstrukten innerhalb von Theorien, die sich zum Zweck der Vorhersage und zum Erstellen von Technologien als erfolgreich erweisen können. Doch auch wenn Theorien großen Erfolg haben, wird nicht angenommen, dass ihre theoretischen Begriffe auf etwas Reales referieren.

Die Wissenschaftler selbst hingegen, ihre Handlungen, ihre Labors und Geräte werden hierbei als real aufgefasst, und es wird angenommen, dass es möglich ist, über deren Tätigkeit etwas zu wissen, z. B. indem man mit den Methoden der Soziologie und der Ethnomethodologie erforscht, wie Wissenschaftler ihre theoretischen Wirklichkeiten konstruieren.

Es scheint allerdings, dass die meisten Richtungen des Konstruktivismus diesen Lösungsweg nicht gehen können, da sie ihre antirealistische These durchaus nicht auf den Bereich der theoretischen Entitäten beschränken wollen, sondern sie auch auf die Welt des Erfahrbaren beziehen. Dann stellt sich aber das besagte Widerspruchsproblem erneut ein.

Der Konstruktivismus beispielsweise, der die Welt für eine Konstruktion des Gehirns hält, behauptet, dass wir nichts über die reale Welt außerhalb des Gehirns wissen könnten. Wenn dies zutreffen würde, so wäre es aber kaum zu begreifen, wie wir überhaupt wissen können, dass wir ein Gehirn haben und was sich darin abspielt. Es erscheint kaum durchführbar, das Wissen über das Gehirn von dem Wissen über die übrige Welt abzutrennen und Ersteres zu beanspruchen, Letzteres dagegen zu bestreiten.

Für einen Konstruktivismus, nach dem die Konstrukteure Personen sind, ergibt sich ein vergleichbares Problem. Nach dieser Auffassung sind die Entitäten im Bereich des Physischen, aber auch die im Bereich des Psychischen und des Sozialen gleichermaßen als konstruiert anzusehen, d. h. als etwas, von dem wir nicht annehmen dürfen, dass es real so existiert und so beschaffen ist, wie es uns erscheint und von uns beschrieben wird. Wenn also z. B. die Sozialwissenschaften davon sprechen, dass es soziales Handeln, soziale Rollen, soziale Positionen und

Institutionen gibt, so muss all dies auf die konstruierte Wirklichkeit bezogen werden und nicht auf die reale Welt.

Diese Sicht müsste nun, gemäß dem zweiten Lösungsvorschlag, auf alle Bereiche der Welt angewendet werden, mit Ausnahme der Aussagen, die davon handeln, wie Personen Wirklichkeit konstruieren. Diese Aussagen hätten erkenntnistheoretisch einen Sonderstatus, sie wären so zu interpretieren, dass sie sich auf reale Personen und Konstruktionsprozesse beziehen.

Diejenigen Handlungen, die mit Konstruktionsprozessen zu tun haben, sind aber mit dem übrigen Handeln von Personen eng verbunden. Wie könnte es überzeugend begründet werden, dass wir über reales Konstruktionshandeln etwas wissen können, nichts dagegen über das reale übrige Handeln bzw. über die gesamte übrige soziale Realität. Allgemein kann man vermuten, dass dieser zweite Lösungsweg keine Aussicht auf Erfolg hat, wenn die Objekte und Ereignisse, die zum Konstruktionsgeschehen gehören, denjenigen ähnlich sind, von denen gesagt wird, dass wir über ihre reale Beschaffenheit nichts wissen könnten, oder wenn sie mit diesen verbunden sind. Letzteres dürfte aber fast immer der Fall sein.

Bei dem zitierten Beispiel des Instrumentalismus scheint die Unterscheidung zweier Bereiche, zu denen eine unterschiedliche erkenntnistheoretische Einstellung empfohlen wird, plausibler zu sein. Aber auch hier hat sich das Problem einer Abgrenzung als sehr hartnäckig herausgestellt. Wo genau verläuft die Grenze zwischen den beobachtbaren realen Dingen und den theoretischen Entitäten, von denen wir niemals gerechtfertigt urteilen dürfen, dass sie existieren? Wenn man zur Beobachtung Instrumente zulässt, so verschiebt sich die Grenze mit der technischen Entwicklung ständig, und es ist kaum abzusehen, wo sie künftig einmal liegen wird.

Lässt man andererseits nur die Beobachtung mit dem normalsichtigen Auge ohne technische Hilfsmittel zu, so erweist sich diese Abgrenzung als überaus willkürlich und problematisch. Danach wären z. B. kleine Lebewesen, die man zwar nicht mit bloßem Auge, doch sehr gut unter dem Mikroskop sehen kann, nicht als real einzustufen. Ist dies plausibel? Man versteht die Funktionsweise des Mikroskops so gut, dass es kaum begründet erscheint, die Wahrnehmung mit diesem Hilfsmittel erkenntnistheoretisch ganz anders zu interpretieren als die Wahrnehmung mit dem bloßen Auge. Im Einzelnen gibt es hierzu eine Menge an Abgrenzungsvorschlägen. Eingehend diskutiert worden ist derjenige von van Fraassen (1980), der Teil seines *konstruktiven Empirismus* ist, und der von instrumentalistischen Auffassungen übernommen werden könnte. Doch auch gegen diesen gibt es gewichtige Einwände. Alan Musgrave hat in den Ausführungen van Fraassens einen Widerspruch nachweisen können, der dem Widerspruch ähnlich ist, von dem dieser Vortrag handelt (vgl. Musgrave 1999, 116). Ich kann jedoch hier nicht weiter auf die Problematik der Interpretation wissenschaftlicher Theorien eingehen und komme zum allgemeinen Konstruktivismus zurück. Hierzu meine ich gezeigt zu haben, dass es sehr schwierig sein dürfte, den zweite Lösungsweg zu gehen und plausibel zu begründen, dass man über die Konstruktion der Welt etwas wissen kann, während man über die übrige reale Welt nichts wissen kann.

Ich komme nun zu dem dritten Lösungsversuch. Der Konstruktivismus könnte in Bezug auf das Konstruktionsgeschehen einen mäßigen Erkenntnisanspruch erheben, und die antirealistische These so abschwächen, dass sie mit diesem mäßigen Erkenntnisanspruch, vereinbar ist. Man kann etwa die antirealistische These so verstehen, dass sie sich nur gegen einen sehr starken Wissensanspruch richtet, etwa gegen eine Position, die eine völlig sichere Erkenntnis der Realität für möglich hält. Der Konstruktivismus könnte dann für sich selbst einen bescheideneren Wissensanspruch erheben und diesen auf die gesamte Realität einschließlich des Konstruktionsgeschehens beziehen.

Ein Autor, der diesen Weg beschritten hat, ist z. B. der Konstruktivist Gerhard Roth (vgl. Roth 1994). Ich weiß nicht, ob Roth diese Auffassung heute noch vertritt, aber das spielt für das Folgende keine Rolle. Wenn er sie nicht mehr vertritt, dann kann seine frühere Auffassung dennoch dazu dienen, diesen dritten Lösungsvorschlag zu illustrieren. Roth stellt in seinem Buch „Das Gehirn und seine Wirklichkeit" zunächst ausführlich dar, wie sich das menschliche Gehirn in der Evolution entwickelt hat, wie es funktioniert und wie im Detail die Prozesse aussehen, die an der Konstruktion der Wirklichkeit beteiligt sind. In den letzten Kapiteln des Buches geht er dann auf die philosophischen Probleme ein und wirft die Frage auf, ob denn nicht auch das Gehirn selbst bzw. der ganze Konstruktionsprozess, von dem das Buch handelt, nur der Erscheinungswelt angehört. Und er bejaht diese Frage: Das Gehirn und der Konstruktionsprozess, mit dem sich die Wissenschaft befasst, gehöre der Erscheinungswelt an, nicht der Realität. (Roth nennt die Erscheinungswelt auch die „Wirklichkeit", im Unterschied zur Realität.) Das Erscheinungs-Gehirn könne nun aber nicht dasjenige sein, das die Konstruktion macht, stellt Roth weiter fest. Die Konstruktion mache vielmehr das reale Gehirn. Über dieses könnten wir aber nichts wissen.

Wie kommt man aus diesem Dilemma heraus? Nachdem er das Problem lange hin und her gewendet hat, ringt sich Roth zu der Entscheidung durch, bedingt doch auch über das reale Gehirn bzw. den realen Konstruktionsprozess etwas aussagen zu können. Man dürfe die Aussagen über die Erscheinungswelt bedingt auf die Realität übertragen. Ein Konstruktivismus, der dies völlig bestreite, gehe zu weit, er sei zu radikal.

Wie soll man sich das näher vorstellen? Roth schreibt: „Obwohl erkenntnistheoretisch die Realität vollkommen unzugänglich ist, muss ich erstens ihre Existenz annehmen, um nicht in elementare Widersprüche zu geraten." (Roth 1994, 321) Und er fährt fort, dass es auch erlaubt sei, sich Gedanken über die

Beschaffenheit der Realität zu machen, und zwar zu dem Zweck, „die Phänomene *in meiner Wirklichkeit* besser erklären zu können. Ich darf nur keine objektive Gültigkeit hierfür beanspruchen."

Roth fragt weiter, was er denn für die Aussagen in seinem Buch, die ja, wie er nun zugibt, auch vom realen Gehirn und realen Konstruktionsprozess handeln müssen, beanspruchen könne. Es sei nicht „objektive Gültigkeit", sondern, „gehobene Ansprüche an Plausibilität und interne Konsistenz" (Roth 1994, 326).

Es wird leider nicht ganz klar, was in diesem Zusammenhang die Begriffe „objektive Gültigkeit" und „gehobene Ansprüche an Plausibilität" genau bedeuten. Aber wenn sie überhaupt etwas zur Problemlösung beitragen sollen, dann müssen sie wohl dazu dienen, so etwas wie einen *bescheidenen Erkenntnisanspruch* auch für Aussagen über die Realität zu erheben. Ich interpretiere sie so: Unter „objektiver Gültigkeit", die für Roth nicht erreichbar ist, versteht er, dass eine Aussage in sehr hohem Maße gerechtfertigt ist, dass sie als sicher, oder als fast sicher gelten kann. Die Formulierung „gehobene Ansprüche an Plausibilität" meint dagegen etwas Schwächeres, etwa, dass es rational gerechtfertigt erscheint, eine Aussage vorläufig zu akzeptieren bzw. sie den konkurrierenden Hypothesen vorzuziehen. Als geeignete Rechtfertigungsgründe nennt Roth die Erklärungsleistung. Wenn eine Hypothese A, die sich auf die Realität bezieht, die Phänomene der Erscheinungswelt besser erklären kann, als eine andere Hypothese B, dann sei es gerechtfertigt, Hypothese A vorläufig vorzuziehen. Dies entspricht dem bekannten Prinzip, das man den *Schluss auf die beste Erklärung* nennt.

Wenn es so gemeint ist, dann resultiert daraus eine akzeptable Auffassung. Diese dritte Lösung erscheint überzeugender als die beiden ersten. Aber ist sie eigentlich von einer realistischen Position zu unterscheiden? Wenn aus konstruktivistischer Sicht ein Realismus in Frage gestellt werden soll, so wird diesem oft ein sehr hoher Erkenntnisanspruch unterstellt, wie es z. B. durch den Vorwurf ausgedrückt wurde, der Realismus würde meinen, er könne den Gottesstandpunkt einnehmen. Dass sich ein derartiger Realismus als nicht haltbar erweist, ist klar. Doch wird er in neuerer Zeit von kaum jemandem vertreten. Heutige realistische Positionen sind in der Regel mit einer fallibilistischen Auffassung von Erkenntnis verbunden. Als Kriterium für die gerechtfertigte Akzeptanz einer Aussage wird nicht ihre völlige Sicherheit verlangt, sondern etwas Schwächeres, z. B., dass die Aussage nach bestimmten Regeln geprüft wurde und der Prüfung bisher standgehalten hat. Wenn Realismus so verstanden wird, dann würde sich ein Konstruktivismus, wie ihn Roth vorschlägt, von einem fallibilistischen Realismus gar nicht unterscheiden – jedenfalls nicht in dem Punkt, der den Wissensanspruch über die Realität betrifft.

Wenn der Konstruktivismus diesen dritten Lösungsweg aber nicht akzeptiert, dann bleibt es bei der grundlegenden Differenz hinsichtlich der Realitätserkenntnis: Der Realismus hält sie für möglich, der Konstruktivismus bestreitet sie kompromisslos. Dann bleibt es allerdings dabei, dass der Konstruktivismus mit dem aufgezeigten Widerspruchsproblem weiterhin konfrontiert ist, für das es meines Erachtens im Rahmen der konstruktivistischen Annahmen keine plausible Lösung gibt.

Literaturverzeichnis

Boghossian, Paul (2013): *Angst vor der Wahrheit. Ein Plädoyer gegen Relativismus und Konstruktivismus*. Frankfurt am Main: Suhrkamp.
Gadenne, Volker (2004): *Philosophie der Psychologie*. Bern: Huber.
Gergen, Kenneth J. (1999): *An Invitation to Social Construction*. London: Sage.
Goodman, Nelson (1978): *Ways of Worldmaking*. Indianapolis: Hackett Publishing.
Goodman, Nelson (1980): „On Starmaking". In: *Synthese* 45, 211–215.
Miller, David (1994): *Critical Rationalism: A Restatement and Defence*. Chicago: Open Court.
Musgrave, Alan (1999): *Essays on Realism and Rationalism*. Amsterdam: Rodopi.
Putnam, Hilary (1987): *The Many Faces of Realism*. La Salle: Open Court.
Roth, Gerhard (1994): *Das Gehirn und seine Wirklichkeit*. Frankfurt am Main: Suhrkamp.
Searle, John R. (1997): *Die Konstruktion der gesellschaftlichen Wirklichkeit. Zur Ontologie sozialer Tatsachen*. Reinbek bei Hamburg: Rowohlt.
van Fraassen, Bas (1980): *The Scientific Image*. Oxford: Clarendon Press.
von Glasersfeld, Ernst (1995): „Die Wurzeln des ‚Radikalen' am Konstruktivismus". In: Fischer, Hans R. (Hg.): *Die Wirklichkeit des Konstruktivismus*. Heidelberg: Auer, 35–45.
Wendel, Hans J. (1990): *Moderner Relativismus*. Tübingen: Mohr Siebeck.

Olaf Hoffjann
Die Wahrheitsspieler. Strategische Kommunikation als Spiel

Abstract: Strategic communication plays are 'in between' and their messages have a paradox character. The paper identifies these paradoxes using the example of truth. On the one hand, a basic doubt in the possibilities of recognizing and in absolute concepts such as truth is a condition for entering a strategic communication play. On the other hand, truth is implicitly or explicitly alleged in these situations. And, finally, strategic communication plays can – despite the 'great doubt' – have in medium term at least such an effect that descriptions are recognized as truth. The paper describes the epistemological questions from a non-dualistic perspective (Mitterer 1992, 2001). Thereto, the concept of the strategic communication play is developed with the help of the play term used by Bateson (1956, 1985) and of the frame analysis (Goffman 1980).

Keywords: play, non-dualism, strategic communication

Bei Preisverhandlungen gibt es keinen objektiv richtigen Preis. Der Preis ergibt sich daraus, zu welchem Preis der Verkäufer bereit ist zu verkaufen und welchen Preis der Interessent zu bezahlen bereit ist. Während der Verkäufer die Qualität des gehandelten Gutes anpreist („Etwas Besseres werden Sie nirgends finden ..."), kann der Interessent auf die Verzichtbarkeit des Kaufes verweisen („Eigentlich muss ich jetzt nicht kaufen ..."). Wenn beide Seiten die Instrumentalisierbarkeit all dieser Argumente gegenseitig unterstellen, kann daraus eine paradoxe Situation entstehen: Die Argumente begründen einen spezifischen Preis, ohne einen spezifischen Preis zu begründen.

In einem Gespräch mit einer Journalistin versucht eine Pressesprecherin, Gerüchte zu Korruptionsfällen in dem Unternehmen zu entkräften. Um die Vertrauenswürdigkeit ihrer Aussagen zu unterstreichen, kann sie versuchen, besonders verbindlich aufzutreten, Widersprüche zu vermeiden, unterstützende Meinungen bzw. Erfahrungen Dritter zu benennen usw. Die Journalistin kann all dies akzeptieren oder aber versuchen, durch Nachfragen Widersprüche zu finden, die Pressesprecherin zu verunsichern oder weitere Indikatoren wie die Bewertung der Stimme zur Einschätzung der Vertrauenswürdigkeit zu nutzen. Wenn beide Seiten die Instrumentalisierbarkeit all dieser Vertrauenswürdigkeitsindikatoren gegenseitig unterstellen, kann daraus eine paradoxe Situation entstehen: Die Indikatoren bezeichnen Vertrauenswürdigkeit, ohne Wahrhaftigkeit zu bezeichnen.

Solche Alltagssituationen werden mitunter als Geplänkel bezeichnet, das das Deutsche Wörterbuch definiert als „leichtes Gefecht, scharmützel, bei dem vereinzelt bald hier bald dort Schüsse fallen" (Grimm/Grimm 1854–1971). Solche Situationen erscheinen momenthaft unverbindlich, obwohl sie in einem verbindlichen Gesamtkontext eingebettet sind. Sie erscheinen momenthaft folgenlos, obwohl sie die zu treffende Entscheidung beeinflussen (können). Und sie erscheinen momenthaft leicht, obwohl sie oft mit großem Ernst betrieben werden. Solche Situationen sollen in diesem Beitrag als strategische Kommunikationsspiele bezeichnet werden.

In solchen strategischen Kommunikationsspielen geht es zumeist um die Wahrheit. Sie nimmt dabei eine vermeintlich widersprüchliche Rolle ein. Zunächst ist ein grundsätzlicher Zweifel an den Möglichkeiten des Erkennens und an absoluten Konzepten wie Wahrheit die Voraussetzung für den Beginn eines solchen Geplänkels. Dennoch werden in diesen Situationen Wahrhaftigkeit bzw. Wahrheit implizit oder explizit behauptet. Und schließlich können strategische Kommunikationsspiele trotz des ‚großen Zweifels' mitunter zumindest mittelfristig eine solche Wirkung entfalten, dass Beschreibungen als Wahrheit ausgeflaggt werden.

In dem Beitrag sollen diese erkenntnistheoretischen Fragen aus einer nondualistischen Perspektive (Mitterer 1992, 2001) beschrieben werden. Dazu muss zunächst das Konzept des strategischen Kommunikationsspiels mit Hilfe eines unterscheidungstheoretischen und paradoxiehaltigen Spielbegriffs in Anlehnung an Bateson (1956, 1985) und eingebettet in die Rahmenanalyse von Goffman (1980) entwickelt werden.

1 Unterscheidungstheoretischer und paradoxiehaltiger Spielbegriff

In Abgrenzung zur mathematisch-ökonomischen Spieltheorie hat Bateson seit den 50er Jahren (Bateson 1956, 1985) ein Spielverständnis entwickelt, das als unterscheidungstheoretischer und paradoxiehaltiger Spielbegriff bezeichnet werden kann (vgl. Baecker 1999, 144). Dieses Verständnis hat er am Beispiel von spielenden Affen herausgearbeitet: „Das spielerische Zwicken bezeichnet den Biss, aber es bezeichnet nicht, was durch den Biss bezeichnet würde." (Bateson 1985, 244) Und allgemeiner: „Diese Handlungen, in die wir jetzt verwickelt sind, bezeichnen nicht, was jene Handlungen, für die sie stehen, bezeichnen würden." (Bateson 1985, 244). Die Besonderheit eines Spieles wird deutlich, wenn man die Unterschiede zwischen einem Kampf und einem spielerischen Kämpfen herausarbeitet. In einem Kampf bezeichnet ein Biss eine Aggression. Beim spielerischen Kämpfen kommt mit der Mitteilung ‚Das ist ein Spiel!' eine zweite Ebene hinzu, da ein Kampf imitiert wird: Ein Zwicken bezeichnet einen Biss, ohne ein Biss zu sein. Damit verbindet ein Spiel das ‚Leichte' und das ‚Ernste' miteinander. Der Verweis auf die Unverbindlichkeit des Spiels (‚Ist ja nur ein Spiel!') ermöglicht z. B. ein momenthaft folgenloses Austesten und Probieren. Durch die Imitation (das Zwicken imitiert einen Biss) bezieht sich das Spiel auf den ‚Rest der Welt' und ermöglicht damit einen Lerntransfer (vgl. Abb. 1).

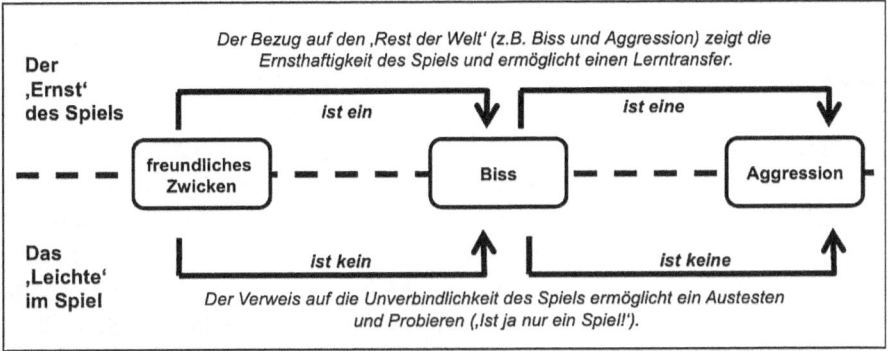

Abb. 1: Die Paradoxie des Spielverständnisses von Bateson (erweitert nach Neuberger 1992, 78)

Ein solches Spielverständnis weist nicht nur Anschlussmöglichkeiten an das bis heute vielfach aufgegriffene Spielverständnis von Huizinga auf (Huizinga 1956, 37), sondern auch an die Sprachspiele von Wittgenstein: Sprachspiele sind für ihn eine ganz zentrale Form des Umgangs mit Bedeutungen, die unabhängig von der Realität und kontextgebunden sind (vgl. PU §43; Römpp 2010, 95, 98; Baecker 1999, 144).

So sehr dieses Spielverständnis das Spielerische in den Vordergrund rückt, so betont Bateson zugleich auch immer wieder die Relevanz von Regeln, die ein Spiel strukturieren. Damit wird die Notwendigkeit deutlich, das Spiel sozialtheoretisch einzubetten. Dies soll mit Hilfe der handlungstheoretischen Rahmenanalyse von Goffman unternommen werden (Goffman 1980, 52). Goffman entwickelt mit seiner Rahmenanalyse einerseits das Rahmenkonzept von Bateson weiter (vgl. Willems 1997, 62f), andererseits knüpft er direkt an das Spielverständnis von Bateson an (vgl. Goffman 1980, 52). Ausgangspunkt seiner Überlegungen sind Rahmen (frames), unter denen er die Definition für Ereignisse und für die persönliche Anteilnahme an diesen gemäß gewisser Organisationsprinzipien versteht (vgl. Goffman 1980, 19). Da man in der Regel immer mehrere Rahmen gleichzeitig anwendet, liefert der primäre Rahmen die Antwort auf die Frage, welcher Rahmen momentan im Vordergrund steht: „Was geht hier eigentlich vor?" (Goffman 1980, 35). Die Eigenschaften des Rahmens sind meist nicht bewusst und können auch nicht annähernd vollständig beschrieben werden – was aber nicht verhindert, dass man ihn mühelos und vollständig anwendet (vgl. Goffman 1980, 31). Preisverhandlungen oder Interviews sind Beispiele für primäre Rahmen, die eine soziale Situation definieren und handlungsentlastend wirken.

Spiele verortet Goffman auf der Ebene von so genannten Moduln, die auch als sekundäre Rahmung bezeichnet werden können (vgl. Lauer/Handel 1977, 414; Willems 1997, 52). Moduln sind „ein System von Konventionen, wodurch eine bestimmte Tätigkeit, die bereits im Rahmen eines primären Rahmens sinnvoll ist, in etwas transformiert wird, das dieser Tätigkeit nachgebildet ist, von den Beteiligten aber als etwas ganz anderes gesehen wird" (Goffman 1980, 55). Spiele sind ein Beispiel für das Modul des So-Tun-als-ob, die eine offene Nachahmung oder Ausführung einer weniger transformierten Handlung ist und bei der alle Beteiligten wissen, dass es zu keinerlei praktischen Folgen kommt (vgl. Goffman 1980, 60). Bei Modulationen wird u. a. vorausgesetzt, dass die Beteiligten wissen und offen aussprechen, dass eine systematische Umwandlung erfolgt ist, die das, was in ihren Augen vor sich geht, grundlegend neubestimmt (vgl. Goffman 1980, 57).

Zur Beschreibung des Spiels arbeitet Goffman die spieltheoretischen Überlegungen von Bateson aus und entwickelt Regeln bzw. Voraussetzungen, wenn ernsthaftes, wirkliches Handeln in etwas Spielerisches transformiert werden soll: Dazu zählen u. a. die Ausführung der spielerischen Handlung in einer Weise, dass ihre gewöhnliche Funktion nicht verwirklicht wird, das Übertreiben der Expansivität mancher Handlungen, die Vielzahl an Wiederholungen sowie ein Abweichen der Handlungsabfolge: „Die Handlungsabfolge, die als Vorbild dient, wird weder genau befolgt noch vollständig ausgeführt, sondern wird angefangen und abgebrochen, neu begonnen, kurz unterbrochen und mit Abfolgen aus anderen Zusammenhängen vermischt." (Goffman 1980, 53) Damit konkretisiert Goffman die spieltheoretischen Überlegungen von Bateson nicht nur, sondern bettet sie auch in einen größeren sozialtheoretischen Rahmen ein. Modulationen und damit Spiele ermöglichen es Individuen, typische Handlungsverläufe zu verändern (vgl. Miebach 2010, 128) und damit nicht zuletzt ein Lernen.

2 Strategische Kommunikationsspiele

Strategische Kommunikationsspiele können als Alltagsspiele in Wettkampfsituationen verstanden werden. Strategische Kommunikation wird hier verstanden als bewusster Versuch, Verhalten durch Zeichen zu beeinflussen (vgl. Schönbach 2009, 26) bzw. mit Habermas als Kommunikationshandlung, in der „der Aktor Mittel und Zwecke unter Gesichtspunkten der Maximierung von Nutzen bzw. Nutzenerwartung wählt und kalkuliert" (Habermas 1999, 127). Da der strategische Kommunikationscharakter das definierende Element ist, interessieren hier nur Kommunikationssituationen, in denen allen Beteiligten der strategische Charakter bewusst ist – wie z. B. in einer Preisverhandlung. Ein verdecktes strategisches Handeln im Sinne Habermas wird hier folglich nicht berücksichtigt.

Genau diese Unterstellung des strategischen Charakters einer sozialen Situation führt dazu, dass man Täuschungen wenn schon nicht unterstellt, so doch zumindest als möglich erachtet. Mit diesem „Unglaubwürdigkeitsstigma" (Willems 2007, 231) muss jede Form strategischer Kommunikation rechnen.

Damit können strategische Kommunikationsspiele auf Basis des entscheidungstheoretischen und paradoxiehaltigen Spielbegriffs wie folgt definiert werden: *Beide Seiten nehmen (a) die Kontingenz und damit die Instrumentalisierbarkeit von Argumenten bzw. Indikatoren an. Zudem unterstellen sie, dass (b) die andere Seite es ebenfalls annimmt und (c) dass beide Seiten es der Gegenseite unterstellen. Diese Kontingenz bzw. die Unverbindlichkeit der Situation – und damit der Spielcharakter – werden in der Regel allenfalls implizit thematisiert bzw. mitgeteilt.* In der einleitend beschriebenen Interviewsituation betreiben die Akteure mithin ein Spiel mit der Vertrauenswürdigkeit und mit den Vertrauenswürdigkeitsindikatoren. Sie nutzen und testen Vertrauenswürdigkeitsindikatoren, die Vertrauenswürdigkeit bezeichnen und wiederum nicht bezeichnen, die wiederum Wahrhaftigkeit bezeichnen sollen – und wiederum nicht bezeichnen.

In der hier beschriebenen Form ist das strategische Kommunikationsspiel ein zweiseitiges Spiel, das folglich von beiden Seiten als solches interpretiert und betrieben wird. Von einem einseitigen Spiel kann gesprochen werden, wenn nur ein Akteur die Kontingenz der Indikatoren unterstellt, zugleich aber unterstellt, dass der andere Akteur dies nicht tut. Der Spieler kann solche Situationen in eingeschränkter Form als Spiel betreiben – er sollte es nur nicht zu offensichtlich tun, um die andere Seite nicht zu irritieren.

So unterschiedlich und vielfältig strategische Kommunikationssituationen sind, so unterschiedlich und vielfältig sind auch strategische Kommunikationsspiele. Während bislang ein strategisches Kommunikationsspiel immer am Beispiel einer Kommunikationssituation von zwei Anwesenden beschrieben wurde, können auch massenmedial vermittelte strategische Kommunikationsspiele betrieben werden. Dazu zählt zum Beispiel die Mediawerbung, in der sowohl die Werbetreibenden als auch ihre Publika die Ausblendungsregel (Schmidt/Spieß 1994, 18) und damit die Kontingenz von Argumenten und Vertrauenswürdigkeitsindikatoren gegenseitig unterstellen.

Zudem werden viele strategische Kommunikationsspiele öffentlich vor einem Publikum betrieben – zum Beispiel in Politik-Talkshows. Mit Goffman (vgl. Goffman 1980, 176) kann dies als weitere Transformation einer Transformation konzipiert werden. Nachdem im ersten Schritt eine politische Debatte (zeitweise) in ein strategisches Kommunikationsspiel transformiert wurde, wird hier ein strategisches Kommunikationsspiel in die öffentliche Aufführung eines strategischen Kommunikationsspiels, das eine politische Debatte imitiert, transformiert. Pointierter formuliert: Die Politiker führen ein Spiel auf. Die öffentliche Aufführung verändert ein strategisches Kommunikationsspiel in gleichem Maße wie ein Nicht-Spiel. Das ‚In-Szene-Setzen' – verstanden als kalkuliertes Auswählen, Organisieren und Strukturieren von Darstellungsmitteln, um eine beabsichtigte Publikumswirkung zu erzielen (vgl. Ontrup/Schicha 1999, 7) – der eigenen Person und der Argumente ist in beiden Fällen in vergleichbarer Weise zu beobachten. Im Gegensatz zum Theaterpublikum sind bei den Zuschauern von Politk-Talkshows die Rezeptionsmodi deutlich heterogener. Insbesondere kann hier zwischen einem naiven und aufgeklärten Rezeptionsmodus unterschieden werden. Ein naives Publikum glaubt an die Kraft der Argumente und der Vertrauenswürdigkeitsindikatoren und unterstellt, dass dies die diskutierenden Politiker ähnlich sehen. Ein aufgeklärtes Publikum hingegen unterstellt sowohl den Inszenierungs- als auch den Spielcharakter. Eine vergleichbare Unterscheidung haben Paus-Haase und Hasebrink (vgl. Paus-Haase/Hasebrink 2001, 147) bei ihrer Untersuchung zur Rezeption von Daily Talks getroffen: Bei der naiven Rezeption wird das Geschehen in der Talkshow als Abbildung der Realität verstanden, während bei der reflektierten Rezeption Inszenierungsmuster hinterfragt und durchschaut werden.

3 Strategische Kommunikationsspiele und Wahrheit

3.1 Der ‚große Zweifel' als Voraussetzung strategischer Kommunikationsspiele

Wenn strategische Kommunikationsspiele so definiert wurden, dass beide Seiten die Kontingenz und damit die Instrumentalisierbarkeit von Argumenten bzw. Indikatoren unterstellen, dann wird deutlich, dass Alltagsrealisten nicht in der Lage sind, strategische Kommunikationsspiele zu betreiben. Zur Erläuterung dieser Hypothese soll im Folgenden ein strategisches Kommunikationsspiel in einer prozessorientierten Perspektive beschrieben werden (vgl. Tab. 1).

Die einleitend skizzierte Situation ist von beiden Akteuren als strategische Kommunikationssituation in der Form des Nicht-Spiels definiert: Die Pressesprecherin möchte ihre Lesart so darstellen, dass die Journalistin sie glaubt. Und sie unterstellt der Journalistin, dass diese ihr genau dies unterstellt sowie ihr zusätzlich unterstellt, dass sie dies der Journalistin unterstellt. Umgekehrt gelten diese Unterstellungsvermutungen für die Journalistin. Diese „Strukturvermaschung" (Merten 1977, 166) macht das weitere Gespräch zu den Korruptionsgerüchten nicht leichter. Die Journalistin hat ihre Zweifel und die Pressesprecherin versucht, diese Zweifel durch eine vertrauenswürdige Darstellung auszuräumen.

Tab. 1: Der Übergang vom Nicht-Spiel zum Spiel in einer strategischen Kommunikationssituation

Nicht-Spiel	Übergang	Strategisches Kommunikationsspiel	Übergang	Nicht-Spiel
Möglicher Ausgangspunkt: Dissens zur Wahrhaftigkeit einer Beschreibung	Mit zunehmender Dauer wird es wahrscheinlicher, dass den Akteuren die Kontingenz z. B. von Vertrauenswürdigkeitsindikatoren bewusst wird. Dieses „Tasten im Dunkeln" (Flusser 1993, 20) ist die Voraussetzung für ein strategisches Kommunikationsspiel.	Beide Seiten nehmen (a) die Kontingenz und damit die Instrumentalisierbarkeit von Argumenten bzw. Indikatoren an. Zudem unterstellen sie, dass (b) die andere Seite es ebenfalls annimmt und (c) dass beide Seiten es der Gegenseite unterstellen. Diese Kontingenz bzw. die Unverbindlichkeit der Situation – und damit der Spielcharakter – werden in der Regel allenfalls implizit thematisiert bzw. mitgeteilt.	Der Übergang ist geprägt von dem Problem, dass irgendwann eine Entscheidung getroffen werden muss.	Nach dem Spiel wird eine Entscheidung z. B. zur Wahrhaftigkeit der Beschreibung getroffen. Der Spielverlauf beeinflusst, determiniert aber nicht diese Entscheidung.

Der Übergang zum strategischen Kommunikationsspiel ist mit einem wachsenden Zweifel und einer zunehmenden Ratlosigkeit verbunden. Um die Wahrscheinlichkeit von Vertrauenswürdigkeitszuschreibungen zu erhöhen, können Vertrauenswürdigkeitsindikatoren wie z. B. eine konsistente Darstellung, Stimme oder das Anführen unabhängiger Dritter genutzt werden (vgl. ausführlich Hoffjann 2013). All diese Indikatoren können aber vom Wahrhaftigen wie vom Lügner in gleichem Maße genutzt werden und verlieren damit ihre Funktion als zuverlässige Indikatoren. Wenn dies in solchen Situationen erkannt wird, kommt es zum ‚großen Zweifel'. Flusser beschreibt dies im historischen Kontext:

> Bei dieser Schilderung fällt vor allem ein fortschreitender Vertrauensverlust auf, eine sich verdichtende ‚Krise des Glaubens'. Nach seinem Austritt aus der ihn konkret angehenden Welt hat sich der Mensch zuerst auf seine Hände verlassen. Dann kontrollierte er die Hände mit seinen Augen. Dann traute er seinen Augen nicht mehr und kontrollierte sie mit Fingern und Ohren. Jetzt aber traut er auch den Fingern und Ohren nicht mehr und tastet im Dun-

keln herum, um überhaupt etwas herauszufinden. Und dieses Tasten im Dunkeln nennt er ‚spielen'. (Flusser 1993, 19f)

Ähnlich konstatiert Bolz: „Nicht nur erkenntnistheoretisch, sondern auch sozialpsychologisch sind wir heute offenbar bereit, die große Lektion der Gegenaufklärung zu lernen: Es geht nicht ohne Fälschung." (Bolz 2005, 102) Wenn jemand seinen Fingern und Ohren nicht mehr traut oder Fälschung unterstellt, wird aus einem Alltagsrealisten momenthaft ein Alltagskonstruktivist. Ein Alltagskonstruktivist geht zwar von der Dualität von konstruierter Wirklichkeit und einer beschreibungsunabhängigen Realität aus, zweifelt aber an den Möglichkeiten des Erkennens. Er hinterfragt in der Situation seine Beobachtungen, schlimmstenfalls kann es zu einer „lähmenden Dauerreflexion" (Schmidt 2008, 45) kommen. Da in strategischen Kommunikationssituationen naturgemäß zwei divergierende Meinungen bzw. Weltbilder aufeinandertreffen, erhöht dies die Wahrscheinlichkeit der Einsicht in die Kontingenz. Strategische Kommunikation trägt als Kontingenztreiberin mithin dazu bei, dass selbst ‚eingefleischte' Alltagsrealisten immer häufiger momenthaft zu Alltagskonstruktivisten werden (vgl. Tab. 2).
Welche Sinnhaftigkeit haben strategische Kommunikationssituationen noch, wenn beide Akteure den ‚Boden unter den Füßen' verlieren, weil sie nicht mehr wissen, was sie glauben können oder sollen? Im Grunde könnten Verhandlungen und Interviews hier beendet werden – und sie werden es in einigen Fällen vermutlich auch. Wenn nicht, spricht viel dafür, dass die Akteure ein strategisches Kommunikationsspiel beginnen.

Der *Übergang* zum Nicht-Spiel ist von der Frage geprägt, dass insbesondere die Journalistin irgendwann die Frage beantworten will, ob sie der Pressesprecherin glaubt. Diese Entscheidung wird in der beschriebenen Situation wiederum im Nicht-Spiel bzw. nach Ende des Gesprächs getroffen. Der Spielverlauf beeinflusst, determiniert aber nicht diese Entscheidung.

3.2 Der Wahrheitsanspruch strategischer Kommunikationsspiele

Strategische Kommunikationsspiele können als Wahrheitsspiele verstanden werden, weil jeder Akteur trotz der unterstellten Kontingenz den eigenen Wahrheitscharakter implizit oder explizit behauptet und darauf zielt, dass sich die eigene Sichtweise durchsetzt. Denn nach dem Spiel muss eine Entscheidung zu einem Wirklichkeitsmodell getroffen werden: Die Journalistin selbst muss die Darstellung der Pressesprecherin nicht glauben. Sie muss aber glauben können, dass ihre Leser es glauben könnten. Im Idealfall setzt sich das Wirklichkeitsmodell

Tab. 2: Alltagsrealisten und Alltagskonstruktivisten in nicht-strategischen und strategischen Kommunikationssituationen

	Alltagsrealist	Alltagskonstruktivist
Nicht-strategische Kommunikation	– Realität kann erkannt werden. – Kommunikationsprobleme gehen zurück auf Inkompetenz, Hinterhältigkeit, Verrücktheit o. ä. (vgl. Krippendorf 1994, 87)	– Unzugänglichkeit der ‚Realität' – Kommunikationsprobleme sind alltäglich und werden durch die gemeinsame Suche nach der Definition einer Situation, eines Begriffs etc. gelöst.
Strategische Kommunikation	– Möglichkeit 1: Selbstbeschreibungen sind direkt überprüfbar. – Möglichkeit 2: Die instrumentalisierten Vertrauenswürdigkeitsindikatoren, mit denen die Wahrscheinlichkeit von Vertrauenswürdigkeitszuschreibungen erhöht werden sollen, können überprüft werden. – Mögliche Ergebnisse: (a) Man glaubt es; (b) Vorwurf der Lüge	– Die mitgeteilten wünschenswerten Wirklichkeiten (vgl. Merten 1992, 44) sind kontingent und nicht überprüfbar. – Auch die instrumentalisierten Vertrauenswürdigkeitsindikatoren, mit denen die Wahrscheinlichkeit von Vertrauenswürdigkeitszuschreibungen erhöht werden sollen, sind nicht überprüfbar. – Mögliche Konsequenz: Beginn eines strategischen Kommunikationsspiels

im Sinne Mitterers (vgl. Mitterer 1992, 71f) mittelfristig als konsensuell und damit nicht mehr oder kaum noch ernsthaft hinterfragt durch. Wie Spiele allgemein so können auch strategische Kommunikationsspiele mithin als „Zwischen" (Adamowsky 2000, 26) charakterisiert werden, als „Schwebezustände zwischen Wirklichkeit und Unwirklichkeit" (Baecker 1999, 141), die sich zwar der Leichtigkeit einer fiktiven Situation erfreuen, aber den Ernst am Horizont haben, da sie auf das ‚ernste' Leben verweisen.

Im Gegensatz zum Spieler ist ein Nicht-Spieler als Alltagsrealist von der objektiven Richtigkeit von Argumenten und Indikatoren überzeugt. Für ihn geht es immer ‚ums Ganze', um das Absolute, um *die* Wahrheit. Das Risiko einer solchen Perspektive ist offenkundig: Wenn beide Seiten von der ‚objektiven' Richtigkeit ihrer Perspektive überzeugt sind, werden sie dem Gegner eine Lüge oder krankhafte Züge unterstellen. Das ist die beste Voraussetzung für ein Scheitern einer Verhandlung: Denn wer will schon gerne von einem Lügner über den Tisch gezogen werden?

Hingegen ermöglicht die Unverbindlichkeit strategischer Kommunikationsspiele den Akteuren ein Austesten und Üben von Argumenten und Vertrauenswürdigkeitsindikatoren. Ähnlich wie Affen beim spielerisches Kämpfen etwas für den ‚richtigen' Kampf lernen, können in strategischen Kommunikationsspielen Vertrauenswürdigkeitsstrategien getestet und eingeübt werden.

3.3 Wie verändern strategische Kommunikationsspiele Wahrheit?

Wie verändern strategische Kommunikationsspiele Wahrheit? Diese Frage soll im Folgenden auf einer non-dualistischen Grundlage (Mitterer 1992, 2001) beantwortet worden. *Wirklichkeit* soll mit Mitterer als die Summe aller Beschreibungen *so far* verstanden werden, also der jeweils letzte Stand der Dinge (Mitterer 1992, 110). Jede neue Beschreibung ändert die Wirklichkeit um eben diese Beschreibung. Dies gilt selbst dann, wenn sie nicht als breiter Konsens aufgefasst wird. Wenn Beschreibungen weitgehend konsensuell sind – also nicht mehr oder kaum noch ernsthaft hinterfragt werden –, wird aus ihnen so etwas wie eine neutralistische Ausgangsbasis bzw. ein Basiskonsens für weitere Beschreibungen (Mitterer 1992, 71 ff). Dies kann auch als *Wahrheit* bezeichnet werden. Dazu zählen Auffassungen, „die wir vertreten müssen, um in unserer Gesellschaft überleben zu können" (Mitterer 2001, 106). Ein solches Wahrheitsverständnis unterstreicht auch noch einmal die soziale Funktion von Wahrheit. Menschen geht es bei der Wirklichkeitskonstruktion letztlich weniger um Wahrheit im klassischen Sinne, sondern vielmehr um Gewissheit im Sinne sozial anerkannter Darstellungen und Deutungen (vgl. Westerbarkey 2000, 215). Hinsichtlich *Wahrhaftigkeit* und *Lüge* gibt es in non-dualistischer Lesart im Grunde keinen relevanten Unterschied zur realistischen und konstruktivistischen Perspektive. Eine Lüge definiert Mitterer wie folgt: „Du redest anders, als ich denke, dass du denkst." Und Wahrhaftigkeit entsprechend: „Ich rede so, wie ich denke." (Mitterer 2001, 66)

Wie können strategische Kommunikationsspiele auf dieser erkenntnistheoretischen Basis Wahrheit verändern? Diese Frage soll für zwei Formen strategischer Kommunikationsspiele erörtert werden.

In *(a) direkten strategischen Kommunikationsspielen* determiniert der Spielverlauf zwar nicht die anschließend zu treffende Entscheidung, sie beeinflusst sie aber durchaus. Wenn in dem beschriebenen Beispiel die Pressesprecherin elegant und souverän Einwände der Journalistin pariert, ist zu vermuten, dass es der Journalistin am Ende schwer fallen wird, die Pressesprecherin der Lüge zu bezichtigen – und umgekehrt. Je nach Spielverlauf wird sie die Version der Pressesprecherin in ihrem Bericht also vermutlich als Wahrheit oder Lüge bzw. in abgeschwächter Form als wahrscheinlich oder unwahrscheinlich bewerten, obwohl sie selbst die Kontingenz der Beschreibung unterstellt. Je wichtiger das journalistische Medium ist, desto wahrscheinlicher ist es, dass diese Beschreibung mittelfristig als Wahrheit ausgeflaggt wird.

In *(b) massenmedial vermittelten strategischen Kommunikationsspielen* wie der Werbung wird die enorme Wirkkraft von strategischen Kommunikationsspielen trotz ihres vermeintlich unverbindlichen Charakters noch deutlicher. So besteht die Kunst der Werbung ja gerade darin, bislang irrelevante bzw. unbekannte Verkaufsargumente zu behaupten und zu penetrieren, bis sie irgendwann vom Publikum, das ja um die Ausblendungsregel weiß, geglaubt werden. Was hat das Rauchen einer Zigarette mit Abenteuer zu tun? Nach jahrzehntelanger Rezeption der *Marlboro*- und *Camel*-Werbung erscheint dies heute für viele ganz und gar selbstverständlich. Obwohl man um die Ausblendungsregel bzw. die Kontingenz der Argumente und damit den Spielecharakter weiß, gelingt es Werbung offenkundig mitunter, Produkten Eigenschaften bzw. Nutzen zuzusprechen, die ihnen ursprünglich nicht zugeschrieben wurden. Anschlussfähig sind hier Erkenntnisse der kommunikationswissenschaftlichen Kultivierungsthese von Gerbner (Gerbner/Gross 1976), die u.a. belegen konnte, dass die regelmäßige Rezeption von fiktionalen TV-Programmen das Wirklichkeitsverständnis beeinflusst. Hier könnten zudem Aspekte von Kommunikationsspielen eine Rolle spielen, die bislang noch nicht erwähnt wurden: Strategische Kommunikationsspiele haben auch einen unterhaltenden Charakter, der dazu führen kann, dass kognitive Filter unterlaufen werden: Die Werbung möchte unterhalten, spielt mitunter mit ihrer eigenen Unglaubwürdigkeit und schafft so zumindest Sympathie bei ihren Publika. Und die Journalistin mag die Version der Pressesprecherin für wenig wahrscheinlich halten, aber das gemeinsame Spielen ist etwas Verbindendes, dass ein positives Urteil zumindest wahrscheinlicher werden lässt.

4 Fazit

Strategische Kommunikationsspiele sind ein „Zwischen" (Adamowsky 2000, 26) und ihre Mitteilungen haben ein paradoxen Charakter. Diese Paradoxie ist in dem Beitrag am Beispiel der Wahrheit herausgearbeitet worden. Einerseits ist ein grundsätzlicher Zweifel an den Möglichkeiten des Erkennens und an absoluten Konzepten wie Wahrheit die Voraussetzung für den Eintritt in ein strategisches Kommunikationsspiel. Andererseits werden in diesen Situationen Wahrhaftigkeit bzw. Wahrheit implizit oder explizit behauptet. Und schließlich können strategische Kommunikationsspiele trotz des ‚großen Zweifels' mitunter zumindest mittelfristig eine solche Wirkung entfalten, dass Beschreibungen als Wahrheit ausgeflaggt werden. Gerade diese potenziellen Wirkungen zeigen den Bezug strategischer Kommunikationsspiele zum ‚Ernst des Lebens'. Strategische Kommunikationsspiele sind eine Möglichkeit, in Konfliktsituationen zusammen zu finden: „Der Mensch benötigt die Wahrheit nicht um der Erkenntnis willen, sondern aus sozialen Motiven. Die ‚Wahrheit' ist ein anderes Wort für die Notwendigkeit, dass sich Menschen auf etwas einigen müssen, wollen sie halbwegs friedlich zusammenleben." (Liessmann 2005, 10) Das zärtliche Festhalten an den durchschauten Illusionen ermöglicht uns, geselliger, politisch handlungsfähiger und auch glücklicher zu werden (vgl. Pfaller 2005, 232).

Für die strategische Kommunikationsforschung zeigen sich insbesondere zwei Aspekte. Obwohl insbesondere die Philosophie den Konstruktionscharakter menschlicher Wahrnehmungen bereits seit vielen Jahrhunderten beschreibt, ist es bislang allenfalls ein Randthema gewesen, welche Konsequenzen sich für soziale Interaktionen ergeben, wenn Akteuren die Einsicht in die Kontingenz von Beschreibungen und damit verbunden der Vertrauenswürdigkeitsindikatoren bewusst wird. Wie verändert der ‚große Zweifel' Alltagssituationen, in denen aus Alltagsrealisten Alltagskonstruktivisten werden? Mit der Theorie strategischer Kommunikationsspiele ist ein Erklärungsrahmen vorgestellt worden, in dem der ‚große Zweifel' der Ausgangspunkt ist. Es spricht viel dafür, dass es zunehmend mehr aufgeklärte Akteure gibt: Der ‚große Zweifel' ist nicht mehr nur auf akademische erkenntnistheoretische Diskussionen beschränkt, sondern hat nach den Feuilletons auch Stammtischgespräche erreicht. Nicht zuletzt professionelle strategische Kommunikatoren wie PR und Werbung haben mit ihren sich widersprechenden Beschreibungen dazu beigetragen, dass die Einsicht kontingenter Wirklichkeitsbeschreibungen heute weit verbreitet ist. Das führt dazu, dass auch die Zahl strategischer Kommunikationsspiele deutlich zunehmen wird.

Literaturverzeichnis

Adamowsky, Natascha (2000): *Spielfiguren in virtuellen Welten*. Frankfurt am Main: Campus.
Baecker, Dirk (1999): *Die Form des Unternehmens*. Frankfurt am Main: Suhrkamp.
Bateson, Gregory (1956): „The message ‚This is play'". In: Schaffner, Bertram (Hg.): *Group Processes: Transactions of the Second Conference, October 9–12.1955, Princeton*. New York: Josiah Macy, Jr. Foundation, 145–242.
Bateson, Gregory (1985): *Ökologie des Geistes. Anthropologische, psychologische, biologische und epistemologische Perspektiven*. Frankfurt am Main: Suhrkamp.
Bolz, Norbert (2005): *Blindflug mit Zuschauer*. München: Wilhelm Fink Verlag.
Flusser, Vilem (1993): *Lob der Oberflächlichkeit. Für eine Phänomenologie der Medien*. Mannheim: Bollmann.

Gerbner, George; Gross, Lynne (1976): „The scary world of TVs heavy viewer". In: *Psychology Today* 4, 41–45.
Goffman, Erving (1980): *Rahmen-Analyse. Ein Versuch über die Organisation von Alltagserfahrungen.* Frankfurt am Main: Suhrkamp.
Grimm, Jacob; Grimm Wilhelm (1854–1971): *Deutsches Wörterbuch.* http://woerterbuchnetz.de/cgi-bin/WBNetz/wbgui_py?sigle=DWB&lemid=GG08173 &mode=Vernetzung&hitlist= &patternlist=&mainmode=, visited on 15 September 2015.
Habermas, Jürgen (1999): *Theorie des kommunikativen Handelns. Band 1: Handlungsrationalität und gesellschaftliche Rationalisierung.* Frankfurt am Main: Suhrkamp.
Hoffjann, Olaf (2013): *Vertrauen in Public Relations.* Wiesbaden: Springer.
Huizinga, Johan (1956): *Homo Ludens. Vom Ursprung der Kultur im Spiel.* Reinbek: Rowohlt.
Krippendorf, Klaus (1994): „Der verschwundene Bote. Metaphern und Modelle der Kommunikation". In: Merten, Klaus; Schmidt, Siegfried J.; Weischenberg, Siegfried (Hg.): *Die Wirklichkeit der Medien. Eine Einführung in die Kommunikationswissenschaft.* Opladen: Westdeutscher Verlag, 79–113.
Lauer, Robert H.; Handel, Warren H. (1977): *Social Psychology: the Theory and Application of Symbolic Interactionism.* Englewood Cliffs, NJ: Prentice Hall.
Liessmann, Konrad P. (2005): „Der Wille zum Schein. Über Wahrheit und Lüge". In: Liessmann, Konrad P. (Hg.): *Der Wille zum Schein. Über Wahrheit und Lüge.* Wien: Paul Zsolnay Verlag, 7–33.
Merten, Klaus (1977): *Kommunikation. Eine Begriffs- und Prozessanalyse.* Opladen: Westdeutscher Verlag.
Merten, Klaus (1992): „Begriff und Funktion von Public Relations". In: *PR-Magazin* 23 (11), 35–46.
Miebach, Bernhard (2010): *Soziologische Handlungstheorie. Eine Einführung.* Wiesbaden: VS-Verlag.
Mitterer, Josef (1992): *Das Jenseits der Philosophie. Wider das dualistische Erkenntnisprinzip.* Wien: Passagen.
Mitterer, Josef (2001): *Die Flucht aus der Beliebigkeit.* Frankfurt am Main: Fischer.
Neuberger, Oswald (1928): „Spiele in Organisationen, Organisationen als Spiele". In: Küpper, Willi; Ortmann, Günther (Hg.): *Mikropolitik. Rationalität, Macht und Spiele in Organisationen.* Opladen: Westdeutscher Verlag, 53–86
Ontrup, Rüdiger; Schicha, Christian (1999): „Die Transformation des Theatralischen". In: Ontrup, Rüdiger; Schicha, Christian (Hg.): *Medieninszenierungen im Wandel.* Münster: LIT, 7–18.
Paus-Haase, Ingrid; Hasebrink, Uwe (2001): „Talkshows im Alltag von Jugendlichen. Zusammenfassung der ‚Talkshow-Studie'". In: Göttlich, Udo; Krotz, Friedrich; Paus-Haase, Ingrid (Hg.): *Daily Soaps und Daily Talks im Alltag von Jugendlichen: Eine Studie der Landanstalt für Rundfunk Nordrhein-Westfalen und der Landeszentrale für private Rundfunkveranstalter Rheinland-Pfalz.* Opladen: Leske und Budrich, 137–156.
Pfaller, Robert (2005): „Das Unglaubliche. Über Illusion, Lust und Kultur". In: Liessmann, Konrad P. (Hg.): *Der Wille zum Schein. Über Wahrheit und Lüge.* Wien: Paul Zsolnay Verlag, 218–234.
Römpp, Georg (2010): *Ludwig Wittgenstein. Eine philosophische Einführung.* Köln: Böhlau.

Schmidt, Siegfried J. (2008): *Systemflirts. Ausflüge in die Medienkulturgesellschaft.* Weilerswist: Velbrück.

Schmidt, Siegfried J.; Spieß, Brigitte (1994): *Die Geburt der schönen Bilder. Fernsehwerbung aus der Sicht der Kreativen.* Opladen: Westdeutscher Verlag.

Schönbach, Klaus (2009): *Verkaufen, Flirten, Führen. Persuasive Kommunikation – ein Überblick.* Wiesbaden: VS-Verlag.

Westerbarkey, Joachim (2000): *Das Geheimnis. Die Faszination des Verborgenen.* Berlin: Aufbau.

Willems, Herbert (1997): *Rahmen und Habitus. Zum theoretischen und methodischen Ansatz Erving Goffmans: Vergleiche, Anschlüsse und Anwendungen.* Frankfurt am Main: Suhrkamp.

Willems, Herbert (2007): „Glaubwürdigkeit und Überzeugung als dramaturgische Probleme und Aufgaben der Werbung". In: Fischer-Lichte, Erika; Horn, Christian; Pflug, Isabel; Warstat, Matthias (Hg.): *Inszenierung von Authentizität.* Tübingen und Basel: Francke, 209–232.

Wittgenstein, Ludwig (1971): *Philosophische Untersuchungen.* Frankfurt am Main: Suhrkamp. [PU]

Sebastian Kletzl
Who Wants to Be a Non-Dualist and Why?

Abstract: In this paper I argue that Josef Mitterer's non-dualizing mode of discourse and Richard Rorty's ironist philosophy should team up. After an introduction (1), my starting point is the portrayal of anti-representationalism which is of central importance in Rorty's philosophical project (2). Then I argue that the non-dualizing mode of discourse is the best available way to cash out anti-representationalism (3). To close this paper I will describe a type of philosopher who will most likely be sympathetic towards such a non-dualizing project (4). Here I will make use of Rorty's ideas in calling this figure the *edifying ironist*. My claim is that edifying ironists should consider adopting the non-dualizing way of speaking and that non-dualists should consider becoming edifying ironists.

Keywords: Non-dualism, Richard Rorty, Josef Mitterer, edifying philosophy, irony

1 Introduction

Creativity is an important value in philosophy. Numerous philosophical ideas we deem to be canonical today were once unforeseen acts of imagination. This shows that philosophy is more than bureaucratic puzzle-solving and that the way the philosophical conversation goes can neither be controlled nor predicted. But it is not only a pleasure to do imaginative intellectual work, it can also be useful for society. New ideas in philosophy can directly or indirectly have great impact on our lives, for better or for worse, for example concerning the question how a driverless car shall react in precarious situations, or philosophical ideas fueling political views.

This paper is about the back and forth between a kind of imaginative undertaking and the attempt of controlling and administering the ways in which we think and speak. To be more exact it is an attempt to provide a picture of how we can understand this tension. Although this shall not imply that the other side is not equally important, I will here focus on the side of creativity and imagination. In order to do so I will bring together two of the – in my opinion – most imaginative philosophers of the last years, Richard Rorty and Josef Mitterer. The choice may seem arbitrary since Mitterer's work is much less discussed and known but I will show that there are good reasons to merge those two together. I will argue that both not only provide means for the same end but that they also do so in complementary manner. While Mitterer brings in the philosophical seriousness and accuracy, Rorty brings in a light-heartedness and a broader scope. The followers of both may profit from this conjunction.

2 Anti-Representationalism

Richard Rorty's philosophical work is as complex as it is far-fetched. He repositioned himself regularly through constant change of self-applied 'Isms'. Nonetheless we can trace one nest of ideas against which he argued at least since *Philosophy and the Mirror of Nature.* We can call this nest which – according to Rorty – held captive philosophers since Plato and which determined their self-perception ever since the 'metaphysical picture'. It says that there are philosophical problems which arise as soon as rational beings start to reflect. The answers to such problems lie in the discovery of truths which we can use to transcend our cultural limitations and get in touch with the world as it *really is*. Philosophers, as they like to see themselves provide a specific and unique method of finding, administering and correlating such truths. The metaphysical picture expresses "a desire for constraint – a desire to find 'foundations' to which one might cling, frameworks beyond which one must not stray, objects which impose themselves, representations which cannot be gainsaid" (Rorty 1979, 315). In philosophy rational beings want to find out how the world really is and not merely how things appear to us.

For various reasons Rorty opposed this self-portrayal of philosophy. The central line of argument against the metaphysical picture is what Rorty calls his anti-representationalism.[1] The metaphysical picture states that our knowledge of the world consists in accurate (inner or linguistic) representations of how things really are independent of us. However we are to understand the details, the central idea is that of representation, the idea that there is something – usually called "the world" – which has to be represented adequately by us. The way the world is dictates which representations of it are correct, that is, what is knowledge about the world and what is mere opinion.

According to anti-representationalism knowledge is not a matter of getting reality right but a matter of finding better ways to cope with the world (see Rorty 1991, 2). But how can we make sense of this claim without presupposing the idea of correct representation?

---

[1] The names vary; sometimes he calls it anti-essentialism (Rorty 1990, 50 ff) or simply holism (Rorty 1998, 105 ff). But all three aspects are part of the same philosophical move although they shed light on different things.

Anti-representationalism generalizes the anti-realist idea that statements of a certain domain do not represent reality to the claim that no part of language should be seen as representing language-independent objects. Language is better described as a worldly tool humans employ among others to be able to cope with the environment. A hammer does not represent the nail, a brake lever does not represent the slowdown of the vehicle and likewise words do not represent the world, they are not a way of representing the world as it really is but another way of modifying our environment. Put differently, anti-representationalists follow Donald Davidson in arguing that we should drop the scheme-content distinction (Davidson 1974). Language should not be conceived of as a scheme, which structures or represents a content, the undescribed world. Seen this way there is no categorical, ontological gap between descriptions and the world being described, no objects with inner essences on the one hand and language correctly depicting them on the other. Descriptions are part of the world like everything else is, hammers, apples, tables, cats and causal interactions do not belong to a fundamentally different category than light, sound, feelings, the self, concepts, sentences, social interactions. "The only difference between such interactions is that we call interactions 'linguistic' when we find it helpful to correlate the marks and noises being produced by other entities with the ones we ourselves make" (Rorty 1998, 96).[2]

This is a fundamental change of how to understand language which is why the following questions become pressing: "Why should we even seriously consider this proposal?" and second "Given we accept anti-representationalism, how should we describe what we are doing when we are using language?" I will begin with a discussion of the latter question in the next section since a relatively straight forward answer can be given.

3 Non-Dualism

Admittedly, Rorty's answers to the question of how we should formulate anti-representationalism as a serious alternative are not overly convincing because

---

[2] Note that this does not deem any talk about representation to be useless. The kind of anti-representationalism discussed here is a claim how to conceive of language in general. There is no problem with saying that in the context of a specific theory x represents y as being z or that this photograph represents a park. The central point with the latter is that we can change the representational function at will. This kind of representation is a useful tool but not a necessity which forces itself upon us "as soon as we start to reflect" (see for example van Fraassen 2008).

they are sketchy at best. I am using the plural term 'answers' because at different stages his instructions vary. Sometimes he suggests that anti-representationalists should simply deny an answer to general questions concerning how language works and change the topic. At other times he proposes to replace the talk about the representational connection between language and world by causal connections (Rorty 1990, 33) and for this purpose makes free use of Davidson's work.

I want to allude to two problems with Rorty's behavior. First, as an example of how an anti-representationalist way of talking would look like Rorty at one occasion recommends that we understand everything we talk about as being modeled on numbers. As he argues, we will not be prone to investigate the true intrinsic essence of the number seventeen and we have not found out anything essential about seventeen as it really is, independent of our talking about it if we learn to take its square root (see Rorty 1990, 52ff). When it comes to numbers, nobody thinks that our descriptions represent the number seventeen as it *really* is in its seventeenishness. We are not puzzled by the question why our way of talking about numbers is nonetheless useful. No one is tempted to say that numbers don't exist just because they are not seen as having an inner essence. Numbers are purely relational things, and according to Rorty everything else should be understood in the same way. This proposal is rather sketchy and the plausibility of the analogy needs to be backed up by arguments. Isn't it counter-intuitive to put tables and numbers on par in this manner? Aren't there important distinctions to be preserved even if we agree that neither may possess an inner essence? I think Rorty could provide us with arguments but he does not do it. Rather this is the point where he usually shifts the strategy. He claims that the anti-representationalist should simply refuse to answer general questions about the nature of reality, world, mind, language, reference and the like. So while maybe understandable from his point of view, this shift remains rather unsatisfying to many. To me it appears a sensible demand to require an argumentative basis for answering at least some of those questions, at the very least in order to persuade people to adopt an anti-representational stance.

The second problem is that in his attempts to spell out his anti-representationalism Rorty often wants to replace the representational with a causal vocabulary. While he maintains that with our language we do not stand in a representational relation to intrinsic properties of things he emphasizes that our words and sentences stand in causal relation to the world exactly like other tools. As I take it, the concept of causality and its central role have an unfortunate realist ring to it and it would prevent confusion if we were able to replace it. Also, as for example Diego Marconi has pointed out, central concepts of Rorty's anti-representationalism like "intrinsic property" and "representational relation" are not clear (see Marconi 2015, 120 ff). This makes it difficult to spot the differences between representational and causal relations as envisioned by Rorty. In my opinion, Marconi's presentation of Rorty's view is not as benevolent as one may wish, and it seems that this is in part due to the haziness in Rorty's terminology which makes it possible for critics to bring home their points all too easy.

Fortunately we can make a stronger case for anti-representationalism. There is an anti-representationalist way of speaking readily available which comes with a lot less of controversial conditions, is worked out in philosophical detail, and goes well together with what I have presented so far: the non-dualizing mode of discourse developed by Josef Mitterer. Also his work can be understood as directed against the metaphysical picture and provides us with both, an argument against representationalism and a proposal of how to talk as anti-representationalists.

The latter is what Mitterer in his *The Beyond of Philosophy* calls a non-dualizing mode of discourse. He begins his project by discussing Wittgenstein's views on aspect seeing. Take the following triangle:

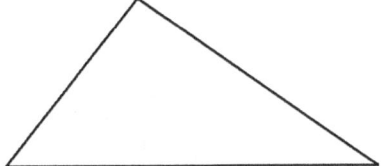

We can imagine that two different people see different aspects of it, A sees it as an arrow, B sees it as a body. It seems intuitive to say that there is one thing, the triangle that can be seen under different aspects. This sounds harmless but leads into the heart of the matter since it imposes on us a specific view of how our language works. Namely that those different aspects all have their foundation in a *real* triangle which is then seen in a certain light – the light-metaphor is very instructive.

Let's change the focus. Which of the two descriptions of the triangle can be justified? How can something be part of such a justification at all? Here a dualist – who assumes a categorical difference between undescribed world and the language we use to talk about the world – grants the undescribed, language-different object, such as the triangle itself, the central place. We are justified if our description matches the undescribed, real object. But, as Mitterer points out, it is already a description if something is described as undescribed and language-different. Even a dualist has to provide us with a *rudimentary description* of the triangle, a minimal starting point in a given situation, in order to make the triangle a part of her justification.

Here then is the problem for the dualist: If the triangle shall be the part of the undescribed world which gives rise to different descriptions, the triangle is either already given as a rudimentary description (otherwise it cannot enter our justificatory practice) or it is a Kantian thing-in-itself (which can by definition never enter our justificatory practices). "The attempt to distinguish the indicated object from the rudimentary description releases an infinite regress that always leads to further rudimentary descriptions, but not to the object 'itself'." (Mitterer 1992, §57, my translation) This infinite regress bewitches every attempt of dualizing (and hence representational) speech (see Weber 2013). A language-independent object *must* remain unrecognized and cannot play any role in justification. The dualizing mode of discourse – and thus representationalism – slides into deep conceptual problems on its own terms.

As an alternative Mitterer proposes to replace the spatial metaphors surrounding our understanding of language with temporal metaphors. Where dualism uses the dichotomy between world and language, he proposes to understand the 'object of description' and the 'description of the object' as an ever-changing ensemble: "The object of description is not description- or 'language-independent' but the part of the description that has been already carried out. *The description is not directed at the object but emanates from the object of description*; it continues the already made description, it is the continuation of the previously available description." (Mitterer 1992, §13, original emphasis, my translation) In the non-dualizing mode of discourse the term 'object of description' is therefore replaced by 'description *so far*' and the 'description of the object' by 'description *from now on*' (see also Mitterer 1999, §140).

Imagine A and B starting a discussion over how to proceed concerning the triangle given above. The description *so far* is relatively meager and consist of everything relevant that is in their shared portion of descriptions, their starting basis or *introductory description*[3] with which /the object/ is introduced into discourse, in our case /that triangle/. Both acknowledge this as the description *so far*, as a starting point for further inquiries. Then A says "That triangle is an arrow" and B says "No, that triangle is a body". Now we have two different descriptions *from now on*, the triangle as arrow or as body. A tries to mediate and says "But it can be both, a body and an arrow?!" and B agrees. Structurally the following happened: At t1 we started with an agreement, a description *so far*,

---

3 The German original reads "Angabebeschreibung" which is difficult to translate in all its meanings.

/x1/. At t2 this description *so far* was continued in two different ways in two different descriptions *from now on*, /Ax/ and /Bx/. Then, at t3, A and B both agreed to accept a mediatory description which turned into the new description *so far*, /x2/. This new description so far can again fall prey to doubt. If this happens the discussants search for the last shared agreement and evaluate how and why their descriptions began to diverge.[4] But at no point a "beyond of discourse" which is said to contain the things as they really are and which dictates what the right or true descriptions are, will be used to stop the conversation. Descriptions will follow descriptions and at the outset introduced /objects/ gain contour as the conversation goes on.

At this point a flabbergasted dualist will exclaim that the triangle has an essence, it is in a certain way, which licenses some descriptions but not others. To say otherwise would amount to language idealism, to the idea that things are nothing but descriptions (for this kind of criticism see for example Kügler 2017 in this volume). The dualist might go on: "This view has the absurd consequence that we cannot distinguish between our descriptions and the things as they are independent of our description. But there is a fundamental distinction because we aren't driving to work with our description of a car but with the car itself! And dinosaurs dominated life on earth billions of years before the first human could describe them. Dinosaurs as well as apples and tables are resistant to our descriptions, they are causally independent of them; they are *as they are* even if we do not describe them!" Usually this is also the part of the discussion in which a dualist will hit the table to show that here we have an ontologically different relation to the table as when we describe it as ugly or too big (see Rorty 1990, 55 f). Therefore non-dualism (and also anti-representationalism) is wrong because of such absurd consequences.

We find a helpful way of putting the problem and its answer in the following quotation:

> Once you describe something as a dinosaur, its skin color and sex life are causally independent of your having so described it. But before you describe it as a dinosaur, or as anything else, there is no sense to the claim that it is 'out there' having properties. *What* is out there? The thing-in-itself? The world? Tell us more. Describe it in more detail. Once you have done so, but only then, are we in a position to tell you which of its features are causally independent of having been described and which are not. If you describe it as a dinosaur, then we can tell you that the feature of being oviparous is causally independent

---

[4] It is important to note that agreement does not have the same significance as in dualistic ways of thinking and speaking. I cannot go into the details here but see (Cyzman 2017) in this volume for details.

of our description of it, but the feature of being an animal whose existence has been suspected only in recent centuries is not. (Rorty 1998, 87 f, original emphasis)

Interestingly enough these are Rorty's words. He too emphasizes that to describe something as undescribed (or as causally independent) is already a description. Only in a language game we can determine if it is part of the description of something to be causally independent. Causal independence is a part of a description and after we accepted it we will use the description in specific ways (for this point see also Rorty 1990, 56). For example, a piece of wood is not a bishop before it was put in the context of chess. Specific pieces of wood do not carry the intrinsic feature of being bishops while others are rooks and so on. Only after we described chess pieces, cars or dinosaurs, but only then, it makes sense to say that their behavior is in certain respects causally independent to the existence of human beings – wood can be burned – while in other respects it is not – you must move a bishop diagonally. If a keen constructivist argues that the existence of dinosaurs is causally dependent on there being humans, she is not able to use the concept of dinosaurs in our language game and she will have severe problems of justifying her claims concerning dinosaurs.

But if this is the case, if descriptions are part of our world in the same way as anything else is, then it becomes unclear what it means for dinosaurs or apples to exist independent of our descriptions in the sense assumed by the dualist (see Rorty 1990, 55 f and 1998, 98 ff). The only possible way to substantiate this claim is to state that dinosaurs have an intrinsic, non-descriptional core or essence which dictates what they really are, apart from being described by us. But this only means to dig in heels and insist on the dualist presupposition. In other words the situation then is that the non-dualist proposes to not make a categorical difference between world and descriptions and the dualist answers "But *I want to make such a distinction*, therefore your proposal has absurd consequences" (see Neges 2013 for discussion of this unsatisfactory dialectic).

I conclude that the non-dualizing way of speaking provides a sensible and worked out version of anti-representationalism which can be fruitfully conjoined with the scattered fragments found in Rorty's texts.

4 Edifying Irony

I want to turn to the first question mentioned above, namely "Why should we consider a non-dualizing way of speaking seriously?" Of course, no answer will amount to a reason which will, if correctly understood, by its rational force turn everyone into a non-dualist. This is why I want to reformulate the question to *"Who is likely to consider this idea seriously?"* Who would want to abandon our safe harbor of certainties and sail for vague promises? Mitterer himself gives a hint what could be the promise of a non-dualizing mode of speech: "Instead of a longing for invariance, truth, deadlock, maintenance of a status quo the non-dualizing mode of discourse longs for change and transformation." (Mitterer 1992, §97, my translation) and he says that maybe "we should prefer a nondualistic 'pursuit of change', a philosophy of alteration over a 'pursuit of truth', a philosophy which is oriented towards truth" (Mitterer 2015, §25, my translation). But why is a pursuit of change desirable especially if it involves the above described fundamental changes? Again, Mitterer gives a hint:

> The employment of the rhetoric of truth, of the conceptual instrumentation of dualistic philosophy does not help to decide in cases of conflict and to establish a 'dominance-free' discourse – but rather they are exacerbate and solidify them. Proponents and opponents of a position, of a theory have mastered this rhetoric and argumentation technique. In applying them we are lead into stalemates and argumentative dead-ends of which we can often escape only by power of interpretation and discursive violence. (Mitterer 2015, §24, my translation)

Here we see what I want to call a political or ethical reason for trying out a new way of speaking. The rhetoric of truth lead all too often into dead-ends which can only be escaped by ignoring other people's opinions or silence them by discursive or physical violence. As Mitterer hopes – as well as Rorty[5] – to swear off the idea that there is only one way the world is and one correct description of it can prevent the exhibition of discursive power and physical violence.But many philosophers, especially those fond to the idea of the importance of truth, will abnegate this claim. According to them truth does not lead to violence but unifies our inquiries and ultimately is the gateway to peace and understanding.

On both sides of this dispute we find deep rooted convictions and intuitions and I shall not even try to alter any of them. Instead I want to describe a figure which will share Mitterer's (and Rorty's) political and ethical outlook and for that reason tries to find and alternative way of discursive behavior, one that is not directed towards a *beyond of discourse*. In order for doing so I will borrow ideas from Rorty to implement an anti-representational non-dualist way of speaking into a broader philosophical outlook. In short I propose that what I will call *ed-*

---

5 Compare this to the final paragraph of Rorty's *Mirror of Nature*, where he says that the "only point on which I would insist is that philosophers' *moral concern* should be with continuing the conversation of the West, rather than with insisting upon a place for the traditional problems of modern philosophy within that conversation" (Rorty 1979, 394, my emphasis).

ifying ironists will be especially interested to try out the non-dualistic mode of discourse.

The first aspect of such a philosopher can be found in the third part of Rorty's *Philosophy and the Mirror of Nature*, the figure he calls the *edifying philosopher*. Making use of Kuhn's terminology Rorty describes progress in philosophy as the succession of normal discourses which sometimes change in revolutionary ways. For example, the normalized discourse of Aristotelian metaphysics was challenged by mechanical philosophy in a revolutionary attempt to change our metaphysical outlook. Other successors are Kant's transcendental philosophy and the linguistic turn. After some time the radical new ideas find followers and they become normalized, until enough problems and dilemmas stack up in order for a new revolution to seem worthwhile.

On a meta-level, Rorty describes another important distinction, that between systematic and edifying philosophers. Systematic philosophers – in normal or in revolutionary discourse – hope that in the end all theories and conversations can be made commensurable, that there is one set of rules, one theory about everything to be found under which every meaningful attempt to say something can be subsumed. They may disagree on the question which vocabulary this is – that of Aristotelian metaphysics, mechanistic empiricism, the analysis of language and so on – but all systematic philosophers are driven by the hope of commensuration, the hope of arriving at the one true worldview. For them the paradigm of philosophy is science and accordingly every philosophical exchange has the form of a scientific inquiry. Such philosophers usually take concepts like 'truth' or 'rationality' to be of central importance because they hope that they can be used to achieve commensuration. They will bring forward arguments to the effect that all philosophical discourse needs to be rational to be significant and responsible and that rational discourse needs the idea of truth because the idea of one world which has an inner essence seems to ensure the possibility of commensuration.

Edifying philosophers are skeptical concerning the idea of commensuration and its philosophical worth. They are on the periphery of mainstream philosophy by mocking traditional problems and traditional attempts to answer them. On a more positive note they also propose new topics of philosophical interest. What differentiates them from revolutionary systematics is that edifying philosophers are not tempted to establish their newly introduced problems as a new normalized discourse which finally will be the true one. They do not strive for commensuration at all. If their revolutionary discourse normalizes they will again become its commentators. In other words they are commenting and discussing problems of the normal discourse to show that alternatives are possible, that we may well take different problems seriously. Their leading idea is that of an ongoing conversation, not of scientific inquiry which finally terminates at a true theory. Her aim is not to reduce, to commensurate all discourse to one true discourse but her goal is the growth of more and more possibilities.[6]

While the central goal of systematic philosophers is commensuration, the goal of an edifying philosopher is to show that the last word has not been spoken, that new ideas cannot be suppressed by the status quo, that commensuration cannot be achieved by force. Such philosophers will argue against the idea that the world has a unifying inner essence which we have to correctly represent with language and they will take concepts like rationality and truth as mere attempts to stop the conversation with an argumentative abort. They argue against the idea that there exists something which dictates and forces us to talk in specific ways. Their ideal is not correct representation of a language-different world but to find better ways of coping with our environment, with ourselves and others.

It is important to note that Rorty emphasizes that this edifying view *only* has its place in contrast to systematic philosophy (see Rorty 1979, 365 f and also Rorty 1989, 87 f, for a similar relation between metaphysicians and ironists). Systematic philosophers provide the material for the edifying philosopher to reflect upon and react to. Edifying philosophers try not to become systematic, they do not want to establish a normal discourse or replace older ones but try to add further possibilities to the conversation. But they also take their point of departure from well established, normalized ways of description and try to engage in arguments and persuasion in – from the systematic viewpoint – radical, revolutionary ways. Such an edifying view depends crucially on the systematic viewpoint since one cannot have a (sane) conversation all for oneself. Without systematic conversational partners the edifying critique would become useless and self-contradictory. Take away the systematic philosopher and the edifying commentator would sooner or later produce the same claim of absoluteness she seeks to prevent. In order for preventing the establishment of a normalized discourse we need someone who tries to establish it. But with every attempt to establish a new theory the edifying philosopher will be there to remember us how human, all too human those world-views are and that alternatives are possible.

As mentioned earlier, Rorty argues that our ideal of philosophical practice should not be science but a conversation. When such a conversation concerns the most fundamental philosophical beliefs it will depend on what Rorty calls a person's "final vocabulary" (see Rorty 1989, 73). This is, what she can accept

---

[6] It seems that Paul Feyerabend is the arch-example of such an edifying philosopher but I cannot go into details here because of limitations of space.

as descriptions so far concerning her own fundamental beliefs. "It is 'final' in the sense that if doubt is cast on the worth of these words, their user has no noncircular argumentative recourse. Those words are as far as she can go with language; beyond them there is only helpless passivity or a resort to force." (Rorty 1989, 73) Rorty's philosophical paragon at this point is what he calls the *ironist*. An edifying philosopher has an ironic relationship to her own final vocabulary if she constantly puts it under scrutiny and tries to be open for change and growth. No belief in her web of beliefs is save from revision, in other words, she is also an edifying commentator of her own final vocabulary.

Since her goal is not truth, not a match of the *real* world and her descriptions she strives for something else. She is aware of the plethora of descriptions by many different people in different times and places which are coagulated in philosophical as well as in literary and poetic works. This awareness turned her into a thoroughgoing historicist. Given this, the only goal such an ironist can imagine as being worth pursuing is that of making creative use of the thought material provided so far and being open minded for future prospects from now on.

An *edifying ironist* hopes that no absolutization of a discourse will ever be successful but that there is an ongoing growth of possibilities and – this is the important point – she embodies this hope in her philosophical behavior. I want to allude to three aspects. First, it shows in her never ending attempt to adopt the language of a given discourse, to be its commentator, and show by its own means that other ways of thinking and acting are possible. She reminds us that what has been said here and now is not true once and for all (see Mitterer 1999, §159). Second, it shows in laying her focus not on getting reality right but on possible future achievements, not on knowledge but on the hope to be more interesting and to live in a more interesting world in the future. Third, it is embodied in her refusal to use conversation-stoppers such as 'truth' or a 'beyond of discourse' and to engage in ongoing conversation without them. When pressed hard enough concerning the question why she holds her final vocabulary, she will respond by shrugging and saying something like "Well, I have exhausted the justifications; I have reached bedrock, and my spade is turned" (PI §217). But she will not try to anchor it in a beyond of discourse, in the way the things are which made her to come to belief what she does.

Non-dualism is a good way of exhibiting this behavior since it is a view designed against deadlock and dogmatization. Non-Dualists are interested in proposing new problems instead of clinging to the old ones come what may. As Mitterer puts it: "This problematization [of dualistic presuppositions, S.K.] leads to a shift in problems. The point is no longer to propose new solutions for the same, traditional problems but to make new problems attractive." (Mitterer 1999, §23). Moreover non-dualism can be understood as a position which shall keep the conversation going, it is not about normalizing a discourse and establish it as the one true theory. Again Mitterer: "The 'pursuit of change' shall not be established as a new paradigm, its aim is to prevent the establishment of paradigms." (Mitterer 2015, §25, my translation) Therefore a non-dualistic way of speaking might be a good modus operandi for an edifying ironist.

But maybe there is also a reason for convinced non-dualists to become ironists in this sense? Edifying irony provides an answer to the question what could be our goal if we decline truth to be the end of discourse. According to edifying ironists we should aim at self-creation and the attempt to wave our web of beliefs in the most interesting ways. We could be interesting, instead of right. It seems to me that this provides a fruitful outlook for non-dualists for at least two reasons. First, as Katharina Neges argues in a Rortyan spirit, ontological questions arise only given dualistic presupposition and that within "the non-dualizing mode of discourse one may [...] leave such questions undecided in a relaxed manner." (Neges 2013, 164) To be an edifying ironist could help to develop such a relaxed attitude towards questions that seemed to be of central importance for decades. Second, it equips the non-dualist with a positive aim apart from criticizing dualistic presuppositions. Correct representation of the world beyond our descriptions as goal is replaced by producing ever more interesting descriptions of the world and ourselves, by becoming more interesting persons.

On a final note I want to consider how the dispute between dualists and non-dualists looks for an edifying ironist. Supposedly both sides argue that the other side should change their final vocabulary accordingly – the systematic dualist because his own view represents how things really are; the edifying, ironistic non-dualist because her view promises interesting future achievements. The problem is indeed fundamental: Should truth be the goal of all our longing or should we strive for the ability to produce more interesting descriptions? In a stalemate on such a fundamental level arguments lose most of their power because they presuppose a shared final vocabulary, an agreement over desirable aims and sensible ends. A change at this point will not be brought about by one master argument but by many arguments, discussed in many conversations combined with attempted persuasion by pointing to future prospects. Such change does not happen all too often, usually we stick to ideas we have come to love and philosophers are not different. All an edifying ironist has to say at this point is: keep the conversation going, listen to each other and hope for the best!

Acknowledgements: I want to thank Katharina Neges for extended discussion and critical remarks throughout the process of writing this paper. Also I want to thank Josef Mitterer for his help in questions of translation which unwittingly turned into philosophical discussions more than once.

References

Cyzman, Marzenna (2017): "On the Non-Dualizing Rhetoric. Some Preliminary Remarks". In: Kanzian, Christian; Mitterer, Josef; Neges, Katharina; Kletzl, Sebastian (eds.): *Realism – Relativism – Constructivism*. Proceedings of the 38th Ludwig Wittgenstein Symposium. Berlin: De Gruyter.
Davidson, Donald (1974): "On the Very Idea of a Conceptual Scheme". In: *Proceedings and Addresses of the American Philosophical Association* 47, 5–20.
Kügler, Peter (2017): "Ontological Relativism as Transcendental Nominalism". In: Kanzian, Christian; Mitterer, Josef; Neges, Katharina; Kletzl, Sebastian (eds.): *Realism – Relativism – Constructivism*. Proceedings of the 38th Ludwig Wittgenstein Symposium. Berlin: De Gruyter.
Marconi, Diego (2015): "Minimaler Realismus". In: Gabriel, Markus (ed.): *Der Neue Realismus*. Frankfurt am Main: Suhrkamp, 110–130.
Mitterer, Josef (1992): *Das Jenseits der Philosophie. Wider das dualistische Erkenntnisprinzip*. Wien: Passagen.
Mitterer, Josef (1999): *Die Flucht aus der Beliebigkeit*. Klagenfurt: Drava Verlag.
Mitterer, Josef (2015): "Wahrheit oder Problemlösung? Welchen Stellenwert hat Wahrheit in den Wissenschaften?". In: Österreichische Forschungsgemeinschaft (ed.): *Wahrheit in den Wissenschaften*. Wien/Köln/Weimar: Böhlau Verlag, 30–43.
Neges, Katharina (2013): "Non-Dualism and World: Ontological Questions in the Non-dualizing Mode of Discourse". In: *Constructivist Foundations* 8 (2), 158–165.
Rorty, Richard (1979): *Philosophy and the Mirror of Nature*. Princeton: Princeton University Press.
Rorty, Richard (1989): *Contingency, Irony, and Solidarity*. Cambridge: Cambridge University Press.
Rorty, Richard (1990): *Philosophy and Social Hope*. London: Penguin Books.
Rorty, Richard (1991): *Objectivity, Relativism and Truth. Philosophical Papers Vol. I*. Cambridge: Cambridge University Press.
Rorty, Richard (1998): *Truth and Progress. Philosophical Papers Vol. III*. Cambridge: Cambridge University Press.
van Fraassen, Bas (2008): *Scientific Representation*. Oxford: Oxford University Press.
Weber, Stefan (2013): "Non-dualism, Infinite Regress Arguments and the 'Weak Linguistic Principle'". In: *Constructivist Foundations* 8 (2), 148–157.
Wittgenstein, Ludwig (2009): *Philosophical Investigations*. London: Blackwell. [PI]

Albert Müller
Jean Piaget und die Erfindung von Radikalem Konstruktivismus und Kybernetik Zweiter Ordnung

Abstract: It is not unusual to associate the rise of Radical Constructivism and Second Order Cybernetics. For example Ranulph Glanville equalized the two terms in his formula "Radical constructivism = Second order cybernetics".

The works of Jean Piaget were absorbed by three (co)founding fathers of Radical Constructivism, namely Ernst von Glasersfeld, Heinz von Foerster and Ranulph Glanville and gained massive influence since the early seventies. While von Glasersfeld coined the term Radical Constructivism, von Foerster and Glanville spelled out many of its implications.

Von Foerster quotes Piaget since 1973/74 in his discussions concerning cognition and the construction of reality. Also in the work of von Glasersfeld Piaget took a key role. Piaget's work stands at the very beginning of his Radical Constructivism. Also Glanville's dissertation, which was concerned with the concept of 'object' took many hints from Piaget's works on the constancy of objects.

Keywords: Radical Constructivism, Cybernetics, Jean Piaget, Heinz von Foerster, Ernst von Glasersfeld, Ranulph Glanville

Im Jahr 1987 wurde im deutschsprachigen Raum der Begriff des Radikalen Konstruktivismus einem breiteren akademischen Publikum gewissermaßen schlagartig bekannt. Der damals an der Universität Siegen forschende und lehrende Literaturwissenschaftler, Philosoph und Erkenntnistheoretiker Siegfried J. Schmidt publizierte einen Sammelband mit dem Titel „Der Diskurs des Radikalen Konstruktivismus" (Schmidt 1987) in einer der damals unangefochten führenden Wissenschaftsreihen „suhrkamp taschenbuch wissenschaft"[1]. Dieser Band hatte bald mehrere Auflagen. Weitere Bände sollten, einer klugen Publikationsstrategie folgend, erscheinen (Schmidt 1992), darunter auch eine Reihe von Übersetzungen, zum Beispiel zentraler Arbeiten von Heinz von Foerster (1993), Ernst von Glasersfeld (1996), Humberto R. Maturana (1998), Francisco Varela oder Gregory

---

[1] Siehe dazu die prägnanten Bemerkungen bei (Felsch 2015).

Bateson (1985, 1987) und anderen.[2] In den 1990er Jahren sodann war Radikaler Konstruktivismus durchaus so etwas wie eine intellektuelle Mode im deutschsprachigen Raum, auch die Zeitschrift „Delfin" erschien als Jahrbuch bei Suhrkamp. Konferenzen, bei denen Protagonisten des Radikalen Konstruktivisten vortrugen, hatten nicht selten viele Hunderte Besucherinnen und Besucher. Dieser Erfolg in der Theorielandschaft ging Hand in Hand mit dem Erfolg der Systemtheorie Luhmann'scher Prägung. Auch Niklas Luhmann initiierte im Übrigen Übersetzungen, so zum Beispiel eine Sammlung von Artikel des englischen Kybernetikers und Konstruktivisten Ranulph Glanville (Glanville 1988)[3], viele Jahre bevor eine englischsprachige Ausgabe dessen Werke publiziert werden konnte (Glanville 2009, 2012a, 2014).

Wenigstens zwei Jahrzehnte dauerte die Erfolgsgeschichte des Radikalen Konstruktivismus im deutschsprachigen Raum an. Heute scheint seine Popularität reduziert, wenn nicht gar gebrochen, er ist eher ein Thema für Spezialistinnen und Spezialisten (vgl. inter alia Scott 2011) – und für die Wissenschaftsgeschichte.

Im anglophonen Raum erzielte der Radikale Konstruktivismus keineswegs jene Popularität, die er im deutschsprachigen Raum genoss, er wurde und wird eher in intellektuellen Nischen diskutiert, populärer waren hier Sozialkonstruktivismen in der Nachfolge von Peter Berger und Thomas Luckmann (1966) nach Vorgaben von Alfred Schütz (1932) oder des Symbolischen Interaktionismus (vgl. Blumer 1969, Steinert/Falk 1973) oder der Konstruktionismus in der Nachfolge von Kenneth Gergen (2001). Dennoch hat etwa die von Alexander Riegler besorgte Online-Zeitschrift *Constructivist Foundations* derzeit rund 10.000 Subscribers.

Für den Rückgang des Einflusses des Radikalen Konstruktivismus wurde von manchen eine Veränderungen des Zeitgeistes nach dem „Einbruch der Wirklichkeit"[4] oder „der Realität" in Gestalt von 9/11 (oder auch des „Neuen Realismus") verantwortlich gemacht. Ich selbst würde aber den Umstand, dass die charismatischste Protagonisten des Radikalen Konstruktivisten, wie Heinz von Foerster, Ernst von Glasersfeld oder Ranulph Glanville verstorben sind, für bedeutender.

---

2 Es erscheint im Nachhinein als bemerkenswerter Irrtum, dass von Seiten der Verlage und Herausgeber damals eine Übersetzung der Arbeiten von Gordon Pask offenkundig nicht in Erwägung gezogen wurde. (vgl. Pask 1961). Ross Ashby's Einführung (Ashby 1956) war hingegen bei Suhrkamp erschienen, in allerdings betont technischer Ingenieurssprache, die viel von Ashbys Witz verloren gehen lässt.

3 Vgl. das Vorwort des Autors, auch wenn ein bei (Felsch 2015) abgedrucktes Dokument dem zu widersprechen scheint.

4 Wie vielfältig diese Phrase einsetzbar ist, zeigt beispielhaft die Bestseller-Reportage von (Kermani 2016).

Hier ist aber nicht die Frage einer zutreffenden Diagnose des heutigen Zustandes das Thema, sondern das, was man die (Be-)Gründungsphase des Radikalen Konstruktivismus nennen kann. Der Terminus selbst wurde bekanntlich von Ernst von Glasersfeld 1974 in einem Forschungsbericht geprägt. Der Titel von Ernst von Glasersfelds Artikel lautete: „Piaget and the Radical Constructivist Epistemology". Mit dieser Überschrift war der Begriff Radikaler Konstruktivismus erfunden und zugleich der Anreger dazu, Jean Piaget, benannt. Von Glasersfeld hat sich mehrmals zur Entstehungsgeschichte dieses Artikels geäußert. Als mehrsprachig aufgewachsenes Kind, später dann als Übersetzer, auch in der Emigration in Irland, sei ihm die Inkonsistenz von Bedeutungen früh bewusst gewesen. Ihm sei bald klar gewesen, dass Spracherwerb und Weltkonstruktion in einem Zusammenhang gesehen werden müssen. Von einem Kollegen an der University of Georgia, Charles Smock, sei er schließlich auf das Piagetsche Werk aufmerksam gemacht worden, wie er in seinen autobiographischen Schriften darlegte. (vgl. von Glasersfeld 2009)

Dennoch hatte der Radikale Konstruktivismus mehrere, vorerst weitgehend voneinander unabhängig agierende Urheber, die sich fast alle im Umfeld der Kybernetik befanden. Die Kybernetik war seit Anfang der 1970er Jahre in einer Krise, welche in den Vereinigten Staaten vornehmlich eine Finanzierungskrise war (Müller 2000, 2007, 2015a; Umpleby 2003). In den 1950er und 1960er Jahren war Kybernetik vor allem auch mit meist kostenintensiver Laborforschung einhergegangen, etwa am Massachusetts Institute of Technology (MIT) oder am Biological Computer Laboratory (BCL) an der University of Illinois (dazu Müller/Müller 2007). Die dort betriebenen Grundlagenforschungen waren seit den 1950er Jahren vor allem auch durch die Förderung durch militärische Stellen ermöglicht worden, ohne dass die Empfänger dieser Forschungsmittel notwendigerweise einen Beitrag zur militärischen Forschung im engeren Sinne zu leisten gehabt hätten. Rund um 1970 bereitete das sogenannte *Mansfield Amendment* dieser großzügigen Förderung von Grundlagenforschung durch militärische Stellen in den USA ein nachhaltiges Ende. Paradoxerweise konnte Senator Mansfield, ein politischer Gegner der USA-Involvierung in den Vietnamkrieg, durchsetzen, dass militärische Forschungsmittel nur mehr für nachweisbar kriegs-relevante (kriegswichtige hätte man einige Jahrzehnte zuvor in Deutschland gesagt) Projekte eingesetzt werden sollten. (Müller 2000; Umpleby 2003)

Dieses politische Detail wird deshalb erwähnt, weil es unmittelbare Auswirkungen auf die Forschungspraxis der Kybernetik hatte. Der Möglichkeit, kostenintensive Laborforschung weiter zu betreiben, beraubt, führte Teile der Kybernetik-Forscher/innen zu einer Hinwendung zu Fragen der Epistemologie und im weiteren Weg zu Second Order Cybernetics. Wir könnten auch sagen, die Kybernetik zweiter Ordnung war wenigstens teilweise das Resultat einer Evaluation der Ergebnisse der vorangegangenen Laborforschung. (Müller 2000)

Es ist keine ungewöhnliche und keine neue Position, die Entstehung beziehungsweise Formulierung von Radikalem Konstruktivismus und Kybernetik Zweiter Ordnung in einem engen Zusammenhang zu sehen. Ranulph Glanville etwa ging so weit, die beiden Begriffe gleichzusetzen: „Radical constructivism = Second order cybernetics" (Glanville 2012b).

Dieser Artikel, welcher in der von Soren Brier herausgegebenen Zeitschrift *Cybernetics and Human Knowing* mit dem Untertitel „A journal of second order cybernetics, autopoiesis and cyber-semiotics" erschien, war ein entschiedener Einspruch gegenüber Versuchen, Radikalen Konstruktivismus unabhängig von der Tradition der Kybernetik zweiter Ordnung zu sehen.

Spätestens an dieser Stelle soll erläutert werden, worum es sich bei Kybernetik zweiter Ordnung handelt. Die kürzeste Definition stammt von Heinz von Foerster, die er 1974 einem von ihm herausgegebenen und von Fachkollegen und Studierenden mitverfassten Kompendium der Second Order Cybernetics voranstellte:

First Order Cybernetics: The Cybernetics of Observed Systems
Second Order Cybernetics: The Cybernetics of Observing Systems (von Foerster 1974, 1)

Diese Definition entstammt dem Buch *Cybernetics of Cybernetics, the Communication of Communication and the Control of Control* (von Foerster 1974), das aus einer zweisemestrigen Lehrveranstaltung an der University of Illinois Champaign/Urbana hervorgegangen ist. Rund 500 Seiten stark, in ungewöhnlichem Format, auf ungewöhnliches Papier gedruckt, mit Parabook und Metabook versehen, handelte es sich um ein „Ereignis" der Mediengeschichte, nicht zuletzt aufgrund partizipatorischer AutorInnenschaft. Das Ergebnis war jedoch gar nicht untypisch für den Anfang der 1970er Jahre. Von Foerster replizierte ein früheres Experiment – den Whole University Catalogue – und brachte es zur Perfektion.

Mit von Foersters Definition rückt die Beobachter-Kategorie in das Zentrum der Aufmerksamkeit (vgl. Müller 2008b). Die von George Spencer Brown benutzte Anweisung: „Draw a distinction!" setzte den Beobachter ja schon in seine Allmachtsposition. Jene Omnipotenz, die von Foerster dem Beobachter zuschrieb, setzte er in Ausgleich zu dessen Verantwortung gegenüber der Welt. Von Glasersfeld hatte genau diese Verantwortung, oder Verantwortlichkeit, wiederum auf ein humanes Maß reduziert. Sein Begriff der Viabilität erlaubt das Agieren und Interagieren „within constraints".

Es wäre im Übrigen irreführend, aus dem etwas seltsam klingenden Titel auf ein einfaches Spiel mit Meta-Ebenen – a la Russell's und Whitehead's *Principia Mathematica* – schließen zu wollen, mit Meta-Ebenen, auf die eine Metameta-

Ebene, eine Metametameta-Ebene etc. gesetzt werden könne. Obgleich es einzelne Versuche gab, derartiges aus den Second Order Cybernetics abzuleiten, stellte es sich heraus, dass diese beiden Ebenen, First Order und Second Order, vollkommen ausreichen.

Der ins Auge fallende Titel des Kompendiums *Cybernetics of Cybernetics* hatte einen Vorläufer in jenem Hauptvortrag, die die Sozialanthropologin Margaret Mead 1968 anlässlich des ersten Annual Meeting der American Society of Cybernetics beitrug. Auch der Titel dieses Vortrages, die unter anderem eine These enthielt, wonach eine Gesellschaft für Kybernetik gehalten sei, ihre Problem und Geschäfte kybernetisch zu lösen und zu betreiben, lautete „Cybernetics of Cybernetics" (Mead (1968)). Allerdings bekannte von Foerster später, dass er selbst diesen Titel angeregt hatte.[5] Der Vollständigkeit halber soll noch erwähnt werden, dass auch von Foerster auf einem späteren Annual Meeting der ASC einen Hauptvortrag beitrug, die den Titel „Cybernetics of Cybernetics" hatte (von Foerster 1979).

Schon zuvor, 1973, hatte von Foerster eine kurze, thesenartige Arbeit veröffentlicht, die den Titel trug: „On Constructing a Reality". Der Artikel, dem man das Attribut nicht-dualisierend mit einigem Recht zuschreiben kann, endete mit zwei strategischen Äußerungen: „The Ethical Imperative: Act always so as to increase the number of choices. The Aesthetical Imperative: If you desire to see, learn how to act." (von Foerster 1973)

Dieser Artikel ging auf einen Vortrag auf Einladung des Designers Wolfgang Preiser zurück, von Foerster hat in einem Interview die Entstehungsgeschichte folgendermaßen dargelegt:

> Ich denke, es ist immer gut zu wissen, wie solche Sachen entstehen. Ich habe also meinen Vortrag gehalten. Wolfgang Preiser war der Organisator. Ich habe überhaupt nicht gewußt, daß man ein Buch aus dieser Konferenz machen wollte und bin nach meinem Vortrag gleich wieder nach Hause gefahren und habe meine Arbeiten gemacht. Auf einmal ruft mich der Wolfgang Preiser an, und sagt: ‚Heinz, wo ist Dein Beitrag?' ‚Was für ein Beitrag?' ‚Du hast doch einen Vortrag gehalten.' ‚Was für einen Vortrag?' ‚Da war doch die große Konferenz vor einem halben Jahr. Wir warten noch auf Deinen Beitrag!' ‚Ich habe überhaupt nicht gewußt, daß ich diesen Beitrag schreiben soll.' ‚Ja, um Himmels willen, in drei Wochen müssen wir das ganze dem Verleger geben.' ‚Drei Wochen? Du bist ja verrückt! Das ist unwahrscheinlich!' ‚Ja, aber unbedingt! Dieser Beitrag wird der erste Artikel sein. Ich habe Dir zwölf Seiten zur Verfügung gestellt. Die sind ausgespart. Also die Seiten zehn bis zweiundzwanzig. Auf zwölf Seiten! Bitte, schreib! Zwei Wochen!'
>
> Ich hatte zu der Zeit eine Sekretärin, die war ein Genie. Ich hab gesagt: ‚O.k., jetzt schreibe ich und wir werden schauen, daß ich das auf zwölf Seiten reduziere.' Damals druckte man die Aufsätze direkt von einem Manuskriptpapier mit vorgedruckten Rändern.

---

5 In einem Interview mit Albert Müller Heinz von Foerster, Pescadero.

Also mußte ich meine Ideen auf diese Papiere bringen. Ich begann zu schreiben, und das ergab gleich achtzehn Seiten. Zuviel! Also: Wie soll ich das reduzieren? Was soll ich rausstreichen? Da ist meine Sekretärin auf eine geniale Idee gekommen. Sie sagte: ‚In jedem Paragraphen verlieren wir zwei Zeilen. Also machen wir keine Paragraphen, sondern deuten die Paragraphen nur durch einen dicken schwarzen Punkt an. Dann können wir eine Seite vollschreiben. Ein dicker schwarzer Punkt, das ist ein visueller Paragraph, und wenn wir dreißig Paragraphen haben, können wir schon sechzig Zeilen gewinnen. Da haben wir schon einmal zwei Seiten eingespart.' ‚O.k., very good! Aber ich muß noch weiter reduzieren, weiteres herausstreichen!' So kamen wir bis zum Schluß, aber ich konnte ihn einfach nicht mehr umdrehen, und hatte doch noch zwei Seiten zuviel. Da habe ich gesagt: ‚Nun reduziere ich diese zwei Seiten auf zwei Sätze!'

Ich glaube, es ist wichtig, daß solche Sachen verstanden werden: Die Größe ist vorgeschrieben! Die Zeit drängt! Dort mußt du hinein! Du mußt einen Gedanken in die kürzeste Form bringen! So sind meine Imperative entstanden.[6]

Soweit der Autor des wahrscheinlich bekanntesten Artikels zum Radikalen Konstruktivismus.

Die hier wiederkehrende quasi genitivische Konstruktion wie Cybernetics of Cybernetics, Kybernetik der Kybernetik, für die man erst in der Syntax des Deutschen einen Genitiv benötigt, kommt aber – ungefähr zeitgleich und relativ unabhängig von den Debatten der ASC und am BCL an einer anderen Stelle zum Tragen. Der absolvierte Architekt und Doktorand der Kybernetik Ranulph Glanville schrieb 1973/74 an einer Dissertation mit dem Titel: *The Objects of Objects (The Points of Points) Or Something About Things. (Also Known As: A Cybernetic Development On Epistemology and Observation. Applied to Objects in Space and Time.)* (Glanville 1975, vgl. Müller 2015b). Glanville, als dessen Betreuer Gordon Pask fungierte, arbeitete an seinem anspruchsvollen Projekt in tendenzieller Abgeschiedenheit vom Universitätsbetrieb. Er entwickelte die ungewöhnlichen Thesen seiner Arbeit weitgehend selbständig. Als seine Prüfer und Gutachter fungierten übrigens 1975 Pask gemeinsam mit von Foerster.

Es wurde schon erwähnt, dass von Glasersfeld einen entscheidenden Hinweis auf Piaget von seinem Kollegen Charles Smock erhielt, der Ähnlichkeiten der Ideen von Glasersfelds und Piagets erkannt hatte. Im Werk von Foersters wird Piaget erstmals in einem 1972 publizierten Artikel zitiert. Ein noch früherer Hinweis auf den Namen Piagets findet sich in von Foersters Tagebuch aus dem Jahr 1970.[7] Glanville führte das Thema der Objekte zu Piaget, in dessen Werk ja „Objektkonstanz" eine zentrale Rolle spielt (vgl. Glanville 1975, 1988, 2009, 2012a, 2014).

---

6 Interview Albert Müller mit Heinz von Foerster, Pescadero.
7 Zu finden im Heinz von Foerster-Archiv am Institut für Zeitgeschichte der Universität Wien.

Jeder dieser drei Autoren, von Foerster, von Glasersfeld, Glanville, gelangte also unabhängig von den anderen zu Piaget. Schon ein oberflächlicher Blick in eine Bibliographie des Werks von Piaget führt die Ausgedehntheit seiner Schriften vor Augen. Trotzdem war es nur ein Buch, das im Kontext von Radikalem Konstruktivismus und Second Order Cybernetics ausführlich – in seinen englischen und französischen Versionen – rezipiert wurde: Die erstmals 1937 erschienene Arbeit *La construction du réel chez l'enfant*. Auf Deutsch: *Der Aufbau der Wirklichkeit beim Kinde*.

> Als ich in den Jahren danach Kurse über Piaget für Studenten veranstaltete, die nur Englisch lesen konnten, stellte ich fest, daß es schwierig, wenn nicht unmöglich war, die Position Piagets allein aus Übersetzungen verständlich zu machen. Mit sehr wenigen Ausnahmen [...] scheinen seine Übersetzer eine ganz naive (das heißt naiv-realistische) Erkenntnistheorie zu haben und daher unbewußt alles, was sie in Piagets Originaltexten lesen, so zurechtzubiegen, daß es mit ihrer Weltanschauung zusammenpaßt. Da dies nicht immer möglich ist, vermitteln ihre Übersetzungen oft Vorstellungen, die mit der Theorie Piagets unvereinbar oder schlicht unverständlich sind. (von Glasersfeld 2005)

‚Assimilation' und ‚Accomodation' sind die beiden Schlüsselbegriffe, sie stehen bei Piaget in einem zirkulären, einander wechselseitig begründenden und bedingenden Verhältnis. Für Kybernetiker haben sie notwendigerweise einen hohen Wiedererkennungswert, stand doch das Thema der Kreiskausalität, der zirkulären Kausalität bereits am Beginn der Geschichte der Kybernetik als zentrales Anliegen der sogenannten Macy-Konferenzen. (Pias 2003/2004) Warren S. McCulloch unternahm im Jänner 1953 den Versuch, Piaget zu einer der Macy Konferenzen einzuladen – im Übrigen neben Albert Einstein, Bertrand Russell, Alan Turing, Grey Walter oder Rudolf Carnap (vgl. Pias 2004, 419 ff). Ein bloß reisetechnisch zu begründendes Hindernis schien die Ursache für eine verspätete Piaget-Rezeption unter den Kybernetikern zu sein.

Während jedoch in den 1940er Jahren Piagets Werk von Kybernetikern weitgehend unbeachtet blieb, wirkte Anfang der 1970er Piaget katalytisch bei der Erfindung von Kybernetik zweiter Ordnung und Radikalem Konstruktivismus. In der Folge war von Glasersfeld mehrfach Gast an Piagets Institut, von Foerster lernte auf einer Konferenz Bärbel Inhelder, die wichtigste Mitarbeiterin und Koautorin Piagets, kennen und wurde zu einer Konferenz anlässlich Piagets achtzigstem Geburtstag eingeladen. Sein dafür geschriebener Vortrag „Objects – Tokens for (Eigen-)behaviour" verlieh Piagets Konzepten der senso-motorischen Schließung einen mathematisch-formalen Rahmen und führte die Begriffe Eigenwert und Eigenverhalten nachhaltig in die Diskussion der Kybernetik ein. Der Mathematiker Louis Kaufman und Glanville entwickelten von Foersters an David Hilbert anknüpfende Idee in vielfältiger Weise weiter. Schließlich publizierte

Glanville mehrere Arbeiten, in den er das Werk Piagets zum Gegenstand machte (Glanville 2009, 2012b, 2014).

Ich versuche folgende Zusammenfassung: Radikaler Konstruktivismus wurde wie Second Order Cybernetics auf der Grundlage bereits vorhandener Ideen erfunden. Zentral waren dabei – neben der Arbeit der Kybernetikerinnen und Kybernetiker – die Arbeiten zweier sehr unterschiedlicher Wissenschaftler: George Spencer Brown (mit den *Laws of Form*) und Jean Piaget (mit *La construction du réel chez l'enfant*). Beide hatten eine vor allem katalytische Wirkung auf die Ausformulierung des Radikalen Konstruktivismus.

Literaturverzeichnis

Ashby, Ross (1956): *An Introduction to Cybernetics*. London: Chapman & Hall.
Bateson, Gregory (1985): *Ökologie des Geistes. Anthropologische, psychologische, biologische und epistemologische Perspektiven*. Frankfurt am Main: Suhrkamp.
Bateson, Gregory (1987): *Geist und Natur. Eine notwendige Einheit*. Frankfurt am Main: Suhrkamp.
Berger Peter; Luckmann, Thomas (1966): *The Social Construction of Reality. A Treatise in the Sociology of Knowledge*. Garden City, NY: Anchor Books.
Blumer, Norbert (1969): *Symbolic Interactionism. Perspective and Method*. Berkeley et al.: University of California Press.
Felsch, Philipp (2015): *Der lange Sommer der Theorie. Geschichte einer Revolte 1960–1990*. München: C. H. Beck.
Gergen, Kenneth (2001): *Social Construction in Context*. London, Thousand Oaks: Sage.
Glanville, Ranulph (1975): *The Objects of Objects (The Points of Points) Or Something About Things. (Also Known As: A Cybernetic Development On Epistemology and Observation. Applied to Objects in Space and Time*. Unpublished Thesis. London: Brunel University.
Glanville, Ranulph (1988): *Objekte*. Herausgegeben und übersetzt von Dirk Baecker. Berlin: Merve.
Glanville, Ranulph (2007): „Grounding Difference". In: Müller, Albert; Müller, Karl (Hg.): *An Unfinished Revolution? – Heinz von Foerster and the Biological Computer Laboratory*. Wien: Echoraum, 361–406.
Glanville, Ranulph (2009): *The Black Box Vol. 3. 39 Steps*. Wien: Echoraum.
Glanville, Ranulph (2012a): *The Black Box Vol. 1. Cybernetic Circles*. Wien: Echoraum.
Glanville, Ranulph (2012b): „Radical Constructivism = Second-order Cybernetics". In: *Cybernetics & Human Knowing* 19 (4), 27–42.
Glanville, Ranulph (2014): *The Black Box Vol. 2. Living in Cybernetic Circles*. Wien: Echoraum.
Kermani, Navid (2016): *Einbruch der Wirklichkeit. Auf dem Flüchtlingstreck durch Europa*. München: C. H. Beck.
Maturana, Humberto (1970): „Neurophysiology of Cognition". In: Garvin, Paul (Hg.): *Cognition. A Multiple View*. New York, Washington: Spartan Books, 3–23.
Maturana, Humberto (1998): *Biologie der Realität*. Übersetzt von Wolfram Köck. Frankfurt am Main: Suhrkamp.

Mead, Margaret (1968): „Cybernetics of Cybernetics". In: von Foerster, Heinz; White, John; Peterson, Larry; Russel, John (Hg.): *Purposive Systems. Proceedings of the First Annual Symposium of the American Society of Cybernetics*. New York & Washington: Spartan Books, 1–11.
Müller, Albert (2000): „Eine kurze Geschichte des BCL. Heinz von Foerster und das Biological Computer Laboratory". In: *Österreichische Zeitschrift für Geschichtswissenschaften* 11 (1), 9–30.
Müller, Albert (2007): „The End of the BCL". In: Müller, Albert; Müller, Karl (Hg.): *An Unfinished Revolution? – Heinz von Foerster and the Biological Computer Laboratory*. Wien: Echoraum, 303–321.
Müller, Albert; Müller, Karl H. (Hg.) (2007): *An Unfinished Revolution? – Heinz von Foerster and the Biological Computer Laboratory*. Wien: Echoraum.
Müller, Albert (2008a): „Zur Geschichte der Kybernetik. Ein Zwischenstand", In: *Österreichische Zeitschrift für Geschichtswissenschaften* 19 (4), 6–27.
Müller, Albert (2015a): Avec un „s": Histories of Cybernetics and the ASC. In: *Kybernetes* 44 (8–9), 1341–1349.
Müller, Albert (2015b): „Ranulph Glanville's Thesis on the Theory of Objects and the Invention of Second-order Cybernetics". In: *Cybernetics and Human Knowing* 22 (2–3), 21–25
Müller, Albert (Hg.) (2008b): „Computing a Reality. Heinz von Foerster's Lecture at the A.U.M. Conference in 1973". In: *Constructivist Foundations* 4 (1), 62–69.
Müller, Albert; Müller, Karl H. (2011): „Systeme beobachten. Über Unterschiede und Gemeinsamkeiten von Kybernetik zweiter Ordnung und Konstruktivismus". In: Pörksen, Bernhard (Hg.): *Schlüsselwerke des Konstruktivismus*. Wien/New York: Springer, 564–582.
Pask, Gordon (1961): *An Approach to Cybernetics*. London: Hutchinson.
Pias, Claus (Hg.) (2003): *Cybernetics/Kybernetik. The Macy-Conferences 1946–1953, Bd. I, Transactions/Protokolle*, Zürich u. Berlin: diaphanes.
Pias, Claus (Hg.) (2004): *Cybernetics/Kybernetik. The Macy-Conferences 1946–1953, Bd. II, Essays and Documents/Essays und Dokumente*, Zürich u. Berlin: diaphanes.
Piattelli-Palmarini, Massimo (Hg.) (1980): *Language and Learning. The Debate between Jean Piaget and Noam Chomsky*. London and Henley: Routledge & Kegan Paul.
Schmidt, Siegfried J. (Hg.) (1987): *Der Diskurs des Radikalen Konstruktivismus*. Frankfurt am Main: Suhrkamp.
Schmidt, Siegfried J. (Hg.) (1992): *Kognition und Gesellschaft. Der Diskurs des Radikalen Konstruktivismus 2*. Frankfurt am Main: Suhrkamp.
Schütz, Alfred (1932): *Der sinnhafte Aufbau der sozialen Welt. Eine Einleitung in die verstehende Soziologie*. Wien: Springer.
Scott, Bernard (2011): *Explorations in Second-Order Cybernetics. Reflections on Cybernetics, Psychology and Education*. Wien: Echoraum.
Steinert, Heinz; Falk, Gunter (1973): *Symbolische Interaktion. Arbeiten zu einer reflexiven Soziologie*. Stuttgart: Klett.
Umpleby, Stuart (2003): „Heinz von Foerster and the Mansfield Amendment". In: *Cybernetics and Human Knowing* 10 (3–4), 161–163.
von Foerster, Heinz (1972/74): „Notes on the Epistemology of Living Things". In: von Foerster, Heinz: *Understanding Understanding. Essays on Cybernetics and Cognition*. New York: Springer, 247–259.

von Foerster, Heinz (1976): „Objects: Tokens for (Eigen-)behaviors". In: *Cybernetics Forum* 8, 91–96.
von Foerster, Heinz (1979): „Cybernetics of Cybernetics", in: Krippendorf, Klaus (Hg.): *Communication and Control*. New York: Gordon & Breach, 5–8.
von Foerster, Heinz (1993): *Wissen und Gewissen. Versuch einer Brücke*, Frankfurt am Main: Suhrkamp.
von Foerster, Heinz (Hg.) (1974): *Cybernetics of Cybernetics. The Control of Control and the Communication of Communication*. Urbana: University of Illinois.
von Glasersfeld, Ernst (1974): „Piaget and the Radical Constructivist Epistemology". In: Smock, Donald; Glasersfeld Ernst von (Hg.): *Epistemology and Education*. Athens, GA: Follow Through Publications, 1–24.
von Glasersfeld, Ernst (1990): „An Exposition of Constructivism: Why Some Like It Radical". In: *Journal for Research in Mathematics Education*. 19 (2), 195–210.
von Glasersfeld, Ernst (1996): *Radikaler Konstruktivismus. Ideen, Ergebnisse, Probleme*. Übersetzt von Wolfram Köck. Frankfurt am Main: Suhrkamp.
von Glasersfeld, Ernst (2005): *Radikaler Konstruktivismus – Versuch einer Wissenstheorie*. Herausgegeben von Albert Müller und Karl H. Müller, Wien: Echoraum.
von Glasersfeld, Ernst (2007): *Key Works of Radical Constructivism*. Herausgegeben von Marie Larochelle. Rotterdam: Sense Publisher.
von Glasersfeld, Ernst (2009): *Partial Memories. Sketches From an Improbable Life*. Exeter: Imprint Academic.

Karl H. Müller
Two Ways of Exploring the World

Abstract: This article deals with the research tradition of Radical Constructivism and proposes four central claims for its theoretical, methodological and epistemic orientation and status. First, Radical Constructivism should be viewed as a comprehensive empirical research tradition with an emphasis on cognition, learning, living systems and organization which, in addition, developed a new general methodology for scientific operations. Second, the main opponent of Radical Constructivism, especially in the research program of Heinz von Foerster, does not lie in philosophical or epistemological terrains but in the area of the general scientific methodology and in its conventional mode of exploring the world. Third, Radical Constructivism proposed a new and alternative way for scientific explorations and world-making which produces, additionally, tangible and non-trivial effects with respect to scientific outcomes. Fourth, due to this new way of scientific world-making and due to its novel scientific methodology Radical Constructivism was only marginally interested in epistemological issues. Instead, the empirical research tradition of Radical Constructivism offered intriguing answers why the varieties of scientific realism and its allies like scientific objectivity seem so appealing and almost self-evident.

Keywords: Radical Constructivism, general scientific methodology, exo-mode, endo-mode, anti-realism

For a considerable number of philosophers Radical Constructivism seems to pose a challenge to the varieties of philosophical realism and can be regarded as a specific version of an anti-realist tradition. At first sight, radical constructivist authors, most notably Ernst von Glasersfeld, provide sufficient materials in their writings to support such a philosophical assessment of Radical Constructivism. In this short article a series of general claims will be put forward which separate Radical Constructivism from epistemological discussions of a philosophical nature and specify the main target of the criticisms of Radical Constructivism which lies in the general methodology of science. Radical Constructivism, especially in the work of Heinz von Foerster, offered and still offers a new way of doing and practicing science and exploring the world which, moreover, is gaining more and more momentum within science itself.

1 Radical Constructivism as an Empirical Research Tradition

Initially, the two core concepts of a research program and a research tradition, require a few comments. Starting with the notion of an empirical research program, Figure 1 shows the typical building blocks like a theoretical core (TC), a set of methods, models and mechanisms (MMM), linked to the theoretical core, the embeddedness of TC and MMM within a wider background-knowledge BK, the bridge-modules BM which link the theoretical domain with applications, a class of paradigmatic examples and sets of observations, data and measurements (DT).

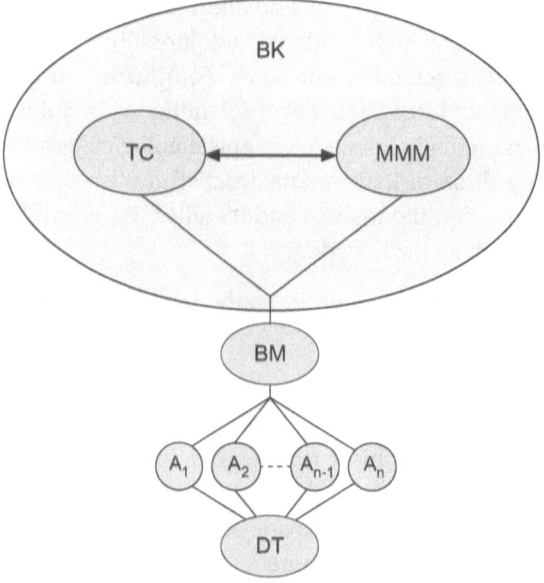

Figure 1. Mapping Empirical Research Programs
BK: Background Knowledge; TC: Theoretical Core; MMM: Models, Mechanisms, Methods; BM: Bridge Modules; A: Applications; DT: Data and Measurements

In Figure 1, no arrows have been used in order to stress the duality of top-down and bottom up flows. Theoretical concepts, generative mechanisms or transfer-modules are as much shaped by the DT-segment as observations, methods and data are determined by the theoretical core, the MMM-segment or the BM-domain.

Radical Constructivism can be introduced as a research tradition where research traditions can be described as a network of empirical research programs and can be visualized in the way of Figure 2. Here one can see networks of theoretical cores T, of methods, mechanisms and models, of bridge modules BM on the one hand and a rich network of different classes of observations, methods and data (DT) and a network of wider application domains (D) on the other hand. The application area changes into larger application domains D_1 to D_n where each domain captures a set of paradigmatic examples.

Radical Constructivism, due to its large set of application domains and to its heterogeneous composition of theories, generative mechanisms or models, can best be characterized as a trans-disciplinary research tradition. The application domains D_i cover unusually wide areas, ranging from cell-biology or cognition to organizations and societal evolution.

It is highly important to stress the empirical orientation of Radical Constructivism as a research tradition and the search for testable and empirical based models and theories of cognition, communication, learning, living systems or organizational developments.

Ernst von Glasersfeld was involved in several major research projects, most notably in chimpanzee communication and the construction of Yerkish language (von Glasersfeld 1977) and the formation of numerical concepts in children (von Glasersfeld 1983). Heinz von Foerster advanced second-order cybernetics in a number of articles throughout the late 1960s and 1970s (see von Foerster 1982, 2003). The theory of autopoietic systems (Varela/Maturana/Uribe 1974; Maturana/Varela 1980; Varela 1979) evolved in an impressive number of books and articles. Between 1975 and 1976, Gordon Pask, in co-operation with Ranulph Glanville and Bernard Scott, finished three volumes (Pask 1975, 1975a, 1976) which highlighted the rich potential of conversation analysis and laid the foundation for a potential revolution in learning and teaching environments. Stafford Beer (Beer 1972, 1975, 1979) developed an intriguing new perspective on management cybernetics. Beer effectively brought a brain-based perspective to the study of organizations and constructed a highly complex formal framework for organizational analysis.

Inside the diversified empirical research tradition with its focus on cognition, learning, organization and living systems Radical Constructivism also advanced a new general method and methodology of science to pursue its empirical agenda. This new method of exploring the world and its underlying methodology were promoted most forcefully by Heinz von Foerster, but were also supported with contributions of Humberto R. Maturana, Ernst von Glasersfeld or, in later years, by Ranulph Glanville, Louis H. Kaufman, Bernard Scott or Stuart A. Umpleby.

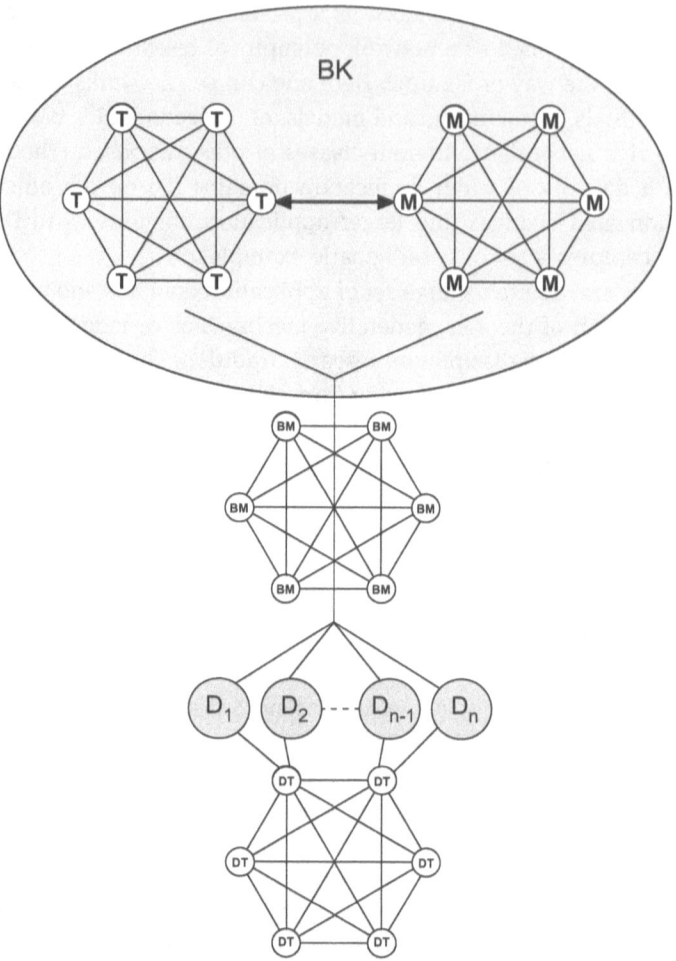

Figure 2. Mapping a Research Tradition as a Network of Research Programs
BK: Background Knowledge; T: Network of Theoretical Cores; M: Network of Models, Mechanisms, Methods and Special and General Methodologies; BM: Network of Bridge Modules; D: Application Domains; DT: Network of Data and Measurements

These two components of Radical Constructivism should and must be evaluated in strict independence from one another. Both strands were advanced from the 1960s and 1970s onwards, although the methodological component was never systematized in a comprehensive manner.

2 The Traditional Way of Scientific World-Making

The next step in this article will lead to the domain of the general scientific method and methodology and to the conventional rules of scientific operations across fields and disciplines.

The traditional ways of scientific world making and their dynamics start with the configuration in Figure 3. Here, a single scientist or a team of researchers RE conduct an investigation on the topic or domain X, guided by various scientific rules RS from the general scientific methodology, from special disciplinary methodologies, from methods relevant for the analysis of X, from the particular research design which was selected for the study of X and from the relevant scientific knowledge base. The researchers are aware of previous publications on X, they have initial expectations and they proceed in their studies of X according to their design and goals.

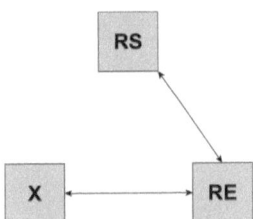

Figure 3. The Initial Configuration of a Traditional Scientific Production Process

Eric Kendel provides a very short summary of the general scientific methodology in the following way. Scientists make models of elementary features of the world that can be tested and reformulated. These tests rely on removing the subjective biases of the observer and relying on objective measurements and evaluations. (Kendel 2012, 449)

Thus, researchers adhere to the rule of objectivity as a gradual replacement of initial subjective biases and expectations as well as of observer-induced effects on observations, measurements and the like.

In dynamic terms, a traditional scientific production process starts with a single or a group of researchers RE, a research problem X to be pursued, a laboratory as the physical work space and, finally, initial and mostly implicit assumptions and expectations on the part of researcher(s). The research process involves, depending on the research problem, experiments, observations, data collections and compilations, the framing of hypotheses or explanations, the building of models as well as various sequences of testing, falsifications, testing, confirmations, etc. in accordance with general and special methodological rules as well as other relevant rules in the analysis of X.

Over time, the scientific production process generates a gradual "blackening" of the researchers involved and their initial biases and expectations. Moreover, researchers and possible researcher effects on X become delinked from the actual outcomes. Another dynamic development concerns the "blackening" of the actual rules which were relevant during the production process. Finally, the research process ends with an account of X which can be a model, an explanation, a theory, a description, a simulation, a scenario, etc. Due to the dual blackening and delinking this account (X) can be seen as strictly independent from the researchers and from the underlying rule systems. Due to the empirical base and due to the test procedures the account (X) relies on objective measurements and evaluations only. Figure 4 presents the final stage of a research process within the traditional scientific methodology where the account (X) becomes delinked from researchers and rule systems.

Figure 4. The Goal of the Traditional Scientific Production Process

Natalie Angier, based on interviews with dozens of eminent scientists, concludes that the evolution and the long-term success of science depends on the implicit and explicit acceptance by scientists

> that there is a reality capable of being understood, and understood in ways that can be shared with and agreed upon by others. We can call this 'objective' reality if we like, as opposed to subjective reality, or opinion, or 'whimsical set of pridelictions'. (Angier 2007, 22)

Angier describes a common sense-understanding of the scientific process and the general scientific method as 'empirical universalism' which includes all the subjective and private realities.

> Science is effective because it bypasses such binaries in favor of what might be called empirical universalism, the rigorously outfitted and enormously fruitful premise that the objective reality of the universe comprises the subjective reality of every one of us. (Angier 2007, 22)

Thus, the traditional scientific production process is organized in a way that additional options like accessibility of relevant data for the scientific community, intersubjective reproducibility of results or peer-reviews guarantee a sufficient element of quality control.

Consequently, the traditional mode of world-making operates by way of self-elimination, reducing the potential impact of researchers to a point or level until all biases and subjective evaluations or traces are removed and "objective measurements and evaluations" prevail.

Due to this gradual elimination of subjective biases of researchers in the research process the traditional way of scientific world-making can be classified as exo-mode, excluding the subjective impacts of researchers in the course of the research processes. The subsequent table summarizes the characteristic rules for the traditional mode of scientific world-making with its corresponding operational features.

Table 1. A Summary of the Traditional Scientific Mode of Exploring the World

Exo-Mode (Exploring from Without)	Operational Features
Objectivity	Exclusion of Researchers
Researcher-Effects Excluded	Elimination of Researcher-Related Effects in Measurements, Observations, etc.
Elimination of Subjective Elements	Inter-subjective Criticisms as a Means for a Successful Goal Attainment of Objectivity
Researchers Untraceable	The Operations by Researchers Remain Hidden
Researchers Implicit in Research Designs and in Research Processes	No Explicit Roles and Functions for Researchers in Research or Research Designs
Non-Participatory	No Interactions and Consensus Formations between Researchers and Research Domains
Central Focus on World/Environments	Descriptive and Explanatory Accounts of the "World as It Is"

3 Radical Constructivism *versus* the General Scientific Methodology

From the early 1970s onwards Heinz von Foerster proposed a radical change of the general scientific methodology and of the way of practising science. For Radical Constructivism, especially in the version of Heinz von Foerster, the main opponent from its early days onwards was not an epistemological tradition like philosophical realism or philosophy of science, but the general scientific methodology which was to be substituted by a different way of scientific world-making. The scientific production process was to be pursued by a new organization.

At various points, Heinz von Foerster characterizes the traditional scientific method with the postulate of objectivity: "The properties of the observer shall not enter the description of his observations" (von Foerster 2003, 285). It is important to note that other core elements of the scientific method like testability, empirical confirmation or falsification as well as statistical test methods were not questioned, but mainly the postulate of objectivity. Heinz von Foerster concludes that the scientific method is "counter-productive in contemplating any evolutionary process, be it the growing up of an individual, or a society in transition". (von Foerster 2003, 204)

A general replacement of this hegemonic method was required because its *modus operandi* excludes and blackens researchers in the research process. In his later writings from the 1970s onwards Heinz von Foerster built and assembled the minimal components for an alternative way of conducting scientific research processes.

4 A New Way of Scientific World-Making

Heinz von Foerster based his new alternative on a distinction of two fundamentally different attitudes in exploring the world. In his lecture on "Ethics and Second-Order Cybernetics" from around 1990 he posed the following two questions.

> 'Am I *apart* from the universe?' Meaning whenever I *look*, I'm looking as if through a peephole upon an unfolding universe or 'Am I *part of* the universe? Meaning whenever I *act*, I'm changing myself and the universe as well. (von Foerster 2003, 293)

Moreover, Heinz von Foerster characterizes these two alternatives as most profound and as

> a fundamental change, not only in the way we conduct science, but also how we perceive teaching, learning, the therapeutic process, organizational management, and so on and so forth, and I would say, of how we perceive relationships in our daily life. One may see this fundamental epistemological change if one first considers oneself to be an independent observer who watches the world go by, as opposed to a person who considers oneself to be a participant actor in the drama of mutual interaction of the give and take in the circularity of human relations. (von Foerster 2003, 289)

From there Heinz von Foerster expanded this distinction to an intriguing list of characteristic differences between two fundamentally different ways of interacting with research domains or the environment in general like "world and I: separated", "world and I: one", schizoid versus hominoid, denotative versus connotative, etc. From these distinctions Heinz von Foerster emphasizes especially two differentiations as most significant, namely the splits between "Say how it is" *versus* "It is how you say it" and "standing outside" *versus* "standing inside" (von Foerster 2014, 129).

The dichotomy of "standing outside" and "standing inside" can be transferred directly to the domains of scientific operations, methods and methodologies where the traditional and still hegemonic approach follows the configuration and practices of science from outside whereas the new alternative corresponds to the organization of a science from inside.

Obviously, these two scientific modes of world making cannot be decided on scientific grounds and belong, thus, to the group of undecidable questions which, according to Heinz von Foerster, have to be decided by ourselves (von Foerster 2003, 293).

The new general scientific method as an alternative *modus operandi* must be organized in a highly interactive and recursive manner as shown in Figure 5. Here, a triadic ensemble between a research domain X, a multiplicity of scientific rule systems RS and an inclusive researcher or a team of inclusive researchers I[RE] is based on generative G, instead of causal relations.

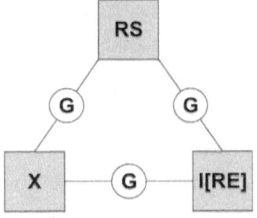

Figure 5. The Transformation of the Transitional Scientific Production Process into a Generative Triadic Configuration

The main differences between Figure 3 and Figure 5 can be specified in the following way.

First, the researchers RE become IRE], the I of researchers as first person actors in research processes and designs. I[RE] must be present in these research processes and designs in a maximally interactive and explicit form.

Second, the research domain X becomes likewise a highly interactive unit whose interaction potential must be fully used during research processes and designs.

Third, rule systems RS in particular and the scientific and societal knowledge base are to be used in an explicit manner.

Fourth, the three nodes in Figure 5 are interlinked in a generative manner and they reproduce each other.

The change from Figure 3 to Figure 5 has apparently lost all the charms of objectivity and closes the gate to the "objective reality of the universe". A triadic and generative configuration or, as Louis H. Kauffman characterizes it (Kauffman 2016), a reflexive domain is organized in a way that various forms of solipsisms, unrestricted subjectivisms and prejudices of all sorts must arise. Operating from within simply implies an "Anything goes" as the necessary outcome.

However, Radical Constructivism offers an alternative way for practicing science because the admission of the full subjectivity of single researchers becomes the starting point and not the end point. Moreover, the configuration of Figure 5 becomes recursively closed and researchers can and must operate recursively where the result R of the ith step is generated by a specific operation Op on R^{i-1}: $R_i = Op\ R_{i-1}$

Additionally, research in a closed and triadic ensemble requires high levels of interactions between the three nodes, especially between the domain under investigation X and the I[RE] of researchers. Thus, the subjective ingredients of a single researcher I[RE] must be matched with the equally subjective components of other researchers I[RE] as well as with the interactive domain under investigation X.

The most important consequence of the recursively closed operations in triadic and generative formations lies in its dynamics and the necessary emergence of eigenforms. The notion of eigenforms or eigenbehaviors was first introduced by Heinz von Foerster in a lecture on the occasion of Jean Piaget's 80th birthday in Geneva on June 29, 1976 (von Foerster 2003, 261ff). Here, Heinz von Foerster developed a remarkable formalism, based on infinite recursions, which produces, by necessity, stable objects or fixed points as the necessary results of recursively closed operations. Louis Kauffman gives a different proof, namely the Church-Curry Fixed Point Theorem which states that in a reflexive domain D there exists an element X such that X is a fixed point for D.

> Let D be a reflexive domain and let T be any element of the domain D. Then there is an element X in D such that X is a fixed point for T. That is, $TX = X$ (Kauffman 2016).

Eigenforms in recursively closed scientific operations can be of various types like experiments, theories, models or even as seemingly trivial as survey questionnaires. In the apparently simple case of a survey questionnaire QU on a particular topic like living conditions OU^L or quality of life QU^{QU} a survey questionnaire like QU^{QU} becomes a transformation QU^{QU} which includes survey researchers SRE and a specific outcome O. O becomes an eigenform so that

$$QU^{QU} (SRE, O) = O.$$

In principle, O could be an eigenform for QU^{QU} which is independent of the composition of survey researchers SRE and could be reproduced whenever a group of survey researchers develops a questionnaire on quality of life. But this particular example shows that the eigenform O is highly sensitive to group compositions and their goals because O turns out to be a local eigenform under a specific group composition only. Other survey researchers in different cultural contexts may produce a new eigenform O* which becomes another local variant, etc. These highly context and composition-sensitive eigenforms reflect the current situation that quite independently from the endo-mode more than 500 different survey questionnaires on quality of life QU^{QU} are already available and their number will be increasing in the future. More generally, survey research in particular and the social sciences in general are usually confronted with local and short-term eigenforms only.

Quite a different situation arises in the case of physical experiments E where a physical experiment includes physicists P and an experimental result R so that the eigenform becomes

$$E(P,R) = R.$$

In many instances of physical experiments the result R turns into a stable and long-term eigenform so that R becomes, unlike in the case of survey questionnaires, independent of the group composition of physicists. In other words, R is the result under various compositions P worldwide. R becomes repeatable and the permanent repeatability under different compositions P makes R a stable eigenform for a particular physical experiment E.

Obviously, the endo-mode is not based on a mechanical model of operation, but on a high degree of interactions and on consensus formations within its triadic and generative formations for each of its recursively closed operations. These processes of consensus-formation need to be organized in specific ways for which Gordon Pask (Pask 1975, 1975a), Ranulph Glanville (Glanville 2012) or Bernard Scott (Scott 2011) presented advanced schemes already.

In this way the endo-mode produces descriptive and explanatory accounts under which conditions long-term and global eigenforms can emerge, local and short-lived eigenforms are reached and under which conditions no eigenforms can be produced, due, for example, to frequent changes in the initial team composition or to an arbitrary termination of the research process.

Figure 6 shows the final stages for the endo-mode in which eigenforms in a triadic and generative configuration or in a reflexive domain X must emerge.

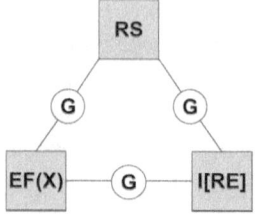

Figure 6. The Goal of Recursively Closed Scientific Production Processes from Within

Table 2 presents a summary for the new endo-mode and its operational features.

Table 2. A Summary of the New Mode for Scientific Production Processes

Endo-Mode (Exploring from Within)	Operational Features
Researcher-effects included	Expectations, initial assumptions are specified
Researchers traceable	Steps and rules of operations need to be documented
Researchers explicit in research processes and in research designs	Goals of researchers and operations by researchers become explicit
Intersubjective Reproducibility	Reproduction of outputs must be achievable Open access to data, to documentations, etc.
As much participation as possible (between researcher and research domains)	Utilization of various participatory research designs
Higher degree of compositional complexity (Endo-Mode: X + RS + I(RE))	Inclusive configuration, plus I of researcher(s) and rule systems RS
Higher degree of relational complexity	Triadic and generative configurations; interacting in reflexive domains
Endo-mode: relations $R^{I\mid X, RS}$ between the I of the researcher(s), X and RS as admissible)	First-person science admissible
Eigenforms as Goals of the Endo-Mode	Specifications of eigenforms under special conditions of scientific discourse
Generative Triadic Configurations between I[RE], X, RS	
Central Focus on the Interactions between I[RE], X, RS	Descriptive and explanatory accounts of "It is as you say it"

5 Potential Advantages for the Endo-Mode

While, following Heinz von Foerster, the decision for the exo- or the endo-mode remains in the responsibility of individual researchers a few arguments can be provided that these two modes also produce significant differences in their research outputs and that, in general, the endo-mode becomes a more complex way of exploring the world than the traditional exo-mode.

The first argument for significant effects between the two modes leads to different cultural contexts and their role in research processes. In general, scientific researchers of the social worlds with different cultural backgrounds exert significant effects on the scenes under observation and are, at the same time, strongly affected by these contexts as well. To a lesser extent, these effects can also become relevant for medical research, the environmental sciences, the life-sciences or the technical sciences. In all these instances the scope, the composition of social ensembles, including the I[RE] of researchers as well as the interaction potentials with a particular domain X, can lead to very different results. Here, the endo-mode addresses these differences in an explicit and open manner which is difficult to pursue within the traditional exo-mode.

A second argument points to measurements and observations where observers can have a strong impact for the results of the measurements and observations obtained. In social psychology a rich literature is available on the effects of experimenters on their experiments (Rosenthal/Fode 1963). In survey research the role of survey researchers has been studied for more than sixty years. At the societal level, predictions may generate self-fulfilling or self-destroying processes, following the publication of a specific forecast. Outside the social sciences the role of researchers has been intensively investigated in medical research, leading within the exo-mode, to double-blind and even triple-blind experimental designs.

A third line of arguments emphasizes the role of the goals of observers in determining the outcomes of research processes. Gordon Pask defined second-order cybernetics with respect to the goals of the modelers, in contrast to first-order cybernetics as goals of the models (Pask 1975, 1975a) Including the goals of observers exerts a powerful impact on the specification of research designs, on levels of abstractions, on classification schemes (Haag/Müller 1992) and on conducting research processes.

A fourth rather strong argument points to new perspectives for the goals and types of scientific problem solutions. The diffusion of an endo-mode can be accompanied by a radical widening of the space of scientific problem solutions and by a shift in scientific problem solutions towards inducing changes in the society and its environments. Thus, the endo-mode should lead to a significant rise in practical problem solutions which are aimed at eliminating or significant reducing societal or environmental problems especially at the community level. Under the old regime of the exo-mode a research problem was solved once it was successfully modeled, explained and the theoretical problem solution allowed for additional features like forecasts or scenarios. Practical solutions require an effective reduction or elimination of a societal problem and this practical problem solution requires an endo-mode where the practical solution must be agreed upon and have observable and positive consequences for the well-being or the quality of life of affected target groups or communities.

Fifth, wicked problems (Ackoff 1974; Alrøe/Noe 2014) are usually defined for complex problems in business and management research, socio-economic policy research or environmental research. These wicked problems are time-consuming and very difficult to solve and require special heuristic strategies. Bringing researchers in and constructing and organizing communication networks in an endo-mode seems to be a promising general strategy for reaching at least temporally limited solutions and eigenforms.

Sixth, a more general argument can be provided which stresses the increasing importance of the reproduction of scientific results and its necessary documentations. Here, a general shift to the endo-mode should make it much easier to replicate investigations, due to the availability of recipes and a record of explicit operations of researchers. This traceability of researchers especially in the context of complex research processes is accomplished much easier within the endo-mode and helps to reach consensus formations and to increase transparency.

Finally, the endo-mode as a highly interactive form of research becomes also a powerful strategy towards more participatory ways of research organizations and to closer ties between science and society. Additionally, the dominance of the exo-mode has generated a high accumulation of theoretical scientific knowledge which was accompanied by wide deficiencies in extension or translational knowledge and an under-developed knowledge of implementing new and highly advanced technologies. The endo-mode can become a vital element in pursuing research to close these asymmetries and deficiencies (Umpleby 2016).

For all these instances, the endo-mode cannot become an easy solution, a quick fix and a trivial cure for everything. But the endo-mode, as opposed to the exo-mode, opens new paths and perspectives for experimenting with and for solving or re-constructing these research problems in the long run.

6 Radical Constructivism and Epistemology

The traditional scientific way of world making can be linked to a relevant background epistemology. For the conventional approach varieties of contemporary realism or empiricism become the obvious candidates for a suitable and coherent epistemology.

It was highly unfortunate that academic philosophers whose overwhelming majority adheres to a realist epistemology de-qualified the rich research tradition of Radical Constructivism as a philosophical epistemology. Although Radical Constructivism was not interested in ongoing philosophical debates on realism and anti-realism philosophers constructed a radical constructivist epistemology as an antirealist account with central claims like an unattainable "knowledge of an independent objective reality" (Gadenne 2010, 77) or a closed system hypothesis in which the brain becomes "operationally closed" (Gadenne 2010, 77). Against this self-constructed straw man of Radical Constructivism several genuinely philosophical counter-arguments were presented, like, for example, the openness of the mind. "The brain can be a closed system while the mind is not." (Gadenne 2010, 78)

But Radical Constructivism started a deep search for the mechanisms of the brain and the neuro-system irrespective of a philosophy of mind. This deep search was looking for the mechanisms of perception and other cognitive faculties and culminated, for example, in the thesis of the inseparability of cognitive faculties like perception, memory and inference (von Foerster 2003, 195).

Radical Constructivism followed along a path which was specified by Willard Van Orman Quine in 1969.

> The stimulation of his sensory receptors is all the evidence anybody has had to go on, ultimately, in arriving at his picture of the world. Why not just see how this construction really proceeds? Why not settle for psychology? (Quine 1969, 75)

Radical constructivism showed, over and over, "how this construction proceeds" and provided, in addition, several explanations on the wide-spread popularity of realism and why a realist epistemology appears so natural and obvious. Moreover, Radical Constructivism with its emphasis on the endo-mode and on the necessary emergence of eigenforms offers also a theoretical account why and how scientific objectivity can occur. And as an empirical research tradition the main target was not epistemology or philosophy of science, but science itself and its usual and traditional paths of exploring the world.

7 Future Horizons

The endo-mode as a new way of scientific world-making and the general scientific methodology of Radical Constructivism are still sufficiently new and unfamiliar within the overall science community. In John Brockman's recent book on scientific ideas which block scientific progress and are bound to die within the next years and decades (Brockman 2015) a total of 175 suggestions were presented from scientists worldwide. Representatives from philosophy of science, logic or science studies presented 36 conceptions which should be abandoned in the future, among them the scientific method, the way of producing and advancing science or science as a self-correcting process. But the arguments offered were extremely weak and did not affect the core of the scientific method or the organization of scientific production processes. The death of objectivity as a blackening of researchers, the death of causality, cause and effects as the primary explanatory scheme, the death of delinking researchers from their fields of research, the death of scientific problem solutions as the only format of problem solutions by scientists and several other ingredients of the exo-mode are still held in high esteem for the future ahead. Here, Radical Constructivism started a still unfinished revolution in reflexivity which is ongoing and which points to the new horizons of the endo-mode as an alternative way of exploring the world which is very likely to expand in the future (Müller 2016).

References

Ackoff, Russell (1974): *Redesigning the Future: A Systems Approach to Societal Problems.* New York: John Wiley & Sons.

Alrøe, Hugo F.; Noe, Egon (2014): "Second-Order Science of Interdisciplinary Research. A Polyocular Framework for Wicked Problems". In: *Constructivist Foundations* 10 (1) 65–76.

Angier, Natalie (2007): *The Canon. A Whirligig Tour of the Beautiful Basics of Science.* London: Faber and Faber.

Beer, Stafford (1972): *Brain of the Firm: a Development in Management Cybernetics.* New York: Herder and Herder.

Beer, Stafford (1975): *Platform for Change.* London, New York: Wiley.

Beer, Stafford (1979): *The Heart of Enterprise.* New York: Wiley.

Brockman, John (ed.) (2015): *This Idea Must Die. Scientific Theories That Are Blocking Progress.* New York: Harper Collins.

Gadenne, Volker (2010): "Why Radical Constructivism Has not Become a Paradigm?" In: *Constructivist Foundations* 6 (1), 77–83.

Glanville, Ranulph (2012): *The Black B∞x.* Vol. I: *Cybernetic Circles.* Wien: Edition Echoraum.

Haag, Günter; Müller Ulrich (1992): "Employment and Education as Non-Linear Network Populations. Part I and II". In: Haag, Günter; Müller, Ulrich; Troitzsch, Klaus (Eds.): *Economic Evolution and Demographic Change. Formal Models in Social Sciences.* Heidelberg: Springer, 349–409.

Kauffman, Louis H. (1987): "Self-Reference and Recursive Forms". In: *Journal of Social and Biological Structures* 10, 53–72.

Kauffman, Louis H. (2016): "Cybernetics, Reflexivity, and Second-Order Science". In: *Constructivist Foundations* 11 (3), 489–497.

Kendel, Eric R. (2012): *The Age of Insight. The Quest to Understand the Unconscious in Art, Mind, and Brain, from Vienna 1900 to the Present.* New York: Random House.

Maturana, Humberto R.; Varela, Francisco J. (1980): *Autopoiesis and Cognition: The Realization of the Living.* Dordecht: Reidel.

Müller, Karl H. (2016): *Second-Order Science. The Revolution of Scientific Structures.* Wien: Edition Echoraum.

Pask, Gordon (1975): *The Cybernetics of Human Learning and Performance. A Guide to Theory and Research.* London: Hutchinson Educational.

Pask, Gordon (1975a): *Conversation, Cognition and Learning. A Cybernetic Theory and Methodology.* New York: Elsevier.

Pask, Gordon (1976): *Conversation Theory, Applications in Education and Epistemology.* New York: Elsevier.

Quine, Willard van Orman (1969): *Ontological Relativity and Other Essays.* New York: Columbia University Press.

Rosenthal, Robert; Fode, Kermit L. (1963): "The Effect of Experimenter Bias on the Performance of the Albino Rat". In: *Behavioral Science* 8, 183–189.

Scott, Bernard (2011): *Explorations in Second-Order Cybernetics. Reflections on Cybernetics, Psychology and Education.* Wien: Edition Echoraum.

Umpleby, Stuart A. (2016): "Second-Order Cybernetics as a Fundamental Revolution in Science". In: *Constructivist Foundations* 11 (3), 455–465.

Varela, Francisco J. (1979): *Principles of Biological Autonomy.* New York: North Holland.

Varela, Francisco J.; Maturana, Humberto R.; Uribe, Ricardo (1974): "Autopoiesis. The Organization of Living Systems, Its Characterization and a Model". In: *Biosystems* 5 (4), 187–196.

von Foerster, Heinz (1982): *Observing Systems.* Seaside: Intersystems Publications.

von Foerster, Heinz (2003): *Understanding Understanding. Essays on Cybernetics and Cognition.* New York: Springer.

von Foerster, Heinz (2014): *The Beginning of Heaven and Earth Has No Name. Seven Days with Second-Order Cybernetics.* New York: Fordham University Press.

von Glasersfeld Ernst (1983): "Learning as a Constructive Activity". In: Bergeron J. C.; Herscovics N. (eds.): *Proceedings of the 5th Annual Meeting of the North American Group of Psychology in Mathematics Education.* Vol. 1. Montreal: PME-NA, 41–101.

von Glasersfeld, Ernst (1977): "The Yerkish Language and Its Automatic Parser". In: Rumbaugh, Duane (ed.): *Language Learning by a Chimpanzee.* New York: Academic Press, 91–130.

2 Epistemology/Epistemological Relativism

Hans-Herbert Kögler
The Truth of Social Constructivism

Abstract: In the course of this essay I attempt to situate truth in social constructivism. I shall first discuss the post-structuralist rejection of truth as a mode of discursive power (1) to then move to the need for a coherent grounding for social constructivism (2). This will lead us to a hermeneutic position which situates the epistemic subject in the social world in which it encounters different historical and cultural perspectives (3). The methodological and ontological problems that beset social constructivism are analyzed with regard to Michel Foucault's discourse analysis (4) and John Searle's intentionalistic ontology of social facts (5). These problems provide evidence for the need for a conception of truth-oriented dialogue in which the other's meaning is approached from one's own situated perspective. The orientation towards understanding the other truthfully is here situated in the social background that undergirds all interpretive efforts. It thereby allows for the reconciliation of the interpreter's truth claim to a justified interpretation with the equally important need to unmask pervasive power relations inherent in discursive practices.

Keywords: social constructivism, truth, hermeneutics, discourse analysis, social ontology

1 Contesting Truth: The Post-Structuralist Rejection

For post-structuralism, truth is the enemy, the nemesis per se, the privileged object of a discursive rejection that is deeply embedded in its cognitive fabric. I shall reconstruct the grounds of this anti-truth attitude to see in which epistemic position it leaves social constructivism. Yet contrary to any quick rejection of post-structuralism itself, I want to show that its rejection of truth is based on insights that reveal problematic features of *truth discourse*. What is at stake in this *discursive dismantling of truth* is a certain account of truth, one that is based on a tight and unreflexive conjunction of truth with a realism that sidesteps the issue of the discursive mediation of reality. The post-structuralist critique of truth discourse rightly suggests that the intrinsic connection of truth and realism may have a detrimental effect on how we approach interpretive and scientific perspectives with truth claims.

The dominant source of this *verito-phobia* is the fact that truth can function to safeguard and immunize a discourse from challenge or contestation. Post-structuralists employ this strategy with a particular view concerning social power. Our access to reality is socially constructed, which concretely means that it is discursively mediated (Hacking 2000). Discourses are part of social reality, and social reality is substantively defined by power struggles among diverse agents and groups (Foucault 1972a). Thus the way in which discourses disclose reality is always an issue of power, a struggle over which view, which conceptual perspective, which articulation of interests and values carries the day. The assignment of truth to one's discourse is seen as an authoritative act that has the function to exempt one's own discourse from further challenge and critique (Foucault 1972b). The focus of truth-oriented discourse is to represent the truth, say, about 'homosexuality.' The post-structuralist critique entails that if the discourse is solely focused on truths about the object, the *conceptual disclosure of 'homosexuality' as an object* is never adequately questioned. Discourses on women/gender, negroes/race, Orientals/Westerners, homosexuals/heterosexuals, etc. accordingly project intentional objects as pre-existing to discourse and about which the discourses are to produce 'the truth.'[1] Truth in this realist sense can thus be shown to be the function of a 'will to knowledge' (Foucault 1994) which immunizes a more radical reflection on the symbolic constructions that disclose the object-domains in the first place.[2]

We can support this discursive criticism of the problematic conjunction of truth and realism from another angle. We may thus point to the vacuous nature of the claim that some discursive statement is 'true.' Truth discourse is empty with regard to the content that is conveyed in a discourse: To learn that it is true that 'the rose is red' does not add anything to my concept of a red rose, just as little as knowing that 'God is perfect' has any consequence for the existence of God.[3] Any existence claim only refers to something as such-and-such, but does not add anything to the definition. The truth predicate merely 'adds'

---

[1] As Edward Said has shown with regard to Orientalism, 'the Oriental' was constructed as a pre-existing reality with which the West had to cope; the discursive construction was intertwined with colonialism finding its legitimacy in the scientific-discursive construction of their object (Said 1975)

[2] It is for this reason that attempts to alleviate the post-structuralist concern about truth with an endorsement of fallibilism, however justified, do not go far enough, as they leave out the need for a reflexive thematization of the counter-productive discursive function of truth.

[3] On these grounds, Kant and Russell were able to reject the ontological argument about God's existence, since concepts fulfill their function in defining content but do not reach beyond themselves to existence.

the existential qualifier to a discourse, stating that such-and-such *exists*. Yet since the disclosure of what is taken to exist is always and insurmountably conveyed in conceptual and discursive form, it is *this form*, and *not the claim to truth*, that provides content. Truth is thus at best a compliment, in Rorty's famous phrase, which we assign to those discourses we already endorse.[4] But if this is so, the reference to truth has no bite with regard to gaining knowledge about the world. The signifying vacuity of the truth predicate may thus complement the power utilization of truth discourse, since an existing practice of discursive world-disclosure can now be declared the authoritative representation of reality without any change in its internal configuration.

2 Follow-up Problems of Rejecting Truth

What post-structuralists (and neo-pragmatists) thus reject is an *extra-discursive conception of truth*. 'Truth' is a marker that makes discourses unchallengeable, that cements their authority and proclaims their reign instead of enabling critical reflexivity or radical transformation. For social constructivists it follows that we should abandon any reference to truth altogether. The deconstruction of truth is seen as allowing an open-minded world-view, as the ground for a pluralism according to which each perspective embraces with open arms any other perspective.[5] Yet this argument from the rejection of truth faces the problem that the endorsement of all perspectives as equally valid goes too far. If the externalist conception of truth leads to a rejection of truth altogether, then discourse-internal modes of disclosure would be solely defining what counts as 'true' according to their respective perspectives. Folding truth entirely into the discourse would mean that *the discursive mediation itself defines what exists* (according to its discursive disclosure). We would arrive at an *intra-discursive conception of reality* according to which all objects and states of affairs would be determined by the discourses themselves. There are at least three unhappy consequences of such an account.

First, if all perspectives would be deemed as equally valid and only responsible to their own internal standards, then the proposed pluri-worldview would itself be just another perspective, and neither more or less valid than a truth-ex-

---

4 See (Rorty 1979) for a full-blown critique of any realist or correspondence-theoretical notion of truth.
5 Sociological accounts of the social structuration of our cognitive dispositions, like Pierre Bourdieu's habitus, are welcomed by many for establishing such a pluri-verse of equally valid and productive perspectives; see (Bourdieu 1984).

ternalist account. Yet it seems pertinent that we do not undermine the general validity of the crucial premise of social constructivism that entails the discursive mediation of our understanding of reality.

Second, the identification of truth as 'whatever the discourse constructs as truth' would amount to idealism. If we reject an externalist view and now embrace that the respective ontologies are discourse-dependent, we seem to engage in the obviously absurd assumption that all the intentionally disclosed objects and states of affairs are themselves discursive. Yet we can neither claim with good reason that reality as such is discursive or conceptual, nor can we overcome the intentional nature of our discourses which are defined by referring to entities and structures in the world that are not themselves discursive.[6]

Third, the rejection of truth argued that truth would immunize discourses from critique. But abandoning the truth concept altogether has in the end the same effect! If we define the world as a landscape of equally valid perspectives, we *de facto* insulate all such perspectives from challenges and criticism. If we define every view as valid, as internally constituted by its own 'truth,' we exempt every view from challenge, critique, and transformation.[7] Accordingly, on the one hand, we would have to accept those views that deem themselves superior to others (based on their access to truth!), and on the other hand, we could not challenge any view via the reference to a better understanding of the issue at stake, which would entail that existing discourses go unchallenged as to how they construct their respective realities.[8]

---

[6] This statement entails two points. First, our understanding is defined by intentionality which displays the cognitive structure to be 'directed towards something.' This directionality means that we refer to something as something. This intentional reference to some content is a feature of every sign and as such defines the basic symbolic mediation of reality. Second, we need to make space for the fact that we may refer to both discursive and non-discursive, material and social realities. To reject this second claim would amount to linguistic idealism.

[7] This view amounts to a conflation of social validity and epistemic validity. This view is untenable because within social practices, agents criticize beliefs and claims based on evidence, and thus challenge accepted beliefs and assumptions. Social validity is thus challenged from within social reality, which means that we need some concept to account for this trans-social validity that is invoked in social practices themselves.

[8] We can see a real-life consequence of this consequence when religious fundamentalist discourse proclaims that its 'truth' is defined by its own standards and as such deems itself both capable of constructing valid views concerning external reality as well as capable to compete with scientific discourses while based on a different standard of 'evidence.'

3 The Hermeneutic Way: From Transcendental to Social Constructivism

In order to show that this impasse should convince us to reconstruct a *hermeneutic conception of socially situated and truth-oriented understanding*, I propose a set of steps that trace the transformation from transcendental (Kantian) constructivism to a social constructivism that understands itself in this context. Social constructivism here becomes a reflexive acknowledgment of one's own epistemic situatedness, but this situatedness is not epistemically castrating and neutralizing, but rather seen as an enabling ground for trans-discursive criticisms and challenges.

For a Kantian constructivism, the issue of realism is a nonissue. For Kant, the objects of experience are transcendentally constituted such that the epistemic subject is capable of knowing the truth (Kant 1999). Truth is seen as correspondence between belief and object, but the object is constituted by the subject's own cognitive operations, which Kant calls 'transcendental apperception.' The ghost of objective idealism is kept in check by the invocation of the thing itself, which is seen as the ultimate essence of reality but irrelevant for the constitution of truth. Truth is about the objects of (our!) experience and as such relates to phenomena that are within the realm of knowledge.

The movement from transcendental to social constructivism is prepared by two historical developments in which the grounding of the epistemic subject undergoes a dramatic transformation. First, this transformation fuses elements of Kantian constructivism with historical, cultural, and social factors, which puts the *social situatedness* of the knowing subject in the center. In the Kantian conception, knowledge is understood as mediated by conceptual or symbolic schemes of understanding (Kant to Cassirer), which emerge from universally shared cognitive structures of the mind. Yet now *the knowing subject becomes the socially situated subject*. The force of synthesis is now derived from social sources, is now located in an empirical agent who is shaped by history and culture. This development is owed to the overcoming of the empirical/transcendental divide of the subject in German idealism, to the materialism of Young Hegelians like Marx, to emerging sociological classics, and finally reaches its culmination in the movement from phenomenology to a "hermeneutics and facticity" (Heidegger 1999).

Second, this movement entails the discovery of a whole new realm of knowledge in the new human sciences (*Geisteswissenschaften*). Here the epistemic subject encounters an 'object' which is itself a subject, which has understanding and knowledge based on categories and conceptions just as herself, and understands itself and the world according to its own conceptual frames and assumptions. The new epistemological challenge, articulated by Schleiermacher, Dilthey, historicism, Neo-Kantianism up to philosophical hermeneutics, is how to address this situation given that *the other knows according to her own conceptual frames and assumptions*. (Schleiermacher 1998; Dilthey 1989; 2004) How is the reality of those different historical epochs and cultural worlds to be construed in the human sciences? How is a true representation and understanding of the other possible? Crucial for the epistemic situation of social constructivism is that *the encountered worlds are recognized as structured by symbolic mediation:* understanding encounters (another) understanding, and thus requires a reflexive taking-into-account how the agents understand themselves. The encountered epochs or worlds are seen as different exemplifications of world disclosure, which means that they cannot simply be 'assimilated' to one's own categories or assumptions if one truly wants to understand *them*.

The lesson of this development is that the *epistemic situation of the social constructivist* is defined by (1) the symbolic mediation of her background beliefs and assumptions, (2) practical embeddedness of this background in social practices and institutions, and (3) dialogical openness vis-à-vis intentional beliefs that are encountered against such a background (Kögler 1999). The point is a hermeneutic one: the social constructivist is *forced to reflexivity* with regard to this background condition of her own analysis of social meanings and practices. The hermeneutic grounding of this view allows for a non-contradictory endorsement of epistemic situatedness because it avoids the problems that haunt the full-blown rejection of truth. The claim that *all beliefs are symbolically mediated* can be presented as universally valid while still recognizing that every concrete act of understanding takes off from one's concrete background assumptions. The claim of *practical embeddedness* makes sure that we avoid linguistic idealism, since we understand discourses to be embedded in *real* social practices and institutions and through them connected with the *external* natural environment. Finally, the linguistic mediation of our beliefs entails that we have to reconstruct meanings and practices as intentional expressions that require our *dialogical engagement*, i.e. that we disclose by investing our own beliefs and assumptions as starting points to understand and interpret the other meaning as a possibly true view about a shared subject matter. The criticism of other beliefs, assumptions and practices thus becomes possible as a challenge that does not simply impose external standards but takes the self-understanding of the other into account.

Yet while I can thus present in broad strokes how this position avoids the pitfalls that plague the rejection of truth, I cannot possibly believe that such a statement suffices to establish this position. What I can do, however, is to show that this position is presupposed by major representatives of social constructivism. I claim that these *hermeneutic conditions of understanding* present a quasi-transcendental presupposition of social-constructivist accounts of social reality. I want to make this claim plausible by reconstructing the contradictions into which the approaches of Michel Foucault and John Searle lead without it.

4 Overcoming Methodological Positivism: Foucault's Discourse Analysis

Foucault's discourse analysis is a paradigm of social constructivism, both with regard to its radical thesis and with regard to its pervasive reception. Discourses for Foucault constitute the symbolic frameworks through which social reality is both understood and produced. In conjunction with power practices, discourses create 'regional ontologies' that disclose phenomena like madness, health, life, economy, 'man,' crime and sexuality, etc. (Foucault 1988, 2003, 1970, 1979, 1994). Discourses are composed of *statements* which are distinguished from grammatical sentences, logical propositions, and normative speech acts; they derive their force from their position in a discursive field. As such, discourses determine the position of the knowing subject, its experiential objects, the conceptual realms, and they are associated with a strategic field (Foucault 1972a). Discourse analysis is thus, by embedding the knowing subject as well as the known object within the realm of (diverse, different) discourses, diametrically opposed to an account of truth that locates it either in a transcendental subject (like Kantian constructivism) or in a realism of objective states of affairs (like empirical realism) (Foucault 1972b).

What interests us is this: How—from which epistemic position—can the discourse analyst reconstruct these discourses? How can one access these rules and practices such that one avoids problematic ontological assumptions regarding a constitutive subject or a pre-existing metaphysical realism? How can one claim to represent and reconstruct these discourses such that one establishes a social-constructivist position vis-à-vis one's own epistemic position, and thus maintains a coherent position?

Foucault aims to reconstruct the *discursive mediation of reality*. This analysis itself, however, it to take place as a 'pure description' of 'discursive facts,' capturing the statements in their particular purity as events.

> One is led therefore to the project of a pure description of discursive events as the horizon for the search for discursive units that form within it... we must grasp the statement in the exact specificity of its occurrence; determine its conditions of existence; fix at least its lim-

its, establish its correlations with other statements that may be connected to it, and show what other statements it excludes. (Foucault 1972a, 26f)

This positivistic self-understanding ultimately means that Foucault does not succeed in delineating *his own specific discursive position*. Foucault may think that he has sufficiently prepared his positivistic move by rejecting all problematic pre-conceptions that would undermine the 'pure description of discursive events.' Foucault lists a whole range of broad-scale meta-historical concepts, such as tradition, influence, development and evolution—and we could easily add progress, epoch, people, class—as categories which obscure rather than disclose historical reality. We are to get rid of all concepts that construct discourses as expressions of a deeper sense or reality, of anything "which allows the sovereignty of collective consciousness to emerge as the principle of unity and explanation." (Foucault 1972a, 21) Foucault's target is a pre-discursive conception of intentionality that can take many forms: as grounding subjectivity (Kant, Husserl), world spirit (Hegel), authorial text-meaning (pre-Gadamerian hermeneutics), value-orientations within social fields (Weber), etc. In all these moves, Foucault detects a pre-discursive, thus pre-analytical attempt to 'subjectivize' or rationalize the historico-social world: to imbue it with a sense, a meaning, an intentional teleology.

Instead of retrieving meaning and truth in discourses, Foucault embeds meaning and truth *within* discursive formations, such that they precede the cognitive control and awareness of situated agents. Yet now the question about the *epistemic identifiability of discourses* poses itself all the more forcefully: From which position is Foucault himself able to undertake the analysis of discursive events and orders? How is his own epistemic position, within discourses and with regard to discursive formations, poised to generate the necessary access to the internal organization of the discourses at stake? The demarcation of the 'discursive statement' as the most elementary level of discourses can in the end only re-articulate the intuition of the concrete embeddedness of statements in existing discursive contexts. The question remains how one is able to get *epistemic access* to the uniquely discursive level of reality—to the level of the discursive mediation of reality in different constellations—given that Foucault himself must speak from within the context of a discursive formation, must acknowledge that he is bound by certain rules and assumptions of the discourse he is part of. If the analysis of discourse is to achieve an adequate level of reflexivity, one that applies the same standards to itself that it projects onto discursive formations, the question how one's own discursive context mediates the analysis of discourses as objects needs to be answered with full rigor. How does he envision to solve the riddle to give a shared and valid account of specific discursive formations, one that is not limited to just some contextual assumptions of his own discourse, if (a) discourses limit *a priori* what agents can state and experience, and if (b) the discourse analyst is herself *positioned* within a definite discursive context?

Foucault's positivism of a 'pure description of discursive events' would, if driven to its methodological extreme, entail that Foucault describes discourses without being himself bound by one: he would then hover, like a historicist helicopter, above all discursive formations, equally close to all, so as to record their internal configurations. If he, on the other hand, would endorse the historicist-constructivist claim that all historical knowledge is bound by its own discursive rules, according to which reality is internally determined, he would fall into the trap of methodological subjectivism, as now the reconstruction of other discursive formations could not claim to be more than an internally constructed projection dependent on his own contingent standards. What Foucault therefore needs is a conception of discursive understanding that allows him (a) to reconstruct the internal order and boundary of existing discourses, (b) to situate his own discourse vis-à-vis its own boundaries, (c) to show that discourse can serve as a medium that enables the reconstruction of other discourses as well as social practices and external reality (since discourses are embedded in 'strategic fields,'), such that (d) he is able to justify that a reconstruction of discursive boundaries could sustain an intersubjective test by other discursive analysts.

5 Overcoming Metaphysical Realism: Searle's Intentionalistic Ontology

However, we may now ask: Could we not sidestep the issue of the epistemic position of the analyst by projecting a social ontology that outlines the basic features of social reality in general? This is the project of John Searle who sets out to make Intentionality the core metaphysical ground of all social being. Searle does *not* introduce a methodology how to understand social realities but presents an *ontology of the 'building blocks' of social reality*. He thereby demarcates the unique space of social reality by placing it nevertheless within one materialistically understood world, yet without reducing its unique ontology to that of natural or material processes. Searle aims to give an *ontological* account of social constructivism via Intentionality to avoid a reductionistic view of social reality, but I shall argue that his account is not sufficiently *epistemologically* constructivist. I argue that there is a conflict between Searle's theory of linguistic understanding, in which he endorses the discursive mediation of reality, and his ontological account of social reality, which I consider to be an intentionalistic version of a metaphysical realism.[9]

Searle argues in his speech act theory that language is comprised of symbolic acts which entail constitutive rules which prescribe for situated speakers how to express, understand, and communicate meaning (Searle 1969). 'Locutionary' expressions entail a 'propositional' content which is modally defined by 'illocutionary' speech act types (as assertive, directive, commisive, expressive, and declarative acts); the particular acts may have 'perlocutionary' effects in the world. In his turn to a social ontology, Searle now claims that linguistic meaning is derivative of Intentionality (Searle 1985). Language is now generated by the intentional projection of content onto phonetic or semiotic units, thereby generating these as meaningful units. Speech acts are thus the model for Searle's general theory of social construction, as they present *in nuce* what happens in any process of social construction: Intentional meaning is projected onto an otherwise material and 'meaningless' being, thus generating social facts or institutions like money, wars, marriages, etc. The intentional understanding of such-and-such, which Searle considers as the assignment of status-functions onto material reality, represents his core idea with regard to the construction of social reality. The intentionalistic account toward linguistic meaning is extrapolated to all social facts: social reality is created by having "X count as Y in context C." (Searle 1995, 28; see also Searle 2010).[10]

Yet the social-ontological approach faces the methodological issue of how access to the constructed meaning-contexts is possible. Agents can only understand the beliefs, assumptions, and practices of other agents (a) if they are able to immerse themselves as possible participants within the intentional contexts and thereby come to share the orientation of situated speakers, picking up how things are taken and meant in the respective contexts, which (b) is only possible by taking into account one's own immersion in practically situated and symbolically mediated contexts, i.e. by drawing on one's own situated and insurmountable pre-understanding of the concepts at stake (Gadamer 1989).

The hermeneutic pre-understanding is a general condition of understanding and yet it is always situated and contextual. Intentional acts are therefore always

---

9 The concept of metaphysical realism is of course borrowed from Hilary Putnam (Putnam 1981)
10 Searle's further development of his position in *Making the Social World* (Searle 2010) re-emphasizes the role of language, compared to Intentionality, because the declarative speech act type is now seen to enable the constitution of status assignments that represent and create a normative reality with 'deontic powers.' Regardless, as we will see, Searle maintains his distinction between the epistemological and ontological meanings of the subjective and the objective, without the slightest sense for the hermeneutic issues that emerge from this.

already discursively mediated, and access to any pure intentionality is ruled out. Searle's pro-claimed 'intentional meaning-constitution' is not phenomenologically accessible, as we obviously live and move within our linguistically mediated sets of beliefs and assumptions when articulating and communicating content. We do not first present content intentionally to ourselves to subsequently assign some otherwise meaningless sound-bites or visible scribbles with 'meaning.' Furthermore, as Searle himself emphasized, all intentional meaning draws on background *assumptions* (the network) and practical *skills and capabilities* (the Background) (Searle 1985). The understanding of the meaning and practices of social realities—the constructed reality Searle's 'building block' approach was supposed to explain—can thus only be achieved via the mediated access through one's own socially defined context. The understanding and interpretation of the meaning of money, marriage, voting, and other social phenomena is thus only possible due to the epistemic subject's situated immersion in a socially constructed context. Searle's ontological account gives us a general story how social reality is constructed, but the ontological foundation of all social reality in an Intentionally writ large—in pre-contextual Ur-acts, as it were—cannot account for the unique epistemic situation that derives from the social situatedness of the knowing subject.

This hermeneutic objection is further supported by several problematic distinctions regarding social facts. According to Searle, we need to distinguish 'intrinsic' from 'observer-relative' facts; observer-relative facts are ontologically subjective, while intrinsic ones are ontologically objective. The intentional ontology makes social reality thereby ontologically subjective, because here "*seeming to be F* is logically prior to *being F*" (Searle 1995, 13) However, *this* distinction between subjective and objective ontology should not be confused with *epistemic* subjectivity or objectivity: "… ontological subjectivity does not prevent claims about observer-relative features from being epistemically objective." (Searle 1995, 13) Yet a closer look at how such an alleged 'epistemic objectivity' is to be achieved leads us right back to the hermeneutic fact that all understanding of the 'observer-relative,' 'ontologically subjective' social reality has to be proceed from the interpreter's own socially situated pre-understanding. It is misleading to invoke an unrevised standard notion of epistemic objectivity when the disclosure of meaning by the situated self is constituted by the contextual horizons provided by particulate beliefs, assumptions, and practices.

Searle's unwillingness to reform his epistemic framework in line with social constructivism is further displayed by his related distinction between brute and institutional facts. For Searle, brute facts exist independently of human institutions, while the latter are required for social facts. Searle acknowledges that the *knowledge* of brute facts requires at least one institutional fact to be possible, namely language: "Brute facts require the institution of language in order that we can *state* the facts, but the brute facts *themselves* exist quite independently of language or of any other institution." (Searle 1995, 27) Note that the distinction between 'stating the facts' and 'the facts themselves' can only be made from within the institution of language. But it gets truly interesting once we realize that with regard to the knowledge of the social world, *stating of the facts and the facts themselves* form an indivisible unity. While social reality cannot be reduced to mere discourse (as this would entail linguistic idealism and neglect the materiality of social practices and environments), the constitution of social facts is essentially maintained by means of socially shared projections of intentional meaning which are linguistically articulated. Thus the respective meaning of social facts is necessarily mediated by contextual background assumptions, and the epistemic access to it has to proceed from one's own situated pre-understanding. The lack of reflexivity concerning epistemic access to social meanings in Searle's account establishes, just as much as it did with regard to Foucault, the need for a hermeneutic grounding of social constructivism.

References

Bourdieu, Pierre (1984): *Distinction*. Cambridge: Harvard University Press.
Dilthey, Wilhelm (1989): *Introduction to the Human Sciences*. Princeton: Princeton University Press.
Dilthey, Wilhelm (2004): *The Construction of History in the Human Sciences*. Princeton: Princeton University Press.
Foucault, Michel (1970): *The Order of Things*. New York: Random House.
Foucault, Michel (1972b): *The Discourse on Language*. In: Foucault, Michel (1972a): *The Archaeology of Knowledge*. New York: Pantheon Books, 215–237.
Foucault, Michel (1979): *Discipline and Punish*. New York: Pantheon Books.
Foucault, Michel (1988): *Madness and Civilization*. New York: Pantheon Books.
Foucault, Michel (1990a): *The Use of Pleasure*. New York: Vintage Books.
Foucault, Michel (1994): *History of Sexuality. Vol. 1*. New York: Vintage Books.
Foucault, Michel (2003): *The Birth of the Clinic*. London: Routledge.
Foucault, Michel (1972a): *The Archaeology of Knowledge*. New York: Pantheon Books.
Gadamer, Hans-Georg (1989): *Truth and Method*. New York: Crossroad Publishers.
Hacking, Ian (2000): *The Social Construction of What?* Cambridge, MA: Harvard University Press.
Heidegger, Martin (1999): *Ontology: Hermeneutics of Facticity*. Bloomington: Indiana University Press.
Kant, Immanuel (1999): *Critique of Pure Reason*. Cambridge: Cambridge University Press.
Kögler, Hans-Herbert (1999): *The Power of Dialogue*. Cambridge, MA: The MIT Press.
Putnam, Hilary (1981): *Reason, Truth, and History*. Cambridge, MA: Harvard University Press.

Rorty, Richard (1979): *Philosophy and the Mirror of Nature.* Princeton: Princeton University Press.
Said, Edward (1975): *Orientalism.* London: Penguin Books.
Schleiermacher, Friedrich (1998): *Hermeneutics and Criticism.* Cambridge: Cambridge University Press.
Searle, John (1983): *Intentionality.* Cambridge: Cambridge University Press.
Searle, John (1995): *The Construction of Social Reality.* New York: The Free Press.
Searle, John (2010): *Making the Social World. The Structure of Human Civilization,* Oxford: Oxford University Press.
Searle, John, (1969): *Speech Acts.* Cambridge: Cambridge University Press.

Gerhard Schönrich
The Objectivity of Epistemic Values and the Argument from Immersion

Abstract: Alethic relativism seems implausible to many philosophers, because it is incompatible with the persistent intuition that truth cannot be relative to an assessment (see for example McFarlane 2014). Justification relativism, however, is rather approved. The hyperbolic demands of relativism seem to be more acceptable if relativism only concerns our beliefs, judgments or claims about the world, but not if it concerns truth or even the world itself. In this paper, it will be argued that justification relativism has some lacunae. It cannot be defended in a strong, externalist version, and it fails with respect to the normative implications of our epistemic practice and a factual understanding of reasons.

Keywords: Normativity, relativism, values, argument from immersion

1 Epistemic Normativity

We aim at truth when we form beliefs, make assertions or give a judgement. Something has gone wrong, if they turn out false. How strictly is this reference to truth to be taken? What distinguishes a propositional attitude such as believing from other propositional attitudes such as guessing, wishing, imagining, etc.? Are these latter attitudes not also aiming at truth? Even if we only want something, we conceive it as true after all; and if we imagine something, such as the land of plenty, we imagine it to be true that roasted pigeons are flying into our mouth. Such attitudes, therefore, seem to be directed to propositions which we regard as true – regardless of whether they are actually true or not.

In the specific case of belief formation, we are to believe a proposition only if it is actually true (see Velleman 2000, ch. 11). Truth is taken as a *final* goal which we aim at for its own sake, and not for the sake of something else, as it is the case with wishful thinking, imaginations, suppositions, etc. In the latter cases, we conceive something as true for the sake of something else, for instance in order to test the consequences of an assumption or to envision a sought-after situation. Truth is sought only *instrumentally*, not for its own sake. Of course, there are other candidates for final epistemic values, such as knowledge or understanding. Whether truth is the only final epistemic value, or whether it has to share this place with other values, may remain open in this paper (Convincing arguments for truth are provided by David 2001). The formation of belief, by all means, is concerned with the unraveling of the truth for its own sake. It is – so to speak – about truth as truth.

The normative structure of *truth regulation* looks like this:

> (TT) Out of the propositions which S considers, it is good (valuable) for S to believe only those which are true.

> (CS) Out of the propositions which S considers, it is correct for S to believe only those which are true.

There is a close relation between the target of truth (TT) and the correctness standard (CS), which allows for at least two different interpretations. According to the *teleological reading*, (CS) is explained by (TT): It is correct to believe only true propositions *because* truth is a goal of our epistemic practices. The *normativistic reading* reverses the direction of explanation: Truth is an epistemic value and to be pursued as a goal *because* it is correct to believe only true propositions. The principle of justification of our beliefs:

> (JB) S may believe that p iff S is justified to believe that p.

will help to reach (TT), or to comply with (CS) respectively. Justification – other than truth – is sought not for its own sake. It is valuable because it is beneficial for achieving the truth. The idea behind (JB) is that truth should not be gained randomly. That's why (JB) stands in an instrumental relationship to (TT) as well as to (CS); and it has been formulated as a permission rule, because we are not to believe any and all true propositions, but only relevant ones.

(TT) and (CS) describe different things. Being valuable is an axiological property, correctness, however, a normative one (see for example Lynch 2009 and Engel 2013). (TT) says that it is valuable to believe only true propositions, while (CS) ascribes the property of correctness to a propositional attitude. It should remain irrelevant for the following considerations which direction of explanation is to be preferred. Within our epistemic practice, both aspects are necessary for the regulation of truth. The notion of belief formation aiming at truth includes a correctness standard in any case.

Epistemic relativists vehemently deny that there are absolute values, absolute correctness, or absolute facts with regard to the justification of belief. They, therefore, should accept the following qualifications:

> (TT-rel) According to S's epistemic system: Out of the propositions p which S considers, it is good (valuable) for S to believe only those which are true.

(CS-rel) According to S's epistemic system: Out of the propositions p which S considers, it is correct for S to believe only those which are true.

(JB-rel) According to S's epistemic system: S may believe that p iff S is justified to believe that p.

2 Justification Relativism and Scepticism

According to Boghossian's much discussed proposal, justification relativism is to be understood as follows (Boghossian 2006, 84f):

> 1. There are no absolute facts about what belief a particular item of information justifies. (Epistemic non-absolutism)
>
> 2. If a person, S's, epistemic judgements are to have any prospect of being true, we must not construe his utterances of the form "E justifies belief B" as expressing the claim: *E justifies belief B* but rather as expressing the claim: *According to the epistemic system C, that I, S accept, information E justifies belief B* (Epistemic relationism).
>
> 3. There are many fundamentally different, genuinely alternative epistemic systems, but no facts by virtue of which one of these systems is more correct than any of the others. (Epistemic pluralism)

Justification relativism is strengthened by making as many externalist stipulations as possible. An internalist conception makes it too easy for scepticism. As evidence, therefore, count facts, measurements, indications etc., which stand in a supportive relation to the content p of the thus justified belief. Evidence is not purely psychological. We need to assume that evidence has a truth capable propositional content in order to stand in inferential relations to other propositional contents. But evidence is not equivalent to reasons. In order to play a role in the truth regulated formation of belief, it must be brought into a relation to S's belief formation and not only to the content of the belief (see Section 3).

An epistemic system consists of beliefs, of logical principles (induction, modus ponens, etc.), and of prima facie principles such as:

> (Observation) If S has observational evidence E that p, then S is *prima facie* justified to form a belief with content p.
> *or*
> (Revelation) If S has evidence E that p such that E has been revealed as God's word, then S is *prima facie* justified to form a belief with content p.

If evidence is understood externally, why then count E as evidence in one system but not in the other? The relativity of evidential support is best to be explained with respect to a way of conceiving something, i.e. a perspective. A perspective consists in selecting a certain set of facts. A perspective can, therefore, be conceived as a mapping from a set of principles (defined by an epistemic system) into a set of facts. It selects or determines – in accordance with the rules and principles prevailing in an epistemic system – those facts, which count as evidence. For relativists, this selection mechanism explains how there can be a situation in which two different parties, let's call them "B" and "G", are equally well justified with respect to one and the same subject matter. (Because we are not concerned with the complex historical controversy between Galileo and Bellarmine here, but use it only as a stylized dispute, the placeholders "B" and "G" are used. However, the historical situation remains useful as an allusion horizon.)

G claims that the earth revolves around the sun (= p); B, however, that the sun revolves around the earth (= non-p). G observes apparent retrograde motions of Mars through a telescope, and he evaluates his observations as evidence e_1 for the fact that Mars revolves around the sun and not around the earth, a fact counting as evidence e_2 for the heliocentric worldview. B, however, is convinced that the sun revolves around the earth. His evidence consists in the revealed word of God which counts as evidence e_1^* for the harmony of the heavenly bodies which in turn counts as evidence e_2^* for the geocentric worldview. In a situation in which the two fundamentally different principles (observation and revelation) select the relevant evidence in a different way, it can happen that two incompatible beliefs p and non-p appear equally well justified:

> (Observation Perspective) The rules of the system that G accepts select the evidence $\{e_1, e_2, ...\}$ which supports the belief that p.
> (Revelation Perspective) The rules of the system that B accepts select the evidence $\{e_1^*, e_2^*, ...\}$ which supports the belief that non-p.

Neither party seems to have made a mistake. Their beliefs are regulated by truth, they react to evidence, and both subject themselves to the correctness standards of their respective epistemic systems. Such a relativity to a way of conceiving things allows us to spell out epistemic non-absolutism in a way that is consistent with our *objectivity* intuition:

> The world as a total set of facts with subsets $\{e_1, e_2, ...\}$ and $\{e_1^*, e_2^*, ...\}$ cannot be such that p and not-p are equally well supported.

The objectivity intuition is not called into question as long as the sets of evidence which support p and non-p respectively are different sets. If we stay within this picture, the two parties could tolerate each other epistemically, without interfering in the cognitive affairs of the other party. (Whether this quietism also holds in political, social, economic, etc. situations would be a different question.) Paying closer attention, we can see, however, that such an epistemic peace does not hold. This is due to a principle which relativism has to accept as well:

> Every justification of contingent truths is fundamentally defeasible.

That the evidence E justifies a proposition p means that E provides enough support to give p a certain degree of justification. This level is usually high, but not too high. It is too high if the belief that p is logically implied by a justification on the basis of E. E, therefore, should not logically imply p (see Huemer 2001). And this is why the support that p gets from E can be challenged by new information. So any justification based on E is logically compatible with the falsity of p. The alternative is an infallibilism according to which the truth of p or the falsity of non-p is logically implied by E. In this case, either G or B (or both) made a mistake; and justification relativism is losing its strongest motive.

The principle of defeasibility of justification is a precondition and – at the same time – a serious threat for relativism. It can be understood as an invitation for skepticism. As long as the evidence which supports p is logically compatible with non-p, the relativist is exposed to countless possible alternatives to p, which he cannot rule out in principle. This, however, would not only put justification relativism into question, it would also render our objectivity intuition moot. The sceptic wants to show – with the help of radical scenarios, such as the Cartesian dream or brain-in-the-vat situations – that all evidence which suggests that we are not in such a scenario, is compatible with the hypothesis that we are in such a scenario (see Huemer 2001). Our beliefs about the world would then be in principle (and not only relatively) incorrect; and justification would not be truth conducive.

The relativist indeed wants to deny absolute facts, but he by no means wants to abstain from relative facts. He insists that there are relatively justified beliefs based on non-absolute facts. In order to fight back against the sceptic, he needs to invest more into his epistemic system as a mere relativity to ways of conceiving something. If the supportive evidence for p is logically compatible with the truth of non-p, the relativist needs to explain why G prefers p (and accordingly: why B prefers non-p) in the face of logically possible alternatives. Such an explanation, however, cannot be based on evidence selected relatively to a way of conceiving things: The conjunction of the sets $\{e_1, e_2, ...\}$ and $\{e_1^*, e_2^*, ...\}$ is compatible with both p and non-p.

In order to give such an explanation, a separate and independent second level evidence about the nature of the selected evidence is needed – evidence which supports the subjects in believing that their first level evidence $\{e_1, e_2, ...\}$ or $\{e_1^*, e_2^*, ...\}$ is truth conducive for p or non-p respectively. Evidence – of course – can justify implicitly, whatever level is concerned. The epistemic agent doesn't need to reflect on his own epistemic situation and form a meta-justification taking the shape of an explicit belief about the reliability of his evidential support. Even the simple possession of second-level evidence can justify him and his system compared to all other alternatives. The situation so far is normatively relaxed and stable. What would then motivate a party tampering with the cognitive affairs of the other party? Obviously the parties are driven by the normative forces of truth regulation, and it is for this reason that they evaluate the beliefs of each other as inadequate and untruthful.

3 The Argument from Immersion and Its Normative Preconditions

According to Boghossian, immersion has to be defined in the following way:[1]

> 1. If it is – according to the Observation perspective – correct for G to believe that p, then it is – according to G's Observation perspective – also correct for G to believe that it is incorrect to believe that non-p.
>
> 2. If it is – according to the Observation perspective – correct for G to believe that p, then it is also correct for G to believe that it is according to B's Relevation perspective incorrect to believe that non-p.
>
> 3. If it is – according to the Observation perspective – correct for G to believe that p, then it is also correct for G to believe that it is according to any perspective incorrect to believe that non-p.

For B *mutatis mutandis*. The argument is successful only if the following three conditions are met: First: The parties G and B must engage in meta-justification, second: they both must be engaged in the pursuit of truth, and third: they must understand the reasons for their beliefs in a factual way. The transitions from step (1) to step (2) and then from step (2) to step (3) can only be understood if the preconditions of this argument are clear.

The first condition: The argument refers to a normatively charged situation: Both parties challenge the other's beliefs by discussing to what extent each other's

---

[1] The argument has been condensed. See more explicitly (Boghossian 2014, 382).

supportive evidence will lead to the truth of their respective belief. The starter of the argument is the truth regulation. Facing the possibility that beliefs might be wrong and justifications might be not truth-conducive, no participant of an epistemic practice can remain quiet. Now, the correctness standard can only be applied if all participants actually form meta-beliefs about the justification of their beliefs. Evidence and even second level evidence is no longer sufficient as soon as competing selective perspectives come into play. According to (CS-rel), it is correct for G to believe that p only if G's belief (p) is supported by $\{e_1, e_2, ...\}$. So G can only assess the correctness of his belief by forming an explicit meta-belief concerning the truth conduciveness of the evidence he selected.

But why – in the perspective of Observation – is it also incorrect for G to believe that non-p, as claimed in the argument from immersion? Why is this move which wasn't allowed in a skeptical context suddenly possible within a normative setting? If it were only for the evidential support of p, G could not even dismiss alternatives as incorrect. G (and B respectively) would have to refrain from any judgement about the correctness of the beliefs of the other party. Some authors claim that it is all right to hold on to your own epistemic system – even blindly – when you are confronted with an alternative (Goldman 2010). This answer, however, is unsatisfactory in a normative context.

The second condition: If we want to understand what it means to engage in an epistemic practice, we should start with the more fundamental question: How is it possible that evidence E is a *reason* to believe p at all? 'True' is not the same as 'correct'. Only propositions are true or false. Beliefs as attitudes are mental states which are neither true nor false, but they can be evaluated normatively. It is correct to adopt a belief, if its content is indeed true; and it is wrong to adopt it, if its content is false. Evidence provides *propositional justification*. Related to the content p of a belief evidence doesn't justify the attitude of believing as such but rather the propositional content of that attitude. Strictly speaking, a belief isn't justified by evidence, but its content is. In order to explain how we come from evidence to the correctness of an attitude, a transmission principle is needed linking the truth of a proposition with the act of adopting an attitude towards that proposition. We arrive at *doxastic justification*:

(DJ) S ought to adopt the belief that p, if
i. E supports p sufficiently,
ii. S has formed a meta-belief about the reliability of E, and
iii. p (or the exclusion of non-p) are relevant.

With respect to S and S's mental states evidence transforms into a reason. In contrast to evidence, reasons are irreducibly normative (Scanlon 2014). If S has undefeated reasons to believe that p but does not form a belief that p, something went wrong normatively. Only by engaging in an epistemic practice of giving and taking reasons, we are on the pursuit of truth and complying with the norm of correctness. As long as B is just being informed about G's heretic beliefs by some reliable henchman or whistle-blower, he is not engaged in the pursuit of truth. B indeed becomes acquainted with the evidence G uses to support his beliefs. B might even realize that G considers himself doxastically justified according to G's epistemic system. B may also have evidence for G's imperturbable belief towards p. And B can report this information to the sacred college of cardinals without ever engaging in the normative obligations of G's epistemic practice.

But as an engaged participant of an epistemic practice, B is obligated to believe that it is indeed – according to G's perspective – incorrect to believe that p. As an informant about G's beliefs, B has no such obligation. He has some different obligations, however, deriving from his role as an informant: B has evidence and maybe even explicit meta-beliefs about the correctness of his report. He does for example trust the testimony of his henchmen. But such beliefs are not meta-beliefs about the correctness or incorrectness of G's beliefs. Not in his role as disengaged receiver of reports, but only in engaging in the pursuit of truth, B will take G's belief that p seriously, i.e. as something that can be evaluated as a correct or incorrect attitude in the perspective of G.

Now, the second step of the argument requires that we apply our own perspective to the perspective of the other party. Why is it correct according to the perspective of Revelation to believe at the same time that it is incorrect for G according to the perspective of Observation to believe that p? Suppose that B would not assign his standard of correctness to the perspective of G. In this case, B would act incoherently since he is obligated to the regulation of truth in its relativistic form (TT-rel) and (CS-rel). B cannot condemn G for the evidence G is using to support his belief that p. The selection of evidence with respect to a perspective is normatively neutral. B can only condemn G's attitude towards p. To believe that p, then, has to be incorrect for G as well – according to G's perspective, if there is a regulation of truth at all. As an active participant in an epistemic practice, B has formed a meta-belief about the truth conduciveness of his own evidence; and he adopts it as a reason for his belief as soon as he is engaged in doxastic justification. He cannot accept G's reasons as equally truth conducive since he cannot withdraw from the (relative) truth regulation to which he is normatively bound. B must insist that it is incorrect for G to believe p according to the perspective of Observation. The same applies to G, *mutatis mutandis*.

Both parties transcend the scope of their relative perspectives in applying (CS-rel) to the evidence of the other party selected by a fundamentally different perspective. If they are pressed to apply their relative standards to the perspective of the other party, why not apply it to any perspective whatsoever? Can the relativist escape this problem if he claims that the meta-beliefs about the truth conduciveness of one's own reasons are only relatively justified, i.e. relatively to the perspective of Observation or the perspective of Revelation or some entirely different perspective? This would amount to a quietism on a meta-level. Step (3) of the argument has the purpose to prevent an argumentative escape towards a meta-level regress: If it is correct for a subject to believe p, then it is incorrect for the same subject to believe non-p in any perspective whatsoever. In order to perform the generalization demanded in step (3), it must be allowed to ignore logically possible alternatives that are incompatible with p. This leads us to the third precondition of the argument. Which alternatives are relevant and by virtue of which reasons?

4 The Problem of Relevance and the Grounding of Reasons

Which of the countless incompatible alternatives to p are the relevant ones? Which can be ignored? Do reasons supporting non-p undermine p's plausibility? Under which circumstances are they potential defeaters for p? The correctness of a belief is closely correlated to the truth conduciveness of its reasons. The sceptic claims that all non-p variants (and their supporting evidence) are always compatible with p (and its supporting evidence). Ought we to ignore these variants? When is it time to consider them as objections that have to be taken seriously in the context of truth regulation? David Lewis proposed seven rules dedicated to these questions (Lewis 1996). For the purpose of this paper, the following three are the most important ones:

(1) According to the *Rule of Method* we are entitled to ignore the possibility that our inferential operations fail in general. G and B both use inductive inferences, avail of *modus ponens* etc. If they did not agree on the validity of those methods, they would not even be able to point out each other's inconsistencies. Those methods are justified by a kind of a transcendental argument. Whoever wants to challenge them, needs to accept them while doing so.

(2) According to the *Rule of Attention*, we cannot ignore an alternative to p if it has our attention. As soon as we focus on an alternative, it becomes irrelevant how absurd the alternative may seem to us. Actual attention is decisive here, and the possibility that we might have ignored the same alternative under other circumstances is not important at all. Because of the *Rule of Attention* one would have to consider even the skeptical scenario of god deceiving G, so that looking through the telescope it seems to G to have evidence for the heliocentric view. Given B brings up that scenario, G would be forced to develop counter arguments against that possibility. (Putnam has shown that it is possible to argue effectively against such a skepticism.)

The *Rule of Attention* fits well with our distinction between propositional and doxastic justification, and respectively with our distinction between evidence for belief and the correctness of adopting such an attitude. Once confronted with an alternative (even an absurd one), our opponents have to deal with the reasons in favor or against it. They cannot remain in the mode of an disengaged observer or informant: Once they learn about the other parties' beliefs, they are committed to intervention – triggering a process of giving and asking for reasons that cannot be stopped anymore.

(3) The *Rule of Actuality* is the most important one. It demands that any facts which are part of the actual world cannot be ignored by one of the parties. Every fact of the actual world is always a relevant alternative to the belief that p. We would be in a different situation if both parties would discuss counterfactual cases or modal questions. If B and G would live in different worlds, we would not need to ask beforehand how the evidence of B might have turned out if he had looked through a telescope, and neither would we need to discuss the possibility that god might have manipulated the evidence of G deceiving G systematically. The *Rule of Actuality* leads to a factualism of reasons. Evidence must be grounded in facts which function as truth-makers for the content of our beliefs. According to this rule, it is impossible that there might be a truth conducive justification for p if non-p is true at the actual world.

From a relativistic point of view it is hard to see why we should accept this rule. Relativism holds that G and B might be justified equally well as long as their selection of evidence for p and non-p is based on different perspectives. But complying with the *Rule of Actuality*, we are not postulating those absolute facts denied by the relativists. We rather take the relativist denial seriously and examine the nature of the relative facts which are used as reasons for their respective beliefs. Even misleading evidence can be a justifier under the right circumstances. The opponents of relativism, therefore, can admit that is possible, even in the actual world, that B and G might seem equally well justified. One does not need to perceive the other party's reasons as possible defeaters to his own beliefs, as long as the sets of evidence are so small that they do not overlap. Up to a particular time, evidence like the retrograde motions of Mars or the harmony of the heavenly bodies might therefore be compatible to each other. But as the scientific endeavor goes on, enlarging the body of evidence, it will become more and more obvious that it is not possible that two sets of truth conducive reasons support p and non-p equally well with respect to our actual world. One of those justified beliefs must be false because it relies on evidence that is not (entirely) grounded in facts of the actual world. Such a dissent is never faultless.

If the justification relativist doesn't – as an act of desperation – opt for the more consistent position of alethic relativism, he has to recognize a non-relative (ontological) principle such as the following:

> (OP) Evidence E does only support a proposition p if E is grounded in the truth-makers for p.

That the sun revolves around the earth and that the earth revolves around the sun would then – as the *reductio ad absurdum* – be grounded in the same movement of the same celestial bodies. Their movement or immobility makes p or non-p true. This claim is not relying on an absolute fact, but merely on the notion of belief and truth regulation. If the relativist takes truth regulation seriously, then reasons must be truth conducive in the respective epistemic system too. And they are not truth conductive, if they are no longer connected to the piece of the world which makes them true in an appropriate way. According to the *Rule of Actuality*, G and B can no longer dismiss the reasons of the other. They are obligated to address the question whether the reasons offered are adequately connected with what makes them true or not.

The *Rule of Actuality* can be combined with a reliabilistic criterion suggested by Goldman:

> System C is better than system C* iff the compliance with C leads in the long run to a higher proportion of true beliefs than the compliance with C*. (Goldman 2010, 194)

Although, we cannot say that G is better justified than B at time t_1, there might – at a later time t_2 – be an advantage for G or B.

How stable perspective-relative justifications are, and how quickly they erode, depends epistemically on the quality of the arguments and counterarguments exchanged within the small-scale reciprocal efforts of convincing the opponents. Successfully defeated or permanently undermined beliefs also undermine the principles whose instances they are, and thus the alternative epistemic system itself. If one endorses the principles of truth regulation and the factualism of reasons one cannot defend a justification relativism. Rejecting these principles does not stand for relativism, but for an alternative epistemology.

References

Boghossian, Paul (2006): *Fear of Knowledge. Against Relativism and Constructivism*, Oxford: Oxford University Press.
Boghossian, Paul (2014): "Der Relativismus des Normativen". In: Gabriel, Markus (ed.): *Der Neue Realismus*. Frankfurt am Main: Suhrkamp, 362–395.
David, Marian (2001): "Truth as the Epistemic Goal". In: Steup, Michael (ed.): *Knowledge, Truth, and Duty. Essays on Epistemic Justification, Responsibility, and Virtue*. Oxford: Oxford University Press, 151–169.
Engel, Peter (2013): "In Defence of Normativism about the Aim of Belief". In: Chan, Timothy (ed.): *The Aim of Belief*. Oxford: Oxford University Press, 32–63.
Goldman, Alvin (2010): "Epistemic Relativism and Reasonable Disagreement". In: Feldman, Richard; Warfield, Ted (eds.): *Disagreement*. Oxford: Oxford University Press, 187–215.
Huemer, Michael (2001): "The Problem of Defeasible Justification". In: *Erkenntnis* 54, 375–397.
Lewis, David (1996): "Elusive Knowledge". In: *Australian Journal of Philosophy* 74 (4), 549–567.
Lynch, Michael (2009): "Truth, Value and Epistemic Expressivism". In: *Philosophy and Phenomenological Research* LXXIX, 76–97.
McFarlane, John (2014): *Assessment Sensitivity. Relative Truth and its Applications*. Oxford: Oxford University Press.
Scanlon, Thomas (2014): *Being Realistic about Reasons*. Oxford: Oxford University Press.
Velleman, David (2000): *The Possibility of Practical Reason*. Oxford: Oxford University Press.

Erwin Tegtmeier
Epistemological Realism, Representation, and Intentionality

Abstract: Epistemological realism is anti-idealism. Idealism was dominant the 18th century and is still very influential, particularly in its Kantian version. The rise of idealism is the consequence of a change of paradigm made by Descartes. In the classical tradition cognition was understood as transfer. Descartes conceived it as representation of objects by ideas in the mind. Already the Cartesians were aware the difficulty to connect idea and object. The idealists then solved it in their way by collapsing both. An epistemologically realist view was developed by the later Brentano who rejected the representational analysis of cognition and assumed a direct and specific intentional relation between mental states and objects. Brentano's new view has been misconstrued by those who introduced the subject of intentionality into mainstream analytical philosophy. It was even portrayed as a kind of representationalism although Brentano's explicit aim was to overcome it.

Keywords: Epistemological realism, idealism, representation, Franz Brentano

1 Epistemological Realism versus Epistemological Idealism

Epistemological realism is realism concerning cognition. It is the opposite of epistemological idealism. According to the latter the objects of cognition are made by mind. According to the former they are merely apprehended by mind. Idealism divides into subjective and objective idealism. The former claims individual minds make the objects of cognition (following common principles though) while the latter holds that a single world mind makes all cognitive objects, indeed everything, and that everything is mental. The subjective idealist assumes something non-mental, which is, however, completely unknowable.

Kant, who is doubtlessly the most influential subjective realist, calls that unknowable non-mental entity "the thing in itself" ("Ding an sich"). The antonym of "thing in itself" would be "thing for us". Kant prefers the term "appearance" although he does not contrast it with and does not relate it to a knowable reality. He characterises the thing in itself as the unknown cause of our sensations arguing that the respective causation cannot serve as cognitive relation because it is not the familiar causal relation which holds only between appearances.

It is crucial for the subjective idealist that all the material objects we perceive are mere appearances. That is strange all the more since as appearances they must be mental since they are produced by mental activity. This is particularly strange because those objects stand as paradigms of material objects. To understand that epistemological metamorphosis one has to consider what has been called "the argument from physics".

2 The Argument from Physics

There was a dismissal of Aristotelianism since the 15th Century partly due to its condemnation by the Archbishop of Paris and to internal difficulties of Aristotelian metaphysics. Nevertheless its categories were more or less still in use explicitly, even in Descartes who is considered the father of Modern European Philosophy. After the downfall of Aristotelianism scepticism with respect to metaphysics but also with respect to perception, Aristotle's epistemological basis, spread out.

The decisive impulse for Descartes came from the new atomistic physics. Descartes himself was also (according to some scholars even in the first place) physicist. The new physics was thought to imply a dissolution of material objects into swarms of particles and a removal of most of their qualities we perceive. Galileo Galilei made a particularly strong case against what became to be called secondary perceptual qualities. Secondary are those qualities which have no place in the theories of particle physics. It turned out that most of the qualities we perceive have to be classed as secondary. That was taken to imply that material objects don't have those qualities and that they are merely reactions of our senses and sensations in our minds.

Later on, it was argued (by Berkeley) that primary qualities are also mind dependent. Thus, it transpires how philosophers have arrived via the argument from physics at the strange view that the paradigms of material objects are actually mental.

3 The Legacy of Representationalism

The argument from physics implies a falling apart of mind and matter. Descartes advocates the view that both are different categories of substances with different essences. This view entails a break with the Aristotelian tradition according to which there is an identity between mind and object in perception. However, as Grossmann emphasises, Descartes and his successors kept a crucial premise of the older tradition, namely that the mind knows (directly) only what is in it. Grossmann calls it "the Principle of Immanence" (Grossmann 1990). Consequently, Descartes held that we don't know material objects directly but only by ideas in the mind as their representatives. That is why his view has also been called "representationalism". Ideas are distinguished from sensations. Both are in the mind but the former represent while the latter do not, as the argument from physics implied.

Representationalism is a form of epistemological realism. However, it is an indirect realism. It holds that we are cognitively related to the thing in itself by a representative of it (an idea or a concept). According to the representationalist view we apprehend a thing by having an idea or concept representing it. The nature of the representation is obscure even to the followers of Descartes because of the categorial disparity between knowing mind and known matter. But it is clear that it cannot be conventional, because it is our primary cognitive connection to things. A case can be made for interpreting the representation as falling under a concept (Bergmann 1967, 132).

Although the difficulties of representationalism were discovered soon and alternative realist views have been developed since, almost all philosophers still think in the representationalist way. However, representationalism is mostly implicit and is taken for granted, particularly by mainstream analytical philosophers. A case in point is Putnam who made himself a name on arguing that what he called "metaphysical realism" is impossible. His argument hinged on a well-known difficulty of representationalism which will be discussed in the next paragraph. But it depended on the presupposition that realism has to be representational. Putnam was completely unaware of this implicit presupposition and has only years later been brought to realize it and drop it. Naive representationalism, as it might be called, may be due to the language orientation of analytical philosophers. Language is, of course, a representation, even though cognition may not and, as I argued, cannot be.

4 The Fatal Difficulty of Representationalism

According to representationalism we are acquainted with the concepts we have but not with the things which fall under them. We know how things are (concepts are in a way descriptions of them) which fall under our concepts but we cannot know whether there are any things falling under them. Thus we cannot compare concepts and things and we cannot know the world beyond our concepts. The corollary of representationalism is scepticism and even agnosticism.

Taking the representatives as concepts or descriptions one is in the comfortable situation of having a representation relation available, namely the relation of falling under a concept or the relation of satisfying a description. But it presupposes a conceptualistic or nominalistic ontology. With a universal realistic ontology there is not only the opacity of the representation of particulars but also that of universals. There is no suggestion by what relation a representative in the mind represents a universal outside the mind. It is obvious that the relation cannot be conventional by designation because for that the universal has to be given. For that the universal had to be in the mind because of the representationalist principle that mind knows directly only what is in it. But the opposite is assumed by the universal realist in this case, namely that some universals are outside of the mind. The conclusion and difficulty would be the same if the qualities outside mind would be tropes instead of universals.

Since in no case do we know whether the representation relation holds and with most ontologies we cannot even know what relation holds between representation in the mind to the represented entities outside of the mind representationalism is not an adequate ground for epistemological realism, not even of indirect epistemological realism.

5 The Idealist's Way Out

The difficulty discussed in the previous paragraph was not discovered by the Cartesians themselves. Rather, it was pointed out by contemporary critics. However, Cartesians felt that their epistemological analysis implied scepticism even without being aware of that fatal difficulty. That was because it seemed inscrutable to them how something mental could represent something physical in spite of the categorial disparity between them. Descartes advocated, as was mentioned already, in contrast to Aristotle that the mental and the physical are different substances. Hence, the assumption of a disparity and gap between them.

The subjective idealist offers as a way out of the representationalist scepticism that was indicated already, namely that the complexes of concepts we have when we perceive material objects such as clouds and cars are not merely representatives of those objects but they *are* nothing but complexes of concepts, which are constructed by us by applying certain forms of intuition and certain principles concerning objects. This way out leads to a blurring of the distinction between the mental and the physical and to making the physical a subclass of the mental. Thus it is an implausible way out.

However, subjective idealism would not only offer a way out of scepticism but also a way out of the fatal difficulty of representationalism by turning the object of knowledge in all cases into something mental and that is to say also into something in the mind. Idealists in contrast to representationalists have no problem with the traditional principle of immanence. They avoid also obviously a gap between the mental and the physical.

For Common Sense subjective idealism is hard to swallow. It may even drive someone into deeper scepticism and despair about knowability of the world in itself, as reading Kant did with the German playwright and novelist Heinrich von Kleist. And the epistemological realist may experience a shudder when he learns about Kant's proclamation of a Copernican Revolution in epistemology according to which the objects are assumed to be determined by the laws of the knowing subject, rather than the other way round.

6 Return to Direct Realism

There were several fundamental criticisms of representationalism and attempts to return to direct realism which even spotted its fatal difficulty but they did not exert much influence. However, in the 19th century it was Franz Brentano who started another and more successful endeavour to overcome representationalism. Brentano began as representationalist (see Chrudzimski 2001, 37f). At first, he reverts to Descartes, and sharpens again the distinction and opposition between the mental and the physical blurred already by the Empiricists and finally repealed by Kant. As is well-known, in the Early Brentano a distinction between the mental and the physical looms large. he distinctive criterion of the mental is its directedness to an object, its intentionality. That does not yet imply some direct epistemological realism. It can be interpreted in terms of representationalism.

Which theorems in Brentano's later epistemology make it a direct realism?

1. The assumption of an intentional relation which holds between mental acts and their objects even if the objects are not mental. Thus Brentano scraps what Grossmann calls "Principle of Immanence". He even makes it one of his central tenets that the object is on no account part of the respective mental act.

2. The rejection of representational contents (concepts) (Brentano 1956, 48). That prevents him from taking them as mediators of cognition. Actually, Brentano is quite clear that cognition is an affair between mental acts and their objects and that no third mediating party is involved.

Thus the introduction of contents of mental acts by Brentano's student Twardowski is a step backward to representationalism (Twardowski 1894). The argument for contents is this: a mental act is firstly of a certain kind, for example, a presentation. Secondly, there must be something which determines the object of the mental act. That the argument is not sound transpires if one as asks whether the holding of the intentional relation to the respective object is not sufficient to ground its being object of that mental act. The suggestion of a content determining or selecting the object amounts to a concept as representation of the object.

7 The Intentional Relation

Crucial for Brentano's direct epistemological realism is his intentional relation which he takes to hold between mental acts and their objects. It is assumed to be a simple relation not based on something else. It is specific to mental acts. The Cartesians took into consideration only similarity and causality as possible relations connecting mind and matter and discarded them while not coming up with the idea of a specific, not yet known relation. Anyway, the principle of immanence which they took for granted would have been an insurmountable impediment.

Putnam writes with respect to Brentano and other Phenomenologists: "These philosophers (who ascribe to the mind intentionality) did not want to claim that we can think about external things without representations at all." (Putnam 1981, 17) Well, that is their crucial claim. That is the main point of their intentional relation. Contrary to what Putnam thinks when he calls theories of intentionality magical theories of reference intentionality is not representational reference. It is more fundamental than representational reference. The first term of the relation of intentionality is not a representation but rather a mental act. Representation is in any case parasitical on the givenness of signs and represented objects. Therefore it cannot be our primary cognitive relation which the intentional relation is meant to be.

Without presumably intending it, Searle actually thwarted and reverses Brentano's attempt to overcome representationalism by explicating intentionality in terms of falling under a concept or satisfying a description (Searle 1981, ch. 1). Seemingly, Searle takes representationalism for granted as most mainstream philosophers today do.

8 Intentional Relation and Correspondence Theory of Truth

It reveals the nature of intentionality to take into account the correspondence theory of truth. Mostly, this theory is associated with epistemological realism; it is even frequently taken to be the core of it. However, it does not fit with intentionality as analyzed by Brentano for the simple and obvious reason that there are according to the intentionality view no two sides that could correspond. The mental act has the object it has only by standing in the intentional relation to it.

Correspondence theory of truth is notoriously a wide term. But it explicates truth in terms of some kind of similarity or fitting on top of each other. Now, without the intentional relation holding between a mental act and its object there is no basis of fit between the two. There is no ground for that mental act to be intentionally related to that object apart from the actual holding of the intentional relation. In other words: Brentano's intentional relation is not an internal relation. It cannot be grounded on the nature of its respective two relata. Therefore, it does not furnish a starting point for a representationalist interpretation and for an explication of truth in terms of some kind of correspondence.

9 Direct Realism Does Not Exclude Error

It is not far to seek and well known that direct realism has a hard time to deal satisfactorily with error. Brentano faced the difficulty from the start. Does an analysis of knowledge in terms of the intentional relation then not imply that a mental act cannot go wrong? If it did it would fail because error actually occurs. The difficulty for a relational analysis of knowing is that in all or in some cases of error there seems to be no second relatum of the intentional relation.

Originally, Brentano argued that because of error intentionality is not a proper relation but only something relation-like ("relativlich" in German) since a second relatum is lacking. The Later Brentano tries to show that relations are such that they can hold with respect to non-existents, not as an exception but typically. He analyses error ontologically as the standing of the intentional relation to a thing which does not exist and claims that all relations allow that. The late Brentano acknowledges only very few relations and rejects most of the relational phenomena as merely relations of comparison which are reducible to conjunctions.

Brentano's explanation of error thus depends greatly on the ontology of relations. The late Brentano adopts Aristotle's view that two-term relations are basically accidents of the fundamentum thing and are only verbally related to the terminus thing (the second relatum). This one-sidedness of relations allows for a relation to hold even if the terminus does not exist.

According to Brentano's Aristotelian view of relations the intentional relation of a mental act m to an object o is an attribute of m whose designation mentions o. One may wonder whether there is not a matching between mental act and object here which would support a representationalist interpretation of this intentionality after all. To see that the answer is negative on needs to know that the attribute (Brentano's term is "Akzidenz") involves ("modalbefasst") the thing (the mind with the mental act) and would thus in ontologies with facts be a relational fact. Thus the relational attribute which is the intentionality of the mental act involves the intentional relation as well as the holding of that relation between the respective act and object. In Brentano's ontology which is strictly reistic and tropist there are no abstract relations, no relational universals.

References

Bergmann, Gustav (1967): *Realism. A Critique of Brentano and Meinong.* Madison. University of Wisconsin Press.
Brentano, Franz (1956): *Die Lehre vom richtigen Urteil.* Bern: Francke.
Chrudzimski, Arkadiusz (2001): *Intentionalitätstheorie beim frühen Brentano.* Dordrecht: Springer.
Grossmann, Reinhardt (1990): *The Fourth Way. A Theory of Knowledge.* Bloomington: Transaction Publishers.
Putnam, Hilary (1981): *Reason, Truth, and History.* Cambridge: Cambridge University Press.
Searle, John (1983): *Intentionality. An Essay in the Philosophy of Mind.* Cambridge: Cambridge University Press.
Twardowski, Kazimir (1894): *Zur Lehre vom Inhalt und Gegenstand der Vorstellungen—Eine psychologische Untersuchung.* Wien: Hölder.

Martin G. Weiss
Angelina's Truth: Genetic Knowledge, Preventive Medicine, and the Reality of the Possible

Abstract: Due to the shift from genetic determinism to genetic probabilism the translation of genetic knowledge from the realm of science into the realm of real-life decision-making paradoxically results in the production of radical uncertainty. My thesis is that although genetic knowledge does not produce certainty or propositional truth it perhaps allows to "touch" (Aristotle) the phenomenological truth of the singular, this is, to understand the primordial "pre-predicative" or non-propositional (hermeneutical), meaning of that "which shows itself from itself" (Heidegger) and thus constitutes the condition of possibility of any explicit (apophantical) proposition.

Keywords: Genetic probabilism, genetic determinism, Aristotle, Martin Heidegger, "Angelina effect"

1 Introduction: The Power of Genetic Knowledge

In 2013 Angelina Jolie published an article in the *New York Times* in which she explained the reasons behind her decision to undergo a preventive double mastectomy after a genetic test had revealed a genetic predisposition to develop breast cancer, which increased her relative cumulative risk to develop breast cancer before turning 80 to about 85 percent. Her message was clear: "Cancer is still a word that strikes fear into people's hearts, producing a deep sense of powerlessness. But today it is possible to find out through a blood test whether you are highly susceptible to breast and ovarian cancer, and then take action." (Jolie 2013) In 2015 she underwent additional preventive ovariectomy to reduce her risk further and explained: "It is not easy to make these decisions. But it is possible to take control and tackle head-on any health issue. You can seek advice, learn about the options and make choices that are right for you. Knowledge is power." (Jolie 2015)

In the years after Jolie's appeal to be proactive many women followed her example in what has been labeled "The Angelina effect" (Park 2013). But what kind of knowledge is the genetic knowledge allegedly empowering women to responsibly manage their own health?

On average a women born today has a cumulative relative risk of 10.2 percent of being diagnosed with breast cancer before her 80th birthday; if she does not die earlier. In absolute numbers this means that out of 1000 about 100 will be diagnosed with breast cancer. (Kürzl 2004) But this cumulative relative risk does tell very little about the actual absolute risk of developing breast cancer at a certain point of life, for example, in the coming year. Thus the individual (absolute) risk of a 55 years old woman to develop breast cancer is 0.2 percent. This means that out of 1000 women aged 55 two will develop breast cancer in the next 12 months. Diagnosed with the Breast Cancer Gene (BARCA) 1 gene-mutation the relative risk to contract breast cancer before one's 80th birthday on average increases from 10.2 to about 65 percent. But the absolute risk for a 55 old women with the BARCA 1 mutation to develop breast cancer in the next 12 month is still only 1.3%. What kind of knowledge is this knowledge? And is this knowledge still power?

2 Genetic Probabilism and the Dynamics of Gene Expression

This example shows that scientific risk analysis, which promises control and manageability by measuring and calculating probabilities, produces "radical manmade uncertainty" (Beck 1992) when translated into our everyday lifeworld (Husserl 1970).

The debate on the BRCA-Gene illustrates that what is at the center of current discussions concerning the influences knowledge about our "genes" has on our daily live, is not genetic determinism, but genetic probabilism. What is at stake is not the truth of the gene, its reality and necessary effect, but the probability of its phenotypic expression and the prevention of possible undesired outcomes. At the same time the medical focus has moved from disease and healing to predisposition and prevention (Rose 2007 and Weiss 2009).

That the classic model of Genetics, based on James Watson's "central dogma of molecular biology" "one gene – one protein, one protein – one function" is no more valid, as today we do not even know exactly what a "gene" is supposed to be, is convincingly claimed by Evelyn Fox Keller in her book *The Century of the Gene*.

According to Keller the century of the gene – which began with the rediscovery of Gregor Mendel's experiments in the garden of his Brünn Monastery in the early 20th century – ended in 2000, with the publication of the first results of the *Human Genome Project*, which was widely expected to confirm the "one gene –

one protein" hypothesis. On the basis of Watson's dogma in combination with the until then known proteins in the human body, it was expected that the *Human Genome Project* would lead to the discovery of about 100.000 protein-coding sequences, this is, genes. But instead of 100.000 the *Human Genome Project* detected only 30.000 "genes", which further more equaled only about 1% of the entire DNA-Code. The era of post-genomics, this is the era after the decoding of the full human genome, began with the end of genetic determinism.

Instead of validating the concept of genetic determinism, underlying not only the central dogma of molecular biology, but also the *Human Genome Project* itself, the very results of the project made clear, that it would become extremely difficult to deduce any phenotypic feature from specific genes. What became evident instead was that there simply was no unidirectional causal relation between genotype and phenotype. What had to be acknowledged was, that the expression of phenotypic features had to be interpreted as a highly complex process of interactions and feedback-loops between DNA, RNA, proteins, and cell plasma. In this process what we usually term "genes", this is the protein-coding sequences of the DNA-string, often play only a subordinate role.

> If the genes are "essentially the same", what then is it that makes one organism a fly and another a mouse, a chimp, or a human? The answer, it seems, is to be found in the structure of gene networks – in the ways in which genes are connected to other genes by the complex regulatory mechanisms that, in their interactions, determine when and where a particular gene will be expressed. But unlike the sequence of the genome, this regulatory circuitry is not fixed: it is dynamic rather than static, a structure that is itself changing over the course of the developmental cycle. (Keller 2000, 100)

The paradigm of classical genetics – "one gene: one protein, one protein: one function" – according to Fox Keller today cannot be upheld any longer, as recent discoveries suggest a new paradigm of genetics: "one gene – many proteins, one protein – many functions."

2.1 Nüsslein-Vollhard's Gradient Hypothesis and McClintock's Jumping Genes

The paradigm shift in molecular genetics described by Fox Keller has been prepared by the theories of two other female biologists, namely Christiane Nüsslein-Vollhard's "Gradient Hypothesis" and Barbara McClintock's discovery of "jumping genes" and her description of DNA as an "organ" of the cell.

The gradient hypothesis, for which Nüsslein-Vollhard received the Nobel prize in Physiology or Medicine in 1995, stresses the central role the cell-plasma plays in the translation of the information contained in the genetic code of the DNA into actual structures of the cell. Her discovery is so important, because it makes clear that the DNA can no more be conceived as some sort of Aristotelian unmoved mover (the master-gene of classical genetics), but that the realization of the genetic information inscribed in the DNA is the result of complex intra- and intercellular feedback-loops in which the DNA is only one of multiple players. Originally prefigured by Theodor H. Bovari the Gradient Hypothesis claims that the influence of the cytoplasm of an zygote on gene expression, is based on different grades of concentrations of specific "morphogenes" in different parts of the cell at different stages of cell development. (Nüsslein-Vollhard 1995)

That gene-expression is influenced by intercellular feedback-loops lead Nüsslein-Vollhard also to reconsider the meaning of human embryonic development, which according to her findings, cannot be traced back to some sort of potentiality enclosed in the isolated zygote, but must be conceived as the result of complex interactions between the developing embryo and the body of the mother. (Nüsslein-Vollhard 2004)

Twelve years before Nüsslein-Vollhard it was Barbara McClintock's turn to receive the Nobel prize in Physiology or Medicine for her discovery of the "jumping genes", or "Transposons", which allowed her to demonstrate that the DNA was no unchangeable blue print, but rather a adaptable organ and the cell not a mechanical machine, but an active Organism capable of reacting to its environment. In her Nobel price lecture she says:

> A goal for the future would be to determine the extent of knowledge the cell has of itself and how it utilizes this knowledge in a 'thoughtful' manner when challenged. [...] In the future attention undoubtedly will be centered on the genome, and with greater appreciation of its significance as a highly sensitive organ of the cell, monitoring genomic activities and correcting common errors, sensing the unusual and unexpected events, and responding to them, often by restructuring the genome. (McClintock 1983)

What strikes in this quote is not only its content, but also the peculiar language, the unusual images, it evokes, showing, that the way in which we speak about an object, reflects, and perhaps shapes, how we conceive it.

Beneath her discovery of the "transposons" McClintock became known as one of the founders of Epigenetics, a theory that further destabilized genetic determinism.

2.2 Epigenetics

Reminiscent of Lamarck and Lysenko, Epigenetics sustains, that the phenotypic expression of the genotype can not only be influenced by environmental factors, but that this epigenetic changes in the phenotype can be passed on to future generations without changing the DNA and therefore following non-Mendelian patterns, so that instead of speaking of hereditary epigenetic effects, it is preferable to speak of trans-generational responses (TGR).

Two studies carried out by the research team of Gunar Kaati in 2002 and 2007 showed a interdependence between the childhood nutrition condition of grandfathers and the living expectancies of their sons and grandsons: If the grandfathers enjoyed a good nutrition between their 8th and 12th year, in their so called "slow growth period" (SGP), a specially sensitive period in phylogenetic development, the living expectancy of their male descendants decreased. If the grandfathers instead had little to eat in their slow growth period, the living expectancy of their male descendants increased. The tentative explanation of this effect goes as follows: The human biology adapts to the dire environmental situation (lack of nutrition) by improving the organism resilience in the next generation:

> The observed TGR's on food availability during ancestor's SGP seemed to be the main mover in determining the probands longevity. The results provide further support for the hypothesis that a sex-specific, male-line TGR-system exists in humans, capturing nutritionally related information from the previous generation(s), resulting in differential mortality depending on ancestors' exposure during the SGP. The transgenerational effects remain after taking account of the genetic relatedness and early life circumstances of the probands. (Kaati 2007, 789)

Thus the stress caused to the grandfather's organism by the lack of proper nutrition, seemed to have prompted a reaction in the next generation, somehow bettering their genes, as a german newspaper put it (Willmann 2002). To be exact however not the genes became "better", but their functionality changed. In fact epigenetic effects are not due to changes in the actual genetic code, the sequence of DNA-bases, but are caused by the sedimentation of methyl-molecules along the DNA-string. This "methylization" of certain sections of the DNA is called "genetic imprinting", or "modification" and influences the activity of the affected genes. Although epigenetic research is relatively young, epigenetic effects are quite common; thus for example in the process of cell differentiation. How is it possible that a single zygote can develop into 200 different types of specialized cells? And why is it that not every cell of the body develops into a full human being, as it entails all the necessary information in its DNA? The answer is: epigenetic effects make sure, that every cell expresses the right genes in the right place and in the right moment.

The master-gene has abdicated. A network of complex inter-depending inner- and inter-cellular feedback-loops influenced by epigenetic factors has taken its place. As the Angelina-effect shows, the paradigm of classical genetics with its implication of genetic determinism (this is, the concept of an unilateral chain of cause and effect from the gene to the somatic feature), has been replaced by a post-genomic, probabilistic-model, which conceives the genome merely as predisposition, a genetic disposition, to develop certain phenotypic features, predictable only by means of statistical probabilities. The genome today is no longer an unchangeable program, but only a hint towards possibilities and probabilities, which further more are suggestible to environmental influences due to epigenetic mechanisms. In the age of post-genomics biology thus is no more fate, but risk. Controlling this risk is the task of the individual as well as of politics.

On the other side it is also clear that the transition from classical genetics to post-genomics and epigenetics does not necessarily mean an end to determinism, also if it is mostly seen as that. Thus Thomas Lemke stresses that post-genomics is not the end of the genomic-discourse, but only a transformation of it as it is very well possible to conceive the entire complex inner- and intra- cellular feedback system, which has taken over the role of "the gene", as determined as a whole. Therefore replacing the master-gene by a complex system of interacting causes does not per se exclude determinism. And also epigenetics does not necessarily coincide with reinforcing the role of nurture in the nature-nurture debate, as epigenetics could also be read as radical biologization, or naturalization, of nurture, because the discourse of epigenetics now inscribes every real-world experience a person makes into her body. Genetic determinism is replaced by physiological determinism (Lux 2012).

The mainstream interpretation of post-genomics and epigenetics however, at least in mainstream media, emphasizes their potentially emancipatory outcome. But also this liberation from genetic determinism, this is from nature, is a double-edged sword. Thus breast cancer until recently considered a stroke of fate and met with compassion, nowadays is considered an illness for which the patient is, at least in part, responsible since it is possible to undergo regular screenings and genetic tests to determine ones predisposition to develop this illness, this is knowing ones "risk", and undergo preventive surgery, if necessary. The possibility of preventive intervention makes the patient co-responsible for its condition, if she chooses preemptive diagnosis or not.

3 Real Possibilities

What this example shows is that the de-materialization of the body, dissolved in genetic predispositions graspable only by means of statistical probability, have not striped the body of its reality, in the sense of effectiveness, of its possessing the power of causation. On the contrary the de-materialization of the biological asset of the human being in genetic predispositions and (un)calculable probabilities of its phenotypic expression, has lead to a "realization" or "actualization" of the immaterial mere possibility.

In the age of genetic testing, facts are no longer distinguishable from probabilities and predispositions, because what makes them real, their effects, are the same (Weiss 2009).

As Nikolas Rose has shown, the mere knowledge of "risk", for example of genetic predisposition, can lead to the same consequences as the actual outbreak of a disease, so that the differences between "pre-symptomatic patients", or "pre-patients", and effectively ill persons is blurred; and with it the Aristotelian difference between "dynamis" and "energeia", "possibility" and "reality".

The philosophic tradition distinguishes three content independent, modes of being which are deemed as "not real" (Kant): possibility, reality, and necessity. The difference of this three modes of being is succinctly illustrated by Martin Heidegger contrasting the characteristics of what is possible to that which is real or necessary: "As a modal category of presence-at-hand, possibility signifies what is *not yet* actual and what is *not at any time* necessary. It characterizes the *merely* possible. Ontologically it is on a lower level than actuality and necessity." (Heidegger 2005, 183, original emphasis)

This changes with post-genomics, because the transition from genetic determinism to post-genomic probabilism urges us to rethink the ontological status of the possible. If we follow Aristotle then reality is conceived as that which possesses the power of causation, it possesses "activity" (*energeia*, actus). But then unwanted possibilities like for example all sorts of risks which are the topic of genetic diagnosis, are eminently real. The fact that in the wake of the probabilistic shift in genetics, mere potentiality gains an unexpected "reality", this is effectiveness, is palpable also in the cases put forward by Thomas Lemke:

> As studies in the US have shown, [...] 'virtual patients' [...] are already confronted with very real forms of genetic discrimination. Thus couples are banned from adopting a child, if one partner is diagnosed with a disposition for a genetic disease. The 'disablement' can manifest itself also in the denial of a job, due to the risk of a possible future illness of the applicant. It also happens that health or life insurance-contracts are cancelled or denied if

genetic testing reveals that a (potential) customer is at risk for developing certain diseases. (Lemke 2000, 246)

To distinguish what is possible from that which is real becomes more and more difficult in a context in which the possible has the same effect, as the real and potential patients are treated in the same way actual patients are.

Another aspect of the leveling of the differences between the possible and the real, is a peculiar concretization of the three modes of time: past, present, and future. Commonly necessity is associated with the past, reality with the present and possibility with the future. Early on however, Augustine has shown, that presence, the time of the real, is not conceivable as extensionless instant passing from a state of future inexistence in a state of past inexistence, but that presence must be conceived as duration, as concurrence of retrospection and expectation. The past exists only in the form of present memory and the future only in the form of present anticipation. What Augustine, and after him Bergson and Heidegger, have grasped conceptually – that the possible exists and is effective as present expectation –, becomes real-life experience in the very moment future possibilities have the same effects as present realities. Preventive mastectomies and ovariectomy give Heidegger's abstract notion of "being-toward-death" an uncanny all to concrete meaning.

The liberation from genetic determinism thus does not lead necessarily to an emancipation from the corporeal body and to more freedom of the subject, but on the contrary to new forms of dependency, that may weight even more than the old fashioned biological fate, one at least could hope not to share or learn to accept. Confronted with possibilities which unfold their effects irrespective of whether they come true or not, this is confronted with a possible future which is real (present) whatever it realizes itself or not, thus confronted with a possibility which is always yet reality, there is no space for hope. In the frame of general risk-discourse where the possible and the real are the same, the only remaining mode of being is necessity. Thus prevention realizes the possibility it wanted to prevent.

Additionally genetic probabilism combined with prevention strategies, strips the biologic constitution of the human being of its "naturalness", in the sense of contingency, as their positive or negative outcomes can be influenced by personal life style. On the one hand genetic determinism had fixed the subject in its (abnormal) physiology, but on the other side genetic determinism freed the subject of any responsibility for her condition. Paradoxically the concept of genetic determinism liberated the subject, at least from the sensation of being responsible for her pathological condition, whereas the age of post-genomics loads the subject with the burden of being the master of her own fate, of "taking control" over health issues, as Angelina Jolie put it.

But on what basis should the post-genomic subject take control of her own life? On the grounds of what kind of knowledge should the post-genomic subject change her life? What kind of individual responsibility is here invoked?

> The appeal to 'responsibility' is the cynicism with which the institutions whitewash their own failure. However – and this is also part of the tragic irony of this individualization process – the individual, whose senses fail him and her in the face of ungraspable threats [...], who, thrown back on himself, [...], remains at the same time unable to escape the power of definition of expert systems, whose judgment he cannot, yet must trust. Sustaining an individual self of integrity in world risk society is indeed a tragic affair. (Beck 2006, 336)

The position of the individual having to deal with genetic knowledge is tragic mainly due to its probabilistic nature, which escapes the classical dichotomy of true versus false.

For Aristotle there was only one object capable of been known in the eminent sense of the word: the necessary. Only the necessary can be known: "We all suppose that what we know is not even capable of being otherwise; of things capable of being otherwise we do not know, when they have passed outside our observation, whether they exist or not. Therefore the object of scientific knowledge is of necessity." (EN, 1139b15) If only the necessary can be known, than what is true must be necessary, at least if by truth we mean "to say of what is that it is, and of what is not that it is not" (Met. 1011b25).

On the basis of this strict concepts of knowledge and truth the mere probable propositions of post-genomics cannot be true, but neither false, as they escape the underling dichotomy of true and false.

Thus what does it mean to 'know' that one has a change of 65 percent to develop breast cancer before turning 80? What does it mean to be told, than one is "with virtual certainty", the father of a child? What form of knowledge is this probabilistic knowledge? And how do we cope with this knowledge that is per definition never certain, although almost? Thus the actual genetic discourse with all its testing and prediction does not lead to more certainty; on the contrary the actual probabilistic genetic discourse produces uncertainty. Ironically producing almost certain propositions about specific facts is possible only at the price of renouncing to "truth". The findings of genetic probabilism can never be true, and only because they are never true they can be almost certain.

Whereas Ulrich Beck distinguishes between two meanings of risk, referring it "in the first place to a world governed entirely by the laws of probability, in which everything is measurable and calculable" and secondly "to non-quantitative uncertainties, to 'risks that cannot be known', suggesting that what defines the "risk society" we live in, is foremost the latter, I would argue that the calculable risk of science is not different from the manmade radical uncertainties we experience in our life-world, but that the two are different appearances of the same phenomenon, which in the realm of science appears as calculable incalculability, whereas transposed in real-life situations appears as radical uncertainty.

The modern concept of risk defines risk on the one hand as quantifiable, controllable and therefore governable probability, but on the other hand experiences the same risk as radical, unmanageable uncertainty in real-life. Politics, economy and science (knowledge) reveal themselves not only to be unable to cope with risk, but to be its main origin, unveiling the true (real-life) nature of modern risks, which are not calculable probabilities, but "non quantitative manufactured uncertainties" creating a "culture of fear" deriving "from the paradoxical fact that the institutions that are designed to control produced uncontrollability." (Beck 2003, 99)

But is this situation really new? Has the human condition not always been confronted with risks? That is certainly true, but what has changed is the meaning of the term "risk". The "risks" we are dealing with today are *radical virtual-real uncertainties involuntarily produced by rational human activity meant to increase the controllability of (human) nature.*

Risks in this sense are incalculable, often (beforehand) unknowable, by-products of techno-science. Techno-science, originally meant to dominate nature, including human nature, by means of "quantitative thinking" (Beck 1992), or "calculating thinking" (Heidegger 2006) paradoxically leads (if combined with a probabilistic notion of knowledge) to a culture of fear in which virtual, i.e. mere possible, events are real (i.e. effective), as actual ones; be it breast cancer or terror attacks (Beck 1992).

4 Conclusions: Post-Genomic Knowledge and the Notion of Primordial Truth (*aletheia*)

As we have seen the probabilistic gene discourse does not produce knowledge and truth but ignorance and uncertainty, this is knowledge of the probable.

Aristotle defines the probable as "a thing that usually happens" and as "that which is not necessary but, being assumed, results in nothing impossible." (An. Pr. II 27, 70a4f)

The knowledge of the possible is knowledge of contingency. In this peculiar sense also the post-genomic knowledge is knowledge, although not of the type expressed in a true proposition. Rather probabilistic genetic knowledge resembles what Aristotle calls *aletheia*, this is truth understood as primordial "concealment" of the singular being before any explicit propositional determination or explicit description. In fact according to Aristotle the singular intelligible object cannot be grasped by conceptual thinking but only be "touched" (*thigein*) by an intuitive non-propositional thinking, in the same way the singular sensual thing is beyond true or false, because as singular object before any determination it can only or appear or remain disclosed: "With respect, then, to all things which are essences and actual, there is no question of being mistaken, but only of thinking (*noein*) or not thinking them." (Met, IX, 10, 1051b, 31–32)

The primordial givenness of beings is beyond the dichotomy of true and false, because this primordial givenness of something, be it the singular sensible thing or the singular intelligible object of thought, is (conceived as the primordial appearance of something before any explicit propositional determination) the condition of possibility of true or false.

Thus according to Aristotle that which primordially "shows itself" cannot be true or false in the same way the object of a proposition is described (by this very proposition) as true or false, but only be known, be "touched", or be unknown, be "non-touched". Accordingly that which is grasped in this intellectual "touching", in this intuition, cannot be expressed in an explicit proposition, but only be "uttered":

> Concerning that which is true (*alethes*) and that which is false (*pseudos*) it is as follows: touching (*thigein*) and uttering (*phainai*) are truth – for utterance (*phasis*) is not the same as affirmative proposition (*kataphasis*) –, and ignorance is non-touching. (Met. IX, 10, 1051b, 24–25)

According to Aristotle only propositions, the combination of a grammatical subject with a grammatical predicate in an act that is *synthesis* and *diairesis* (separation) in one, can be true or false. Only the explicit affirmation of a proposition, the *logos apophanticos*, can be true or false. In accordance for Heidegger this propositional truth, explicit propositions in general, predications that explicitly attribute something to something, rest on a more original truth: the primordial understanding of meaningful entities beyond (and "before") explicit propositions, this is, they rest on the *logos hermeneuticos*.

According to Heidegger, the "theoretical," or "logic" description of "something as something" (the *logos apophanticos)* in an explicit proposition is based on a primordial practical meaning that he calls, with Aristotle, *logos hermeneuticos*. In *Being and Time* Heidegger explains:

> Prior to all analysis, logic has already understood 'logically' what it takes as a theme under the heading of the 'categorical statement' – for instance, 'The hammer is heavy.' The unexplained presupposition is that the 'meaning' of this sentence is to be taken as: 'This thing – a hammer – has the property of heaviness.' In concern full circumspection [the practical everyday approach to reality, MGW] there are no such assertions 'at first.' […] Interpretation is carried out primordially not in a theoretical statement but in an action of circumspective concern – laying aside the unsuitable tool, or exchanging it 'without words.' From the fact that words are absent, it may not be concluded that interpretation is absent. […] When an assertion has given a definite character to something present-at-hand, it says something about it as a 'what'; and this 'what' is drawn from that which is present-at-hand as such. […] Thus assertion cannot disown its ontological origin from an interpretation which understands. The primordial 'as' of an interpretation (*hermeneia*) which understands circumspectively we call the 'existential-hermeneutical as' in distinction from the 'apophantical as' of the assertion. (Heidegger 2005, 200)

This primordial truth (*aletheia*), conceived as mere non-propositional givenness of the meaningful is not only the condition of the possibility of whatsoever proposition and correspondence theory of truth, but if "touched" (which means intuitively experienced), a way to understand what it means, that reality "shows itself from itself" (Heidegger) beyond human proficiency. Thus the intuition of truth, understood as experiencing the process of "unconcealment" (this is what Heidegger and Aristotle call *aletheuien*) is always also an experience of contingency, a "touching" of finitude. In this sense the probabilistic knowledge of post-genomics is true in an imminent way.

References

Aristotle (1984): *The Complete Works of Aristotle*. Edited by Jonathan Barnes. Princeton: Princeton University Press.
Beck, Ulrich (1992): *Risk Society: Toward a New Modernity*. London: Sage.
Beck, Ulrich (2003): "An Interview with Ulrich Beck on Fear and Risk Society (by Joshua Yates)". In: *The Hedgehog Review: Critical Reflections on Contemporary Culture* 5, 96–107.
Beck, Ulrich (2006): "Living in the World Risk Society". In: *Economy and Society* 35 (3), 329–345.
Fox Keller, Evelyn (2000): *The Century of the Gene*. Cambridge: Harvard University Press.
Heidegger, Martin (2005): *Being and Time*. Oxford: Blackwell.
Heidegger, Martin (2006): *Was ist Metaphysik?* Frankfurt am Main: Klostermann.
Husserl, Edmund (1970): *The Crisis of European Sciences and Transcendental Phenomenology*. Evanston: Northwestern University Press.
Jolie, Angelina (2013): "My Medical Choice". In: *The New York Times*, May 14, A25.
Jolie, Angelina (2015): "Diary of a Surgery". In: *The New York Times*, March 24, A23.

Kaati, Gunnar et al. (2007): "Transgenerational Response to nutrition, early life circumstances and longevity". In: *European Journal of Human Genetics* 15, 784–790.

Lux, Vanessa (2012): "Epigenetik als Molekulare Bio-Graphie". In: *Gen-ethischer Informationsdienst* 213, 33–35.

McClintock, Barbara (1983): "The Significance of Responses of the Genome to Challenge". Nobel Lecture, http://www.nobelprize.org/nobel_prizes/medicine/laureates/1983/mcclintock-lecture.pdf.

Nüsslein-Vollhard, Christiane (1995): "The Identification of Genes Controlling Development in Flies and Fishes". Nobel Lecture, http://www.nobelprize.org/nobel_prizes/medicine/laureates/1995/nusslein-volhard-lecture.pdf.

Nüsslein-Vollhard, Christiane (2004): *Von Genen und Embryonen*. Stuttgart: Reclam.

Park, Alice (2013): "The Angelina Effect: Why Her Mastectomy Raises Key Issues about Genes, Health and Risks". In: *Time Magazine,* May 27, 28–33.

Rose, Nikolas (2007): *The Politics of Life Itself: Biomedicine, Power, and Subjectivity in the Twenty-First Century.* Princeton: Princeton University Press.

Lemke, Thomas (2000): "Die Regierung der Risiken". In: Bröckling, Ulrich (ed.): *Gouvernamentalität der Gegenwart.* Frankfurt am Main: Suhrkamp, 227–264.

Weiss, Martin G. (2009): "Die Auflösung der menschlichen Natur". In: Weiss, Martin G. (ed.): *Bios und Zoë: Die menschliche Natur im Zeitalter ihrer technischen Reproduzierbarkeit.* Frankfurt am Main: Suhrkamp, 34–55.

Willmann, Urs (2002): "Feist, Opa! Wenn die Ahnen hungerten, haben die Enkel bessere Gene". In: *Die Zeit,* October 31.

3 **Realism versus Relativism**

Heike Egner
Neither Realism nor Anti-Realism: How to approach the Anthropocene?

Abstract: Taking the hypothesis of the Anthropocene as a starting point, the paper challenges traditional epistemologies and indicates fundamental changes within scientific concepts.

Initially suggested in 2000, the hypothesis that we have entered the new geological era of the Anthropocene has started an intense debate on its plausibility and on the evidence the era could be based on. The hypothesis of the Anthropocene implies a concept fundamentally different from many precursors: It is assumed that humans and their societies no longer have a symbiotic relationship with nature but rather modify and transform natural processes to such an extent that humans have to be acknowledged as a natural force. Taking the assumptions of the Anthropocene seriously, a fundamental revision of almost every concept of the relation of societies, humans and nature would be required, as well as of our concepts of ourselves as humans and our responsibilities as scientists. The paper focuses on the question of epistemology and argues that epistemologies rooted in dualistic thinking are not suitable in the Anthropocene. Thus, neither realistic nor anti-realistic approaches are adequate any longer.

Keywords: Anthropocene, epistemology, non-dualism, Niklas Luhmann, Karen Barad

1 Introduction

At a UN conference in Mexico in 2000, the atmospheric chemist and Nobel Prize winner Paul Crutzen almost incidentally declared our present times to be the new geological era of the Anthropocene. The hypothesis of the Anthropocene implies a concept fundamentally different from many precursors such as the concept of sustainability, for instance: It assumes that humans and their societies no longer have a symbiotic relationship with nature but rather modify and transform natural processes to such an extent and in such a fundamental way that humans have to acknowledges as a "natural force", or, to be more specific, a "geophysical force". Since publishing the idea (Crutzen/Stoermer 2000, Crutzen 2002), an intensive debate has emerged on the plausibility of this statement and on the evidence the era of the Anthropocene could be based on (see for example Steffen et al. 2007, Zalasiewicz et al. 2008, Zalasiewicz et al. 2010, Steffen et al. 2011, Austin/Holbrook 2012, Smith/Zeder 2013, Ruddiman et al. 2015, Waters et al. 2016).

Meanwhile, "the Anthropocene is everywhere in academia" (Moore 2016, 1). However, so far, the term Anthropocene has not yet been officially approved, i.e. integrated into the Geological Time Scale, the official "rock record" which geoscientist use to distinguish the Earth's past into named segments, each marking shifts in the Earth's state. There seems to be little doubt among geoscientists that we have already entered a new geological epoch, it is obviously rather a question of how and on which level to integrate it into the Geological Time Scale (Edwards 2016).

What seems to be a debate in geosciences at first glance, and thus of little interest for the humanities and social sciences, turns out to be a fundamental question with the largest possible reach. The decision, whether or not we are living in the Anthropocene, is not only a question of semantics, but rather it will influence most – if not all – of our scientific concepts in a fundamental way and may even have legal implication for our daily lives. The historian Dipesh Chakrabarty points out that the anthropogenic explanations of climate change have already spelled "the collapse of the age-old humanist distinction between natural history and human history" (Chakrabarty 2009, 201); even more the current geological debate about the hypothesis of the Anthropocene "requires us to put global histories of capital in conversation with the [much longer] species history of humans" (Chakrabarty 2009, 212). Additionally, the Anthropocene radically questions our neoliberal, capitalistic approach of the last two centuries.[1] All this is going to change our ways of looking at ourselves in a fundamental manner: We have reached a new starting point in science and the humanities in general.

This chapter aims at exploring the implications of the era of the Anthropocene for epistemology. I am going to argue that by accepting us humans as a natural force, which modifies the Earth's surface so extensively, neither realist nor anti-realist approaches are sufficient epistemologies any longer. Chapter 2 focuses on a thorough understanding of the Anthropocene by sketching the rough idea of the suggested new geological era, its formal requirements and some general consequences. Chapter 3 explores why traditional epistemologies rooted in realistic and anti-realistic approaches can hardly be applied to the new era of the

---

[1] The sociologist Jason Moore is in the centre of a related debate about the naming of the fundamental changes (see for example Moore 2015a, Moore 2015b, Haraway 2015), suggesting the term "Capitalocene", since the hypothesis of the Anthropocene might indeed give a good description of "what is", but so far fails in providing an understanding of "how" humans have become that kind of force (Moore 2015a, 70).

Anthropocene, while the closing chapter points to first attempts in non-dualistic ontologies and epistemologies.

2 A Short Introduction to the Era of Humankind

The creation of a new geological era is nothing one can just do incidentally. For several years, the International Commission on Stratigraphy (the scientific body that maintains the official Geologic Time Scale) has been working on a proposal to formalize a definition of this term; an announcement of the results of their discussion is to be expected in 2016. A new geological era has to meet crucial requirements and this is: a) to mark a fundamental difference to the prior sequence in the sediment layers and b) to do so over the long term.

ad a) Since traces and remnants are of such an extraordinary significance for any geological argumentation, the debate focuses on the question which of our activities will remain over the long term and could be used as a marker to determine the beginning of the Anthropocene (i.e. marking the fundamental change to prior sediment layers). Moreover, the distinction between Holocene and Anthropocene must be detectable on a global scale, mere local or regional markers will be insufficient. Geoscientist are investigating various materials and or other outcomes of human activities on their potential to serve as evidence for a clear distinction between Holocene and Anthropocene. They seek for evidence comparable to the Permian-Triassic extinction event about 252 million years ago or the Triassic-Jurassic extinction event some 200 million years ago. Waters et al. for instance, sum up what they assume as evidential for the Anthropocene:

> The appearance of manufactured materials in sediments, including aluminium, plastics, and concrete, coincides with global spikes in fallout radionuclides and particulates from fossil fuel combustion. Carbon, nitrogen, and phosphorus cycles have been substantially modified over the past century. Rates of sea-level rise and the extent of human perturbation of the climate system exceed Late Holocene changes. Biotic changes include species invasions worldwide and accelerating rates of extinction. These combined signals render the Anthropocene stratigraphically distinct from the Holocene and earlier epochs. (Waters et al. 2016, 137)

However, the hypothesis of the Anthropocene is still contested and functions as a "rough place-holder for an undefined and arguably unprecedented historical condition underpinned by environmental uncertainties" (Johnson/Morehouse 2014, 440). Lucy Edwards (Edwards 2016, 6) collected the various arguments within the current debate and compared different timeframes.

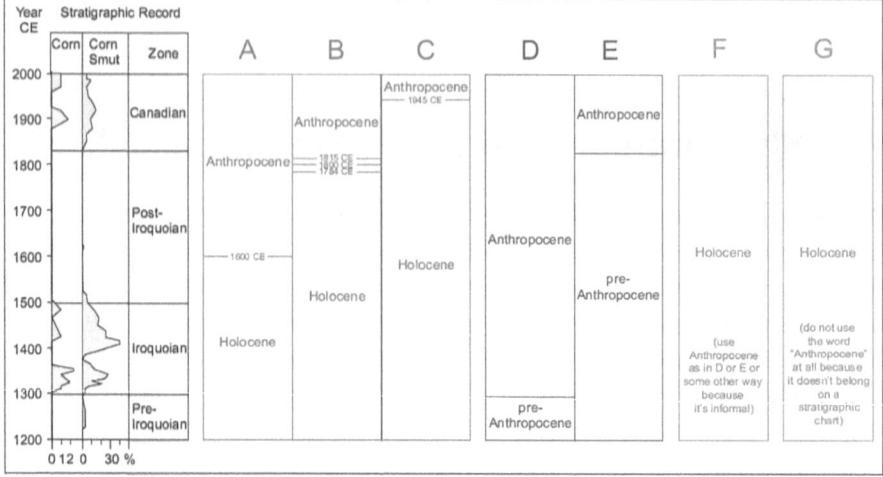

In this figure we see a comparison of different geological arguments according to Edwards:

> (left) A simplified pollen/spore diagram (redrawn from McAndrews/Turton 2010) of the record from a lake sediment core with annual layers in southern Ontario, Canada. Variations in percentage of corn pollen (labeled 'corn') and spores from a corn smut fungus serve as a proxy for human impact. Chronology comes from layer counts and radiocarbon dating. (right) Seven of the many concepts of the word 'Anthropocene' (A–G) that divide this record. CE = Common Er [...] (Edwards 2016).

In the figure, Edwards relates various concepts of the Anthropocene to specific sedimentation records, showing that in any case, "no matter how you use the term 'Anthropocene,' others are using the same word with a very different meaning":

> If you answered A, B, or C, you probably think you favor including the Anthropocene as a formal part of the Geologic Time Scale—especially if your particular choice of start date is selected. If your choice is not selected, you may not favor formalization at all. If you answered D or E, you probably oppose formalization. The choice you made is based on cultural considerations—here with either a First Nation (D) or Eurocentric (E) emphasis. You probably don't want a subset of geologists to co-opt the word "Anthropocene" for their concepts. If you answered F or G, you probably mildly (F) or strongly (G) oppose this inclusion. (Edwards 2016, 6)

However, the debate about a potential starting point of the Anthropocene is still running high (e.g. Waters et al. 2016, Lewis/Maslin 2015, Ruddiman et al. 2015, Steffen et al. 2015). Two timeframes in particular are discussed for the shortlist:

the onset of the age of industry some 250 years ago (as the starting point and driver of the "Great Accelaration", which has definitely and unambiguously has gathered speed from 1950 onwards) and the time of the nuclear bombing of the mid 20th century. Whatever the International Commission on Stratigraphy is going to decide, the rest of us will have to live with it. However, the huge amount of contributions to the debate already show that one can be fairly certain that the Anthropocene will live on, even if it should not be formally added to the Geological Time Scale. Its function as a place-holder for a yet to be defined unprecedented historical-environmental condition offers a good starting point for cultural narratives using it as a kind of holistic concept, indicating that humankind significantly alter the global environment.

ad b) The second requirement for a new geological era refers to time, i.e. the sediment markers have to preserve "over the long term". This means for instance: When, in 10 million or 100 million years, someone arrives on our planet, the traces of our existence should have endured and not have become erased by then. This argument indicates that humans are expected to be extinct; if we were still be around at that point, nobody would be surprised to find traces and remnants of our activities. The hypothesis of the Anthropocene, thus, poses the question whether we might "have left some faint, enduring mark on the universe" (Weisman 2007, 4), which continue to persist once there is "a world without us", as Alan Weisman has put it in his thought-provoking bestseller.

However, the question of time, especially the understanding of geological time, is intriguing when it comes to the Anthropocene. Geological timespans are so far beyond the usual human imagination, that they have to be transferred into a more common scale for the measurement of time: Taking a 24-hour clock representing the Earth's history, the time we start to know more about in terms of its history begins a little after than 9 pm (about 541 million years ago). The youngest geological era (the Quarternary, covering 2.5 million years), would be represented by the last 47 seconds on the clock. The final period, the Holocene, marking a phase of global warming, started some 11,700 years ago, or 0.2 seconds on the 24-hour clock. Hominides have been around almost since the Quarternary started, for 2.5 million years or 45 seconds, while homo sapiens has been playing on earth only in the last 4 seconds (some 200,000 years). For the sake of comparison, I introduce a non-geological event: the blink of a human eye takes 100 milliseconds (0,01 seconds), which is 50 times longer than the time that is discussed as that starting point of the Anthropocene, some 200 years ago (0.002 seconds).

Against this backdrop of timeframes, the development of the hypothesis of the Anthropocene is at the very least: astonishing. The dinosaurs (to introduce another strong species in Earth's history for the sake of comparison) were the dominant terrestrial species for some 170 million years (51 minutes on the 24-hour clock) – but no geological epoch is named after the dinosaurs. Quite obviously, it is not our presence on Earth, but rather our restlessness[2] that has made us into *the* transforming and modifying force within our short presence on Earth, finally leading to the current crisis, which is acknowledged with the hypothesis of the Anthropocene.

To date, much of the research of the Anthropocene has focused on interpreting past and present developments (as also argued in this chapter). However, its even greater "significance lies in how it can be used to guide attitudes, choices, policies and actions that influence the future" (Biermann et al. 2015, 2). It still is an open question how the hypothesis of the Anthropocene can contribute to *desirable* futures, which seem to be so crucial in the current debate on the future of crisis and catastrophe.

3 Realistic and Anti-Realistic Epistemologies and the Anthropocene

Classic epistemologies follow the long established dualistic distinction, dividing our world (and with it scientific disciplines) into disconnected spheres separated by an insurmountable gap (e.g. nature/culture, body/mind, matter/meaning). Despite ongoing research and debate, the gaps between different epistemologies have not yet become any smaller, mostly due to the point that epistemological questions are "as a matter of principle: undecidable" and are, thus, a question of decision as Heinz von Foerster (von Foerster/Bröcker 2002, 1f) has pointed out. By acknowledging the new geological era as a fruitful description of our present times, the established dualistic approaches are going to collapse. What does this mean for epistemology? The following focuses on observation, as the question of whether (and to what extent) the observed is a representation or whether, instead, it is disconnected from the material world, plays a crucial role, which in the end result in realistic and anti-realistic epistemologies.

---

[2] The philosopher Ralf Konersmann points to the "ontological gap" (in German: "das ontologische Gefälle," Konersmann 2015) as the source of the "restlessness" of us humans: It is one of our fundamental assumptions that the world fails to be ideal and thus, cannot stay the way it is, but has to be adjusted and modified in an unceasing and ever on-going process.

Ever since the stunning and counter-intuitive experiments of quantum physics of the 1920s, the process of observation as well as the role of the observer in the observation process is still an open field. The experiments showed that the materialization of quantum objects depends on the fact whether they are observed and how they are observed, i.e. with what *theory* or which *expectation* the result of the materialization is interpreted (e.g. in the case of the experiments with light: whether light is expected to be a "wave" or to be a "particle", see for example Green 1995, 108 ff; Zeilinger 2005, 29 ff). Although these striking contributions were already made in the early 20th century in physics, their disturbing consequences and their irritations for our traditional epistemologies and the philosophy of science are not yet well developed. Interestingly enough, the quantum physics experiments support *neither* realist *nor* (radical) constructivist positions (see Egner 2012). So far, the experiments in quantum physics only show the central role of observation and the exposed position of the observer. To date, quantum physics is still quite desperately in need of an appropriate theory of observation to explain the unexplained phenomena of their experiments (see Stapp 2011). A comprehensive theory of observation must be capable of answering crucial basic questions: How is observation carried out, i.e. how to describe the process of observing? What exactly is the role of the observer in the observation process? Does observation necessarily require a consciousness or are other entities also able to observe?

These questions are not new at all, but against the background of the hypothesis of the Anthropocene the matter becomes all more urgent. Its strong case for human agency placing it right in the centre of the world's development implies that hardly any activity on Earth takes place without human participation (in the broadest sense). Classical epistemological and ontological assumptions are based on an autonomously existing world (e.g. Newtonian physics), which can be described independently from our experimental research and, thus, independently from any observer. This has led to the long-established idea of an Archimedean point as a position "outside" from which a different, perhaps objective or "true" picture of something will be obtainable. The hypothesis of the Anthropocene, in contrast, puts us humans in the middle, not only in the observation process, but rather in the Earths' chemical, biological, biophysical and geophysical processes. As a result, the notion of a possible observation from an "outside" can no longer persist. In the Anthropocene, "observation" turns into "participating observation", with an observer who is inseparably entangled with the observed (for more see chapter 4). In other words, we have to rid our imagination of a view from a satellite and embed the starting point for any observation in ourselves. With this, the hypothesis of the Anthropocene appears to be evidence of a statement by Ernst von Glasersfeld: "We have no one but ourselves to thank for the world the way it is" (Lochhead 2013, 39). In consequence, this leads to a rejection of realistic approaches.[3]

What about the obvious next choice: anti-realism? Working on the interface of natural and social sciences, I have been pondering on system theoretical approaches for quite a while. In most, observation also plays a central role, while it is somewhat unclear whether systems theories are to be understood in terms of realism or rather anti-realism. Niklas Luhmann's *Theory of Social Systems*, for instance, it mostly perceived as a constructivist approach,[4] but some of the examples he uses for what he calls "the operation of observation" (Luhmann 2002) are difficult to comprehend in terms of constructivism. In his theory, observation is understood as the operation of distinguishing and indication at the same time: A certain distinction is applied to be able to determine something within this distinction and to mark one side of a thing (and not the other) as the starting point for further operations (see Luhmann 1986b, 112, Luhmann 1988, 52). According to Luhmann, *all* autopoietic and self-referential systems can observe, meaning all living, psychic and social systems. As both psychic (meaning individuals) and social systems refer to and utilize meaning (Sinn) in their operations (see Fuchs 2004), it seems to be self-evident that they can observe. Unsurprisingly, the constraints and consequences of the observation as an operation of psychic and social systems more or less matches the argument of (radical) constructivism (see Luhmann 1986a, Luhmann 2002).

The capability to observe of Luhmann's third category – the living systems (meaning all entities of the living, from cells to bodies or plants) – is not that self-evident. Thinking of animals, the understanding of observation of psychic systems might be transferred (pet owners would probably deny any differences anyway). However, Luhmann gives some curious examples to illustrate the difference of "observation" and "understanding" using living systems: "The stomach, for instance, can observe since it digests only food but not itself; but it cannot understand how the food is affected when it is digested and it probably would be confusing for the stomach to understand this and to deal with these differentiations." (Luhmann 1986a, 91)

According to this, our stomach is able to observe. Going forward from this point, a further argument can be drawn (see Egner 2008, 62): Living systems,

---

[3] Admittedly, this is a very general, if not crude, statement (and most probably illicit in philosophical arenas), lacking a detailed and thorough elaboration for the different approaches of realism. For the sake of argumentation (and due to limited space), I want to leave it as crude as it is and ask for the readers' indulgence and patience

[4] Although Luhmann's own elaborations seem to oscillate between realistic and constructivist standpoints (see Scholl 2012).

such as chemical, biological or physical systems, cannot only distinguish but can also describe and thus: learn. For instance, when a hangover (as the physical defence reaction against high-strength booze) gradually disappears following regular application or when the efficacy of pharmaceuticals diminishes over time. How can an example like this be understood in terms of constructivism? To my knowledge, there are no concepts of constructivism that can deal with operations without a consciousness.

Within physics, the concept of observation is driven even further, when not only applied to autopoietic and self-referential systems, but rather to all "complex adapting systems", which is, in short, for most of the physical world. In an attempt to answer the question why the physical world around us seems (or better: proves?) to be solid even if there is no (human) observer to hold it stable and in its place by observation, Murray Gell-Mann and Jim Hartle understand natural or physical systems as "actors" (calling them "Information Gathering and Utilizing Systems", in short IGUS) (Gell-Mann 1995, 155f) that can observe and, thus, fulfil the task of stabilizing the world by mutual observation. But again: Looking at the physical world around us with its chemical, biophysical and geophysical manifestations, there is no consciousness whatsoever involved, which seems to be a crucial point. Quite obviously, we simply do not have an appropriate theory of observation available to include such phenomena as an observing stomach or "Information Gathering and Utilizing Systems" of the material world. There is still much to be done to gain an understanding of the "who" and "how" in observational processes.

4 First Steps Towards Non-Dualistic Epistemologies

The term Anthropocene points to a world of complex dynamic structures, self-organised and self-referential developments, several intertwined drivers with surprising emergences and unintended consequences across different scales. Pointedly, one could argue that traditional epistemologies and ontologies have been developed in a world that appeared to be simpler, slower and could be more easily divided in sectors, spheres or fields. The Anthropocene throws us into a fuzzy, vague, indeterminate domain with manifold entanglements and uncertainties on different scales. This requires adaptations (if not new) epistemologies. Concurrently, ontologies are needed that allow a focus on processes rather than on objects or separated entities (see for example Sohst 2009 and, of course, Whitehead 1987).

Karen Barad, coming from theoretical particle physics and philosophy and now working on feminist studies and history of consciousness, tries to bridge dualism by grasping matter and meaning together in her notion of agential realism (Barad 2007, Barad 2015). She suggests taking a look at "phenomena" (instead of independent objects with inherent boundaries and properties) as the primary ontological unit. According to her agential realist elaboration, phenomena do not merely mark the epistemological inseparability of observer and observed [...]; rather, *phenomena are the ontological inseparability / entanglement of intra-acting "agencies"*. That is, phenomena are ontologically primitive relations without pre-existing relata. The notion of *intra-action* (in contrast to the usual "interaction", which presumes the prior existence of independent entities or relata) represents a profound conceptual shift. It is through specific agential intra-actions that the boundaries and properties of the phenomena become determinate and that particular concepts (that is, particular material articulations of the world) become meaningful (Barad 2007, 139, emphasis in original).

With her notion of agential realism, Barad proposes an ontology that "does not take separateness to be an inherent feature of the world" (Barad 2007, 136). This notion appears consistent with the fuzzy, vague and indeterminate fields coming into view through the hypothesis of the Anthropocene. It allows us to capture a world in which matter is not fixed or given and at the same time not the mere result of specific processes. It is a world, in which differences, of course, matter, but cannot be taken for granted. "Mattering is differentiating, and which differences come to matter, matter in the iterative production of different differences" (Barad 2007, 137). With her notion of entanglements as the fundamental characteristic of "phenomena", in which all is intra-acting (instead of interacting), Barad offers a stunning and very promising way of bridging the so far seemingly insurmountable gap between nature/culture, body/mind, matter/meaning, etc.

While we elaborate ontologies and epistemologies adequate to the era of humankind, we could begin bridging established dualisms by practising a non-dualistic manner of speaking as proposed by Josef Mitterer (Mitterer 2001, Mitterer 2011). Since various chapters of this volume address his sophisticated considerations in detail, it might suffice to note that Mitterer's approach focuses on the conditions of change and progress rather than on being right or wrong. A notion, that fits to the uncertain fields we are about to enter. Twisting Mitterer's wording: We have come *so far*, but the Anthropocene opens up surprising new questions of how we shall proceed *from now on*.

Acknowledgements: First of all, I am very grateful to Josef Mitterer for his boldness in inviting a geographer to a philosophers' conference. I am indebted to

Egon Becker for many entangled discussions on society and nature, philosophy, quantum physics, observation …, in short: on the conditions of the possibility of the world. I also owe many thanks to the Institute of Advanced Study, Durham University, for granting me a fellowship in the Michelmas term 2015 that allowed so many fruitful discussions, influencing my argumentation.

References

Austin, Witney, J.; Holbrook, John M. (2012): "Is the Anthropocene an issue of stratigraphy or pop culture?" In: *GSA Today* 22 (7), 60–61.
Barad, Karen (2007): *Meeting the Universe Halfway. Quantum Physics and the Entanglement of Matter and Meaning.* Durham and London: Duke University Press.
Barad, Karen (2015): *Verschränkungen.* Berlin: Merve.
Biermann, Frank; Bai, Xuemei; Bondre, Ninad; Broadgate, Wendy; Chen, Chen-Tung Arthur; Dube, Opha Pauline; Erisman, Jan Willem; Glaser, Marion; Van Der Hel, Sandra; Lemos, Maria Carmen; Seitzinger, Sybil; Seto, Karen C. (2015): "Down to Earth: Contextualizing the Anthropocene". In: *Global Environmental Change*, in preparation.
Chakrabarty, Dipesh (2009): "The Climate of History. Four Theses". In: *Critical Enquiry* 35, 197–222.
Crutzen, Paul (2002): "The Geology of Mankind". In: *Nature* 415, 23.
Crutzen, Paul; Stoermer, Eugene F. (2000): "The 'Anthropocene'". In: *Global Change Newsletter* 41, 17–18.
Edwards, Lucy E. (2016): "What is the Anthropocene?". In: *EOS Earth & Space Science News* 97 (2), 6–7.
Egner, Heike (2012): "Jenseits der Dichotomie von ‚Sinn' und ‚Materie'. Ein neues Metaparadigma am Horizont?". In: Weixlbaumer, Norbert (ed.): *Anthologie zur Sozialgeographie.* Wien: Institut für Geographie und Regionalforschung, 35–51.
Fuchs, Peter (2004): *Der Sinn der Beobachtung. Begriffliche Untersuchungen.* Weilerswist: Velbrück.
Gell-Mann, Murray (1995): *The Quark and the Jaguar. Adventures in the Simplex and the Complex.* London: Abacus.
Green, Brian (1995): *The Elegant Universe. Superstrings, Hidden Dimensions, and the Quest for the Ultimate Theory.* London: Vintage Books.
Haraway, Donna (2015): "Anthropocene, Capitalocene, Plantanionocene, Chthulucene: Making Kin". In: *Environmental Humanities* 6, 159–165.
Johnson, Elizabeth; Morehouse, Harlan (2014): "After the Anthropocene: Politics and Geographic Inquiry for a New Epoch". In: *Progress in Human Geography* 38 (3), 439–456.
Konersmann, Ralf (2015): *Die Unruhe der Welt.* Frankfurt am Main: Fischer e-Books.
Lewis, Simon L.; Maslin, Mark A. (2015): "Defining the Anthropocene". In: *Nature* 519, 171–180.
Lochhead, Jack (2013): "Constructing the Construction of Constructions: How Ernst became Ernst". In: Hug, Theo; Schorner, Michael; Mitterer, Josef (eds.):

Ernst-von-Glasersfeld-Archiv. Eröffnung – Inauguration. Innsbruck: Innsbruck University Press, 37–40.
Luhmann, Niklas (1986a): "The Autopoiesis of Social Systems". In: Geyer, Felix; van der Zouwen, Johannes (eds.): *Sociocybernetic Paradoxes. Observation, Control and Evolution of Self-Steering Systems.* London: Sage, 172–192.
Luhmann, Niklas (1986b): "Systeme verstehen Systeme". In: Luhmann, Niklas; Schorr, Karl Eberhard (eds.): *Zwischen Intransparenz und Verstehen. Fragen an die Pädagogik.* Frankfurt am Main: Suhrkamp, 72–117.
Luhmann, Niklas (1988): "Selbstreferentielle Systeme". In: Simon, Fritz B. (ed.): *Lebende Systeme. Wirklichkeitskonstruktionen in der systemischen Therapie.* Berlin u.a.: Springer, 47–53.
Luhmann, Niklas (2002): *Theories of Distinction. Redescribing the Description of Modernity,* Stanford, CA: Stanford University Press.
McAndrews, John; Turton, Charles (2010): "Fungal Spores Record Iroquoian and Canadian Agriculture in 2nd Millennium A.D. Sediment of Crawford Lake, Ontario, Canada". In: *Vegetation History and Archaeobotany* 19, 531–544.
Mitterer, Josef (2001): *Die Flucht aus der Beliebigkeit.* Frankfurt am Main: Fischer.
Mitterer, Josef (2011): *Das Jenseits der Philosophie. Wider das dualistische Erkenntnisprinzip.* Weilerswist: Velbrück.
Moore, Amelia (2016): "The Anthropocene. A Critical Exploration". In: *Environment and Society* 6 (1), 1–3.
Moore, Jason W. (2015a): "Putting Nature to Work. Anthropocene, Capitalocene & the Challenge of World-Ecology". In: Wee, Cecilia; Schönenback, Janneke; Arndt, Olaf (eds.): *Supramarkt. A Micro-Toolkit for Disobedient Consumers, or How to Frack the Fatal Forces of the Capitalocene.* Gothenburg: Irene Books, 69–117.
Moore, Jason W. (2015b): *Capitalism in the Web of Life. Ecology and the Accumulation of Capital.* New York: Verso.
Ruddiman, William F.; Ellis, Erle C.; Kaplan, Jed O.; Fuller, Dorian Q. (2015): "Defining the Epoch We Live In. Is a Formally Designated 'Anthropocene' a Good Idea?" In: *Science* 348 (6230), 38–39.
Scholl, Armin (2012): "Between Realism and Constructivism? Luhmann's Ambivalent Epistemological Standpoint". In: *Constructivist Foundations* 8 (1), 5–12.
Smith, Bruce D.; Zeder, Melinda A. (2013): "The Onset of the Anthropocene". In: *Anthropocene* 4, 8–13.
Sohst, Wolfgang (2009): *Prozessontologie. Ein systematischer Entwurf der Entstehung von Existenz.* Berlin: xenomoi.
Stapp, Henry P. (2011): *Mindful Universe. Quantum Mechanics and the Participating Observer.* Berlin, Heidelberg: Springer.
Steffen, Will; Broadgate, Wendy; Deutsch, Lisa; Gaffney, Owen; Ludwig, Cornelia (2015): "The Trajectory of the Anthropocene: The Great Acceleration". In: *The Anthropocene Review* 2, 81–98.
Steffen, Will; Crutzen, Paul J.; McNeil, John R. (2007): "The Anthropocene: Are Humans Now Overwhelming the Great Forces of Nature?" In: *Ambio* 36 (8), 614–621.
Steffen, Will; Persson, Asa; Deutsch, Lisa; Zalasiewicz, Jan; Williams, Mark; Richardson, Katherine; Crumley, Carole; Crutzen, Paul; Folke, Carl; Gordon, Line; Molina, Mario; Ramanathan, Veerabhadran; Rockström, Johan; Scheffer, Marten; Schellnhuber, Hans

Joachim; Svedin, Uno (2011): "The Anthropocene: From Global Change to Planetary Stewardship". In: *Ambio* 40, 739–761.
von Foerster, Heinz; Bröcker, Monika (2002): *Teil der Welt. Fraktale einer Ethik – oder: Heinz von Foersters Tanz mit der Welt.* Heidelberg: Carl Auer.
Waters, Colin N.; Zalasiewicz, Jan; Summerhayes, C. P.; Barnosky, Anthony D.; Poirier, Clément; Gałuzka, Agniezka; Cearreta, Alejandro; Edgeworth, Matt; Ellis, Erle C.; Ellis, Michael E.; Jeandel, Catherine; Leinfelder, Reinhold; McNeil, J. R.; Richter, Daniel; Steffen, Will; Syvitsky, James; Vidas, Davor; Wagreich, Michael; Williams, Mark; Zhisheng, An; Grinevald, Jaques; Odata, E. O.; Oreskes, Naomi; Wolfe, Alexander P. (2016): "The Anthropocene is Functionally and Stratigraphically Distinct from the Holocene". In: *Science* 351 (6269), 137–147.
Weisman, Alan (2007): *The World Without Us.* New York: Virgin Books.
Whitehead, Alfred North (1987): *Prozess und Realität. Entwurf einer Kosmologie.* Frankfurt am Main: Suhrkamp.
Zalasiewicz, Jan; Williams, Mark; Smith, Alan; Barry, Tiffany L.; Coe, Angela L.; Brown, Paul R.; Brenchley, Patrick; Cantrill, David; Gale, Andrew; Gibbard, Philip; Gregory, F. John; Hounslow, Mark W.; Kerr, Andrew C.; Pearson, Paul; Knox, Robert; Powell, John; Waters, Colin; Marshall, John; Oates, Michael; Rawson, Peter; Stone, Philip (2008): "Are We Now Living in the Anthropocene?" In: *GSA Today* 18 (2), 4–8.
Zalasiewicz, Jan; Williams, Mark; Steffen, Will; Crutzen, Paul (2010): "The New World of the Anthropocene". In: *Environmental Science & Technology* 44, 2228–2231.
Zeilinger, Anton (2005): *Einsteins Schleier. Die neue Welt der Quantenphysik.* München: Goldmann.

Hans Rudi Fischer
Ein Bild – ohne Betrachter – hielt uns gefangen. Wittgensteins ambivalenter Abschied vom Realismus

Abstract: Often Wittgenstein compares his style of working with that of a painter and he takes thinking (and speaking) as analog to drawing. The concept of a drawing is central to his thinking and is developed in the *Tractatus*. Explaining how a picture (or a sentence) depicts reality is the paradigm case with which Wittgenstein wants to clarify how reality can be depicted at all. Depiction in a literal as well as in a linguistic sense is understood explicitly as a process of construction in the *Tractatus*, the sentence is a "projection method".

The method of representing visual objects in a picture in a realistic, this is, perspectival, way was developed in the 15th century on the basis of geometrical and optical laws. Albertis theory of pictures, consisting of the velum as projection technique, is analog to the picture theory of the *Tractatus*. Making use of Albertis theoretical work and of some pictures I want to show that (1) the *Tractatus* makes use of the logic of the method of using perspectivity, (2) that the *Tractatus* shall be read as being constructivistic in spirit, and (3) how Wittgenstein's own, ambivalent relation to the logic of the *Tractatus* looks like.

His ambivalence with respect to the binary logic he brilliantly exposed in the *Tractatus* remains to be the creative source of his later philosophy which is better understood as being constructivist in spirit. But: the decision between realism and constructivism is not to be determined rationally, it remains ambivalent until the last passages of *On Certainty*.

Keywords: Wittgenstein, picture-theory, Tractatus, contemplating subject, constructivism

1 Ein Bild – vom Bild – hielt uns gefangen. Ein Rückblick

Wittgenstein vergleicht im Vorwort der *Philosophischen Untersuchungen* seine Bemerkungen mit Landschaftsskizzen, „die auf langen und verwickelten Fahrten entstanden sind. […] mit allen Mängeln eines schwachen Zeichners behaftet […] daß sie dem Betrachter ein Bild der Landschaft geben." Diese Formulierung ist aufschlussreich, weil sie sowohl den Zeichner *als auch* den Betrachter des Bildes einführt. Relativ häufig vergleicht er das Denken mit dem Zeichnen von Bildern und seine Arbeitsweise mit der eines Malers, der Zusammenhänge *nach*zeichnen will. Das Bild (bzw. die Metapher) wird dabei zum Medium zwischen Maler und Betrachter und ist der Schlüssel zu Wittgensteins Sprachdenken.

Die Maleranalogie führt zur – erkenntnistheoretisch entscheidenden – Frage, *wie* ein Maler Wirklichkeit so ins Bild setzen kann, dass es *dem Betrachter* als (wahres) Bild von der Wirklichkeit erscheint bzw. es mit ihr „übereinstimmt". Im *Tractatus Logico-Philosophicus* wird Erkennen als Abbilden verstanden. Die Frage, wie es möglich ist, dass ein Bild uns etwas über das Abgebildete, die Wirklichkeit, sagen kann, ist analog zur Frage, *wie* ein Satz etwas über die Wirklichkeit aussagen kann. Diese Fragen wollte Wittgenstein mit der Abbildtheorie im *Tractatus* beantworten, wobei er Begriffe darstellender Geometrie nutzt, um zu klären, *wie* ein Bild (das heißt „Satz") Wirklichkeit abzubilden vermag. Abbildung im bildlichen wie sprachlichen Sinne wird dabei explizit zum *Konstruktionsprozess*, der Satz zur „Projektionsmethode" des Denkens. Wenn Wittgenstein in dekonstruktiver Weise vom Bild spricht, das nach „exakten Projektionsregeln" mit der Wirklichkeit zu vergleichen sei (PG §123), dann führt das zur Bildtheorie Leon Battista Albertis (1436) und der Funktion des Velums als Technik, das Bild *nach* der Wirklichkeit zu malen. Wittgenstein verwendet in seiner frühen Bildtheorie – so meine These – das realistische Erkenntnismodell der Renaissance, nach dem der Betrachter *durch* das Bild auf die Welt blicken kann. Damit wird das Bild (wie der Satz) ambivalent, denn es liegt auf der Grenze zwischen Sprache und Wirklichkeit, es ist Realität und Fiktion zugleich. Ich möchte zeigen, dass im *Tractatus* die Projektionstechnik der Perspektivtheorie in Gestalt der *logischen Form* auftaucht, der jedes Bild (jeder Satz) genügen muss, um etwas über Wirklichkeit aussagen können.

Wittgensteins Rückblick auf seine „Irrtümer" im *Tractatus* offenbaren die Perspektivtheorie als Schlüssel zur Abbildtheorie. Worin liegt seine Kritik? Betrachten wir, wie er einen seiner „Denkfehler" im *Tractatus* zitierend markiert: „Log. Phil. Abh. (4.5): ‚Die allgemeine Form des Satzes ist: Es verhält sich so und so.' – Das ist so ein Satz von jener Art, die man sich unzählige Male wiederholt. Man glaubt wieder und wieder der Natur nachzufahren, und fährt nur der Form entlang, durch die wir sie betrachten." (PU §114)

Der Abbildungsprozess (der „Natur") besteht darin, der Form *nachzufahren, durch* die der Betrachter/Maler (per spicere) das abzubildende Objekt betrachtet. In dieser Formulierung klingt die Perspektive als *symbolische Form* der Abbildung an. Die Etymologie des Verbs *nachfahren* führt in die „Nähe von etwas" (hier der Form), verwandt mit nach*h*men (mhd. amen), was zu „ausmessen", „visieren" und „*nachmachen*" führt, das im 16. Jahrhundert „nach*messen*" bzw. dem „*Maß des Vorbilds* entsprechend nachgestalten" bedeutete (Kluge 1989). Wenn wir *visieren* etymologisch verfolgen (vis, altfranz. Gesicht, videre (visum), visus (visage),

i. e. Blick, Anblick, ins Auge fassen), kommen wir zu Termini der Geometrie, die zu Zeiten Albrecht Dürers mit „Messkunst" übersetzt wurde. Wie muss eine Form beschaffen sein, *durch* die man der Natur nach*fahren*, diese nach*messen* oder „dem *Maß* des Vor-Bilds" (!) nachgestalten kann? An einem Holzschnitt Dürers möchte ich illustrieren, wie sich Wittgensteins Bemerkung verstehen lässt.

Abb. 1: Albrecht Dürer, Der Zeichner des sitzenden Mannes, Holzschnitt, 1525, aus: Underweysung der Messung.

Das Beispiel zeigt das Glastafelverfahren, wobei der Zeichner auf einer durchsichtigen Fläche (Glastafel), der *Form* des Vorbilds *nachfahren* kann. Der Augenpunkt ist fixiert.

Im folgenden Paragraphen (PU §115) nennt Wittgenstein – wieder metaphorisch – die eigene, vom „Vorurteil der Kristallreinheit" (PU §108) eindeutiger Logik geprägte Bild- bzw. Satzauffassung im *Tractatus* als Grund seines Irrtums: „Ein Bild hielt uns gefangen. Und *heraus* konnten wir nicht, denn es lag *in unserer*

Sprache, und sie schien es uns nur unerbittlich zu wiederholen." (PU §115, Hervorhebung hinzugefügt)

Ist die Sprache ein Gefängnis, wie Wittgenstein einmal fragt? Ja und Nein. Ambivalenz – und diese auszuschließen – ist die Grundtönung in Wittgensteins Denken, auch was erkenntnistheoretische Positionen betrifft – und das zeigt sich schon im *Tractatus*, der gemeinhin realistisch interpretiert wird (vgl. Fischer/ Lüscher 2014 und Lüscher/Fischer 2014).

Doch schon im *Tractatus* erleidet der Versuch, die Welt (mit sprachlichen Mitteln) aus *einem* rationalen, logischen Guss zu begreifen, Schiffbruch; es ist ein Schiffbruch mit Wittgenstein als Zuschauer. Die Wirklichkeit des Realismus war dort bereits von konstruktivistischen Ideen kolonisiert. Denn der Tractatrealismus enthält nicht nur den Keim der Selbsttranszendenz, sondern auch die Leiter, um den Dualismus von Realismus und Konstruktivismus zu transzendieren. Der Schlüssel zu diesem Überstieg liegt im Mystischen, im Unbegrifflichen, im Zeigen dessen, was nicht gesagt werden kann, im Ich, das auf der Grenze situiert wird.

Bevor ich konstruktivistische Aspekte der Abbildtheorie herausarbeite, möchte ich als historisches Vorbild die Perspektivtheorie der Renaissance skizzieren.

2 Das geöffnete Fenster – zur Logik der „Costruzione Legittima"[1]

Die Methode, sichtbare Dinge im Bild so darzustellen, dass sie als vom Betrachterblickwinkel abhängiges Bild erscheinen, wurde im 15. Jahrhundert auf Grundlage geometrischer und optischer Gesetze erfunden. Auf Experimente des Architekten Brunelleschi zurückgreifend definierte Alberti in seinem Buch *Über die Malkunst* (Alberti 2002) das Bild als *senkrechte Schnittfläche* durch die Sehstrahlpyramide, deren Spitze im Auge des Betrachters liegt. Was auf der Schnittfläche (dem Bild) erscheint, wird als lineare Projektion der realen Gegenstände von der Basisfläche aufgefasst. Stellt man sich das Bild (Schnittfläche) aus durchsichtigem Glas vor (siehe Abbildung 1), wird klar, wie es dem Maler möglich

---

1 Der Begriff „Construzione legittima" tauchte im 17. Jahrhundert für Albertis Methode auf. Ich kann hier nicht auf Wittgensteins Spätphilosophie eingehen, auch dort finden sich viele Belege für seine perspektivistische Grundposition. Ein Beispiel, wo er Begriffe darstellender Geometrie auf Sprache überträgt, möge genügen: „Ein *Satz* ist sozusagen ein *Schnitt* durch eine Hypothese in einem *bestimmten Ort*." (PB 286, Hervorebung hinzugefügt)

ist, „die Formen gesehener Gegenstände" (Alberti 2002, 83f) auf dem Bild darzustellen.

Auf dieser Grundlage formuliert Alberti die Metapher vom Bild als *offenstehendem Fenster* (finestra aperta), dessen Logik, wie ich zeigen möchte, im *Tractatus* wiederkehrt. Wie definiert Alberti die Voraussetzungen, die eine „gesetzmäßige" Perspektivkonstruktion ermöglicht?

> Als Erstes zeichne ich auf der zu bemalenden Fläche ein rechtwinkliges Viereck *von beliebiger Größe*; von diesem nehme ich an, es *sei ein offenstehendes Fenster*, durch das *ich betrachte*, was hier gemalt werden soll; darauf *lege ich nach Belieben fest*, von welcher Größe ich die Menschen in meinem Gemälde haben möchte; [...] Dann bringe ich innerhalb dieses Rechtecks, *wo es mir richtig scheint*, einen *Punkt* an, der den Ort einnimmt, auf welchen der Zentralstrahl trifft, und den ich deshalb ‚Zentralpunkt' nenne. (Alberti 2002, 93, Hervorhebung hinzugefügt)

Alberti lässt keinen Zweifel an seinem point of view: Der Maßstab der Messung ist 1. „nach Belieben", 2. *vor* der Messung festzulegen und 3. ist auch der Fluchtpunkt willkürlich vorzugeben, er korrespondiert mit dem Augenpunkt des Betrachters und repräsentiert ihn (Welsch 2004).

In der Bildmetapher steckt ein realistisches Erkenntnismodell: Das gemalte Bild öffnet dem Betrachter den *direkten* Blick nach draußen, *in die Wirklichkeit*. Das Bild sehen, heißt auf die Wirklichkeit blicken, weil im Bild (der gedachten Schnittfläche) die realen, dreidimensionalen Gegenstände „dahinter" projiziert sind.

Damit schafft Alberti die Grundlage für die Erfindung der Technik, die die perspektivische Konstruktion ermöglicht: das Velum. Mit dem Velum (lat. Segel)[2], einem hauchdünnen, durchsichtigen Tuch, vereint Alberti die Vorstellungen vom Bild als *Schnitt* durch die Sehpyramide *und* als durchsichtiges Fenster. „Dieses Velum stelle ich *zwischen* das Auge und den gesehenen Gegenstand und zwar so, dass die Sehpyramide das lose Gewebe des Tuches durchdringt." (Alberti 2002, 115)[3] Wittgensteins Metapher der Brille führt ebenfalls ein Drittes ein, das der Funktion des Velums analog ist: „Die Idee sitzt gleichsam als Brille auf unserer Nase, und was wir ansehen, sehen wir durch sie." (PU §103) Bei Albertis Velum bilden dickere Fäden ein Fadengitter aus Quadraten, durch das die Gegenstände projiziert erscheinen.

---

2 Vgl. zum Velum (Alberti 2002, 115f). Und den instruktiven Kommentar der Herausgeber Oskar Bätschmann und Sandra Gianfreda in (Alberti 2002, 16ff).
3 Bätschmann und Gianfreda schreiben, laut Filarete habe Brunelleschi die zentralperspektivische Konstruktion bei der Analyse eines Spiegelbildes entdeckt (Alberti 2002, 13).

Das Velum hat eine Janusfunktion, die vaszilliert: 1. als gedachter Schnitt *durch* die Sehpyramide, als geöffnetes Fenster ist es optische Projektions- und Messebene (der Gegenstände „draußen" in der Wirklichkeit) und 2. ist es – mit Fadengitter/netz und/oder diaphaner Fläche – die materialisierte Zeichenfläche, die die perspektivische Konstruktion der Anschauung (als vermessene Form) ermöglicht.

Mit *dem fixierten Auge* des Betrachters ist das Velum Projektionsmethode, um die „natürliche" Anschauung in den zweidimensionalen Bildraum zu transponieren. Die Welt wird so zum Bild, das sich nach geometrischen Gesetzen *konstruieren* lässt.[4]

Im Bild erscheint die Wirklichkeit, wie sie sich der Anschauung des Malers darstellt, sein *Augenpunkt* ist Maßstab und Konstruktionszentrum des Bildes. Die Gegenstände und ihre Beziehungen im Bild korrespondieren *seinem Blick*. Da dieser Blick mit geometrischen Gesetzen beschrieben werden kann, glaubte man *die* Form der Darstellung gefunden zu haben, in der Gegenstände „natürlich" gesehen und dargestellt werden mussten.

Ein Blick auf Rodlers Darstellung dieser Konstruktionsmethode (1531) zeigt, warum diese Abbildungsmethode den Nimbus von „realistisch", mithin von „objektiv" im Sinne von beobachterunabhängig erhalten konnte. Der Maler kann die Messpunkte der zu malenden Gegenstände vom Fadengitter (Velum ist Fenster) auf ein analog quadriertes Blatt übertragen, aber die Fixierung des Augenpunktes (point of view) und damit der Beobachter sind getilgt. Damit wird diese Form der Abbildung – ohne Betrachter – zur vermeintlich „objektiven" *Norm der Abbildung* verabsolutiert. Betrachter und Zeichner sind im geschlossenen Raum eins. Wir haben einen durchsichtigen Realismus.

Zusammenfassend lassen sich die folgenden Prinzipien des Renaissancerealismus beschreiben:

1. Die Bildfläche wird als durchsichtig verstanden, aufs Bild blicken heißt, die dargestellte Realität „dahinter" erblicken. Das Bild wird ambivalent (Büttner 2003)[5], es ist faktische Basis der Sehpyramide des Betrachters, zugleich „zeigt" es in seiner Vorstellung auf den abgebildeten Gegenstand *als gedachte Basis der*

---

4 Ich vernachlässige, dass das Sehen auf ein Auge und einen ausdehnungslosen Punkt reduziert wird, dass die Retina konkav und nicht eben ist, auf der ein Bild sich „einschreibt" etc. Alberti greift auf Euklids geometrische und optische Gesetze zurück.

5 Für Büttner wird in Albertis Fensteridee das Ambivalente des neuzeitlichen Bildes anschaulich, weil „das mit der Schnittebene erzeugte Bild zugleich faktisch und fiktiv ist." (Büttner 2003, 25) Das kommt im *Tractatus* zum Ausdruck, indem das Bild (der Satz) eine Tatsache *bezeichnet* und zugleich selbst Tatsache *ist*.

Abb. 2: Hieronymus Rodler, Ein schön nützlich Büchlein der Kunst des Messens (Simmern 1531).

In Rodlers Versuch, Dürers *Unterweisung der Messkunst* allgemeinverständlich darzustellen, fehlt die notwendige Fixierung des Augenpunktes. Perspektive und Abstände der abzubildenden Objekte zueinander wären so nicht stabil, es könnte nicht zu einer korrekten Abbildung kommen. Bei der Begründung der „wissenschaftlichen" Perspektive wird der Beobachter zunächst auf Euklids „ausdehnungslosen" Punkt reduziert, bevor er seine Schwundstufe erreichte. Wittgenstein rückt ihn – mit allen Ambivalenzen – wieder in den Blickpunkt, positioniert ihn nicht „draußen", sondern zwischen Drinnen und Draußen: auf der Grenze (Tractatus 5.64ff.). Wobei das Draußen unsagbar wird.

Sehpyramide. So vaszilliert das Bild zwischen Realität und Fiktion bzw. Illusion, der Betrachter schaut auf das Bild *vor* sich und blickt zugleich in die (virtuelle) Realität *dahinter*.

2. Vom Blickwinkel des Auges referieren Bildpunkte auf Gegenstandspunkte (der abgebildeten Wirklichkeit), das führt zu einer Isomorphie zwischen Bild und Abgebildetem.

3. Der Augenpunkt (i. e. der Beobachter) ist das Konstruktionszentrum des Bildes; er spiegelt sich als Fluchtpunkt im Bild und bestimmt die Perspektive. Der Augenpunkt ist willkürlich festzulegen und nicht theoretisch (rational), allenfalls pragmatisch zu legitimieren (wie Anamorphosen zeigen).

3 Die Bildtheorie und der Abschied vom Realismus

Bereits im Vorwort des *Tractatus* werden die philosophisch zentralen Begriffe genannt: Sprache, Welt und Grenze. Das Buch soll dem Denken eine Grenze ziehen „oder vielmehr – nicht dem Denken, sondern dem Ausdruck der Gedanken: Denn um dem Denken eine Grenze zu ziehen müssten wir beide Seiten dieser Grenzen denken können (wir müssten also denken können, was sich nicht denken lässt). Die Grenze wird also nur in der Sprache gezogen werden können [...]". Grenze (lat. finis, verwandt mit *fenestra*, Fenster) ist ein geometrischer Begriff und spielt in der „Messkunst" der Perspektivtheorie eine große Rolle. Im *Tractatus* taucht der Begriff an vielzitierten Stellen auf, wenn es heißt, dass die *Grenzen der Sprache die Grenzen meiner Welt bedeuten*; für meine Zwecke wichtiger sind die Passagen, in denen Wittgenstein das Subjekt, das Auge oder das Ich auf der Grenze verortet. Betrachten wir diese Positionierung.

Die Quintessenz des Vorwortes: alle erkenntnistheoretischen oder semantischen Fragen – wie die der Korrespondenz von Sprache und Wirklichkeit, der Bedeutung unserer Wörter etc. – nur *innerhalb eines sprachlichen Raumes* gedacht werden können, der durch eine Ja/Nein-Logik geprägt ist, die keinen Raum für Vieldeutigkeit oder Ambivalenz zulässt. Schon dort schließt Wittgenstein die Möglichkeit eines Blickes von der anderen Seite, von „draußen", einen „god's eye view" kategorisch aus. Dies ist eine entscheidende Grundlegung mit weitreichenden Konsequenzen.

Die ersten Sätze lassen die ontologische Verrückung erkennen, die die konstruktivistische Position seiner Spätphilosophie ausarbeiten wird. Die ontologische Frage, was ist die Welt *ist*, wird perspektivisch zur Sprache gewendet. Der Realismus geht – wie es das Wort nahelegt – von res, von Dingen aus. Nicht so

Wittgenstein: „Die Welt ist alles, was der Fall ist. Die Welt ist die Gesamtheit der Tatsachen, nicht der Dinge." (T 1) „Was der Fall ist, die Tatsache, ist das Bestehen von Sachverhalten." (T 1.1) Sachverhalte haben eine Struktur, die in prädikativen Sätzen (Urteilen) formuliert werden können, die wahr oder falsch sein können.

Die Unterscheidung zwischen Dingen und Tatsachen belegt, dass Wittgensteins Blick von Anfang an *durch* eine sprachliche bzw. sprachlogische Perspektive auf die Welt gerichtet ist.[6] Ihn interessiert nicht, was an sich „existiert", was abstrakt „Ding" genannt wird, um eine beobachterunabhängige Außenwelt vorauszusetzen, sondern Tatsachen. Das ist wörtlich zu lesen: Tat-Sachen, Hergestelltes, Gemachtes (lat. *factum*, vo *facere*). Mit diesem Tatsachenbegriff spricht Wittgenstein zwar über die Welt, legt den Fokus aber auf *Zusammenhänge*, auf Relationen *zwischen* den Gegenständen, die in Sachverhalten auftreten können:[7] Mit dem Strukturgedanken (lat. struere, hiervon abzuleiten *construere*, zusammenbauen) bereitet er seine Satztheorie vor, in der sich Namen (Worte) auf Gegenstände beziehen, aber nur im Satzzusammenhang Bedeutung haben. So lässt sich zwischen der Bedeutung von Namen (sie referieren auf Gegenstände) und dem Sinn von Sätzen unterscheiden. Wörter haben Bedeutung, wenn sie auf „Gegenstände" verweisen, Sätze haben Sinn, wenn sie wahr oder falsch sein können. Sätze sollen so von der logischen Struktur her Sachverhalten entsprechen. Der Zusammenhang zwischen Sprache und Welt wird begreifbar, indem der Welt eine Struktur (Tatsachen, nicht Dinge) *unterlegt* wird, die für die Struktur sprachlicher Logik schon vorbereitet ist. Die Logik wird dabei als Art „kognitiver Landkarte" verstanden, die die Strukturen des Territoriums (Welt) draußen – mittels Isomorphie – *im Denken* spiegelt: Die Logik wird zum „Spiegelbild der Welt" (T 6.13).[8]

Wittgenstein verlegt die sprachliche Logik *in den Augenpunkt*; Sprache wird zum Medium (Grenze/Velum), das eine bereits *logisch formierte* Durchsicht auf die Welt ermöglicht.[9] Die bei Alberti willkürliche Bestimmung des Augenpunktes und des Blickwinkels ist damit in *nur einen* möglichen point of view überführt, der

---

6 „Meine ganze Aufgabe besteht darin, das Wesen des Satzes zu erklären. Das heißt, das Wesen aller Tatsachen anzugeben, deren Bild der Satz *ist*. Das Wesen alles Seins angeben. (Und hier bedeutet Sein nicht existieren – dann wäre es unsinnig." (Wittgenstein 2001, Tagebuch 22.1.1915).
7 Wittgenstein formuliert das von ihm *Vorausgesetzte* so: „Die Welt hat eine feste Struktur." (Wittgenstein 2001, Tagebuch 17.6.1915)
8 Auch diese Metapher ist mit der Renaissancetheorie assoziiert, wie Albertis rhetorische Frage zeigt: „Wie anders könnte man die Malerei beschreiben als dadurch, daß dem Original ein Spiegel vorgehalten wird [...]?" (vgl. Abrams 1978, 49)
9 In der Spätphilosophie wiederholt sich dieses Bild, wenn Wittgenstein Ontologie als Schatten der Grammatik bzw. Logik begreift. Die Struktur der Wirklichkeit ist dann Ergebnis der Projektion in die Wirklicheit.

Abb. 3: Yes – No, 2003, Grauguss (28 x 41 x 30 cm) Markus Raetz. © Markus Raetz, Bern.

Drei Fotos derselben Skulptur. Raetz visualisiert die zwangsläufige Ambivalenzerfahrung eines Denkens, das sich im dichotomen Ja/Nein-Raum bewegen möchte. Das war Wittgensteins Projekt einer idealen, ein-eindeutigen Sprache im Tractatus. Die vermeintliche Eindeutigkeit der Skulptur verändert sich mit der Perspektive, der Zeit und dem Standort des Betrachters. Abhängig vom Blickwinkel wird aus Yes, über viele, sprachlich nicht einzuordnende und damit nicht erkennbare Zwischenstufen der Gegenpol: No. Das gilt aber nur für ein Bewusstsein, das durch das „Velum der Sprache" den Gegenstand schon als sprachliches Zeichen sehen kann. Dass und wie Ambivalentes aus der Tractatlogik ausgeschlossen werden muss, zeigt sich insbesondere an den „intentionalen" Sätzen (wie A glaubt, dass p), die er als nicht-wahrheitsfähig ausschließt. Diese Sätze, deren „Gegenstände" nicht im sichtbaren Raum sind (wie Gefühle, Haltungen, Schmerzen), stehen im Zentrum der philosophischen Psychologie des Spätwerkes und sie offenbaren eine noch viel größere Abhängigkeit vom Beobachter.

notwendig ist. Diese Logik sitzt wie eine Brille auf der Nase, und wo auch immer wir hinsehen, wir sehen *durch* sie. Es ist analog zum Sehen. Wir sehen perspektivisch, sehen aber nicht, dass wir perspektivisch sehen. Daher kann es auch keine Metaposition geben, von der aus wir auf beide Seiten der Grenze blicken können. Zwei Prämissen werden hier schon klar: Der Beobachter hat weder *direkten Zugang* zur „Realität", noch einen außerweltlichen Blickwinkel, von dem aus er eine Übereinstimmung von Sprache und Wirklichkeit erkennen könnte.

Kommen wir zum Bild, das den frühen Wittgenstein „gefangen hielt". „Bild" ist im *Tractatus* – und später – Metapher für Sprache schlechthin. Bilder sind immer Bilder *von etwas*, von Jemandem für Jemanden; dem entsprechend wird das *aktive Subjekt* eingeführt, das Bilder (ebenso wie Sätze) erzeugt, bildet bzw. konstruiert. Ich zitiere einige Sätze aus dem *Tractatus*, um Analogien und konstruktivistische Facetten aufzuzeigen:

> 2.1 *Wir machen* uns Bilder der Tatsachen.
> 2.11 Das Bild *stellt* die Sachlage *im* logischen Raume, das Bestehen und Nichtbestehen von Sachverhalten vor.
> 2.12 Das Bild ist ein *Modell* der Wirklichkeit.
> 4.01 Der Satz ist ein Bild der Wirklichkeit.
> 4.021 Der Satz ist ein Modell der Wirklichkeit, so *wie wir sie uns denken*.
> 2.141 Das Bild *ist eine Tatsache*.

2.201 Das Bild *bildet* die Wirklichkeit *ab*.
2.15 Daß sich die Elemente des Bildes in bestimmter Art und Weise zueinander verhalten, *stellt vor*, daß sich die Sachen so zueinander verhalten.

Hier fungiert das vom Zeichner *konstruierte* Bild *als Fenster*, das die *Vorstellung* (!) des Sachverhaltes im „logischen Raum" „draußen" ermöglicht. Wittgenstein verwendet auch perspektivtheoretische Begriffe: „Das Bild stellt sein Objekt *von außerhalb* dar (sein Standpunkt ist seine Form der Darstellung), darum stellt das Bild sein Objekt richtig oder falsch dar." (T 2.173) Die oben diagnostizierte Ambivalenz des Bildes als Fenster zur Realität zeigt sich auch hier: Das Bild stellt Sachlagen vor (fiktiv), zugleich ist es selbst Tatsache (T 2.141).

Mit dem „Standpunkt" (= Augenpunkt perspektivischer Konstruktion) *als Form der Darstellung* sind wir in der Perspektivtheorie Albertis und weil das Bild (der Satz) sein Objekt *von außerhalb* (!) darstellt, ist nicht entscheidbar, ob es richtig oder falsch ist. Daraus folgt das erkenntnistheoretische Problem: „Um zu erkennen, ob das Bild wahr oder falsch ist, müssen wir es mit der Wirklichkeit vergleichen. Aus dem Bild allein ist nicht zu erkennen, ob es wahr oder falsch ist." (T 2.223) Wie ist dieser Vergleich möglich?

Die Bildtheorie folgert, dass wir keinen direkten Zugang zur Wirklichkeit haben. Das Bild (der Satz) *vermittelt* zwischen der Welt *für uns*, nämlich dem, was für uns der Fall ist, und der postulierten Realität der Welt. Die perspektivische Konstruktion erzeugt einen *internen Realismus* und zeigt die Ambivalenz, in die wir geraten, weil wir prinzipiell nur Bild mit Bild vergleichen können und die Welt nur von einem „außerhalb" darstellen können, das ein „innerhalb" ist.

Fludd illustriert diese Vorstellung anhand des perspektivischen Abbildungssystems.

Wenn wir fragen, worin die abbildende Beziehung zwischen Sprache (Bild/Satz) und Welt besteht, so können wir nur sagen, im Blick des Beobachters (dem Subjekt, dem Ich), den Wittgenstein immer wieder verschwinden und auftauchen lässt. Auf die Passagen, wo das Auge – der Beobachter – oder das philosophische Ich wieder thematisch werden, komme ich zurück.

Wenn Wittgenstein (T 4.023) schreibt, dass der Satz mithilfe eines logischen Gerüstes *eine* (!) Welt *konstruiert*, dann ist bemerkenswert, dass nur von *einer* und nicht von *der* Welt die Rede ist. Im „logischen Gerüst" lässt sich Albertis Velum sehen. Eine damit verwandte Metapher ist die des Netzes, wie sie T 6.341 einführt. Das Gedankenexperiment geht von einer weißen Fläche (die eine Leinwand evoziert) mit unregelmäßig darauf verteilten schwarzen Flecken als zu beschreibender Wirklichkeit aus. Wird ein *feines quadratisches Netz darauf projiziert*, dann lässt sich von jedem Quadrat sagen, ob es schwarz oder weiß ist. So könnte die Fläche – die Wirklichkeit – vollständig beschrieben werden.

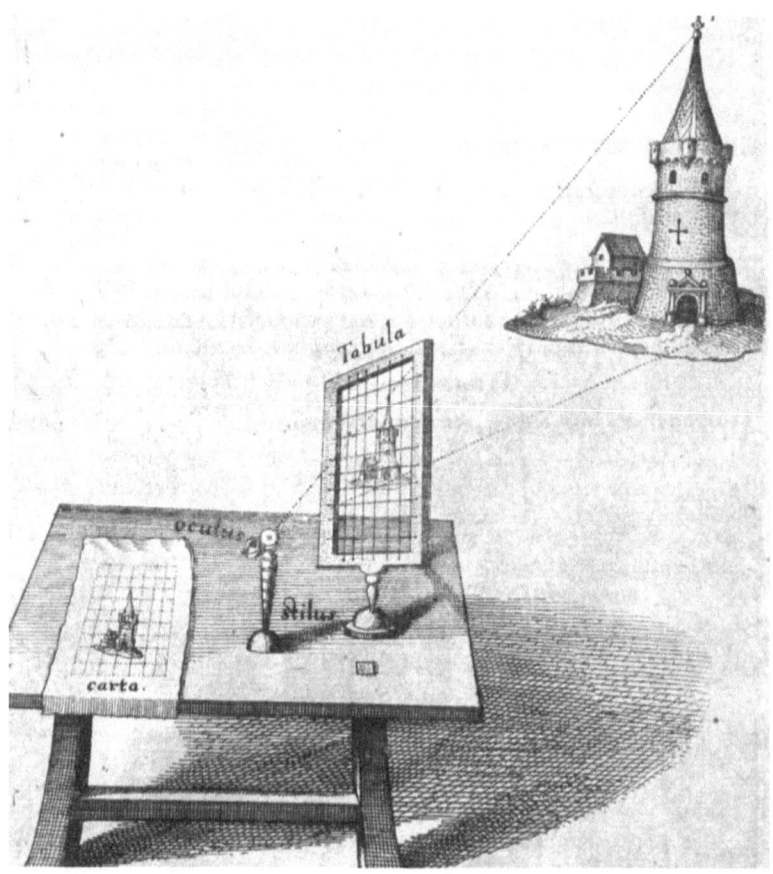

Abb. 4: Robert Fludd (1618): Utriusque cosmi mairois salicet et minoris metaphysica, S. 308.

Perspektivkonstruktion dargestellt als System aus Motiv, Velum (Tabula, Bildschirm); auf Stilus fixiertem Augen(-punkt) (oculus) und Blatt (carta) mit Netzstruktur des Velums, auf dem das Objekt schon „abgepaust" ist.

Das Netz fungiert dabei als Projektionsmethode oder *Form der Darstellung* und als solches ist es *beliebig*. Hier haben wir die Struktur des Velums vor Augen: „Den verschiedenen Netzen entsprechen verschiedene Systeme der Weltbeschreibung. Die Mechanik bestimmt eine Form der Weltbeschreibung." (T 6.341, vgl. Fischer 1999) Die Metapher vom Netz verdeutlicht, dass das, was gefischt (abgebildet), was beschrieben, was abgebildet werden kann, davon abhängt, wie das Netz, das Beschreibungs- bzw. Referenzsystem (Koordinatensystem) aufgebaut bzw. strukturiert ist. „Sätze des Netzes" öffnen den geschlossenen, logischen Horizont der Tractatus-Philosophie und weisen den Weg zum Verständnis der Logik und

Grammatik der Umgangssprache. In den „Sätzen des Netzes" ist eine Brücke zu erkennen, die aus dem Glauben, die aristotelische Logik sei *die Zentralperspektive* unseres Denkens, in Richtung Multiperspektivität (Multiplizität der Sprachspielmethode) und Pluralität von Logiken weist.

Die beste Illustration von Wittgensteins Tractatuslogik scheint mir Dürers Perspektivapparat zu sein. Dürer versucht (Dürer 1525) sieht in „Kunst der Messung"die Legitimation aller guten Malerei und legt Wert auf die Vermittlung perspektivischer Projektionen und deren Berechenbarkeit. In *Der Zeichner der Laute* wird der Perspektivapparat als System gezeigt, das analog zu Wittgensteins „logischem Apparat" erklärt, wie sich ein perspektivisches Bild konstruieren lässt. Damit möchte ich die Abbildungslogik und Projektionsmethode des *Tractatus* illustrieren.

Das „logische Gerüst", mit dem ein Satz (Bild) „eine Welt konstruiert" (T 4.023), lässt sich hier gut visualisieren. Andere Formulierungen verweisen ebenfalls auf den begrifflichen und metaphorischen Kontext der Perspektivtheorie (T 2.1 ff.): Das Bild ist *wie ein Maßstab ... angelegt*, die äußersten Punkte *berühren* den zu *messenden Gegenstand, die Zuordnungen sind Fühler, mit denen das Bild die Wirklichkeit berührt; Namen gleichen Punkten, Sätze Pfeilen; der Satz ist wie ein Pfeil, er steht in projektiver Beziehung zur Welt u.v.a.*

Die Abbildungsmöglichkeiten zeigen sich an den Variablen, die sich für den Konstruktionsprozess verändern ließen: dem Augenpunkt, dem Rahmen und der geometrischen Relationen zwischen Augenpunkt und Velum/Rahmen. Das führte u. a. zu Abbildungen, die nicht erkennen lassen, was abgebildet wird (wie Anamorphosen oder unten bei Markus Raetz „Yes – No" dargestellt). Dürers Blick durchs Fenster in die Malerwerkstatt zeigt: Das „Auge" (der Augenpunkt) ist im selben Bildraum wie das entstehende Bild der Laute und die Laute. Diese Vorstellung führt in jenes Dilemma, das Wittgenstein dazu bringt, den Beobachter auf der Grenze und *nicht* „draußen" zu verorten. Der Augenpunkt wird zum blinden Fleck der Beobachtung, er kann sich selbst nicht sehen, was Wittgenstein in seiner Augenanalogie verdeutlicht:

5.6331 Das Gesichtsfeld hat nämlich nicht etwa eine solche Form:

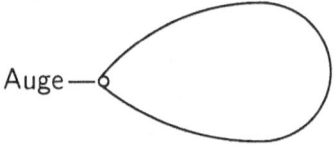

Wenn wir die Drinnen-Draußen-Dichotomie einführen, wird deutlich, dass das Fenster geschlossen werden muss, damit wir hinausschauen können. Aus dem

Abb. 5: Albrecht Dürer (1525): Der Zeichner der Laute (aus Underweysung der Messung).

Der in die Wand geschlagene Nagel markiert den Augenpunkt, der Faden (mit Blei beschwert) symbolisiert den „Sehstrahl". Die weiße Fläche illustriert die ambivalente Funktion des Schnitts durch die Sehpyramide: Als zu bemalende Tafel (oder Leinwand) ist sie optische Messfläche zum Eintragen der Messpunkte; sie lässt sich wie ein Fenster in einem Holzrahmen öffnen und schließen. Im Rahmen sind zwei waagrecht und zwei senkrecht verschiebbare Stäbe angebracht. Der Geselle führt den Faden mit dem Stift durch den Rahmen und zeigt auf die für die Form der Laute im perspektivischen Bild relevanten Punkte. Der Ort, an dem der Faden (Sehstrahl) den Rahmen durchdringt, fixiert der Zeichner durch verschieben der Stäbe als Kreuzungspunkt; der Faden wird zurückgezogen, um das Fenster (i.e. die Tafel) in den Rahmen zu drehen und den Punkt auf der Zeichenfläche einzutragen. Dieser Prozess wird wiederholt, bis ein perspektivische Form der Laute entstanden ist. Bild und Abgebildetes erhalten (im Auge des Betrachters) so die gleiche Form. Abbilden lässt sich so als Metalepsis verstehen.

Blickwinkel des Malers – rechts vor dem Rahmen – wird das Fenster geöffnet, um „hinaus" zu schauen, dann wieder geschlossen, um den Punkt zu berechnen und einzutragen. Ist das Bild fertig, erblickt der Maler *durch* das „geschlossene Fenster" (= Bild), das Alberti geöffnetes Fenster nannte, hinaus auf die Wirklichkeit im Bild. Klar ist, ob Bild der Laute oder „wirkliche" Laute, beides sind

Schnitte durch dieselbe Sehpyramide des Betrachters/Malers im Bild. Wittgenstein bemerkt, dass sein *durchsichtiger* Realismus nicht durchzuhalten ist.[10]

4 Was ist drinnen, was ist draußen? – Das Auftauchen des Betrachters

Das vergessene Subjekt (für uns hier: der Beobachter) taucht in unterschiedlichem Gewande dann mit allen Ambivalenzen auf und der Abschied vom „reinen Realismus" wird explizit.

Die Rolle des Subjektes wird an der Augenanalogie deutlich. Das Auge, das mit dem metaphysischen Ich („ausdehnungsloser" Punkt) gleichzusetzen ist, ist Grenzpunkt (T 5.6331) des Wahrnehmungsfeldes und *nicht* im Bereich des Erfahr- oder Beschreibbaren, daher lehnt Wittgenstein die Rede von einem denkenden Ich *im empirischen* Sinne ab.

Die Relation des Auges zu seinem Wahrnehmungsfeld lässt sich nicht ausdrücken, sie ist *intern*. Warum?

Weil wir dazu einen point of view (eine Metaposition) außerhalb bräuchten, den es nicht geben kann. Die Grenze ist nur *in der Sprache* zu ziehen ... Dürers Fenster in die Malerwerkstatt (Abb. 5) zeigt die Beziehung zwischen Bildpunkten und Referenzpunkten auf der Laute als – perspektivlogisch – korrektes, aber dennoch *bildinternes* Verhältnis. Aus der Perspektive des „Augenpunktes" als Konstruktionszentrum wären fertiges Bild und „wirkliche" Laute nur zwei verschiedene Schnitte durch dieselbe janusköpfige Sehpyramide: zwei faktische *und* fiktive Bilder *im Bild*. Wo bleibt die beobachterunabhängige Realität?

Wenn gefragt wird, wo *in* der Welt ein „metaphysisches Subjekt" (*meta physica*, hinter der Natur) zu merken sei, greift er auf die Augenanalogie zurück: „Aber das Auge siehst du wirklich nicht. Und nichts am Gesichtsfeld lässt darauf schließen, dass es von einem Auge gesehen wird." Der Beobachter ist auf dem Augenpunkt, der sich selbst nicht sieht, verschwunden. Daher – so Wittgenstein – gehört das Subjekt nicht zur Welt, es ist *eine (!)* Grenze der Welt (T 5.632).

Dann führt Wittgenstein die Kontingenz ein, für die es in der Ja/Nein-Logik keinen Platz gibt. Kein Teil unserer Erfahrung sei a priori, weil „Alles, was wir sehen, [...] alles, was wir überhaupt beschreiben können, könnte auch anders sein. *Es gibt keine Ordnung der Dinge a priori.*" (T 5.634, Hervorhebung hinzuge-

---

10 Beispielsweise: „Die Grenze der Sprache zeigt sich in der Unmöglichkeit, die Tatsache zu beschreiben, die einem Satz entspricht [...], ohne eben den Satz zu wiederholen. (Wir haben es hier mit der kantischen Lösung des Problems zu tun)." (VB 27)

Abb. 6: Markus Raetz, Zeichnung (1970): Meine unsere Sprache. Füllfeder und Tinte. © Markus Raetz, Bern.

Die ambivalenten Grenzen meiner Welt. Was ist innen, was ist außen? Markus Raetz setzt sprachliche Ambivalenzen ins Bild: Ein hermeneutischer Zirkel? Meine Sprache ist unsere Sprache? Oder ist unsere Sprache meine Sprache? Wo ist der Eingang ins Verstehen? Versteht ein jeder den anderen nur in seiner Sprache? Babel scheint allgegenwärtig. „Daß die Welt *meine* Welt ist, das zeigt sich darin, daß die Grenzen *der* Sprache (der Sprache, die allein ich verstehe) die Grenzen *meiner* Welt bedeuten." (T. 5.62, Ludwig Wittgenstein)

fügt) Was soviel heißt, dass diese Ordnung durch eine sprachliche Logik in die Welt gebracht werden muss, die der *Tractatus* entwickeln sollte. Im Folgesatz wird eingeschränkt: „Hier sieht man, dass der Solipsismus, streng durchgeführt, mit dem reinen Realismus zusammenfällt." (T 5.64)

Der reine Realismus, der Glaube, die Welt öffnete sich unseren Augen in ihrer wahren Gestalt, führt zum – erkenntnistheoretischen – Solipsismus: Ich kann die Welt nur erkennen, was und wie sie für mich ist. Was bleibt? „Das Ich des Solipsismus schrumpft zum ausdehnungslosen Punkt zusammen, und es bleibt die ihm koordinierte Realität." (T 5.64) Hier dreht sich Wittgenstein im dualistischen Kreise seiner Voraussetzungen. Er legt die erkenntistheoretische Basis (den Ursprung) aller Beschreibung von Realität auf eine Grenze, die nicht hinter sich schauen kann, den Augenpunkt des Beobachters. Grenzen erzeugen ein Diesseits und ein Jenseits. Das Fenster hinaus in die Welt scheint wieder geschlossen zu werden. Wenn er schreibt: „es bleibt die ihm koordinierte Realität", dann fragt sich, *wer* diese Realität (die keine Ordnung *aprori* hat) dem Ich des Solipsismus *koordiniert* hat? Und was wird aus diesem Ich, das in die Philosophie dadurch eintritt, dass die „Welt meine Welt ist"? Man merkt Wittgensteins Ringen, das notwendige Pendant seiner Projektionsmethode – die bewusstseins*un*abhängige, „reale" Welt draußen – retten zu müssen, gleichwohl zu wissen, dass das nur ein Gedanke desselben Ichs drinnen ist. Jetzt wird deutlich, dass nicht der Satz, sondern *wir* mithilfe des Satzes (einer Sprache) „eine Welt konstruieren".

Im Folgesatz bestimmt er, dass das philosophische Ich *nicht* der Mensch, nicht der menschliche Körper oder die Seele ist, „sondern das metaphysische Subjekt, die Grenze – nicht ein Teil der Welt." (T 5.641) Mit dieser Verortung des philosophischen Ichs auf die Grenze (der Augenpunkt der Perspektivtheorie) ist der Beobachter aus der Welt verschwunden.

Das, was wir *voraussetzen* müssen, um eine Welt zu konstruieren, ist *in* der konstruierten Welt nicht zu haben. Bekanntlich mündet das im Mystischen, worüber wir schweigen müssen. Dennoch erhebt sich die Frage nach dem Grenzort, der wie ein Fenster zwischen zwei Räumen liegt, von denen nur einer gedacht werden kann.

Die Gretchenfrage bleibt: Bin ich in der Welt oder die Welt in mir?

Die Frage führt – ob realistisch oder konstruktivistisch beantwortet – in unauflösbare Paradoxien, weil das, was je nach Ausgangspunkt voraus*gesetzt* wird, in der Beschreibung nicht eingeholt werden kann. Denkt sich das philosophische Ich Wittgensteins nicht als Teil der Welt, dann ist die Welt in mir, in meinem Bewusstsein (Ich bin meine Welt). Denkt sich das philosophische Ich[11] – entgegen Wittgensteins Annahme – *als Teil der Welt* (Ich bin in der Welt), so ist diese Vorstellung, dass ich in der Welt bin, außerhalb dieser Welt u.s.w. Diese Entscheidung ist vorher zu treffen und als solche rational unentscheidbar; sie ist Quelle von Wittgensteins Ambivalenzen gegenüber Realismus und Metaphysik, alias Ontologie.[12]

Abschließend möchte ich an zwei Beispielen zeigen, dass der Abschied vom Realismus, im *Tractatus* begonnen, bis in die letzten Passagen seines Werkes ambivalent bleibt.

---

11 Die Unterscheidungen Wittgensteins in empirisches/metaphysisches Ich/Subjekt sind Versuche, die Ambivalenz zu bewältigen; sie führen allerdings zu weiteren Ambivalenzen. Denn als empirisches Ich denke ich mich als philosophisches Ich, das sich nicht als Teil der Welt denkt, und das empirische als Teil der Welt usw.
12 Auswege aus den Sackgassen dualistischen Philosophierens scheinen nur Ansätze zu bieten, wie sie Josef Mitterer (Mitterer 1992, 2001) in seiner non-dualistischen Philosophie unternimmt.

Ein Beispiel für Wittgensteins Ambivalenz, die sich in einem Sowohl-als-auch bei einer ontologischen Frage ausdrückt, möchte ich erwähnen:

> Wir haben ein System der Farben wie ein System der Zahlen. Liegen die Systeme in unserer Natur oder in der Natur der Dinge? Wie soll man's sagen? *Nicht in der Natur* der Zahl oder Farben. Hat denn dieses System etwas Willkürliches? *Ja und nein.* Es ist mit Willkürlichem verwandt *und* mit Nichtwillkürlichem. Ja aber hat denn die Natur hier gar nichts mitzureden?! Doch – nur macht sie sich auf andere Weise hörbar. (PG Nr. 355–357, Hervorhebung hinzugefügt, ausführlich in Fischer 1991 und 1999)

Die Unterscheidungen, die Diskurs erst ermöglichen, sind nicht durch Bezug auf „Gegebenes" oder Ontologie (Natur, Realität oder wie wir das nennen) zu rechtfertigen, weil wir diese immer a priori – vor dem Messen – in Anspruch nehmen müssen. Am Ende des begründeten Glaubens, den wir *Wissen* nennen, steht der unbegründbare Glaube, der „Spaten biegt sich zurück, so handle ich eben" (wie es in den *Philosophischen Untersuchungen* heißt, PU § 217).

Die Festlegung jedes Maßstabes muss der Messung vorausgehen und der Maßstab selbst ist *nicht* wahr/falsch, sondern nur mehr oder minder nützlich für unsere Zwecke. Richtige (i. e. sinnvolle) und falsche Spielzüge (im Perspektivapparat: Punkte, die auf Punkte referieren) gibt des erst *innerhalb dieses Rahmens*. Es gibt also einen logischen Unterschied zwischen der Wahrheit *im Spiel* und der Wahrheit *des Spiels* (bzw. der Theorie). Und von der Wahrheit des Spiels im Sinne eines externen Realismus hatte sich schon der *Tractatus* verabschiedet, denn die dazu nötige Metaposition ist nicht zu denken.

Wenn Wittgenstein schließlich sagt: „Alles Wesentliche ist, dass die Zeichen sich [...] am Schluss doch auf die unmittelbare Erfahrung beziehen und nicht auf ein Mittelglied (ein Ding an sich)" (PB §282) wird offensichtlich, dass ich meine Wirklichkeit nur auf meine *unmittelbare* Erfahrung aufbauen kann. Nichts anderes hat der große Psychologe Ernst von Glasersfeld mit seinem „radikalen" Konstruktivismus gemeint (siehe von Glasersfeld 1997).

Literaturverzeichnis

Abrams, Meyer Howard (1978): *Spiegel und Lampe. Romantische Theorie und die Tradition der Kritik.* München: Fink.
Alberti, Leon Battista (2002): *Della Pittura. Über die Malkunst.* Lateinisch/Deutsche Ausgabe. Herausgegeben, eingeleitet, übersetzt und kommentiert von Oskar Bätschmann und Sandra Gianfreda. Darmstadt: Wiss. Buchgesellschaft.
Büttner, Frank (2003): „Die Macht des Bildes über den Betrachter". In: Osterreicher, Wulf; Regn, Gerhard; Schulze, Winfried (Hg.): *Autoriät der Form – Autorisierungen – institutionelle Autoritäten.* Münster: LIT, 17–36.

Dürer, Albrecht (1525): *Underweysung der Messung, mit dem Zirckel und Richtscheyt, in Linien, Ebenen unnd gantzen corporen.* Nüremberg, Online-Ausgabe der Sächsischen Landesbibliothek – Staats- und Universitätsbibliothek Dresden.
Fischer, Hans Rudi (1991): *Sprache und Lebensform. Wittgenstein über Freud und die Geisteskrankheit.* Heidelberg: Carl-Auer.
Fischer, Hans Rudi (1999): „Rationalität als offene Ordnung. Zur Logik und Evolution neuer Sprachspiele". In: Schneider, Hans J.; Kroß, Matthias (Hg.): *Mit Sprache spielen. Die Ordnungen und das Offene nach Wittgenstein.* Berlin: Akademie Verlag, 149–168.
Fischer, Hans Rudi; Lüscher, Kurt (2014): „Ambivalenz ergründen. Philosophische und anthropologische Ursprünge eines Begriffs". In: *Familiendynamik. Systemische Praxis und Forschung,* Heft 2/2014, 122–133.
Kluge, Friedrich (1989): *Etymologisches Wörterbuch der deutschen Sprache.* 22. Auflage, Berlin/New York: de Gruyter.
Lüscher, Kurt; Fischer, Hans Rudi (2014): „Ambivalenzen bedenken und nutzen". In: *Familiendynamik. Systemische Praxis und Forschung.* Heft 2/2014, 84–95.
Mitterer, Josef (1992): *Das Jenseits der Philosophie. Wider das dualistische Erkenntnisprinzip.* Wien: Passagen Verlag.
Mitterer, Josef (2001): *Die Flucht aus der Beliebigkeit.* Frankfurt am Main: Fischer
Rodler, Hieronymus (1531): *Perspektiva. Eyn schön nutzlich büchlin und underweisung der kunst des Messens, mit dem Zirckel, Richtscheidt oder Linial.* Simmern: Hofdruckerei von Rodler.
von Glasersfeld, Ernst (1997): *Radikaler Konstruktivismus. Ideen, Ergebnisse, Probleme.* Frankfurt am Main: Suhrkamp.
Welsch, Wolfgang (2004): „Die Kunst und das Inhumane". In: *Grenzen und Grenzüberschreitungen. Deutscher Kongress für Philosophie.* Berlin, Akademie Verlag, 730–751.
Wittgenstein, Ludwig (1970): *Philosophische Bemerkungen.* Frankfurt am Main: Suhrkamp. [PB]
Wittgenstein, Ludwig (1977): *Vermischte Bemerkungen. Eine Auswahl aus dem Nachlass.* Herausgegeben von Georg Henrik von Wright und Heikki Nyman. Frankfurt am Main: Suhrkamp. [VB]
Wittgenstein, Ludwig (1993): *Philosophische Grammatik.* Werkausgabe Band 5. Frankfurt am Main: Suhrkamp. [PG]
Wittgenstein, Ludwig (2001): *Logisch-philosophische Abhandlung. Kritische Edition.* Herausgegeben von Brian McGuinness und Joachim Schulte. Frankfurt am Main: Suhrkamp. [T]
Wittgenstein, Ludwig (2003): *Philosophische Untersuchungen.* Auf der Grundlage der kritisch-genetischen Edition neu herausgegeben von Joachim Schulte. Frankfurt am Main: Suhrkamp. [PU]

Michael Krausz
Relativisms and Their Opposites

Abstract: This paper unpacks variables embedded in the following definition of relativism: "Relativism is the view that values such as truth, goodness, or beauty are relative to a reference frame, and no absolute overarching standards to adjudicate between reference frames exist." When unpacked and combined in various ways, the embedded variables give rise to a myriad of relativisms. In turn, strands of absolutism may be realist, universalist, or foundationalist. While I remain neutral about the plausibility of these strands of absolutism, I find that when absolutism is disambiguated according to them, the self-referential argument against relativism is shown to be invalid.

Keywords: Relativism, absolutism, self-refutation argument

My principal aim in this paper is to show the relationships between varieties of relativism and their absolutist opposites. In so doing, I will reveal the invalidity of the classical self-referential argument against relativism. At the same time, it is not my aim to endorse any particular variety of relativism or absolutism.

1 A Definition of Relativism

Let us begin with a working definition of relativism, which I believe captures its characteristic usages.[1] For present purposes, I shall define relativism as the

---

[1] Note that relativism is a cluster concept. So no one definition can be definitive. Accordingly, my effort to disambiguate its variables applies to my definition without presuming that it will apply to other reasonable definitions with their own respective variables. Accordingly, while I take the present working definition of relativism to capture its characteristic uses, it cannot be comprehensive. Among non-standard definitions, I include that of Joseph Margolis, which characterizes "robust relativism" in terms of "two essential doctrines: (1) that, in formal terms, truth values logically weaker than bipolar value (true or false) may be admitted to govern otherwise coherent forms of inquiry and constative acts, and (2) that substantively, not merely for evidentiary or epistemic reasons, certain sectors of the real world open to constative inquiry may be shown to support only such weaker truth-values." (see Margolis 2010, 100) For a discussion of Margolis' view see (Krausz 1999). In turn, Richard Bernstein provides a more standard definition of relativism when he says: "In its strongest form, relativism is the basic conviction that when we turn to the examination of those concepts that philosophers have taken to be the most fundamental—whether it is the concept of rationality, truth, reality, right, the good,

claim that *such values as truth, goodness, or beauty is relative to a reference frame, and no absolute overarching standards to adjudicate between competing reference frames exist.*

This definition embeds numerous variables, which include: *values* (such as truth, goodness, or beauty); *reference frames* (such as points of view, symbols systems, paradigms, cultures); *domains of inquiry* (for example, nature, or culture); *levels* (namely ontic or epistemic); standards of *adjudication*; and *varieties of absolutism* that a relativist might oppose (namely realism, universalism, or foundationalism). When unpacked and combined in various ways, these variables yield a myriad of relativisms. As we shall see, relativism is no one doctrine. So, let us examine more closely these variables of relativism. I shall offer brief comments about each of them in turn.[2]

1.1 Values

Notice that our working definition of relativism allows that relativism may range over, for example, "truth, goodness, *or* beauty." One reason for the "or" rather than the "and" is that it allows for either *global* or *piecemeal* treatments of relativism. That is, one might affirm a relativism with respect to all values or with respect to only one or some values. For example, one might affirm relativism with respect to any of the following combinations: truth, goodness, and beauty; with respect to goodness and beauty, but not truth; with respect to goodness, but not truth or beauty; with respect to beauty, but not truth or goodness; with respect to truth, but not goodness or beauty; or with respect to neither truth, goodness, nor beauty. In short, one might take one's relativism on a value-by-value basis. (Were one to admit yet more values – such as "indeterminate" or "undecidable" – the permutations could be expanded still further.)

---

or norms—we are forced to recognize that in the final analysis all such concepts must be understood as relative to a specific conceptual scheme, theoretical framework, paradigm, form of life, society, or culture. [...] For the relativist, there is no substantive overarching framework or single meta-language by which we can rationally adjudicate or univocally evaluate competing claims of alternative paradigms." (Bernstein 1983, 8)

2 While I speak of "no absolute standards" to adjudicate, Bernstein speaks of "no substantive overarching framework" by which to adjudicate" (see note 1). The difference is significant. I understand absolutism not to invoke an absence of some "substantive framework" of adjudication. For even if a substantive framework for adjudication existed, we would still have a *framework* in virtue of which adjudication would operate. The concept I oppose to relativism is the absolutist one—at least in its realist version—that standards of adjudication are beyond "framedness" altogether.

Second, relativism as to truth typically takes truth in a bivalent way. That is, truth and falsity are typically taken as mutually exclusive and exhaustive. Yet, "truth-like" values may be multivalent. For example, pairs such as reasonableness and unreasonableness, aptness and inaptness, or appropriateness and inappropriateness are not mutually exclusive. In the moral realm, for example, we may speak of fairness or praiseworthiness in a multivalent way; in the aesthetic realm we may speak of "interesting" or "convincing" in a multivalent way.

Joseph Margolis, for example, urges that opposing judgments that would be contradictory on a bivalent logic would turn out not to be so on a multivalent logic. In this sense, opposing judgments based on a multivalent logic would be "incongruent" rather than contradictory. Accordingly, two incongruent judgments may be reasonable, appropriate, or apt (see Margolis 1976).

Third, note that while some values are typically associated with particular domains of inquiry – for example, beauty, with respect to the aesthetic domain – such values may also apply to other domains. For example, a solution to a mathematical or scientific problem may be considered to be "beautiful", while moral or aesthetic claims may be taken to be "true". So, no necessary line-up between certain values and particular domains exists. Values and domains may overlap, but they need not be co-extensive.

1.2 Reference Frames

Now consider reference frames. They come in many varieties. Their cognates may include paradigms, symbol systems, world-versions, systems of belief, languages, points of view, perspectives, standpoints, forms of life, or conceptual schemes. They may include cultures, tribes, communities, countries, civilizations, societies, historical periods, religions, races, or genders. This list of cognates is not exhaustive. Neither are they mutually exclusive. Some of these cognates of reference frames overlap; some do not. Some of their boundaries are easily delineable; others are not. Sometimes we can easily distinguish what is inside and what is outside a reference frame; sometimes we cannot. For example, the boundaries between Hindu and Buddhist traditions are vague, while those between Medieval, Renaissance, and Baroque periods are indeterminate. Boundaries between guilt and shame cultures are difficult to delineate.[3]

---

[3] In passing, we may note that Donald Davidson famously argues for the incoherence of the very idea of a conceptual scheme. If he is right, a relativism that deploys the idea of a conceptual scheme is incoherent. But even if Davidson is right, it is an open question how wide ranging

Absolutists might argue that the very diversity of reference frames could show up in the first place only if such diversity itself is frame-independent. Correspondingly, relativists could not even assert relativism without first transcending it. That is, to affirm that truth, goodness, or beauty is frame-relative, for example, one must rise above frame-relativity altogether. In this way, an absolutist might argue that relativism actually presupposes absolutism. But this argument is invalid because frame diversity may be noted within some larger reference frame. It does not follow that the relativist must rise above frame-dependence *as such*. Relativists would need only to transcend their immediate reference frame to note the diversity of reference frames. It does not follow that one must rise above "reference-framedness" per se. Put otherwise, "rising above" does not entail frame-independence.

Absolutists might press their case by observing that frames of reference are attached *onto* something, and that to which a frame attaches must be frame-independent. Yet a relativist may counter by suggesting that frames may attach on to other frames. Accordingly, it would be a mistake to presume that there must be some frame-independent *thing* that reference frames are *of*. For example, there is no frame-independent fact of the matter whether the shortest distance between two points is a straight line, that is, independent of a given geometry. The shortest distance between two points *is* a straight line in Euclidean geometry, but it *isn't* so in a non-Euclidean geometry, say in a Riemannian geometry.

Yet absolutists might press their point by affirming that such geometries are still "about" some frame-independent thing, namely space. That is, there must be some thing that diverse geometries are *of*. But the relativist might respond that space is but a postulated abstraction with no absolutist standing. It may be a subject without ostensive reference.

Absolutists might press their point still further by conceding that while we may understand the world via reference frames, such frames *distort* or *falsify* our knowledge of the world. That is, frames negatively filter our access to the world – much like dirty eyeglasses might. Nevertheless, those who concede

---

his conclusions are. Whether, to be vulnerable to his arguments, all the varieties of reference frames I have mentioned are—in a sufficiently strong sense—cognates of conceptual schemes, remains an open question. Does the absence of criteria to individuate one would-be conceptual scheme from another entail the same absence with regard to one or another religion, one or another historical period, and so on? If these reference frames are not cognates of conceptual schemes, Davidson would have had to provide supplemental arguments with regard to such other sorts of reference frames. That assumes that in the first place, his arguments against the idea of conceptual schemes are sound. I will not rehearse his arguments here. See (Davidson 1974) and also (Krausz 2006).

that reference frames may distort or falsify their vision of the world still must postulate a frame-independent world, without which they could not understand the very idea of distortion or falsification in the first place. In reply, the relativist may insist that the idea of distortion or falsification does not require an absolutist construal of the world, because what we take to know is always already framed. Put otherwise, one who embraces a "coherentist" rather than a "correspondist" theory of truth can agree that some statements are truer than others – truer, that is, in virtue of their fittingness with a constellation of other entrenched frame-dependent beliefs. Such an approach would disallow talk of "getting at" or "not getting at" frame-independent matters.

1.3 Domains

I turn now to domains of inquiry to which relativism might apply. One might be relativist with respect to all domains or with respect to only some domains. In this sense, a relativist might be *global* or *piecemeal*. Depending upon our purposes and interests, we may divide domains in numerous ways. For example, we may distinguish between such domains as nature and culture. Or, we might broadly distinguish between such domains as logic and mathematics, natural sciences, social sciences, the humanities, or the arts. Or, more narrowly, we may divide domains according to "departmental" disciplines such as mathematics, physics, chemistry, biology, economics, sociology, anthropology, philosophy, law, politics, history, religion, languages and literatures, art, music, and so on. According to such a departmental scheme, an individual could be a relativist with respect to language and literature, art, or music, but absolutist with respect to mathematics or physics, for example. Whichever taxonomy one might favor as regards domains, some domains might be thought to be compatible with relativism while other domains might be thought to be compatible with absolutism.

Yet, in applying relativism in such a piecemeal way, an impediment arises: How should we separate pertinent domains? What "joints" exist that would separate them? Are the characterizations of such joints meant to capture frame-dependent facts of the matter or are they meant to capture constructed cultural achievements? Are such joints found or made? For example, moral absolutists might object to characterizing morality in relativist terms, and scientific constructivists might object to characterizing science in absolutist terms. Indeed, might the construal of pertinent domains and their joints itself implicate relativist or absolutist dispositions to start with? Does question-beggingness loom?

In this connection, we should note that relativism is not pluralism. "Pluralism," as here defined, affirms that for a given reference frame, a distinct subject matter or "world" exists. A pluralist could hold that for any scientific paradigm, for example, another world exists. In contrast, insofar as relativism is concerned at all to deny absolutist standards for adjudication, relativism requires that, with respect to the *same* subject matter, competing reference frames exist. If a systematic plurality of subject matters or "worlds" answered to different reference frames, then as I have suggested pertinent frames could not compete. Different frames would address different worlds.

Thomas Kuhn's remarks are instructive here. He says, "there is, I think, no theory-independent way to reconstruct phrases like "really there"; the notion of a match between the ontology of a theory and its "real" counterpart in nature now seems to me illusive in principle." He says further, "The transition from Newtonian to Einsteinian mechanics illustrates with particular clarity the scientific revolution as a displacement of the conceptual network through which scientists view the world." (Kuhn 1970, 102)

However, Kuhn verges on the *pluralist* view when he adds, "Two groups, the members of which have systematically different sensations on receipt of the same stimuli, do in some sense live in different worlds." (Kuhn 1970, 193) Kuhn's last remark hints that if different paradigms invoke different concepts to structure their respective subject matters, they cannot be about the same subject matter. Accordingly, they cannot compete.

As opposed to pluralists, relativists need to reject the pluralist assumption that difference in concepts mandates difference in subject matter. Otherwise, adherents of different reference frames would talk past each other. Under that condition, the relativist claim that no absolute standards exist to adjudicate between pertinent reference frames would be inconsequential.

1.4 Levels

Another variable embedded in our definition of relativism involves "ontic" versus "epistemic" *levels*. A relativist at the *ontic* level embraces the relativity of objects of inquiry to reference frames. A relativist at the *epistemic* level embraces the relativity of our knowledge of objects of inquiry. A *global* relativist at the ontic level affirms that *all* objects of inquiry are frame-dependent, while a *piecemeal* relativist at the ontic level affirms that only *some* such objects are frame-dependent. In contrast, a relativist at the *epistemic* level embraces the relativity of our knowledge of such objects to reference frames. Further, a *global* relativist at the epistemic level affirms that our knowledge of *all* objects is frame-dependent, and a *piecemeal* relativist at the epistemic level affirms that our knowledge of only *some* objects is frame-dependent.

Yet the distinction between ontic and epistemic levels itself is contentious. A relativist may hold that if we have no access to objects of inquiry *as such* – that is, frame-independent objects – we cannot compare our descriptions of such objects with those objects as such. At best, we have access to the world and its objects only through some description or depiction of them. We can know them only as conceptualized in one way or another. Therefore, we can compare our descriptions only with other descriptions. The most that we can establish is a relationship between descriptions, not a relationship between descriptions and the world's supposed objects as such. Thus, one might conclude that the notion of the world and its objects as such is of no use in the conduct of inquiry. Correspondingly, one might argue that the very distinction between ontic and epistemic levels is of no use in the conduct of inquiry.

An ontic absolutist might counter that positing the notion of a frame-independent world does indeed serve a useful purpose. Without it, there would be no point at all in pursuing cognitive inquiries. Without it, one could make no sense of the idea of progress in the history of science, for example. Ironically, realist-absolutist Karl Popper concedes how limited his own realist-absolutism is in matters of methodology. He says:

> within methodology we do not have to presuppose metaphysical realism; *nor can we, I think, derive much help from it, except of an intuitive kind.* For, once we have been told that the aim of science is to explain, and that the most satisfactory explanation will be the one that is most severely testable and most severely tested, we know all that we need to know as methodologists. That the aim is realizable we cannot assert, neither with nor without the help of metaphysical realism which can give us some intuitive encouragement, *some hope, but no assurance of any kind.* And although a rational treatment of methodology may be said to depend upon an assumed, or conjectured, aim of science, it certainly does not depend upon the metaphysical and *most likely false assumption that the true structural theory of the world (if any) is discoverable by man, or expressible in human language.* (Popper 1985, 170, emphasis added)

1.5 Adjudication

Let us now turn to the variable of adjudication in our definition of relativism. Notice that our definition allows the possibility of a single frame of all frames, an "imperial" reference frame, so to speak. An imperial frame would subsume all lower-level reference frames. For the relativist, such a possibility would amount to an anomaly. For, as our definition suggests, relativism concerns the non-adjudicability by absolutist standards *between* reference frames. If only one imperial reference frame exists, the relativist's claim about the non-adjudicability between reference frames becomes inapplicable. That would not be a bad thing for relativists, for they are concerned to deny the existence of absolute standards to adjudicate among a plurality of reference frames. That the question of adjudication does not arise in the case of an imperial reference frame is no demerit for the relativist. If in that case no plurality of reference frames exists, the question of adjudication just does not arise.

Now we should ask what sort of existents one might appeal to in order to adjudicate between reference frames. What about an indeterminate frame-independent order – an "undifferentiated unity" – like Kant's noumenon? Can its invocation adjudicate between frames of reference? I suggest that saying, with Kant, that an indeterminate order – an "I know not what" – exists, provides no praxial basis to *adjudicate* between reference frames. Interestingly, a relativist could – without contradiction – embrace such an indeterminate order. That is, a relativist might affirm the existence of something like Kant's noumenon, recognizing that such an order is unable to adjudicate between reference frames.

This finding also holds for the Brahman or the Oneness, as invoked by Advaita Hindus. More fully, Advaitists embrace the notion that ultimate reality is the undifferentiated, non-countable ineffable One (see Roy 1993). That Advaitist notion affirms that ultimate reality is the totality of existence, and not any or all of its conventionally constituted countable objects. Appeals to that Advaitist notion would be ineffectual as regards adjudication between competing reference frames.[4] Yet, as I have suggested, insofar as the relativist is concerned with adjudication, a relativist could without contradiction embrace the Advaitist notion of Oneness. Further, to some, the noumenon of Kant or the Oneness of Advaita may look "absolutist" in some loose sense of that term. But it is not the sense of absolutism that is invoked in our definition of relativism. *That* sense of absolutism concerns adjudication between reference frames.

2 Absolutisms Negated by Relativists

So then, what sense of absolutism do relativists characteristically oppose? Recall that the second part of our definition states, "no *absolute* overarching standards to adjudicate between competing reference frames exist." What, more precisely, might a relativist oppose?

---

[4] Douglas Duckworth, Assistant Professor of Religion at Temple University, has suggested to me in personal communication that my point about the non-adjudicability of Advaita's Brahman also extends to the Tibetan Buddhist's principle of emptiness of inherent existence.

Absolutism can be variously comprised of at least three bundled strands: *realist, universalist,* or *foundationalist*. At first glance, it is tempting to say that a strong absolutist bundle will affirm all three strands, and it is tempting to say that a strong relativism will oppose all three absolutist strands. I shall return to these first temptations after defining salient terms.

2.1 Realism

By "realism", I mean the view that frame-independent facts of the matter exist. This view accords with that of John Searle, who says, "realism is the view that there is a way that things are that is logically independent of all human representations. Realism does not say how things are but only that there is a way that they are" (Searle 1995, 155).[5]

Now relativists – or at least non-realists – may be allowed to talk of "facts". But when they do so, they clearly mean it in a sense quite different from the realist's sense. The non-realist is free to say, for example, that "it is a 'fact' that the shortest distance between two points is a straight line", understanding by that that such a claim is made within the reference frame of Euclidean geometry. So, we should not presume that any talk of "facts" mandates a realist construal. We should not force a realist's construal of facts upon the non-realist. Accordingly, Nelson Goodman – who calls himself a "radical relativist with restraints" – says, "[we] cannot find any world-features independent of all versions. Whatever can be said truly of a world is dependent on the saying [...] informed by and relative to the language or other symbol system we use" (Goodman 1996, 144).

2.2 Universalism

The second strand sometimes associated or bundled with absolutism is universalism. Universalists hold that certain non-trivial characteristics apply to all peoples, at all times, and in all cultures. Such characteristics at the ontic level may or may not be frame-independent. For example, universalists hold that human rights exist for all peoples, regardless whether such rights are frame-dependent. In contrast, anti-universalists hold that some non-trivial characteristics may

---

[5] Compare Searle's definition of realism with Hilary Putnam's characterization of realism when Putnam says, "the world consists of some fixed totality of mind-independent objects. There is exactly one true and complete description of 'the way the world is'" (Putnam 1981, 49).

apply only to some peoples at some times in some cultures. They may claim that some human rights, for example, exist for some people and not for others.

At its epistemic level, universalists assert that peoples in all cultures and at all times can *know* whether all peoples share pertinent characteristics, for rationality itself is universally exemplified. At the epistemic level, anti-universalists hold that such knowledge does not obtain for all peoples. They could argue that sometimes incommensurability between reference frames blocks universalism. For example, those of shame cultures in traditional Japan cannot fully understand those of guilt cultures in contemporary America, and vice versa. At the epistemic level, anti-universalists may conclude that the search for a universal language is futile. At that level, an anti-universalist could affirm that there are no universal grounds for deliberation shared by all peoples at all times in all cultures.

I distinguish between universalism as an *existential* claim from universalism as a *regulative* principle. While the existential universalist asserts that universal commensurating resources exist, the regulative universalist affirms that it is useful to conduct one's inquiries *as if* the existential condition exists—without actually assuming that the existential condition exists. For, even if we do not embrace universalism in its existential version, if we adopt universalism as a regulative principle, we might overcome cross-cultural antagonisms. Regulative universalism may at least encourage cross-cultural dialogue.

2.3 Foundationalism

By way of introducing our third strand characteristically bundled with absolutism, namely foundationalism, I distinguish between two kinds of universalism – "foundational" and "nonfoundational." Foundational universalism holds that all peoples share some common characteristics by virtue of what – *inherently or intrinsically* – it is to be a human being. Nonfoundational universalism holds that all peoples share common characteristics without presuming that they do so by virtue of what, inherently, it is to be a human being. Foundational universalism is a claim of inherence or intrinsicality. In contrast, non-foundational universalism is a claim of historical or cultural or biological contingency. In short, foundationalism is the view that characteristics of pertinent subjects are what they are in virtue of their being inherent or intrinsic to those subjects. At the epistemic level, *knowledge* of foundational conditions can be acquired in virtue of first principles of rationality, such as the principle of non-contradiction.

They are self-evident and not further reducible. They constitute the rock-bottom basis for argumentation and justification.[6]

Consider this example of foundational universalism at the ontic level. Consider the claim, "All persons have biological mothers". This example would amount to a foundational universalism if it were conjoined to the further claim that having a biological mother is an inherent or intrinsic feature of what it is to be a human being. In contrast, a nonfoundational universalist might urge that the fact that all persons have biological mothers is contingent and – considering possible developments in human cloning – it could be otherwise. Contingently understood, universal commonality does not amount to a foundational universalism. A foundationalist might reply that the universal instantiation of characteristics that all peoples share needs to be foundationally grounded in order to explain the otherwise miraculous fact of universality. That is, without foundational universalism, the commonality of shared characteristics seems miraculous.

To reiterate the relationships between realism, universalism, and foundationalism thus far, let us consider their exemplifications in an aesthetic example. Some say that the geometric proportions exhibited in the cross section of the chambered nautilus shell – as formalized in the Fibonacci number series – exemplify aesthetically perfect proportions. Starting with 1 + 1, each following number is the sum of the previous two numbers. Here is the sequence: 1, 1, 2, 3, 5, 8, 13, 21, 34, 55, 89, 144, and so on. The aesthetic realist takes the series as embodying a perfect proportion independent of reference frames. In contrast, anti-realists hold that the series is frame-dependent. Whether frame-independent or frame-dependent, universalists take the series to be universally instantiated, while anti-universalists deny such universality. Moreover, the foundationalist takes the series to be inherent or self-evident. The non-foundationalist denies such inherence or self-evidence.

2.4 Polymorphism

Consider now a kind of non-foundationalism that I call "polymorphism". The polymorphist affirms that no description nested in any reference frame can be

---

6 Notice that the distinction between foundationalism and non-foundationalism presupposes the distinction between inherence and non-inherence, or between necessity and contingency. So, if the distinction between inherence and non-inherence or between necessity and contingency were denied, the distinction between foundationalism and non-foundationalism would be vulnerable.

taken to capture a presumed inherent or ultimate constituent of reality. For example, if we describe water in a glass as thirst quenching, a realist might take that description as a truth about a frame-independent way of the world. Yet a polymorphist emphasizes that the water understood only as a middle-sized phenomenon is what affords satisfactions to middle-sized organisms such as human beings, dogs, and cats. Yet, when we redescribe the water in terms of electrons in empty space, the property of thirst-quenchingness does not apply. In this way, polymorphism holds that relevant properties must be understood elliptically, that is, within one reference frame or another, and no level of description captures an inherent or ultimate constituent of what there is.[7]

Here is another example of a polymorphist handling. In everyday contexts one might say, "This is my hand" while a cell biologist might say that it is a collection of cells, or, a particle physicist might say that it is a collection of subatomic particles in empty space.

The polymorphist allows that cells are *most basic in cell biology*. Similarly, the polymorphist allows that subatomic particles are *most basic in physics*. But neither cells nor subatomic particles need be regarded as inherent constituents of reality irrespective of domains of inquiry. While designated basic claims – or basic presuppositions – can be taken as most *basic* within a given inquiry, polymorphism refuses to make a claim about the inherent or ultimate nature of things as they might otherwise be taken to be. What appears to be basic in an inquiry is basic only after a choice has been made about what reference frame one wishes to pursue in accord with one's purposes and interests.[8]

Now, if we accept the polymorphist idea that we choose our reference frames in accord with our purposes and interests, we must ask, "What kind of being is it that has purposes and interests?" Typically, but not perhaps necessarily, it is a human being who has purposes and interests. I leave open whether other sentient beings are capable of choosing reference frames in accord with their purposes and interests.[9]

---

[7] Interestingly, such diverse thinkers as Nelson Goodman and Tibetan Buddhists share this polymorphic view. Tibetan Buddhists hold that nothing exists *inherently*. All is "empty" of inherent existence. That does not mean that nothing exists. It only means that what does exist does so conventionally. See (Goodman 2001). See also (Gyatso 1992) and (Duckworth 2011, especially chapter 7). I tentatively offer polymorphism as non-foundationalist, non-realist, and possibly universalist.

[8] Polymorphists may embrace Collingwood's misleadingly called "absolute presuppositions". Collingwood would better have called them "basic" presuppositions, for they are basic with respect to a systematic inquiry, see (Collingwood 1998, 23ff) and also (Skagestad 2005).

[9] Catherine Elgin has pointed out that it is not so much human beings as such that have purposes and interests as the consciousness they embody (personal communication, December 14,

2.5 Strands

I have characterized realism, universalism, and foundationalism as possible strands of an absolutist bundle. Now we should consider whether any or all of them are invariantly necessary for any absolutist bundle. In addition, we should consider whether the negation of any or all of them is necessary for any relativist bundle.

While realism, universalism, and foundationalism are compatible with each other, each of them is logically distinct. Realism entails neither universalism nor foundationalism; universalism entails neither realism nor foundationalism; and foundationalism entails neither realism nor universalism. More fully, realism is compatible with foundationalism or non-foundationalism – because frame-independence requires no assumption of inherence. Realism is compatible with universalism or non-universalism – because frame independence may be instantiated in some but not all domains. Universalism is compatible with realism or non-realism – because all peoples may share certain non-trivial properties, regardless whether they are frame-dependent or frame-independent. Universalism is compatible with foundationalism or non-foundationalism – because all peoples may share certain non-trivial properties regardless whether they are inherently shared. Foundationalism is compatible with universalism or non-universalism – because inherence may be instantiated in all or some peoples, at either or both ontic or epistemic levels. Finally, foundationalism is compatible with realism or non-realism – because inherence may be instantiated with frame-independence or frame-dependence in some but not all domains or at either or both levels.

Since the three strands and their negations are logically distinct, might some of the strands initially associated with absolutism be bundled with strands initially associated with relativism? For example, one might insist that at least realism is necessary for absolutism. As well, foundationalism might be thought to strengthen realism in an absolutist bundle. But a realist-foundationalist need not be universalist. In piecemeal fashion, realist-foundationalists might apply such a bundle to a natural domain (like Newtonian physics) but not to a cultural domain (like art history). Alternatively, in the cultural domain, one might be both non-realist and universalist. One might hold that all cultures exemplify some form of music appreciation without affirming that such appreciation is

---

2014). This leaves open the possibility that consciousness not uniquely embodied in human beings might have purposes and interests. The pursuit of this fruitful suggestion goes beyond the reach of this paper. See also (Nida-Rümelin 2014)

frame independent. Notice also that in some domains, or at the epistemic level, foundationalism is compatible with non-realism and non-universalism. At the epistemic level, for instance, one may hold that only certain tribes – according to principles inherent to rationality – can understand some frame-dependent practices. For example, only those of certain tribes have the capacity to understand certain religious practices without at the same time violating the law of non-contradiction.

Here, then is a puzzle about labeling. Should we call non-foundational universalism an absolutist or a relativist bundle? If we are realist in certain domains but not others, are we absolutist or relativist? Does subtracting universalism from a realism or foundationalism weaken one's absolutist credentials? Does adding universalism to a foundationalism strengthen one's absolutism? Does subtracting realism from universalism weaken one's absolutist credentials? Indeed, given these heterodox possibilities, at least in such cases, does a sharp demarcation between relativism and absolutism exist at all? And is there a compelling reason to label such heterodox bundles as either relativist or absolutist?

3 The Self-Referential Argument

However we might answer these questions of labeling, we are now in a position to revisit the classical argument against relativism. That argument holds that *relativism is self-refuting*, according to which if someone asserts "Relativism is true" we may inquire in what sense of truth the claim is intended. That is, in what sense of "true" is the assertion supposed to be true? If the sense of truth our interlocutor invokes is absolutist, the claim is self-referentially contradictory. This charge of self-contradiction is often taken to be decisive. It is this apparent contradiction that is my main concern now.

In passing though, we may note limited ways a relativist might try to avoid the putative contradiction. A relativist may affirm that "Relativism is true" is true in a relativist sense, not in an absolute sense. While this strategy would avoid the threatening contradiction, it has its own challenge. For, to say that relativism is relatively true, can carry with it no recommendation why someone outside the relativist's reference frame should take the relativist seriously. Relativism, so modified, ceases to have wide argumentative traction.[10]

---

[10] The present taxonomy details the relationships between realism, universalism, and foundationalism. So, how should we situate the taxonomy within its own terms? I suggest that as a taxonomy, it may but need not answer to non-realism, non-universalism, and non-foundationalism.

Alternatively, to avoid the problem of contradiction, a relativist might seek to limit the scope of application of the claim of relativism. The relativist might urge, "All statements are relatively true except for the statement that all statements are relatively true". But this self-exempting strategy seems arbitrary and ad hoc.

So let us return to the charge of self-contradiction when relativism is said to be absolutely true. Having untangled the possible strands of absolutism – into realism, universalism, or foundationalism – we are now equipped with the resources to unseat the charge of contradiction. More fully, recall our initial definition of relativism: "relativism is the claim that such values as truth, goodness or beauty is relative to a reference frame, and no *absolute* overarching standards of adjudication between competing reference frames exist".

Now, for the term "absolute" in the latter part of our definition, let us substitute the disentangled strands, "realist, universalist, or foundationalist". Such a substitution yields the following more explicit formulation of relativism as the view that "such values as truth, goodness or beauty is relative to a reference frame, and no *realist, universalist, or foundationalist* overarching standards to adjudicate between competing reference frames exist".

Whatever one's philosophical misgivings might be about varieties of realism, universalism, or foundationalism as they stand, clearly *no contradiction* follows when the relativist negates any one or all of them. Neither the negation of realism, nor the negation of universalism, nor still the negation of foundationalism is self-contradictory. Put otherwise, *if we conceive of relativism as a negation of one or more of the offered strands of absolutism, relativism is not self-refuting.* Under this condition, the self-refuting argument against relativism dissolves. QED. Of course, this argument does not establish the rightness of either absolutism or relativism. It only shows the invalidity of the classical self-referential argument against relativism.

Here, then, is my overall conclusion. We should defer the question, "Who is right – the relativist, or the absolutist?" Rather, we should first ask, "Which relativism?" and "Which strand of absolutism does it negate?"

Acknowledgements: I am indebted to Catherine Elgin, Michael Forster, and Markus Gabriel for their helpful comments on a previous version of this paper, "Relativism as Opposed to What?" delivered at the "Conference on the Coherence of Relativism" at the University of Bonn, December 14, 2014. This paper overlaps with the Bonn paper, and with new material it redirects the overall argument. For their further comments I thank David Bloor, Gaza Kallay, and Josef Mitterer.

References

Bernstein, Richard (1983): *Beyond Objectivism and Relativism: Science, Hermeneutics and Praxis*. Oxford: Blackwell.

Collingwood, Robin (1998): *An Essay on Metaphysics*. Edited by Rex Martin. Oxford: Clarendon Press.

Davidson, Donald (1974): "On the Very Idea of a Conceptual Scheme". In: *Proceedings and Addresses of the American Philosophical Association* 47, 5–20.

Duckworth, Douglas (2011): *Jamgon Mipam: His Life and Teachings*. Boston and London: Shambala Press, 99–117.

Goodman, Nelson (1996): "On Starmaking". In: McCormack, Peter (ed.): *Starmaking: Realism, Anti-Realism, and Irrealism*. Cambridge, MA: MIT Press.

Goodman, Nelson (2010): "Just the Facts, Ma'am!". In: Krausz, Michael (ed.): *Relativism: A Contemporary Anthology*. New York: Columbia University Press, 80–85.

Gyatso, Lobsang (1992): *The Harmony of Emptiness and Dependent-Arising*. Dharamsala: Library of Tibetan Works and Archives.

John Searle (1995): *The Construction of Social Reality*. New York: Free Press.

Krausz, Michael (1999): "Interpretation, Relativism, and Culture: Four Questions for Margolis". In: Shusterman, Richard; Krausz, Michael (eds.): *Interpretation, Relativism and the Metaphysics of Culture: Themes in the Philosophy of Joseph Margolis*. Amherst, NY: Humanity Press, 105–124.

Krausz, Michael (2006): "Relativism and Its Schemes". In: Mou, Bo (ed.): *Davidson's Philosophy and Chinese Philosophy: Constructive Engagement*. Amsterdam: Brill Publishers, 37–53.

Kuhn, Thomas (1970): *The Structure of Scientific Revolutions*. Second Edition. Chicago: University of Chicago Press.

Margolis, Joseph (1976): "Robust Relativism". In: *The Journal of Aesthetics and Art Criticism* 35 (1), 37–46.

Margolis, Joseph (2010): "The Truth about Relativism". In: Krausz, Michael (ed.): *Relativism: A Contemporary Anthology*. New York: Columbia University Press, 100–123.

Nida-Rümelin, Martine (2014): "Basic Intentionality, Primitive Awareness, and Awareness of Oneself". In: Reboul, Anne (ed.): *Mind, Values and Metaphysics: Philosophical Papers dedicated to Kevin Mulligan*. New York: Springer, 261–290.

Popper, Karl (1985): *Popper Selections*. Edited by David Miller. Princeton, NJ: Princeton University Press.

Putnam, Hilary (1981): *Reason, Truth, and History*. Cambridge, UK: Cambridge University Press.

Roy, Khrishna (1993): *Hermeneutics East and West*. Calcutta: Allied Press.

Skagestad, Peter (2005): "Collingwood and Berlin: A Comparison". In: *Journal of the History of Ideas* 66 (1), 99–111.

Martin Kusch
When Paul Met Ludwig: Wittgensteinian Comments on Boghossian's Antirelativism

Abstract: This paper tries to make plausible the following claims: The paragraphs §608–612 of *On Certainty* do not speak in favour of what Boghossian construes as the Master Argument for Relativism; that *On Certainty* introduces various relativistic themes; and that Boghossian and Wittgenstein conceptualize epistemic systems in rather different ways that lead to very different views on three candidate cases for radical difference in epistemic systems.

Keywords: Wittgenstein, relativism, Paul Boghossian, On Certainty

1 Introduction

This paper will discuss, from a Wittgensteinian perspective, some key aspects of Paul Boghossian's influential anti-relativist arguments. My starting point is the observation that Boghossian sometimes presents Wittgenstein as a key influence behind much contemporary relativism, while on other occasions he borrows elements from Wittgenstein in order to construct antirelativist positions. Is Boghossian right to do so? And what would Wittgenstein make of Boghossian's arguments for and against relativism?

1.1 The Master Argument for Relativism (MAR)

Boghossian construes the opposition between epistemic absolutist and relativist as follows. The former affirms what the latter denies: that there are absolute epistemic facts. Both sides agree, however, that if there are absolute epistemic facts, then it is in principle possible to have justified beliefs about them. Of course, the relativist thinks it is not possible to have such justified beliefs about absolute facts. How can the relativist establish this view? Boghossian suggests the following five-step argument (MAR) (Boghossian 2006, Chapter VII):

> Step 1: We encounter "genuine alternative epistemic systems".

Epistemic systems are systems of epistemic principles. A genuine alternative to our own system is one that differs from ours in at least one fundamental principle.

Step 2: When encountering such alternative, the onus is on us to justify our epistemic system.

According to the relativist, we are tacitly committed to such "Demand for Justification".

Step 3: In this task we have no resources but our own epistemic system.

Call this insight "Ethnocentric Justification": Epistemic justification must be based on one's own epistemic principles.

Step 4: But we are not allowed to use our own epistemic system for this task of justification.

According to the relativist, we should accept "No-Self-Certification": the justification of a given form of reasoning must not make use of this very form of reasoning.

2 *On Certainty* and Relativism of Distance

Boghossian sees *On Certainty* §608–12 as gesturing towards MAR (Boghossian 2006, 69, 78–79, 95). Before looking at §608–12 directly I want to briefly explain what I take to be an important relativistic strand of the book. This strand is its attempt catalogue our – primarily Wittgenstein's own – responses to people who (seem to) deny one of our, or his, certainties. The point of the exercise is to emphasise the variety of our responses to such denials. Some such responses are dismissive, some educational, some sceptical, some relativist. There are about thirty of such scenarios in *On Certainty*.

Here are some examples. When a friend denies a certainty then Wittgenstein is inclined to regard him as "demented" or "insane" (OC §71). Wittgenstein treats other adult members of his own culture similarly (OC §271, 257). Children receive a more charitable treatment. In their case Wittgenstein is willing to offer arguments, explanations, and education (OC §310, 322). Turning to the categories of strangers that are not members of our culture, Wittgenstein thinks that sometimes we are willing to dismiss them as ignorant. Thus the tribesmen who in 1950 insist that someone has been to the Moon – and who thereby deny one of our fundamental empirical-scientific beliefs – are "people who do not know a lot that we know" (OC §286). But other paragraphs suggest that this response is natural only as long as we treat the claim "someone has been to the moon" as a direct denial of one of our scientific certainties. Thus §92 considers a king who has been told since childhood that "the earth has only existed [...] since his own birth." Wittgenstein likens the king's belief to magical beliefs about one's ability to make rain. This suggests to Elizabeth Anscombe that the king is best thought of as a religious leader like the Dalai Lama (see Anscombe 1976). Wittgenstein imagines George Edward Moore trying to convince the king that the earth has existed since long before our birth. And he goes on: "I do not say that Moore could not convert the king to his view, but it would be a conversion of a special kind; the king would be brought to look at the world in a different way." What is striking here is the absence of any "they are wrong and we know it" (OC §286). In a related passage (OC §238) Wittgenstein insists that sometimes, when someone contradicts "my fundamental attitudes" I can do no better than "put up with it". And in §108 Wittgenstein speaks of people who claim to have been to the moon: "We should feel ourselves intellectually very distant from them."

Having convinced himself that this is indeed the proper response to certain disagreements concerning magic and religion, Wittgenstein then draws an analogy between the disagreements between believers and nonbelievers on the one hand, and our response to past periods with their different conceptions of the reasonable and the unreasonable, on the other hand: "But what men consider reasonable or unreasonable alters. At certain periods men find reasonable what at other periods they found unreasonable. And vice versa." (OC §336) This suggests that Wittgenstein assumes that our response to disagreements over some other certainties too might be treated on the model of the religious certainties.

I propose calling the relativistic theme that emerges in these passages "relativism of distance"; a term coined by Bernard Williams in a different context (see Williams 1981). A relativism of distance has two key elements. On the one hand, we have a "confrontation" of epistemic or moral systems that is "notional" rather than "real". A confrontation is notional if going over to the other side is not a "real", a live option; it demands a conversion. On the other hand, "for a *reflective* person the question of appraisal does not genuinely arise ... in purely notional confrontation". Her terms of appraisal appear to her inappropriate or without traction regarding the beliefs and actions of members of the other culture.

Relativism of distance can be enriched with an idea central in the work of another relativist moral philosopher, David Wong. He suggests that a relativistic attitude is triggered by "moral ambivalence" (Wong 2006). This is an experience of an encounter in which "our sense of the unique rightness of our own judgment gets destabilized". We encounter someone too much of an intellectual peer to be dismissed as insane or foolish, and yet acting or judging in a way that makes us suspect or realize that our sense of right and wrong is not uniquely correct.

There are thus three features that set Wittgensteinian "relativism of distance" apart from other versions of relativism. First, it focuses on specific experiences triggering relativistic reactions. Second, it centers on conceptual difficulties of appraisal. And third, it has a "particularist" orientation: it can apply to much smaller units than whole cultures or epistemic or moral systems.

3 On Certainty §602–612

We can now return to the question how these paragraphs stand vis-à-vis relativism. They belong to a train of thought that begins in §602. §602 states the problem to be discussed: there is something about our trust in physics that seems to undermine its objective character. §603 points out that physical knowledge is *systematic*, and that my knowledge of it is merely *partial*, overwhelmingly *testimonial*, and largely based on *blind trust*. §604 reminds us of two things. First, the trust in physics is embedded and enforced by important social institutions like the law. Second, someone who is not a credentialed physicist is unable to challenge the results of physics. §605 expresses a worry relating to the idea that our reliance on physics is grounded in blind trust: what if the physicists' statements were "superstition"? Would we be able to detect this? §606 rejects this worry. Ordeal by fire was a bad epistemic tool, though people did not realize this at the time. This is no reason for suspecting that physical methods might likewise be bad. §607 lets a judge emphasize a point that Wittgenstein himself wants to insist on: that the blindness of the trust underlying physics does not make physical knowledge impossible.

§608 restates the concern: does the blind trust rob me of the rationale to rely on physics? And the reassuring answer is that we treat the propositions of physics as "good grounds" almost by definition. This thought is followed, in §609, by a question that structures the rest of the discussion: how do we who trust in physics react to people who put their trust in oracles instead? The initial reply is that we call "them" "primitive" and "wrong". These evaluations are forms of "combat" based on our language-game. In §610 Wittgenstein raises the question whether this combatting is right. Leaving this question open, he notes that our case for superiority is based on "slogans". The important implication is that we have got nothing better. §611 adds to this that the clash between the oracle-following tribe and us is a clash of two irreconcilable principles, and that invectives like "fool" or "heretic" are markers of such conflicts. It seems that instead of convincing the other side, all we can do is dismiss it. §612 confirms the suspicion of §611: some reason-giving is possible but in the end there is only combat, persuasion and conversion.

§602 to 612 do not argue that the oracle is as reliable as is ours physics. But nor do they seek to establish that we invariably fail in justifying our epistemic systems, and that hence there are no absolute epistemic facts. The ideas hinted at in these paragraphs part and parcel of an investigation into the foundation of the (ultimately blind) trust upon which science is based. That science is so based, is a shortcoming only in the eyes of someone who has mistaken excessively rationalist standards.

Moreover, one of the upshots of these paragraphs is that our aggression towards the oracle-users tells us something about the strength of our socially-sanctioned trust in our experts. And part of our aggression may spring from the fact that in the encounter with the oracle-users we might be realising the role of blind trust in our belief system for the first time. But that our belief system is based in blind trust, is not an argument for relativism – not even for a relativism of distance. On the contrary, Wittgenstein wants to remind us of how natural it is for us to reject those who deny our scientific certainties in a systematic way.

§602–612 thus are a sketch of an analysis of our natural antirelativism (in certain domains) and its social and social-psychological foundations. And the message is not what Boghossian formulates as MAR. Wittgenstein would not accept steps 2 and 4. He does not think that we have to defend our epistemic system when we encounter another; for him there is no such demand. There is only the natural attitude of dismissing challenges to our science. And concerning "No-Self-Certification" Wittgenstein would remark that we simply use our epistemic system when it comes to the purposes of combatting, persuading and converting.

And yet, while I deny that Wittgenstein offers §602–612 as a Master Argument for epistemic relativism, I still think that the epistemic relativist is able to use §602–612 in defence of a relativist position. Let me explain. Peter Strawson once suggested that "[a]ccording to Hume [...] sceptical doubts are [...] powerless against the force of nature, of our naturally implanted disposition to belief" (Strawson 1985, 19). Strawson went on to observe "a profound community" on this point between Wittgenstein and Hume. Michael Williams later objected that on this reading, Wittgenstein and Hume would "concede [...] the sceptic's theoretical invulnerability" (Williams 1988, 416). It may be impossible to live scepticism, but it may still be right.

The central issue before us is not scepticism, but relativism. We saw that §602–612 suggest that between us and a relativism about the results of current science stands our ultimately blind trust in our scientists. This trust makes it difficult for us to live such a relativism. This is analogous to Strawson's reading of Wittgenstein on scepticism. And now the relativist can argue in parallel with Michael Williams: it may well be true that we cannot live this kind of relativism, but this consideration leaves the relativist's position theoretically invulnerable. Relativism about our currently best science is impossible to live – but it has not been defeated as a theoretical outlook of, say, the anthropologist or sociologist of knowledge. Once more, Wittgenstein does not reason in this way – but we could.

How does my interpretation of §602–612 relate to relativism of distance? It is a fact about us that we feel epistemic or moral ambivalence in some cases and not in others. We do not feel epistemic ambivalence about the best current physics when we meet the tribe who trusts oracles. But some of us feel such ambivalence when we encounter, say, the religious beliefs of intellectual peers.

4 Blind Entitlement

Boghossian does not only take Wittgenstein to gesture towards MAR in §608–612; he also holds that elsewhere in Wittgenstein's oeuvre we find an idea that blocks MAR from going through. This idea Boghossian calls "Blind Entitlement": "each thinker is entitled to use the epistemic system he finds himself with, without first having to supply an antecedent justification for the claim that it is the correct system" (Boghossian 2006, 99). The inspiration for this principle in §219 of the *Philosophical Investigations:* "When I obey a rule, I do not choose. I obey the rule blindly." (PI §219) Blind Entitlement disables MAR in cooperation with two other principles, "Coherence" and "Demand for Impressiveness":

> (Coherence) Any ES that fails constraints of coherence is incorrect.
> (Demand of Impressiveness) For an alternative ES to trigger Demand for Justification, its "*actual* achievements [...] have to be *impressive* enough to make us legitimately doubt the correctness of our own [epistemic system]." (Boghossian 2006, 101)

Coherence radically restricts the number of genuine alternatives to our epistemic system. Blind Entitlement together with Demand for Impressiveness dislodges the Demand for Justification. And Blind Entitlement contradicts No-Self-Certification.

I am not convinced that this is in the spirit of Wittgenstein's position. Note, first of all, that his remark about obeying a rule blindly is not a remark about an *entitlement*. It is an observation about what we do. Second, while *On Certainty* too frequently speaks about systems of beliefs, it does not couch our relationship to such systems in terms of entitlements. Instead Wittgenstein speaks of this relationship as "something animal" (OC §359) or "trust" (OC §509). Third, it seems to me that Wittgenstein would be likely to regard Blind Entitlement as no more than a "slogan" that we use to sublimate our gut response. And fourth, Wittgenstein would also object to the all too narrow range of outcomes that Boghossian allows for the encounter between two epistemic systems. To wit, that either one of the two is judged superior to the other, or else that they are taken to equal, and equivalent to one another.

More generally, Wittgenstein would also object to the ways in which Boghossian renders the relativist and the anti-relativist positions. For Wittgenstein, the best way to make some forms of relativism plausible would not be an in-principle argument like MAR. A better route would be to focus on our responses to certain types of encounters. Perhaps we can capture the difference by distinguishing between "generalist" and "particularist" versions of relativism. The generalist wants an in-principle argument as to why a whole domain of judgments has to be understood in relativist terms. The particularist insists that we have relative intuitions about quite specific questions within domains. If the Wittgenstein of *On Certainty* is a relativist, he surely is a relativist of the latter sort.

5 Epistemic Systems

For Boghossian an epistemic system consists of epistemic principles. Some of these are fundamental, some are derived (Boghossian 2006, 67). "Observation" is fundamental: "For any observational proposition p, if it visually seems to S that p and circumstantial conditions D obtain, then S is prima facie justified in believing p." (Boghossian 2006, 64) The distinction allows Boghossian to specify a criterion for being a "genuine alternative to our epistemic system". The criterion is that the alternative must be different in *at least one* fundamental principle. Boghossian argues that a couple of often-cited examples of such alternatives – the Azande and Cardinal Bellarmine – do not in fact meet his criterion.

Wittgenstein too talks about epistemic systems of sorts (OC §105, 108, 144, 410, 411). Beliefs in our belief systems are more or less fundamental. The more fundamental they are, the less likely it is that they are wrong. The most fundamental beliefs are certainties. The key idea is that some "sentences (or beliefs) of the form of empirical judgments (or beliefs)" can in some contexts be as fundamental as are judgments or beliefs about the meanings of words, or mathematical beliefs. And not all beliefs about the meaning of words or mathematical propositions are as certain as are "sentences of the form of empirical judgments". Furthermore, there is structural reason why certainties cannot be proven true: "My having two hands is, in normal circumstances, as certain as anything that I could produce in evidence for it. That is why I am not in a position to take the sight of my hand as evidence for it." (OC §250) Finally, Wittgensteinian epistemic systems are dynamic, they change over time (OC §96, 99). This dynamic aspect is missing in Boghossian's work. Note also that whereas Boghossian's principles are an analyst's idealizations, abstract, and separable from specific contents and contexts, Wittgenstein's certainties are actor's paradigms, concrete and inseparable from specific contents and contexts. Finally, other than Boghossian, Wittgenstein does not offer a criterion for what constitutes a genuine alternative epistemic system. We can see what difference these differences make when we turn to the examples discussed by Boghossian.

The first example is the epistemic system of Robert Bellarmine, Galileo's opponent, and defender of a geocentric universe. According to Boghossian, Bellarmine adhered to the following principle:

> (Revelation) "For certain propositions p, including propositions about the heavens, believing p is prima facie justified if p is the revealed word of God as claimed by the Bible." (Boghossian 2006, 69)

This interpretation can be supported by the fact that Bellarmine defended Ptolemy's system with passages from the *Bible:* "The words 'The sun rises and the sun sets, and hurries back to where it rises, etc.' were those of Solomon, who not only spoke by divine inspiration but was a man wise above all others" (Bellarmine 1615).

But did Bellarmine use an epistemic system that can be categorized as a genuine alternative to our own? For Boghossian this hinges on whether Bellarmine followed a fundamental epistemic principle that we do not recognize as binding. The most plausible candidate for such fundamental principle is Revelation. Boghossian is not convinced that Revelation qualifies. If Revelation were fundamental then it would trump Observation with respect to some statements about the heavens (e.g. Jupiter has moons) but not with respect to others (e.g. there are clouds in the sky). The problem is that the dividing line would not be epistemologically motivated; it would be arbitrary. And arbitrary distinctions make an ES incoherent. Ergo it is more charitable to assume that Revelation is derived; and that Bellarmine and us share the same epistemic system.

I am not convinced. It is not obvious that if Revelation were a fundamental principle for Bellarmine, he would then let Revelation trump Observation in an epistemically unprincipled way. On the one hand, Bellarmine believed that no "true demonstration" of the Copernican system had been presented; and that therefore doubts about its truth were justified. On the other hand, he also held that "in a case of doubt, one may not depart from the Scriptures as explained by the holy Fathers" (Bellarmine 1615). That is to say, the situations in which Revelation was the dominant principle with respect to the heavens were restricted in a principled way. Revelation was to be relied upon when no true demonstration of a scientific theory was possible. We thus do not have to treat Revelation as a derived principle in order to save Bellarmine's epistemic rationality.

This is not to deny that the history of Bellarmine's adoption of Revelation involved other principles to do with sensory observation or testimony. But this need not conflict with its fundamental status. Here it helps to think of epistemic systems as dynamic, and hence in accordance with *On Certainty*. Initially Bellarmine may well have justified Revelation in terms of norms and standards that he shared with Galileo and with us. But he may then have gone further: he may have found further evidence for Revelation from reading the Bible. Maybe the Bible told him to take Revelation as fundamental. This evidence may have lead him to boost the standing of Revelation to a position as strong as any fundamental principle.

Remember also that for Bellarmine King Solomon "spoke by divine inspiration". So maybe Bellarmine accepted ...

> (Mystical Perception): If it seems to S that God is telling him that p, and circumstantial conditions D obtain, then S is *prima facie* justified in believing that God is telling him that p.

Trust in Mystical Perception may, or may not have been based on the Bible. Either way, it could well have been fundamental.

Boghossian's second example concerns exotic, real or imagined, tribes, like the oracle-using Azande or Wittgenstein's "odd woodsellers" that price piles of wood by the area covered, disregarding the height of the piles. Boghossian's central question is again whether we have here genuine alternative epistemic systems. His treatment of the Azande's oracle is swift. Even though the Azande have an epistemic principle that they do not share with us – "(Oracle) For certain propositions p, believing p is prima facie justified if a Poison Oracle says that p." (Boghossian 2006, 71) – this principle is not fundamental. If Oracle were fundamental then the Azande would let Observation be trumped in an arbitrary fashion (Boghossian 2006, 105). In the same context, Boghossian also addresses an old chestnut about the Azande's reasoning. Recall that the Azande accept a principle according to which if a father is/was a witch, then so are his sons. And yet, confronted with, say, Jones, whose father was a witch, the Azande are unwilling to draw the conclusion that Jones is a witch, too. Is this a sign that the Azande have a different logic? Do they reject Modus Ponens? Boghossian justifies a negative answer in the following way. Assume we translated some elements, E, of the Zande language as "if-then". And suppose further that on this translation the Azande would be committed to denying Modus Ponens. As Boghossian has it, this would be very strong evidence that our translation of "E" as "if-then" had been incorrect. And he concludes that this demonstrates the difficulty of describing a fundamentally different logic, or a genuine alternative to our epistemic system. Allegedly Wittgenstein conceded this point when he admitted that the odd woodsellers "simply do not mean the same by 'a lot of wood' and 'a little wood' as we do [...]" (RFM §150): "[...] they may not be denying anything that we regard as obviously true and the attempt to describe a genuine alternative to our [ES] will have failed once again." (Boghossian 2006, 109)

What would Wittgenstein make of Boghossian's arguments? First of all, are the Azande arbitrary in letting Oracle trump Observation on some occasions but not on others? This is far from obvious. They consult their oracles primarily in those areas of life where it is hard to obtain hard and fast evidence: adultery and causes of illness, mishaps and death. Why is this not a plausible epistemic category? Turning to Boghossian's translation-theoretic argument against the possibility of a different logic, what if the best translation of the Azande's expression E were the *if-then* of "relevance" or "linear logic"? Or what if on our translation a tribe's logic were "paraconsistent" or "dialethist" or "defeasible"? Or what if the Azande restricted Modus Ponens to certain domains – on the basis of plausible epistemological considerations? Would all these not count as different logics, leading to different conclusions? It is true that in such cases E would not mean "if-then" in the sense of the material conditional in classical logic. But its meaning might still be "close enough" for us to see the similarities and to appreciate the differences.

Finally, consider the odd woodsellers. Is their system of measuring wood a genuine alternative to our own? Wittgenstein makes three observations on this imagined tribe. The first is that such tribe could easily be exploited by us. Consider two piles of wood, A and B, of identical area, but of different height: B is higher than A. Assume that the Azande possess B and we own A. We could then say: "Let's swap: I'll give you my Pile B for your Pile A." Second, Wittgenstein asks whether the odd woodsellers suffer from "logical madness". And third, Wittgenstein addresses the question whether the practice of the odd woodsellers is "pointless". Here are his replies: "Pointless"? Well, much is pointless in our culture, too. Think of coronations. Concerning logical madness he writes: "We might call this a kind of logical madness. But there is nothing wrong with giving wood away. So what is wrong with this? We might say, 'This is how they do it.'" (LFM 202) And thirdly, yes, the Azande are exploitable by us, but not by each other, provided they do not live by selling wood. And thus their practice may well be functional in their society. The upshot is that although their way of measuring the value of wood is very different from ours, theirs is not irrational. And thus Wittgenstein thinks that there is a perspective from which the odd woodsellers' practice can be treated as equal to our own – each is functional given the social arrangements in the society.

Nevertheless, Boghossian's worry remains: do the Azande really draw conclusions that differ from ours? Or do they simply mean different things by "little wood", and "a lot of wood", and would we be in full agreement with them, once these differences on meaning were properly taken care of? In other words, is there any disagreement, or any sort of exclusiveness, between us and them? One response to this might be to say that the differences between us and the odd woodsellers must run much deeper than the simple distinction between two senses of "a lot of wood" and "a little of wood". A community whose thinking differs from our with respect to these terms is also likely to deviate from us in many other respects. We do not simply disagree over whether pile A is a little wood or lots of wood; rather, the consequences of their perspective include actions that are incompatible with the actions that are consequences of the our perspective. On this line of reasoning Wittgenstein would reply to Boghossian: 'you are right, the Odd Woodsellers do mean different things by "a lot of wood" and "a little wood", but this does not remove the tension between their judgments and actions and ours.'

Another response – less Wittgensteinian – might be to insist that Boghossian's distinguishing between two meanings of say "a lot of wood" does not get rid of the disagreement. Assume we say (I) '(Pile) A is a little wood' and the Azande say (II) 'A is a lot of wood.' That surely looks like a disagreement. But if we mean different things by 'little wood' and 'a lot of wood', the disagreement seems to disappear. (I) might then turn out to mean (I') "If one goes by area covered, A is a little wood", and (II) might become (II') "If one goes by the number of logs, A is a lot of wood." And yet, does this really remove the tension? Nelson Goodman (Goodman 1978, 114–115) suggests that the answer must be negative: in replacing (I) with (I') and (II) with (II') we have stripped away the speakers' commitments to claims about an amount of wood. And we have replaced these commitments with commitments about conditionals. To put the commitment back in, we have to add "and this is the correct way" to (I') and (II') respectively. And then disagreement is back.

6 Conclusions

I have tried to make plausible the following claims: §608–612 do not speak in favour of MAR; *On Certainty* introduces various relativistic themes: Relativism of Distance; antirelativism as the natural attitude in the case of certain challenges to current science; and Particularist Relativism. Boghossian and Wittgenstein conceptualize epistemic systems in rather different ways. These differences find expression in their different views on three test cases. In these cases Wittgensteinian challenges to Boghossian seem promising.

Acknowledgements: For comments on a first draft and constructive questions after my talk, I am grateful to Paul Boghossian, Robin McKenna and Martha Rössler. Work on this paper was supported by the ERC Advanced Grant 339382 "The Emergence of Relativism – Historical, Philosophical and Sociological Perspectives".

References

Anscombe, Elizabeth (1976): "The Question of Linguistic Idealism". In: *Acta Philosophica Fennica* 27, 188–215.
Bellarmine, Robert (1615): "Letter to Foscari", http://www.historyguide.org/ earlymod/foscarini.html, accessed February 18th, 2016.
Boghossian, Paul (2006): *Fear of Knowledge. Against Relativism and Constructivism*, Oxford: Oxford University Press.
Goodman, Nelson (1978): *Ways of Worldmaking*. Indianapolis: Hackett.
Strawson, Peter (1985): *Skepticism and Naturalism: Some Varieties; The Woodbridge Lectures 1983*. London: Methuen.
Williams, Bernard (1981): "The Truth in Relativism". In: Williams, Bernard: *Moral Luck*. Cambridge: Cambridge University Press, 132–143.
Williams, Michael (1988): "Epistemological Realism and the Basis of Scepticism". In: *Mind* 97, 415–439.
Wittgenstein, Ludwig (1953): *Philosophical Investigations*. Oxford: Blackwell. [PI]
Wittgenstein, Ludwig (1969): *On Certainty*. Oxford: Blackwell. [OC]
Wittgenstein, Ludwig (1976): *Wittgenstein's Lectures on the Foundations of Mathematics, Cambridge 1939*. Edited by Cora Diamond. Chicago: Chicago University Press. [LFM]
Wittgenstein, Ludwig (1978): *Remarks on the Foundations of Mathematics*. 3rd ed. Oxford: Blackwell. [RFM]
Wong, David (2006): *Natural Moralities*. Oxford: Oxford University Press.

Danièle Moyal-Sharrock
Fighting Relativism: Wittgenstein and Kuhn

Abstract: As Ilham Dilman puts it: 'language is the source of the system we find in nature'. There is no *conception* of reality independent of language. There are at least three problems with this – Kuhn's and Wittgenstein's – way of thinking: (1) the problem of incommensurability; (2) the problem of idealism – in the case of Kuhn and Wittgenstein, a *linguistic* idealism; (3) the problem of conceptual relativism. In this paper, I argue that 'incommensurability' is a non-problem. I then defend Kuhn and Wittgenstein against the charge of linguistic idealism by showing that and how, on their view, our concepts attach to the world. Finally, I deflate the charge of conceptual relativism by arguing that although they reject the existence of an objective basis lying outside all human conceptual frameworks and world-pictures, neither Wittgenstein nor Kuhn endorses an indiscriminate acceptance of all conceptual schemes. In conclusion, however, we shall see that only Wittgenstein finds the stopping-place of relativism – in his *naturalism*.

Keywords: Wittgenstein, Kuhn, incommensurability, idealism, relativism

Wittgenstein and Kuhn[1] believed there are no joints already in the world;[2] but that we, human beings, make them up. As Wittgenstein writes: "One thinks that one is tracing the outline of a thing's nature over and over again, and one is merely tracing round the frame through which we look at it" (PI §114). This, however, is not to say that the world is an invention or construction of the creatures that inhabit it, but that languages – not the world – are responsible for the frame: our concepts: "Creatures born into [the world] must take it as they find it", writes Kuhn, "it is entirely solid: not in the least respectful of an observ-

---

[1] I will be concerned only with the later Wittgenstein; as for Kuhn, I have made no effort in this paper to keep track of the changes in his thought, helping myself simply to what I considered he did best. Alexander Bird notes that Kuhn mentions Wittgenstein just twice in his writings (Kuhn 1996, 44f; Kuhn 1977, 121), but that he may well have absorbed much Wittgenstein indirectly from discussions with Stanley Cavell at Berkeley (Bird 2000, 295n11).
[2] No attempt was made in this paper to define or distinguish the terms 'world', 'reality' and 'nature' used by philosophers quoted in the paper to refer, more or less metaphorically, to unconceptualized or raw reality – or what Wittgenstein refers to as the 'reality lying behind the notation' (PI § 562). My use of these terms usually follows theirs but I have also tried to navigate as best I could to avoid confusion (1) with the sense of 'reality' as comprising and often constituted by our conceptual constructions; and (2) with the sense of 'nature' about which our accounts or conceptualisation would sound too close to those of a botanist or zoologist.

DOI 10.1515/9783110524055-016

er's wishes and desires; quite capable of providing decisive evidence against invented hypotheses which fail to match its behaviour". There *is* a language-independent world; it is the world about which we speak; the world our languages cut up. What there is not is a *conception* of the world independent of language; and inasmuch as there are different languages, there will be different conceptions of the world: "languages cut up the world in different ways" (Kuhn 2000, 164).

Having eliminated from our concern the extreme or absolute idealism which takes the world itself to be a human creation, we can focus on the kind of idealism which *should* concern us: that which results from the claim that our language does not follow, or attempt to follow, an existing, though inconspicuous, outline in the world which it is science's business to render more conspicuous; language is itself responsible for the outline. There are at least three problems with this way of thinking:

> 1. If our accounts of the world are relative to the language in which they are couched, how do different linguistic communities understand each other's respective accounts? The problem here is that allegedly resulting from *incommensurability*;
>
> 2. If our accounts of the world are nothing but linguistic projections, how do they attach to the world at all? This is the problem of *idealism* – in the case of Kuhn and Wittgenstein, it would be an "idealism with a linguistic turn" or what has been called *linguistic* idealism;
>
> 3. If there is no neutral, language-independent way of depicting the world, to which our linguistic accounts can refer or appeal to for correction or guidance, *anything goes* – however a particular culture sees fit to describe the world cannot be gainsaid, becomes a benchmark in its own right. There will be as many so-called 'objective' accounts as there are languages. And here we face the problem of *conceptual relativism*.

I'll address these problems in turn.

1 Incommensurability, not Incommunicability

For Kuhn and Wittgenstein, there is no objectivity in the Nagelian sense – that is, no "view from nowhere". For a view from nowhere requires the absence of a place from which to view, and without a place, there can be no viewer either, and thus no *view*. This isn't to say there would be nothing there, but that it cannot be called a view, a perspective. Removing the perspective is precisely the point of Nagel's image, for a *perceived* reality is necessarily a distorted reality, and the ensuing account of reality will be equally distorted, or subjective. So that, in their quest for an objective basis for knowledge, philosophers have sought to eliminate not so much the viewer, for that would defeat the epistemic enterprise altogether, but the viewer's input into the account: they have sought as impersonal an account as possible. This has meant looking for a basic language or 'brute data vocabulary' consisting of words attached to the world in ways that are unproblematic and independent of theory – a language which would provide a 'common measure' or neutral, mind-independent description of the world against which to evaluate our scientific, mind-dependent descriptions and theories. For both Kuhn and Wittgenstein, this philosophers' quest for such a language is of no avail.[3] As Kuhn writes:

> The heavens of the Greeks were irreducibly different from ours. [...] the difference is rooted in conceptual vocabulary. [It cannot] be bridged by description in a brute data, behavioural vocabulary. [...] No more in the natural than in the human sciences is there some neutral, culture-independent, set of categories within which the population – whether of objects or of actions – can be described. (Kuhn 2000, 220; see also 162)

What we are left with then is a view, necessarily, from somewhere. And that somewhere, for linguistic creatures, is language. As Putnam says: "We have no other place to stand but within our own language" (Putnam 1995, 54); and in Kuhn's words: "we have no access to a neutral sublinguistic means of reporting" (Kuhn 2000, 164). The essential theory-ladenness of language,[4] Kuhn argues, is responsible for incommensurability; that is: for the absence of a common, neutral language in which our theories could be fully expressed, and which could therefore be used in a point-by-point comparison between them (Kuhn 2000, 189). This, however, does not imply that different languages are *utterly* impenetrable to each other; nor does it imply that they are incomparable[5] or have noth-

---

3 As Norman Malcolm writes: "To suppose that there is an 'objective basis' in terms of which one language-game could be judged to be more adequate or more 'true' than the other, is to suppose that the true concept of pain is stowed away somewhere like the standard meter, available for comparison when differences arise between merely human concepts. But we may be certain that there are no principles of justification which lie outside of all human conceptual frameworks and world-pictures." (Malcolm 1982, 99)
4 Wittgenstein would not speak of theory-ladenness, but he views language as necessarily conditioned by, and embedded in, our forms of life; they are therefore, one could say "reality-soaked" (on this, see Moyal-Sharrock 2016). I am not concerned in this paper with the conceptuality of *perception*. Suffice it to say that for Kuhn, there is no access to a nonconceptualized world; even observation is theory-laden. Wittgenstein would not go that far: animals and pre-linguistic children are concept-free (e.g., "As children we learn concepts and what one does with them simultaneously" (LWPP II 43). Kuhn can go this far in that he believes a prelinguistic "mental module" or "taxonomic module" is possessed also by animals (Kuhn 2000, 93). This brings Kuhn much closer to Kant than Wittgenstein could ever be.
5 Kuhn repeatedly corrects his readers' assumption that when he spoke of theories as incommensurable he meant that they could not be compared (e.g. Kuhn 2000, 189).

ing at all in common. The one thing they do *not* have in common is a neutral language from which they might all have emerged or to which they might all refer.[6]

Incommensurability precludes total translatability, but that does not prevent intelligibility, communication, comparability or learnability. Anything lost in translation can be approximated via interpretation, hermeneutics or paraphrase (Kuhn 2000, 45); indeed "anything that can be said in one language can, with imagination and effort, be *understood* by a speaker of another" (Kuhn 2000, 61). So Kuhn does not think that incommensurability is "ever total or beyond recourse" (Kuhn 2000, 124); there *is* communication between schemes – certainly, sufficient communication for a member of one scheme to realize *that* the other scheme is different and, often, precisely *where*. We *can* know that the heavens of the Greeks were irreducibly different from ours, in the same way we know that the ancient Greek concept of happiness (*eudaimonia*) was different from ours; we can know this because although their concepts of the heavens and of happiness "cut across ours", as Wittgenstein would put it (Z §379), the rest of the language is sufficiently transparent, sufficiently close to ours, for us to get the drift. In comparative judgments, notes Kuhn, shared beliefs serve as a platform from which unshared or alien beliefs can be distinguished and evaluated (see Kuhn 2000, 96), though not necessarily *thoroughly* understood or translatable.

For Kuhn, then, two scientific systems are neither wholly opaque, nor fully translatable into one another. As to Wittgenstein, his holding that there are different conceptions of reality in different languages and cultures does not prevent him from asserting that we can and do imaginatively or empathically enter into alien practices, and what is more, that we can see *sense* in them, even where we could hardly see *ourselves* in them (e.g. OC §594f; Z §368f; §383–390). On Kuhn and Wittgenstein's view, then, although our conceptual schemes are internally related to our languages, there is sufficient overlap between languages to allow for non-trivial communication, comparison and understanding (see OC §524). But if what is sought is something like a Gadamerian 'fusion of horizons', then more is needed; according to both Kuhn and Wittgenstein, something like a 'conversion' must be effected – a conversion, in that a whole world picture would have to be assimilated (OC §92; Kuhn 1996, 151; Kuhn 2000, 175), and for that to occur, there must be *participation* in the *practice* or *practices* of the other (OC §315; Kuhn 2000, 54). So that when Wittgenstein writes, in *On Certainty*, that in combatting the man who "instead of the physicist" consults an oracle, he

---

6 Of course, many languages (most European and many Asian ones) may have derived from a common Indo-European one, but the latter isn't a *neutral* language.

would give reasons as far as they go, but that "[a]t the end of reasons comes *persuasion*" (OC §612), there is no suggestion here of an abandonment of position or communication, but of a maintenance of position in another, more fundamental, mode of communication.

2 No Linguistic Idealism

Now that we have ascertained the possibility of communication across conceptual schemes, we are better equipped to ward off conceptual relativism. But first we should try and clarify Wittgenstein and Kuhn's view of the relationship between world and language. For both thinkers, there is no such thing in nature as an outline, a system or a concept; nature is conceptually unmarked; nature simply *is*. The system does not reside in the nature of things, writes Wittgenstein (Z §357). It is we who, with our language, cut paths or inroads of salience and understanding – concepts – that allow us to harness the wild, the contingent, in ways that make and govern sense for us. Wittgenstein takes this harnessing to be not metaphysical, but grammatical.[7] At the *conceptual* basis of our confrontation with experience are not bare particulars, but grammar: "grammar is a preparation for description" (MWL 72), and it is *grammar* that tells us what *kind* of object anything is (PI §373). *As linguistic beings*, we come to experience and grapple the world *always already* with language, and there is no getting out of language (grammar) to compare or measure our system/outline/beliefs against bare particulars.

Kuhn believed that "a lexical taxonomy of some sort must be in place before description of the world can begin" (Kuhn 2000, 92), and it is this 'lexicon' which – like Kantian categories, though not fixed – constrains any description of experience. He rejects the idea that we attach or learn to attach scientific concepts to the world by strict correspondence, and claims that *paradigms* or *exemplars* are determined by our drawing *similarities* (or resemblances) and *patterns* from concrete examples that we are exposed to.[8]

---

[7] Grammatical *or* conceptual. Though these are not synonymous, Wittgenstein often uses them interchangeably to refer to our modes of classification, and I shall also do so here. On Wittgenstein's connected use of grammar and concepts, see (Moyal-Sharrock 2013).

[8] There is a possible debt here to *family resemblance*, but the reference to 'patterns' is not likely to have been inspired by Wittgenstein, though he, too, spoke of *patterns of experience* – a term he used with specific regard to psychological concepts (cf. LWPP I, 211; LWPP II, 42).

So that, for both thinkers, it is *what we say* counts as 'real' or 'similar' and what does not that determines whether the experience is 'real' or 'illusory'; 'similar' or 'different'.[9] The multifarious distinctions we make between what is real and what is not; what is similar and what is not; the systems of classification that enable us to speak of empirical reality in terms of 'real' or 'illusory', 'good' or 'bad', 'same' or 'different', 'high' or 'low', 'true' or 'false', *belong to language* (grammar), not to the world. It is our language, then, that determines the world's conceptual outline. But "[i]s there some reality lying behind the notation, which shapes its grammar?" (PI §562), asks Wittgenstein. And his answer is: yes.

3 How Nature makes Herself audible

Granted, what we make of the solid, biological niche we find ourselves in, is internal to our language; as soon as we begin to reflect on the world as we find it, it becomes a world of *our making*; however, this conceptual outline is not disconnected from the world. Language does not operate in a vacuum. The empirical world has its word to say; it is not a silent partner:

> but has nature nothing to say here? Indeed she has – but she makes herself audible in another way. "You'll surely run up against existence and non-existence somewhere!" But that means against facts, not concepts. (Z §364)

Facts, not concepts, he stresses.[10] The formation of our concepts must be impacted by existence, by nature, but this impact does not come in the form of *concepts* in nature (such as 'gravity'); it comes in the form of *facts* of nature:

> What we have to mention in order to explain the significance, I mean the importance, of a concept, are often extremely general facts of nature: such facts as are hardly ever mentioned because of their great generality. (PI 56 – bottom note)

---

9 Ilham Dilman writes: 'Think of the similarity we may find between a deep well and a deep sorrow. Is it not clearer here that were it not for our language we would not find a similarity here? (Dilam 2002, 71)

10 Suggesting he knows full well that the problem is that empiricists confuse facts and concepts, and so take sentences like 'The earth is a planet' to express a fact or an empirical proposition. This confusion between the empirical and the formal (or grammatical) is at the heart of what both Wittgenstein and Kuhn are combating.

"Indeed, doesn't it seem obvious that the possibility of a language-game is conditioned by certain facts?" (OC §617), that "very general facts of nature" are "favourable" to the formation of certain concepts (Z §352)?[11] Facts such as human beings experience pain; have the visual apparatus they do; cannot fly unaided; or that mountains don't sprout up in half an hour and apples fall from trees. His acknowledgement of such 'basic facts' – the "basic worldly dough", as Paul Boghossian calls it, on which our classifications can get to work – estranges the later Wittgenstein from fact-constructivism.[12] For Wittgenstein, such basic contingent facts inform our classifications – and were those facts different, so would our concepts be:

> It is a fact of experience that human beings alter their concepts, exchange them for others when they learn new facts; when in this way what was formerly important to them becomes unimportant, and *vice versa*. (Z §352)[13]

While this acknowledgement of the rootedness of our concepts in the world puts Wittgenstein outside the idealist camp, it does not thereby place him in the Realist camp (realist, here, with a capital 'R'). Our conceptualization of the world is made, not found, and so the 'realism' that is operative here cannot be of a strict correspondence kind.[14] The difference is subtle, but crucial. Wittgenstein writes: "The rule we lay down is the one most strongly suggested by the facts of experience" (AWL 84) – *suggested, not dictated*; and so the autonomy of grammar is, in spite of nature's input, maintained: although what gives a rule its importance are the facts of daily experience a "rule *qua* rule is detached; it stands as it were alone in its glory" (RFM §357). Though nature provides the basic dough, it is we

---

11 Wittgenstein even speaks here of correspondence – "Indeed the correspondence [*Entsprechung*] between our grammar and general (seldom mentioned) facts of nature does concern us" (RPP I, 46) – however, as all his other formulations and descriptions make clear, not in the sense of a strict or veridical correspondence.

12 Or indeed from nominalism; see Hacking: "The realist, in the sense that matters here, may well echo the first half of Wittgenstein's first sentence in the *Tractatus:* 'The world is made up of facts'. The nominalist retorts that we have a good deal to do with organizing what we call a fact. The world of nature does not just come with a totality of facts; rather it is we who organize the world into facts." (Hacking 1999, 174)

13 This does not mean that *all* our concepts are susceptible of change: our *basic* concepts are unalterable: 'Sometimes it happens that we later introduce a new concept that is more practical for us. – But that will only happen in very definite and small areas, and it presupposes that most concepts remain unaltered. / Could a legislator abolish the concept of pain? / The basic concepts are interwoven so closely with what is most fundamental in our way of living that they are therefore unassailable.' (LWPP II 43–44).

14 "Not empiricism and yet realism in philosophy, that is the hardest thing" (RFM VI, §23).

who cut it up into concepts; we are not *answerable* to nature for these concepts but to ourselves, to our epistemic endeavours and successes. A concept may be inadequate – it may fail to cohere with our other concepts or fail to enable the desired predictions – and we may need to change it. Gravity is not something we have observed; it is a concept we have formulated in an effort to order specific empirical events – events that we *have* observed; and the concept of 'gravity' is not *internally* linked to such events: we may find that what we have defined as 'gravity' is better defined by a new concept. To think that this inadequacy is due merely to our epistemic deficiency is to think that the right concepts are in nature, waiting to be discovered; but Kuhn and Wittgenstein would reply that nature has no concepts for nature has no language. Concepts are linguistic constructs and, as such, internal to language. Though nature has its impact, it is through *our* rules and *our* concepts that she "makes herself audible".[15]

We don't read off our concepts from nature, but this doesn't mean that these have no basis at all in nature. Only, nature's connection to our concepts is not to be thought of in terms of correspondence, isomorphism, derivation, inference, or justification: "What is laid down depends on facts, *but is not made true or false by them*" (AWL 162, my emphasis). For, what is laid down – our grammar – is not susceptible of truth or falsity; it is a way of classifying reality, not a truth-evaluable description of it. There is no truthful correspondence between our concepts and the world, but there is a live connection: "Would it be correct to say our concepts reflect our life? They stand in the middle of it." (LWPP II, 72)

Our concepts are immersed in our life, intertwined with it in a dynamic interaction: the fabric of our life provides the milieu in which our concepts are formed; in turn, our concepts order the fabric of life. And so the only sense we *find* in nature is the sense we *put* in nature, although that sense is necessarily influenced by that nature.

Kuhn, like Wittgenstein, sees a give-and-take between our paradigms and the world; or what he calls an "accommodation of language and experience" (Kuhn 2000, 207), so that the changes or

> alterations in the way scientific terms attach to nature are not [...] purely formal or purely linguistic. On the contrary, they come about in response to *pressures* generated by observation or experiment, and they result in more effective ways of dealing with some aspects of some natural phenomena (Kuhn 2000, 204; my emphasis).

---

[15] "[...] we lay down the rule, we hold the measuring-rod: The certainty with which I call the colour "red" is the rigidity of my measuring-rod, it is the rigidity from which I start" (RFM § 329).

There is then nothing idealistic in saying that our account of reality is language-dependent because 1) it leaves room for a language-*in*dependent reality – that about which we speak and think; and 2) the fact that our concepts (our grammar) are not *veridically grounded* in experience does not mean that they are totally divorced from or impervious to it. Our concepts are not *empty*, but how they are informed by the world is not how realists and empiricists think they are; that is, they are not rationally linked to a veridical, absolute account, though they may be rooted, and certainly they have their life, in the natural conditions in which human beings are ensconced. The difficulty in making that difference clear is, I think, encapsulated in this sentence of Wittgenstein's: "Not empiricism and yet realism in philosophy, that is the hardest thing" (RFM VI, 23, 325). The hardest thing for a philosopher is to show that not everything that is of the world, and not everything that is *experienced*, is *empirical*.

It is our concepts, our grammar, that lie at the foundation of knowledge, but these are impacted by what exists outside language. Kuhn and Wittgenstein share this view, and this is what prevents them from being any kind of idealist. We have seen that the view that our conceptual schemes are embedded in language neither implies that reality is our construct nor that we are not in touch with reality, but does it preclude objectivity? Are we doomed to conceptual relativism? I think not.

4 No Conceptual Relativism

The tendency is to think that if there is no theory-free account of reality in which our various accounts are anchored and to which they might appeal for comparison, justification or verification, any evaluation of schemes can only ever involve a comparison between schemes. Our evolving schemes would not therefore take us closer to the truth; they would simply be *other* schemes, other world-pictures (see Kuhn 1996, 118). If relativism is defined as

(1) the view that there are no absolute truths about the world,

then Kuhn and Wittgenstein *are* relativists – the notion of 'absolute truths' being decisive.[16] Both reject the existence of a language-independent benchmark or

---

[16] Indeed, Kuhn does not believe that scientific progress is truth-related (unless truth be taken intra-theoretically); that we can compare theories as statements about 'what is really there' (Kuhn 2000, 159), but this absence of *truth* as a goal, does not mean that science has no goal at all, and therefore that any theory is as good as another: Kuhn sees the progress of science

'true' concepts towards which our ordinary concepts are thought to strive.[17] But relativism can also be defined as

(2) the claim that any theory is as true/acceptable/good as the other; or
(3) the claim that there is no objective, universal basis to knowledge claims.

I will argue that while neither Wittgenstein nor Kuhn can be charged with (2), only Wittgenstein can steer clear of (3); on his view, there *is* a universally objective basis to knowledge claims – where 'universally' means 'humanly', not 'super-humanly'; not across 'all possible worlds', but across all forms of human life.

4.1 Kuhn and Wittgenstein Against Theory Equivalence

Neither Wittgenstein nor Kuhn believes that any theory is as true/acceptable/ good as the other. As we have seen, Kuhn thinks that incommensurability does not prevent intelligibility, but nor does intelligibility entail acceptability: semantic understanding does not eliminate the clash between paradigms. For Kuhn, we cannot accept an alien point of view as true, but only appreciate it.[18] Kuhn has no problem applying the label 'truth' intra-theoretically; he agrees

---

in evolutionary and pragmatic terms. For Kuhn, science is a cognitive empirical investigation of nature that exhibits a unique sort of progress – that is, it does not progress towards some goal (truth), but instead progresses away from its primitive, earlier stages (cf. Bird 2000, 27). Kuhn defined this progress as increasing fitness over time, including the fitness of the exemplars themselves, where fitness means consonance with the state of the art as defined by the scientific community, not directly to reality itself (cf. Nickles 2003, 169). Not truth, but 'accuracy, precision, scope, simplicity, fruitfulness, consistency, and so on, simply *are* the criteria which puzzle solvers must weigh in deciding whether or not a given puzzle about the match between phenomena and belief has been solved' (Kuhn 2000, 251).

17 Kuhn and Wittgenstein, in their rejection of a human-independent objective description of the world, explicitly and implicitly hold that correspondence and causal theories of truth are not valid. Kuhn: '… what is fundamentally at stake is rather the correspondence theory of truth, the notion that the goal, when evaluating scientific laws or theories, is to determine whether or not they correspond to an external, mind-independent world. It is that notion, whether in an absolute or probabilistic form, that I'm persuaded must vanish together with foundationalism. What replaces it will still require a strong conception of truth, but not, except in the most trivial sense, correspondence truth.' (Kuhn 2000, 95)

18 Sharrock and Read clarify this aspect of Kuhn and Peter Winch's position, which makes them, they write, "the true 'anti-Relativists'" (as we shall see, Wittgenstein can be added to the picture): "Far from arguing that we have to accept that the convictions of the pre-Copernicans or those of believers in magic are true, Kuhn is in fact arguing that we *cannot possibly* make their way of thinking our own. [...] Kuhn and Winch aspire to present the point of view

with Popper that each historical theory was believed true in its time but later abandoned as false, and that the later theory was the better of the two 'as a tool for the practice of normal science': "One scientific theory is not as good as another for doing what scientists normally do. In that sense, I am not a relativist" (Kuhn 2000, 160).

Similarly, although Wittgenstein's appreciation of other cultures is deep (as evidenced in his *Remarks on Frazer*), his *inability* – and by implication ours – to treat some beliefs as right or acceptable and some behaviours as human or normal is also clear. In *On Certainty*, he often calls people who do not share our basic certainties "mad" or "demented"(OC §217, §420; §155): "If someone said to me that he doubted whether he had a body, I should take him to be a half-wit" (OC §257); and that includes philosophers: "If Moore were to pronounce the opposite of those propositions which he declares certain, we should not just not share his opinion: we should regard him as demented" (OC §155). And in the following passage, theory equivalence is ruled out:

> We all believe that it isn't possible to get to the moon; but there might be people who believe that that is possible and that it sometimes happens. We say: these people do not know a lot that we know. And, let them be never so sure of their belief – they are wrong and we know it. If we compare our system of knowledge with theirs then theirs is evidently the poorer one by far. (OC §286)[19]

As to there being an objective, universal basis to knowledge claims, as earlier suggested, where objectivity is defined in absolutist, human-independent terms, Kuhn and Wittgenstein would both have to be seen as relativists. But on a more down-to-earth version of objectivity – which would be *objectivity, humanly speaking*[20] – Wittgenstein and Kuhn would be deemed relativists only if they denied the existence of a foundation upon which all *human* knowledge logically rests. Here, Kuhn parts company with Wittgenstein in that he considers objectivity to be culture-linked.

---

of 'the Other' to us in such a way that we can understand how that point of view could be compelling to them, how, *in those same circumstances and under those conditions*, we ourselves would have thought ... in exactly those same ways – and how, in the circumstances in which we actually are, those other/older ideas *are complete non-starters*." (Sharrock/Read 2002, 161)
19 Wittgenstein wrote this fifteen years before Armstrong set foot on the moon.
20 Putnam uses this phrase, which he attributes to David Wiggins (Putnam 1981, 55).

4.2 Wittgenstein: the Human Form of Life as the Stopping-place of Relativism

Although Kuhn comes very close to Kant's transcendentalism when he speaks of the shared taxonomic categories that must be in place before description of the world can begin as "a particular operating mode of a mental module prerequisite to having beliefs, a mode that at once supplies and bounds the set of beliefs it is possible to conceive"; taking some such taxonomic module to be prelinguistic and possessed by animals (Kuhn 2000, 94), he makes clear that the position he is developing is an evolutionary one; his, as he writes, is "a sort of post-Darwinian Kantianism", with the difference that "lexical categories, unlike their Kantian forebears, can and do change, both with time and with the passage from one community to another", with their lexical structures overlapping in major ways so as to enable communication between communities (Kuhn 2000, 104). So that Kuhnian categories differ from Kantian categories in that they are lexical and in that they are not fixed: "I am a Kantian with movable categories" (Kuhn 2000, 264), he writes.

As for Wittgenstein, he speaks in *On Certainty* of the bedrock of our thoughts as consisting "partly of sand, which now in one place now in another gets washed away, or deposited", but also "partly of hard rock subject to *no alteration*" (OC §99; my emphasis). This means that some of our basic certainties "underlie *all* questions and *all* thinking" (OC §415; my emphasis); such certainties as "I have a body", "The world exists" or "Human beings express feelings" are examples. So that were we to meet a tribe of people brought up from early youth to give no expression of feeling of any kind, we could not see these people as human:

> "These men would have nothing human about them." Why? – We could not possibly make ourselves understood to them. Not even as we can to a dog. We could not find our feet with them. (Z §390)

That humans express feeling is part of the 'substratum' of human thought (OC §161); it is one of those "universal certainties"[21], as I have called them, that logically or grammatically underpin anything any normal human being

---

[21] See (Moyal-Sharrock 2007, chapter 7). It is worth reminding that by "universal" I mean "across the human world", not across "all possible worlds".

can say or think about her peers.²² Universal certainties are conditioned by *universally basic* facts of nature. Such facts importantly include what Wittgenstein calls "the common behaviour of mankind"; e.g. we are creatures who are born and will die; have the potential of evolving from infanthood to adulthood; require nourishment, air, sleep; inhabit and interact in a world peopled by other beings; (excepting pathological cases) acquire and use language, have and express feelings and emotions.²³ These facts logically condition the concepts or grammar of all normal human beings. Indeed, Wittgenstein writes that this "common behaviour of mankind is the system of reference by means of which we interpret an unknown language" (PI §206) – by which he means any *human* language. What we have here, then, is the system of reference that marks the stopping-place of relativism.

Whereas difference, pluralism, and disagreement thrive in *the various forms of human life*, there is no pluralism, but only unquestionable unity as regards our *one human form of life*.²⁴ It is our universally-shared form of life that informs Wittgenstein's realism by constituting the system of reference which logically underpins any meaningful account of ourselves and our world. It logically (grammatically) rules out a thoroughgoing relativism by ensuring that there are some things about which we, humans, cannot disagree if we are to make sense. To use one of Wittgenstein's examples: we cannot cut off someone's head and expect them to go on living (OC §274) – not in 'real life' anyway. And the fact that we can conceive of it – say, in fictional contexts, or in our magical or religious forms of human life – does not make it a real possibility in our human form

---

22 Universal certainties are *universally grammatical*; they "underlie *all* questions and *all* thinking" (OC § 415; my emphasis). For a discussion of the grammatical nature of Wittgensteinian certainty, see (Moyal-Sharrock 2007, Chapter 4).
23 See Carpendale & Lewis: "It might seem that if we endorse the Wittgensteinian idea that children learn about the mental world through learning how to express their feelings, plans, and goals, etc. in language, and learning the criteria for the third person use of various psychological terms, then we must endorse an enculturation position in which mentalistic concepts are imported from the social world to the individual. As mentioned above, this is one interpretation of Wittgenstein and it implies a cultural relativism, by which children would just learn the mental concepts used in their particular culture. However, we do not endorse this interpretation for two reasons. First, at the basic level of social understanding (e.g., seeing, looking, intentions, desires and beliefs) children's understanding is built onto shared practices that we expect would be common across cultures because these are common aspects of human experience [...]. This does not rule out that there may be cross-cultural variability, such as in complex emotions." (Carpendale/Lewis 2004, 20)
24 For a discussion of the difference, see (Moyal-Sharrock 2015).

of life. A brief look at the *Remarks on Frazer's Golden Bough* will help illustrate this point.

As is clear from the *Remarks*, Wittgenstein is a relativist as far as religion and magic are concerned, but not where science or knowledge are concerned. Though a tribe's 'magic' may seem to contradict our universal certainties, Wittgenstein is clear that it does not *in fact* do so:[25]

> The same savage, who stabs the picture of his enemy apparently in order to kill him, *really* builds his hut out of wood and carves his arrow skilfully and not in effigy. (RFGB 125; my italics)

That is, he knows what *really* will kill his enemy, and what will act as protection in case that fails: a skilfully carved arrow and a hut built out of wood (RFGB 125). Contrary to what Frazer alleges, the "savages" do not have "a completely false (even insane) idea of the course of nature ... Only their *magic* is different" (RFGB 141).

Having denounced Frazer's interpretation of magic as "essentially false physics" (RFGB 129), Wittgenstein wants to underline that magic cohabits with science in the lives of the savages (as it does in twentieth century societies) without their being confused about the two. Indeed, Frazer's belief that they confuse the two makes him, writes Wittgenstein, "much more savage than most of his savages, for they are not as far removed from the understanding of a spiritual matter as a twentieth-century Englishman" (RFGB 131):

> The nonsense here is that Frazer represents these people as if they had a completely false (even insane) idea of the course of nature, whereas they only possess a peculiar interpretation of the phenomena. That is, if they were to write it down, their knowledge of nature would not differ *fundamentally* from ours. Only their *magic* is different. (RFGB 141)

To Wittgenstein's consternation, "Frazer would be capable of believing that a savage dies because of an error" (RFGB 131). That is to say, Frazer would be capable of believing that, say, the women in the Trobriand Islands called *Yoyova* or flying witches, who are believed to have the capacity to fly, *really* believe they can fly. But of course they don't believe this, and that is why they have fireflies do it for them.[26] Were a *Yoyova* to actually attempt to fly off a cliff, it wouldn't be the savage in her but the deluded person who acted: her attempting

---

[25] "... it belongs to the logic of our scientific investigations that certain things are *in deed* not doubted" (OC § 342).
[26] Malinowski in (Young 1979, 207).

to fly off a cliff would not be an error but a pathological act. What Wittgenstein says of the Rain King in the following passage also applies to the flying witch:

> It is, of course, not so that the people believe that the ruler has these powers, *and the ruler knows very well that he doesn't have them, or can only fail to know if he is an imbecile or a fool.* But the notion of his power is, of course, adapted in such a way that it can harmonize with experience – the people's as well as his own. That some hypocrisy thereby plays a role is true only insofar as it generally lies close at hand with most things people do. (RFGB 139; my emphasis)

Some hypocrisy but mostly, as he will say, symbolism. In any case, Wittgenstein is clear that there is no confusion between ritual and scientific belief. As regards the Rain-King in Africa to whom the people pray for rain when the rainy period comes, he writes: "But surely that means that they do not really believe that he can make it rain, otherwise they would do it in the dry periods of the year" (RFGB 137).

Their magic notwithstanding, the "savages" share our basic acceptance of the "very general facts of nature" and the "common behaviour of mankind". When it comes to their basic beliefs and ordinary ways of acting, their magic does not trump their science, but vice-versa: "If the adoption of a child proceeds in such a way that the mother draws it from under her clothes, it is surely insane to believe that an *error* is present and that she believes she has given birth to the child." (RFGB 125) The mother cannot be in error because, magical rituals notwithstanding, she never believed she was in fact giving birth to the child. The adoption ritual is something she may believe *in*, not something she believes *that*. Or better, it is simply something symbolic.[27] As Wittgenstein insists, magic is not based on opinion but on symbolism.[28]

The "savages" have science as well as magic, as do we.[29] It is not their magic that we should compare with our science, but their science that we should com-

---

[27] Wittgenstein also sees the purpose of some ritualistic action as expressivist: "Burning in effigy. Kissing the picture of one's beloved. That is *obviously not* based on the belief that it will have some specific effect on the object which the picture represents. It aims at satisfaction and achieves it. Or rather: it *aims* at nothing at all; we just behave this way and then we feel satisfied." (RFGB 123)
[28] "... the characteristic feature of ritualistic action is not at all a view, an opinion' (RFGB 129); 'magic is always based on the idea of symbolism" (RFGB 125).
[29] "I should like to say: nothing shows our kinship to those savages better than the fact that Frazer has on hand a word as familiar to himself and to us as 'ghost' or 'shade' in order to describe the views of these people. ... much too little is made of the fact that we count the words 'soul' and 'spirit' as part of our educated vocabulary. Compared with this, the fact that we do not believe that our soul eats and drinks is a trifling matter." (RFGB 133)

pare with our science (e. g. how they build their huts and carve their arrows) and, here, there is a better or worse way of doing things that they could learn from us, or us from them.[30] There is then only one benchmark when it comes to science. Wittgenstein would share Kuhn's anti-relativistic view of scientific progress – progress not in terms of truth but in evolutionary and pragmatic terms – as increasing fitness over time, where fitness means consonance with the state of the art as defined by the global scientific community.

The point is that magic – when it does not slide into madness – never overrides science. What ritual calls for is one thing – it has its role and its impact – but it does not trump the universal bedrock of human thought. Such certainties as "Human beings can't fly unaided" or "Human beings feel and express pain" (pathologies excepted) are part of the objective, universal foundation of knowledge claims – that to which Wittgenstein refers when, to the question "Could a legislator abolish the concept of pain?", he replies: "The basic concepts are interwoven so closely with what is most fundamental in our way of living that they are therefore unassailable".

5 Objectivity, humanly speaking

Gertrude Conway calls Wittgenstein's position an *objectivism without absolutism:* the absence of absolutism doesn't mean that objectivity is lost, but that it is *conditional* on our human form of life – 'species-relative', as it were (Conway 1989, 94, 141–142).[31] Yet rather than speak of Wittgenstein's notion of objectivity as 'species-relative', and given the puzzling nature of the notion of a *human or mind-independent* objectivity, I suggest we no longer think of the latter as the benchmark of objectivity and refer to it as 'absolutism', while using 'objectivity' to refer exclusively to *objectivity, humanly speaking*.

---

[30] "As simple as it sounds: the distinction between magic and science can be expressed by saying that in science there is progress, but in magic there isn't. Magic has no tendency within itself to develop." (RFGB 141).

[31] For a discussion of the nonsensicality of equating possibility with conceivability (all possible worlds), see (Moyal-Sharrock 2003). In brief, I oppose the chimera of a superhuman, supernatural, imperturbable absolute logical necessity which, by dint of being applicable to all possible worlds, makes a farce of ours – forcing us, as it does, to consider evil geniuses, brains in vats, and zombies as real possibilities in our world. Logical necessity is not less compelling or objective for being specifically human. It is *objective, humanly speaking*. And this is the only objectivity we ought to appeal to if we want to stop being philosophically distracted by zombies or, more generally speaking, 'the illusion of possibility'.

Acknowledgements: I am grateful for helpful comments from my Kirchberg audience and from participants in an Academia session. Particular thanks go to Paul Standish, John Preston, Richard Gipps and Amin Rabinia.

References

Bird, Alexander (2000): *Thomas Kuhn*. Princeton: Princeton University Press.
Carpendale, Jeremy; Lewis, Charlie (2004): "Constructing an Understanding of Mind: The Development of Children's Social Understanding within Social Interaction". In: *Behavioral & Brain Sciences* 27, 79–96.
Conway, Gertrude D. (1989): *Wittgenstein on Foundations*. New Jersey: Humanities Press International.
Dilman, Ilham (2002): *Wittgenstein's Copernican Revolution: The Question of Linguistic Idealism*. Basingstoke: Palgrave Macmillan.
Hacking, Ian (1999): *The Social Construction of What?* Cambridge: Harvard University Press.
Kuhn, Thomas (1977): *The Essential Tension: Selected Studies in Scientific Tradition and Change*. Chicago: University of Chicago Press.
Kuhn, Thomas (1996): *The Structure of Scientific Revolutions*. 3rd Edition. Chicago: University of Chicago Press.
Kuhn, Thomas (2000): *The Road since Structure: Philosophical Essays, 1970–1993*. Edited by James Conant and John Haugeland. Chicago: University of Chicago Press.
Malcolm, Norman (1982): "Wittgenstein and Idealism". In: Malcolm, Norman: *Wittgensteinian Themes: Essays 1978–1989*. Edited by Georg Henrik von Wright. Ithaca: Cornell University Press, 87–108.
Moyal-Sharrock, Danièle (2003): "Logic in Action: Wittgenstein's *Logical Pragmatism* and the Impotence of Scepticism". In: *Philosophical Investigations* 26 (2), 125–148.
Moyal-Sharrock, Danièle (2007): *Understanding Wittgenstein's On Certainty*. Basingstoke: Palgrave Macmillan.
Moyal-Sharrock, Danièle (2013): "Realism, but not Empiricism: Wittgenstein versus Searle". In: Racine, Timothy; Slaney, Kathleen (eds.): *A Wittgensteinian Perspective on the Use of Conceptual Analysis in Psychology*. Basingstoke: Palgrave Macmillan, 153–157.
Moyal-Sharrock, Danièle (2015): "Wittgenstein's Forms of Life, Patterns of Life and Ways of Living". In: *Nordic Wittgenstein Review*, Special Issue October 2015, 21–42. http://www.nordicwittgensteinreview.com/article/view/3362/pdf.
Moyal-Sharrock, Danièle (2016): "Wittgenstein, no Linguistic Idealist". In: Greve, Sebastian; Macha, Jakub (eds.): *Wittgenstein and the Creativity of Language*. Basigstoke: Palgrave Macmillan, 117–140.
Nickles, Thomas (ed.) (2003): *Thomas Kuhn*. Cambridge: Cambridge University Press.
Putnam, Hilary (1981): "Two Philosophical Perspectives". In: Putnam, Hilary: *Reason, Truth and History*. Cambridge: Cambridge University Press, 49–74.
Putnam, Hilary (1995): *Pragmatism: An Open Question*. Oxford: Blackwell.
Sharrock, Wes; Read, Rupert (2002): *Kuhn: Philosopher of Scientific Revolution*. Cambridge: Polity Press.
Wittgenstein, Ludwig (1953): *Philosophical Investigations*. Oxford: Blackwell. [PI]

Wittgenstein, Ludwig (1967): *Zettel*. Edited by Elizabeth Anscombe and Georg Henrik von Wright, translated by Elizabeth Anscombe. Berkely: University of California Press. [Z]

Wittgenstein, Ludwig (1969): *On Certainty*. Oxford: Blackwell. [OC]

Wittgenstein, Ludwig (1978): *Remarks on the Foundations of Mathematics*. 3rd ed. Oxford: Blackwell. [RFM]

Wittgenstein, Ludwig (1979): *Remarks on Frazer's Golden Bough*. Edited by Rush Rhees. Newark: Brynmill Press. [RFGB]

Wittgenstein, Ludwig (1980): *Remarks on the Philosophy of Psychology, Vol. 1*. Translated by Elizabeth Anscombe. Chicago: University of Chicago Press. [RPP I]

Wittgenstein, Ludwig (1993): *Last Writings on the Philosophy of Psychology, Vol. 2*. Edited by Heikki Nyman and Georg Henrik von Wright. London: Blackwell. [LWPP II]

Wittgenstein, Ludwig (1996): *Last Writings on the Philosophy of Psychology, Vol. 1*. Edited by Heikki Nyman and Georg Henrik von Wright, translated by C. G. Luckhardt. Chicago: University of Chicago Press. [LWPP I]

Wittgenstein, Ludwig (2001): *Wittgenstein's Lectures, Cambridge 1932–3*. Edited by Alice Ambrose. Amherst: Prometheus. [AWL]

Wittgenstein, Ludwig (2016): *Wittgenstein's Lectures 1930–33. Georg Edward Moore's Notes from Wittgenstein's Lectures*. Edited by David G. Stern, Brian Rogers and Gabriel Citron. Cambridge: Cambridge University Press. [MWL]

Young, Michael (ed.) (1979): *The Ethnography of Malinowski: The Trobriand Islands 1915–18*. London: Routledge & Kegan Paul.

Franz Ofner
Wissenschaftstheoretische Überlegungen jenseits von Realismus, Relativismus und Konstruktivismus

Abstract: My thoughts regarding the theory of science take up Josef Mitterer's non-dualizing way of speaking according to which it is not justifiable to refer to language-different objects if there are diverging or contradictory research findings. The consequence of this is that – in contrast to realistic, constructivist, and relativistic positions – we cannot differentiate between true and false descriptions. In the view of science, the question arises as to what status objects have in the context of empirical research and how research activities and descriptions of research results are interrelated. In what follows I would like to present a proposal on how these questions can be answered in a non-dualistic way. In doing so, I rely on the pragmatist view of science as well as the action and communication theory of George Herbert Mead. I would like to show that it is possible to develop a conception which allows linking research as linguistic and non-linguistic activities in a non-dualistic way. This concept contains some realistic, constructivist and relativistic elements, but without the reference to true/false.

Keywords: Non-dualism, George Herbert Mead, science, non-dualistic empirical research

1 Fragestellung

In meinem Beitrag möchte ich Überlegungen zu einer Wissenschaftstheorie vorstellen, die mit der non-dualisierenden Redeweise kompatibel ist, die von Josef Mitterer entwickelt worden ist. Die Wissenschaftstheorie interessiert mich aus der Perspektive der Soziologie. Von der Soziologie wird erwartet, dass sie empirische Forschung betreibt und empirisch gestütztes Wissen über soziale Prozesse und gesellschaftlichen Verhältnissen hervorbringt. Das Konzept der non-dualisierenden Redeweise Mitterers stellt jedoch eine starke Verunsicherung und Herausforderung für das Selbstverständnis empirischer Forschung dar.

    Mit dem Begriff der *Dualisierung* charakterisiert Mitterer Wahrheitsdiskurse, d. h. Diskurse, bei denen es aufgrund von Auffassungsunterschieden um die Richtigkeit oder Adäquatheit von Beschreibungen geht (vgl. Mitterer 2001). Mit

Dualisierung meint er alle Positionen, die eine *kategoriale Unterscheidung* zwischen der Beschreibung und dem, was beschrieben wird, voraussetzen oder, anders gesagt, eine *dichotome Trennung* der Beschreibung eines Objekts von dem Objekt der Beschreibung, zwischen Sprache und Wirklichkeit. *Kategorial* ist die Unterscheidung insofern, als vorausgesetzt wird, dass die Objekte unabhängig von der Beschreibung eine Identität besitzen und das Kriterium für wahre oder adäquate Beschreibungen sind.

In seinen Untersuchungen zeigt Mitterer, dass nicht nur realistische Positionen dualisierend vorgehen, sondern auch konstruktivistische und relativistische:
- Laut *Realismus* hat die Welt, die beschrieben wird, ohne jegliche Beteiligung der beschreibenden Subjekte eine Identität.
- Im *Konstruktivismus* erzeugt die Funktionsweise unseres Erkenntnisvermögens aus der Realität eine bestimmte Welt und diese Welt enthält die Objekte, die wir beschreiben; worauf das Erkenntnisvermögen beruht, dazu gibt es verschiedene Versionen: etwa unsere biologische Ausstattung, das Zentralnervensystem, psychologische Gegebenheiten u. a.
- Im *Relativismus* werden durch unterschiedliche Zugangsweisen zur Realität, etwa durch die Sprache, durch Theorien oder Kulturen, unterschiedliche Weltversionen erzeugt, innerhalb derer Beschreibungen vorgenommen werden.

Das Argument Mitterers gegen die Dualisierung lässt sich etwa folgendermaßen formulieren: Wir geraten in einen infiniten Regress, wenn wir im Rahmen eines Diskurses um die Wahrheit, die Adäquatheit oder die Viabilität von Beschreibungen versuchen, von unseren Beschreibungen sprachunabhängige Objekte zu unterscheiden, auf die sich unsere Beschreibungen beziehen, denn wir können Objekte nicht ohne Beschreibung angeben. Demgemäß, so Mitterer, sei das Objekt einer Beschreibung selbst eine Beschreibung und die Beschreibung eines Objekts die Fortsetzung einer bereits durchgeführten Beschreibung. Die Unterscheidung wahr/falsch im Sinn der Übereinstimmung einer Beschreibung mit einem beschreibungsunabhängigen Objekt mache daher keinen Sinn. Für die empirische Forschung heißt dies: Wenn wir einem Forschungsergebnis, das dem unseren widerspricht, nachweisen wollen, dass es falsch ist, so können wir dies nur mit unserem eigenen sprachlich formulierten Forschungsergebnis tun und nicht dadurch, dass wir unmittelbar auf ein Jenseits der Forschung verweisen.

Welche Konsequenzen sollen wir daraus für die empirische Forschung ziehen? Müssen wir den Anspruch aufgeben, mittels empirischer Forschung etwas über eine sprachunabhängige Realität auszusagen? Oder ist kein Verständnis von Forschung möglich, das mit der nicht-dualisierenden Redeweise Josef Mitterers kompatibel ist? Worin genauer besteht das Problem?

2 Das Problem des Verhältnisses von Non-Dualismus und empirischer Forschung

Wenn wir mit Mitterer davon ausgehen, dass die Beschreibung eines Objekts die Fortsetzung einer bereits geleisteten Beschreibung ist, so ist es die *Fortsetzung* von Beschreibungen, wo die empirische Forschung zu verorten ist. Es stellt sich nämlich die Frage, aus welchen Quellen der Inhalt für die Fortsetzung geschöpft wird, und eine dieser Quellen ist – zumindest nach wissenschaftlicher Auffassung – die empirische Forschung: mit ihr kommen wir zu neuen Erkenntnissen und Beschreibungen.

Die Argumentation Mitterers gegen das Dualisieren ist eine Auseinandersetzung mit dem Wahrheitsdiskurs. Mit der Frage nach der Forschungstätigkeit verlassen wir den Wahrheitsdiskurs, d. h. es geht nicht um die Frage wahr/falsch von bereits vorliegenden Beschreibungen, sondern um das Hervorbringen von Beschreibungen. Während der Wahrheitsdiskurs zweigliedrig ist, durch die Frage nach dem Verhältnis von Objekt und Beschreibung charakterisiert ist, ist der Forschungsprozess dreigliedrig: zwischen Objekt und Beschreibung schiebt sich die Forschungstätigkeit (Objekt – Forschungstätigkeit – Beschreibung).

Die traditionelle Auffassung des Forschungsprozesses ist dualistisch:
- Die *Objekte* mit ihren Eigenschaften und Beziehungen sind *unabhängig* von unserer Untersuchungstätigkeit.
- Mit unserer Untersuchung *analysieren* wir die Objekte und stellen ihre Eigenschaften fest.
- Die Forschungsergebnisse *transformieren* wir mit Hilfe der Sprache in Beschreibungen.

Die Frage ist nun: Lässt sich die Beziehung zwischen Objekt, Forschungstätigkeit und Beschreibung so konzipieren, dass Dualisierungen vermieden werden? Die non-dualisierende Redeweise erweckt den Eindruck, als verträte sie einen Sprach- und Beschreibungsmonismus. Dieser Eindruck könnte nahelegen, einen Dualismus dadurch zu vermeiden, dass wir Forschungstätigkeit als rein sprachliche Tätigkeit auffassen. Zwei Varianten sind diesbezüglich vorstellbar:
- Der *Inhalt der Fortsetzung* einer vorliegenden Beschreibung ist in dieser Beschreibung bereits vorhanden, war aber bisher verborgen, wird jetzt entdeckt und der vorliegenden Beschreibung explizit hinzugefügt, oder
- der *Inhalt* wird aus einem externen Reservoir existierender Beschreibungen ausgewählt und der vorliegenden Beschreibung hinzugefügt.

Bei beiden Varianten befinden wir uns in einem sprachlichen Solipsismus. Allerdings erhebt sich dabei die *Frage*, ob die Vermeidung des Dualismus gelingt. In der einen Variante ist Beschreiben an das *Entdecken* von Beschreibungen gebunden und in der zweiten Variante an das *Auswählen* von Beschreibungen. *Entdecken und Auswählen sind jedoch keine sprachlichen Tätigkeiten.* Offensichtlich verlassen wir damit die Sprachwelt und landen, ganz gegen unsere Absicht, in einem Dualismus, wenn wir empirisches Forschen als rein sprachliche Tätigkeit auffassen möchten.

Welchen Schluss sollen wir daraus ziehen? Dass es kein Entkommen daraus gibt, die Objekte der Forschungstätigkeit und der Beschreibungen als sprachunabhängig aufzufassen? Oder dass wir in der Forschung einen Zugang zu einer sprachunabhängigen Realität haben, und diesen Zugang verlieren, sobald es in der Diskussion um die Forschungsergebnisse geht?

Im Folgenden möchte ich einen Ansatz skizzieren, der die Beziehungen zwischen Forschungsobjekt, Forschungstätigkeit und Beschreibung als nichtkategorial verschieden auffasst. Die Schlüsselposition nimmt dabei der Begriff der Forschungstätigkeit ein, der zwischen Objekt und Beschreibung vermittelt. Ich setze mich zunächst mit dem Verhältnis Forschungstätigkeit und Beschreibung auseinander und anschließend mit dem Verhältnis Forschungstätigkeit und Objekt. Ich schließe dabei an die pragmatistische Erkenntnis- und Kommunikationstheorie von George Herbert Mead an (vgl. Mead 1938).

3 Zur Beziehung von Forschungstätigkeit und Beschreibung

George Herbert Mead hat am Beginn des 20. Jahrhunderts eine Konzeption des Zusammenhangs von Handeln und Sprechen entwickelt, die als non-dualistisch verstanden werden kann. Es ist eine phylogenetische Konzeption, insofern Mead Sprache als etwas auffasst, das sich aus dem Gestenaustausch bei Tieren entwickelt hat. Diese Konzeption wurde zu Meads Zeiten eher schwach durch empirische Forschung gestützt, da die Verhaltensforschung bei Tieren damals erst am Beginn stand. Die Konzeption Meads ist aber so formuliert, dass sie einer empirischen Überprüfung zugänglich ist. Michael Tomasello untersucht am Max-Planck-Institut für Evolutionäre Anthropologie seit vielen Jahren die Genese der Kommunikation bei Menschenaffen und Kleinkindern; seine Untersuchungen können als Unterstützung von Meads Konzeption der Genese von Sprache aus der tierischen Gestenkommunikation gelesen werden (vgl. Tomasello 2009).

Ich kann hier auf Meads Konzeption der Sprachgenese nicht näher eingehen, sondern bloß mit einigen Stichworten versuchen, den nicht-dualistischen Charakter des Verhältnisses von Handeln und Sprechen plausibel zu machen (für eine detaillierte Darstellung vgl. Ofner 2013):
- Mead sieht den Beginn der Sprachentwicklung bei den *tierischen Gesten*; diese sind die *Anfangsphasen* von Handlungen, die ein Individuum an ein anderes richtet; sie leiten eine Handlung gegenüber einem anderen ein, sind demnach Elemente von sozialen Handlungen.
- Aus der Reaktion des Adressaten erfährt ein Individuum die soziale Bedeutung seiner Geste.
- Der Schritt zur sprachlichen Kommunikation erfolgt durch die Verwendung von Lauten als Gesten. Die Relevanz dieser Umstellung für die Sprachentwicklung besteht darin, dass das Lebewesen die Laute, die es macht, selbst wahrnehmen kann, sich dadurch selbst adressiert und zu einer Reaktion stimuliert. Durch die Selbststimulierung kann das Lebewesen die Reaktion des Interaktionspartners mitvollziehen und die Bedeutung seiner Geste erfahren.

Auf diese Weise bilden sich nach Mead in der Interaktion gemeinsame sprachliche Symbole mit gemeinschaftlichen Bedeutungen heraus. Grundlegend für die Ausbildung einer Sprache und gemeinsamen Bedeutungen sind die gemeinsame Praxis und die gemeinsamen Erfahrungen. – Wittgensteins Sprachauffassung in den *Philosophischen Untersuchungen* ist Meads Konzeption insofern ähnlich, als auch er die Einbettung von Sprache in praktische Lebensformen betont (vgl. Wittgenstein 1984). Allerdings beinhaltet Wittgensteins Theorie nicht die Einheit von Handeln und Sprechen, nicht die Genese des Sprechens aus dem Handeln, wie das bei Mead der Fall ist.

Für die Frage des Non-Dualismus hat die Meadsche Konzeption von Sprache folgende Relevanz: Handeln und Sprechen sind nicht kategorial verschieden, sondern beides ist Handeln. Man kann auch sagen: Sprechen ist initiiertes Handeln, Handeln in der Vorstellung und Aktivieren von Handlungserfahrungen. Auf den wissenschaftlichen Forschungsprozess bezogen, heißt dies: Beschreibungen aktivieren die Erfahrungen, die beim Forschungshandeln erzeugt worden sind.

4 Zur Beziehung von Forschungstätigkeit und Objekt

Auch hinsichtlich der Beziehung von Handlung und Objekt ist Mead non-dualistisch. Seine Unterscheidung von Individuum und Umwelt ist nicht kategorial: Individuen sind Elemente ihrer Umwelt, Individuen und Umwelt sind ihm zufolge keine voneinander getrennten und unabhängigen Entitäten, die in einem äußerlichen Verhältnis stehen, sondern durch Austauschprozesse miteinander verbunden und bilden eine Einheit. Demzufolge beobachten wir die Umwelt nicht von außen, gewinnen wir kein Wissen darüber, wie die Umwelt unabhängig von unseren Interaktionen mit ihr ist, sondern die Inhalte unseres Wissens sind Interaktionserfahrungen. Mead lehnt ontologische Aussagen über die Welt, d. h. darüber was Dinge sind und welche Eigenschaften sie an sich haben, strikt ab.

Dementsprechend ist auch Meads Konzept der Forschungs- und Erkenntnistätigkeit strikt non-dualistisch. Zur Forschungstätigkeit kommt es seiner Auffassung nach in Situationen, in denen unser Handeln gehemmt, blockiert oder behindert ist, also in Problemsituationen. Solange ein Handlungsprozess problemlos läuft, gibt es keinen Anlass, Nachforschungen und Untersuchungen anzustellen, dies geschieht erst, wenn Probleme auftreten. Im Einzelnen unterscheidet Mead folgende Schritte bei der Forschungstätigkeit:

- Durch die Hemmung zerfällt die Handlung in Teile: Durch die Hemmung wird Handeln auf Handlungsimpulse reduziert und andererseits entsteht gegenüber den Handlungsimpulsen eine Umwelt, die die Ausführung der Handlungsimpulse nicht zulässt.
- In der Folge wird die Umwelt analysiert: Es werden jene Eigenschaften identifiziert, die die Handlungsausführung hemmen, und von denen getrennt, die zur Handlungsausführung passen. Diese Analyse erfolgt mit Hilfe der Sprache, denn diese zeigt, wie vorher ausgeführt, Handlungen und mit ihnen verbundene Erfahrungen auf.
- Durch experimentierendes Verhalten werden neue Handlungsmöglichkeiten erkundet, auch dies erfolgt mit Hilfe der Sprache.
- Es folgt die Synthese von Handlungsmöglichkeiten zu einem Handlungsentwurf, d. h. die Bildung von Hypothesen darüber, wie die Handlung ausgeführt werden kann; auch dabei ist die Verwendung von Sprache zentral.
- Schließlich werden die Hypothesen getestet, d. h. darauf geprüft, ob die entworfene Handlung erfolgreich durchgeführt werden kann.

Objekte entstehen diesem Meadschen Konzept gemäß in der Phase der Analyse und Synthese (Hypothesenbildung): Objekte sind die durch die Handlungshemmung abgespalteten Umweltmerkmale, auf die sich Handlungsimpulse richten. Es sind also Objekte, die im Handlungsprozess entstehen und nicht unabhängig vom Handeln vor dem Handeln bereits existieren. Und sie sind an Sprache gebunden. Dieses Konzept von Forschungstätigkeit ist demnach non-dualistisch.

Aus dieser Sicht ergibt sich ein Dualismus dann, wenn das Objekt, das im Zuge der Hemmung im Prozess der Analyse und Synthese entsteht, nachträglich vorausgesetzt wird als etwas, auf das sich das Handeln gerichtet hat. Dieser Akt des nachträglichen Voraussetzens ist dem ähnlich, was Mitterer im Wahrheitsdiskurs aufzeigt, wonach die Teilnehmer die eigene Beschreibung im Nachhinein den Beschreibungen der anderen voraussetzen, um deren Inadäquatheit nachzuweisen.

5 Conclusio

Ich wollte unter Bezugnahme auf George Herbert Meads Handlungs- und Sprachtheorie zeigen, dass sich sowohl die Beziehung „Objekt und Forschungstätigkeit" als auch die Beziehung „Forschungstätigkeit und Beschreibung" auf nicht-dualisierender Weise verstehen lassen. Objekte werden im Zuge des Forschungshandelns gebildet, Sprache ist eine Weise des Handelns und bereits an der Objektbildung beteiligt und nicht erst an der Beschreibung von Forschungsergebnissen.

Es liegt auf der Hand, dass in dem vorgestellten wissenschaftstheoretischen Konzept kein Platz für eine Wahrheit ist, die sich auf beschreibungs- und erfahrungsunabhängige Objekte beruft. Worauf es in diesem Konzept ankommt, ist die Beziehung zwischen einem Handlungsentwurf und dem Versuch, ihn auszuführen. Beide Elemente dieser Beziehung sind Elemente des Handelns und keines der beiden Elemente ist beschreibungsunabhängig, d.h. es stellt sich nicht die Frage, ob Beschreibungen mit beschreibungsunabhängigen Elementen übereinstimmen, sondern ob Beschreibungen, die zu unterschiedlichen Zeitpunkten gemacht werden, miteinander übereinstimmen.

Der Beschreibungsbegriff der non-dualisierenden Redeweise von Josef Mitterer wird in meiner Konzeption um die Dimension des Handelns und der Erfahrung auf nicht-dualisierende Weise erweitert – nicht-dualisierend deshalb, weil Beschreiben eine Weise von Handeln ist. Auf Mitterers Objekt der Beschreibung so far folgt in meinem Konzept nicht unmittelbar die Beschreibung des Objekts from now on, sondern die beiden sind durch den Forschungsprozess und die Beschreibung von *Handlungsentwürfen* vermittelt.

Damit ergeben sich neue Möglichkeiten für den Umgang mit Auffassungsunterschieden von Beschreibungen. Der eine Punkt ist: Die Diskussion von strittigen Forschungsergebnissen beruft sich nicht auf handlungs- und sprachverschiedene Objekte, beruht also nicht auf dem Gegenüberstellen bzw. gegenseitigen Unterstellen von Beschreibungen, sondern bezieht sich auf Handlungsmöglichkeiten und Handlungserfahrungen. Der andere Punkt ist: Da sich Sprache aus sozialem Handeln, aus gemeinsamer Praxis entwickelt, ist in ihr die Möglichkeit enthalten, die Handlungserfahrungen der anderen mitzuvollziehen. In einem nicht-dualisierenden Forschungsverständnis wird sich daher die Diskussion von Auffassungsunterschieden darauf richten, das eigene Handeln den anderen nachvollziehbar zu machen.

Im Titel meines Vortrags spreche ich von wissenschaftstheoretischen Überlegungen jenseits von Realismus, Relativismus und Konstruktivismus. Dies bezieht sich darauf, dass ich den Dualismus dieser drei Positionen vermeiden möchte. Andererseits kann man sehen, dass die drei Positionen als Elemente in der vorgestellten Konzeption enthalten sind, allerdings nicht mit ihrem Bezug auf eine externe Wirklichkeit, sondern auf das Handeln:

- Beim Zerfall des Handelns in der Problemsituation tritt ein unproblematischer Bereich der Umwelt auf, der einfach da ist und als gegeben hingenommen wird; dies kann man als realistischen Aspekt der Erfahrung ansehen. Realistisch heißt in diesem Fall, das kein Handlungsproblem vorliegt.
- Der unproblematische Umweltbereich ist jedoch nicht unabhängig vom Handeln vorhanden, sondern ergibt sich aus dem Handlungskontext. Dies kann man als relativistischen Aspekt der Erfahrung auffassen.
- Und schließlich hat der Entwurf von Handlungsmöglichkeiten, um aus der Problemsituation herauszukommen, also die Hypothesenbildung, konstruktiven Charakter.

Literaturverzeichnis

Mead, George Herbert (1938): *Philosophy of the Act*. Edited by Charles W. Morris with John M. Brewster, Albert M. Dunham and David Miller. Chicago: University of Chicago Press.
Mitterer, Josef (2001): *Die Flucht aus der Beliebigkeit*. Frankfurt am Main: Fischer.
Ofner, Franz (2013): „'Bewusstseinslücken' – Meads Konzeption der Genese des Selbst-Bewusstseins – Probleme und Lösungsvorschläge". In: *Österreichische Zeitschrift für Soziologie*, Sonderheft 12: Potentiale einer pragmatistischen Sozialtheorie. Beiträge anlässlich des 150. Geburtstags von George Herbert Mead, 155–180.
Tomasello, Michael (2009): *Die Ursprünge der menschlichen Kommunikation*. Frankfurt am Main: Suhrkamp.
Wittgenstein, Ludwig (1984): *Philosophische Untersuchungen*. Frankfurt am Main: Suhrkamp.

Peter Strasser
Realism without Foundation

Abstract: The question whether or not there is an external world consisting of a subject independent realm of objects, facts and laws is neither trivial nor a pseudo-problem. Today, this question is facing the challenge of neurological reductionism. If we are in essence our brain, then we are entangled in a paradox: on the one hand, our brain is part of the external world and so creates our subject-dependent pictures of the external world. This leads on the other hand to the result that our brain itself is a brain-internal 'construction' completely composed of neurologically coded data. It seems we are trapped in an onto-epistemological circle, which is the main reason that realism does not have a solid foundation. Plato and his followers claimed that there is, nevertheless, a way out of the cave of subjectivism. Their credo is objective idealism. According to this ontology, brain imprisonment and its viciously circular consequences can be avoided by idealistic realism, which postulates not the priority of matter but of mind – in the sense of 'Geist' in German. Idealistic realism itself, however, does not provide an alternative to scientific knowledge of the world's basic laws, nor does it fit into the ontological framework of naturalism.

Keywords: Mind-body problem, brain-fundamentalism, metaphysics of the human person, radical constructivism, objective idealism

To expose my crucial point, I want to discuss in the first section some well-known, rather conventional aspects within the realism-debate under the leading question: 'Is there an outer world paradox?' I will answer this question in the positive while demonstrating in the second section that today's favored brain fundamentalism urges an alarming suspicion: 'Does brain-fundamentalism lead to a vicious circle?' Finally, in my third section, I would like to ask, 'Is the concept of objective idealism an ontological *cul-de-sac*?' This question is to provoke some considerations whether or not the concept of objective idealism could be helpful to overcome the disastrous consequences of brain-fundamentalism.

1 Is there an Outer World Paradox?

In his famous article *Proof of an External World* of 1962, George Edward Moore assures us that there is an external world. After a long consideration of Kant's transcendental realism, Moore gives a stunning demonstration of his common-sense view: "I can prove now, for instance, that two human hands exist. How? By holding up my two hands, and saying, as I make a certain gesture with the right hand, 'Here is one hand', and adding, as I make a certain gesture with the left, 'and here is another'". (Moore 1962, 44)

Moore's aim is to demonstrate under which conditions realism is true. Simple enough, realism is, according to our common-sense evidence, true if there are things that belong to the so-called external or outer world. Now, holding up both of his hands, Moore asserts that there cannot be any doubt that, at least, two things do really exist. But if so, there also must be an external world. By the way: Moore assures us that – while holding up his hands under the given, reliable circumstances – he is justified in believing that his senses are working well, his mental condition gives no cause for complaint, and, generally speaking, he is not under the spell of any manner of erratic influences.

Let us assume Moore is right in his exclusion of all possible sources of sensual errors, psychic deceptions and mental defects: then – as is the case with common-sense thinking – Moore's hands would not disappear if there were neither Moore nor any other observer perceiving Moore's hands. In other words, by referring to his hands, Moore talks about entities whose existence does not depend on being perceived.

All these aspects are well known. Nevertheless, not all of them are philosophically transparent. Rather the contrary is the case. At this point it may be helpful to remember Rudolf Carnap's verdict. Carnap declares the outer world question to be a pseudo-problem (Carnap 1928). Why? Since – according to Carnap's neo-positivistic credo – it does not make any factual difference whether a scientist is, ontologically speaking, an idealist or a realist. Idealists do not believe in a mind-independent world, whereas realists take such a world for granted. To disqualify both of these views, Carnap runs the following argument: Given all of the possible questions that could be answered on the basis of observation and experiment, neither idealists nor realists need refer to their ontological credo. Idealism as well as realism is of no relevance for any rational decision concerning the existence of certain empirical facts.

Take, for instance, the question of whether there are two hands that belong to the philosopher Moore. If the right answer is yes, then a simple examination of Moore's body will settle the issue. Yet, as for the allegedly crucial question whether there is an external world or not – the point at which the realist differs from his idealistic counterpart – this question, Carnap says, is completely irrelevant. The existence of Moore's hands seems to be compatible with each ontological conviction – be it realistic or not. For in this case, the ontological conviction is a metaphysical one. It cannot be verified (or falsified) by applying empirical methods. Therefore, Carnap concludes, the issue of realism cannot be settled – not because it is so difficult a problem but because it does not have any factual content (*Sachgehalt*).

Carnap is right insofar as the problem of realism cannot be dealt with empirically. Yet does this lead to the consequence that Carnap's verdict ought to be accepted? Does the philosophical realist unknowingly defend a meaningless issue? Is it – figuratively speaking – an empty gesture when Moore shows his hands in order to demonstrate that there are at least two things which must, beyond any reasonable doubt, be qualified as outer world entities? And finally – is Moore's comment "Here is one hand, and here is another" nothing more than thoughtless talking, a *façon de parler*? I think the right answer to this question should be in the negative; but to demonstrate this point, we must gain a deeper understanding of the *constructive nature* of ontological realism.

First of all, the scientific idea of knowledge presupposes that there are insights into the realm of nature that ought to be expressed in a subject-neutral manner. Talking about the facts of nature implies talking about facts which can, in principle, be experienced from any conceivable perspective. Each perspective is subject-bound – being dependent on some observer – but all of them together *represent the objectivity of our observations*. Objectivity itself cannot be experienced. Instead, it is a *highly constructive idea*; at the same time it is a *threshold concept* to signify our realistic discussion of facts. According to this concept, facts stimulate our senses, whereas the facts themselves, as objective elements of the external world, are independent of our senses. Facts do not depend on any subject-bound representations, especially the contents of our perceptions.

To sum up by stating the obvious: Philosophical realism is based on the constructive principle of subject-neutrality. This principle rules not only our common-sense concept of reality but, more sophisticatedly, the external-world concept of sciences, too. At this point, however, we are confronted with a puzzling question: If all the contents of our perceptions are necessarily subject-*bound* – how, then, could the constructive idea of a subject-*neutral* fact ever be more than a pseudo-concept? This is reminiscent of Carnap's verdict, and once again there is an answer derived from our common-sense concept of reality. Although we cannot take a subject-neutral point of view in experiencing reality, it is often the case that – while taking different perspectives – we do not have the slightest doubt that we perceive the same subject-neutral facts. In other words, our evidence of a common world we refer to by referring to facts is indispensable. It is the indubitability of such a world that enables us to communicate successfully with each other, from small talk to scholarly speculation.

Granted that we intuitively understand the principle of subject neutrality, any further deliberation confronts us with a deep riddle. Thomas Nagel once expressed this riddle by using an ingenious metaphor that also formed the title of one of his most influential books, *The View from Nowhere*. The view from nowhere is the view from which the world is perceived in a subject-neutral manner. As Nagel himself has pointed out, this 'view' implies a profound paradox concerning the *essence* of our common concept of reality. 'The view from nowhere' is a formula which strives to make intelligible a highly metaphysical idea – the idea of a subject-independent world that *transgresses* intelligibility.

I do not know if Nagel chose his metaphor because it is well known in traditional theology, circumscribing God's infinite capacity of perceiving his creation. According to classical tradition, God's sensitive mind is everywhere and, therefore, nowhere in particular. God's eye is all embracing and all pervasive. While continually perceiving all things from all perspectives at the same time, God never needs to change his point of view. Given this notion of God's infinite capacity, finite creatures whose perceptions are inherently subject-bound do not have an intelligible, non-contradictory idea of God's experience – an experience embedded in the view from nowhere or, anyway, everywhere. Nonetheless, the paradoxical metaphor reflects the main requirement for thinking of outer world facts as parts of objective reality.

To negate our concept of reality means to get trapped in solipsism – or even worse, because solipsism knows at least one real entity, namely me, the sensitive, sensible and self-conscious center of the whole world. I and only I do not depend on a 'bundle of perceptions,' to use David Hume's term. Seen in this way, there *is* a kind of view from nowhere – the view, so to speak, from me to me myself. My self-evidence of having, or being, an 'I' proves – as René Descartes would argue – beyond any doubt that I exist objectively as a self-conscious being: an immaterial *res cogitans*.

May be this sounds strange, but there is no other view than the view from nowhere – or everywhere – in order to provide our experiences with a *fundamentum in re*. Otherwise, my consciousness would be like a fantastic movie screen delivering sensory data that would be already the world instead of representing only a *picture* of the world. Hume has argued that if we had to start with nothing else than a 'bundle of perceptions' – as is the doctrine of classical empiricism – then we would neither get hold of a material world nor could we have evidence of a ghostly substance be it labelled 'Ego' or 'I' or 'Me'.

Now, for the benefit of our further considerations let us assume we are able to build up a subject-neutral theory of the external world by using the inter-subjective methods and theoretical concepts of natural sciences. Then we have to face the results of neurosciences that are being widely acknowledged by today's brain researchers. In a nutshell, these results are often summarized, at least in fairly popular publications, by stating that we *are* our brain. For instance,

Nagel says: "The brain, but not the rest of the animal, is essential to the self. Let me express this with mild exaggeration as the hypothesis that I am my brain [...]" (Nagel 1988, p. 40).

Nagel admits 'with mild exaggeration,' that he is inclined to accept that he is his own brain. Why? Since, according to Nagel, the 'hypothesis' that he is his own brain has become strongly confirmed by scientific knowledge. In this line of argument, our brain does *not* only contribute to our personality and physical appearance but, far more than that, is *the very essence of our being a self-conscious person*.

The same argument is affirmed by many brain researchers, but often with a mental reservation. Imagine the neuroscientist Prof. Schmitt who, as an acknowledged member of his profession, assures his scholarly audience that he is, in essence, his brain. Contrary to that, if talking to himself, he does not tell his – so to speak – private ego, that he, Prof. Schmitt, is his own brain. For Prof. Schmitt is proud to be a distinguished member of neuroscientists' community. He does not earnestly believe that his scientific reputation is his brain's achievement instead of his own. Generally speaking, he is proud to be the distinguished Prof. Schmitt and not Prof. Schmitt's distinguished brain, although Prof. Schmitt's reputation is, ironically enough, based on his contribution to a neurological doctrine which seemingly confirms that he, Prof. Schmitt, is his own brain.

The doctrine that I am my brain is, of course, supported by the fact that my consciousness is dependent on my brain's neurological activities. This implies that my evidence of being an individual – in my case, my evidence of being P. S. – is caused by my brain's activities, too. My brain is networking while dealing with millions and billions of data encoded into the electrochemical language of neurons. If my brain is networking in the right way, then, so the neurological doctrine tells us, my brain produces the long-term evidence that is best expressed by stating that I am the person called 'P. S.'

Now, I think there is a strong argument against the doctrine of my being my brain without presupposing a *res cogitans*. This argument, less ambitious than Descartes' 'Cogito sum,' *je pense donc je suis,* stresses our common-sense point of view: *it takes for granted that we are more than our brain*. Simply enough, there are two reasons: in order to have personal identity I need not know anything about my brain; and, furthermore, in order to be a person my knowledge of my brain has to be accompanied by a peculiar sort of first-person evidence: it is necessary *that I know that I am the one* who knows something about his brain.

The same is true of all of my experiences. All of them are intrinsically related to my self-consciousness. Let us say they are *I-related*. Then it is necessarily true that all of my experiences are I-related, otherwise they would not be *my* experiences. Consequently, the evidence of I-relatedness cannot be an experience among others. I-relatedness constitutes the whole range of my experiences by building up the framework of self-consciousness, thereby providing me with personal identity.

2 Does Brain-Fundamentalism Lead to a Vicious Circle?

Working as a neuroscientist I get neurological evidence of how my brain causes I-relatedness. But my evidence that all of my experiences are I-related, otherwise they would not be *my* experiences – this evidence is a trans-empirical or, to use Kant's term, a transcendental phenomenon. Contrary to that, neurological facts, if truly understood, are to be described as empirical phenomena not dependent on being perceived; there is also no need for I-relatedness. Neurons, clusters of neurons and neurological networks, regardless of how complex and multi-centered, must never be conceptualized as facts presupposing consciousness, let alone self-consciousness.

From that follows, then, the *neurological paradox*. On the one hand, my self-consciousness necessarily entails, and is built up by, I-related experiences. On the other hand, all of my experiences are caused, or – metaphorically speaking – 'fabricated,' by electro-chemical or hormonally based processes taking place in my brain. None of these processes is conscious of itself. Given my brain as a part of my body, there is no such phenomenon as my brain's self-awareness. Yet only the self-awareness of my brain could justify Nagel's 'hypothesis.' Contrary to that, if it were true that I am my brain, then my being my brain would be a pure neurological fact – that means, a fact which could not be expressed in terms of I-relatedness. Ergo, if I were really my brain, then I would never be a person who could have reasons, neither good nor bad ones, for claiming to be his or her brain.

Let us assume our society has taken a *neurological turn*, leading to the result that we live in some sort of – let us say – *neurosociety*. What does the neurological turn amount to? Now, neurosociety's people think about their own personal identity in terms of being their own brain. They are inclined to do so because of their common belief that all of the primary causes that form a self-conscious mind are impersonal facts mainly located in the neurological activities of the brain.

Therefore, each neurosociety is submitted to the neurological paradox. For neurosociety's people *theorize* about themselves as if they were really – to use a bulky term – *non-I-related entities*. They would have been taught (or should I better say: conditioned to believe?) that the reductionist's view as favored by naturalism represents a highly confirmed, even indisputable truth. Nevertheless, neurosociety's people would theorize about their being non-I-related entities *against a transcendental background of I-relatedness*. What else?

I-relatedness is a relation that plays an indispensable role as soon as an empirical fact gets perceived by a self-conscious human being; but I-relatedness itself cannot be perceived in this way. Kant has pointed out that this relation is the most formal, all-embracing, all-covering condition of the possibility of having perceptions at all – therefore, it does not fit into the framework of scientific reductionism.

As long as being entangled in the neurological paradox, the cognitive attitude of neurosociety's people with respect to themselves fosters a deeply irrational state of mind. For as a mentally sane person I cannot bring myself to earnestly believe that I am my own brain. If I were truly convinced that I am my own brain, then doctors would have a very good reason for having me admitted to a psychiatric ward.

This leads me to a provocative question: Should philosophers or scientists who *earnestly and firmly* insist on being their own brain not be the first ones to be put into a lunatic asylum ...? The question needs, of course, no answer. According to their neurological doctrine, those experts may tell us, 'I am my brain,' but they never could *literally believe* that they are their brain as long as they reason in an I-related manner. People who try hard to believe that they are their own brain should be considered – according to their self-alienated way of thinking about themselves – as *would-be brains*. Would-be brains are, according to my suggestion, people who are determined to harmonize the naturalist's framework with the transcendental phenomenon of I-relatedness – *although it is obvious that they cannot but fail*. To stress this point: the I-relatedness-phenomenon leads to the common-sense evidence that mentally sane persons *have* a brain but *are not* one.

Given this mental constraint – or capacity –, we must now take into consideration the connection between common-sense realism and neurological reductionism. There cannot be any doubt that our brain – in contrast to our perceptions – is part of the outer world. My brain, in any intelligible meaning, does *not* depend on my consciousness understood as the inner world of me, the 'brain-bearer.'

The existence of human brains is the evolutionary product of a very long process embracing physical, chemical and biological components. On this fundamental level, there are no phenomena that could be considered to be immaterial. In our academic tradition, it has often been said – thereby underlining the naturalistic approach – that all of the phenomena belonging to our consciousness are no more than *epi*-phenomena.

An epiphenomenon, for instance my perception of the sentences and words I am producing on my computer-screen, may cause some further events like other words and sentences that also will become elements of my stream of perceptions. Given the common-sense mode of thinking about the real, the words and sentences on my computer screen are, under normal circumstances, simple facts of the external world. But given the naturalistic view, all contents of my perceptions – in our example, words and sentences on my computer screen – are primarily brain-processed neurological facts which become, in a completely mysterious way, perceived facts. These consciousness-bound facts are *intimately linked with* the ontological belief that they are elements of the outer world. And therefore, they *are*, as long as not falsified, elements of the subject-neutral outer or external world.

What follows from that? According to brain fundamentalism, all of our ontological beliefs – like all the other elements of our consciousness – are fundamentally caused by our brain; our brain itself, however, belongs to the outer world, being independent of our consciousness. Yet if so, it seems inevitable that our idea of an outer or external world is a misshapen, if not self-contradictory, concept. For, as we have seen, all of our seemingly objective knowledge about our brain is *a construct based on consciousness-bound data*. According to the neurologic doctrine that is favored by today's naturalism, these data belong to the epiphenomenal sphere of subjectivity.

3 Is the Concept of Objective Idealism an Ontological *Cul-de-Sac*?

By contrast, we should think of Plato's parable – or analogy – of the Cave (Plato 2007, 514 A – 517 B). The Cave is a place of imprisonment. There people are chained from childhood on. They cannot move in their seats. So they are forced to look at an opposite wall where only shadows of the real things can be seen. No wonder the chained people believe that they are looking at real things.

Plato's parable would not work at all if there were not *an external point of view* being taken by Socrates. It is this philosopher, Plato's hero, who tells his audience about the Cave. There are, on the one hand, shadows and all sorts of illusions moving across the wall; and there are, on the other hand, the real things, illuminated by a fire while being moved behind the prisoners' backs.

Furthermore – as we, the *external onlookers*, can easily imagine – there is an exit: a way out of the Cave. The way is steep, a *rîte de passage* that is destined for the philosophical mind only. Beyond and above the cave there is, as we are told, the empire of the sun. In Plato's world the sun is a symbol of the highest reality – the reality of ideas. Worldly things represent only drab and sallow images of those eternal ideas.

The choice of words, like parable and allegory, indicates that Plato's Cave is not to be taken literally; nor is the Cave's construction flawless. Firstly, there are the shadows on the wall symbolizing the subject-bound world, the place of perceptions and sensations. Then, secondly, there is the realm of entities, 'objects and puppets of men and other living things,' carried on a walkway behind the backs of the chained. These objects are, seen from a common-sense point of view, elements of the external world, physically located in space and time. But, as we know from Plato's idealism, objects common to us through our senses do not have full reality. They are only real in a dependent and subdued sense. Their reality depends on the existence of immaterial entities, namely Platonic ideas represented by universal concepts. Therefore, thirdly, reality in the full sense can only be found in the god-like ideas culminating in the highest idea – the divine Good.

There is no clear understanding of how the three ontological dimensions are connected, though in one respect the Cave's account of reality is definite. In Plato's view we are not enclosed in our brain like the oyster in its shell. Our imprisonment in sensuality is not inevitable; it is not an inherent constraint of our human nature. At least some people are able to shake off their chains. If they are courageous and spirited enough, they will unmask the shadows of things by looking at their real appearance recognizable in the Cave's background. But the most important step in the process of acknowledging the true reality of things is symbolized by the ascent to higher regions of the mind – that means out of the Cave's darkness and into the light of the sun.

By virtue of our mind's immaterial eye we are connected with the universe of eternal ideas. Most humans are too weak-minded to get a clear picture of pure ideas. Fortunately, there are exceptionally strong-minded individuals among us, philosophical natures whose passion for knowledge opens to them – metaphorically speaking – the door to heaven. Only the true philosopher gets full insight into the core of absolute reality.

Now, we should compare this idealistic panorama with our naturalistic concept of reality. There seems to be no way out of *our* kind of ontological cave. Apparently we are forced to go round and round in a huge epistemic circle. Our brain is thought of as a part of the external world; at the same time, our concept of the external world, which should guarantee a subject-neutral ontology, is derived from our subject-bound world of consciousness. There is no degree of abstraction that would lead to Plato's sun or Nagel's view from nowhere, at least in the mode of approximation. As soon as we realize that we are inescapably imprisoned in the naturalistic construct of reality, we became aware that the circle we are trapped in is a vicious one. It foils any justification of real things like those two hands Moore is holding up to prove that there is an external world.

At this crucial point let us shortly reconsider two approaches of how we could reach justified knowledge about the subject-neutral reality, even if all our primary data are subject-bound.

The first approach works with the criterion of coherence. According to this criterion the following assumption would be reasonable: The more our empirical and theoretical data fit together, being tightly linked, without producing contradictions or other conceptual distortions, the more we are justified to believe that our knowledge represents an approximation to the subject-neutral reality. Yet harmony within the elements of a conceptual system does not guarantee a cognitive outcome which would be more than a coherent fantasy. This argument could be successfully rejected only by taking an external point of view – a view, so to speak, beyond our brain-internally generated data. For only then we could compare our subject-bound data with the outer world facts in order to decide whether or not there is an adequate kind of correspondence between both.

The second criterion is often said to be supporting the first one. It is the criterion of efficiency, being part of the evolutionary approach. However, if most or even all of our allegedly truths were no more than fantasies or illusions 'produced' by our brain, how, then, could they be of any use in our struggle for life? Furthermore, prognoses derived from imaginary and therefore invalid natural laws could surely not be helpful in developing successful outer world technologies, could they?

Now, all of these considerations lead us to the result that we do not have sound arguments to reject the skeptical conclusion. Without being able to take a brain external point of view, we simply do not know why our allegedly knowledge works as it works – that means, why it helps us to survive and, more than that, increase our well-being given the permanent challenge of a Darwinian world.

But is there really no way out? No – not if our ontological starting point is naturalistic reductionism. To get out of the circle, we have to dismiss the 'hypothesis' or, stronger yet, the neurological credo according to which I am my brain. Instead, we would have to revive the idealistic approach in its objective version. This version postulates, contrary to our recent world-view, the priority of mind. If so, then there would have to be a kind of *mind-based affinity* between the contents of our consciousness and the outer world facts from the very beginning.

To indicate this fundamental affinity of ontological features inside and outside consciousness, Goethe used to talk metaphorically about *Wahlverwandtschaft*, elective affinity, which in modern chemistry means the phenomenon whereby certain molecules or chemical species have the tendency to aggregate or bond. The great poet exemplified his understanding of the term by a somewhat enigmatic sentence – however, what else could be more clear-sighted at this point? –: "If the eye were not sun-like, it could not see the sun" (*"Wär nicht das Auge sonnenhaft, die Sonne könnt es nie erblicken"*) (Goethe 2014, Book III).

Given the priority of mind as it is emphasized by objective idealism, the term 'mind' must also be understood in an objective manner. Unfortunately, there is no English equivalent to the German word *Geist*. But one has to bear in mind: Mind in the meaning of Geist could deliver a metaphysical foundation of realism only, if our ontology were based on some kind of *Weltgeist* – a world-founding and even world-creating substance that had to be seen as the ontological source as well as the essence of facts, whether they are located in the physical or the conscious sphere. Consequently, particular entities would be – so to speak – embodiments or representations of this trans-individual mind.

Obviously, the idealistic approach – highly speculative as it is – cannot offer an alternative to scientists' theorizing in their efforts to explain the world. If objective idealism appeals despite its metaphysical abyss, then it does so because of the same principle that guides Sherlock Holmes in solving hard cases: 'When you have eliminated the impossible, whatever remains, however improbable, must be the truth.' When we try to realize the view from nowhere, we end up in the vicious circle of neurological paradox; what remains, however improbable, is the priority of mind which, then, must be the truth.

Idealistic realism suggests, at least in its moderate versions, that it does not seem impossible to gain approximately true knowledge of the world. Contrary to German idealists like Hegel or Fichte, objective idealism, as long as it does not strive to be absolute truth, also does not claim that we, as finite beings, could ever attain full insight into the truth of the *Weltgeist*. To achieve such a godlike insight we would have to overcome our human limits. But humbly aware of our limits, our common-sense based realism – even in its scientifically sophisticated version – is connected to a kind of ontological promise or even metaphysical hope. It urges us to look for *truth that would be more than a conceptual construct within an epistemological circle.*

No doubt, philosophical constructivism is, in its postmodern design, the legitimate successor of the great tradition of enlightenment. Given the dogmatists' manifold sins against humanity in claiming exclusive ownership of true knowledge, constructivists are deconstructivists in the name of human life's inborn variety and the right of mutual tolerance on which it is based. The Austrian philosopher Josef Mitterer coined the term 'non-dualism' or, more explicitly, 'non-dualizing mode of speaking' to refer to his philosophical credo. According to Mitterer there is, as far as human faculties are concerned, no description-independent reality – and more than that: reality itself is nothing beyond the total sum of descriptions *so far*, by virtue of discourse continually transformed to descriptions *from now on*, thereby always changing the so-called 'truth' (cf. Mitterer 1992; Mitterer 2001).

One understands the anti-dogmatic ambition. But following the constructivist's line of argument – at least in its radical version – there is, in the end, no reality at all but only our reality-imitation game played by fabricating descriptions. As non-dualists we are, tongue in cheek, playful truth-seekers like Boy Scouts playing treasure hunters. In my opinion, there is far too much human-centered ontology around. At last it seems that man is comparable to a godlike spider spinning a huge web of concepts to generate a whole world. On the contrary, some sort of idealistic realism that does not offend our common sense will last as long as human nature urges us on to look for meaning inherent in our world – despite the naturalistic picture of a meaningless universe. But this, the heavy question of meaning as a feature of objective reality, is – to use a light-spirited phrase – already another story ...

... and now
BACK TO SQUARE ONE, AS THEY SAY!

Acknowledgements: I am indebted to Eugenia Lamont for improving my paper, especially for contributing the last sentence, which seems to me to express a truly philosophical thought.

References

Carnap, Rudolf (1928): *Scheinprobleme in der Philosophie*. Leipzig/Berlin: Weltkreis Verlag.
Goethe, Johann Wolfgang (2014): *Zahme Xenien*. Munich: C.H. Beck.
Mitterer, Josef (1992): *Das Jenseits der Philosophie*. Vienna: Passagen.
Mitterer, Josef (2001): *Die Flucht aus der Beliebigkeit*. Frankfurt/Main: Fischer.
Moore, George Edward (1962): *Philosophical Papers*. New York: Collier.
Nagel, Thomas (1988): *The View from Nowhere*. Oxford: Oxford University Press.
Plato (2007): *Politeia*. Translated by Joe Sachs. Newburyport: Focus Publishing.

4 Ontology/Ontological Relativism

Ludger Jansen
Constructed Reality

Abstract: A popular argument goes thus: This is a construction, hence it is not real. Adding an appropriate adjective (social, mental, human, ...) in front of "construction" or cognate terms like "(legal) fiction" yields a whole family of related arguments, all of which, or so I will argue, are fallacious. Contrary to popular opinion, these arguments fail both on the epistemic and the ontic sense of construction. Ontic constructions exist at least at one point in time, while epistemic constructions may well correspond to reality. The motivation behind these fallacious arguments can often be found in a misconceived conception of ontology and reality. A full theory of reality must take constructed entities into account because important domains of reality (mental life, social reality, technical artefacts, art and fiction) essentially depend on mental or social constructions.

Keywords: Constructivism, epistemic constructions, fiction, realism, ontology

1 Introduction: A Popular Argument

In some quarters it is a popular argument to argue for some sort of non-being from the fact that it is a construction. Something does not exist or, depending on jargon, is not real because it is constructed. Many authors referring to this argument do not hesitate to continue with the remark that being a construction does not, in fact, imply non-reality, and I will side with these authors with respect to the evaluation of this argument.[1] The common scheme of these arguments is:

(1) Premise: x is a construction.
    Conclusion: x is not real.

This argument scheme may be applied to a large variety of entities. Popular subjects to which the argument scheme is applied are social categories like gender, class and race (Fitzgerald 2014, xiv and 18), but it can also be applied to diseases like ADHD (Pickering 2006, 123) and even atoms (Romanyshyn/Whalen 1989, 20). There are various flavours of constructivisms, constructionisms or similarly

---

[1] See for example (Sprague 2005, 51), (Gergen 2009, 4 and 161) using the examples of death, the sun and a chair, (Dumouchel 2014, 127) about economic scarcity and (Vogel 2015, 37).

named theories on offer on our library shelves; for the purpose of this paper I stay mainly content with the term "constructivism". The flavours of these theories range from social or cultural to radical constructivism. Depending on the flavour of the constructivism motivating the popular argument, different modifying adjectives could be inserted in front of "construction". The premise may refer to a social construction, mental construction, human construction, cognitive construction – or a fiction. The conclusion, however, is invariably that the phenomenon in question is not real or does not exist. I will first explain why this argument is not logically valid (§2) and argue that it is just the other way round: Construction is a hallmark of existence; what has been constructed exists at least at one point in time (§3). Then, of course, the question arises whence the popularity of the argument. I will argue that its popularity is due to a misconception of reality and, connected with this, a misconception of the task of ontology (§4). I will go on to argue that similar objections are due if we replace the word "construction" in the premise by phrases containing the word "fiction" (§5).

It should be noted that, in a way, I am in good company in constructivist quarters. Many among the best constructivists do not see their project as opposed to realism.[2] Dave Elder-Vass has dedicated a whole book on *The Reality of Social Construction* (Elder-Vass 2012) and already Peter Berger and Thomas Luckmann assure their reader that society "does indeed possess objective facticity" exactly because it is "built up by activity that expresses subjective meaning" (Berger/Luckmann 1966/1991, 30). However, the realist and the constructivist are often divided on how to deal with epistemic constructions like theories or concepts. I will argue that they are often intended to fit to a pre-existing reality and may well do so successfully (§6). In a word, I will argue in this paper that constructions exist, that they are real. As I will add by way of conclusion, this is important because important parts of reality are constructions which would get lost if we only consider mind-independent entities as real (§7).

2 The Popular Argument is Fallacious

As popular as argument scheme (1) might be, it is, alas, a fallacy. An argument scheme can be shown to be fallacious if there is at least one instance of the

---

[2] Similarly, Hacking's analysis of talk about "social construction" presupposes the present existence of the socially constructed phenomenon. The point of calling something a "social construction" is rather, according to Hacking, that its existence is neither necessary nor inevitable, and may even be a bad thing (Hacking 1999, 6). This analysis is compatible with my present account.

scheme such that all premises are known to be true while the conclusion is known to be false. Here is such an instance:

(2) Premise: Trump Tower has been constructed.
    Conclusion: It is not real.

The Trump Tower was, indeed, constructed in 1983 in New York under the direction of architect Der Scutt and it has existed ever since. It is there to be seen, to be walked in, to sit in, and to go up the floors in the elevator. It is a real building; it exists. Hence the Trump Tower argument is an instance of the popular argument scheme with a true premise and a wrong conclusion. Thus it is shown that the popular argument scheme is fallacious.

There are, of course, ways to defend the popular argument. Are there not philosophers like Peter van Inwagen who deny the existence of artefacts (van Inwagen 1990)? According to such nihilism about material artefacts, the conclusion of our purported counterexample would just be false and thus not a counterexample against the validity of the argument scheme at all. But, first, there are important arguments against nihilism about artefacts (Jansen 2013). Second, even Peter van Inwagen insists that some constructions exist: bioengineered organisms, for example, are composed of material simples that participate in a very special complex event, a life, and hence they exist (van Inwagen 1990, 82). Likewise, there could be a "self-maintaining club of automata" who would also be candidates for real existents according to van Inwagen (van Inwagen 1990, 85 ff, 95, 137, 149). Hence, other counterexamples would be readily available for proving the non-validity of the popular argument. Whoever wants to dispose of these arguments would need to negate not only the existence of material artefacts, but also of living beings – and as we are living beings ourselves, this is a dangerous position playing with our own existence.

3 Construction and Reality

On closer inspection it can be seen that argument scheme (1) can be turned into a valid modus ponens by adding the following conditional sentence as an additional premise:

(3) If x has been constructed, x does not exist.

From a commonsense perspective, this is an odd principle. It seems to be just the other way round: Being object of an act of construction is evidence for existence rather than for non-existence; and non-existence is evidence for not having been constructed. We could, in fact, be tempted to argue as follows:

(4) Premise: x does not exist.
Conclusion: x has not been constructed.

(5) Premise: x has been constructed.
Conclusion: x exists.

Neither of these is, however, a valid inference, as can be seen from the example of the Twin Towers: Argument scheme (3) is not valid, because the Twin Towers do not exist today (true premise), but they have, of course, been constructed (false conclusion). Argument scheme (4) is not valid, because the Twin Towers have been constructed (true premise), but today they do not exist (false conclusion), though they existed up to September 11, 2001.

In order to exclude these counterexamples, we could give the verb "exist" a de-tensed interpretation:

(6) Premise: The Twin Towers have been constructed. (true)
Conclusion: The Twin Towers existed, exist or will exist. (true)

It would be a bit odd, though, to have a tensed premise and a de-tensed conclusion in the same argument. Alternatively, we can retain the tensed interpretation of "exist" and quantify over all times in the premise and conclusion:

(7) Premise: The Golden Tower never existed. (true)
Conclusion: The Golden Tower has never been constructed. (true)

And by contraposition:

(8) Premise: The Golden Tower was at some time constructed.
Conclusion: The Golden Tower existed at some time.

The reason for this is, of course, that construction processes are events in space and time, and that the mode of existence for constructed entities is temporal existence, this is existence in time. In both respects constructed entities differ from mathematical entities like the number 2 or an ideal rectangular triangle, which are normally conceived of as not coming into being by an act of construction, but as existing in a non-temporal way.[3] For this reason we need a temporalised version of the argument from non-existence, which is represented in the following scheme:

(9) Premise: x does not exist at any $t^* \leq t$.
     Conclusion: x has not been constructed at t.

Again, by contraposition we get:

(10) Premise: x has been constructed at t.
      Conclusion: x does exist at some $t^* \leq t$.

This is true because the process of construction is a process of bringing into existence: if an artefact never comes into existence, its construction process has never been completed. Hence, it is never true that this artefact has been constructed. Hence, the completion of the construction process guarantees that there is at least one point in time at which the constructed object exists. It obviously does not guarantee eternal existence, though. Constructed objects can later be deconstructed. They can be destroyed, deteriorate, scramble down, etc. There are many ways a constructed object can go out of existence. Hence, if we want to infer the present existence from the completion of a past construction process, we would have to exclude that any of these possible ways of ceasing to exist occurred. We would, that is, proceed as follows:

(11) Premises: x has been constructed.
                x has not been destroyed.
                x has not deteriorated.
                x has not scrambled down.
                …
     Conclusion: x exists now.

---

[3] Florian Fischer, in personal communication, asked me how I deal with geometrical constructions. This depends on whether we think of constructions on paper or in an idealized Euclidean plane. What we construct with real-world edge and compass is not an ideal rectangular triangle, but a paper diagram of it, whereas so-called constructions with ideal edge and compass do not bring an ideal triangle into existence, but rather identify which of the infinitely many triangles pre-existing in the Euclidian plane is the one we were referring to.

Without these additional premises we can only infer the existence of the constructed object for some point in time – more precisely, for the first moment of its existence:

(12) Premise: x has been constructed at t, and there is no $t^* < t$ at which x has already been constructed.
Conclusion: x exists at t.

The work here is, of course, done by the second clause in the premise. By requiring that t is the first time at which x has been constructed, i.e. at which the process of construction has been completed, it can be secured that there was no time interval, however short, in which x could have ceased to exist again. There is, of course, no logical need for artefacts to cease to exist after a short time. Some artefacts, like the Venus de Milo, the Great Wall of China or the Stonehenge monument, do, in fact, exist for a very long time. But neither is there a logical guarantee for their persistence, which we would need for a stronger version in lieu of argument scheme (12).

4 Why is the Fallacious Argument so Popular?

Now, if the popular argument is obviously fallacious and its premise is not so much evidence for its purported conclusion, but rather for its negation, then the question arises as to why the fallacious argument is so popular.

My guess is that its popularity is based on confusion between reality and banality, between reality in general on the one hand and the level of ontologically basic entities on the other hand. In the end, this comes down to a misconception of ontology itself. Let me explain. Ontological debates are often built around certain dichotomies like, for example, matter vs. mind, matter vs. form, nature vs. culture, matter vs. construction, simple vs. complex, small vs. big, basic vs. derived. But, of course, it would be an impoverished image of reality to think that it consists only of the material, natural, simple, basic or small. Reality consists, of course, of matter and mind, form and construction. It consists of nature and culture, the simple and the complex, the small and the big, the basic and the derived. Finally, it would be a misconception of ontology to think that it has only to deal with the basic, natural or small things. A full picture of our world has also to account for the derived, non-natural, complex and big things, and the way they depend on the basic etc. things. An adequate ontological theory of the world may thus not stop short of the description of the ontologically complex and derived bits of reality, in particular of constructed beings.

5 The Case of Fiction: Linguistic Therapy

A near relative of the popular argument from construction is the popular argument from fiction. What is fictitious, or so the argument goes, cannot be real. To call something a fiction normally goes along with ontological degradation: it is not real, but only human fiction.[4]

Some of the motivation behind this argument is perhaps that the false is sometimes called fiction. But, as Peter Strawson rightly says, "Fiction is not the same thing as falsehood, though we sometimes politely disguise the nature of falsehood by calling it fiction." (Strawson 1952, 69)[5]

The word "fiction" gained particular prominence in the context of the so-called fiction theory of juridical persons (Savigny 1840), as well as with Arnold Gehlens "Fiktionstheorie" of social institutions. However, Gehlen did not intend to ontologically degrade institutions, but referred to their origin. He discusses, for example, that some cultures allow for the change of gender by assuming the roles that are standardly ascribed to the opposite sex: "Fictive status representations have no diminished theoretical-anthropological relevance. Fiction that has become obligatory is a reality in its own right." (Gehlen 1956, 210)[6] And hence, we can add, fiction has no diminished ontological relevance.

But can fictions be real? If we consider the etymology of the word, the answer is clearly yes. In contemporary everyday language, the word "fiction" is mostly used in the meaning "(literary) invention", as in "science fiction", "fan fiction" and so on. In Latin, these are only two among many other possible meanings of the verb "fingere", its participle "fictum" or the noun "fictio" (see Georges 1958, I 2747 (s.v. fictio) and 2764–2766 (s.v. fingo)). In Latin, you can, of course, also speak about the inventions of the poets ("poetarum fictiones"), in particular the invention of a person or the personification of a non-person ("fictio personae", the equivalent to the Greek term *prosôpopoia*). But the Latin word *fictio* refers to any kind of making or becoming, be the generation of an individual body ("fictio nostri corporis") or of human beings in general ("fictio hominis") or the formation of words ("vocum fictiones"), in particular by onomatopoiesis after a natural sound ("fictio nominis"). In the juridical lan-

---

4 Witness the report of the argument as applied to social groups in (Gilbert 1989, 433 f): "There are no plural subjects *really*. It is a human *fiction* that there are." (italics in the original)
5 I am indebted to Petter Sandstad for pointing me to this reference.
6 My translation of: "Die fiktiven Statusdarstellungen haben keine geringe theoretisch-anthropologische Bedeutung. *Die obligatorisch gewordene Fiktion ist eine Realität eigenen Rechtes.*" (italics in the original).

guage, *fictio* is already used as a technical term in ancient times ("fictio legis"). The verb *fingo* (from whose participle, *fictum*, the noun *fictio* has been derived) means originally as much as "forming a mass" – such that Cicero can summon the orator to create his speech out of words as one forms and "feigns" malleable wax with one's fingers.[7] In Latin, bees "feign" the wax like artists "feign" a sculpture and birds "feign" their nests ("fingere et construere"), and nature is said to "feign" man. Hardly anybody wants to claim that the wax of the bees, the nests of the birds or human beings are mere inventions or not real. Even the laws, the fictions of jurists, are no shams or literary inventions. True, they do not exist by nature, are not grown on trees – this is a feature they share with the fictions of the poets. But there is an important difference: the content of a law is a valid and effective guideline for social interactions. Against this background, it is no wonder that Thomas Hobbes used the word "fictitium" more or less synonymously with "artificiall" – which does not connote unreality.[8]

The upshot of all this is that in our normal use of the word "fictive" we are used to applying it to literary inventions, while there are other uses of the word that do not have the same implication. When we accuse fictive entities of not being, we take this special use of the word as representative for all its uses. But it is not. This is also true for the English verb "to feign", which is derived from the Latin "fingere". It can still have the general meaning of "to fashion, form, shape", but judging from the space dedicated to the various meanings in the *Oxford English Dictionary*, the general meaning has been superseded by the narrower meaning "to fashion fictitiously or deceptively". Hence a rediscovery of the old general meaning of the verb is a good therapy against the linguistic bewitchment that makes us combine fiction with non-existence.

We could, thus, say that the argument from fiction falls prone to the fallacy of the wrong opposite, for the correct opposite of the fictive is not the real, but the non-fictive. What is fictive, however, is made and thus exists. Once we have seen this, we may also revise our stance on literary fictions. Even literary fictions, one could argue with Peter van Inwagen, must exist in a way, for the best analysis of true sentences about literary fictions (like "Sherlock Holmes is a male character") must quantify over them (see van Inwagen 1977). Hence, fictions exist; they are real. Or, to put it in a slogan: fictions are facts.

---

[7] See (Cicero 1963, III 177): "molissimam ceram ad nostrum arbitrium formare et fingere".
[8] See (Hobbes 1991, ch. 15) "persona fictitia" and (Hobbes 1996, 111): "Feigned or Artificiall person".

6 Epistemic Constructions

In the introduction I mentioned that many constructivists refer to the popular argument only to distance themselves from its conclusion. They rightly point out that constructions are, in a way, mind-dependent, but nevertheless exist. This position can well be called "realist constructivism" (Barkin 2010) or "realist constructionism" (Elder-Vaas 2012). Though this is, in a way, a realist position, metaphysical realism can still be in conflict with realist constructionism because many constructivists do not distinguish between ontic and epistemic constructions.[9] In the preceding sections I have discussed ontic constructions, i.e. constructions that bring things into being. Epistemic constructions, on the other hand, are constructions that bring into existence very special things like knowledge, theories, conceptual schemes or discourses – which, however, may well be about things that are not themselves constructions.

The constructivist's stress on epistemic constructions is a justified reaction to the positivist paradigm, according to which the world is something simply given to us in perception. It is a truism that there can be no knowledge without epistemic constructions. To know trees and atoms is to have a matching epistemic construction of them, while they exist independently of our mental states. But states and policemen are in need of acts of ontic constructions in order to exist in the first place. Once states and policemen exist, children can learn about them just like they learn about trees and atoms. But before this stage, states had to be established and policemen had to be appointed. This difference is not always observed. For example, Berger and Luckmann do not distinguish between the sociology of knowledge about already existing institutions (or other worldly entities) and the establishment of new social entities (Berger/Luckmann 1966/1991). These are, however, distinct phenomena. We need to distinguish between a child being socialised in a society with policemen or a police cadet being trained in a police academy on the one hand, and a police force being established or a policeman being appointed by the authorities on the other hand.

---

9 See for example (Patton 2015, 121): "[...] the world of human perception is not real in an absolute sense; for example, the sun is real but is 'made up' and shaped by cultural and linguistic constructs, for example, the sun as a god." The statement oscillates strangely between talk about human perception and the objects perceived. The sun obviously is all the same whether someone perceives it as a god or not; the difference is only in the perception.

In a nutshell, theories that conflate ontic and epistemic constructions treat trees[10] and atoms[11] in the same way as states and policemen. Trees and atoms, however, are mind-independent entities. True, sceptical arguments tell us that it may well be that they do not exist. This is particularly true for so-called theoretical entities like atoms, which we do not perceive with our naked eye, but whose existence we only infer from experimental observations. Thus, it might well be that atoms do not exist. But if they exist, their existence does not existentially depend on our minds. In fact, trees and atoms existed long before human minds evolved. Words like "tree" and "atoms" are, of course, human constructions, as well as cognitive schemata of trees and physical theories that deal with atoms. Our physical and chemical theories are well entrenched; nevertheless, it might well be that, in the future, still better theories will no longer talk about atoms, as we today no longer talk about ether or phlogiston.

But this does not imply that atoms are human constructions. The physical theories talking about and the linguistic entities referring to atoms are, indeed, human constructions, but not the atoms talked about or referred to. What is at stake here is a special kind of constructions, for which I use the term "epistemic constructions." Epistemic constructions can be of quite different ontological categories. They can be mental entities like thoughts and mental representations; abstract entities like theories or hypotheses; and even material documents like books, diagrams and pictures. What all these different epistemic constructions have in common is their semiotic character: they are signs representing some state of affairs. Such a semiotic character comes with a potential fit between representation and thing represented. There is, of course, also the possibility that representation and thing represented do not fit to each other, or that it turns out that there is no such thing that is purportedly represented. Today we consider the theories about the ether or phlogiston to be of this nature, but not the theories about atoms.

---

10 See (Crotty 1998, 43): "What the 'commonsense' view commends to us is that the tree standing before us is a tree. It has all the meaning we ascribe to a tree. It would be a tree, with that same meaning, whether anyone knew of its existence or not. We need to remind ourselves here that it is human beings who have construed it as a tree, given it the name, and attributed to it the associations we make with trees. It may help if we recall the extent to which those associations differ even within the same overall culture. 'Tree' is likely to bear quite different connotations in a logging town, an artists' settlement and a treeless slum."

11 See (Romanyshyn/Whalen 1989, 20): "We tend, however, to regard the atom as a discovered reality and, in this sense, as a real thing that already exists in nature. But the atom does not exist *in* nature. Atoms are not real but are ways of *realizing* nature. They are not only a something to be seen but are also ways of seeing. The observed is what it is in relation to the attitude of the observer. In this sense, the atom can be called a *construction*."

There is an important similarity between trees and atoms on the one hand and states and policemen on the other, but there is also an important difference. In all of these examples, our linguistic terms for them and our theories about them are constructions. But states and policemen are themselves constructions and trees and atoms are not. While we invariably use epistemic constructions for all domains of reality, only some domains of reality are ontic constructions and other domains – like many trees and atoms – are not.

7 Conclusion

I have shown that the arguments from construction and fiction are fallacious. Instead of being evidence for not being, being constructed is evidence for existence: all constructions exist at least at some time. Indeed, important parts of reality are not only constructed, but essentially constructed, among which are social reality, technical artefacts, art and fiction.

Ontic constructions always exist at least at some point in time, or else they would not have been successfully constructed. This also applies to epistemic constructions. Epistemic constructions always exist at least at some point in time – but they may or may not represent the world correctly.

Some of the quarrels between constructivists and realists seem to be of terminological nature. For the realist it is unacceptable that everyone "constructs their own reality". There is only one reality, though everyone may contribute to this reality by constructing things on their own or collectively. So I would advise adhering to the integrity of reality, but say that everyone has their own perception of it. Also, there is no departmentalization of reality: if something is real, it is real – full stop. Hence, instead of saying that something is "not real in the absolute sense" (Patton 2015, 121), say that it is ontologically dependent on other entities. Instead of saying that something is "not real in a biological sense" (Fitzgerald 2014, 18), say that it depends on social attitudes, collective intentions, social or legal norms or human actions. Do not say "trees are construction" when you mean that our perceptions of trees depend on culture; and do not say that "atoms are constructions" if you mean that our acceptance of them and the way we talk about them depends on language and theory. This will also provide an opportunity for being more precise: What exactly do these entities depend on ontologically? On intentions, rules, practises, actions or documents?

Without such cautious language, it will not be possible to distinguish between, for example, ontic and epistemic constructions. This will, however, be crucial in order to develop a unified theory of constructed entities. Currently there is no ontology of constructions as such. But important work has been done on various special kinds of constructions. Exciting new debates are going on about social reality (Gilbert 1989, Searle 2011, Jansen 2016), material culture in general (Dipert 1993, Preston 2013) and technical artefacts in particular (Houkes/Vermaas 2010, Kroes 2012), on the ontology of art works (Schmücker 2014, 2009) and fictional entities (Reicher 2010, Daiber et al. 2013). Further work is required to bring together these different strands of discussions into a unified theory of constructed reality – a general ontology of artefacts. In particular, there is need for an elucidation of the relationship between ontic and epistemic constructions. That they cannot simply be treated alike has been argued for in this paper, but the exact nature of their relation is still in the dark.

References

Barkin, J. Samuel (2010): *Realist Constructivism. Rethinking International Relations Theory.* Cambridge: Cambridge University Press.
Berger, Peter; Luckmann, Thomas (1966/1991): *The Social Construction of Reality. A Treatise in the Sociology of Knowledge.* London: Penguin.
Brett, David (1996): *The Construction of Heritage.* Cork: Cork University Press.
Cicero, Marcus Tullius (1963): *De Oratore.* Edited by Augustus Wilkins. Oxford: Clarendon Press.
Crotty, Michael (1998): *The Foundations of Social Research: Meaning and Perspective in the Research Process.* Los Angeles: Sage.
Daiber, Jürgen; Konrad, Eva-Maria; Petraschka, Thomas; Rott, Hans (eds.) (2013): *Fiktion, Wahrheit, Interpretation. Philologische und philosophische Perspektiven.* Münster: Mentis.
Dipert, Randall R. (1993): *Artifacts, Art Works, and Agency.* Philadelphia: Temple University Press.
Dumouchel, Paul (2014): *The Ambivalence of Scarcity and Other Essays.* East Lansing: Michigan State University Press.
Elder-Vaas, Dave (2012): *The Reality of Social Construction.* Cambridge: Cambridge University Press.
Fitzgerald, Kathleen (2014): *Recognizing Race and Ethnicity. Power, Privilege and Inequality.* Boulder CO: Westview.
Gehlen, Arnold (1956): *Urmensch und Spätkultur. Philosophische Ergebnisse und Aussagen.* Bonn: Athenäum.
Georges, Karl Ernst (1958): *Ausführliches Lateinisch-Deutsches Handwörterbuch.* Hannover/Leipzig: Hahn.
Gergen, Kenneth J. (2009): *An Invitation to Social Construction.* Second edition. Los Angeles: Sage.
Gilbert, Margaret (1989): *On Social Facts.* London/New York: Routledge.
Hacking, Ian (1999): *The Social Construction of What?* Cambridge MA: Harvard University Press.
Hobbes, Thomas (1991): *Man and Citzen.* Edited by Bernhard Gert. Indianapolis: Hackett.

Hobbes, Thomas (1996): *Leviathan*. Edited by Richard Tuck. Cambridge: Cambridge Universite Press.
Houkes, Wibo; Vermaas, Pieter E. (2010): *Technical Functions. On the Use and Design of Artefacts*. Dordrecht: Springer.
Jansen, Ludger (2013): "Warum sich Artefakte ihrer Marginalisierung widersetzen". In: *Deutsche Zeitschrift für Philosophie* 61, 267–282.
Jansen, Ludger (2016): *Gruppen und Institutionen. Eine Ontologie des Sozialen*. Wiesbaden: Springer.
Kroes, Peter (2012): *Technical Artefacts: Creations of Mind and Matter. A Philosophy of Engineering Design*. Dordrecht: Springer.
Patton, Michael Quinn (2015): *Qualitative Research and Evaluation Methods. Integrating Theory and Practice*. Fourth Edition. Los Angeles: Sage.
Pickering, Neil (2006): *The Metaphor of Mental Illness*. Oxford: Oxford University Press.
Preston, Beth (2013): *A Philosophy of Material Culture. Action, Function, and Mind*. New York: Routledge.
Reicher, Maria E. (ed.) (2010): *Fiktion, Wahrheit, Wirklichkeit. Philosophische Grundlagen der Literaturtheorie*. Paderborn: Mentis.
Romanyshyn, Robert D.; Whalen, Brian J. (1989): "Psychology and the Attitude of Science". In: Valle, Ronald S.; Halling, Steen (eds.): *Existential-Phenomenological Perspectives in Psychology: Exploring the Breadth of Human Experience*. New York/London: Plenum Press, 17–40.
Schmücker, Reinold (2009): *Identität und Existenz. Studien zur Ontologie der Kunst*. Paderborn: Mentis.
Schmücker, Reinold (2014): *Was ist Kunst? Eine Grundlegung*. Frankfurt am Main: Klostermann.
Searle, John R. (1995): *The Construction of Social Reality*, New York: Free Press.
Searle, John R. (2010): *Making the Social World. The Structure of Human Civilization*. Oxford: Oxford University Press.
Sprague, Joey (2005): *Feminist Methodologies for Critical Researchers. Bridging Differences*. Walnut Creek CA: Altamira.
van Inwagen, Peter (1977): "Creatures of Fiction". In: *American Journal of Philosophy* 14, 299–308.
van Inwagen, Peter (1990): *Material Beings*. Ithaca: Cornell University Press.
von Savigny, Carl (1840): *System des heutigen römischen Rechts*, Vol. 2. Berlin: Veit.
Vogel, Steven (2015): *Thinking like a Mall. Environmental Philosophy after the End of Nature*. Cambridge MA: MIT Press.

Peter Kügler
Ontological Relativism as Transcendental Nominalism

Abstract: Ontological relativism denies metaphysical realism and thus the assumption of natural kinds. Instead, it postulates a pre-conceptually given reality or experience that is sometimes envisaged as an unstructured domain (unformed matter, raw experience) ready to be structured by concepts. This paper argues that ontological relativism is best interpreted as transcendental nominalism and that the latter is to be distinguished from metaphysical nominalism, which is a limiting case of metaphysical realism. Transcendental nominalism construes the pre-conceptual as an experience of individuals. Following a suggestion by Dominik Perler, we may understand this experience, which medieval nominalists called "sensory intuitive cognition", as encoding information about individuals in analog form (Dretske). Conceptual schemes classify individuals, particularly objects of experience. They do not structure an unstructured something, nor do they "carve nature at the joints".

Keywords: Relativism, realism, transcendental nominalism, conceptual schemes

1 Ontological Relativity

What kinds of things are there? Ontological relativity is the idea that any answer to this question depends on conceptual decisions and has therefore only relative validity. We cannot ask or answer ontological questions independently of conceptual schemes. Different schemes imply different ontologies.

It is important to distinguish this relativity of ontology – of *kinds* of things – from the constructivist idea that the existence of *things* depends on concepts. Existential relativity of this sort would raise an objection that Paul Boghossian calls the "problem of causation": Many things have existed before the appearance of human beings on earth; if the existence of these things depended on our concepts, we would have to be able to do the impossible: to create our own past by speaking about it (Boghossian 2006, 38).

Ontological relativity is closely associated with the name of Willard van Orman Quine. An article from 1968 bears this title as well as the anthology in which this article reappeared (Quine 1969). Yet the idea of ontological relativity is already present in Quine's earlier essay "On What There Is" (Quine 1948). Later, Hilary Putnam incorporated Quine's idea into his "pragmatic" or "internal realism", replacing "ontological relativity" with "conceptual relativity", which he defines in one place as "the fact that the logical primitives themselves, and in particular the notions of object and existence, have a multitude of different uses rather than one absolute 'meaning'" (Putnam 1987, 19).

Here is one of Putnam's examples: suppose you see three individuals, let's say, three dice. The question as to how many things there are obviously depends on what we mean by "thing", that is, on how we identify and count things. If you understand things as individual cubes, you will count three. If your concept of thing covers mereological sums, too, you will count seven things, namely three cubes plus three sums of two cubes, plus the sum of all three cubes. These are just two of many possible interpretations of "thing" that yield different descriptions of the situation.

The above seems rather trivial; it is no surprise that the meanings and truth-values of statements about things depend on what the word "thing" means. This only becomes interesting when we assume that the various descriptions are ontologically on a par and that none of them represents reality "as it is in itself". In other words, conceptual relativity gets its force by the denial of what Putnam has called "metaphysical realism".

2 Metaphysical Realism

On this perspective, the world consists of some fixed totality of mind-independent objects. There is exactly one true and complete description of "the way the world is". Truth involves some sort of correspondence relation between words or thought-signs and external things and sets of things (Putnam 1981, 49).

This is how Putnam described metaphysical realism before he would replace "mind-independent" with the less misleading term "language-independent" (Putnam 1990, 27). The history of philosophy includes many classical examples of metaphysical realism. The following is a more recent account from Theodor Sider's book *Writing the Book of the World:*

"Metaphysics, at bottom, is about the fundamental structure of reality. [...] Discerning 'structure' means discerning patterns. It means figuring out the right categories for describing the world. It means 'carving reality at its joints', to paraphrase Plato." (Sider 2011, 1)

There is no doubt that metaphysical realism provides some theoretical benefits. Among others, it suggests a straightforward account of the truth-values of assertions about reality. Reality makes some of these assertions true and others false. On the other hand, however, metaphysical realists tend to downplay problems of meaning and reference, for example by claiming that concepts refer to reality by "carving nature at the joints", even if we are not able to explain the meanings of these joint-carving concepts.

The metaphysical realist typically thinks that reality comprises *natural kinds* or entities akin to these (universals, natural properties, structures), and that general terms refer to these entities. This view of semantics has been called "reference magnetism" (Sider 2011, 23 ff), a metaphor expressing the idea that semantic reference is caused by something like an "attraction" between words and natural kinds. Sider goes as far as to claim that *existence* is a natural kind to which the word "existence" refers (Sider 2006, §4; 2009, §11). (I will return to this at the end of section 4.)

Reference magnetism raises the difficult problem of how natural kinds manage to "magnetically attract" words. Garry Merrill (1980) and David Lewis (1984) did not answer this question when they proposed reference magnetism *avant la lettre* in criticizing Putnam. Sider however invokes the assumption that the notion of reference has a function in explaining linguistic behavior (Sider 2011, 28): when I utter or write a sentence, the fact that the words in this sentence refer to reality is part of the explanation of my behavior. In short, I am using the word "cube" *because* it refers to cubes. According to Sider, this implies that reference is a "joint-carving relation", for otherwise it would not really be explanatory.

Unfortunately, Sider seems to miss the circularity of his argument. As he readily admits (Sider 2011, 23), language use is essential for explaining reference, which means that the reverse of the above explanation is also true: the word "cube" refers to cubes *because* we use it in the way we do. Sider thinks that language use is not sufficient for determining reference; the rest is supplied by the "magnetism" of natural kinds. Nevertheless, the question remains how reference can explain linguistic behavior given that the latter is part of the explanation of the former. It is much more plausible to explain linguistic behavior, like other kinds of behavior, by psychological factors, including reasons, beliefs, motives, and sense impressions.

3 The Pre-conceptual

Ontological relativism rejects natural kinds and denies any predetermined ontological structure to which concepts would refer. Even ontological relativists, however, postulate something that exists prior to and independent of descriptions. Ontological relativism shares with metaphysical realism the distinction between concepts or conceptual schemes on the one side, and that to which concepts are applied on the other. Putnam refers to the latter, somewhat loosely, as "reality" or "world", whereas Quine prefers sense experience in this role, at least in the following statement from "On What There Is":

> Our acceptance of an ontology is, I think, similar in principle to our acceptance of a scientific theory, say a system of physics: we adopt, at least insofar as we are reasonable, the simplest conceptual scheme into which the disordered fragments of raw experience can be fitted and arranged. (Quine 1948, 35f)

This emphasis on experience is reminiscent of Immanuel Kant, who famously distinguished between matter and form of appearance in the *Transcendental Aesthetic* of the first *Critique* (Kant 1929, B 34, A 20). Just as philosophers after Kant have wondered what an unformed matter of appearance (*Empfindung*) might be, we may ask ourselves what Quine means by "disordered fragments of raw experience". It is true that Quine favored the term "stimulation" later on (Quine 1969), but this preference for a particular conceptual scheme – of physics or behavioristic psychology – is arguably in conflict with the notion that different conceptual schemes are ontologically on a par.

The analogous question for Putnam is this: what is the nature of the pre-conceptual *reality*, of the world prior to and independent of descriptions? But whether the pre-conceptual is construed as raw experience (Quine) or as some external reality (Putnam), the obvious problem is that neither of these can be conceptually characterized without losing its pre-conceptual status. As Putnam puts it, "what we cannot say – because it makes no sense – is what the facts are independent of all choices." (Putnam 1987, 33) This, in turn, raises the question if we understand the notion of the pre-conceptual at all, given that we cannot understand it by means of concepts and descriptions.

Some might try to avoid this problem by abandoning the notion of the pre-conceptual altogether, which would lead to a position that deserves to be called "constructivism". We already know, however, that constructivism runs into Boghossian's "problem of causation". What is constructed did not exist prior to construction, yet the world did not begin with us. Consider the following statement by Richard Rorty, which is an affirmative comment on Donald Davidson's well-known criticism of the distinction between scheme and content:

> [Davidson] suggests that we stop trying to say *anything* general about the relation between language and reality, that we stop falling into our opponents' trap by taking seriously problems that owe their existence to the scheme-content distinction. We should just refuse to discuss such topics as "the nature of reference." [...] This strategy dictates that whenever we are asked a question like "*Was* the solar system waiting around for Kepler?" we decline to answer. (Rorty 1998, 90f)

This is hardly convincing, however, for it is difficult to see why it would not make sense to ask whether the solar system existed before Kepler (or Copernicus, or Aristarchos of Samos, for that matter). This question is certainly intelligible, and we have every reason to answer it with "yes".

Unlike Rorty and other constructivists, the ontological relativist will admit the existence of the solar system before Kepler (Copernicus, Aristarchos). Objects are not constructed by concepts. The real theoretical challenge is to identify the conditions of the construction of *ontologies* and, in particular, to give a satisfactory account of the relationship between a conceptual scheme and the pre-conceptual domain to which the scheme is applied.

4 Metaphysical and Transcendental Nominalism

To conceive of the pre-conceptual in a nominalistic fashion is probably the best way to approach the theoretical challenge just mentioned. Here we may draw on Ian Hacking's interpretation of Putnam's viewpoint:

> Kant called himself a transcendental idealist. I would call Putnam a transcendental nominalist. [...] Idealism is a thesis about *existence*. In its extreme form it says that all that exists is mental, a production of the human spirit. Nominalism is about *classification*. It says that only our modes of thinking make us sort grass from straw, flesh from foliage. The world does not have to be sorted that way; it does not come wrapped up in "natural kinds". (Hacking 1983, 108)

It is rather obvious that at least some forms of idealism are forms of constructivism, but we can put idealism aside, as this is not our topic. Regarding nominalism, Hacking notes that it includes the rejection of natural kinds (which comes along with Putnam's denial of metaphysical realism). It is not clear, however, what Hacking means by "transcendental" in this context. Above all, he fails to explain what distinguishes transcendental nominalism from other types of nominalism, which I shall subsume under the term "metaphysical nominalism".

The defining thesis of metaphysical nominalism is that only individuals exist, but no abstract or universal objects. Regarding the meaning of "individual", we may employ Rudolf Carnap's explanation of this term:

> [T]he so-called individual objects have in common that they are temporally determined, either as belonging to a given time point or a connected time stretch. Furthermore, there is always a definite space point or a connected spatial area to which they belong, if they can be spatially determined at all. On the other hand, the sense quality brown, for example, has many unconnected space-time areas assigned to it [...]. (Carnap 2003, 248, §158)

Carnap was *not* a metaphysical nominalist, however. For him, the choice of elementary experiences (*Elementarerlebnisse*) as basic elements (*Grundelemente*) of the constructional system (*Konstitutionssystem*) was merely a matter of convention (Carnap 2003, 107 ff). It is always possible to choose other elements. For the metaphysical nominalist, by contrast, the aim of such conceptual choices is to establish a correspondence between concepts and pre-existing types of things. These types do not exist by convention, and it is the function of concepts to represent them.

William of Ockham, for example, the paradigmatic nominalist of medieval philosophy, reduced Aristotle's ten categories to substance and quality, implying that reality is made up of individuals of these two types. Modern nominalists go even further in terms of reduction, assuming, for example, that reality consists of concrete particulars (Rodriguez-Pereyra 2002) or of abstract particulars, also known as tropes (Campbell 1990). The metaphysical nominalist may as well opt for particular events or particular processes, or any combination of ontological types, as long as these are supposed to be types of *individuals*.

Metaphysical nominalists do not think that these categorizations are mere conventions. They intend to map the ontological structure of the world by finding the right categories of individuals, which is what makes this nominalism *metaphysical*, after all. Reality in itself consists of specific individuals, and only a conceptual scheme that posits the right types of individuals can provide a true description of reality.

Assuming the traditional distinction between species and genus, ontological categories such as "substance" and "quality" denote genera, more precisely, *supreme genera*, the most general natural kinds. In other words, metaphysical nominalism does postulate natural kinds, if only very few of them. It follows that metaphysical nominalism is a weak version of metaphysical realism. When we think of natural kinds, we usually think of elementary particles, chemical elements, biological species, and the like. Yet in the context of metaphysical nominalism, the relevant kinds are ontological ones – substance and quality, or whatever categories the metaphysical nominalist prefers.

Let us turn to *transcendental* nominalism, which proceeds from the idea that pre-conceptual experience is an experience of individuals. As many philosophers have observed, however, experience does not present an assemblage of unconnected individuals. Carnap, for example, who based his constructional system on elementary experiences, rightly noted that these items are not epistemically primary. What comes first in the epistemic order is what he calls the "stream of experience" (*Erlebnisstrom*) (Carnap 2003, 102).

It is well-known that the interrelatedness of experiences is especially prominent in the philosophy of William James. In "A World of Pure Experience", for example, James argues that "the relations that connect experiences must themselves be experienced relations, and any kind of relation experienced must be accounted as 'real' as anything else in the system" (James 1912, 42, italics removed). For James, experienced relations include qualitative similarity and difference, as well as spatiotemporal relations such as simultaneity and spatial distance.

Nominalists would want to remark that all these relations are individual relations, or relational individuals, if you will. In addition, they would resist the temptation to include qualia (sense qualities) among the objects of pre-conceptual experience. Qualia have been postulated to explain qualitative similarity and difference, but qualia are experiential kinds. If every kind is created by conceptual classification, this must also be true of qualia.

Insofar as ontology deals with ontological categories, it depends on the availability of conceptual schemes that classify experienced individuals. We may express this by saying that the pre-conceptual experience of individuals is a *transcendental condition* of ontology. Considered by itself, pre-conceptual experience is ontologically neutral, which is the reason why it is compatible with different conceptual schemes and different ontologies.

Finally, I come back to Sider's claim mentioned above: that existence is a natural kind to which the word "existence" refers. Obviously, this alone does not tell us what existence is. It is an advantage of transcendental nominalism over metaphysical realism that it suggests a promising strategy to analyze the notion of existence (which I can only outline here). The basic idea is that the presence of individuals as objects of experience is the paradigm case of existence. This is not to say that "presence in experience" covers the full range of the concept of existence, since many objects are not objects of experience. Nevertheless, we may conjecture that other meanings of "existence" can be derived from its primary meaning.

5 Intuitive Cognition

Pre-conceptual experience is not just a source of suitable material that is handed over to cognition. It is neither an unformed matter of perception (Kant), nor does it consist of "disordered fragments of raw experience" (Quine). Rather, it is a type of cognition itself, namely experiential cognition of individuals. Ockham referred to it as "intuitive cognition", *cognitio* or *notitia intuitiva*, borrowing a term from John Duns Scotus (Pasnau 2003, 296 ff).

Intuitive cognition divides into sensory and intellectual intuitive cognition. For our purposes, the first type is more interesting than the second one, since medieval nominalists construed it as pre-conceptual. In the cognitive process, sensory intuitive cognition precedes conceptual classification and judgement. In an article on Ockham and his pupil Adam Wodeham, Dominik Perler explains the interaction of *cognitio intuitiva sensitiva* and *cognitio intuitiva intellectiva* by way of an example:

> As long as I have a mere sensory intuitive cognition of the apple, I see it as something existent, and I am able to distinguish it from other objects present to me, given the specific shape, size and color I grasp. Yet I do not use the mental term "apple" or any other term to categorize the apple. This is why I am not yet able to come up with the judgment that there is an apple in front of me. For such a judgment, I clearly need mental categorematic and syncategorematic terms that come into existence only as soon as I engage in an intellectual activity. [...] This distinction between a pre-conceptual act of seeing (sensory intuitive cognition) and a conceptual act of apprehending (intellectual intuitive cognition) inevitably raises the question of how we should understand pre-conceptual seeing. (Perler 2008, 155f)

Answering the question in the final sentence, Perler alludes to Fred Dretske's distinction between analog and digital coding of information. According to Dretske,

> a signal (structure, event, state) carries the information that *s* is *F* in *digital* form if and only if the signal carries no additional information about *s*, no information that is not already nested in *s*'s being *F*. If the signal *does* carry additional information about *s*, information that is *not* nested in *s*'s being *F*, then I shall say that the signal carries this information in analog form. (Dretske 1981, 137)

The term "nesting" needs a bit of explanation. Dretske states that a particular information is "nested in *s*'s being *F*" if and only if *s*'s being *F* carries this information. A signal carrying the information that *s* is *F* also carries any information nested in *s*'s being *F* (Dretske 1981, 71). For example, if a signal carries the information *that there is an apple*, it also carries the nested information *that there is a piece of fruit*.

How does this help to understand the difference between sensory and intellectual intuitive cognition? Consider again the information that there is an apple. My *seeing* the apple, *qua cognitio intuitiva sensitiva*, carries this information in *analog* form, because it also carries additional information *not* nested in the information that there is an apple: information about the color of the apple, its size, shape, and so on. The *judgment* that there is an apple, by contrast, carries its information in *digital* form, as it does *not* carry additional information not nested in the information that there is an apple. For example, it does not carry information as to the apple's color, size, and shape.

The judgment belongs to *cognitio intuitiva intellectiva*. It is the intellect's contribution to cognition and involves conceptual classification of individual things. *Sensory* intuitive cognition, on the other hand, is a condition of the possibility of conceptual classification and therefore of ontology.

To complete this brief tour into medieval nominalism, I should mention that the opposite of intuitive cognition is abstractive cognition, *cognitio abstractiva*. The word "abstractive" has more than one meaning in Ockham, including "a wide sense in which all acts of cognition that are not intuitive are abstractive" (Karger 1999, 206). Abstractive cognition in this sense covers all judgements about objects that are not actually experienced, such as memory judgments and judgments about distant objects or imperceptible constituents of objects.

It is safe to assume that there can be no abstractive cognition without intuitive cognition. Ockham's contemporary Peter Aureol describes this dependence as follows: "an abstractive cognition presupposes an intuitive one. For the universal is abstracted only insofar as the singular has been under sense and intuition" (Peter Aureol 2002, 48): Concepts emerge in the context of intuitive cognition and are then used to describe non-present parts of reality or to develop, by various logical means, appropriate concepts for describing these parts.

References

Boghossian, Paul (2006): *Fear of Knowledge. Against Relativism and Constructivism*. Oxford: Oxford University Press.
Campbell, Keith (1990): *Abstract Particulars*. Oxford: Blackwell.
Carnap, Rudolf (2003): *The Logical Structure of the World and Pseudoproblems in Philosophy*. Translated by Rolf A. George. Chicago: Open Court.
Dretske, Fred I. (1981): *Knowledge and the Flow of Information*. Cambridge, MA: MIT.
Hacking, Ian (1983): *Representing and Intervening: Introductory Topics in the Philosophy of Natural Science*. Cambridge: Cambridge University Press.
James, William (1912): *Essays in Radical Empiricism*. New York: Longmans, Green, and Co.
Kant, Immanuel (1929): *Critique of Pure Reason*. Translated by Norman Kemp Smith. London: Macmillan.
Karger, Elizabeth (1999): "Ockham's Misunderstood Theory of Intuitive and Abstractive Cognition". In: Spade, Paul Vincent (ed.): *The Cambridge Companion to Ockham*. Cambridge: Cambridge University Press, 204–226.
Lewis, David (1984): "Putnam's Paradox". In: *Australasian Journal of Philosophy* 62, 221–236.
Merrill, Garry (1980): "The Model-Theoretic Argument against Realism". In: *Philosophy of Science* 47, 69–81.
Pasnau, Robert (2003): "Cognition". In: Williams, Thomas (ed.): *The Cambridge Companion to Duns Scotus*. Cambridge: Cambridge University Press, 285–311.

Perler, Dominik (2008): "Seeing and Judging: Ockham and Wodeham on Sensory Cognition". In: Knuuttila, Simo; Kärkkäinen, Pekka (eds.): *Theories of Perception in Medieval and Early Modern Philosophy*. Dordrecht: Springer, 151–169.
Peter Aureol (2002): "Intuition, Abstraction, and Demonstrative Knowledge". In: Pasnau, Robert (ed.): *The Cambridge Translations of Medieval Philosophical Texts. Volume 3: Mind and Knowledge*. New York: Cambridge University Press, 178–218.
Putnam, Hilary (1981): *Reason, Truth and History*. Cambridge: Cambridge University Press.
Putnam, Hilary (1987): *The Many Faces of Realism*. LaSalle, IL: Open Court.
Putnam, Hilary (1990): *Realism with a Human Face*. Edited by James Conant. Cambridge, MA: Harvard University Press.
Quine, Willard van Orman (1969): *Ontological Relativity and Other Essays*. New York: Columbia University Press.
Quine, Willard van Orman (1948): "On What There Is". In: *Review of Metaphysics* 2, 21–38.
Rodriguez-Pereyra, Gonzalo (2002): *Resemblance Nominalism: A Solution to the Problem of Universals*. Oxford: Clarendon.
Rorty, Richard (1998): *Truth and Progress: Philosophical Papers. Volume 3*. Cambridge: Cambridge University Press.
Sider, Theodore (2006): "Quantifiers and Temporal Ontology". In: *Mind* 115, 75–97.
Sider, Theodore (2009): "Ontological Realism". In: Chalmers, David; Manley, David; Wasserman, Ryan (eds.): *Metametaphysics*. Oxford: Oxford University Press, 384–423.
Sider, Theodore (2011): *Writing the Book of the World*. Oxford: Oxford University Press.

Martine Nida-Rümelin
Realism about Identity and Individuality of Conscious Beings

Abstract: According to the realist view, conscious beings are perfect individuals: their Identity across time (what it takes for them to continue existing) and their individuality (what it takes for them to exist under counterfactual circumstances) has no informative explication. Nonetheless we can understand, engaging in a specific mode of thought (conceptually taking the perspective of others) what the identity and individuality of a given conscious individual consists in. This particular version of realism about the identity and individuality of conscious beings can be used to motivate a non-materialist view about conscious individuals. The argument is based on the premise (to be justified) that thinking about others in the specific mode at issue is to manifest genuine understanding of what being a conscious individual amounts to.

Keywords: Consciousness, identity, realism, experience, subject-body dualism

1 Introduction

The aim of this talk is to defend and motivate a realist view in a specific sense of 'realism' and with respect to a very specific domain: I will argue that we should regard the question of identity between conscious individuals existing at different moments in time as a question about an objective feature of reality which does not in any sense depend on our conceptualization, which cannot be ruled by convention and which always has – independently of whether there is a way to find it out – a determinate answer. An analogous thesis will be defended for counterfactual circumstances: it is a factual question about considered counterfactual circumstances in which role a given conscious individual A exists under those circumstances (if at all) and the question can only be answered saying of *that* individual A (rigidly referring to A) which role it is supposed to occupy under the circumstances imagined. – The conference to which this talk contributes focusses on realism in a different and broader sense. Its central theme is the issue about whether or in what sense there is a mind-independent reality consisting of objects having properties and standing in relations to one another independently of the way we conceptualize that reality. The realist view here sketched about transtemporal identity and individuality of conscious beings is however not unrelated to that broader topic. It could be used to argue for a radical position with respect to the issue about realism in the broader sense. It is a natural consequence of the view here defended that conscious individuals are the *only* genuine individuals in the sense that only of them is it right to say that they exist independently of our conceptual schemes. These far-fetching consequences will however not be addressed here in any explicit manner.

Identity and individuality of conscious beings is usually only addressed in philosophy with respect to the special case of people or human beings. According to the view here presented this is a mistake. All reasons one may have for adopting a realist position with respect to the identity and individuality of people are equally well justified for and applicable to the general case of conscious beings. These deeper reasons speaking in favor of the realist view can be easily overlooked or misunderstood when one focuses on the special case of human beings.

Realism about the identity and individuality of conscious beings is deeply incorporated in our thinking.[1] Upon reflection the realist view about what it takes for a conscious being to exist across time (transtemporal identity) or to exist in counterfactual circumstances (transworld identity) turns out to be intuitively forced upon us. One might suspect, as it is often claimed, that we are led astray here by our natural intuitions. I will argue that this is not so. I will first explicate the realist position by several claims and explain their intuitive motivation. I will then sketch the conceptual basis of the realist intuition and briefly sketch how one may argue that the relevant intuition should be trusted. The aim of the overall argument is to show that realism should be adopted as adequate to the nature of conscious individuals.[2]

---

[1] See for more on this issue (Nida-Rümelin 2006), sections 3.10 and 3.15–3.20.
[2] Realism about transtemporal personal identity can be attributed to Bishop Butler and to Thomas Reid (see Butler 2008 and Reid 1984). In contemporary philosophy the view has been defended among others by Roderick Chisholm, Richard Swinburne and Geoffrey Madell (see Chisholm 1970, Swinburne 1984, Madell 1981). Swinburne integrates the view into a variant of substance dualism according to which a person consists of a material and an immaterial part, the latter being the soul which is composed of immaterial stuff. According to Chisholm the person is not a composed entity and he rejects the idea of immaterial stuff. (I side with Chisholm on this issue and cannot make sense of the idea of an immaterial stuff). Parfit famously rejects realism despite his explicit endorsement of the claim that our natural intuitions favor the realist view about transtemporal personal identity compare (Parfit 1984 and 1999). Realism about transtemporal identity of conscious beings in the sense here presented is elaborated in (Nida-Rümelin 2006, 2008, 2012b and in forthcoming, chapter 6.

2 Realism about Transtemporal Identity of Conscious Beings

The core intuition of realism about transtemporal identity of conscious beings can be captured by the following claims R1 to R5. R1 expresses the intuition that a description of the world which does not specify for conscious beings existing at different moments whether or not they are one and the same is, by that token, an incomplete description of the world; it leaves open a factual question. Here is a way to formulate the idea a bit more precisely:

> R1 (non-reducibility + determinate answer): If A (existing at m) and B (existing at m') are conscious individuals and if D is a complete description of the world, then D explicitly contains or logically implies either "A = B" or "A ≠ B".

The intuitive motivation behind this claim can be put as follows: it is a factual question about the earlier existing individual A which fate it will live trough at the later moment m' considered; and it is a factual question about the later existing individual B what it is that B experienced at the earlier moment m under consideration. But these factual questions depend on the question of identity between A and B. Furthermore, in order to answer them it must be explicitly specified if A and B are one and the same (or something explicitly said in the description must logically imply this information). No description of bodily or psychological relations between A and B formulated in 'identity-neutral' terms (that is in a way which does not explicitly mention or logically imply whether or not they are identical) gives an answer to these factual questions. This motivation makes use of the following conceptual truth (it is presupposed that A exists at moment m and B at moment m'):

> (1) A = B if and only if
> (2) B's life at m' is part of A's future at m; A's life at m is part of B's past at m'.

The relevant intuition is this: A description which does not explicitly mention whether or not A and B are identical does not answer the factual question about whether (2) is true or false. Therefore, such a description is not complete.

The following claim R2 is arguably implied by R1 but highlights a different aspect of the realist view. According to R2 there are no metaphysically possible cases in which there is no answer to the question whether an earlier existing conscious individual A is or is not identical to a later existing individual B. The claim that there is no such answer does not just mean that the answer cannot be found. It means, literally, that no such answer exists; the claim is, in other words, that the real features of the world do not determine which answer adequately describes the real situation. The realist about transtemporal identity of conscious beings says that there is no such metaphysical possibility because the existence of such a case is incompatible with what it *is* to be a conscious individual. Using the definition D below, this claim can be briefly formulated in the following way:

> R2 (no under-determination): there is no metaphysically possible case such that, if the case were actual, then the identity of a conscious individual A (existing at m) with a conscious individual B (existing at m') would be under-determined by that case.
>
> Definition D: The proposition p is underdetermined by a given actual case if and only if the real features of the case neither determine that p is true nor that p is false.

The motivation for accepting R2 is analogous to the motivation for accepting R1. The basic intuition here is that there must be an answer to the question about what the individual A will experience at the later moment m' and that there must be an answer to what the individual B experienced at the earlier moment m. It cannot be, in other words, that even an omniscient being could not give an answer to A's question about his or her future or to B's question about his or her past. But, given the above formulated equivalence between (1) and (2), if there must be an answer to those questions, then there must be an answer to the question of identity between A and B as well.

The following claim R3 could be seen to be implied by R2 with the help of further premises. R3 concerns conventional decisions. In a case where an ordinary non-conscious object has two successors which both appear to be equally good candidates for being considered identical to the original object (like, perhaps, in the case of the division of a plant which for the present purposes is assumed not to be conscious), one might well take a conventional decision about which successor should be considered identical with the original object. Such a conventional decision may rule legal issues and one does not risk getting things wrong by adopting such a conventional decision. In the case of a conscious being conventional decisions may be taken in order to rule practical issues as well; but in those cases one *does* take an epistemic risk: by adopting the convention one might miss-describe the world. One might rule, by convention, that A is to be regarded as identical with B and yet it may be that, *in fact*, A is not identical to B and vice versa. The claim just sketched may be formulated as follows:

> R3 (no decision by convention without epistemic risk): The question of identity between a conscious individual A (existing at m) and a conscious individual B (existing at m') cannot be decided by convention without thereby taking the risk of miss-describing the actual situation.

In order to see how R3 is intuitively motivated one must again use the above mentioned equivalence between (1) and (2) and focus on (2) first. The intuition is that (2) describes an objective feature of the world which does not depend on anybody's arbitrary decision about how to describe the case. It follows that (1) cannot depend on such a decision either.[3]

A related and yet slightly different claim characterizing the realist view about the identity of conscious beings is a thesis about the nature of the question we are asking when we reflect upon the question of transtemporal identity between conscious individuals. In other cases, concerning non-conscious objects such as plants, tables, watches or socially constituted objects, the question about whether the considered objects existing at different moments are numerically identical may not be something one can decide by convention without the risk of getting it wrong and yet it may be no factual question either in the following sense: to search an answer to the question is not to try to *learn* something about the *real* features of the case considered; these real features are already assumed as known or as completely described in all relevant respects by the description given. It is rather a question about what description of the case (the features of which are taken to be fixed) is adequate given the meaning of the concepts involved or the established language conventions; or it is a question about which philosophical ontology one should adopt where adopting one or another ontological option commits one to describing the case in different manners. The realist insists that the question about transtemporal identity of conscious individuals is always a factual question in a sense which excludes that it can be rationally answered by linguistic consideration or by theoretical arguments about philosophical ontology in the manner just sketched. This is the idea the following thesis R4 is intended to capture.

> R4 (no linguistic issue / no issue about adopting philosophical ontologies): The question of identity between a conscious individual A (existing at m) and a conscious individual B (existing at m') is – in all metaphysically possible cases – a factual question. It is never a question which can be decided by reflection on language or by metaphysical arguments about what philosophical ontology one should adopt.

Once again the motivation for adopting R4 is based on the intimate relation between (1) and (2): it is, according to the realist intuition, a question about objec-

---

[3] The term 'realism about personal identity across time' is not very common as a label for the view here explained and defended (more often philosophers refer to the view calling it "the simple view" following the terminology of (Parfit 1984)). The term is, however, used by Trenton Merrick who uses it as a name for all views including the thesis here formulated as R3, compare (Merricks 2001).

tive features of the world whether (2) obtains. Neither linguistic considerations nor general theoretical arguments about which philosophical ontology one should chose can be relevant to the simple question about what A will in fact experience in the future and what B in fact experienced in the past. Therefore the question about whether (1) obtains cannot be decided in such a way either.

Furthermore, a realist about transtemporal identity of conscious beings will have to insist that whether or not A (living at the earlier moment m) and B (living at the later moment m') are one and the same experiencing subject only depends on the relation between A and B taken in isolation; it cannot depend on events which have no causal influence at all on how the later individual evolves from the former. For instance, if A is the person who enters at m an operation room in order to undergo a medical surgery and if B is the person who, after that operation, wakes up at m' in the adjacent wake-up room, then the question about whether A and B are one and the same person cannot depend on happenings during that operation in some other operation room which have no influence on how B develops from A. Here is a way to formulate this intuition:

> R5 (no dependence on external factors): The question of identity between a conscious individual A (existing at m) and a conscious individual B (existing at m') cannot depend on factors external to the way in which B (or B's body) has evolved from A (or A's body). Factors having no influence on how B has evolved from A cannot be responsible for whether or not A and B are identical.

In order to understand why R5 is intuitively undeniable from the realist point of view one must again reflect about (2). The realist takes is as obvious that the question whether (2) obtains is a factual question. If this is so then it would be 'magical' if events which have no causal influence on the way in which B develops from A could nonetheless determine whether B, at m, had the experiences associated to A's life at m and whether A at the later moment does not exist anymore or rather has the experiences associated with B's life. If B is the person who has developed from A through a surgery and who wakes up after the operation, then A has the experiences associated with B's life just in case A, after the operation, perceives the walls of the wake-up room from the relevant perspective, hears the voice of the nurse, worries about whether the operation was successful etc. Whether A's life is over or continues in the wake-up room in the way described after the operation cannot depend (according to the realist) on distant happenings having no causal influence on the way the later person develops from the former. Since the future A has at m and the past B has at m' cannot depend on such external factors, the identity of A and B cannot depend on such external features either.

R5 excludes so-called closest continuer theories of personal identity and their generalization to conscious individuals.[4] R3 excludes all those accounts that take conscious beings to be temporally extended four-dimensional entities capable of fission and fusion.[5]

3 Realism about the Individuality of Conscious Beings[6]

For each real individual we may ask: what is it that makes it the case that *this* individual is the one it actually is? This question sounds puzzling and one might doubt at first that is has an understandable meaning. But the question can be given a clear sense when it is reformulated in the following way: what are the conditions in virtue of which a considered counterfactual situation would be one in which *that* individual (existing in the real world) exists as well? Let us call this the *individuality question* for a given individual. Realism about the individuality of conscious beings is a close relative to realism about transtemporal identity and it says that the individuality question does not have an informative answer when conscious beings are concerned. In order to answer the factual question about counterfactual circumstances whether a given real individual exists under those circumstances we must say *of that real individual* whether or not it exists under the circumstances considered. In other worlds: there is no other way to answer the question; we cannot answer it by describing conditions which supposedly constitute A's existence.

The view here called realism about the individuality of conscious beings is a close relative of realism about their transtemporal identity and the two views can serve to clarify each other. The following claim R6 parallels R1 and expresses the idea that the description of counterfactual circumstances which, for some specific real conscious human or non-human being, does not specify whether and in

---

[4] According to closest continuer theories of personal identity in a case of 'fission' we should accept the best candidate for identity with the original person as identical to the original person. However, whether in a given case a person B existing at m' is the best candidate for identity with the original person A existing at m can depend on external factors having no causal influence on the way B develops from A. Therefore such theories violate R5. The closest continuer theory is defended, for instance, in (Nozick 1981, ch. 1).
[5] For a discussion of the view that people are temporally extended entities see (Sider 2001, section 3). The paper defends an anti-realist view in the sense here introduced.
[6] Realism about the individuality of conscious beings is developed in (Nida-Rümelin 2012a and forthcoming, ch. 7).

which role that experiencing subject exists under those counterfactual circumstances is, in virtue of this fact, an incomplete description of those circumstances; a factual question about them is left open.

> R6 (non-reducibility + determinate answer): If D is a complete description of a metaphysically possible counterfactual situation, then D explicitly mentions with respect to every real conscious individual A whether and in which role it exists in the counterfactual situation. (The latter cannot be done without rigid reference to the real conscious individual at issue).

The intuitive motivation behind R6 is analogous to the one given earlier for the corresponding realist claims about transtemporal identity. It makes use of the following two assertions which are, on their intended understanding conceptually equivalent:

> (1') A exists and has role R in a counterfactual situation C under consideration
> (2') A has access to the world through experience in the counterfactual situation C and A has that access in the way described or implied by R.

The second assertion (2') is formulated in a metaphorical manner but perhaps this is how its underlying intuition can be rendered most obvious: the description of a counterfactual situation must describe for each real conscious individual whether and from what perspective it has access to the world under those circumstances; otherwise, a factual question about the considered situation remains unanswered. So any complete description of counterfactual circumstances includes for each real conscious being an answer to the question about whether there is some role R such that (2') is a correct description of the situation considered. Given the above equivalence it follows that the same applies to (1').

According to (R6) (1') must be explicitly mentioned. This claim is motivated by the following insight: if one describes the distribution of properties over conscious individuals in a considered counterfactual situation in the most detailed way but does not thereby refer to the specific conscious individual A existing in the real world specifying whether *it* exists and what *its* properties are in the counterfactual situation, then the description does not allow us to conclude whether or not (for some R) (2') applies to the situation considered.

The following realist claim about the individuality of conscious beings may be taken to be just another way to express the same idea:

> R7 (objective feature of the situation described): If D is a description of a metaphysically possible counterfactual situation and if, for some actually existing conscious individual A, D does not explicitly mention whether A exists in the situation so described and (if so) which is A's role, then

(a) adding an assumption about A's existence and A's role in the circumstances so described must be interpreted as a *stipulation* concerning an *additional objective feature* of the situation so described;

(b) no assumption about A's existence and A's role in the circumstances so described can be motivated, on the basis of D by considerations about linguistic issues or about the ontology to be adopted or by 'best counterpart' considerations.

4 The Conceptual Basis of Realism about the Identity and Individuality of Conscious Beings[7]

Let us come back to the intuitive motivation of realism with respect to the identity across time of a conscious being and let us now ask: what is its conceptual basis? In other words: what are the facts about the way we conceptualize transtemporal identity behind that intuitive motivation? Can we understand what it is about our conceptual architecture in virtue of which realism is intuitively forced upon us?

The motivation, as sketched above, is based on a certain way of conceptualizing what it is for A (the earlier existing individual) to live B's life at the later moment m'.[8] Our positive understanding of that feature is furthermore based on a particular understanding of what it is for B to be the one who lived A's life at the earlier moment. In thinking about what is said in

(2) B's life at m' is part of A's future at m; A's life at m is part of B's past at m'.

We take up, so to speak, A's perspective. We think about A's future in terms of what it means for A, what it is 'from his or her perspective' to live B's life 'from the inside' so to speak. Analogously, we take up B's perspective and consider what it is for B, from his or her perspective, to have the past associated to A's life. The example illustrates what it is to engage in that specific conceptual activity. By understanding (2) in this particular way, we gain a *positive understanding* of what it is for the world to be such that (1) is true. A parallel observation applies to (2'):

---

[7] For more on the theme of the present section, compare (Nida-Rümelin 2012b, 2016 and forthcoming, ch. 7 and 10).

[8] The person B living at the later moment is of course always 'picked out' here in a way which leaves it open weather he or she is A.

(2') A has access to the world through experience in the counterfactual situation C and A has that access in the way described by R.

We have a *positive understanding* of the specific objective feature of a counterfactual situation which would make it a situation fulfilling (2') by an analogous conceptual activity. We consider the question from A's perspective and thereby understand what it is for *him* (or *her*) to live, in a counterfactual situation, a specific human life 'from the inside'.[9] Developing a positive understanding of (2') in such a way amounts to developing a positive understanding of (1') as well. The conceptual claim just expressed about how we understand claims of identity over time of conscious beings and about how we understand claims about identity of conscious individuals in the real world with conscious individuals in counterfactual circumstances can be summarized as follows:

> Thesis C1 (Positive understanding of the relevant feature of the future and the past / of counterfactual situations by taking up perspectives): We have a positive understanding of the feature which renders (1) (resp. (1')) true by our positive understanding of (2) (resp. (2')); we have a positive understanding of (2) (resp. (2')) due to our *capacity to take up the perspective of another conscious individual in our thoughts*.

It is impossible to give an account here of what it is to take up perspectives. I will limit the exposition to a few remarks about T1 which might help to avoid misunderstandings and help to convey a clearer understanding of the conceptual activity the locution is intended to refer to.[10]

> (a) Thesis C does not imply that (1) (resp. 1') is reducible to (2) (resp. 2'). The proposal to analyse (1) (resp. (1')) by (2) (resp. (2')) would be hopelessly circular. According to realism there is no conceptual or metaphysical reduction available for (1) and (1'). (2) and (2') are introduced as a first step in explaining how we develop a positive understanding of what renders (1) true (resp. of what makes a counterfactual situation into one to which (1') applies).
>
> (b) Due to our capacity to take up perspectives of others in thought, third person thought and first person thought share their special conceptual features; the distinction between

---

[9] This is again a metaphorical way to describe what is going on and the metaphor is only partially adequate. We need not fill in any assumptions about what it is like to live a life specified by R in order to develop a positive understanding of the feature of a counterfactual situation which renders (2') true but that such a 'filling in' is necessary is somehow suggested by the metaphor.
[10] The relevant notion of 'taking up perspectives' is further developed in chapter 10 and 11 of (Nida-Rümelin forthcoming). Some material on what it is to take up perspectives can be found in (Nida-Rümelin 2012a).

"third person thought" and "first person thought" as standardly understood in the literature is therefore misleading.

(c) Taking up perspectives of others is a conceptual activity; it is not to be confused with empathy; it is not to be confused with imagining being in the situation of another.

(d) Taking up perspectives is involved, however, not only in thought but also in other-directed emotion and in social perception. It is therefore deeply incorporated and omnipresent in our conscious life.

(e) The capacity to take up perspectives concerning other conscious individuals is a manifestation of our understanding of what it is to be a conscious individual.

The last claim (e) is a crucial premise in the argument presented in the next section.

5 The Route from Conceptual Observation to Realism as a Metaphysical Claim: Understanding One's Own Nature as an Experiencing Subject

I started with a few claims that characterize the realist view and I described their intuitive motivation. I then gave a brief sketch of how one may explain why this intuitive motivation is appealing.[11] According to this explanation, realism is intuitively attractive in virtue of our capacity to take up perspectives in our thought. But this raises the following question: why should we trust the intuitions which are based on that capacity? Couldn't it be that when we think about conscious beings by taking up their perspectives we think about them in a way which creates illusions about what their identity and individuality consists in? Taking up perspectives might be, after all, a mode of thinking which does not lead to deep metaphysical insights but rather to fundamental metaphysical errors.

In order to answer replies along these lines one must give a positive argument for the claim that the relevant intuitions manifest *genuine understanding*

---

[11] It will be controversial whether the intuitive motivation is in fact appealing and many people in particular philosophers tend to deny that they share the intuition. This is a serious threat to the view here presented but it can hopefully be met by further clarification of the precise content of the intuition at issue. I tend to think that deeply incorporated intuitions are more difficult to verbalize and easier to be overlooked or denied than others that are closer to the surface.

of what it *is* to be an experiencing subject. According to our natural understanding of what it is to be an experiencing subject, experiencing subjects are, by their nature, such that it is *adequate* to think about them by taking up perspectives in the relevant sense. If one wishes to defend realism about the identity and individuality of conscious beings then one must develop an argument for the view that our natural understanding of what it is to be a conscious individual is right in this respect.

The only argument that I hope can convincingly show this is rather complex and each of its premises is controversial. Here I would just like to describe the structure of the argument and its central ideas in order to give a rough picture of how one may try to proceed in order to defend realism as a metaphysical thesis.[12] The argument starts with the phenomenological claim that we are aware of ourselves in every experience in a pre-reflective manner. On that basis, so the argument goes on, we are able to develop, a *general concept* of what it is to be an experiencing subject and that general concept partially reveals to us what it *is* to be an experiencing subject. In a further step the claim is developed that the capacity to take up the perspective of another conscious being is a manifestation of having the general concept of an experiencing subject. In order to reach the desired conclusion one then only has to assume that a conceptual capacity which is the manifestation of a having a nature-revealing concept (a concept that gives access to the nature of the phenomenon it refers to) does not lead astray in the way suggested by the opponent. The argument can thus be summarized as follows:

> Thesis PH (pre-reflective self-awareness): When a conscious being undergoes an experience, thinks or acts, then it is (necessarily) pre-conceptually, non-reflectively and in a non-objectual manner aware of itself as the subject who undergoes the experience, thinks or acts.
>
> Thesis C2 (the basis of the implicit general concept of conscious beings): Sufficiently developed thinking subjects form – on the basis of their pre-reflective self-awareness (see thesis PH) – an implicit general concept of what it is to be a conscious being.
>
> Thesis CM1 (an essence revealing concept): The implicit general concept (developed in the way described in thesis C2) of what it is to be a conscious being is 'essence revealing' (and it is 'essence revealing' because it is acquired in that particular way): having the concept is to have acquired an adequate partial understanding of what being a conscious individual amounts to.
>
> Thesis CM2 (manifestation of having a concept): Taking up perspectives in one's thought about others is a manifestation of the implicit general concept of an experiencing subject.

---

12 The argument here described is developed in (Nida-Rümelin forthcoming, ch. 10).

Thesis CM3 (genuine understanding via manifestations of essence revealing concepts): Since taking up perspectives is a manifestation of an essence revealing concept, the understanding of (2) and (2') (and thereby of (1) and (1')) provided by taking up perspectives is *genuine* understanding: it provides an adequate understanding of what identity across times and across possible worlds for conscious individuals consists in.

Thesis CM3 implies that the realist claims formulated above should be accepted as correctly describing the metaphysical nature of conscious individuals. If the argument just sketched can be defended then realism about transtemporal identity and individuality cannot be reasonably limited to the human case. It must be broadened to every being which deserves to be thought about by taking up its perspective and this, I claim, is true for every conscious individual, for every individual to which the metaphor of 'having a perspective' in the relevant sense correctly applies.

6 Realism about the Identity and Individuality of Conscious Beings and Subject Body Dualism

Realism about the identity and individuality of conscious beings is a central element of a broader view about consciousness which puts the special metaphysical status of experiencing subjects in its center. According to that view the ontological irreducibility of identity and individuality of conscious beings is not the only special feature of experiencing subjects which should motivate acknowledging that conscious beings belong to an ontological category of their own. Further elements that characterizes their special ontological status is their capacity to be active and their capacity of experiencing. Subject-body dualism regards experiences as necessarily involving an experiencing subject whose identity across time and whose individuality must be understood along the lines here presented. Dualism is quite often regarded as an anti-scientific doctrine and rejected for that reason. Subject-body dualism of the kind here at issue is, however, not anti-scientific at all. It is rather part of the view that only on the basis of a dualist theory which fully acknowledges the special ontological status of conscious beings would it be possible to adequately formulate the most central questions a science of consciousness should ultimately be able to address: under what physical conditions do experiencing subjects emerge? And what is the physical basis for their continued existence?[13]

---

[13] Compare for how subject body dualism can be integrated into a scientific world view (Nida-Rümelin forthcoming).

References

Butler, Joseph (2008): "Of Personal Identity". In: Perry, John (ed.): *Personal Identity*. Berkeley: University of California Press.
Chisholm, Roderick (1970): "Identity through Time". In: Kiefer, Howard Evans; Munitz, Milton Karl (eds.): *Language, Belief, and Metaphysics*. Albany: State University of New York Press, 163–182.
Madell, Geoffrey (1981): *The Identity of the Self*. Edinburgh: Edinburgh University Press.
Merricks, Trenton (2001): "Realism about Personal Identity Over Time". In: *Philosophical Perspectives* 15, 173–187.
Nida-Rümelin, Martine (2006): *Der Blick von innen. zur transtemporalen Identität bewusstseinsfähiger Wesen*. Frankfurt am Main: Suhrkamp.
Nida-Rümelin, Martine (2008): "An Argument from Transtemporal Identity for Subject Body Dualism". In: Bealer, George; Koons, Robert (eds.): *The Waning of Materialism*. Oxford: Oxford University Press, 191–211.
Nida-Rümelin, Martine (2012a): "The Non-descriptive Nature of Conscious Individuals". In: Gasser, Georg; Stefan, Matthias (eds.): *Personal Identity. Complex or Simple?* Cambridge: Cambridge University Press, 157–176.
Nida-Rümelin, Martine (2012b): "The Conceptual Origin of Subject Body Dualism". In: Colliva, Annalisa (ed.): *Self and Self-Knowledge,* Oxford: Oxford University Press, 39–73.
Nida-Rümelin, Martine (2016): "Self-awareness". In: *Review of Philosophy and Psychology,* Special Issue: *Consciousness and Inner Awareness*, in print.
Nida-Rümelin, Martine (forthcoming): *Conscious Individuals. Sketch of a Theory"*. Oxford: Oxford University Press.
Nozick, Robert (1981): *Philosophical Explanations*. Cambridge, MA: Harvard University Press.
Parfit, Derek (1984): *Reasons and Persons*. Oxford: Clarendon Press.
Parfit, Derek (1999): "Experiences, Subjects, and Conceptual Schemes". In: *Philosophical Topics* 26, 217–270.
Reid, Thomas (1984): *Philosophical Works*. Edited by William Hamilton. Hildesheim: Georg Olms.
Sider, Theodore (2001): "Criteria of Personal Identity and the Limits of Conceptual Analysis". In: *Philosophical Perspectives* 15, 189–209.
Swinburne, Richard (1984): "Personal Identity: The Dualist Theory". In: Shoemaker, Sydney; Swinburne, Richard: *Personal Identity*. Oxford: Basil Blackwell, 1–66.

Nikos Psarros
What is the Thing Whose Measure is Money?

Abstract: The received view defines money by four basic functions: unit of account, store of value, a medium of exchange, and standard of deferred payment. The two main grand views on the nature of money regard either its function as a unit of account (*chartalism*), or its function as a general medium of exchange (*metallism*) as the fundamental characteristic of money and try to derive the other functions of money from the proposed fundamental characteristic. Both chartalism and metallism fail to see, however, that all four accepted functions of money are rather necessary expressions of the nature of money and not elements of its definition. My thesis is that all four basic functions of money can be explained by regarding money as an instrument for measuring an extensive magnitude of things and poietic actions that is called commonly 'value'. However, value is not a fundamental magnitude, but is in a certain way the representation of human freedom in the material world. Thus money is in fact an indirect instrument for determining and measuring at least an aspect of human freedom. From this definition of the nature of money also the obligation for the institution of a conditionally guaranteed minimal income can be defended.

Keywords: Money, freedom, measure, chartalism, metallism

1 Money as Measure of Value

The received view defines money by four basic functions: unit of account, store of value, a medium of exchange, and standard of deferred payment. The two main grand views on the nature of money regard either its function as a unit of account (*chartalism*), or its function as a general medium of exchange (*metallism*) as the fundamental characteristic of money and try to derive the other functions of money from the proposed fundamental characteristic (for a full account on chartalism and metallism see Ingham 2000 and Wray 2000). Both chartalism and metallism fail to see, however, that all four accepted functions of money are rather necessary expressions of the nature of money and not elements of its definition. For, if we accept that either one, or some, or even all of the above mentioned functions of money are elements of its definition then we cannot explain a) why this list is confined to those four functions only and cannot be extended by adding more properties, and b) why those four characteristics are attributed to the one entity called 'money'.

We can call the common equivalent that enables the commensurability of 'amount of duty' and 'value of a good or a service' the 'value simpliciter'. Money is then defined as the instrument of measuring 'values simpliciter'. In order to fulfill its fundamental function a mode of measurement has to be established and it has to be ascertained that the unit of measure has the same property in common with the magnitude that is measured. Thus the fundamental property of money is its value simpliciter. The value simpliciter is an extensive magnitude because the concrete values simpliciter (i.e. the prices) of things, services, duties, etc. can be added linearly and expressed as a sum of money. (For example, from a given credit on a bank account the various amounts for payments of goods, services, taxes etc. are removed linearly and at the end the remaining amount is just the rest after the subtraction of the sum of the payments, regardless of their 'quality').

However, value simpliciter is not a primitive property of things or actions, since, if this were the case, its importance for human life would be mysterious and opaque. Additionally, value simpliciter as an extensive magnitude can only be distributed quantitatively and the 'correctness' of the distribution can be only understood in terms of the so-called 'distributive justice'. On the other hand, the common sense mandates to apply on value distributions also the concept of 'commutative justice'. In order to comply with both aspects of justice, value simpliciter has then to be an expression or a representation of (or at least a phenomenon that is related to) a more fundamental trait of human nature that has an intrinsic relationship both to distributive and to commutative justice, and has nevertheless the properties of a magnitude. The idea of commutative justice imposes a qualitative aspect on value simpliciter that cannot be measured by means of a purely extensive magnitude. Thus the property, of which value simpliciter is the expression or representation, has to have an intensive magnitude that enables the projection of qualitative differences in quantitative ones.[1] Because of the necessity of compliance with commutative justice, the property, of which value simpliciter is a representation or an expression, has then to be an intensive magnitude.

---

[1] A similar problem occurs in the metrication of colors. Despite the fact that colors have primarily a qualitative character it is possible to establish quantitative relationships between the primary colors and the colors that result from the mixing of the primary colors by treating them as intensive magnitudes (Psarros 1999).

2 The Current Theories of Money are Reductionist

My thesis is then, that the above mentioned basic functions of money do not determine the nature of money, but are rather determined by its nature, which has then to be defined without recurring to them. Nevertheless the functions of 'unit of account' and 'medium of exchange' that are regarded by chartalism and metallism respectively as fundamental can give a clue about the nature of money. Namely, both functions attribute to money the nature of an instrument of measurement: chartalism claims that money originally measured something like the extent of duties of the subjects toward the (autocratic) state, while metallism regards it as a means for comparing a property of goods and services exchanged at the market, which is called 'value'. Since chartalism and metallism put both functions in relation, claiming either that money was originally introduced as a unit of account of duties (taxes, levies), but in the course of time became a medium of exchange (chartalism), or vice versa (metallism), we can conclude that both the 'amount of duty' and 'the value of a good or a service' are constituted in such a way that enables their measurement by the same instrument, namely money.

In the philosophy of economics there have been many attempts to determine the fundamental property of human life that is represented by (or expressed as) value simpliciter. In the Marxist-Lockean tradition this property is defined as the amount of human labour that is consumed for the production of a thing that is necessary for human life. Classical 'liberal' economic theories accept a multitude of equivalent sources of value simpliciter (prominent representatives are Adam Smith, David Ricardo and Jean-Baptiste Say), and the so-called 'Physiocrats' stipulated that there is a kind of 'natural source' of value simpliciter, which is identified with the power of the soil to produce food.

The problem with all these approaches is that they reduce value simpliciter to the material and factual aspect of the world and fail thus to give a proper account of the normative and ethical aspect of the sphere of economy: In the Marxist theory there is no explanation for the allegation that the contractually agreed appropriation of the surplus value produced by the wage worker is ethically wrong and must be abolished by giving up the institution of the property on means of production, the classical economic theory comes only with a relativist and voluntarist concept of value, and finally a physiocratic concept of value can be justified only on the background of a theory of nature that evaluates every natural thing with respect to its utility for human life.

3 The Alternative: Money as Measure of Human Freedom

The desiderate is then a foundation of value simpliciter that has both a factual and a normative aspect and that allows, i.e. does not exclude categorically, its projection or representation as an extensive magnitude. To my opinion, the best candidate for this anthropological foundation of value simpliciter is human freedom. This is so for following reasons (which will not be examined or justified further here):
1. Human freedom is an essential and characteristic trait of human beings.
2. Human freedom is an actual trait of human beings.
3. Human freedom needs for its actualization the interaction with the material world.
4. The individual range of human freedom in the material world can be constrained and extended quantitatively, but not purely extensively.

The factors that determine the degree of constraint resp. extension of human freedom are:
1. The individual exercise of human freedom is subject to the judgment of the acting person.
2. The individual exercise of human freedom is constrained by its obligations toward the other human beings in general and the human beings who share the social environment, in which the acting person is situated.
3. The exercise of the individual freedom is constrained by the duties of the acting person toward the state, to which she owes allegiance as a citizen. These duties of a person toward the state are both material and moral.
4. Under the rule of law (i.e. within the framework of a state or a law governed community) the exercise of the individual freedom of a person with respect to the freedom of the other persons is regulated by various kinds of licenses. Such licenses can be issued either by the state or they can be accepted by social convention.

On the background of this description of human freedom *money* can be defined as a state-issued or as a socially accepted license able to constrain human freedom that
   a. regulates the fulfillment of duties toward the state regarding the provision of certain material resources (taxes, levies, fees etc.), and
   b. regulates the access of a person to material resources and services of other persons (or institutions) depending on the ability of the person to

provide specific material resources or services to other persons or institutions.

The specific shape of such licenses, i.e. of money, which are recognized in a given state or in an area defined by international treaties (as for example the Euro-zone) defines the so-called *legal tender* that is in circulation in this state or area.

The value simpliciter of a given thing or a service or a duty is then determined as the impact of the production of this thing, the performance of this service, or the fulfillment of this duty on the freedom of the persons who live under a given rule of law, in which a legal tender is specified as the realization of money. The value simpliciter of an entity is expressed as a certain amount of money, i.e. as a price, so that in a given social or legal environment entities with the same price exert the same constraint on the freedom of the persons living and acting in this environment in order to produce, perform or fulfill them.

Since the individual freedom of a person is subject both to the subjective judgment of the acting person and to the structure of the social environment, in which this person is situated, the value simpliciter of an entity has both a subjectively and a socially determined component. On the other hand, the various socially determined aspects of value simpliciter are not interculturally or internationally incommensurable, since every particular society and every state or internationally defined area are populated by human beings and every human being is the actualization of the human form.

Summarizing the results of our analysis, we can see that money is an instrument of measuring human freedom as far as human freedom is essential element of the actualization of human life. Depriving a person totally of monetary funds is then equal to the total constraint of this person, a situation that cannot be allowed to take place – at least not when the person in question is innocent of any judicially punishable deed. It is a thus a moral duty of every person to allow to any other person a minimum of freedom expressed in terms of value simpliciter, i.e. debt bondage is morally wrong even in the state of nature, because also in the state of nature, i.e. in absence of state-imposed legal structures, a person is under the obligation to treat herself and every other person as actualization of the human form. This obligation relies on the very fact that persons as rational beings have the knowledge that they have a form, and having a knowledge of something is manifested by treating this something according to its nature.

In the civic state this obligation toward the preservation of a minimum of freedom that enables the proper conduct of a human life is expressed as the right of every person living under a given rule of law to a conditionally guaranteed minimal income. The guarantee is conditional in the sense that the minimal income shall be granted only upon the condition that the person benefiting from it is not capable of maintaining her minimal freedom by her own power. Historically this right was not always exercised in form of receiving a certain amount of money as a stipend or a subsidy, but also in form of inalienable land property, or as property rights on ships, as dowry or even in other more exotic forms.

The concept of money as a measure of human freedom is compatible with the prevailing monetary phenomenology and the macroeconomic practice, especially with the concept of a central regulation of the volume of money by the national central banks by means of determining the basic interest rates.

References

Ingham, Geoffrey (2000): "'Babylonian Madness': on the Historical and Sociological Origins of Money". In: Smithin, John (ed.): *What is Money?* London: Routledge, 16–41.
Psarros, Nikos (1999): *Die Chemie und ihre Methoden – eine philosophische Betrachtung*, Weinheim: Wiley-VCH.
Wray, Larry (2000): "Modern Money". In: Smithin, John (ed.): *What is Money?* London: Routledge, 32–66.

5 Values and Value Relativism

Paul Boghossian
Relativism about Morality

Abstract: Many philosophers and non-philosophers are attracted to the view that moral truths are relative to moral framework or culture. I distinguish between two versions of such a view. I argue that one version is coherent but not plausible, and I argue that the second one can't be made sense of. The upshot is that we have to make sense of at least some objective moral truths.

Keywords: Moral relativism, normativity, thoroughgoing relativism, absolutist relativism, rationality

1 Introduction

Many people, philosophers and non-philosophers alike, think of themselves as moral *relativists:* they deny that there are absolute truths about morality, and insist that moral truth, when it obtains, is relative to a cultural (or possibly even individual) perspective.

Others reject moral relativism and assert the existence of at least some absolute truths about morality.[1]

Both parties to this dispute assume the *coherence* of moral relativism. They merely disagree about its correctness. My own view, by contrast, is that there is no coherent position that deserves the label 'moral relativism.' Or, to put the matter a bit more precisely since anything can be called by any name one likes, there is no position that coherently expresses the *motivations* that moral relativists typically say drive them to their relativism.

The worry that relativism might not be a coherent view is a familiar one. But it is familiar largely in application to the idea that *all* facts are relative – *global relativism*. Here the worry is a familiar one about self-refutation. If all truths are relative to perspectives, what about the truth of global relativism itself? Either it is itself only true relative to the perspective of relativists, in which case we non-relativists may ignore it; or it is itself true absolutely, in which case at least one truth is absolute and global relativism stands refuted.

Powerful as this familiar worry is, it doesn't apply in any obvious way to *local* relativisms – relativistic views about particular domains, such as that of

---

[1] See, for example, (Benedict 2009), although it is by no means only theists who are attracted to at least some moral absolutism.

morality. Since those views don't commit themselves to *all* facts being relative, but only those in a specified domain, the familiar threat of self-refutation does not apply, at least not obviously.

Perhaps not obviously, but I believe that, in the end, there is a substantial worry about how relativistic views of *normative* domains, such as that of morality, could be coherent. I will illustrate with the especially important case of morality, but my argument is more general.

2 Motivations for Moral Relativism

Let me first start by asking about the *motivations* for moral relativism. Why would someone recoil from moral absolutism and be attracted to moral relativism?[2]

The view I aim to discuss stems from the conviction that it is hopelessly mystifying to suppose that an act could be *simply* right or wrong; that all you need to do is say what act is in question, and then the world takes over and pronounces on its moral status as either right or wrong. Why would such absolute facts about moral right and wrong be mystifying?

The crucial feature of moral judgments is that they are *normative* or *evaluative*. Moral judgments do not say how things *are*, but, rather, how they *ought* to be, or how there is *reason* for them to be or how it would be *good* for them to be.

And it can seem pretty mysterious – especially to a naturalist, but not only to a naturalist – how there could be normative, prescriptive or evaluative facts just sitting out there. Where would they come from? Where do they reside?

Furthermore, there seems to be a difficulty explaining how we might come to *know* what such facts are, assuming they exist. By what sensory means might we access facts about oughts and value? Can we just see that something is right or wrong, in the way that we can see whether it is flat or spherical? And why, if these facts are just sitting out there, is there so much disagreement about them?

One way of responding to these sorts of puzzle about absolute facts about morality is to think of moral truths as not merely sitting out there, but somehow or other grounded in the dictates of an almighty being: the facts don't just sit out there; they are God's commands. However, few philosophers would be willing to resort to theism these days in order to defend moral realism. Moreover, if some-

---

[2] As I said above, it's important to attend to the underlying philosophical motivations, because 'relativism' is a technical term that has been applied to a wide variety of positions. Without a specification of the work it's supposed to do, the goals it's supposed to fulfill, one can get bogged down in pointless terminological squabbles.

one were so tempted we could fairly quickly show that it would not be a very good defense.

Another way of responding to the puzzles is to think of moral truths as delivered not by the judgments of an almighty being, but rather by the judgments of a certain sorts of idealized *human* judge. David Hume has a famous theory of aesthetic truths that assumes this form (see Hume 1757/1987). But this sort of 'ideal observer' view, as applied to morality, has turned out to be very difficult to spell out in a non-vacuous manner. (It is only slightly less problematic in the case of aesthetic truth.)

Against the background of these failed attempts to make sense of absolute moral truths, a relativistic view of morality can come to seem quite appealing. By relativizing moral facts it seems to enable us to hang onto moral discourse, while avoiding a commitment to mysterious absolute normative truths.

3 Relativizing the Facts of a Given Domain

How, exactly, does a relativistic view of morality do this? We need to formulate the view more precisely and then show that, so formulated, it indeed does have the advantages that are claimed for it.

Let us start with the question of formulation. What does it mean to 'relativize' the facts of a given domain? Well, science has provided us with some prominent examples in which a rejection of an absolute conception of a given domain in favor of a relativized conception of that domain has led to important advances in our understanding.

For example: Before Galileo, we used to think that there was such a thing as *absolute motion:* either an object was moving or it wasn't. Galileo taught us, however, that there is no such thing as absolute motion, but only motion relative to a specified frame of reference; and that none of these frames is more privileged than any of the others.

To take another example: Before Einstein's Special Theory of Relativity, we believed that there was such a thing as absolute *simultaneity:* either two events were simultaneous, or they weren't. Einstein taught us that we should not think that there is any such thing as the absolute simultaneity of two events separated in space, but only simultaneity relative to a (variable) spatio-temporal frame of reference; and that none of these spatio-temporal frames of reference was any more privileged than any of the others.

To illustrate with Einstein's famous thought experiment: suppose you are standing on the platform of a train station, and another observer is on a boxcar on a train moving past you, facing you. At the moment when you and the observer on the train are lined up, he releases a light beam both to his left and to his right. To him, the light beams will seem to hit the front and back walls of his boxcar simultaneously; but to you, the light will seem to hit the back of the box car, which is moving towards the beam, earlier than it hits the front of the box car which is moving away from it. On Einstein's theory, no one of these spatio-temporal frames is more privileged than the other. So we have to say that simultaneity is *relative* to your frame of reference. Judgments of simultaneity are relative to variable frames of reference and no particular frame of reference is more privileged or correct than any of the others.

In both of these famous cases, we start out with an absolute predicate – 'moves' or 'is simultaneous with' – which we believe we can truly apply to the world. We become convinced, however, for good reason, that nothing in the world answers to that absolute predicate, and that the most we can claim is that a close *higher-degree cousin* of the predicate applies – "moves relative to F" or "is simultaneous relative to F". So we recommend that people stop talking in terms of the absolute predicate and start talking only in terms of its higher-degree relativistic cousin.

> "Moves" gives way to: "Moves relative to F"
> "Is simultaneous with" gives way to: "Is simultaneous relative to F"

And we add: None of these F's is more privileged than any of the others.[3]

4 Formulating Moral Relativism

Now, these cases seem to provide us with a template that we can apply to the moral case in order to generate a coherent moral relativism. Thus, to formulate a relativism about morality we take the predicate

> "is morally right (wrong)"

and we replace it with:

> "is morally right (wrong) relative to F."

---

[3] This "no privilege clause" is important for otherwise it would not have been secured that there are no absolute facts of the type at issue.

For example, instead of simply saying

(1) It is right to educate girls

we would have to say

(2) It is right to educate girls relative to F.

What is "F" going to be in the moral case? We know what we were relativizing to in the case of motion and simultaneity. But what are we relativizing to in the case of morality? Here there are two importantly different options and they determine two very different types of view.

On the first, we relativize to some *moral code* or other – that is, to some person's, or some community's, background set of moral values; and we add: and none of these moral codes is more privileged than any of the others. On this view, which I will call, for reasons that will emerge, a

(3) *Thoroughgoing Relativism* about morality, we replace talk of
x is morally right
    with
x is morally right relative to moral code M.

This is the most common formulation of a relativistic view of morality. And I think there is a deep reason why it is the most common formulation, a reason that I will explain in a moment.

On the second option, which I will call, for reasons that will emerge, an Absolutist Relativism, we relativize not to background moral codes, but to the *circumstances*, broadly conceived, in which the act is performed. On this

(4) *Absolutist Relativist* view, we replace
x is morally right
    with
x is morally right relative to its circumstances C

These circumstances are to be conceived very broadly: any fact that might be relevant to the moral status of the act can be included in them, including facts about what moral codes the various agents involved endorse.

When people talk about moral relativism, they sometimes mean the one view and sometimes the other, often not distinguishing between them. But they are very different views.

5 Absolutist Relativism

Let's look first at the case where we relativize to *circumstances*. Given what I said at the start, you may be surprised to learn that I think that there is *nothing* incoherent about this view. More than that: I believe that, sometimes, moral claims that are relativized to circumstances in this way are actually *true*. For example if we ask:

> (5) Should I stop to help a motorist who has broken down on the side of the road? – The answer is not a straight "yes" or a straight "no". The correct answer is: It depends on the circumstances.

For example: If it's the middle of night and there is no one else around and you don't yourself have a medical emergency, then you ought to stop; but if you yourself need to be somewhere else urgently and there are lots of other friendly people around, etc., then you are permitted not to stop.[4] There are lots of other examples.

> Should I leave someone who has served me a tip? – It depends on the local customs.
> Should I eat noisily or quietly? – It depends on the cultural setting you are in.

We can also cite examples of such relativized claims that, while coherent, seem *false:*

> May I abuse children for fun? – It depends on whether you will get caught.
> May I kill an innocent person in order to harvest their organs and save a larger number of people? – It depends on how important the person in question is.

Finally, there are examples of circumstance-relative claims that are *controversial* – people argue about them:

> May I torture someone to obtain information? – It depends on how large a calamity is at stake …

So, given that I started out saying that I was going to argue *against* the coherence of moral relativism, how can I say that this sort of relativization to circumstances is not only coherent, but is even sometimes *true?*

The answer is that, while it may be perfectly legitimate to call this a type of 'moral relativism', (as I said, 'relativism' is a technical term so you have a lot of

---

4 A similar example can be found in (Scanlon 1998).

leeway in how you get to use it) it is not the sort of moral relativism that can accommodate the metaphysical and epistemological motivations that typically motivate relativists and which I outlined at the beginning of this paper.[5]

Why would relativization to circumstances not be capable of meeting the original metaphysical and epistemological concerns?

The reason is that such a relativism does *not* escape a commitment to absolute (and universal) moral facts. For what a statement like:

> If circumstances are C, then you ought to stop and help the broken-down motorist; but if they are C*, then you are permitted to keep on going.

says is that:

> (6) It holds for everyone that he/she ought to do help if circumstances are C; and holds for everyone that he/she is permitted to carry on if circumstances are C*.

This is the sort of content that moral claims have when they are relativized to circumstances.

So, if you were worried about how there could be impersonal normative facts, this sort of relativization would not allay those concerns. There is just as much of a problem seeing how there could be impersonal normative facts of the form

> (7) You ought to Φ if circumstances are C

as there is about facts of the form:

> (8) You ought to Φ no matter what the circumstances.

6 Thoroughgoing Relativism

This helps explain why a moral relativist, like Gilbert Harman, relativizes not to a person's circumstances but rather to his/her background moral code, adding that none of these codes is any more privileged than any of the others (see Harman 1996). With this relativization, which I called a *Thoroughgoing Relativism*, we

---

[5] To reiterate: this explains why it is so important, in explaining the position that concerns you, to specify what philosophical work you take it to do. Without such a specification one can get bogged down in pointless terminological disputes.

have a real chance of getting away from a commitment to absolute moral facts of a kind that we were worried about. For when we say that the only moral facts there are, are facts of the form

(9) According to moral code M, one ought to Φ if C,

while insisting that none of these codes is any 'truer' than any of the others, we really do seem to get away from the idea that there are absolute facts about morality. For, if we now ask:

If C, ought we to Φ?

the answer will have to be: That depends, according to moral framework M1, yes, and according to moral framework M2, no. There are only facts about what your background moral values tell you to do, and none of these sets of values is any 'truer' than any of the others.

Naturally, no one will want to deny that people have background moral values, or that some normative claims follow from those and others don't. And since that is all that a Thoroughgoing Relativist is committed to, it looks as though we have finally formulated a relativistic view about morality that is responsive to the concern about the metaphysical strangeness of absolute moral facts.

The problem is that this is not so much a relativism about moral judgment as an eliminativism or nihilism about it, since *any* trace of normativity in the 'relativized' moral judgments has been lost. If all I can say are things like

(10) It's right to educate girls according to my moral code

and

(11) It's wrong to educate girls according to the code of the Taliban

then I've only said things with which everyone can agree, no matter what their moral perspective. Such judgments are *merely descriptive* remarks about what particular moral codes do and do not allow. And the upshot is indistinguishable from an eliminativism or nihilism about moral judgment.

Recall: relativism was supposed to be distinct from nihilism. Relativism was supposed to be a way of *retaining* moral discourse while evading its naïve commitment to absolute moral facts, by accepting only a relativized version of those facts. But if what I've said is right, then real relativism, one that has a prima facie chance of evading commitment to absolute moral facts, does not do that at all:

rather, it ends up eliminating moral discourse replacing it with purely descriptive remarks that are ill-suited to play anything like a normative role.[6]

If one were content with eliminativism about morality, one could achieve that outcome very quickly by putting forward not a relativism about morality but an *error theory* about it: one could just say: this discourse is committed to absolute moral facts; there aren't any; so we should just get rid of this discourse in favor of descriptive remarks about the sort of world we would prefer to live in.

That's in effect what we did with 'witch' discourse. We said there are no witches so we should just get rid of witch discourse. No one would confuse an eliminativism about witch discourse with a 'relativistic' view of witches.

I'm not now arguing that we *shouldn't* be error theorists about morality. I'm just making the point that relativism about morality was supposed to be something *distinct* from an eliminativism about it. But so far we have not found a formulation of relativism that manages both to retain moral discourse and to evade a commitment to absolute moral facts.

Contrast the case of morality with the case of simultaneity. Why do we end up eliminating moral judgments when we relativize them, but do not end up eliminating simultaneity judgments when we relativize them? Is it because moral properties are normative whereas simultaneity is not? That is not the right answer.

Take the case of phlogiston (which I'll safely assume is not a normative notion). Once we give up on the existence of phlogiston, the only real option is to eliminate phlogiston discourse and not use it in application to the world. It's not a real option to 'relativize' phlogiston discourse, urging that it is ok to use it provided we relativize phlogiston discourse to something. There is no useful relativistic cousin of phlogiston that plays anything like the role that phlogiston was supposed to play: the property of "being phlogiston according to theory T" is not a kind of phlogiston, but a kind of content (the content of theory T): it's a way of characterizing what theory T says, not a way of characterizing the world.

The problem, then, seems to derive not so much from *what* we are relativizing, but rather from what we are relativizing *to* – in particular from the fact that we are relativizing to a set of propositional attitudes that are said to contain a 'conception' of the subject matter in question. This makes the relativization look like a complete change of topic – from something about the world, to how things are according to a certain conception of the world.

---

6 Some philosophers have thought that if we worked with an *alethic* version of relativism, rather than a *property* version, as I have been doing, we would evade this difficulty. I explain in detail why that is not so in (Boghossian 2011) and in a longer version of the present paper (Boghossian ms).

By contrast, in the Special Theory of Relativity case, we are not relativizing to a conception, or even to anything mental, but rather to a spatio-temporal frame of reference. This sort of relativization ends up being consistent with a retention of the original subject matter, even if in a somewhat altered form.

Now, you might ask, why don't we relativize moral judgments to something other than moral codes, why don't we relativize to something non-mental, like circumstances? As we already saw in the discussion of relativization to circumstances, however, if we were to apply this strategy to the case of morality, while we retain the subject matter of morality, we do not succeed in evading a commitment to the existence of some absolute moral truths.

So we seem to face a dilemma: we could relativize moral claims to circumstances or to background moral codes. On the first option, we get credible results, but nothing that evades commitment to absolute moral truths. On the latter option, we get avoidance of commitment to absolute moral truths, but we preserve nothing of the original subject matter.

7 What About the Worries that Led to Relativism in the First Place?

All of this suggests that it's in *the very nature* of a normative subject matter that if there are to be moral judgments at all, they have to be meant in an absolutist sense. But what about the original metaphysical and epistemological concerns that made the existence of absolute normative facts so problematic-seeming in the first place?

It would take a large book to address those in a satisfactory way. But let me say some brief things now. I won't be telling you how to solve those problems. I will just indicate my reasons for thinking that we should feel very confident that there are solutions to those problems.

First, the conclusion that I am most directly arguing for here is not

There are absolute moral facts

but, rather,

To make moral judgments is to commit oneself to there being at least some absolute moral facts.

So, most directly, the conclusion I'm defending is only the conditional:

> If you want to continue making moral judgments, you had better be willing to countenance some absolute moral facts. Relativism will not allow you both to hang onto the discourse while distancing yourself from such facts.

But I would want to go further and say that we *should be* willing to countenance absolute moral facts. How, then, might we deal with the metaphysical and epistemological concerns that we raised right at the start?

First, the metaphysical question: how could there be impersonal normative facts 'out there'?

One possible reply is that the facts are not impersonal after all, that they are constituted by the verdicts of a certain sort of ideal judge. As I've already indicated, I don't hold out much hope for such theories, but they have not been definitively ruled out.

But even if we could not make such theories work, I think we have no choice but to acknowledge at least *some* absolute *normative* facts. The absolute facts that we don't have much choice about acknowledging are not facts about morality, but rather facts about *rationality:* facts about what you ought to believe, given the evidence available.

Why do we have no choice but to acknowledge facts about rationality? Because facts about rationality are presupposed by *any* judgment, including the judgment that one ought not to acknowledge facts about rationality.

If you say: facts about rationality should be rejected since, if they existed, they would be problematic normative facts, you are tacitly presupposing that there are facts about rationality, since you are claiming that the rational thing to believe, given your arguments, is to reject facts about rationality.

So, we can't but acknowledge some normative facts, since we can't but acknowledge some rationality facts. And, according to me, to acknowledge some normative facts necessarily entails acknowledging some absolute normative facts.

What about the epistemological problem of *knowing* normative facts? Once more there is a lot to be said, but the point to observe for the moment is that we are here in the domain of the *a priori*. And we know once again that we *have* to be able to explain at least how *some* a priori knowledge is possible.

I say this not only because it is overwhelmingly plausible that we have a priori mathematical knowledge. But also because, once more, it is not really an option for us to claim that we don't have knowledge of at least some a priori propositions since it is not an option to claim that we don't know at least some truths about logic – about what follows from what – or some truths about rationality – about what one ought to believe given such and so evidence.

So all of this leads me to be confident that we can solve these deep philosophical problems and so that we should not be afraid of at least some measure of normative absolutism.[7]

References

Benedict XVI (2009): *Caritas in Veritate: Encyclical Letter.* Vatican: The Holy See.
Boghossian, Paul (2011): "Three Kinds of Relativism". In: Hales, Steven (ed.): *A Companion to Relativism.* Oxford: Wiley-Blackwell, 53–69.
Boghossian, Paul (ms): "Relativism about Normative Domains".
Harman, Gilbert (1996): "Moral Relativism". In: Harman, Gilbert; Thompson, Judith Jarvis (eds.): *Moral Relativism and Moral Objectivity,* Cambridge MA: Blackwell, 3–64.
Hume, David (1757/1987): "Of the Standard of Taste". In: Hume, David: *Essays: Moral, Political and Literary.* Indianapolis: Liberty Classics, 226–249
Scanlon, Thomas (1998): *What We Owe to Each Other.* Harvard: Harvard University Press.

---

[7] I am grateful to audiences at the University of Vienna, the Wittgenstein Conference in Kirchberg in the summer of 2015 and to David Velleman, Sharon Street and Yu Guo for helpful comments on the material in this paper. This paper was also included on the 'Silver Dialogues' website maintained by NYU, devoted to representative works by NYU's Silver Professors.

Cora Diamond
Slavery and Justice: Williams and Wiggins

Abstract: David Wiggins argued that there are ethical questions that admit of answers that are substantially true. He considers the case of slavery, and argues that, in response to the question about its moral legitimacy, there is nothing else to think but that it is unjust and insupportable. His view was criticized by Bernard Williams. I examine their disagreement, and consider the views of those who defended slavery, since it is central to Wiggins' argument that discrepancies in belief about a case of this sort need to be accounted for.

Keywords: Moral realism, slavery, justice, Wittgenstein, Elizabeth Anscombe

1 Introduction

My topic is a dispute between Bernard Williams and David Wiggins about ethics. Williams' argument against Wiggins depended on his ideas about thick ethical concepts—concepts like *cruel* and *dishonest*.

Williams claimed that, to get the kind of substantial truth that Wiggins thought there was in ethics, there would have to be some thick ethical concepts that were not local and particular but universal. But there aren't any; there is an irreducible plurality of thick concepts.

Williams did not directly attack Wiggins on truth. He focused instead on a formula that Wiggins uses—the formula: *there is nothing else to think but that p*. Wiggins' idea was that there are various subject matters in which you may consider a question, and may be given the reasons supporting p as the answer to the question,—and, on the basis of these reasons, you may recognize that *there is nothing else to think in response to that question but that p* (see Wiggins 1990, 66). For example, you can be given calculating rules, and shown how to use them, and then come to recognize that the answer to 'what does 7 plus 5 come to?' is 12. You can recognize that, on that matter, there is nothing else to think but that 7 plus 5 is 12. Wiggins then argues that, within ethics, there are cases in which there is nothing else to think but that such-and-such.

Wiggins is not arguing that, on some matters, there is nothing else *for us* to think; he's making the stronger point that there are ethical matters about which there is nothing else *to think* but that so-and-so.

The example he uses is: "there is *nothing else to think*, but that slavery is unjust and insupportable" (Wiggins 1990, 70, original emphasis). His point is that a "wealth of considerations can…be produced", that make it evident *that there is nothing else to think but that slavery is unjust and insupportable*. He says: "At some point in running through these considerations, it will appear that the price of thinking anything at variance with the insupportability of slavery is to have opted out [...] of the point of view that [can be shared] between one person and another." (Wiggins 1990, 70) Here you may want to ask, 'Well, what if, when you say that there is nothing else to think but that p, there are people who think something else?' Wiggins did set out ways to explain what is happening in these cases. Anyway, that view of Wiggins' is what Williams is criticizing.

Williams tried to show that Wiggins can't get what he wants: in ethics, all that you can get is cases where there is nothing else for *us* to think but such-and-such, or nothing else for some other group of people to think but that such-and-such (see Williams 1995). If we take there to be nothing else *to think* but that such-and-such, this presupposes some particular vocabulary of evaluation, but no such vocabulary is universal. Williams' argument is interestingly fishy. So that's the topic of Part 2.

2 Williams' Argument

Williams begins by producing a formula of the same sort as Wiggins'—but using a quite different example. Wiggins' example was "There is nothing else to think but that slavery is unjust and insupportable". The case that Williams sets up is one in which some boys "do a wanton and hideous thing to the cat, [causing] the cat great pain" (Williams 1995, 237). Wiggins' view, Williams says, is that there is nothing else to think but that this was a cruel thing to do; but the boys may nevertheless not think that; they may think that it was fun. So this is meant to go against Wiggins.

But there is already something peculiar going on here, since Wiggins' formula, "There is nothing else to think but that slavery is unjust and insupportable" didn't rule out thinking various other things about slavery, for example that it was profitable. When Wiggins gives the example, "there is nothing else to think *but that slavery is unjust and insupportable*", he is concerned with what there is to think about the moral legitimacy of slavery. If someone thinks that *slavery is profitable*, this is not disagreeing about whether slavery is unjust. It wouldn't be a counter-example to Wiggins. Similarly, if we consider the boys who think that what they did was fun, this doesn't obviously count against Wiggins. Unless you make clear what *question* is being asked, Wiggins' approach doesn't set up any kind of conclusion about what is the only thing to think.

Back to Williams' argument. He says that *if* you use the concept 'cruel', then indeed there is nothing else to think but that what the boys did was cruel. Williams takes it that the boys are *not* users of the concept 'cruel', and this is reflected in their thinking that what they did was fun. But here Williams' approach gets fishier. After all, maybe these boys *are* users of the concept 'cruel'—they might think one of their teachers is horribly cruel. If the concept 'cruel' is in their evaluative vocabulary, they may nevertheless avoid thinking of what *they themselves are doing*, as cruel. This sort of thing happens all the time: you may use some evaluative concept in many circumstances, but may avoid thinking about whether it applies to something you did. There is no inference from the boys' describing what they did as fun to their not being users of the concept 'cruel'. Their evasion of the question might indicate that they *do* use the concept. The main point here then, is that people may *turn off* the issue of the application to themselves of some concept that they do use in an ordinary way in other circumstances.

After Williams has described the boys as not using the concept 'cruel', he says: "This draws our attention to an extremely important form of ethical difference—namely that between those who do and those who don't use a certain concept." (Williams 1995, 237) And he then gives the case of Oscar Wilde, saying that "obscene" is not a word of his. Williams has been leading up to this case, to bring out the differences there are, between people and between cultures, in the thick concepts that people use. His basic argument against Wiggins is then that there is no set of thick concepts that we all share. *If* there were some underlying canonical, homogeneous set of thick concepts, then we might be able to get some kind of truth in ethics that went beyond the appropriate application of the thick concepts of this or that culture, but the idea of such a canonical homogeneous set of thick concepts is utterly unrealistic. And so, therefore, is the idea of getting any kind of substantial truth in ethics, anything beyond the notion of truth that is tied to this or that particular evaluative language. Thus there is no non-relative truth in ethics. What is fishy here is that

Williams has an idea of what the best prospect for substantial truth in ethics *would be:* you'd get it if there were some universal set of thick concepts. But what is striking about his whole approach is that in his argument, he moves further at each step from what Wiggins was trying to do, and specifically further and further from the case that Wiggins gave as his example. So in the next part I want to turn to Wiggins' example, to bring out how far it is from anything that Williams is discussing.

3 There is Nothing Else to Think But that Slavery is Unjust and Insupportable

The first move that Williams made was to replace Wiggins' example of the injustice of slavery with the case of the cruelty of what the boys did. The reason Williams changed the example is that he wanted the focus to be on a case where a thick concept plainly applies to something, in the way the concept of cruelty plainly applies to the wanton thing the boys did, which caused the cat great pain. Williams wanted an example using a concept with much tighter connections to how the world is than the concept of injustice. In the case of injustice, there can be serious disagreement about what the concept does or doesn't apply to. *Justice* isn't a thick concept, on Williams' own view; and Williams' argument against Wiggins depends upon switching to an example involving a thick concept and then showing that that thick concept won't be part of some people's vocabulary. But Wiggins' example is extremely interesting and important, just the way it is, because it brings out that Wiggins is not doing what Williams thinks you have to do if you are trying to set out a substantial notion of truth in ethics. When Williams moves away from Wiggins' example of slavery to the example of what the boys did being cruel, he obscures important features of the case of slavery.

Think about slavery. Slavery in its various forms has involved many kinds of cruelty and brutality. 'Cruel' and 'brutal' are thick concepts, and the application of these thick concepts to slavery is important; but there is a further issue, of a different kind, at the heart of what makes slavery odious, on many people's view. A central thing in the various institutions of slavery is *property in human beings*. If there are considerations that can be brought to bear on thought about slavery —considerations that will leave you with nothing to think but that it is odious, unjust, an intolerable evil,—these often involve showing what is appalling about a man or woman being owned and used and disposed of as a piece of property; they involve showing what is wrong with using another human being as a kind of extension of your own will. The issue about slavery, as it has been thought about, doesn't in any straightforward way depend on thick concepts of the sort that Williams discussed. It's not an accident that the original form of Wiggins' example does not use any thick concept.

I don't at all want to deny the significance of thick concepts applying to slavery, but these are not concepts that those who defend slavery lacked or repudiated; and further, I want to keep in the center here the idea that *property in human beings* is an abomination.

My conclusion so far is that what Williams does when he reads Wiggins is impose *his model* of what you'd have to do if you held that some ethical statements were capable of substantial truth. Williams thinks that the best you can get, if you are looking for truth in ethics, is the kind of truth you get with the application of thick concepts, belonging to this or that particular vocabulary. And this truth has an irremovable kind of relativity—relativity to particular vocabularies of evaluation. But Williams, by imposing this model, misses what Wiggins was doing in his discussion of truth in ethics, and also misses what is at stake in the debate about slavery. I turn in Part IV to Wiggins' reply.

4 Wiggins' Reply

Wiggins' basic idea is that if you deny that slavery is evil, you are at risk of having no workable system of moral ideas, because you will be working *without* such central moral ideas as justice and the significance of not treating human beings merely as means. He said that the issue whether slavery is indeed evil can be joined only if one compares the system of moral ideas that we have, including notions like justice and respect for humanity, with a system of moral ideas dispensing with such notions. Once you've got justice and respect for humanity on board, you have considerations that will lead to recognition of the evil of slavery. So what system do you have without such notions? That's the question Wiggins wants us to ask.

Pro-slavery writers, though, did not in general dispense with such notions; they rather understood them not to lead to condemnation of slavery. One source of their ideas is Aristotle, who held that there were people who were natural slaves, and that enslaving them was no injustice. Starting in the sixteenth century, ideas like Aristotle's about natural slaves were used to defend the subjugation of American Indians and the enslavement of Africans. Pro-slavery writers of the eighteenth and nineteenth centuries held that Africans, identifiable by their race, were naturally fitted to be slaves; and they also made use of a conception very close to Aristotle's, of how slavery benefits a person who is a 'natural slave'. These ideas were central in defences of slavery.

There is a huge disagreement about ethical things that is coming up at just this point. There are disagreements about ethics where one group of people thinks that the other side has got things wrong, but there are also disagreements in which people take some way that other people are thinking about ethics *not just to be wrong,*—but to be a case of *the other people's thinking having gone off the rails*. I'm suggesting that the dispute about slavery involves a disagreement of that sort. That is, one response to all ideas that take some group of people to be natural slaves is: *thinking that way is thinking that has gone off the rails, it is not merely mistaken*. There's a road that you are going down, and thought that goes down that road has gone profoundly astray. Signs ought to be put up saying: don't go down that road.

And indeed there was such a sign that was put up, the statement that men are by nature equal, or the statement that all men are created equal. This was a road-sign for how to think; it says: don't go in search of, or think that you have found, an essential nature that some group of people have—a nature that makes it perfectly in keeping with justice to turn them into slaves, to keep them and use them as slaves.

Statements like 'all men are created equal' have, as part of their meaning, something like this: There are all kinds of differences and inequalities of talents and intelligence and reasonableness and character between human beings, but none of these indicate some inbuilt natural distinction in virtue of which some people may *justly* be owned by others, and may justly be treated merely as means. Hutcheson, for example, made the point this way: "[N]o endowments, natural or acquired, can give a perfect right to assume power over others, without their consent. This is intended against the doctrine of Aristotle, and some others of the ancients, 'that some men are naturally slaves.'" (Hutcheson 1755, 301).

Differences between human beings, whatever they may be, don't ground the subordination of some human beings to others, which is exactly what the defenders of slavery were holding.

I am contrasting two kinds of disagreement in ethics: there is, on the one hand, the kind of disagreement I've been talking about, where one group of people believes that the thinking of the people they disagree with has gone off the rails, and, on the other hand, there are disagreements where you merely believe that what the other people think is wrong, but you don't take their thinking to have gone deeply astray. A good example of the more ordinary sort of disagreement would be over the question whether owning slaves is itself corrupting, as Jefferson, for example, thought, while many pro-slavery thinkers disputed this, and claimed that being a slaveowner was entirely compatible with virtue.

I have been contrasting ordinary moral disagreements and disagreements where one group believes that the thinking of the others has gone totally astray, that it is a kind of mis-use of our thinking capacity. But this is not just the way critics of slavery may treat apologists for slavery: many *pro*-slavery thinkers believed that anti-slavery thinking had gone off the rails, had gone profoundly astray as thinking. This is now what I want to get to: defenders of slavery took abolitionist and other anti-slavery thought not just to be mistaken but to have gone off the rails, to have gone down a path of disastrously tempting but utterly confused thought. If they had been able to read Wiggins, they'd have taken *his* thinking also to have gone down just such a path.

Wiggins' example was that there is no alternative to thinking that *slavery is unjust and insupportable*. He connects that claim with the idea that human beings should not be treated merely as means. Many people would agree that slavery is unjust and insupportable, full stop, total generality. I think this.

Further, many people also would, like Wiggins, connect the general claim with ideas about respect for humanity. One main strand in pro-slavery thought rejects any general abstract treatment of slavery,—as thinking that has gone astray. It's thinking about social and political life in a way that utterly ignores our nature and capacities. It's exactly the kind of thinking that leads to revolutionary destruction of workable though flawed institutions. William Harper, writing in 1837, said: "It is no less a false and shallow than a presumptuous philosophy, which theorizes on the affairs of men as of a problem to be solved by some unerring rule of human reason [...] Man is born to subjection [...] To say that there is evil in any institution, is only to say that it is human" (Harper 1838, 611), and James Hammond wrote that "every attempt by fallible man to extort from the world obedience to his 'abstract' notions of right and wrong, has been invariably attended with calamities dire" (Hammond 1853, 105). Hammond and Harper, like other pro-slavery thinkers, repudiated eighteenth century ideas about equality and liberty. They and other defenders of slavery believed that there is a path of thinking which may be found attractive, but it is a path down which thought is led fundamentally astray,—down that path, *thinking goes adrift from all sense of our limits and fallibility as human beings*. Any general critique of slavery as inconsistent with justice and what is due to human beings has been tempted down that false path.

Where are we now? That's the question to which I turn in Part 5.

5 Some Issues to Think About

i. Wiggins argued that there are notions that cannot easily be dispensed with in any workable system of moral ideas, and that these notions lead to the recognition that slavery is unjust and insupportable. The problem, though, is that defences of slavery do not usually dispense with the notions that Wiggins thinks lead to the conclusion that slavery is unjust and insupportable. From Aristotle on, defenders of various forms of slavery have insisted that certain forms of enslavement are just. Again, there is a problem with Wiggins' point that if you try to deny that slavery us unjust, you will have opted out of any moral viewpoint that can even make sense of the question whether slavery is just. The problem there, at first sight anyway, is that defenders of slavery do apparently make sense of the question whether slavery is just, and provide what they take to be good reasons for the answer that they give. Further, the defences of slavery contain arguments, formulated from what purports to be the moral point of view, that there is no disrespect for human nature inherent in slavery, but rather a realism about the forms that human nature takes.

I've just disputed Wiggins' claims, but isn't there a problem with what I said? Isn't there something right in Wiggins' belief that, if you take 'the moral point of view', there is no alternative to the condemnation of slavery? Do the defenders of slavery really have an alternative system of moral ideas?

Do they really have an alternative answer to the question whether slavery is just? Does it all come apart?

Does their thinking come apart? Is it a kind of miscarriage of thinking?—But I've also suggested that defenders of slavery see a kind of miscarriage of thinking in anti-slavery writings. This sort of issue is one that needs to be argued: if you believe that there is a miscarriage of thinking in the ideas of those who disagree with you, *that* needs to be shown. But what this all does mean is that Wiggins' example of slavery, which he tries to use as a case where there are concepts through which we can categorize a practice, concepts the application of which can make clear that there is only one thing to think about its injustice—that example is problematic. People who defend slavery do not give up the concept of justice; they hold onto the concept but put it to very different work.

ii. What Wiggins says about slavery brings out the inadequacy of Bernard Williams' treatment of truth in ethics. Williams takes as central the application of thick concepts, and the idea that there is no basic shared human vocabulary of thick concepts. Possibly one could reformulate some of the dispute about slavery in Williams' sort of terms,—you would then see the dispute as a matter of pro-slavery people and anti-slavery people having different vocabularies of thick concepts. Anti-slavery thinkers totally reject the concept of *natural slaves*, and you can say that that is a thick concept of pro-slavery thinkers that we don't use. So far as Williams draws that kind of difference to attention, that's fine. But the objection to Williams' kind of presentation of the issue is that the anti-slavery people don't just reject the concept of *natural slaves*; they don't just work with some different evaluative concepts. The disagreement goes deeper. And here Wiggins points us in the right direction. The pro-slavery people and the anti-slavery people have very different systems of moral ideas, and to understand what is involved in their disagreement about slavery, it's not enough to see the heterogeneity of moral vocabulary;—you have to see how their systems of moral ideas as a whole work against each other, despite sharing,—in some sense sharing,—such crucial notions as that of justice. They both *want* the concept of justice; they both take there to be something that is thinking well about justice in relation to slavery; they both want to make plain how they, as opposed to the people they disagree with, are thinking rightly about the justice of slavery.

iii. I have argued that there are disagreements in ethics, in which one or other or both sides hold that the thinking of their opponents is a kind of *miscarriage* of thought. There are two sorts of question about this. First, couldn't one say that, whenever someone disagrees with you about anything, her thinking is miscarrying? That is, one might question what I have said so far, and ask whether it is helpful to conceptualize ethical disagreements, as in *some* cases involving claims about other people's thought having gone off the rails, miscarried, etc, in contrast with *other* ethical disagreements where we merely take other people to be holding a wrong view, but still to be engaged in *thinking*. I'm suggesting that it *is* helpful, because it is a significant feature of ethics that we may want to think of there being tempting paths of thought in ethics, paths that tempt us onwards,—and we may believe that *thought going down those paths has got lost, or gets lost*. Ethics works with *ideas of temptation*, ideas of there being tempting but terribly misleading paths of thought;—and I think such ideas shape our understanding of many of our disagreements.—The other question that comes up is how this all connects with Wiggins' defence of non-relative truth in ethics. When we take his own example of slavery, and follow it up, we can see disagreements between different systems of moral ideas, where each side may want to characterize the other as having gone totally astray in its thinking; but then *can there be truth and falsity about such a matter?*

iv. I want to return to the a quotation that I had from Wiggins in Part I: "At some point in running through these considerations, it will appear that the price of thinking anything at variance with the insupportability of slavery is to have opted out [...] of the point of view that [can be shared] between one person and another." (Wiggins 1990, 70)

One way in which the idea of some people as being 'natural slaves' and of slaves as being a kind of property plays out in practice is that the moral point of view, as understood by pro-slavery thinkers, is not a point of view that can be shared 'between one person and another', but a point of view that can be shared only between some persons and others, not including slaves. Slaves have no point of view that need be taken into account; they have no voice that need be heard. From the pro-slavery point of view, there is nothing unjust in excluding any 'slave point of view', in treating them as not addressed in any discussion of slavery, and as having nothing to say in it. Here we should note that *what the moral point of view is,* is itself one of the things that is in dispute, in the dispute about slavery. You cannot separate the question about the justice of slavery from the question what the moral point of view supposedly is, — the question who can have something to say from that point of view, and whom one is taking oneself to address if speaking from this point of view.

Wiggins' claim that there is nothing else to think but that slavery is unjust was part of his defence of cognitivism in ethics. He was challenging what he called 'the insidious presumption of symmetry' — the idea that, in any ethical dispute in which we might take something to be true, there is a tenable opposing view. Wiggins read the parliamentary debate about slavery as indicating that there was no tenable proslavery position. But he didn't consider a significant range of pro-slavery thinkers, many of whom believed that there was only one sustainable position on slavery, namely, their own. *The idea that there is no symmetry, and that there is only one sustainable view, can be symmetrically held.* Wiggins ends his discussion of the 'insidious' presumption of symmetry by remarking that "Unless the non-cognitivist or the error theorist can show that there is an incoherence in the very idea of enlightenment and of refinement of moral conceptions, it is simply question-begging to make this presumption" (Wiggins 1990, 78). His reference there to 'enlightenment' is particularly striking in relation to the debate over slavery, since many proslavery thinkers rejected central Enlightenment ideas. They thought that there are tempting and deeply misleading impressions of 'enlightenment' in moral thinking. I am not here presuming symmetry, but suggesting that the debate about slavery doesn't deliver any easy defeat to the 'symmetry' view, but rather raises deep questions about what 'the moral point of view' is, and suggests at the same time that there is a danger of a too-easy defeat for the presumption of symmetry, if one reads the pro-slavery view out of moral thought altogether.

Parts 6 and 7 are about Wigginsian, Wittgensteinian and Anscombean responses to the questions in part 5.

6 Wigginsian-Wittgensteinian Things to Think About in Response to the Questions in Part 5

Wiggins has suggested a parallel between the kind of objectivity there can be in ethics and objectivity in mathematics; and he drew on Wittgenstein for this. He said:

for someone who wanted to combine objectivity with a doctrine of qualified cognitivism or of underdetermination, there might be no better model than Wittgenstein's normative conception of the objectivity of mathematics; and no better exemplar than Wittgenstein's extended description of how a continuing cumulative process of making or constructing can amount to the creation of a shared form of life that is constitutive of rationality itself, furnishing proofs that are not compulsions but procedures to guide our conceptions, explaining, without explaining away, our sense that sometimes we have no alternative but to infer this from that. (Wiggins 1998, 128)

In that passage, Wiggins invites us to treat Wittgenstein on mathematics as a model for the kind of objectivity available in ethics; and I want to look further at this *Wigginsian Wittgenstein* as a model for what is going on in the dispute about slavery.

i. One thing we get from the Wigginsian Wittgenstein is the idea of procedures that *guide our conceptions*. Mathematical activities—of giving proofs and working over proofs—can be seen as procedures that *guide our conceptions*, our conceptions of how we have to infer, how we have to think.

Moving over to the case of slavery, and using Wiggins' Wittgenstein as our model, we can think of the arguments given by anti-slavery thinkers as *meant to guide our conceptions*, meant to guide our thinking, away from any paths of thought that allow for there being people whose nature makes it legitimate to enslave them;—we can also think of the pro-slavery arguments as meant to guide our conceptions, meant to guide our thinking, away from any paths of thought that introduce notions of the natural equality and natural liberty of human beings.

ii. On the Wigginsian Wittgensteinian view, the business of giving and working over mathematical proofs has two features. One is that these proofs guide our conceptions; and the second is that this is a cumulative process, a process through which we construct a form of life, including how we understand what is and isn't rational. In this way, we develop the capacity to judge, in particular cases, *that we have no alternative to inferring this from that,—to moving this way, not that, in our thinking*. The idea of a cumulative process through which we shape what we take to be rational involves there being new principles or arguments that we come to take as guides to how to think; but the cumulative process may also involve taking principles or propositions or arguments that we already had, and coming to see their force in new ways. This is particularly relevant to the case of the statement "all men are equal", which I was treating as a guide to thinking,—as a warning against thinking that such-and-such people can justly be enslaved. The statement that all men are created equal has a history: it *comes to be* understood as a standing rebuke to justifications of slavery,—where this, then, is one of the things that feeds into the cumulative process of shaping rationality, shaping how we think *thinking* needs to go.

iii. The model of Wittgenstein on mathematics is useful but has its limits when we think of it as a model for objectivity in ethics, as Wiggins suggests. The model suggests that there is something we might think of as the shared form of moral life, within which we may sometimes have a sense that we have to go this way, not that, in our thinking. But that notion of a shared form of life doesn't go very far when we consider the debate about slavery, and ask whether pro-slavery thinkers and anti-slavery thinkers were answering *the same question*, or whether they weren't, some of them, opting out of the moral point of view. Were they genuinely disagreeing, genuinely contradicting each other, genuinely addressing each other? Where there are the kinds of deep disagreements that there were over slavery, where these disagreements even included disagreements about what color skin you had to have, to have a voice in the disagreement, *Wittgenstein on forms of life provides no answers*. He doesn't give us a theoretical picture of the conditions for genuine disagreement, that we could just plug in to answer our questions here.

7 An Anscombean-Aristotelian But Not Entirely Unwittgensteinian Approach

In that last quotation from Wiggins, he is talking about proofs that guide our conceptions by enabling us to see a path we *need to take* in our reasoning. In the dispute about slavery, each side was trying to indicate a path of thought that we *should not take*. But in both kinds of case, we have *guides to thinking*, or what purport to be guides to thinking. Here I want to suggest a kind of Anscombean view about propositions that guide thinking. Anscombe, in writing about practical truth, appeals to a passage in Aristotle's *Ethics*, where Aristotle says that truth is the business of everything intellectual. Doing well and doing badly in thinking are truth and falsehood, whether we are concerned with purely theoretical thinking or practical thought.—I want to go on from what Anscombe herself says to ask whether we might take it to be part of the business of thinking, part of its job, to guide, or to help put back on track, the business of thinking. If you held that that *was* part of the business of thinking,—*if you held that part of the business of thinking is to help along the business of thinking*—and if you worked with the Aristotelian idea that truth is what you have when the business of thinking is done well, — then statements that guide thinking, or that put thinking back on track, that help it to be done well, could themselves be described as *true*, if they are indeed doing their guiding-job well, if they get right how to guide thought well.

If you say something in response to what someone else has said, that you take to be *thinking that has gone totally off course*, what you say may be thinking *done well*, while what you are responding to is muddle or confusion or miscarriage of thought. There is a kind of asymmetry here: there are not two opposed thoughts, *p* and *not-p*, but failed thought on the one hand, and what we hope is a kind of thinking that guides thought well, on the other hand. Thinking is getting something right, here, but its rightness is that of a right and helpful response to a failure of thought. The response has its sense, its point, from being a response to thought that has failed. We get it, we get what it means, in seeing it a pointful response to something we take to be meant as proper thought, but which is *not that*.

There is a further point here that we can get from Wiggins' Wittgenstein, of there being a kind of cumulative process, as we shape *what thinking is*, what counts as *thinking*, by working our way to this or that thought-guide, and recognizing its usefulness. In this cumulative process, we are making or constructing a shared form of life that is constitutive of rationality. Wiggins' claim that *there is nothing to think but that slavery is unjust and insupportable*, connects with the idea of there being a cumulative process within which we have shaped a form of life constitutive of moral rationality. Within the way this form of life has developed, we can see to be blocked off, as *failed thought*, any conception of justice that excludes some human beings from participating in thought about justice. Wiggins held that, if you keep hold of justice, you will find that there is nothing to think *but that slavery is unjust*; and I'm ascribing to him a conception of the opposition here as having *lost hold of justice*. There are ways of apparently thinking about justice, which are central in pro-slavery thought, and which we have come to be able to recognize as non-thought, failed thought. Some such idea as this underlies, I think, Wiggins' criticism of the 'presumption of symmetry'. A presumption of symmetry in ethics involves failing to see that we may shape well or badly what counts as thinking. Losing hold of justice, as pro-slavery thought did, was shaping thought badly. Here we can see a Wigginsian response to the question "What about Aristotle? Doesn't he illustrate that there isn't just one thing to think about the injustice of slavery?" The answer is that *it can become clear* (though it may not always have been clear) that there is only one thing to think here.

There are connections between Wiggins' attack on 'the insidious *presumption of symmetry*' and Anscombe on Wittgenstein and *On Certainty*. She was thinking about cases where you are confronted with a system of knowledge that you reject. In such cases, there may be the possibility of *persuading* those who accept that other system to change, but *can there be right and wrong here?* Anscombe herself pretty plainly believed that there can be right and wrong in such cases; and she thought that one shouldn't read Wittgenstein as denying it. The Wigginsian Wittgensteinian view is I think similar. Wiggins takes over for ethics the idea of a cumulative process within which we shape what we take to be rational; and he sees this as allowing him to deny 'the presumption of symmetry', the idea that there is always a tenable alternative to any moral view. Against that view, Wiggins insists that there is the possibility of "enlightenment and refinement of moral conceptions", that is, *we can get something right, which we hadn't got right before*. Anscombe and Wiggins, in their different ways, are arguing that the philosophical appearances here can be deeply misleading. The philosophical appearances here seem to lead to forms of relativism or idealism. Bernard Williams' argument against Wiggins, from the plurality of evaluative concepts, is an example of how the presumption of symmetry can work to make truth appear always relative. My argument has been that following out Wiggins on slavery can help us see the issues here.

References

Hammond, James (1853): "Hammond's Letters on Slavery". In: Harper, William; Hammond James; Simms, William; Dew, Thomas: *The Pro-Slavery Argument*. Philadelphia: Lippincott, Grambo & Co, 99–174.
Harper, William (1838): "Memoir on Slavery". In: *Southern Literary Messenger* 4 (10), 609–636.
Hutcheson, Francis (1755): *System of Moral Philosophy*. London: Miller & Longman.
Wiggins, David (1990): "Moral Cognitivism, Moral Relativism and Motivating Moral Beliefs". In: *Proceedings of the Aristotelian Society* 91, 61–85.
Wiggins, David (1998): *Needs, Values, Truth: Essays in the Philosophy of Value*. Oxford: Clarendon Press.
Williams, Bernard (1995): "Truth in Ethics". In: *Ratio* 8 (3), 227–236.

Marie-Luisa Frick
A Plurality of True Moralities? Tracing 'Truth' in Moral Relativism

Abstract: Commonly understood, moral relativism calls into question the capability of moral judgments to be true in an absolute manner. Yet, what truth means in that regard remains contested. If there is no single true morality, as moral relativists typically suggest, does this imply that there are multiple equally true moralities without any nuances of truth and error? By what standards would the assumption that there are no moral truths itself be either true or false? Setting apart moral relativism as a branch of limited or local relativism from types of universal relativism, it can be shown how moral relativism is relying upon a certain notion of truth in order to sweep away another. Far from shying away from it or fearing it, moral relativism embraces truth as a 'weapon' and a criterion of its own adequacy. Without it, moral relativism would not only risk self-defeating inconsistencies; it also would lose its critical potential rendering it a vital enrichment of ethical discourses not only in the eyes of its proponents but also in those of many of its antagonists.

Keywords: Moral relativism, ethics, disagreement, framework, metaphysical truth

Moral relativism is as much controversial as it is afflicted by ambiguities and misapprehensions. In fact, quite a variety of theories or ideas are subsumed under this umbrella term and distinctions between relativism, skepticism, nihilism, contextualism or constructivism are sometimes blurred. Moral relativism, as I understand it, is a complex set of assumptions in three different, yet relating domains: epistemological/hermeneutical, ontological, and normative-practical (see Frick 2010). There is not *the* moral relativism, but – here I agree with Michael Krausz without fully relying on his classification (see Krausz 2010) – various moral *relativisms* are imaginable depending on their peculiar arranging and combining these assumptions. However, at its core moral relativist approaches share a distinct assertion that also is the starting point for reframing the meaning of truth in the context of morality. It is one of my main arguments that understanding "truth" in relativism is crucial in order to assess the traditional charges against moral relativist thought. In particular, two charges have commonly been raised against moral relativism: that it violates the law of non-contradiction and that it is self-refuting. I will argue that both are by no means necessary objections and that reflected and accordingly cautious theories of moral relativism are not affected by them. The key to that finding lies in understanding what notion(s) of truth are applied by moral relativists. This will be the first part of my remarks. In a next step, I will pay attention to implications of such an understanding of truth with regard to moral disagreement and discuss alternative approaches of *non*-metaphysical moral truth.

1 True Morality/True Moralities: The Two Understandings of Truth in Moral Relativism

Having described moral relativism as a complex set of epistemological or hermeneutical, ontological and finally normative-practical assumptions, it is now time to elaborate on this definition a bit more. Not every complex set of such assumptions represents a genuine moral relativist view or theory. To be regarded as such it is necessary that this set involves one proposition in particular which I call the *thesis of ontological relativity*. It can be described in the words of Gilbert Harman as the view that there is "no single true morality" (see for example Harman 2001). The word "single" in that regard seems to suppose that instead of there being no true morality at all; we should imagine at least two or even a plurality of true moralities. In order to understand how relativists like Harman, David B. Wong[1] or also John Leslie Mackie whose antirealist and non-cognitivist stance is a classic example of relativist argumentation,[2] arrive at this assumption, we have to look closely at their path of thought. This starts with what one can call *the observation of an antagonist plurality* of moral views and opinions. This observation, however, is not all at restricted to moral relativists but rather is an anthropological universal at least for those life forms in respective environments where they can encounter diverging judgments, value and moral. What distinguishes the moral relativist from others in that regard is her interpretation of that plurality in general and its inherent disagreement in particular, i.e. the way she makes sense of it (see Frick 2010). From the relativist point of view, moral disagreement

---

[1] Despite his insistence on "universal constraints" Wong can be considered a moral relativist since he argues the case for "an alternative to the universalist view that a single true morality exists" (Wong 2010, p. 245).
[2] Mackie's error theory, although sometimes considered as a version of cognitivism, is not concerning moral but *metaethical* error. Even if, as he admits, the "belief in objective values is built into ordinary moral thought and language", this belief nevertheless is false or implausible when confronted with Mackie's two arguments (from relativity and queerness) (see Mackie 1977, 48 f).

– at least when it comes to uncircumventable axiological-/moral premises – is irresoluble. It cannot be resolved simply by pointing to facts or by demonstrating logical errors. Referring to flaws in such regard, moral relativists argue, is futile since no moral facts do exist which could guarantee the truth of moral judgments. This antirealist view is central to moral relativist thinking and its understanding. If no objective reality is at hand that could be used for testing opposing moral judgments and norms (and moral arguments at large), from this it follows that no true morality exists since no set of moral judgments and norms whatsoever could aspire to match with "moral facts". From the assumption that no true morality exists, it is however quite a way to the claim that no single true morality exists or that a plurality of true morality exists, respectively. How then, does the moral relativist get from here to there? He gets there by changing – implicitly in the most cases – a former *correspondence theory* of truth to something that can best be described as a type of *coherence theory* of truth.

This switch has significance in several important regards: First, it helps clarifying the meaning of the thesis of ontological relativity. In the new understanding, a true morality no longer is something conforming to an external objective reality independent of us; it rather appears as a set of judgments conforming to or capable of being integrated into some non-objective reality, such as a certain worldview or cultural framework. Such non-objective realities do, however, not exist in singular: there are many worldviews – some would argue as many as there are people alive – and there is certainly more than one cultural framework. Any morality then, which has the ability of fitting into such a social reality coherently, is 'true' by the moral relativist. Since many and potentially all moralities that people have adopted can satisfy such standards of framework-coherence, the idea of a plurality of true moralities now appears not only to be meaningful but also inescapable. A moral judgment or a set of moral judgments could then be considered true in the relativistic sense if it is warranted by a respective larger belief system as its justificatory framework of reference. It is important to mind, however, that whereas a plurality of moralities can be considered true in terms of being warranted by their respective frameworks that does not mean that these frameworks are equally flawless. They can still be criticized on the grounds of non-moral truth and logics. But the blade of rational critique is blunt when we get down to the fundamentals of moralities in terms of ultimate values and existential orientations.

Second, with this particular notion of truth, we can now reconsider the charges according to which moral relativism is at risk or even destined (a) to conflict with the law of non-contradiction and (b) to contradict itself. Self-refuting inconsistencies are among the most common charges raised against relativist thinking. Here I will be concerned with a peculiar charge of *theoretical inconsis-*

tency as contrasted with the charge of practical self-contradiction that refers to the alleged impotency of moral relativists to take a stance in terms of normative ethics. In order to answer the charge of theoretical inconsistency, the reference to the notion of truth embedded in moral relativism is important insofar as it sheds light on the nature of this sort of relativism that is no *global* relativism, but only a *local* one. In contrast to the latter which only holds some kind of judgments, e. g. in the context of values and morals, to be relative to a corresponding framework whose truth cannot be established entirely, the former claims that truth is relative in any context. It thus provokes the question if its own assumption is merely a relative one too, i.e. if its form is in accordance with its content. The two horns of the dilemma accompanying any global relativism can be described as follows: In the first case, it might proof difficult convincing someone of the superiority of the all-truth-is-relative-claim; in the second, this claim is obviously contradicting itself since at least one true judgment is said to exist that is above all frameworks-relativity. Being a local relativism only, this dilemma does not apply to moral relativism. Its own truth condition is the *factual* truth according to which no morality (ever entirely) corresponds to an objective reality Another, indeed more serious risk of self-contradiction awaits the moral relativist as soon as he enters the domain of normative ethics. This is especially true for – what Bernard Williams has called – "vulgar relativism" (Williams 1982), i.e. for those moral relativists who propagate tolerance as the only legitimate conclusion of their metaethical insight into the relativity of all morality.[3] Some (see e. g. Schaber 2008) – argue that not only vulgar relativism constitutes an inconsistent position in that regard, but any theory assuming relative moral truths. They claim that once the moral relativist is committed to moral truth relative to framework A, she is also forced to make a *normative* claim regarding the obligation of members or adherents of A to follow this truth's respective norms. Whoever is convinced that a moral judgment is true for members of framework A, is equally convinced that they should act accordingly. I am afraid this argument is misleading. As we have seen, the relativized moral truth in terms of a coherence theory of truth is no genuine moral truth at all. Hence, to say that something is true in that sense does not entail the request to act upon it. Whereas claiming that a moral judgment is true in a non-relative sense equals demanding its compliance and respect, presenting a moral judgment as relatively true to a certain referential belief system is a more complex operation since it has two dimensions: the first one

---

[3] This is why in order to avoid such fallacy I have proposed to regard a hypothetical principle of reciprocity based on the motive of fairness as the only normative implication of the ontological relativity thesis. It works in both directions of tolerance *and* non-tolerance (see Frick 2010).

is a descriptive one: Members of framework A believe judgment X to be true given their respective axiomatic scheme; the second dimension embedded in the assertion according to which a given moral judgment is relatively true to a certain belief system, is indeed a normative one. It is, however, not the *categorical* statement that members of A are obliged to comply with this very judgment, but rather a *hypothetical* imperative. If a member of A would ask the moral relativist: "Shall I act according the judgment X?", the reflective relativist will not answer "Yes!", but tell this person to act according to judgment X *if he wants to conform to the rules of his framework or belong to his moral community*. The relativist could add: "And do not act accordingly if you want to conform to the rules or belong to another". Absolutist, non-relative normative claims are nothing a moral relativist is inevitably committed to as long as she is aware of the fine, but crucial line between categorical and hypothetical imperatives.

Let us now look at the implications of moral relativism's understanding of truth relating to the law of non-contradiction according to which – given the same context – something cannot both be true and non-true at the same time. At a first glance, moral relativism – when applying its coherence moral truth criterion – states exactly that: something, say a moral judgment, is true according to system of reference A and false according to system of reference B. But how could the same judgment be true and false at one time depending on which framework is concerned? Recalling the switch in truth understandings moral relativism has performed after establishing its thesis of ontological relativity, we now see that once truth *has* been relativized to some sort of framework, moral relativists no longer talk about truth in a genuine sense: At the utmost, the moral relativist can speak of a relative truth in question marks. For any judgment, moral and factual alike, coherently fitting into a larger web of judgments means to manifest a sort of "correspondence" with not the slightest metaphysical weight.

To sum up, minding the conception(s) of truth operating in moral relativism, the two charges of violating the law of non-contradiction and of self-refuting inconsistency can be avoided. Yet, other questions arise.

2 Further Questions Discussed: Relative Moral Truth and Genuine Disagreement; Non-Metaphysical Truth

One discomfort with moral relativism's underlying notion of truth has been expressed by Nicolas Sturgeon who confessed to be confused by the way moral relativists seem to "fallback" from the claim that there is no moral truth to the assumption that there are only relative moral truths (see Sturgeon 1994). To him, this maneuver amounts to affirming moral nihilism first and then to diverge into relativism. I am not sure if his confusion could be diminished by the moral relativist's conception(s) of truth as outlined here, but what is more is that his confusion is only part of a larger argument which seems to put the moral relativist into a dilemma since with the fallback from nihilism to relativism, the primarily relativism-inducing disagreement no longer appears to be genuine.[4] If two people disagree about a moral issue and one's judgment is true relative to belief system A and the others' relative to belief system B, can one really say their views conflict? Do they actually *meet*? A genuine disagreement from this perspective would only be possible if the two strive for a single moral truth – which moral relativism just has excluded. In her *The Metaphysics and Ethics of Relativism* Carol Rovane portraits such pseudo-disagreement in quite detail: two women – one from India, one from the USA – "disagree" about the moral relevance of carrying out filial duties, this is, compromising one's own happiness for the sake of the parents' happiness (Rovane 2013). In Rovane's example they both 'agree to disagree': they come to the conclusion that the moral relevance of carrying out filial duties is higher in one and lower in the other society and that it is ok for both of them to see or have it their respective ways. According to Rovane, there is nothing to resolve between the participants in a controversy on moral issues and therefore no genuine disagreement can be said to exist.

I am not convinced by this account and the argument as such. On one hand side, there is the difference between the perspective of the disputants and the perspective of an observer: What might be experienced as a genuine disagreement might not however appear so to a bystander or an expert in moral philosophy – and vice versa. In addition, one should mind the various forms of moral controversies: people can disagree whether a certain judgment is preferable either because it is objectively true or because it is more adequate to one particular belief system. The latter possibility would still exist even if the former seems to be obsolete in a world of moral relativists. Imagine for example the discussion between my friend Caroline and myself. One could say we both more or less share the same system of beliefs – let's call it a secular-human-rights-feminist framework for the sake of argument –, yet we are divided over the extent to which abortion should be allowed. Whereas I tend to argue that the right of

---

[4] This dilemma goes back to David Lyons who described it as follows: Either the moral relativist "seems to endorse logically incompatible judgements as simultaneously true" or he cannot speak of genuinely conflicting moral judgments anymore and thus "forsakes relativism entirely" (Lyons 1976, 292f).

women to reproductive self-determination should be balanced against the unborn child's right to life, Caroline argues for a principle priority of the women's decision. For us, this is not about finding objective moral truth in that matter. It is merely about what position is more in line with a secular-human-rights-feminist framework. This, however, is not simply a question of coherence and norm logic that a more competent third party could resolve for us. This is a question about the weight attached to values and moral principles shared within one general framework of reference. On could even say: It is a question about how an ideal secular-human rights-feminist framework should look like, i.e. a fundamental *intra-framework disagreement*.

In the example mentioned by Rovane, another sort of disagreement is imaginable that in my view is of even greater importance: an *inter-framework disagreement* pertaining to the question which of the (cultural) belief systems of the two women involved is more able to make the world a "better place". Just add to Rovane's example a third women asking the two how to act when confronted with the wish of her parents to get married and found a family instead of pursuing her career. They most probably will advise her according to their own respective systems of belief and try to make it appear more attractive to her than the other. They may not have absolute reasons to do so or any substantial truth on their side of argument, but they nevertheless will be inclined to propagate their respective culture or framework and the way of life it entails. This is all too natural because the disposition to universalize one's own morality in terms of wishing it rather observed by many than by few is by no means peculiar to non-relativists but a key feature of any morality. Seen in that light, the Indian and the US-American women in Rovane's example not only disagree about the right thing to do according to two rivaling belief systems but also about their preferability which they cannot – in the eyes of the moral relativist – decide by resorting to empirical facts and laws of logic only.

Both cases, the extended example of Rovane and my own, finally support the moral relativist's claim that even in ideal situations disagreement would continue over moral issues and that we have no good reason to assume that such disagreement never would be genuine or fundamental. Attempts to show that moral truth as understood by moral relativism does away with genuine disagreement, in generally seem to overestimate the significance of the disagreement argument. Disagreement as such neither is an argument in favor of moral relativism, nor does its absence prove right absolutist theories. Of course, the path of moral relativist thought is – practically speaking – more likely to start with observation of disagreement than universal consensus, but that is not necessarily the case. One could well think of some hypothetical individual who is living in a society where everyone shares the same morality and who starts to ask himself one day what guarantees the truth of their common moral judgments and norms irrespective of their consensus? Or who even imagines a group of people who share another moral code and starts searching for a standard to adjudicate between his and theirs? He can, however, not derive from this factual universal consensus that this consensus constitutes a single true morality because two options would both be perfectly sound: (a) that this consensus constitutes the one and only true morality since consensus is a characteristic mark of moral truth; (b) that this consensus does not constitute the one and true morality since concealment or singularity are characteristic marks of moral truth. Thus, moral relativism would not be defeated just because an antagonist plurality of moral views was absent. Just as uniformity in moral views does not induce the belief that a true morality exists, moral disagreement as such is not relativism-inducing.

Here the question arises why then moral relativists interpret moral disagreement – at least such pertaining to irreducible moral axioms and values – in terms of the thesis of ontological relativity according to which no single true morality exists? We now have arrived at the question of *moral relativism's own truth condition:* Why should we belief in moral relativism at all? The short answer is: because it best explains moral disagreement. People naturally are divided over certain moral issues since there is no single true morality. Being an argument to the better explanation, moral relativism is bound constantly to engage with rivaling perspectives; it can never assume its case to be settled; it can never claim its truth without a minimum of skeptical caution. In the words of Krausz: "The relativist cannot rise up to the absolutist's challenge for a frame-independent argument against the absolutist" (Krausz 2010, 14). I hence suggest the thesis of ontological relativity being moderated to "no single true morality *presumably* exists".

What are then these rivaling perspectives challenging the relativist reading of moral dissent? The most important is the idea of *moral error*. Seen in this light, when people disagree over moral issues, some of them simply do not get it right (see for example Brink 1989). However, one could ask: "do not get it right" in what regard? In regard to empirical facts – then some, by no means all moral dispute would cease. In regard to moral facts – how are we possible aware of them and more importantly, how could we exclude the chance of not getting them right ourselves? I have always wondered why those arguing with moral error virtually without exception assume that those occur to be in error with whom they disagree.[5] Other interpretations of moral disagreement

---

5 Even framing the idea of moral error in terms (im-)partiality, if it is not an ad-hoc argument after all, is itself not an innocent strategy since it rests upon the implicit claim that each person

would be the suppositions of irrationality or evil. Again, they too have considerable flaws (Frick 2010). Another, likewise unconvincing strategy is what can be called a *universalist reduction:* Moral conflicts are 'eliminated' by reducing the apparently contradicting views to shared principles or values. Apart from the fact that it does not succeed in all circumstances, this maneuver raises the question as to what is gained by presenting conflicts about the legitimacy of capital punishment, for example, as a conflict merely about different versions of the shared principle of (criminal) justice?

The problem of moral error accompanies also another question that could be raised in view of moral relativism's antirealism and emphasis on the classical notion of truth in terms of correspondence: Why focus so much on metaphysical truth when there are alternative understandings of (moral) truth? Indeed, several approaches exist to conceive of "moral truth" without relying onto an objective reality or moral facts. Take for example Derek Parfit's version of "non-metaphysical cognitivism". According to Parfit "[t]here are some claims that are, in the strongest sense, true, but these truths have no positive ontological implications" (Parfit 2011, 479). They simply do not exist in some empirical sense, but – like numbers and logical truths – are (sometimes) "self-evident". In Parfit's view we have "intuitive abilities" to recognize such moral truths like: "Torturing children merely for fun is wrong". Some people however – Parfit is referring to psychopaths and sociopaths – lack this faculty: "Most of us can see, though some of us are blind" (Parfit 2011, 544). What are we to make of this approach? I argue it does not bear close examination – no matter how much we are inclined to agree with Parfit that torturing for fun is morally disgusting. It is the problem of all moral-error-theories: Why is Parfit so sure to belong to the seeing camp? He has no (ontological) basis for this. If producing true normative judgments is conditioned by the faculty of intuition and the functioning of intuition is not ascertained otherwise than by producing certain normative judgments, we ultimately have a circle.

In a similar vein already Thomas Nagel has argued for non-metaphysical moral objectivity which nevertheless supports a "normative realism", that is "the view that propositions about what gives us reasons for action can be true or false independently of how things appear to us" (Nagel 1986, 139). This was no truth about the external world, "but rather just the truth about what we and others should do and want" (Nagel 1986, 139). This truth according to Nagel lies in an "impersonal standpoint" that we can reach once "stepping out-

---

is entitled to equal consideration. But why should moralities incorporating selfish or aristocratic ideals be ipso facto false?

side ourselves" (Nagel 1986, 140). The example Nagel gives as moral truth arrived at by this reasoning, is "[t]he objective badness of pain". Anyone "capable of viewing the world objectively [should] want it to stop". Again, I am not convinced that truth talk is adequate here. Apart from the fact that pain, at least the ability to feel it, is not inherently bad seen from an evolutionary or simply medical point of view – just try to live one week without it and then count your bruises –; it also begs the question: Who should have reason to stop whose pain? Why should I have a reason to stop the heartache of an artist, for example, who is dependent on such sort of pain in order to be productive? Should we all have a reason to stop the pain women endure when giving birth even when they refuse anesthesia? Moreover, even if we agree that we should have a reason to stop the pain of elderly patients of Alzheimer disease, wouldn't we soon start quarreling over the pros and cons of euthanasia? What sort of moral truth is this that leaves open so many doors and finally room for contradicting views?

A third approach to do without the classical notion of truth and its metaphysical weight in the realm of morality is Crispin Wright's (Wright 1992). He suggests – similar to Jürgen Habermas' truth analogon "justification" (Habermas 1999) – the criterion of "superassertability" which could function as a truth predicate in moral contexts. A judgment is considered to conform to the standard of superassertability if it is warranted based on all information available and if it continues to be warranted unaffected by any enlargement of that information and any objections raised against it. Wright's attempt is more modest compared to Parfit and Nagel, but his problem is that this theory contains in fact two gateways for moral relativism: first, since superassertability is a formal criterion only, the question when exactly a moral judgment might be warranted, is still open to controversies without any gold standard to adjudicate between different opinions and their corresponding belief systems. The vagueness of the concept of superassertability raises serious doubt whether or not it can really function as an analogon of truth in moral contexts. Second, even if we all could agree on a single clear-cut definition of what makes a moral judgment warrantable – let's say for example a judgment is superassertible if and only if it fulfills the criterion of impartiality – could we really expect that no two moral judgments possibly continue to exist that are not impartial but nevertheless contradict themselves? The question can be put in the following way: Which specific justificatory demands judgments have to meet in order to exclude this sort of pluralism or relativism of moral truths that initially made us wish for an instrument of adjudicating between them? Superassertability seems rather powerless to function as such an instrument.

All in all, it seems to me that nothing is gained by exchanging truth for justifiability, impersonal objectivity or other surrogate truth predicates. They simply don't escape the(ir) framework. Apparently, these three theories of non-metaphysical moral truth dash against the well-known truth (this time it is one) according to which you can't have a cake and eat it at the same time. If – for whatever reasons – you do not want to base your theory of morality on the idea of a mind-independent objective reality ensuring something like moral facts, you better stick to the implications of antirealism and learn to live with the outlook that there is no true morality. You can of course end the journey here and align yourself with moral nihilism (no true morality, no meaning to moral discourse etc.) – or else embrace moral relativism. It is, I would argue, the more daring way given all the snares lurking when handling relative moral 'truth'. However, it *is* a way, and as I hope to have been able to show, a way not necessarily without coherence and not without an element of plausibility.

References

Brink, David (1989): *Moral Realism and the Foundations of Ethics*. Cambridge: Cambridge University Press.
Frick, Marie-Luisa (2010): *Moralischer Relativismus. Antworten und Aporien relativistischen Denkens in Hinblick auf die weltanschauliche Heterogenität einer globalisierten Welt*. Wien/Münster: Lit.
Habermas, Jürgen (1999): *Wahrheit und Rechtfertigung. Philosophische Aufsätze*. Frankfurt am Main: Suhrkamp.
Harman, Gilbert (2001): "Is there a Single True Morality?". In: Moser, Paul K.; Carson, Thomas L. (eds.): *Moral Relativism*. Oxford: Oxford University Press, 165–184.
Krausz, Michael (2010): "Mapping Relativisms". In: Krausz, Michael (ed.): *Relativism. A contemporary anthology*. New York: Columbia University Press, 13–30.
Lyons, David (1976/2010): "Ethical Relativism and the Problem of Incoherence". In: Krausz, Michael (ed.): *Relativism. A Contemporary Anthology*. New York: Columbia University Press, 286–302.
Mackie, John L. (1977/1990): *Ethics. Inventing right and Wrong*. London: Penguin.
Nagel, Thomas (1986): *The View from Nowhere*. New York/Oxford: Oxford University Press.
Parfit, Derek (2011): *On What Matters*. Vol. II. Oxford: Oxford University Press.
Rovane, Carol (2013): *The Metaphysics and Ethics of Relativism*. Cambridge MA: Harvard University Press.
Schaber, Peter (2008): "Ethischer Relativismus: eine kohärente Doktrin?". In: Biller-Andorno, Nikola (ed.): *Gibt es eine universale Bioethik?* Paderborn: Mentis, 159–168.
Sturgeon, Nicholas L. (1994): "Moral Disagreement and Moral Relativism". In: *Social Philosophy and Policy* 20, 80–115.
Wong, David B. (2010): "Pluralism and Ambivalence". In: Krausz, Michael (ed.): *Relativism. A Contemporary Anthology*. New York: Columbia University Press, 254–267.

Williams, Bernard (1982): "An Inconsistent Form of Relativism". In: Krausz, Michael; Meiland, Jack W. (eds.): *Relativism. Cognitive and Moral.* Notre Dame: University of Notre Dame Press, 171–174.

Wright, Crispin (1992): *Truth and Objectivity.* Cambridge MA: Harvard University Press.

Martina Herrmann
Zum Wert von Vertrauen

Abstract: Trust and its value is commonly understood in instrumental terms. But in interpersonal relationships trust has non-instrumental value as well. Indeed, the intrinsic value of trust manifests itself in the fact that trust is part of the point of interpersonal relationships. To understand the intrinsic value of trust requires amending and amplifying existing theories. The account emerging from this critique will focus on esteem and conditional expectations in interpersonal relationships.

Keywords: Trust, intrinsic value, interpersonal relationships, Annette Baier, Philipp Pettit.

Vertrauen, aber auch Solidarität, Achtung bzw. Respekt, Anerkennung, Freundschaft, Liebe, Loyalität, usw. sind wichtige emotional getönte Phänomene. Sie sind wichtig im Sinne von wertvoll in menschlichen Gemeinschaften, in kleinen und großen. Es sind Phänomene, die Beziehungen ausmachen oder Elemente komplexerer Beziehungen sind. Ein Teil ihres Wertes erklärt sich daher, dass sie die Menschen in Beziehungen zusammenhalten, aus einem Paar oder einer Gruppe eine Gemeinschaft machen. Sie sind so etwas wie der Kitt des Sozialen, oder wenigstens ein Teil davon. Und in vertrauensvollen, solidarischen, respektvollen, freundschaftlichen usw. Beziehungen zu stehen ist gut in vielerlei Hinsicht. Das scheint mir auf der einen Seite ziemlich trivial zu sein, insofern als ich erwarte, dass fast alle dem zustimmen und das nicht für kontrovers halten. Auf der anderen Seite ist es nicht trivial auszumachen, worin der Wert dieser beziehungsstiftenden und -tragenden Phänomene in Gemeinschaften bzw. in sozialen Beziehungen besteht. Man kann ihn auf verschiedene Weisen kennzeichnen, explizieren oder erläutern, die wiederum extrinsisch auf andere Werte Bezug nehmen können, aber die Phänomene auch intrinsisch, ohne Bezug auf andere Ziele oder Werte, charakterisieren können.

In diesem Text werde ich mich speziell mit dem Wert von Vertrauen beschäftigen. Es wird sich zeigen, dass die Literatur sich besonders auf den funktionalen Wert von Vertrauen konzentriert hat (siehe McLeod 2015). Der ist hoch und den will ich keinesfalls bestreiten. Ohne Zweifel hält auch der Nutzen, den vertrauensvolle Beziehungen für die Beteiligten haben, diese Beziehungen zusammen. Mein Ziel ist es, etwas Erhellendes zum intrinsischen Wert von Vertrauen in Beziehungen zu sagen. Ich mache plausibel, dass die funktionale, extrinsische Analyse von Vertrauen beschränkt ist, und dass Vertrauen, wenn auch vielleicht nicht in allen Beziehungen, einen intrinsischen Wert hat. Dann unternehme ich erste Schritte, um diesen Wert genauer zu beschreiben. Es ist nicht einfach, etwas Analysierendes oder Erhellendes zu Vertrauen zu sagen, das über den funktionalen Wert hinaus geht, und das die tiefere Bedeutung erläutert, die man vertrauensvollen Beziehungen, insbesondere mit Menschen, an denen man hängt, beimisst. Letztlich werde ich nur etwas Unvollständiges zu den Bedingungen sagen, unter denen Vertrauen in persönlichen Beziehungen intrinsischen Wert hat.

1 Annette Baier: Vertrauen heißt wohlwollenden Personen Güter anvertrauen

Viele Autoren kommen auf Annette Baier zurück, insofern ist ihre Theorie des Vertrauens ein guter Ausgangspunkt (Baier 1986, 2001). Vertrauen wird Baiers Meinung nach gebraucht, weil Menschen Dinge, die ihnen wichtig sind, nicht allein schützen können. Sie benötigen dazu die Unterstützung anderer und müssen sich dabei auf diese Unterstützung verlassen können. Dieses Sich-Verlassen beruht auf der Überzeugung, dass diese anderen einem selbst gegenüber wohlwollend eingestellt sind.

Anke vertraut Berti ein Gut an, z. B. ihr Haustier am Wochenende oder ein Geheimnis, in der Erwartung, dass Berti ihr gegenüber soweit wohlwollend ist, dass er das Gut schützen wird. Er wird das Haustier gut versorgen oder das Geheimnis nicht weitererzählen. Im Vertrauen akzeptiert A, dass B die Möglichkeit hat, ihr zu schaden. Berti könnte das Haustier vernachlässigen oder das Geheimnis ausplaudern. Häufig wird das in einem Schlagwort zusammengefasst als „akzeptierte Verletzbarkeit" (Hartmann 2003).

Vertrauen kann bewusst gebildet werden, z. B. wenn man über mögliche Misstrauensindikatoren nachgedacht hat und glaubt, sie vernachlässigen zu können, oder es kann unbewusst entstanden sein. Als unbewusst entstanden und trotzdem paradigmatisch für Vertrauen versteht Baier das kindliche Vertrauen in die Eltern. Zwischen den beiden Polen des vollkommen unbewussten und des vollkommen bewussten Vertrauens liegen verschiedene Grade der Ausdrücklichkeit, mit denen vertraut wird. Dass A B unbewusst vertraut hat, merkt A manchmal erst nachträglich, nämlich z. B. daran, dass sie enttäuscht ist, wenn B ihr Gut nicht schützt, ohne dass sie vorher darüber je nachgedacht hätte. Im bewussten Vertrauen ist sich A darüber klar, was sie von B erwartet und was nicht.[1]

---

1 Insofern ist es für Vertrauen nicht wesentlich, dass es sich irgendwie anfühlt, und auch nicht, dass es ein Geisteszustand ist. Lagerspetz und Hertzberg schlagen, in Anlehnung an Wittgensteins Ausführungen zu Trauer, vor, dass sich Vertrauen zeigt, und zwar in „an overall pattern in a

As Vertrauen in B ist nach Baier gerechtfertigt, wenn es der Fall ist, dass B wohlwollend A gegenüber ist und das Gut um As willen schützt. Wenn A sich stattdessen auf Anreize verlassen muss, die B unabhängig von ihrem Vertrauen hat, und/oder B sich konform verhält, weil er mit Sanktionen bedroht ist, dann ist As Vertrauen nicht gerechtfertigt. Wenn B A betrügt oder bei bestehender Möglichkeit betrügen würde, ist es ebenfalls kein echtes Vertrauensverhältnis. Das bringt Baier in ihrem kontrafaktischen Vertrauenstest zum Ausdruck: ihr Vertrauen darf nicht gestört werden, falls Anke Genau(er)es über Bertis Einstellungen und Gründe für die Pflege ihres Haustieres oder das Wahren ihres Geheimnisses erfährt und umgekehrt. Vertrauen ist mehr als ein bloßes Sich-Verlassen, dass der andere das Erwartete tun wird. Es wird erwartet, dass es zusätzlich aus den richtigen Motiven getan wird. Der kontrafaktische Vertrauenstest spezifiziert die Komponente des Wohlwollens.

Der eigentlich paradigmatische Fall scheint aber der eines unbewussten oder impliziten Vertrauens zu sein (Lagerspetz 2001). Wenn man anfängt darüber nachzudenken, ob jemand vertrauenswürdig ist, hält man das Wohlwollen des anderen nicht mehr für selbstverständlich – und damit kommt schon ein Moment des Misstrauens hinein. Man vertraut in der Regel unreflektiert, ohne nachzudenken. Das Vertrauen zeigt sich dann im Verhalten (Pettit 1995), wenn z. B. Anke Berti bedenkenlos ihr Geheimnis erzählt. Insofern kalkuliert man nicht strategisch mit dem Wohlwollen. Von außen betrachtet kann man das als Eingehen eines Risikos beschreiben[2]. Von innen betrachtet[3] wird dieses Risiko beim unbewussten oder impliziten Vertrauen nicht gesehen oder zumindest nicht beachtet. Einer vertrauenswürdigen Person vertraut man seine Güter in der Regel bedenkenlos an.

---

person's thinking and acting: a pattern in the weave of life" (Lagerspetz/Hertzberg 2013, 34). Wenn Vertrauen auch ein Gefühl ist, woran ich keinen Zweifel habe, dann ist Vertrauen haben nicht daran gebunden, dass man immer etwas Bestimmtes oder Unbestimmtes fühlt, wenn man vertraut, und auch nicht daran, dass es spezifische Situationen gibt, in denen man etwas fühlen muss, damit Vertrauen zugeschrieben werden kann.
2 Entsprechend Niklas Luhmanns Analyse von Vertrauen als einem Sich-Verlassen unter Eingehen eines Risikos (Luhmann 2000).
3 Gegen Luhmanns Analyse von Vertrauen als einer Abwägung eines Risikos.

2 Die sozialwissenschaftliche Perspektive: Vertrauen als funktional für Kooperation

Autoren aus der Soziologie, Politikwissenschaft, Spieltheorie und den Wirtschaftswissenschaften haben alle eine eher funktionale Perspektive auf Vertrauen. Die deskriptiven Wissenschaften sehen die soziale Pointe des Vertrauens in der Verbesserung von Kooperationsmöglichkeiten und damit in der besseren Befriedigung der eigenen Interessen. Darum ist es gut, selbst eine Disposition zum Vertrauen zu haben. Man wird zwar gelegentlich enttäuscht, wenn man, ohne zu überlegen, in Vorleistung geht oder anderen wichtige eigene Güter zum Schutz anvertraut, aber im Großen und Ganzen verbessert man seine Lebensqualität im Verhältnis zu chronisch misstrauischen Menschen (Hardin 2001, 2006). Annette Baiers Begriffsanalyse leistet dieser funktionalen Sicht Vorschub. Bei Baiers Modell des Anvertrauens von Gütern geht es A im Vertrauen in B um *ihr* Gut, dass B ihr schützen helfen soll. A braucht B für einen bestimmten Zweck, nämlich zum Schutz ihres Gutes. Insofern können sich die Sozialwissenschaften gut auf sie beziehen und viele Autoren tun das auch.

Funktionale Analysen weichen allerdings bei der Einbeziehung der Motivation, aus der heraus sich B als vertrauenswürdig erweist, in der Regel von Baiers Analyse ab. Baier möchte nur eine wohlwollende Einstellung als Vertrauen rechtfertigend zulassen. Funktionale Analysten sehen keinen Grund dagegen, auch bei Egoismus oder Zwang von „Vertrauen" zu sprechen. Wer einen Zweck verfolgt, bei dem ist eher der Aspekt der Zuverlässigkeit in der Vertrauenswürdigkeit wesentlich, aus welchen Motiven auch immer.[4] Sie sprechen auch von Vertrauen, wenn man sich auf Anreize verlässt, die andere haben. Darunter fallen auch langfristige soziale Beziehungen, in denen Zuverlässigkeit aufrechterhalten wird, auch ohne dass Partner sich wohlwollend gegenüberstehen.

Dass Vertrauen das eigene Leben besser macht, scheint mir ohne Frage richtig zu sein. Aber der Vorteil für die Lebensqualität scheint mir nur partiell von den Vorteilen des Vertrauens für die Realisation von eigenen Interessen her zu rühren. Phänomenal macht Vertrauen das eigene Leben auch per se besser, ohne diese Funktion zu erfüllen. Es hat die Funktion, Kooperation zu befördern, aber eine vertrauensvolle Beziehung ist auch wertvoll, wenn A nichts für B tut, oder umgekehrt. Für Anke ist es auch einfach so eine gute Sache, dass sie Berti vertrauen kann, und für Berti, dass Anke ihm vertraut – und umgekehrt. Man möchte, und

---

4 Vgl. auch (Hawley 2012, 31 f) für die Ambivalenz, auch das „Vertrauen" zu nennen, was eher ein Sich-Verlassen auf die Anreize des Kooperationspartners ist.

das scheint mir lebensweltlich evident zu sein, Beziehungen haben, in denen man sich gegenseitig vertraut, auch ohne sich Güter oder wichtige Ziele zum Schutz anzuvertrauen. Ein, wenn auch negatives, Indiz dafür ist, dass man sich bei Vertrauensbruch nicht nur über die verletzten Güter empört, sondern auch – wie man sagt – persönlich enttäuscht ist (Hartmann 2003).

Dass man persönlich enttäuscht ist, und zwar sogar oft unabhängig davon, ob man durch einen Vertrauensmissbrauch einen Schaden erlitten hat, deutet darauf hin, dass eine vertrauensvolle Beziehung auch intrinsische evaluative Aspekte hat. Eine vertrauensvolle Beziehung mag vorteilhafte Folgen haben, aber sie ist, auch unabhängig von vorteilhaften Folgen, etwas Gutes. Das deutet sich auch bei Baier an: ein Gegenüber mit wohlwollender Einstellung ist eines, das dem anderen wohl will, und das heißt ja nichts anderes, als dass das Wohl oder das Gute des anderen einer seiner Zwecke ist. Und jemand, der das Wohl eines anderen vorwiegend um anderer Ziele anstrebt, z. B. um Konflikten aus dem Weg zu gehen, würde man nicht als wohlwollend bezeichnen.

Funktionale Erläuterungen von Vertrauen treffen diesen wesentlichen Teil des Phänomens nicht. Vertrauen kann diverse Funktionen haben, z. B. dass man sich vorübergehend nicht um sein Haustier kümmern muss und es gut versorgt weiß, aber vertrauensvolle Beziehungen werden nicht nur wegen dieser Funktionen gewünscht, sondern auch um ihrer selbst willen. Zumindest manchmal, denke ich, auch *nur* um ihrer selbst willen. Man gibt zwar z. B. intime Informationen preis, ohne deren Weitergabe kontrollieren zu können oder zu wollen, mit der impliziten Erwartung, dass sie nicht weiter gegeben werden. Ein solches Sprechen über sich selbst und andere gerade zu Beginn einer Beziehung schafft nicht nur eine gewisse Nähe in der Situation, es ist vertrauensstiftend für die Zukunft. Auf den Schutz des Geheimnisses kommt es u. U. gar nicht so an. Man denke nur an Klatsch und Tratsch. Oder man leiht dem neuen Bekannten Geschirr und Gläser für sein Fest, und drückt damit nebenbei aus, dass man sich eine Vertiefung der Beziehung wünscht. Dabei kann es ziemlich nebensächlich sein, ob das Leihgut kaputt geht. Sich Informationen, aber auch Güter anzuvertrauen, dient nicht immer dem Schutz dieser Güter, sondern oft dem Aufbau einer Beziehung durch den Aufbau von Vertrauen.

Gerade weil eine vertrauensvolle Beziehung eine gemeinschaftsstiftende Seite hat, wird sie vermutlich zumindest nicht nur um einer Funktion willen aufgebaut und erhalten. Wie kann man Vertrauen so rekonstruieren, dass dessen Wert als ein intrinsischer Wert einer Beziehung deutlich wird? Annette Baiers Begriffsrekonstruktion reicht hier nicht hin, weil sie durch das Modell des Anvertrauens von Gütern einer funktionalen Perspektive Vorschub leistet. Sie deutet zwar durch das Sich-Verlassen auf das Wohlwollen auf Seiten des Vertrauensnehmers einen intrinsischen, ihrer Meinung nach moralischen, Wert an, aber dieses Wohlwollen ist andererseits etwas, das Menschen in ihrem Verständnis zum Schutz aufgrund ihrer Verletzbarkeit brauchen, auf das sie also als ein Mittel angewiesen sind.[5]

3 Philip Pettit: Vertrauen als Motivieren eines Verhaltens durch dessen Erwartung

Weiterführend für das Verständnis des intrinsischen Wertes von Vertrauen ist hier, mit geeigneten Modifikationen, die Analyse von Philip Pettit. Auch Pettit sieht Vertrauen als eine spezielle Unterart von Sich-Verlassen an. A verlässt sich dabei darauf, dass B ein bestimmtes Verhalten zeigen wird. Sich-Verlassen ist so zunächst sehr weit, weiter als das Anvertrauen von Gütern und unabhängig von der Motivation derjenigen, auf die man sich verlässt. Es schließt aber als Unterart Vertrauen ein.

Die Pointe der Unterart „Vertrauen" wird von Pettit nicht in Bezug auf eine Motivation wie Wohlwollen bestimmt. Sie besteht für ihn darin, dass beim Vertrauen sich die Intentionen der Vertrauensgeberin (A) und des Vertrauensnehmers (B) in bestimmter Weise aufeinander beziehen. Ein Sich-Verlassen As auf B ist gerechtfertigtes Vertrauen[6] As in B, wenn zwei Bedingungen erfüllt sind:

> (i) B muss registrieren, dass A sich auf ihn verlässt, ein bestimmtes Merkmal zu haben oder ein bestimmtes Verhalten zu zeigen. Das darf nicht nur zufällig so sein.
> (ii) Für B muss der Umstand, dass A sich auf ihn verlässt, ein (nicht unbedingt der einzige) Grund sein, das Merkmal oder Verhalten zu zeigen – und A weiß das.

Das ist zwar wieder eine Konstruktion, die das Vertrauen auf Situationen eingrenzt, in denen A von B etwas möchte bzw. ihm ein Gut zum Schutz anvertraut. Insofern hat es so nicht den von mir gewünschten breiteren Anwendungsbereich auf durch Vertrauen geprägte Beziehungen, in denen man die meiste Zeit nichts füreinander tut.

Die Bedingung (ii), nämlich dass As Sich-auf-ihn-Verlassen für B ein Grund ist, dem zu entsprechen, fängt aber gut ein, dass A zutreffenderweise glaubt, dass sie selbst und nicht nur ihre Güter und Ziele für B relevant sind. Und das wiederum

---

5 A kann B nach Baiers Analyse aus rein funktionalen Gründen vertrauen. Dass A sich strategisch auf Bs Wohlwollen verlässt, schließt der Vertrauenstest nicht aus. Für Baier verliert A ihr Vertrauen in B nur, wenn sie entdeckt, dass B ihr gegenüber nicht wohlwollend eingestellt ist, sondern verlässlich ist aufgrund anderer Anreize. Auch wenn A Bs Wohlwollen ausnutzt, kann sie das auf der Basis ihres Vertrauens in B tun.
6 Pettit lässt in seiner Ausformulierung offen, ob das Vertrauen gerechtfertigt ist.

heißt mindestens, dass A glaubt, sie bzw. ihr Wohlergehen seien B nicht gleichgültig. Insofern setzt A auch in dieser Analyse auf Bs Wohlwollen. Baiers inhaltlicher Schwerpunkt wird hier mit abgedeckt, ohne die Motivation in die Bedingungen hinein zu nehmen.

Denn es kann ja noch andere Motivationen und Gründe als vorhandenes Wohlwollen geben. Bedingung (ii) sagt aus, dass A glaubt, dass der Umstand, dass sie sich auf B verlässt, für B ein Grund ist, sich als vertrauenswürdig zu erweisen. Vielleicht glaubt A, dass sie Bs Wohlwollen dadurch weckt, dass sie ihm signalisiert, sie verlasse sich auf ihn. Vielleicht glaubt sie aber, dass B Werteinstellungen hat, die unabhängig sind vom Wohlwollen, wie z. B. Pflicht zur Hilfeleistung, und auf ihre Erwartungen ansprechen. Es kann auch sein, dass B gar keine über das bloße Registrieren von As Sich-Verlassen hinausgehende Gründe benötigt. Alltagsbeispiele dazu sind: Wenn jemand nach dem Weg fragt, gibt man eine korrekte Antwort. In Mehrparteienhäusern nimmt man selbstverständlich für die Nachbarn Post an. Man weiß ja, dass die anderen sich darauf verlassen, und das reicht dafür, dass man es tut. A setzt darauf, dass ihr Sich-Verlassen B nicht gleichgültig ist. B liegt etwas daran, sich A gegenüber als vertrauenswürdig zu erweisen. Pettits Bedingungen, unter denen ein Sich-Verlassen ein Vertrauen ist, enthalten so betrachtet noch zusätzlich etwas, nämlich, dass Vertrauen ein Bezogensein der Personen aufeinander ausdrückt, und dass Vertrauen Herstellen ein beziehungsstiftendes Moment hat.

Insofern sind die Motive Bs zwar, anders als bei Baier, aus der Definition herausgenommen. Die Definition ist in dieser Hinsicht weiter als Baiers. Aber das ist für die Rekonstruktion des intrinsischen Wertes von Vertrauen günstig so. Immerhin ist die Motivation durch Bedingung (ii) eingeengt. Pettit nennt drei Möglichkeiten, den Grund Bs zu typisieren: Klugheit, Tugend, Freundschaft. Damit sind drei große Bereiche genannt und mir ist kein weiterer eingefallen, in denen Sich-Verlassen auf der Basis dieser beiden Bedingungen funktioniert. Pettit erläutert das nicht weiter.[7]

---

7 Es liegt nahe, auch „Gewohnheit (einer kulturellen Praxis)" als eine Motivation zu nennen. Das leuchtet mir auf der Seite der Vertrauensgeber ein: die andere Person hat in der Vergangenheit immer zuverlässig getan, was ich von ihr erwartet habe, wenn ich ihr gezeigt habe, dass ich es von ihr erwarte. Aber auf der Seite des Vertrauensnehmers scheint es mir zu kurz gegriffen und auf die anderen drei Typen von Motivationen zu verweisen. Bs Motivation zu tun, was A von ihm erwartet, weil er registriert, dass A es von ihm erwartet, ist seine Gewohnheit, so auf A (und andere) zu reagieren. Das scheint mir etwas dünn zu sein. Man müsste die Gewohnheit genauer spezifizieren: als Praxis der Freundschaft, der Tugend, der Klugheit.

4 Vertrauen als ein geteilter intrinsischer Wert in persönlichen Beziehungen

Meines Erachtens ist es kein Fall von intrinsisch wertvollem Vertrauen, wenn man sich auf die Klugheit des anderen oder seine Tugendhaftigkeit verlässt. Es liegt nur im Fall von Freundschaft weit verstanden ein Vertrauen vor, das sich über die Situationen hinaus, in denen das Merkmal aktiviert wird oder das Verhalten gezeigt wird, als Merkmal der Beziehung erhält.

Wer aus Freundschaft etwas tut, wenn er registriert, dass sich eine andere Person darauf verlässt, der tut es nämlich um des Freundes und um der speziellen Beziehung willen. Er tut es nicht um seines eigenen Wohls willen, aus Klugheit, und er tut es nicht, weil der andere ein Mensch ist und er so etwas für alle Menschen tun würde, egal ob aus Tugend oder Pflicht. Bei Freundschaft geht es darum, dass es dieser bestimmte Mensch ist, der sich auf einen verlässt. Anke kann sich auf ihren Freund Berti verlassen, weil sie und damit ihre Anliegen für Berti relevant sind. Wenn Berti registriert, dass Anke sich auf ihn verlässt, hat er Ankes Wohl und ihre wechselseitige Beziehung als Grund, sich vertrauenswürdig zu zeigen. Gegenseitiges Vertrauen, auch wenn es in seinem Umfang durchaus variiert, gehört zum Cluster von Merkmalen, die Freundschaft kennzeichnen.[8] Sich bei gegebenem Anlass als vertrauenswürdig zu erweisen, erhält und bestärkt dann die Beziehung; es nicht zu tun irritiert und stört sie.

Wenn man andere nicht kennt, vertraut man ihnen manchmal trotzdem. Dann kann man sich nicht so ohne weiteres auf die Klugheit, Moralität oder Freundschaft des anderen verlassen. Pettit hat eine allgemeine Erklärung dafür, warum B immer *einen* Grund hat zu tun, was A erwartet. Es ist ein Grund, den jeder Mensch hat: B wünscht Wertschätzung und A zeigt, dass sie B wertschätzt, indem sie B vertraut. B wünscht diese Wertschätzung auch für die Zukunft, deshalb bestätigt er As Vertrauen in seinem Handeln.

Dieser Grund steht allerdings in einer gewissen Spannung zu meinem Versuch, Pettits Rekonstruktion für die Erläuterung des intrinsischen Wertes von Vertrauen zu nutzen. Pettit betont hier m. E. völlig zu Recht, dass Vertrauen Wertschätzung ausdrückt. Von As Seite aus spricht nichts dagegen, ihr eigenes Vertrauen in B in diesem Aspekt als intrinsisch wertvoll zu beurteilen: sie bringt B damit Wertschätzung entgegen. Aber Pettit selbst interpretiert Bs Gründe letztlich eher soziologisch-psychologisch: Seine Erklärung für Bs Gründe macht, dass trotz

---

8 Freundschaft ist weit verstanden. Es muss keine individualisierte Freundschaft sein, sie kann auch mit einer sozialen Rolle verbunden sein: als Nachbar, als Kollegin, als Tante, usw.

der Wertschätzung, die A B entgegenbringt, umgekehrt B A nicht als intrinsisch wertvoll betrachtet und auch die Beziehung zwischen A und B keinen intrinsischen Wert hat. Wenn B aus dem Wunsch nach eigener Wertschätzung heraus handelt, kann A sich auf B verlassen, aber analog zu der Verlässlichkeit einer Person, die sich als Kooperationspartnerin empfehlen will. Aus dem Wunsch nach zukünftiger Wertschätzung heraus zu handeln ist letztlich ein Klugheitsgrund. Der Wunsch nach Wertschätzung der eigenen Person kann nicht die Basis für ein intrinsisch wertvolles Vertrauen zwischen A und B sein. Denn B handelt dann nicht um As willen und auch nicht um der Beziehung willen, sondern um seiner selbst willen. Dass die Beziehung diesen Wunsch erfüllt, macht die Beziehung für B nicht weniger wichtig, aber es bestimmt den Wert des Vertrauens für B als funktional bzw. instrumentell und damit als extrinsisch.[9]

Pettits Analyse von Vertrauen ist attraktiv, weil sie eine Erklärung dafür bietet, inwiefern es zum freundschaftlichen Verhältnis gehört, dass Anke und Berti sich auf bestimmte Weise aufeinander beziehen, wenn Anke Berti vertraut. Damit hat man ein Beziehungselement in der Erklärung, und nicht nur, wie bei Baier, ein einseitiges Anvertrauen bei erwartetem Wohlwollen unter Akzeptanz von eigener Verletzlichkeit. Pettits eigene Erklärung für Bs Gründe, auf As Wertschätzung zu reagieren, bleiben auf der funktionalen Ebene und reichen nicht aus, um den intrinsischen Wert von Vertrauen zu erklären.

Aber mindestens für persönliche Beziehungen kann man sich auch auf andere Gründe als auf den Wunsch nach zukünftiger Wertschätzung beziehen. Unter Freunden zeigt man das erwartete Charaktermerkmal oder Verhalten um des Freundes willen und um der Beziehung willen. Wenn man sich auf die Elemente der Freundschaft im sehr weiten Sinne von Philia bezieht, gewinnt man eine Beschreibung, die erklärt, inwiefern Vertrauen in einer persönlichen Beziehung zwischen A und B intrinsisch wertvoll für A wie für B ist. Es ist ein intrinsischer

---

9 Für A hat die Interaktion mit B natürlich *auch* einen funktionalen Wert. Sie erwartet, indem sie sich auf B verlässt, von B eine Reaktion, die ihr in irgendeiner Hinsicht zuträglich ist. Aber insoweit As Handeln Wertschätzung der *Person* Bs ausdrückt – und nicht nur für Bs Funktion als Mittel für A –, drückt sie etwas aus, das über den funktionalen Wert hinausgeht. Und es ist ja diese Wertschätzung als Person, von der Pettit meint, dass sie Bs Grund ist, As Erwartung zu entsprechen. – Sollte A sich ausschließlich auf Bs Wunsch nach Anerkennung als Grund verlassen, ist ihr Vertrauen in B nicht mehr intrinsisch wertvoll: weder bringt sie damit ihre Wertschätzung Bs noch eine der Beziehung zum Ausdruck. – Ebenso nimmt ein Wunsch Bs nach Wertschätzung durch A nichts von seiner Vertrauenswürdigkeit soweit sie funktional betrachtet wird, im Sinne von Verlässlichkeit. Aber Bs Grund für seine Zuverlässigkeit trägt nichts zum intrinsischen Wert des Vertrauens bei. Für eine ähnliche Kritik Pettits vgl. (Mäkela 2013). Mäkela meint, es handele sich nicht mehr um Vertrauen im eigentlichen Sinne, wenn beide Seiten auf Bs Wunsch nach Wertschätzung setzen.

Wert aus As Perspektive[10] und ein intrinsischer Wert aus Bs Perspektive. Beiden liegt etwas an der anderen Person *und* an der Beziehung, in der sie sich gegenseitig vertrauen können. Sie sind, um der anderen Person willen und um der vertrauensvollen Beziehung willen, bereit, etwas für die andere Person zu tun, wenn sie registrieren, dass die andere Person es erwartet. Damit ist ein wichtiges Element der Erläuterung, was intrinsisch wertvolles Vertrauen ist, genauer ausgeführt: es bedarf wechselseitiger Wertschätzung aus nicht-instrumentellen Gründen und einer vertrauensvollen Beziehung.

Der Wert ist nach dieser Analyse in Ergänzung zu Pettit aber leider nur mit Einschränkungen das, was für eine Erläuterung des intrinsischen Wertes von Vertrauen (in persönlichen Beziehungen) gebraucht wird. Auch Pettits Rekonstruktion von Vertrauen orientiert sich daran, dass A von B etwas mehr oder weniger Bestimmtes erwartet. B soll für A ein Gut schützen oder A helfen oder B soll für A etwas anderes tun. A erwartet von B ein bestimmtes Verhalten und wäre verletzt, wenn B es nicht zeigt. Sie wäre zum einen persönlich enttäuscht, denn B würde so zeigen, dass er sie nicht so wertschätzt wie gedacht. Zum anderen würde der Wert des Vertrauens, das A in ihre Beziehung zu B setzt, beschädigt. Wenn B das erwartete Verhalten zeigt, wird damit sowohl seine Wertschätzung As als auch die vertrauensvolle Beziehung zwischen beiden bestätigt und bekräftigt.

Ich hatte aber darauf hingewiesen, dass Vertrauen und vertrauensvolle Beziehungen auch wertvoll sind, wenn A und B gerade nichts füreinander tun. Das geht aus den beiden Vertrauensbedinungen Pettits so noch nicht hervor. Um Pettits Rekonstruktion auch auf die Phasen der Beziehungen anwenden zu können, in denen A nichts von B erwartet, kann man die Formulierungen in den kontrafaktischen Konditional bringen. Überzeitlich ausgedehntes Vertrauen zu einer Person hat man und in einer vertrauensvollen Beziehung zu einer anderen Person steht man, wenn der andere ein bestimmtes Verhalten, prima facie, zeigen würde, gesetzt ein Fall tritt ein, in dem die Person registriert, dass man es von ihr erwartet. So lässt sich Pettits Vorschlag für die Erläuterung des Wertes von Vertrauen in Beziehungen für dessen intrinsischen Wert passend abändern und erweitern.

Aber es gibt noch eine offene Stelle in meinem Vorschlag, die meines Erachtens schwerer wiegt: Der so rekonstruierte intrinsische Wert des Vertrauens im Anschluss an Pettit ist bloß perspektivisch. Es ist zum einen ein intrinsischer Wert aus der Perspektive von A – A schätzt B nicht-instrumentell und sie kann sich darauf verlassen, dass es für B ein Grund wäre, etwas von ihr Erwartetes zu tun, falls sie es gegebenenfalls dahin brächte, dass er registrierte, dass sie sich darauf

---

10 Das schließt nicht aus, dass die andere Person, wie auch die Beziehung, darüber hinaus für A und/oder B auch einen extrinsischen, funktionalen Wert hat.

verlässt. Und es ist zum anderen ein intrinsischer Wert aus der Perspektive von B – B schätzt A nicht-instrumentell und das ist ein Grund für ihn, für A gegebenenfalls zu tun, was sie erwartet, wenn er registriert, dass sie sich auf ihn verlässt. Gesucht ist aber eine Erklärung für den intrinsischen Wert einer vertrauensvollen Beziehung, die außerdem verständlich macht, warum eine vertrauensvolle Beziehung auch jenseits der Perspektive der einzelnen auf den anderen, *nämlich aus einer übergreifenden, geteilten oder gemeinsamen Perspektive* intrinsisch wertvoll ist. Der Wert des Vertrauens in der Beziehung oder besser gesagt der vertrauensvollen Beziehung müsste so charakterisiert werden, dass es ein Wert der Beziehung ist, die A und B umfasst. Dazu müsste es gewissermaßen *ein* Wert sein, und nicht der intrinsische Wert für B in Kombination mit oder Addition zu dem Wert für A. Ein intrinsischer Wert für A *und* B, und möglicherweise auch für andere, ist ein Wert, den beide in einem zu explizierenden Sinn gemeinsam haben bzw. den sie teilen. Vielleicht kann man das zu Illustrationszwecken analog dazu auffassen, wie man eine Meinung teilt.[11] Um eine Meinung zu teilen, reicht es nicht, dass zwei derselben Meinung sind. Es reicht auch nicht, dass beide wissen, dass der jeweils andere derselben Meinung ist wie sie selbst. Das entspricht in etwa der Perspektivität. Beide teilen die Meinung des anderen erst, wenn sie sich irgendwie miteinander darüber verständigt haben, dass es jetzt ihre gemeinsame Meinung ist. Das impliziert oft, dass sie sich wieder darüber verständigen werden, wenn sich etwas daran ändert. Dafür, dass ein solches Ausbilden einer gemeinsamen Meinung funktioniert, gibt es eine schon bestehende gemeinsame Praxis, die eine solche Verständigung darüber, dass man einer Meinung ist, ermöglicht. Wenn A dann zu B sagt „Ich teile Deine Meinung, aber ...", dann ist das im Gespräch eine Aufforderung, die gemeinsame Meinung zu überdenken – es sei denn, dass es sich um eine strategische oder anders funktionale Verwendung des Ausdrucks handelt. Auch der geteilte Wert des Vertrauens in einer Beziehung kann durch eine Praxis zustande kommen, die noch beschrieben werden müsste.

Vertrauen wurde in Anknüpfung an Annette Baier zunächst als akzeptierte Verletzbarkeit charakterisiert, bei der wir uns für den Schutz für uns wichtiger Güter auf das Wohlwollen anderer verlassen. Das stimmt, ist aber nur ein Teil der Sache. Den Schutz wichtiger Güter ins Zentrum zu stellen verstellt den Blick darauf, dass Vertrauen auch wertvoll ist, wenn man andere nicht braucht. Es wird auch um seiner selbst willen geschätzt in der Form einer vertrauensvollen Beziehung

---

[11] Man könnte hier auch auf die Diskussion um kollektive Intentionen verweisen. Die hilft aber m. E. nur begrenzt weiter. Das kann ich hier nicht näher begründen Und deshalb habe ich hier eine hoffentlich weniger assoziationsreiche Analogie gewählt.

zwischen zwei Personen. In einer vertrauensvollen Beziehung schätzen sich die beteiligten Personen um ihrer selbst willen und auch die Beziehung, die sie zueinander haben. Vertrauen ist gerechtfertigt, wenn unter geeigneten Umständen auf eine bestimmte Weise gehandelt wird, und Vertrauen liegt vor, wenn die Beteiligten dieses Handeln erwarten. Das kann man kontrafaktisch zum Ausdruck bringen. Zu jedem Zeitpunkt gilt: Falls in einer vertrauensvollen Beziehung eine Person der anderen zeigt, dass sie ein bestimmtes Verhalten von ihr erwartet, dann ist dies für die andere Person ein motivierender Grund, das Erwartete zu tun. Dieser motivierende Grund beruht auf dem intrinsischen Wert des Wohls, den jede Person in den Augen der anderen hat, und dem intrinsischen Wert, den für jede Person die vertrauensvolle Beziehung zwischen ihnen hat. Das zeigt sich in ihren Erwartungen und in ihren motivationalen Handlungsgründen. In einer vertrauensvollen Beziehung ist aber die vertrauensvolle Beziehung auch ein von den Beteiligten gemeinsam *geteilter* intrinsischer Wert. Eine Erklärung dieses Teilens steht noch aus.

Danksagung: Für hilfreiche Kommentare danke ich Diskutanten in Dortmund, Kirchberg, Osnabrück und Essen, außerdem Susanne Boskamp, Nicola Kampa, Rüdiger Bittner, Oliver Hallich und Christian Neuhäuser, und nicht zuletzt Concordia.

Literaturverzeichnis

Baier, Annette C. (1986): „Trust and Antitrust". In: *Ethics* 96, 231–260.
Baier, Annette C. (2001): „Vertrauen und seine Grenzen". In: Hartmann, Martin; Offe, Claus (Hg.): *Vertrauen. Die Grundlage des sozialen Zusammenhalts*. Frankfurt am Main: Campus Verlag, 37–84.
Hartmann, Martin (2003): „Akzeptierte Verletzbarkeit. Elemente einer normativen Theorie des Vertrauens". In: *Deutsche Zeitschrift für Philosophie* 51 (3), 395–412.
Hardin, Russel (2001): „Die Alltagsepistemologie von Vertrauen". In: Hartmann, Martin; Offe, Claus (Hg.): *Vertrauen. Die Grundlage des sozialen Zusammenhalts*. Frankfurt am Main: Campus Verlag, 295–332.
Hardin, Russel (2006): *Trust*. Cambridge: Polity Press.
Hawley, Katherine (2012): *Trust. A Very Short Introduction*. Oxford: Oxford University Press.
Lagerspetz, Olli (2001): „Vertrauen als geistiges Phänomen". In: Hartmann, Martin; Offe, Claus (Hg.): *Vertrauen. Die Grundlage des sozialen Zusammenhalts*. Frankfurt am Main: Campus Verlag, 85–113.
Lagerspetz, Olli; Hertzberg, Lars (2013): „Trust in Wittgenstein". In: Mäkela, Pekka; Townley, Cynthia (Hg.): *Trust. Analytic and Applied Perspectives*. Amsterdam: Rodopoi, 31–51.
Luhmann, Niklas (2000): *Vertrauen: ein Mechanismus der Reduktion sozialer Komplexität*. Stuttgart: UTB.

McLeod, Carolyn (2015): „Trust". In: Zalta, Edward (Hg.): *The Stanford Encyclopedia of Philosophy*, http://plato.stanford.edu/archives/fall2015/entries/trust/.
Mäkela, Pekka (2013): „Desire for Esteem as Reason for Trust?". In: Mäkela, Pekka; Townley, Cynthia (Hg.): *Trust. Analytic and Applied Perspectives*. Amsterdam: Rodopoi, 119–129.
Pettit, Philipp (1995): „The Cunning of Trust". In: *Philosophy and Public Affairs* 24 (3), 202–225.
Pettit, Philipp (2004): „Trust, Reliance and the Internet". In: *Analyse und Kritik* 26, 108–112.

Hans Kraml
Die Erfindung der Sein-Sollen-Dichotomie

Abstract: The dichotomy between 'Is' and 'Ought' is one of the problems that occupied an important place in the debates on Ethics and the possible scientific status of ethical doctrines during the 20th century. The problem was raised by George Edward Moore and is connected with a famous remark by David Hume. Yet the invention of the dichotomy may be traced back to medieval discussions on the character of sentences with respect to the beginnings of an empirical science. The normative content of large parts of every-day talk is from then on thought to be rooted in the will of agents. For the Middle Ages this is the will of god, in a secular context perhaps it is the will of human actors. The paper inquires the impact and some consequences of this development.

Keywords: Fallacy, naturalistic fallacy, is/ought distinction, facts, communication

George Edward Moores *Principia Ethica* aus dem Jahr 1903 (Moore 1959) löste eine Debatte aus, die unter dem Stichwort „naturalistischer Fehlschluss" eine philosophische Diagnose dessen nach sich zog, was es heißt, ein Mensch zu sein. Das ist jetzt mit einem recht hochgestochenen Vokabular formuliert, aber ich glaube, dass die Situation der Menschen seit dem 20. Jahrhundert in einer Weise beschrieben werden kann, die immer auf das Problem von Sein und Sollen zurückführt, auch wenn es recht verschiedene Möglichkeiten gibt, mit dem Thema umzugehen.

Ich möchte im Folgenden versuchen zu zeigen, dass die Problemstellung selber und die damit verbundenen Schwierigkeiten das Ergebnis einer langen Diskussion sind, aus der sich einerseits die Ausbildung enormer technischer Errungenschaften ergeben hat, in der aber auch große Unsicherheit darüber entstanden ist, wie diese Errungenschaften zu bewerten und einzusetzen sind. Diese Form, die Lage darzustellen, ist aber selbst ein Ergebnis der erfundenen Dichotomie, nicht Ausdruck einer Konstante des Menschseins. Man könnte sagen, dass der Rückgriff auf so alte Auffassungen wie die von Moore und Hume, und dann erst recht noch der von mir beabsichtige Rückgriff auf noch viel ältere Autoren, angesichts des erreichten Diskussionsstandes völlig überflüssig ist. Eine solche Feststellung kann man machen, aber manchmal wirft die Entstehung eines Problems doch ein unerwartetes Licht auf die Lage selbst. Meine andere Bemerkung dazu wäre: Was zeichnet Rawls gegenüber Hume, diesen gegenüber Ockham, und diesen gegenüber Al-Ghazali aus? Das Ablaufdatum?

Ich beabsichtige gar nicht, alte Theorien und Lehren stark zu machen, sondern die Herkunft neuer Lehren aus den alten zu verdeutlichen, um damit ihre Stärken und Schwächen zu sehen, ihre Reichweite einschätzen zu können.

1 Moores berühmte Feststellung

Die *Principia Ethica* von George Edward Moore entstanden in einer Umgebung, in der Moral eine besondere Rolle spielte. Um Moores Ethik wirklich besser verstehen zu können, hätte man vielleicht Alan Janik motivieren sollen, *Moores' London* oder wenigstens *Moores' Cambridge* zu schreiben. Es geht aber jedenfalls darum, dass Moore feststellen musste, dass die Bedeutung von Bewertungsprädikatoren, insbesondere von „gut" und „schlecht", nicht auf angebbaren Eigenschaften der bewerteten und zu bewertenden Fälle beruhen kann, sondern etwas zu tun haben muss mit einer Intuition, einem schlichten Erfassen von etwas als gut. Moore besteht darauf, dass sich wertende Prädikate nicht auf rein deskriptive Prädikate zurückführen lassen.

2 Humes Beobachtung

Moore hat einen Vorläufer in David Humes berühmter – eigentlich durch Moore berühmt gewordener – Bemerkung die ich hier wiedergeben möchte:

> Ich kann nicht umhin, diesen Betrachtungen eine Bemerkung hinzuzufügen, der man vielleicht einige Wichtigkeit nicht absprechen wird. In jedem Moralsystem, das mir bisher vorkam, habe ich immer bemerkt, dass der Verfasser eine Zeitlang in der gewöhnlichen Betrachtungsweise vorgeht, das Dasein Gottes feststellt oder Beobachtungen über menschliche Dinge vorbringt. Plötzlich werde ich damit überrascht, dass mir anstatt der üblichen Verbindungen von Worten mit 'ist' und ‚ist nicht' kein Satz mehr begegnet, in dem nicht ein ‚sollte' oder ‚sollte nicht' sich fände. Dieser Wechsel vollzieht sich unmerklich; aber er ist von größter Wichtigkeit. Dies sollte oder sollte nicht drückt eine neue Beziehung oder Behauptung aus, muss also notwendigerweise beachtet und erklärt werden. Gleichzeitig muss ein Grund angegeben werden für etwas, das sonst ganz unbegreiflich scheint, nämlich dafür, wie diese neue Beziehung zurückgeführt werden kann auf andere, die von ihr ganz verschieden sind. Da die Schriftsteller diese Vorsicht meistens nicht gebrauchen, so erlaube ich mir, sie meinen Lesern zu empfehlen; ich bin überzeugt, dass dieser kleine Akt der Aufmerksamkeit alle gewöhnlichen Moralsysteme umwerfen und zeigen würde, dass die Unterscheidung von Laster und Tugend nicht in der bloßen Beziehung der Gegenstände begründet ist und nicht durch die Vernunft erkannt wird. (Hume 1973, 211 f)

Ich meinerseits möchte nun Ihre Aufmerksamkeit, so wie Hume das tut, wenn auch in andere Richtung, darauf lenken, dass viele der Wörter, die wir verwenden, eine – einmal vorsichtig gesagt – Semantik beinhalten, die dem in einem Satz verwendeten „ist" oder „ist nicht" einen Charakter verleiht, der das „soll sein" oder „soll nicht sein" nahelegt.

3 Erfordernisse der Alltagsverständigung

Denken wir an relativ einfache Fälle wie den im letzten Sommer häufig zu hörenden Satz: „Mit heftigen Gewittern und Hagel ist zu rechnen." Worin liegt der logische Fehlschluss, wenn Sie auf diese Nachricht hin versuchen, Ihr Auto in einer Garage oder unter einem Dach unterzubringen?

Ich würde mich selbst für unklug halten, wenn ich daraufhin sagte: Das ist ja nur eine Behauptung, daraus folgt überhaupt nichts darüber, was ich meinerseits tun soll. Aus der Auskunft der Meteorologen folgt nämlich in gewissem Sinn doch, dass ich meine Vorkehrungen treffen sollte.

Ich würde mich allerdings unter den Bedingungen meiner Ausbildung für uninformiert halten, wenn ich behauptete, aus dem von den Meteorologen verkündeten Satz würde „folgen", dass ich mein Auto in Sicherheit bringen sollte. Der Satz beinhaltet ja weder etwas über mich noch über ein Auto noch über Sicherheit und dergleichen. Also folgt daraus auch nichts, das etwas über diese Dinge sagen könnte. Und natürlich erst recht nicht etwas, das über ein Sollen etwas sagen könnte.

Und doch ist es völlig klar, dass aus dem Wetterbericht folgt, dass ich unter bestimmten Umständen ganz bestimmte Dinge unternehmen sollte. Die in diesem Zusammenhang unterstellte Bedeutung von „folgen" ist nicht so weit entfernt von jener, die in einem beliebigen Logiklehrbuch von einigem Niveau definiert zu werden pflegt. Die logische Folgerungsbeziehung macht von der Kenntnis der Bedeutung der in den Sätzen enthaltenen Ausdrücke, insbesondere der logischen Konstanten Gebrauch, während die Folgerungsbeziehung außerhalb des Lehrbuchs im faktischen sprachorientierten Umgang mit den Gegebenheiten der Umgebung von der Kenntnis der Erfordernisse der alltäglichen Lebensführung Gebrauch macht.

4 Die Unterscheidung zwischen Faktischem und Gesolltem als Diskursergebnis

In unserer Alltagssprache und im alltäglichen Reden ist der handlungsleitende Charakter sprachlicher Äußerungen ständig enthalten. Im Rahmen des Philosophierens, das ja in vielen Fällen eine Verständigung und Klärung im Hinblick auf die Sprache anzielt, nicht aber in erster Linie eine Verständigung durch Sprache in Kontexten, die über die Sprache hinausgehen, ist dieser Bezug meist ausgeklammert.

Einem Menschen, der mit der Diskussion des 20. Jahrhunderts mehr oder weniger aufgewachsen ist, ist das Problem der Dichotomie von Sein und Sollen gewissermaßen in Fleisch und Blut übergegangen, und es sieht für ihn so aus, als gäbe es nichts Selbstverständlicheres als diese Dichotomie. Jeder erlebt alltäglich, dass das, was sein soll, nicht unbedingt das ist, was ist, selbst in völlig trivialen Situationen wie dem alltäglichen Straßenverkehr, und dass umgekehrt das, was ist, sicher nicht immer das ist, was sein soll, etwa bei der Lärmeinwirkung der Nachbarn.

Die alltägliche Verständigung ist dadurch bestimmt, dass sie im Zusammenhang der wechselseitigen Abstimmung der Tätigkeiten erlebender und handelnder Wesen steht. Der Anfang des Philosophierens und wissenschaftlicher Bemühungen hatte mit der Verdeutlichung der Situation des Menschen angesichts dessen, was er erlebt, zu tun. Ereignisse und Vorgänge in der Umgebung des Menschen haben in verschiedenem Ausmaß eine Bedeutung für das, was vom Menschen als nächstes zu tun ist, mindestens aber dafür, was er als nächstes zu erwarten hat. Für ein erlebendes und tätiges Wesen wie den Menschen nehmen sich nicht nur die Tätigkeiten anderer Menschen und anderer Lebewesen, sondern auch Erscheinungen in der unbelebten Welt wie Handlungen aus, die zu verstehen sind. „Alles ist voller Götter" (Thales von Milet 1954, 79), das heißt, von allem gehen Handlungsanforderungen aus. Ernst Topitsch hat das als Handlungsförmigkeit des ursprünglichen, metaphysischen Denkens analysiert (Topitsch 1958), und Günter Dux spricht von der subjektivischen Logik, die unsere traditionellen Weltbilder bestimmt (Dux 1982). Epikureer und Stoiker konnten ebenso wie Neuplatoniker und Skeptiker ein Leben im Einklang, im Einverständnis mit sämtlichen Formen der Äußerungen aus der Umgebung eines Menschen als richtige Lebensweise empfehlen. So lange die erlebte Welt mit der erlebten Natur und den natürlich, d. h. naturwüchsig entstandenen Regeln des Umgangs der Menschen miteinander im Zentrum der Lebensgestaltung stand, war es kein Problem, sich auf die Natur der Dinge zu beziehen, um die Anforderungen zu erfassen, denen ein gemeinsames Leben gewachsen sein musste.

Das wird normalerweise im direkten Umgang mit den Dingen gelernt, und in diesem Sinn lernt jeder Mensch von Kind an, was er beim Auftreten bestimmter Situationen tun soll. Woher kommt dann diese uns so selbstverständlich erscheinende Kluft?

Die erste, mir bekannte Formulierung der Unzulässigkeit eines Schlusses vom Sein auf ein Sollen stammt von Johannes Duns Scotus aus der Zeit um 1300 (Scotus 1950, 187). Die Trennung ist meines Erachtens das Ergebnis einer Entwicklung im Zusammenhang mit professionellem Lehrbetrieb. Vollends mit der Gründung der Universitäten als Zunftverbände der Lehrer und Schüler ab 1200 wurde der theoretische Umgang mit Wissen verselbständigt. So finden wir im 13. Jahrhundert bei Roger Bacon die korrekte Erklärung des Zustandekommens des Regenbogens im Jahr 1268 und in kurzer Folge die genauere Darstellung des Strahlenganges in den Regentropfen für die einzelnen Farben bei Witelo (1278) und Dietrich von Freiberg (um 1300) (siehe Kraml 2002, 201 ff). Insbesondere Bacon betont, dass es sich hier um Kenntnisse von Naturvorgängen handelt, die der Mensch jederzeit für seine Zwecke einsetzen kann. Bacon selbst hat ja auch gleich die Phantasie von Fluggeräten und durch Naturkräfte getriebenen Fahrzeugen und von Maschinen zur Bewegung ungeheurer Lasten.

Hier handelt es sich um Kenntnisse, die aus der reinen Feststellung von Tatsachenzusammenhängen und ihrer Darstellung mit Hilfe der Geometrie stammen. Diese Zusammenhänge lassen sich nutzbar machen für Ziele, deren Wahl dem Menschen offen steht. Damit sind diese Kenntnisse sozusagen neutral und mögliche Mittel für ein gutes Leben, aber selbst nicht an etwas Gutem orientiert. Das Gute stammt nicht aus der in diesem Sinn verstandenen Natur der Dinge, sondern braucht eine andere Quelle.

5 Das Wollen als Quelle des Sollens

Als solche Quelle legt sich nun damals wie heute das Wollen nahe. Es ist, so wird gesagt, das der rechten Vernunft konforme Wollen, das allein eine Handlung gut macht. Und wenn man von Dingen sagen kann, dass sie gut sind, so liegt das allein daran, dass sie so sind, wie sie gewollt sind. Damit kommt selbstverständlich im Rahmen mittelalterlicher Vorstellungen die Rede von Gott ins Spiel. Mit Duns Scotus tritt der Gedanke, dass die Welt durch Gottes Wollen besteht, gegenüber dem alten Emanationsgedanken in den Vordergrund. Die nunmehr betonte Kontingenz der Welt wird ausdrücklich damit in Verbindung gebracht, dass die Welt Ergebnis eines Wollens ist, nicht des Seins, weder des göttlichen noch eines universalen kosmischen Seins. Es ist deswegen vielleicht kein Zufall, dass sich ausgerechnet bei Scotus auch die erste Formulierung der Zurückweisung eines

Schlusses vom Sein auf das Sollen findet: „conclusiones enim practicae resolvuntur in principia practica, non speculativa" (Scotus 1950, 187)

Der Gedanke, dass das Gute abhängt vom Wollen, geht zurück auf Peter Abelard, der damit eine heftige Kontroverse ausgelöst hat (Luscombe 1971). Im Lauf des 14. Jahrhunderts beginnt dann eine Bewegung, in der das moralische Sollen zurückgeführt wird auf die Erfüllung des Willens Gottes. Die durchaus kontrovers interpretierte Zentralgestalt dieser Bewegung ist zunächst Wilhelm von Ockham, in dessen Gefolge es eine Reihe von Denkern gibt, die der Idee der Ethik aus göttlichem Gebot folgen. Besonders deutlich formuliert sind bestimmte Grundlagen dieser Auffassung bei einem gewissen Andreas von Neufchateau (ca. 1360). Nach dessen Auffassung ist alles, was außer Gott als ein Gut in Betracht kommt, kontingenterweise ein Gut. Und es ist ein solches Gut, weil Gott es frei als solches Gut will.

Gutsein hängt damit zusammen, dass etwas gewollt wird. Dinge, Eigenschaften an Dingen, Ereignisse und Handlungen sind aus einer bestimmten Perspektive gesehen lediglich etwas, das vorkommt. Dieser Gesichtspunkt wird bei Andreas wohl im Anschluss an Ockham oder an Diskussionen aus dem Umfeld des Denkens von Scotus und Ockham hervorgehoben. Grundsätzlich gilt auch für Handlungen, dass diese für sich und ihrem bloßen Inhalt nach betrachtet, als Vorgänge sozusagen, neutral sind (Ockham 1982, 360, vgl. 384 ff; Neufchateau 1997, 16, 20). Zwar ist im Zusammenhang mit einer Feststellung bei Aristoteles zugestanden, dass etwa Diebstahl oder Mord schlecht sind, Almosengeben oder dergleichen gut, ohne dass hier nach der rechten Mitte gefragt werden müsste. Aber ob ein Vorgang, der als Mord oder Diebstahl bezeichnet wird, als solcher auch tatsächlich Mord oder Diebstahl ist, hängt davon ab, dass es sich dabei um das verbotene Töten eines Menschen oder um die verbotene Aneignung von etwas handelt, nicht schlichtweg um ein Töten oder eine Aneignung. Selbst wenn man sagte, dass jegliches Töten eines Menschen schlecht ist, ist es das eben, weil das Töten als solches verboten ist. Und es wäre dann deswegen schlecht, weil von Gott frei gewollt wurde, dass das Töten diesen Charakter hat und deswegen ein Übel ist.

Man kann das auch als Ausdruck der Einsicht betrachten, dass die Semantik von Werturteilen damit zu tun hat, dass mit ihnen festgestellt wird, dass ein zu bewertender Fall den Anforderungen entspricht, die an die betreffende Sorte von Fällen gerichtet werden. Und solche Anforderungen, so kann man sagen, stammen daher, dass jemand im Hinblick auf die betreffenden Fälle etwas will.

Das hat zu der plausibel erscheinenden Trennung geführt zwischen dem, was an technischen Kenntnissen gewonnen werden kann, und dem, was von diesen Kenntnissen für menschliche Zwecke eingesetzt werden sollte.

6 Vernunftmoral

Auf der Seite der Frage danach, wie nun gelebt werden soll, hat der Einfluss der Ethik des göttlichen Willens eine Betonung der strengen Imperativität des Sollens nach sich gezogen. Rigoristische und prinzipienorientierte Formen der Ethik sind Ergebnis der Gebotsmoral. Man kann durchaus sagen, dass Kants Kategorischer Imperativ als Ausdruck der Vernunft die Vorstellung von Gott als dem Gesetzgeber einfach ersetzt. Die Aufgabe philosophischer Begründung und Reflexion ist es, sich den Anspruch der Vernunft zu vergegenwärtigen und herauszufinden, worin dieser bestehen kann. Wie erkennt der Mensch den durch die Vernunft vorgegebenen Imperativ für das menschliche Handeln? Das ist die entscheidende Frage der praktischen Philosophie. Es sollte nicht verwundern, dass diese Frage genauso im Zusammenhang mit der Ethik göttlicher Gebote auftritt. Wie erkennt der Mensch den Willen Gottes? Nach Auffassung etwa Wilhelms von Ockham ist es in erster Linie die recta ratio (vgl. Ockham 1982, 428), die rechte Vernunft, durch die wir erfassen können, was Gottes Wille sein könnte, auch wenn Ockham natürlich die Möglichkeit einer besonderen Kenntnis des Willens Gottes nicht ausschließt. Dabei knüpft diese Version des Vernunftbegriffs an die alte Vorstellung von Vernunft als Fähigkeit zum Erfassen oder Herstellen des rechten Verhältnisses zwischen einem tätigen Wesen und seiner Umgebung an. Aristoteles hat ja, wie schon früh bemerkt wurde, mindestens einen doppelten Vernunftbegriff: Vernunft als Fähigkeit zum Erfassen des Wesens der Dinge, und Vernunft als Fähigkeit zum Auffinden des rechten Verhältnisses zwischen Möglichkeiten der Lebensgestaltung. Die erste Form, die Vernunft als Fähigkeit zum Erfassen der Bestimmungen der Dinge, wird im 3. Buch von „Über die Seele", dort im berühmten 4. Kapitel, das zahlreiche Kommentierungen im Lauf der Geschichte erfahren hat (Besonders wichtig Alexander von Aphrodisias 1926), behandelt. Die zweite Form, die Fähigkeit, das richtige Verhältnis zu Umständen herzustellen, ist genaugenommen das Gesamtthema der „Nikomachischen Ethik" und der „Politik" des Aristoteles.

Hume spricht in der am Anfang zitierten Passage von der Vernunft im ersten Sinn, die im Lauf der Zeit in der Philosophie bevorzugt worden war. Ein Beispiel für die Festlegung des philosophischen Interesses auf diesen Aspekt der Rede von Vernunft ist die einflussreiche Entwicklung bei den arabischsprachigen Philosophen des 9. und 10. Jahrhunderts, insbesondere bei Al-Kindi (Al-Kindi 1897, 1ff) und Al-Farabi (Al-Farabi 1929, 115ff).

Der zweite Aspekt des Vernunftverständnisses, der etwa in Al-Farabis Traktat „Über die Vernunft" kurz angesprochen, aber zurückgestellt wird, ging in der Geschichte mehr und mehr verloren und erhält erst gegenwärtig wieder Aufmerksamkeit in den Überlegungen im Anschluss an John Rawls zu Reflexionsgleichgewichten (Hahn 2000) und deliberativen Formen der Begründung ethischer Haltungen (Mazouz 2012).

7 Die Beschränkung auf die Wahrheit deskriptiver Sätze

Das hängt meines Erachtens damit zusammen, dass in der Philosophie insgesamt und in den einzelnen Wissenschaften die Devise im Vordergrund stand, nach der Wahrheit zu streben. Die Devise hat im Wesentlichen dazu geführt, dass man sich mehr oder weniger ausschließlich mit dem propositionalen Gehalt von Äußerungen aller Art, einschließlich von Texten, beschäftigt hat und nur wenig mit dem ganzen Feld der Sprechakte insgesamt, und schon gar nicht mit dem Thema der gemeinsamen Lebensführung.

Wo man sich ausdrücklich mit Sprachklärung und mit einer expliziten Einführung sprachlicher Einrichtungen im Rahmen des Bemühens um argumentative und wissenschaftliche Verständigung auseinander gesetzt hat, ist man von der darstellenden und behauptenden Rede ausgegangen. Schon im 14. Jahrhundert trat diese Redeweise in den Vordergrund.

Im letzten Viertel des vorigen Jahrhunderts hat etwa Franz Koppe in *Sprache und Bedürfnis* (Koppe 1977) den Versuch gemacht, die Objektivität und Argumentierbarkeit subjekt- und bedürfnisbezogenen Redens nach dem Muster des darstellenden Redens zu zeigen. Der Grundgedanke war, dass Prädikatoren, die zur Bedürfnisbekundung dienen, ebenso methodisch eingeführt werden können wie Prädikatoren, die im Rahmen der Darstellung von Sachverhalten gebraucht werden. Situationen, in denen Menschen als erlebende Subjekte betroffen werden, können ebenso hergestellt und für das Erlernen entsprechender Unterscheidungen zugänglich gemacht werden wie Situationen, in denen die Prädikatoren zur Beschreibung von Sachverhalten gewonnen werden. Die verwendeten Prädikatoren bringen wesentlich den Charakter subjektiven Betroffenseins zum Ausdruck. Eine Situation kann angenehm oder schmerzhaft sein, und das ist nicht ein Merkmal an einem Gegenstand oder einer Landschaft, auf das man sich als Sprechender beziehen könnte. Es ist damit auch nicht der Verständigungsfestlegung durch Triangulation im Sinne Davidsons zugänglich. Es ist aber etwas, das jemand in bestimmten Situationen erlebt und bei dem man davon ausgehen kann, dass es in vergleichbaren Situationen jedem sprachfähigen Wesen (falls es auch ein Lebewesen ist) zugänglich gemacht werden kann. Insofern kann die entsprechende Prädikation ebenso gemeinsam erlernt und sprachlich festgelegt und geregelt werden wie die Prädikation im Zusammenhang der Verständigung über Gegebenheiten der sogenannten Außenwelt.

Durch die seinerzeitige Arbeit einer Kollegin und durch neuere Diskussionen mit ihr und im Lichte philosophischer Entwicklungen seither bin ich zu der Ansicht gekommen, dass bei aller Verständlichkeit des Gewichts, das von Menschen in wissenschaftlichen Unternehmungen auf die Darstellungsebene gelegt wird, der Ausgangspunkt menschlicher Verständigung in solchen Betroffenheitssituationen liegen muss. Die Verständigung geht mit der Konstituierung einer gemeinsamen Wirklichkeit Hand in Hand. Dabei wird der Umgang mit Situationen, in denen jede einzelne menschliche Person als betroffene beteiligt ist, überhaupt erlernt. Was Frau Falkinger damals vorgeschwebt ist, findet teilweise einen Ausdruck in Michael Thompsons Buch *Leben und Handeln* (Thompson 2011). Die gemeinsame Wirklichkeit der Menschen in diesem Sinn ist gar nicht in erster Linie die beschreibbare und zu den Randbedingungen des Handelns gehörende äußere Umgebung, sondern der Lebenszusammenhang, in dem dafür gesorgt wird, dass überhaupt einmal gelebt und gehandelt werden kann. Tätigkeitsmuster werden zusammen mit den erforderlichen Verständigungseinrichtungen erzeugt, die für das menschliche Leben grundlegend sind. Im Rahmen von Lebenssituationen, auf die mit solchen Tätigkeitsmustern reagiert wird, sind dann der Beobachtung zugängliche Fälle als solche, die jedem so gut wie jederzeit in relativ gut vergleichbarer Weise begegnen, unterscheidbar. Es ist aber klar, dass auch die neutralste Beobachtung und deren Darstellung in jedem Fall eine Erlebniskomponente aufweisen muss, die nicht zur Beobachtung hinzukommt, sondern dieser zu Grunde liegt. Was nicht erlebt wird, kommt überhaupt nicht in Betracht.

Die entsprechenden gemeinsam zu lernenden Muster für Situationsbewältigung und Verständigung beinhalten eine ganze Reihe von Sprechhandlungen, die primär einen Bezug zur Abstimmung des Verhaltens haben. Unter diesen kommen wohl häufig Bekundungen von Anliegen einerseits, von Unsicherheiten und Unkenntnissen andererseits, diesen gegenüber Aufforderungen und Ermunterungen vor, und schließlich wohl auch Hinweise auf Dinge, die getan werden müssen und auf solche die unterlassen werden müssen. Es ist in diesem Sinn der kommunikative Umgang mit Menschen in Situationen, aus denen Anforderungen, Aufforderungen und schließlich Forderungen erwachsen, einfach weil bestimmte Dinge zum Erleben und zur Bewältigung des Lebens gehören. In diesem Zusammenhang werden von den Menschen Fertigkeiten erworben, die zum Leben erforderlich sind. Zu diesen Fertigkeiten gehört auch die Fähigkeit, auf äußere Umstände zu achten, die für das Handeln unerlässlich sind, aber auch die Möglichkeiten des Handelns einschränken können. Im Rahmen des Erlernens der Lebensmöglichkeiten und der Verständigung in diesem Zusammenhang treten deswegen auch

Aufforderungen auf, bestimmte Dinge als Gegebenheiten zur Kenntnis zu nehmen. Davon geht die Möglichkeit, Tatsachen etwa als solche festzustellen, aus.

Insofern die reine Feststellung von Tatsachen und im Weiteren das Betreiben von Wissenschaft sich innerhalb des erlebten und gemeinsam bereits gestalteten, damit auch von Zielen und Bewertungen durchsetzten Lebens abspielt, scheint auch deutlich zu sein, dass die Art von Wirklichkeit, mit der wir in wissenschaftlichen Zusammenhängen rechnen, bezogen ist auf das, was unsere Weise zu leben ausmacht, weil wir eine ganz bestimmte Art von Lebewesen sind, aber auch, sofern wir unter den verschiedenen, für diese Art von Lebewesen, die wir sind, gangbaren Weisen auf einige ganz bestimmte Weisen gekommen sind, auf Lebensweisen, denen wir folgen. Diese haben sich einfach eingebürgert. Die eingebürgerten Lebensweisen sind zwar von vielen Umständen abhängig und nicht in einem einzigen Muster der Lebensführung festgelegt und in diesem Sinn gewissermaßen beliebig und kontingent, aber es ist nicht ins Belieben der Menschen gestellt, solche Muster überhaupt zu entwickeln. Es ist auch nicht ins Belieben der Menschen gestellt, sich eingebürgerten Formen der Lebensgestaltung anzuschließen. Man kann sehr wohl wissen, dass andere als die einem von Kindheit an vertrauten Lebensweisen ebenso sinnvoll sein könnten, und sich doch den Lebensweisen überzeugt anschließen, auf die man sich nun einmal verlassen hat und auf die sich die anderen, mit denen man gemeinsam lebt, ebenfalls verlassen. Wie gesagt, man kann das, wohl wissend, dass die gegebene Weise zu leben nicht notwendig ist, auch wenn es notwendig ist, auf irgendeine Weise sein Leben zu gestalten.

Ich halte das für ein mögliches Verständnis von Richard Rortys Rede von Ironie (Rorty 1992). Ironie in diesem Sinn würde weder Sarkasmus noch Spott oder Verachtung der weniger Aufgeklärten beinhalten, sondern lediglich die Einsicht in die Kontingenz menschlicher Lebensverhältnisse, d. h. die Einsicht, dass diese Verhältnisse auch anders gestaltet sein könnten, und die bewusste Zustimmung zu dieser Kontingenz.

Die Gewohnheiten bilden die Grundlage dafür, wenn auch nicht die Entscheidung darüber, wie wir leben sollen (Aristoteles 1994, Buch 2, Kap. 8 [1269a20]). Wir können uns ja aus der Einsicht in die Gewohnheiten heraus darum bemühen, ungünstige eingebürgerte Formen durch solche zu ersetzen, die unseren Anliegen eher entsprechen. Schon Aristoteles hatte bemerkt, dass die Änderung von Gewohnheiten eine mühsame Angelegenheit ist, zumal im Fall von schlechten Gewohnheiten. Jeder, dem es gelungen ist, das Rauchen aufzuhören, weiß, dass es aber immerhin möglich ist, die Kompatibilität mit den unentbehrlichen gemeinsamen Gewohnheiten vorausgesetzt.

Es ist bekannt, dass es nie funktioniert, etwas zu erforschen und damit Möglichkeiten der Betätigung zu entwickeln, und das Erforschte dann nicht einzusetzen. Man könnte sich aber einmal klar machen, dass die Erkenntnisse, die im Rahmen der Feststellungen von Tatsachenzusammenhängen gewonnen werden, nicht die eigentliche Wirklichkeit wiedergeben, was immer das heißen sollte, sondern durch die spezielle Zugangsweise bereits Kenntnisse sind, die an der technischen Verwendbarkeit des Wissens orientiert sind.

Unser Leben beruht nicht auf den von den Wissenschaften erforschten Tatsachenzusammenhängen mit einem diesen hinzugefügten Wissen um Normen für unsere Verwendung des Tatsachenwissens. Die Rede von Tatsachen und von Normen stammt vielmehr aus der methodischen Beschränkung auf bestimmte Aspekte und Teile unseres Alltagshandelns zur Gewinnung von Wissen, das unserem gemeinsamen Leben behilflich ist. Priorität hat allemal das gemeinsame Leben.

Literaturverzeichnis

Alexander von Aphrodisias (1926): „De intellectu et intellecto". In: Théry, G. (Hg.): *Autour du décret de 1210: II. Alexandre d'Aphrodise. Aperçu sur l'influence de sa noétique.* Le Saulchoir Kain: Revue des Sciences Philosophiques et Théologiques, 74–82.

Al-Farabi (1929): „De intellectu et intelligibili". In: *Archives d'histoire doctrinale et littéraire du moyen âge* 4, 115–126.

Alkindi, Jaqub ben Ishaq (1897): „De intellectu". In: Nagy, Albino (Hg.): *Die philosophischen Abhandlungen des Jaqub ben Ishaq Al-Kindi*. Münster: Aschendorff, 1–11.

Andreas von Neufchateau (1997): *Questions on an Ethics of Divine Commands*. Edited, translated and introduced by Janine Marie Idziak. Notre Dame, Ind.: University of Notre Dame Press.

Aristoteles (1994): *Politik*. Übersetzt und mit einer Einleitung von Franz Susemihl. Reinbek: Rowohlt.

Dux, Günter (1982): *Die Logik der Weltbilder. Sinnstrukturen im Wandel der Geschichte.* Frankfurt am Main: Suhrkamp.

Falkinger, Notburga (1982): *Der handlungsleitende Anspruch von Bekundungen*. Innsbruck: Diplomarbeit.

Hahn, Susanne (2000): *Überlegungsgleichgewicht(e). Prüfung einer Rechtfertigungs-metapher.* Freiburg/München. Karl Alber.

Hume, David (1973): *Ein Traktat über die menschliche Natur*. Hamburg: Meiner.

Koppe, Franz (1977): *Sprache und Bedürfnis. Zur sprachphilosophischen Grundlage der Geisteswissenschaften.* Stuttgart-Bad Cannstatt: Frommann-holzboog.

Kraml, Hans (2002): „The Colors in the Drops: Roger Bacon's explanation of the Rainbow". In: Saunders, Barbara; van Brakel, Jaap (Hg.): *Theories, Technologies, Instrumentalities of Color*. Lanham, New York, London: University Press of America, 201–214.

Luscombe, David E. (1971): *Peter Abelard's Ethics. An edition with introduction, english translation and notes.* Oxford: Clarendon Press.

Mazouz, Nadia (2012): *Was ist gerecht? Was ist gut? eine deliberative Theorie des Gerechten und Guten*. Weilerswist: Velbrück.

Moore, George Edward (1959): *Principia Ethica*, Cambridge: Cambridge University Press.
Ockham, Guillelmus de (1982): „Quaestiones in librum tertium Sententiarum". In: Kelley, Franciscus E.; Etzkorn, Girardus I. (Hg.): *Opera Theologica. Vol. VI.* St. Bonaventure, New York: St. Bonaventure University.
Rorty, Richard (1992): *Kontingenz, Ironie und Solidarität.* Übersetzt von Christa Krüger. Frankfurt am Main: Suhrkamp.
Scotus, Johannes Duns (1950): „Ordinatio". In: Balić, Carolus (Hg.): *Opera Theologica. Vol. 1.* Rom: Editio Vaticana.
Thales von Milet (1954): „Fragment 11". In: Diels, Hermann; Kranz, Walther: *Die Fragmente der Vorsokratiker.* Berlin: Weidmannsche Verlagsbuchhandlung, 67–81.
Thompson, Michael (2011): *Leben und Handeln. Grundstrukturen der Praxis und des praktischen Denkens.* Übersetzt von Matthias Haase. Frankfurt am Main: Suhrkamp.
Topitsch, Ernst (1958): *Vom Ursprung und Ende der Metaphysik: eine Studie zur Weltanschauungskritik.* Wien: Springer.

Peter Schaber
Wird die Moral von uns geschaffen?

Abstract: It is a widely shared view that moral norms are the outcome of our volitional activity. In this paper it is argued that this view should be rejected. It is shown that none of the proposals to understand moral norms as created by volitional activities are convincing. Moral norms are neither the outcome of demands nor the result of hypothetical agreements. This is, it is argued, what distinguishes moral from other norms such as legal and institutional norms.

Keywords: Moral norms, legal norms, institutional norms, constructivism, hypothetical agreements

Verschiedene Autoren vertreten die Ansicht, dass moralische Normen sich nicht einfach in der Welt vorfinden, sondern von Menschen geschaffen werden. So schreibt zum Beispiel Peter Stemmer:

> Das moralische Müssen ist [...] ein Müssen, das nicht einfach aus vorgegebenen Umständen resultiert, sondern durch menschliches Handeln erst geschaffen wird [...] Es ist Menschenwerk und insofern ein in diesem Sinne künstliches Müssen. (Stemmer 2000, 118)

Moralische Normen regeln unsere sozialen Beziehungen. Es ist deshalb naheliegend, sie als etwas zu verstehen, das Menschen für genau diese Zwecke schaffen. Viele, die moralische als von Menschen geschaffene Normen verstehen, meinen zudem, dass die einzig und dabei abzulehnende Alternative die Ansicht sei, moralische Normen seien von einem göttlichen Gesetzgeber geschaffen worden (vgl. Stemmer 2000, 6). Wer diese Ansicht für falsch hält, muss, so diese Autoren, moralische Normen für Menschenwerk halten.

Werden moralische Normen allerdings wirklich geschaffen? Es soll nachfolgend dafür argumentiert werden, dass das nicht der Fall ist. Es ist charakteristisch für moralische Normen, dass sie nicht geschaffen wurden und nicht geschaffen werden, weder von Menschen noch von anderen Wesen. Wenn gefragt wird, ob moralische Normen geschaffen werden, dann stehen die richtigen moralischen Normen im Blick und nicht die, welche fälschlicherweise für moralische Normen gehalten werden. Der Auffassung zufolge, die nachfolgend kritisiert werden soll, sind diese Normen das Resultat menschlichen Handelns und zwar des absichtlichen Handelns derjenigen, welche die Normen befolgen sollten.[1]

---

[1] Für diese Auffassung ist folgende These zentral: „(T)hat all normative facts and principles are

Den unterschiedlichen Interpretationen dieser Doktrin ist die Idee gemeinsam, dass es Normen nur geben kann, wenn Menschen bestimmte Dinge tun und sich in diesem Tun auf die Normen beziehen. Was Menschen dabei tun, ist „truthmaking not truth tracking". Die moralischen Normen, denen wir folgen sollten, kommen durch absichtliches Handeln von Menschen in die Welt.

Ich werde diese Auffassung nachfolgend zurückweisen, indem deutlich mache, dass keiner der Vorschläge, wie moralische Normen als geschaffene Normen verstanden werden könnten, zu überzeugen vermag. Wir verfügen nicht über die normative Fähigkeit, moralische Normen zu erzeugen. Wie wir sehen werden, sind wir in gewissen Situationen durchaus in der Lage, die moralischen Eigenschaften von Handlungen zu verändern, dies aber bloß auf dem Hintergrund schon bestehender moralischer Normen.

Wenn das, wofür hier argumentiert wird, richtig ist, nämlich dass moralische Normen keine geschaffenen Normen sind, dann heißt das nicht, dass es sie auch ohne Menschen geben würde, sondern bloß, dass sie nicht geschaffen wurden. Nicht bloß die Moral, sondern auch andere Dinge gibt es bloß, weil es Menschen gibt: So gibt es z. B. ein Bewusstsein der Zukunft bloß, weil es Menschen gibt. Keine anderen uns bekannten Wesen besitzen ein solches Bewusstsein. Zukunftsbewusstsein haben Menschen aber nicht geschaffen. Wir haben ein Zukunftsbewusstsein aufgrund bestimmter physischer Eigenschaften. Entsprechend denke ich, dass es moralische Normen bloß gibt, weil es Menschen gibt, die bestimmte Eigenschaften besitzen. Genauso wie das Bewusstsein von Zukunft werden moralische Normen allerdings nicht durch Menschen geschaffen.

1 Begriffliche Vorbemerkungen

Moralische Normen würden geschaffen, wenn sie das Resultat intentionalen Handelns wären. Stellen wir uns vor, Menschen würden sich treffen und nach eingehender Diskussion auf die Norm „Man soll Unschuldige nicht töten" einigen. Sie würden sagen, dass diese Norm von denjenigen, welche sich darauf geeinigt haben, nun auch in Zukunft befolgt werden soll.

Die Beteiligten haben der besagten Norm zugestimmt mit der Absicht, ihr in ihrer Gemeinschaft Geltung zu verschaffen. „Töte keine unschuldigen Menschen" ist die Norm, die nun gilt. Sie wäre das Resultat intentionalen Handelns vieler Menschen. Sie könnte aber auch das Resultat intentionalen Handelns einzelner

---

ultimately constructed through the volitional activity of the agents to whom they apply." (Wallace 2012, S. 21)

sein. Wir werden verschiedene Vorschläge, wie moralische Normen durch Menschen geschaffen werden, nachfolgend näher betrachten.

Dabei muss folgendes vorausgeschickt werden: Es gibt verschiedene Arten von Normen: Normen der Klugheit, Höflichkeitsnormen, moralische Normen und andere mehr. Unter Normen verstehe ich das, was wir durch Sollensaussagen zum Ausdruck bringen: „Du sollst mehr Sport treiben", „Du sollst nicht lügen". Diese Sollensformen können in einem schwachen und in einem starken Sinn verstanden werden: Im schwachen Sinn sind Gründe gemeint, die dafür sprechen etwas zu tun oder zu unterlassen. Im starken Sinn sind Dinge gemeint, die zu tun wir verpflichtet sind. Nicht alle Sollen sind dabei moralischer Natur. Wenn ich sage „Hans sollte mehr Sport treiben", dann meine ich, dass es klug von Hans wäre, wenn er mehr Sport treiben würde, und dumm, wenn er dies nicht tun würde, aber nicht verwerflich.

Einige Formen des Sollens sind allerdings moralischer Natur: Ihnen nicht nachzukommen, wäre nicht bloß dumm, sondern verwerflich. Dabei verstehe ich unter *moralischen Normen* solche, deren Beachtung von allen eingefordert werden kann und deren Verletzung alle berechtigt, den moralischen Missetätern Vorwürfe zu machen. Moralische Normen gehen alle etwas an. Wenn Paul Gerda misshandelt, dann darf nicht bloß Gerda, sondern alle dürfen Paul dazu auffordern, damit umgehend aufzuhören. Und nicht nur Gerda darf ihm Vorwürfe, sondern wir alle dürfen ihm Vorwürfe machen. Dass Paul Gerda misshandelt, ist keine Angelegenheit, die bloß Paul und Gerda betrifft. In gleicher Weise sind die Menschenrechtsverletzungen einer Despotenregimes nichts, was bloß die davon Betroffenen und das Regime etwas angeht. Das heißt: Nicht nur die Bürgerinnen und Bürger des Landes dürfen das Regime dazu auffordern, mit den Menschenrechtsverletzungen aufzuhören. Dazu sind vielmehr alle berechtigt; gleichzeitig dürfen auch alle den Missetätern Vorwürfe machen. Das ist das, was ich nachfolgend unter moralischen Normen verstehen werde. Eine Norm wird als eine moralische Norm verstanden, wenn man sie als eine Norm auffasst, die von allen eingefordert werden kann und die alle zu Vorwürfen gegenüber den Missetätern berechtigt.

2 Forderungen und Verpflichtungen

Werden moralische Normen geschaffen? Das ist die Frage: Sind die Normen, denen wir folgen sollten und deren Verletzung alle dazu berechtigt, uns Vorwürfe zu machen das Resultat intentionalen Handelns? Sie könnten, dies der erste Vorschlag, aus Forderungen hervorgehen. Dieser Vorschlag drängt sich auf, weil es Normen gibt, die in der Tat das Resultat von Forderungen sind. Sie bestehen, weil

Menschen Dinge mit der Absicht tun, sie hervorzubringen. Eine Form, das zu tun, besteht darin, von anderen etwas zu fordern. Gewisse Normen bestehen, weil eine oder mehrere Personen von einer oder mehreren Personen etwas fordern. Aus Forderungen – so der Vorschlag – gehen moralische Normen hervor, sofern die fordernde Person dazu berechtigt ist, Forderungen zu stellen.

Betrachten wir dazu ein Beispiel: Wenn der Rektor einer Universität der Seminarvorsteherin des Philosophischen Seminars aufträgt, die Prüfungsordnung zu ändern, dann sollte sie das tun. Wenn das Straßenverkehrsamt mich anweist, mein Auto vorzuführen, dann sollte ich das tun. Genau dasselbe gilt für die Aufforderung des Steueramts, die Steuererklärung für das Jahr 2015 auszufüllen. Das alles sind Beispiele für Dinge, die wir lediglich tun sollen, weil wir dazu aufgefordert worden sind. Dabei mag es unabhängig davon gute Gründe geben, z. B. die Prüfungsordnung des Philosophischen Seminars zu ändern. Verpflichtet das zu tun wird die Seminarvorsteherin jedoch erst durch die Aufforderung des Rektors.

Nicht nur institutionelle, sondern auch rechtliche Normen werden geschaffen. Sie sind das normative Resultat eines intentionalen Handelns von Menschen, und zwar genau von denen, die autorisiert sind, die entsprechenden rechtlichen und institutionellen Normen zu schaffen. So legt die Universitätsordnung der besagten Universität fest, dass der Rektor die Autorität hat, den einzelnen Instituten vorzuschreiben, wie die Dozentinnen und Dozenten die Studierenden prüfen sollen. Und entsprechend kann allein der Rektor die Seminarvorsteherin anweisen, die Prüfungsordnung auf die von ihm gewünschte Weise zu ändern. Würde eine andere Person diese Anweisung erlassen, würde diese normativ ohne Folgen bleiben.

Gehen auch moralische Normen aus Forderungen hervor? Man könnte fragen: Ist die Seminarvorsteherin dem Rektor gegenüber moralisch verpflichtet? Das könnte schon deshalb naheliegen, weil zumindest einige der institutionellen und rechtlichen Normen zugleich auch moralisch gefordert sind. Das Gebot, andere nicht zu töten, ist etwa nicht nur rechtlich, sondern zugleich auch moralisch geboten. Die konkreten Rechtsgebote, andere nicht zu töten, sind zu einem bestimmten Zeitpunkt vom Gesetzgeber erlassen worden. Damit wurde, so könnte man sagen, ein rechtliches und zugleich ein moralisches Gebot geschaffen.

Der Vorschlag ist allerdings mit folgender Schwierigkeit konfrontiert: Andere nicht zu töten, ist rechtlich wie moralisch geboten. Das moralische Gebot, dies nicht zu tun, bestand allerdings schon bevor das Gesetz erlassen wurde. Durch die Gesetzgebung wurde eine moralische in eine rechtliche Norm verwandelt. Das gilt auch für institutionelle Normen: Wenn Dozierende moralisch verpflichtet sind, die Arbeiten der Studenten fair zu beurteilen, dann wird mit der entsprechenden institutionellen Regelung eine moralische in eine institutionelle Norm transformiert.

Die Möglichkeiten, wie moralische Normen durch Forderungen geschaffen werden könnten, sind damit nicht erschöpft. Betrachten wir folgendes Beispiel: Hans tritt Gerda auf die Füße (Darwall 2006, 67). Das tut ihr weh. Hans sollte seine Füße wegnehmen. Er ist moralisch verpflichtet, das zu tun. Gerda kann das von Hans fordern („Nimm deine Füße weg"). Dieses Beispiel könnte so gelesen werden, als erschaffe Gerda hier eine Norm. Dies ist jedoch irreführend. Es ist nicht Gerdas Forderung, die Hans verpflichtet, seine Füße wegzunehmen, was sich durch folgende Überlegung deutlich machen lässt: Stellen wir uns vor, Gerda würde es nicht wagen, das zu fordern, weil sie eine sehr schüchterne Person ist. Ungeachtet dessen hätte Hans dennoch die Pflicht, Gerda keine Schmerzen zuzufügen. Und wenn Gerda Hans auffordert, seine Füße wegzunehmen, dann macht sie Hans bloß auf seine bereits bestehende moralische Pflicht aufmerksam und erzeugt Druck, das auch zu tun.

Es könnte allerdings sein, so ließe sich einwenden, dass das auf Pflichten der genannten Art, nicht aber auf alle moralische Pflichten zutrifft. Es könnte moralische Pflichten geben, so könnte man argumentieren, die mit Erschaffen anderer Pflichten entstehen. Nehmen wir noch einmal die Aufforderung des Rektors, die Prüfungsordnung zu ändern. Er verpflichtet die Seminarvorsteherin damit, diese Änderung vorzunehmen. Dazu war sie davor nicht verpflichtet. Könnte es sich dabei zugleich auch um eine moralische Verpflichtung handeln? Würde die Institutsleiterin moralisch falsch handeln, wenn sie sich weigern würde, die Prüfungsordnung zu ändern? Wenn das der Fall wäre und die Pflicht vor der Aufforderung des Rektors noch nicht bestanden hätte, dann wäre es naheliegend, dass sie ebenfalls durch die Forderung des Rektors erschaffen worden wäre. Handelt es sich um eine moralische Norm, die geschaffen wurde?

Die Seminarvorsteherin ist verpflichtet, die Prüfungsordnung zu ändern. Sie ist dem Rektor gegenüber verpflichtet, das zu tun und sonst niemandem. Er ist autorisiert, von ihr die Einhaltung der Norm, die er erzeugt hat, zu fordern. Andere können sie natürlich darauf aufmerksam machen, dass es eine Norm gibt, die sie zu befolgen hat. Das ist aber nicht dasselbe wie die Einhaltung einer Norm zu fordern. Wer autorisiert ist, dies zu tun, ist nämlich auch autorisiert, den Normadressaten bei Nicht-Einhaltung der Norm zur Rechenschaft zu ziehen. Das kann in dem beschriebenen Fall bloß der Rektor tun. Würde die Seminarvorsteherin der Forderung des Rektors nicht nachkommen, wäre er dazu berechtigt, von ihr zu fordern, sich zu rechtfertigen. Würde sie das nicht tun oder nicht in einer Weise, die er als zufriedenstellend ansehen würde, könnte er ihr auch berechtigterweise Vorwürfe machen. Würde eine Drittperson sie auffordern, sich zu rechtfertigen, könnte sie mit Recht erwidern: „Das geht sie nichts an, kümmern sie sich um ihre eigenen Angelegenheiten".

Daran wird deutlich, dass die Norm, um die es hier geht, keine moralische ist.

3 Hypothetische Einigung 1

Meine bisherigen Überlegungen zeigen nicht, dass moralische Normen nicht geschaffen wurden. Sie zeigen bloß, dass moralische Normen nicht durch Forderungen geschaffen werden. Sie könnten sich aber den Forderungen vorausliegenden intentionalen Handlungen von Menschen verdanken. Man könnte argumentieren, dass sich Menschen vorgängig darauf geeinigt haben, dass wir einander z.B. keine Schmerzen zufügen dürfen. Diese Norm wird im Hans/Gerda Beispiel wirksam. Mit Einigung können dabei unterschiedliche Dinge gemeint sein. Die Einigung kann eine faktische sein: Menschen haben sich zu einem identifizierbaren Zeitpunkt auf die Norm, dass wir uns nicht ohne guten Grund Schmerzen zufügen sollen, geeinigt. Die Einigung könnte aber auch in dem Sinne eine faktisch sein, als Hans, Gerda und die Menschen, mit denen sie es in ihrem Leben im Wesentlichen zu tun haben werden, sich darin einig sind, dass man sich nicht ohne guten Grund Schmerzen zufügen sollte. Der zu diskutierende Vorschlag lautet: Eine moralische Norm besteht, weil wir dieser Norm zustimmen, wenn sie gefragt würden. Moralische Normen sind das Resultat solcher hypothetischer Einigungen unter nicht idealisierten Bedingungen. Ob eine Einigung über diese Norm zu einem bestimmten Zeitpunkt stattgefunden hat, ist fraglich, aber es ist wohl so, dass die meisten Menschen, mit denen wir es in unserem Leben zu tun haben werden, sich darin einig sind, dass anderen nicht grundlos Schmerzen zugefügt werden sollten.

Ist die besagte Norm also das Resultat einer derartigen Einigung? So wie die Seminarvorsteherin die Prüfungsordnung ändern sollte, weil der Rektor sie dazu aufgefordert hat, würde dann gelten: Hans ist verpflichtet, seine Füße wegzunehmen, *weil* wir uns einig sind, dass man das tun sollte (und entsprechend fordern würden, wenn wir gefragt würden). Man könnte dann sagen: Die Norm gilt, weil wir unsere Zustimmung zu dieser Norm geben und dies von Hans fordern *würden*. Bei dieser Idee von Einigung geht es um eine hypothetische Einigung, die im Unterschied zu derjenigen, die wir später noch genauer betrachten werden, unter nicht-idealisierten Bedingungen zustande kommt.

Dieser Vorschlag wirft einige Fragen auf. Was ist der Fall, wenn nicht alle zustimmen würden? Gilt die Norm dann immer noch? Wie viele müssten der Norm ihre Zustimmung geben? Die Mehrheit der Menschen, mit denen wir es zu tun haben werden? Oder reicht eine relativ große Minderheit? Oder müssten alle dieser Norm zustimmen? Unabhängig davon, dass nicht klar ist, ob das wirklich alle tun würden, stellt sich auch die Frage, wieso es denn eigentlich alle sein müssten?

Es ist unklar, welche faktische Einigung eine Norm hervorbringen würde. Das ist ein Problem dieses Vorschlags. Ein anderes ist dies: Wenn faktische Einigungen

Normen hervorbringen würden, dann müssten wir mit unplausiblen Resultaten rechnen. Nehmen wir an, Hans und Gerda lebten in einer stark männerdominierten Gesellschaft, in der die auch von den meisten Frauen geteilte Meinung vorherrscht, auf Schmerzen von Frauen müsse keine Rücksicht genommen werden. Hans müsste in dieser Welt seine Füße nicht von denen Gerdas wegnehmen, da die Norm, anderen nicht grundlos Schmerzen zuzufügen, bloß für Männer gelten würde. Das werden viele für wenig plausibel halten und entsprechend auch nicht bereit sein, diese Norm auf Männer einzuschränken. Wären hypothetische Einigungen unter nicht idealisierten Bedingungen ausschlaggebend, müssten solche Normen als moralische Normen anerkannt werden.

4 Hypothetische Einigung 2

Wenden wir uns dem Vorschlag zu, den die meisten Vertreter der Idee, dass moralische Normen geschaffen würden, für richtig halten. Danach gehen moralische Normen aus einer hypothetischen Einigung unter *idealisierten* Bedingungen hervor. Dieser Vorschlag liegt faktisch in unterschiedlichen Varianten vor und wird von unterschiedlichen Autoren vertreten.[2] Die Bedingungen, die dabei im Blick stehen, sind solche, die sich von den Bedingungen unterscheiden, unter denen wir normalerweise über moralische Normen nachdenken und zum Schluss kommen, bestimmte Normen für richtig und andere für falsch zu halten. Die hypothetische Einigung ist eine, die Menschen unter idealisierten Bedingungen erzielen würden. Und die richtigen moralischen Normen sind solche, auf die wir uns unter diesen Bedingungen einigen würden. Sie sind richtig, dies die Idee, *weil* sie das Resultat eines solchen Verfahrens sind. David Copp sieht dies als die Kernidee einer *konstruktivistischen* Auffassung moralischer Normen: „[A] constructivist theory defines a hypothetical procedure that could in principle be followed, where the outcome of the procedure is a set of standards that the theory holds to be true *because* they are yielded by the procedure" (Copp 2013, 16). Was spricht dafür, sich an Einigungen unter idealisierten Bedingungen zu orientieren?[3] Der Grund, das zu tun, kann nur darin liegen, dass man sich im Vergleich mit den Einigungen unter nicht idealisierten Bedingungen die besseren Resultate verspricht. So wird man vermuten, dass Menschen sich unter idealisierten Bedingungen z.B. nicht auf sexistische oder rassistische Normen einigen würden. Das ist es, was für solche

---

[2] So einschlägig (Rawls 1971), (Scanlon 1998), (Darwall 2006), (Southwood 2010) und auch (Stemmer 2000).
[3] Dazu ausführlich auch (Enoch 2005).

hypothetischen Einigungen spricht. Würden wir sie uns nicht mit den besseren Resultaten versorgen, wäre nicht klar, wieso wir uns nicht an Einigungen unter nicht idealisierten Bedingungen orientieren sollten.

In welcher Hinsicht sind die einen Resultate jedoch besser als die anderen? Die Antwort kann nur lauten: Im Blick darauf, was wir suchen, wenn wir über moralische Normen nachdenken, nämlich richtige Antworten. Die idealisierten Bedingungen versprechen uns die richtigen Resultate. Wir würden die idealisierten Bedingungen auch nach diesem Gesichtspunkt auswählen: Nehmen wir an, wir hätten zwei unterschiedliche Vorschläge für idealisierte Bedingungen. Für welche würden bzw. sollten wir uns entscheiden? Wir würden uns für diejenigen entscheiden, die uns mit größerer Wahrscheinlichkeit auf den richtigen Pfad und zu Einigungen führen, welche die richtigen moralischen Normen hervorbringen.

Damit wird aber vorausgesetzt, dass die richtigen moralischen Normen den Einigungen vorausliegen. Die idealisierten Bedingungen erlauben es uns, die richtigen moralischen Normen zu finden. Wenn es nicht das wäre, was wir uns von den idealisierten Bedingungen versprechen, wäre unklar, wieso wir uns an Einigungen unter idealisierten Bedingungen orientieren sollten. Der Grund, das zu tun, kann nur der sein, dass ein Nachdenken unter diesen Bedingungen uns auf den richtigen Pfad führt, auf den nämlich, der uns zu den richtigen moralischen Normen führt.

Klar, es geht bei idealisierten Bedingungen darum, Faktoren auszuschalten, die auf die Meinungsbildung in moralischen Fragen keinen Einfluss haben sollten. Angst, Wut, Macht und Eigeninteresse sind Dinge, die in diesem Kontext genannt werden können. Wieso aber sollten solche Faktoren auf unsere Meinungsbildung keinen Einfluss nehmen? Es ist nicht so, dass sie Einigungen verhindern. Das tun sie nicht. Es ist vielmehr so, dass sie zu Einigungen zu führen scheinen, die nicht die Resultate hervorbringen, die wir haben möchten: nämlich die richtigen. So sollten Normen nach Ansicht verschiedener Autoren z. B. nicht bloß im Lichte des Eigeninteresses erwogen werden, weil wir annehmen, dass uns das vom richtigen Pfad wegführt. Nur diejenigen Faktoren sollten für unsere moralische Meinungsbildung maßgebend sein, die uns zu den richtigen moralischen Normen führen. Die Rechtfertigung, sich an idealisierten Bedingungen zu orientieren, liegt allein darin, dass sie das zu tun.

Von Autoren wie Stemmer wird argumentiert, dass nur unter idealisierten Bedingungen die Normen gewählt werden, deren allgemeine Geltung im besten Interesse der Normadressaten wären. Eine rationale Moral kann, so Stemmer, „nur eine interessenfundierte Moral, wobei die Interessen [...] konvergieren müssen [...] (Stemmer 2000, 204). Stemmer bezeichnet das als einen hypothetischen Kontraktualismus, von dem er sagt:

Er behauptet nicht wirkliche Agreements, sondern imaginiert einen vormoralischen Raum, um zu zeigen, dass es hier für rationale Individuen im Blick auf ihre eigenen Interessen vernünftig wäre, moralkonstituierende Agreements zu vereinbaren und damit eine Moral zu etablieren (Stemmer 2000, 204).

Das idealisierte Verfahren sichert dabei, dass Menschen die Normen wählen, die sie rationalerweise wählen sollten. So Stemmers Vorschlag.

Damit wird aber kein plausibles Modell des Schaffens von Normen verteidigt, weil nach diesem Vorschlag moralische Normen genau besehen gar nicht geschaffen werden. Stemmer geht vielmehr davon aus, dass die richtigen moralischen Normen diejenigen sind, deren allgemeine Geltung und Befolgung im besten Interesse der Normadressaten sind. Und die idealisierten Bedingungen werden nach Maßgabe dieser Idee richtiger moralischer Normen ausgewählt. Letztere gehen aber dann nicht aus intentionalen Akten von Menschen hervor. Welches die richtigen moralischen Normen sind, ist nach diesem Vorschlag vielmehr vorgängig schon bestimmt. Es sind diejenigen Normen, deren Befolgung im besten Interesse der Normadressaten ist. Die idealisierten Bedingungen ermöglichen es den Normadressaten bloß, diese Normen auch zu entdecken.

5 Versprechen

Damit sind die Möglichkeiten, wie moralische Normen geschaffen werden könnten, noch nicht erschöpft. Mit bestimmten Handlungen können wir die moralischen Eigenschaften von Situationen verändern. Mit Einwilligungen verwandeln wir unerlaubte in erlaubte Handlungen, mit Versprechen erzeugen wir Pflichten. Deshalb ist folgender Vorschlag naheliegend, der Vorschlag nämlich, dass moralische Normen aus Versprechen hervorgehen. So könnte man sagen, dass Menschen diejenigen moralischen Normen erzeugen, die einzuhalten sie einander versprechen. Und da wir das nicht in realen Akten tun, müsste man ergänzen: diejenigen moralischen Normen, die einzuhalten wir einander versprechen würden, wenn wir danach gefragt würden. So sollten wir andere nicht quälen, demütigen, betrügen et cetera, weil wir ihnen das versprechen würden, würden wir danach gefragt.

Erzeugen Versprechen also in diesem Sinne moralische Normen? Es gibt zwei Gründe, dies zu bestreiten:

a) Wiederum müsste man sich hier auf hypothetische Versprechen unter idealisierten Bedingungen beziehen (was Menschen unter idealisierten Bedingungen einander versprechen würden). Und die Probleme, die mit diesem Vorschlag verbunden sind, haben wir oben gesehen.

b) Ein weiteres Problem des Vorschlags besteht darin, dass Versprechen moralische Normen voraussetzen, um normativ bedeutsam sein zu können. Versprechen bringen nämlich nur dann moralische Pflichten hervor, wenn sie sich auf Handlungen beziehen, die moralisch erlaubt sind. Hans verspricht Gerda, ihr beim Umzug zu helfen. Damit verpflichtet er sich ihr gegenüber. Das tut er aber nur unter der Bedingung, dass die fragliche Handlung (Gerda beim Umzug zu helfen) moralisch erlaubt ist. Stellen wir uns vor, er würde ihr versprechen, einen ungeliebten Konkurrenten umzubringen. Er würde sich damit nicht moralisch verpflichten, den Konkurrenten umzubringen, da das, was er verspricht, moralisch verboten ist.

Wer an der Auffassung, dass Versprechen moralische Pflichten erzeugen, festhalten will, müsste sagen, dass Hans durch sein Versprechen eine Pflichtenkollision erzeugt. Er hat nun die Pflicht, den ungeliebten Konkurrenten nicht umzubringen und gleichzeitig die Pflicht, ihn umzubringen. Nun kann man ganz generell bestreiten, dass es Pflichtenkollisionen geben kann. Man kann aber auch im Besonderen bestreiten, dass man Pflichtenkollisionen selbst erzeugen kann. Das aber wäre der Fall, wenn Versprechen in jedem Fall moralische Pflichten erzeugen würden.

Erzeugen Versprechen aber nicht Pflichten? Hans' Versprechen erzeugt in der Tat eine Verpflichtung, aber keine moralische Pflicht.[4] Wenn er sein Versprechen nicht hält, kann Gerda ihm Vorwürfe machen, er hätte sich ihr gegenüber nicht loyal verhalten. Er hat mit seinem Versprechen aber *keine* moralische Pflicht erzeugt, die von allen eingefordert werden kann und alle zu Vorwürfen berechtigt, würde er sein Versprechen nicht halten. In normativer Hinsicht verändert sich durch sein Versprechen bloß etwas zwischen ihm und Gerda. Sein normatives Verhältnis zu allen anderen bleibt durch das Versprechen unberührt. Sie werden von ihm nicht berechtigterweise fordern, den ungeliebten Konkurrenten zu töten, sondern vielmehr das gerade nicht zu tun, also sein Versprechen, das er Gerda gegeben hat, nicht zu halten. Eine *moralische* Pflicht wird mit unmoralischen Versprechen nicht geschaffen.

Mit Versprechen können wir Dinge, die moralisch erlaubt in Dinge verwandeln, die moralisch geboten sind. Auf diese Weise können moralische Eigenschaften von Situationen verändern. Das gilt allerdings bloß für Handlungen, die

---

4 Gilbert redet von einem „commitment", das der Promissar dem Promittenten gegenüber eingeht; vgl. (Gilbert 2011).

moralisch erlaubt sind, etwas, das vorgängig feststehen muss. Moralische Verbote können nicht durch Versprechen in Gebote verwandelt werden. Zudem ist es so, dass Versprechen auch keine moralischen Pflichten erzeugen, wenn sie sich auf Handlungen beziehen, die auszuführen wir unabhängig von unseren Versprechen verpflichtet sind. Wenn Hans Gerda verspricht, sie nicht zu vergewaltigen, erzeugt er damit keine moralische Pflicht. Dazu war er nämlich schon davor moralisch verpflichtet. Wir haben die normative Fähigkeit, die moralischen Eigenschaften von Situationen zu verändern, nicht aber die normative Fähigkeit, Normen zu erzeugen.

6 Eine besondere Autorität?

Aber wie kommen moralische Normen in die Welt? Werden sie wenn nicht von Menschen so doch von einem Wesen, das eine besondere moralische Autorität besitzt, geschaffen? Nein. Sie werden von niemanden geschaffen. Das lässt sich an folgendem verdeutlichen: Wenn moralische Normen von einem Wesen geschaffen würden, wäre die Einhaltung der geschaffenen Normen etwas, das wir dem Normengeber schulden. Er ist berechtigt, uns zur Rechenschaft zu ziehen. Das ist der Fall bei rechtlichen und institutionellen Normen: Wir schulden ihre Einhaltung dem Normengeber: Der Rechtsgemeinschaft im Fall rechtlicher Normen und dem Inhaber normativer Autorität im institutionellen Fall. Wenn man rechtliche und institutionelle Normen verletzt, bringt man dem Normengeber nicht die angemessene Achtung entgegen. Die Seminarvorsteherin schuldet es dem Rektor, die Prüfungsordnung zu ändern. Er hat die Norm geschaffen und er kann entsprechend die Einhaltung seiner Norm einfordern und der Seminarvorsteherin Vorwürfe machen, wenn sie seiner Forderung nicht nachkommt. In gleicher Weise schulden Bürger die Einhaltung der Rechtsnormen der Rechtsgemeinschaft. Und genau das wäre auch der Fall, wenn moralische Normen von einem Wesen mit besonderer Autorität geschaffen würden. Wir würden dem moralischen Gesetzgeber die Einhaltung der moralischen Normen schulden; dieses Wesen allein wäre autorisiert, dies von uns zu fordern und uns im Fall der Verletzung der Norm zur Rechenschaft zu ziehen. Und daran wird deutlich, dass es sich bei den Normen, die durch ein solches Wesen erzeugt würden, um keine moralische Normen handeln würde: Moralische Normen können von allen eingefordert werden und alle sind berechtigt, den moralischen Missetätern Vorwürfe zu machen. Nicht bloß Gerda darf von Hans fordern, seine von ihren Füßen zurückzuziehen. Alle dürfen das von ihm fordern und ihm Vorwürfe machen, wenn er es nicht tut. Die Verletzung moralischer Normen geht uns alle etwas an.

Es lässt sich fragen, ob es die Achtung, die man dem Normengeber auch in institutionellen und rechtlichen Zusammenhängen schuldet, nicht auch Gegenstand einer *moralischen* Achtungsnorm ist. Wenn das allerdings der Fall wäre, könnte die Seminarvorsteherin von allen aufgefordert werden, die Prüfungsordnung zu ändern und von allen zur Rechenschaft gezogen werden, wenn sie es nicht tun würde. Das ist aber nicht so. Nur der Rektor ist berechtigt, das von ihr zu fordern. Daran wird deutlich, dass in einem solchen Fall keine moralische Verpflichtung vorliegt.

Doch wie kommen moralische Normen in die Welt, wenn sie nicht von Menschen geschaffen wurden? Moralische Normen setzen bestimmte Dinge voraus: Dass es Wesen gibt, die in der Lage sind, Normen zu erfüllen und Pflichten zu befolgen; Wesen, die Adressaten von Forderungen sein und Tadel und Vorwürfe verstehen können. Moralische Normen setzen auch voraus, dass es Wesen gibt, die bestimmte Anliegen und Interessen haben, die beeinträchtigt und verletzt werden können; Wesen, denen bestimmte Dinge wichtig sind und die in der Lage sind, Ansprüche geltend zu machen. So setzt die moralische Norm, anderen nicht ohne guten Grund Schmerzen zuzufügen, voraus, dass es Wesen gibt, die Schmerzen haben und unter Schmerzen leiden können. Und die Norm, andere nicht zu demütigen, setzt voraus, dass Menschen sich als Wesen verstehen, welche die gleichen Rechte und die gleiche Würde wie alle anderen haben. Wesen, auf die das zutrifft, erzeugen nicht die Moral. Vielmehr ist es so, dass mit ihnen moralische Normen entstehen: Die Norm, anderen nicht ohne guten Grund Schmerzen zuzufügen, entsteht, weil Menschen bestimmte Eigenschaften haben, nicht durch Menschen. Wie der Zusammenhang zwischen diesen Eigenschaften und moralischen Normen genau beschaffen ist, welche Eigenschaften in welcher Weise moralisch relevant sind, ist der Gegenstand einer substantiellen Theorie moralischer Normen, von Theorien, die zu sagen versuchen, welche Eigenschaften als Gründe zum Handeln und im Besonderen welche als Verpflichtungsgründe anzusehen sind. Genau das ist der Gegenstand normativer Theorien der Moral.

7 Conclusio

Rechtliche Normen und institutionelle Normen sind das Resultat intentionalen Handelns. Moralische Normen, so habe ich argumentiert, sind das nicht. Das heißt: Es gibt zwar Akte, nämlich Versprechen, die auch moralische Normen schaffen. Sie tun das aber bloß innerhalb einer moralischen Ordnung dessen, was moralisch verboten, erlaubt und geboten ist. Interessanterweise ist die Idee, dass moralische Normen geschaffen werden, verbreitet. Verbreitet ist sie, weil es naheliegend ist, moralische Normen in Analogie zu rechtlichen und institutionellen

Normen zu sehen. Wenn letztere geschaffen werden, so die Überlegung, dann auch die moralischen. Doch moralische Normen sollten, so viel sollte deutlich geworden sein, nicht nach dem Modell rechtlicher und institutioneller Normen verstanden werden. Moralischen Normen sind nicht eine Art von rechtlichen Normen, sondern Normen eigener Art, die wir nicht schaffen, sondern vorfinden. Von der Idee, sie seien von jemandem geschaffen worden, sollten wir uns verabschieden.

Literaturverzeichnis

Copp, David (2013): „Is Constructivism an Alternative to Moral Realism?". In: Bagnoli, Carla (Hg.): Constructivism in Ethics. Cambridge: Cambridge University Press, 108–132.
Darwall, Stephen (2006): The Second Personal Standpoint. Harvard: Harvard University Press.
Enoch, David (2005): „Why Idealize?". In: Ethics 115, 759–787.
Gilbert, Margaret (2011): „Three Dogmas about Promising". In: Sheinman, Hanoch (Hg.): Promises and Agreements. Oxford: Oxford University Press, 80–108.
Rawls, John (1971): A Theory of Justice. Cambridge: Belknap Press.
Scanlon, Thomas (1998): What We Owe to Each Other. Harvard: Harvard University Press.
Southwood, Nicholas (2010): Contractualism and the Foundations of Morality. Oxford: Oxford University Press.
Stemmer, Peter (2000): Handeln zugunsten anderer. Berlin: de Gruyter.
Wallace, R. Jay (2012): „Constructivism about Normativity: Some Pitfalls". In: Lenman, James; Shemmer, Yonatan (Hg.): Constructivism in Practical Philosophy. Oxford: Oxford University Press, 18–39.

6 Wittgenstein

David Bloor
The Sociology of the Supernatural: Wittgenstein's *Lecture on Ethics*

Abstract: In his *Lecture on Ethics* Wittgenstein addressed the themes of absolutism and relativism in an explicit fashion. He gave expression to a dramatic form of moral absolutism but, at the same time, developed a revealing sociological analysis of what was involved in the absolutist stance. This analysis ultimately subverted the absolutism that it had been developed to illuminate, but the exercise had fruitful consequences for Wittgenstein's later thinking. My aim is to explore the sociological dimension of the *Lecture on Ethics* and indicate how it was transformed into some of the most characteristic themes of the later philosophy, e.g. the appeal to language games and the analysis of rule following. Wittgenstein's trajectory was from an inconsistent absolutism to a consistent relativism. I shall end by drawing some conclusions about the conditions that should be satisfied by any well-formed definition of the concept of "relativism".

Keywords: Wittgenstein, sociology of knowledge, ethics, absolutism, relativism

In November 1929 Wittgenstein gave a talk on ethics in Cambridge. The talk remained unpublished until after his death. The text eventually appeared in 1965 under the title "A Lecture on Ethics" (see also Wittgenstein 2014). In the lecture Wittgenstein employed the categories of 'relativism' and 'absolutism' in an uncharacteristically explicit way. In fact, Wittgenstein embraced a dramatic form of ethical absolutism and related the category of the absolute to the supernatural, the miraculous, and the sublime. His central thesis was that ethics was at once absolute and inexpressible.

The *Lecture on Ethics* belongs to a transitional period in Wittgenstein's development and the argument of the lecture betrays signs of the flux in his thinking. For example, the analysis that he gave of ethical absolutism ultimately served to subvert that absolutism, but it did so in a way that proved richly suggestive for his later work. It is possible to see in Wittgenstein's account of absolutism the foundations of some of the most characteristic ideas of the later philosophy, for example, the idea of language games and the analysis of rule following.[1]

---

[1] The signs of flux in Wittgenstein's thinking are viewed in different ways by different commentators. E.D. Klemke finds the lecture full of confusion and declares it to be unworthy of publication. (see Klemke 1975, 127). Theodore Redpath finds the lecture an admirable expression of

What were these subversive, but suggestive, themes that emerged in the *Lecture on Ethics*? I shall argue that, in the lecture, Wittgenstein proposed a simple, but unmistakably sociological, model of the phenomena that he designated by the words 'absolute', 'supernatural' and 'sublime'. It was a version of these sociological ideas that later bore fruit in the *Philosophical Investigations*.

1 The Argument from the *Lecture on Ethics*

To establish these claims I need to give an account of the argument developed in the lecture. Any sociologist or anthropologist would recognize Wittgenstein's argument as an application of the distinction between the sacred and the profane (for the classic distinction see (Durkheim 1961). The distinction is sometimes expressed by saying that one can 'touch' the profane but one cannot, and must not, 'touch' the sacred. Everything that is merely empirical comes within the scope of the profane; everything that is mysteriously powerful, and which commands a special respect, belongs to the sacred. Common-sense knowledge, and even the detailed investigation of natural phenomena, can be considered profane, while ethics, aesthetics and religion belong to a more sublime realm. Wittgenstein was emphatic: "Ethics, if it is anything, is supernatural." (LE 6)

The usages of everyday language sometimes blur the distinction between the sacred and the profane so Wittgenstein set about the task of making his audience sensitive to these different registers. He indicated that a number of important words have both 'natural' and 'supernatural' connotations that need to be distinguished. The word 'good', when used to describe a good chair simply means that this object satisfies certain pre-given specifications. This usage is called 'relative' and 'trivial'. When we speak, ethically, of a 'good man' the word is used in a higher and 'absolute' sense.

The same applies to the word 'right'. If we speak of taking the 'right road' to our destination we mean no more than taking the road that meets our mundane requirements e.g. it is the shortest or quickest road. What, then, might be meant by the 'absolutely right road'? Wittgenstein suggests that it would be 'the road which everybody on seeing it would, with logical necessity, have to go, or be ashamed for not going" (LE 7). The same applies to the absolute 'good'. The absolute good, said Wittgenstein, "if it is a describable state, would be one which

---

Wittgenstein's moral seriousness but identifies significant shortcomings and contradictions (Redpath 1972). Rush Rhees has a positive view of the lecture as an expression of the transition between the *Tractatus* and the *Investigations*. He also presents it as a successful expression of what Wittgenstein called "the anthropological method" (see Rhees 1965, 25).

everybody, independent of their tastes and inclinations, would necessarily bring about or feel guilty for not bringing about" (LE 7).

The next step in the argument was to assert that, after all, absolute, ethical, goodness is *not* a describable state. Here Wittgenstein applies the sacred-profane distinction with the utmost rigor. A state of affairs which is deemed good in an absolute sense cannot even be 'touched', or grasped, by profane human language and thought. The claim is that we can make no sense of the embodiment of value in any matter of fact or state of affairs. The point is expressed in a compressed passage which reads as follows: "And I want to say that such a state of affairs is a chimera. No state of affairs has, in itself, what I would like to call the power of an absolute judge" (LE 7).

There are two metaphors here: the chimera and the judge. I shall come back to the chimera shortly but want to concentrate for the moment on the reference to an absolute judge. The thesis is that facts cannot embody values, but where does the power of an absolute judge come in? I take this to be an oblique reference to God's power – the ultimate embodiment of ethical value. Wittgenstein's point was that the fact of power, as such, is intrinsically devoid of moral significance and yet, in the case of God's power, it is typically said to embody absolute moral significance. How are fact and value combined?

We know from some notes taken by Friedrich Waismann (and published along with the lecture) that, for Wittgenstein, the good is what God commands (see Waismann 1965). God does not command something because it is good; rather, it is good because God commands it. Here the power and the goodness become one. But Wittgenstein was saying that the combination of God's power and God's goodness cannot be stated intelligibly: it is literal nonsense. This theology pre-figures the situation on the human plane. Ethics itself is literal nonsense. Wittgenstein put it like this. "And I will make my point still more acute by saying 'It is the paradox that an experience, a fact, should seem to have supernatural value'" (LE 10).

Can this be right? Is there really a paradox? Could the allegedly meaningless character of ethical judgments perhaps have arisen from a failure on Wittgenstein's part to give them a correct analysis? Wittgenstein rejected this. He did not accept that someday an ingenious philosopher might hit upon an analysis of ethical statements that would reveal their inner coherence – any more than an ingenious theologian could ever remove the mystery and paradox of God's power. These expressions, said Wittgenstein, "were not nonsensical because I had not yet found the correct expression, but their nonsensicality was their very essence" (LE 11).

2 Chimeras and Miracles

I now want to focus on one particular part of Wittgenstein's argument: the part in which he discusses miracles. This theme in the lecture grew out of his attempt to solve the problem of how to talk about things which were, in their very essence, said to be nonsensical.

To address this problem Wittgenstein had resorted to the method of evoking mental pictures and feelings in the mind of his listeners. He explained his procedure to his audience by saying that it was like the method used by the scientist Francis Galton to convey the appearance of racial and family types. Galton superimposed a number of photographs to produce a composite image. Wittgenstein encouraged his audience to superimpose a number of experiences and feelings. He asked them to consider, for example, the experience of wonderment at the existence of the world, the feeling of the existence of the world as a miracle, or again, the feeling of being absolutely safe in God's hands.

Wittgenstein insisted that these experiences could not be expressed verbally in coherent terms. Expressions of amazement convey surprise that this event rather than that event has happened, not that anything at all has happened. Feelings of being safe can express a surge of assurance in the face of this or that eventuality. But you cannot truly be said to 'feel safe' *whatever* happens. All the usual discriminations and relative contrasts which give these expressions their purchase on reality have been lost in the attempt to render them absolute. This is why such ideas could only be conveyed by some form of gesture towards their significance in human life.

This takes us back to Wittgenstein's claim that the attempt to talk about the absolutes of ethics is a 'chimera'. But what is a chimera? In Greek mythology, a chimera is a creature with a lion's head, a goat's body and a snake's tail. It is a beast that combines what cannot be combined. It violates categories and this makes it a useful symbol of chaos or of transcendence. This will be why Wittgenstein chose the word. But he did not content himself with simply employing the metaphor. He took the further step of asking his audience to imagine a much more direct confrontation with a chimera. He asked them to think about how they might respond if one of them were suddenly to grow a lion's head and begin to roar, that is, to imagine how they would respond if one of them became a composite beast resembling the mythical chimera.

This may seem a bizarre thought experiment but it was meant seriously and it was a clever way to convey an interesting line of argument. Wittgenstein said, plausibly, that such an event might be called 'miraculous'. The use of this word would be prompted by the fact that no one would have ever seen anything similar before. Of course, we would be shocked by the event, but what would we say when we had got over the shock? There are various possible reactions and these would determine the significance attached to the word 'miracle'. It would determine whether the word 'miracle' was being used in a relative or an absolute sense.

Despite his declared respect for the supernatural character of ethics Wittgenstein took the relativist line in anticipating his own reaction to the so-called miracle. In a down-to-earth way, he said: "what I would suggest would be to fetch a doctor and have the case scientifically investigated". Referring to the victim of the transformation he added, "and if it were not for hurting him I would have him vivisected" (LE 10). Clearly, Wittgenstein was not, for his own part, treating the phenomenon as untouchable.

But now, asked Wittgenstein, if we bring in the scientists, what has happened to the miracle? He argued that if we mobilize the methods of scientific investigation then we are assuming, from the outset, that what is under study is merely an unusual natural phenomenon. The supernatural has been excluded. Wittgenstein put it like this:

> The truth is that the scientific way of looking at a fact is not the way to look at it as a miracle. For imagine whatever fact you may, it is not in itself miraculous in the absolute sense of the term. For we now see we have been using the word "miracle" in a relative and an absolute sense. (LE 11)

To call something a 'miracle', in the relative sense of the word, just means that it is to be regarded as highly improbable. To call something a 'miracle' in the absolute sense of the word is to declare that it is out of bounds to science. It is to be seen as untouchable.

Here is the central point. For Wittgenstein, to be miraculous, in the absolute sense, does not depend on the intrinsic nature of the phenomenon itself. The quality of being 'miraculous' does not inhere in the object itself because it inheres in the reactions and understanding and norms of the persons who are, as it were, standing around the object and mobilizing their collective reaction to it.

Wittgenstein did not deny that a miraculous object, such as an unfortunate human with a lion's head, might have remarkable, and hitherto unknown, empirical properties. He was implying that remarkable intrinsic properties are neither necessary nor sufficient for the object to be a miracle. What then is necessary and sufficient? The form of Wittgenstein's answer was: A characteristic, collective and normative orientation with regard to the object – namely the insistence that it not be treated as profane. For these reasons we can say that Wittgenstein was giving us a sociological or anthropological model of a miracle. To be a miracle is to be accorded a social status. A miracle is an institution. Given that Wittgenstein was identifying the character of the ethical absolute with the character of the miraculous, the sublime and the supernatural, we can draw the conclusion that he was giving a sociological model that was applicable to all absolutes.

3 Natural and Supernatural Predicates

Let me now try to generalize Wittgenstein's account by stripping it down to its naturalistic essentials. At this point I want to move a little beyond what Wittgenstein said in the lecture but I shall stay true to the trajectory of his thinking as it moved towards the formulations he used in the *Philosophical Investigations*.

A person responding to the horrible event that Wittgenstein described has just two sources of information available. The first source derives from the empirical character of the observed event. The second source derives from the response of other people who are also observing the event. These two resources are the same two that all of us have available in responding to any state of affairs. The miracle example merely invites us to reflect on one, extreme, employment of commonplace modes of cognition.

Corresponding to these two sources of information I want to follow Wittgenstein's procedure in the lecture and identify two, simplified, kinds of linguistic predicate. First, there are Wittgenstein's 'natural' predicates that are learned by responding to the observable features of independent objects. But not all predicates applied to an object are prompted by the qualities that can be detected in the object. There is a second sort of predicate that is possible. These exploit the second source of information – the reactions of other people to the object.

Following Wittgenstein's terminology of 'natural' and 'supernatural' we can call the first sort of predicate an 'N-predicate', and the second sort an 'S-predicate'.[2] Like Wittgenstein in the lecture, let us assume for the moment that N-predicates, natural predicates, are unproblematic.[3] The important point is that

---

[2] I am here closely following the work of the sociologist Barry Barnes, see (Barnes 1983).
[3] I am taking over the N-predicate and S-predicate distinction from Barnes' paper cited in footnote 2. Of course, N-predicates are not unproblematic. They are, as Barnes emphasizes, a radical idealization of real descriptive predicates. When due allowance is made for the notion of the right and wrong application of these empirical predicates it becomes clear that a real predicate involves a combination of the two idealized cases. These themes are discussed in more detail in (Bloor 1997).

Wittgenstein was telling his audience that the word 'miraculous,' in its 'absolute' sense, was an S-predicate.

I now want to pose two questions. What do S-predicates, or supernatural predicates, refer to? And what use are S-predicates – why do supernatural predicates exist at all?

First, then, what do S-predicates such as 'miraculous' refer to? If, as Wittgenstein indicated, there is no independent property of the object with which the word can be correlated, then what is it correlated with? There is only one possible answer. When an object is called 'miraculous' the reality with which the speaker engages is the reality of the object being called 'miraculous' by other speakers. Whether knowingly, or unknowingly, when I endorse the description 'miraculous' I am responding to, and referring to, other people calling it 'miraculous'. And the same applies to all these other people and their acts of calling an object miraculous. The upshot of this argument is that S-predicates, i.e. 'supernatural' predicates, when taken collectively, have a self-referring and self-reinforcing character. Unlike natural, N-predicates, in the case of S-predicates there is no object to which the discourse refers that is independent of the discourse itself.

This takes me to my second question. What is achieved by employing words in this way? The answer is that this pattern of self-referential usage serves to mobilize and co-ordinate collective action. The usage conveys information, not about the intrinsic nature of an external object, but about how that object is to be treated and how other people will treat it. Self-referential processes are the means by which information about social order and structure is conveyed and, in being conveyed, that information becomes part of the order and structure itself. This (I am saying) is the story that is beginning to emerge in the *Lecture on Ethics*.

4 Self-Reference and Language Games

The contrast between forms of discourse that relate to an independent object, and forms of discourse that have no independent object, can shed light on the strange idea that ethics is meaningless. It will appear meaningless if it is assumed that meaning is furnished by an independent object, or that meaning presupposes an external object. In order to overthrow this conclusion it is necessary to accept the idea of meaningful, but self-referential, patterns of language use.

I now want to ask the question: Did the emerging theme of self-reference ever become explicit in Wittgenstein's work? The answer is that the idea of self-reference never became fully explicit, but it is implicit in the idea of a language game – the central metaphor of the late work. The word 'game' is an S-predicate. This is because games are social institutions. They are realities that exist in and through the references made to them and the actions oriented towards them. They are not objects that have an existence that is independent of the understanding and orientation of those who participate in them.[4]

The use of the metaphor of a 'language-game' allowed Wittgenstein to combine the idealised N-predicates and S-predicates that were assumed in the *Lecture on Ethics*.

Recall the two sources of information that can inform a response to an independent object: the discernable empirical features of the object, and other people's responses to the object. In the *Lecture on Ethics* these two sources of information were kept separate, but in a real, public language they are typically combined. The metaphor of the language game enabled Wittgenstein to convey, in an intuitive way, how our responses to the empirical properties of the world also, and necessarily, embody responses to one another. This furnishes the normative aspect of the use of a real predicate. This is why, in a real language, every meaningful response is a social response, even if it is a response to an independent object.

5 Two Objections

I now want to look at two objections to my reading of the *Lecture on Ethics*. One of the objections was anticipated by Wittgenstein and addressed in the lecture itself. The other objection comes from Waismann's notes. Waismann recorded a sentence from a conversation in which Wittgenstein appeared to deny that his position in the lecture should be read sociologically. Let me address these two objections in turn.

Wittgenstein imagined his audience jumping to the conclusion that he was offering some version of a subjectivist theory of ethics. Despite his talk of ethical absolutes, he feared that his audience would attribute to him a position like that of Shakespeare's Hamlet – namely, the belief that nothing is good or bad but thinking makes it so. Wittgenstein rejects this as a misunderstanding. Now, it

---

4 Some aspects of self reference were spelled out in considerable detail in papers by Anscombe (see Anscombe 1981, Vol. I, chapter 13 and Vol. III, Chapter 2 and 10). It is important to note, however, that Anscombe opposed all naturalistic accounts of rules, rights and promises and ultimately abandoned the appeal to language games in favor of a theological stance based on Aristotelian and teleological concepts. Anscombe called the self-referential account of social reality by the unfortunate name of 'linguistic idealism' (see Bloor 1996).

may seem that Wittgenstein's rejection of the Hamlet position presents me with a problem. I see him as moving towards a sociological account of ethics, but isn't that just a form of 'subjectivism'? Nothing is good or bad but collective thinking makes it so.

Here it is important to notice that what Wittgenstein rejected as a misunderstanding was the individualistic form of subjectivism, not the collectivist form. The mistake that he said he wanted to avoid was the assumption that ethical qualities reside in individual states of mind. In his reply to the objection, Wittgenstein insisted that, "a state of mind … is in no ethical sense good or bad" (LE 6). Individual states of mind are simply facts in the world and are incapable of generating the qualities of good and bad.

Thus far Wittgenstein's response is consistent with my reading of him as providing a collective and sociological analysis – not an individualistic or psychological analysis. Now I must confront the second problem. Waismann's notes appear to show Wittgenstein rejecting a sociological reading of the position taken in the *Lecture on Ethics*. Waismann quoted Wittgenstein as saying: "*Und hier ist es wesentlich, daß es keine Beschreibung der Soziologie ist, sondern daß ich von mir selbst spreche*" (LE 14). And here it is essential that this is not a sociological description but that I speak *for myself*. What can I say about this? Does the emphasis on speaking for oneself mean that, after all, we should give an individualistic reading to the *Lecture on Ethics?*[5]

I do not think the quoted words contradict my sociological reading. The most plausible interpretation is that Wittgenstein was saying that when a person asserts that "X is good", they are doing something different to asserting "Most people call X 'good'". This is true. Those two formulations do not mean the same thing. A sociologist might report that in some society most people call X good – but a typical, unselfconscious member of that society will simply affirm that X is good. They will speak directly and for themselves, but they will also be responsive to others who are speaking for themselves. In this way they will be actively constructing their shared ethical institutions. In general, they will do this by *participating* in the self-referential process, rather than by *commenting* on it as if they were outsiders. This presents no difficulty for my reading.

Let me rehearse these objections and replies using the miracle example. First, Wittgenstein was clearly rejecting an individualistic analysis of the claim that an event was a miracle. Something has the status of a miracle if it is collectively called a miracle. I may personally call an event a miracle, but if everybody

---

5 Many commentators insist on an individualistic and anti-sociological reading of Wittgenstein, e.g. (Baker/Hacker 1984, 16), (McGinn 1984, 200), (Budd 1989, 41), (Johnston 1989, 128)

else treats the event as a scientific puzzle then it is a scientific puzzle not a miracle. To say 'X is a miracle' does not mean 'Most people call X a miracle', but it is a contribution to collectively defining the object as out of bounds to the scientist.[6]

Wittgenstein's miracle example is an imaginary one, and some philosophers think that it is important that Wittgenstein often used hypothetical, rather than real, examples. They think this is a justification for avoiding any naturalistic and sociological reading of Wittgenstein's work.[7] I do not think this justification is adequate. The initiating event in his discussion of miracles, the lion's head, is fantastical; but the reactions find their counterpart in real life.[8]

When Wittgenstein said he would call in the doctors and physiologists we can accept that he was speaking "for himself". But he was also speaking as a social actor. He was speaking as an informed member of a society containing specialists whose expertise could be invoked in times of crisis. Admittedly, when Wittgenstein explained the essential difference between seeing an event as a miracle rather than a scientific puzzle, he did not say what might bring about one or the other of these outcomes. He did not address the causes of credibility of the two, polarised collective reactions. But it is easy to extrapolate these parts of his example in plausible ways. If the lion's-head episode had taken place in the vicinity of the Department of Physiology in Cambridge it would have been viewed as a scientific puzzle. If it had taken place in (say) a remote village in the south of Italy, it might have been viewed in the other – miraculous – way. The experts to be called in would then be priests rather than professors.

---

6 Wittgenstein's student Theodore Redpath accepts that the scientific study of a phenomenon can very often destroy a person's sense of wonder but asserts that, sometimes, it may not do so. He concludes that Wittgenstein "went too far in assuming that this is what would necessarily happen" (Redpath 1972, 115). I think that Redpath has missed the point. Wittgenstein was not making a claim about what would happen to each and every individual. Whether right or wrong, Wittgenstein was advancing a sociological claim about the relation of two social institutions. Redpath is construing Wittgenstein as making an individualistic and psychological claim.
7 See, for example, (Cerbone 1995), (Friedman 1998), (Stern 2002).
8 On occasion, Wittgenstein was willing to use real-life examples. These were sometimes drawn from the history of mathematics, sometimes from the theological tradition, and sometimes from anthropology. For an example of the latter see (Wittgenstein 2010). It is remarkable that Wittgenstein's critical response to Fraser, and to Fraser's conjectural history of myth, should be glossed by Rhees with the comment: "And clearly he is not discussing history or anthropology" (Wittgenstein 2010, 21). This is *exactly* what Wittgenstein is discussing. Rhees is claiming that black is white.

6 From the Supernatural to the Social

In making the transition from the *Lecture on Ethics* to the position adopted in his later work Wittgenstein systematically replaced supernatural categories by sociological categories. Rule following was explained in terms of custom, convention and habit. A rule was now a social institution. And what became of the coercive power of the absolute judge, as it featured in the earlier picture? The reader of the later work is told that a rule compels like any other law in society. The coercive power turns out to be the power of society.

In the lecture, Wittgenstein declared that absolute and supernatural ideas were meaningless but nevertheless deserved respect. In the later work much of this respect had evaporated. The picture of mathematical rules as roads and rails was dismissed as mythical and unrevealing. It was a mere picture – the sign of a failed analysis, not a sign of reaching the limits of thought. What had previously been a noble attempt to transcend language was now given the unflattering description of 'language on holiday'.[9]

Throughout these changes there are also continuities. There are textual and metaphorical links between the idea of the absolutely right road in the *Lecture on Ethics* and the account of rule following in the *Investigations*. The rule determines what you *must* do while the absolutely right road is the road you *must* travel. In the *Investigations* Wittgenstein was rejecting an absolutist account of rule following but he did so by exploiting the self-referential, sociological mechanisms that first surfaced in the *Lecture on Ethics*.

The links between the earlier and later discussions are easy to see once one knows where to look. Thus, self reference is implicit in Wittgenstein's skillfully dramatized interaction between a school teacher and a pupil who is trying, and failing, to learn how to generate the number sequence 2, 4, 6, 8, ... etc. Wittgenstein portrayed the teacher and the pupil circling around one another within the self-referential reality that constitutes the social institution of the rule. Why do I have to say 2004 after 2002? Because the rule requires it! What does 'the rule requires it' mean? It means you have to say 2004. Why must I say that? Because

---

9 "For philosophical problems arise when language *goes on holiday*". (Wittgenstein PI, § 38). Although it is not germane to my present argument I doubt that Wittgenstein's account of "the absolutely right road" really is 'meaningless'. Talk of an absolutely right road may be based on a teleological picture of nature in which there is an allegedly 'natural' tendency for events in the world to move towards some goal and embody some (supernatural) purpose. Such an Aristotelian vision might be better designated unscientific (by today's standards) than meaningless. I drew attention to this teleological option, and its significance for the analysis of rule following, in (Bloor 1973, 182).

that is what the rule says! And so on, round in a circle. The circle is unavoidable because, throughout these exchanges, the rule is not an independent object of reference. It exists in and through the very interactions that have just been described.

There is a much-discussed paragraph in the *Philosophical Investigations* in which Wittgenstein identified what he called a "paradox" generated by the theory that rule-following must always take place through a process of interpretation. On this theory we are said to give an interpretation to the symbols expressing the rule and then proceed according to the meaning of the interpretation. But then, said Wittgenstein, if an act of interpretation is always necessary, we must interpret the interpretation. This generates a regress and, what is more, if there are no further constraints, the regress could lead anywhere as interpretation follows interpretation. The result of this theory is that, "no course of action could be determined by a rule, because every course of action can be made out to accord with the rule". Wittgenstein said that the "answer'" to this "paradox" was that under these circumstances "there would be neither accord nor conflict here" (PI § 201).

The terminology and structure of this argument resonates with the central themes of the *Lecture on Ethics*. Recall what was said about the experience of being absolutely safe in God's hands. Everything that happens is consistent with this absolute safety, just as every course of action is consistent with the rule on some interpretation. When the word 'safety' is given an absolute significance all the usual discriminations are lost – it becomes 'paradoxical'. There is no difference between being safe and unsafe. In the same way, all the usual discriminations of accord and conflict are lost in the appeal to interpretations – interpretations which are meant to capture meanings and hence absolute notions of logical determination. The difference between the two cases is that in the lecture Wittgenstein embraced the paradoxes of absolutism while in the *Investigations* he rejected them.

7 The Definition of Relativism

I want to end with a specific suggestion drawn from the *Lecture on Ethics*. The suggestion is relevant to the concerns of this conference. It is about how we might best define the words 'relativism' and 'absolutism'. Wittgenstein did not himself define these words because he claimed that they had no literal meaning, but his Galtonian – picture method was employed in a way that carries an important message about the relation of relativism and absolutism.

The message is structural and is embodied in the fact that Wittgenstein worked with a dichotomy between relativism and absolutism – just as he worked with a dichotomy between the natural and the supernatural and the factual and the ethical. Thus he asked: are the words 'good' and 'miracle' being used in their absolute sense or their relative sense? He did not countenance any middle ground. We have also seen that Wittgenstein made a firm connection between absolutism and a religious conception of the world and between relativism and a scientific conception of the world. I think he was right to proceed in this way.

I therefore suggest that we follow Wittgenstein's example when we come to frame our own definitions of relativism and absolutism. There are certain conditions that any such definition should satisfy. We should treat relativism and absolutism as forming a dichotomy. An absolutist need not deny that there are relative truths, but must assert that there is at least one absolute truth that can be grasped. The relativist must believe that there is not one single instance of absolute truth available to us. Like naturalism and supernaturalism, relativism and absolutism should be seen as mutually exclusive and jointly exhaustive.

We learn from Wittgenstein that, ultimately, such a dichotomy has the character of a convention. Human categories express conventions not essences. But that does not mean that we can treat categories such as 'relativism' and 'absolutism' lightly, or define them in haphazard ways – which is what happens when critics impute to the relativist the (so-called) 'equal validity thesis.' Critics should not indulge themselves in this way. As the *Lecture on Ethics* made clear, important matters are at stake, namely our standpoint towards our own established traditions and institutions such as science and religion.[10]

These traditions and institutions may feel as if they embody moral and cognitive essences, as they clearly did to Wittgenstein in 1929. But, as he later came

---

10 Because of the importance of what is at stake it is a pity that Wittgenstein himself did not pay more attention to real rather than hypothetical examples. This is also the reason why it is incumbent on his readers to seek out the naturalistic aspects of his thinking rather than play them down. I have tried to follow the policy of locating this naturalistic dimension in (Bloor 1983). Lively debates have taken place over the past few decades (and are still going on) concerning the proper scope of sociological explanation in the history of science. They show that the sacred-profane distinction is still a live issue. Philosophers of science treat the rational core of science as *sui generis* and, in effect, as 'untouchable' by profane, causal explanation. Science is sacred and the sociology of knowledge is profane. There are revealing parallels to be drawn between these debates over the proper scope of sociological explanation in the historiography of science and nineteenth-century debates over the historiography proper to church history and the history of theology, i.e. the debates over what was called 'the higher criticism'. I have explored these parallels in (Bloor 1988).

to realize, "to the depth that we see in the essence there corresponds the deep need for the convention" (Wittgenstein *RFM* I §74). Given the confused state of the current anti-relativist literature there is a deep need for some conventions here to re-establish order and clarity.[11] For example, many philosophers claim to be neither relativists nor absolutist. They think that they can achieve this goal by making appeal to the category of 'objectivity' – but they omit to tell us whether their favoured form of objectivity is an absolute objectivity or a relative objectivity. Presumably they think it is neither. We should not believe them because such claims are the result of evasion.[12] If we want to avoid obscurity, and focus on what is essential, we should follow Wittgenstein and treat the rejection of absolutism as both a necessary and a sufficient condition for embracing relativism.

Acknowledgements: I am grateful to Andrew Barker both for discussion and for spotting a mistake in an earlier draft. I must also express my gratitude to Barry Barnes whose work I have used so freely. We had a lengthy discussion at an early stage in the writing of the paper. I think that we are in agreement on many, though perhaps not all, aspects of the argument I am presenting. The responsibility for remaining errors is mine alone.

References

Anscombe, Elizabeth (1981): *The Collected Papers of G.E.M. Anscombe*. Oxford: Blackwell.
Baker, Gordon; Hacker, Peter (1984): *Scepticism, Rules and Language*. Oxford: Blackwell.
Barnes, Barry (1983): "Social Life as Bootstrapped Induction". In: *Sociology* 17 (4), 524–545.

---

11 As an illustration of the confusion and vagueness of the anti-relativist literature consider the following passage from the article on 'Philosophy of Science', in (Psillos 2008). Stathis Psillos, is writing in defense of a naturalistic perspective. But, he writes, "naturalism ... seems to lead to epistemic relativism. This concern forces naturalism to adopt an axiology, that is, a general theory of the constraints that govern rational choice of aims and goals. More specifically, naturalism has to accept truth as the basic cognitive virtue. This move blunts the threat of relativism." (Psillos 2008, p. 637) In response, I want to ask: How does this move serve as a counter to relativism? The only way that relativism can be avoided is by endorsing some form of absolutism. The recommended commitment must therefore be to an absolutist axiology. But absolutism is a form of supernaturalism and this makes it incompatible with any thoroughgoing naturalism. In reality, the author of the above passage is compromising the naturalist position, while expressing concern for its wellbeing.

12 For a defense of the dichotomy between relativism and absolutism, and the dire consequences of trying to evade it, see (Bloor 2011).

Bloor, David (1973): "Wittgenstein and Mannheim on the Sociology of Mathematics".
   In: *Studies in the History and Philosophy of Science* 4, 173–191.
Bloor, David (1983): *Wittgenstein. A Social Theory of Knowledge*. London: Macmillan.
Bloor, David (1988): "Rationalism, Supernaturalism, and Sociology of Knowledge".
   In: Hronsky, Imre; Fehér, Márta; Dajka, Balázs (eds.): *Scientific Knowledge Socialised*. Budapest: Akademiai, 59–74.
Bloor, David (1996): "Linguistic Idealism Revisited". In: Sluga, Hans; Stern, David (eds.): *The Cambridge Companion to Wittgenstein*, Cambridge: Cambridge University Press, 354–382.
Bloor, David (1997): *Wittgenstein, Rules and Institutions*. London: Routledge.
Bloor, David (2011): "Relativism and the Sociology of Knowledge". In: Hales, Steven (ed.): *A Companion to Relativism*. Oxford: Blackwell, 433–455.
Budd, Malcolm (1989): *Wittgenstein's Philosophy of Psychology*. London: Routledge.
Cerbone, David R. (1995): "Don't Look But Think. Imaginary Scenarios in Wittgenstein's Later Philosophy". In: *Inquiry* 37, 159–183.
Durkheim, Emile (1961): *Elementary Forms of the Religious Life*. Translated by Joseph Ward Swain. London: Allen and Unwin.
Friedman, Michael (1998): "On the Sociology of Scientific Knowledge and its Philosophical Agenda". In: *Studies in History and Philosophy of Science* 29 (2) 239–271.
Johnston, Paul (1989): *Wittgenstein and Moral Philosophy*. London: Routledge.
Klemke, Elmer D. (1975): "Wittgenstein's Lecture on Ethics". In: *The Journal of Value Enquiry* 9 (2), 118–127.
Koetge, Noretta (2013): "Relativism in Scientific Theories". In: Kaldis, Byron (ed.): *Encyclopedia of Philosophy and the Social Sciences*. Los Angeles: Sage, 808–810.
McGinn, Collin (1984): *Wittgenstein on Meaning*. Oxford: Blackwell.
Psillos, Stathis (2008): "Philosophy of Science". In: Moran, Dermot (ed.): *The Routledge Companion to Twentieth Century Philosophy*. London: Routledge, 618–657.
Redpath, Theodore (1972): "Wittgenstein and Ethics". In: Ambrose, Alice; Lazerowitz, Morris (eds.): *Ludwig Wittgenstein. Philosophy and Language*. London: Allen and Unwin, 95–119.
Rhees, Rush (1965): "Some Developments in Wittgenstein's View of Ethics". In: *The Philosophical Review* 74 (1), 17–26.
Stern, David (2002): "Sociology of Science, Rule Following and Forms of Life".
   In: Heidelberger, Michael; Stadler, Friedrich (eds.): *History and Philosophy of Science. New Trends and Perspectives*, Dordrecht: Kluwer Academic Press, 347–367.
Waismann, Friedrich (1965): "Notes on Talks with Wittgenstein". In: *The Philosophical Review* 74 (1), 12–16.
Wittgenstein, Ludwig (1965): "A Lecture on Ethics". In: *The Philosophical Review* 74 (1), 3–12. [LE]
Wittgenstein, Ludwig (1983): Remarks on the Foundations of Mathematics. Edited by Georg Henrik von Wright, Rush Rhees and Elizabeth Anscombe. Massachusetts: MIT Press. [RFM]
Wittgenstein, Ludwig (2009): *Philosophical Investigations*. Translated by Elizabeth Anscombe. Revised by Peter Hacker and Joachim Schulte. Oxford: Wiley-Blackwell. [PI]
Wittgenstein, Ludwig (2014): *Lecture on Ethics*. Edited by Eduardo Zamuner, Ermelinda Valentina Di Lascio and D.K. Levy. Oxford: Wiley Blackwell.

Rom Harré
Can We Piece Together a Coherent Account of the "Person" from the Writings of Wittgenstein?

Abstract: In this paper I continue to fine-tune a discussion with Peter Hacker as to the ontological status of those members of the species homo sapiens who inhabit environments in which the use of language is a vital means of living. Contrary to Hacker's proposal to root the human world in the generic category of 'highest animal' I will restate and elaborate the claim that the world of human beings is rooted in an array of persons, former, actual and possible, beings who (rather than 'which') inhabit a world shaped by meanings and normative conventions, particularly those that preserve the existence and integrity of persons.

Keywords: Wittgenstein, person, Peter Hacker, mereological fallacy, grammar of personhood

> The clowns would be just as funny if their heads
> were filled with sawdust.
> Attributed to John Gardner

1 Claims

1.1 The Mereology of Persons

It is a mistake, Peter Hacker argues, to ascribe predicates the meaning of which is given in the cultural/historical context of the whole person, to any of the structures that constitute the body of the person. If persons belong to the more fundamental category 'highest animal' then persons have parts, some of which are organic and material. This is not an uncontested claim. Persons are complex in that any person has several powers and capacities but this is not obviously an assemblage of substances. Powers and capacities are not parts of a person. They do not conform to elementary mereology. I will return to deal with the suggestion that the possession of higher order dispositions is depends on certain material structures in the body of the person that is in the highest animal aspect of humanity.

1.2 The Role of the Human Body Human Life

I propose two metaphors. The first is that the body can be thought of as a tool kit used by a person to accomplish projects that originate in the culture of the local tribe. The second is that the body can be thought as a site which in normal circumstances just one person occupies. A proper name is like a street address to guide a visitor to where my house is situated. Just as at an old style boarding school we had Smith Major and Smith Minor so we have 136 A Cap Marti and 136 B Cap Marti after some infill construction.

1.3 Indexical Expressions and the Role of the First Person

First person talk binds a living person, one who can undertake commitments and is morally protected, into the local moral order. A proper name identifies a material being, usually the site for a person, but that name is routinely used for a corpse or even an urn of ashes.

What philosophical arguments and analyses underpin these significant claims?
1. Versions of the mereological fallacy;
2. The role of hinges in the shaping of discourses;
3. The logic of the vocabulary used to make reference to persons.

Once we reach outside the bounds of the impoverished English pronoun system we encounter very complex ways of indexing persons. These can have fateful consequences for a person that may attend their improper use.

The distinctions in modes of personal being that can be seen in pronoun usage are not reducible to intrinsic differences in higher animals in a world of persons but are significant as one person moves from one social context to another. The very same 'high animal' is heavily qualified as a person referred to by 'tu' among family and friends, but 'Usted' to more distant others. These are distinctions among persons.

2 Among the Ruins of Cartesianism

How do we proceed when we realize that the very idea of one of the pair of Cartesian substances, 'matter' and 'mind' is conceptually incoherent?

Escape Route A: We try to proceed by using the idea of the remaining substance as the ground of our analysis of human beings. Its properties and processes become the working basis of researches into all aspects of human life, at least in principle. We may need vernacular concepts to identify processes of interest in the human world but in the end we think we need only material concepts to give a total account of the phenomenon in focus. Much of recent psychology as neuropsychology makes used only of material properties of a higher animal even when the topic at hand is a cognitive, emotional or moral matter.

Escape Route B: We abandon both members of the dichotomy and introduce new pairs of distinctions, for example, living/dead; skilled/unskilled; expressive/stolid, industrious/lazy, contemptible/praiseworthy and so on. These are distinctions both constituents of which are at home, that is gain their meanings, in a world of persons.

I argue that in the *Philosophical Investigations* §281–284 and §302 Wittgenstein follows the second route to escape philosophical confusion that might attend the collapse of the Cartesian dichotomy. In so doing his tactic is to abandon both of the 'big' Cartesian concept-pairs 'mental/material' and 'mind/body'. The former pair involves categories of attributes, the latter categories of substances. We recall that Descartes (used the distinction of attributes as the ground for his argument in favor of a radical distinction of substances (see Descartes 1641).

2.1 Resolving the Mereological Fallacy

It is a fallacy to ascribe attributes to any of a human beings parts by the use of words which get their sense in their use for discourses in which they are ascribed to whole persons. In Hacker's famous argument (see Bennett/Hacker 2003) The parts in question turn out to be anatomical parts of the highest animal. The most relevant for the philosophy of psychology are parts of the brain such as the hippocampus, the frontal lobes and so on. These are often currently described with words such as 'remembers', 'understands' 'has a strongly held belief', 'is anxious about', 'suffers', and so on. Wittgenstein himself discusses attributions of whole person concepts to body parts such as hands (PI §280f). The original context in which meaning is established is that of everyday person-talk in English.[1] Is the category of 'person' also the category of 'highest animal' – not just co-extensive but synonymous with it? Neither Hacker nor I suppose that these terms are synonymous. The argument of this paper is towards something much more fundamental, that the basic particulars of the human world are per-

---

[1] Most psychology published today is in English and uses English vernacular terms to epitomise the significance of the work.

sons. An account is therefore needed of the role of 'higher animal' in the discourses of such a world.

Whatever analysis we develop, a common starting point must be the common observation that there are two vocabularies in use in the management of human life: one for body talk and one for person talk. Those the meaning of which is determined by their use in the human being-as-person talk cannot be ascribed to the parts of the human being-as-an-anatomical-and-physiological-complex (that is the highest animal) as represented in the body talk vocabulary. To do so is to commit a mereological fallacy. But what is basis of the claim that this predication is incoherent?

2.2 Hacker's Conclusion

Instead of taking the seemingly inevitable next step, namely ontologically distinguishing persons from their bodies,

1. Hacker takes the 'highest animal' as the ontological ground of human life, as the logical subject for the whole gamut of descriptive concepts, anatomical, physiological and psychological.
2. The whole person psychological predicates cannot be ascribed to the parts of the human being as higher animal, on pain of committing a mereological fallacy.
3. He declares 'person' to be a forensic concept, introduced when issues like responsibility, blame, praise and so on are at issue.

2.3 An Alternative Route

What makes a predicate a 'whole person' predicate? So far as I can see Hacker's route is based on intuitions about the uses of words that is a claim about criteria of correct use. Why is the 'whole higher animal' able to accept psychological predicates that are forbidden for ascription to its parts? For that is what Hacker's ontology of 'higher animal' seems to require, if it is to be used as part of a critical commentary on neuroscience based on an accusation of the commission of a mereological fallacy, an illegitimate extension of use from a whole to a part of the whole.

What identifies the rules that mark off the predicates that cannot be used ascribed to parts from the rest? It cannot simply be mereological since the person as higher animal has a certain weight and so do many of its parts; such as the right arm of Andy Murray.

Examples suggest that such predicates as 'thinks', 'remembers', 'decides', 'makes a stunning passing shot' and so on involve a normative dimension – for example 'skill' (a claim to a high standard of performance) – or a moral dimension – for example 'remembers' (a claim to authority).

Andy Murray is a skilled tennis player but his right arm is not skilled. A witness claims to remember the great Wimbledon final but neither her larynx nor her hippocampus remembers.

We are in familiar territory – it is a fallacy to infer an 'ought', expressed as a normative predicate, from an 'is', expressed as a descriptive predicate

2.4 Summary

Hacker's proposal for grounding post-Cartesian discourses of psychological import is based on *'highest animal'* (so necessarily embodied) as the ontological basis of human life. In commenting on the pretensions of neuroscience to be some or even all of psychology, he accuses neuroscientists of committing a mereological fallacy. The psychological predicates in question are those the meaning of which is established in the context of the life of persons, whole human beings. So his analysis covertly presupposes that a person has parts, and so must be the highest animal.

My proposal, by contrast, for grounding post-Cartesian discourses: *person*, that is culturally sensitive agent (but not *necessarily* embodied), is a being that has powers and capacities, but no parts, and is the recipient of normative judgements, from skills to virtues and vices.

The argument for this *is* based on taking a closer look at what distinguishes the predicates of the whole person which are not meaningful when used of the body or parts of it? What is the deep issue with the mereological fallacy in this context? Rather than Hacker's semantic argument (those which get their meaning from their use in whole person contexts must not be used for describing parts of persons qua higher animals) I argue that the predicates in question are distinguished from others by having explicit or implicit moral content. Therefore, they get their meaning from their use in whole *person* contexts, because whole persons are subject to assessment in terms of the norms of their culture, be it woodwork or kindness to animals and orphans. But this is not qua higher animals, rather as the creators and inhabitants of cultures. I think this point is foreshadowed by Wittgenstein's closing of his listing of human attributes short of those with normative content. In §281 Wittgenstein lists the distinguishing psychological features of human beings qua 'highest animal'. The list comprises the following attributes: 'Only of a human being and what resembles a human being (behaves like a living human being) can we say it has sensations, it sees, is blind, hears, is deaf, is conscious or unconscious'. These are just the attributes that characterize human beings qua higher animals and which are shared with our primate cousins and some domestic animals. This point is not uncontroversial (see Cook 2010). To distinguish human beings as persons from other primates we need to ask whether we can coherently ascribe such predicates as 'hoping', 'remembering', 'intending', 'willing' and so on, intrinsically normative attributes that are discussed at large by Wittgenstein (cf. his remarks about the psychology of dogs in PI §250). How far down the chain of 'higher animals' may we go without falling into anthropomorphism? Surely we must include chimpanzees, such as Washoe, and perhaps some pigs among the morally protected beings and thus legitimate recipients of some of the above predicates.

To reiterate: Predication in post-Cartesian discourses concerning the world of human beings are disciplined by none other than Hume's declaration that one cannot infer an 'ought' from an 'is'. (Hume 1972, Book III, Part 1, Sect 1).

Reminder: Intelligibility Frames. Wittgenstein's progressive identification of the sources of the rationality of discourses has a part to play in this discussion. In the *Tractatus* logic is the exclusive source of discursive rationality. Contrary to Russell logic is not a super science, but a group of rules for maintaining the intelligibility of a discourse through various transformations. In the *Philosophical Investigations* the 'grammar' of everyday uses of language is the source of discursive rationality, introducing the distinction between descriptive and expressive uses of language. To a large extent, 'grammar' is independent of matters of fact. In *On Certainty* hinges are the sources of rationality of many kinds of common discourses, realized in the norms of hinge practices (material, ceremonial etc.) and expressed in their *doppelgängers*, hinge propositions, unexamined empirical generalities (Moyal-Sharrock 2004).

3 The Role of the Human Body in Human Life

To interpret the role of the body in a discursive/cultural philosophy we need to assemble various metaphors and analogies, since this is a sui generis concept.

What are the person hinges, as expressed in propositional and attitudinal *doppelgängers* to practices?
A. Hinges at the root of the display of feelings (and the *doppelgänger* hinge propositions with displayed attitudes)
B. Hinges at the root of the practices that require the use of body parts (and the *doppelgänger* hinge propositions and displayed attitudes).

3.1 Could a Stone be a Person?

We return to the 'logic' of important regions of person talk, in particular the Private Language Argument. It shows that talk apropos one's feelings is not just talking *about* one's feelings but a way of expressing them. What it is to have such and such a feeling is not just to be in certain psychic state but to be disposed to display them such and such expressions, current in one's culture.

In §302 of the *Investigations* Wittgenstein says: "Pain behavior can point to a painful place – but the subject of pain is the person who gives it expression A stone cannot 'give pain an expression'." Suppose one were turned to stone? One's feelings are irrelevant to life as a stone among stones, because they cannot be expressed. And it follows from the from the Private Language Argument such a being could not even have words for a private soliloquy apropos of his/her/its feelings.

3.2 Moral Contexts

In first part of §284 of the *Investigations* we see that the question of the feelings of a stone is a matter of expression. The fly expresses something that can be connected with human pain expressions – but the stone lies inert. So the question of whether or not it can feel pain is empty. In short *a stone cannot be a person*. He says: "And so, a corpse seems to be quite inaccessible to pain – Our attitude to what is alive and to what is dead is not the same. All our reactions are different" (PI §284). In short *a corpse cannot be a person*.

Note the moral dilemmas of the treatment of the brain dead – when to disconnect the support system depends on whether the body is the site for a person. Bodies per se are not morally protected but persons are.

3.3 What a Person does with Her Body

A human being considered as a site for a person is not just an assembly of parts. An arm, even if detached, is always *someone's* arm. We must ask what *that person* once used it for – as we try to devise a prosthetic limb, or decide upon a suitable transplant. Body parts are the topic of two distinct vocabularies – as material systems, and as tools for performing tasks. Note that a person's use of body parts to accomplish culturally defined tasks is embedded in layers of normative presumptions and explicit standards of 'good work'.

3.4 Person Hinges

The attitude we take to stones and corpses in differentiating them so readily from persons can be linked to the idea of a hinge. In Moyal-Sharrock's expansive account, hinges, whatever they are, are manifested in practices and in *doppelgänger* propositions. I suggest that displaying an attitude is like uttering a *doppelgänger* proposition, relative to relevant practices. Let us see how hinge propositions would fit in with the metaphors of embodiment.

Basic Metaphor 1
Take a person's body as a kit of tools for accomplishing tasks.
An example of a *doppelgänger* hinge proposition could be 'the opposable thumb can be used for grasping'.

Basic Metaphor 2
Take a person's body as a site or location for a person. A relevant hinge proposition might be: sending a person to jail by sending their body to be locked into a prison. Some philosophers, for example Peter Strawson in exploring the idea of sounds as criterial for same person, have argued that what it is to be this or that person is bound up with having this or that body (see Strawson 1954). 'Same body' in the sense of numerically the same physical object is criterial for being the same person. It might be objected however that we can easily imagine a site in a city renovation project being occupied first by one house and then by another. Can numerically the same body be a site for two different persons? The cases of long lasting amnesia, schizophrenic episodes and so on could be taken as examples of a human body being the site for different persons at different times. We do not have to illustrate this phenomenon in practice – it may never have actually occurred – but we can show the conceptual possibility in the intelligibility of cases like these.

4 Grammar of Person Centered Talk

In § 410 of the *Investigations* Wittgenstein opens a topic which he did not pursue much further, though it is a key matter when we are discussing how persons figure in everyday discourse. He says "'I' is not the name of a person, nor 'here' of a place, and 'this' is not name. [Russell's <logically proper names>] But they are connected to names. Names are explained by means of them. It is also true that it is characteristic of physics not to use these words." (PI § 410) Recent interest in the social and person factors in the running of research programs in the physical and biological sciences has thrown doubt on the last sentence of this paragraph. But this strengthens the importance of indexical devices.

4.1 Anaphoric Pronouns

Anaphoric pronouns (third person, for example) get their meaning from something internal to the discourse and its well understood reference to an extra-discursive matter of fact. We know the person who is meant by the existence of a definite description or proper name somewhere nearby in the discourse. 'Ludwig said that *he* wanted to see a cowboy film'. This picks out the person because we already know who Ludwig is, whether he is here present or not.

4.2 Indexicals

If we agree with Wittgenstein that 'I' is not a name what role do first and second person pronouns play in an utterance? As indexicals they get their sense from something external to the discourse. They enrich the content of the utterance with some fact about the occasion of that utterance and the standing of the speaker min the local community. Knowledge of such facts allows the hearer to complete the sense of the utterance. Expressions such as 'here' and 'there' are indexicals of place, just as 'now' and 'then' are indexicals of time. To grasp their content on any particular occasion of utterance we must know whether what is referred to is near or far from the speaker (usually at the moment of utterance) or whether it is occurring while the speaker is talking or at some other time. Indexical pronouns not only index an utterance with the speaker's location in space and time relative to that of the hearer, but they are also expressions of the speaker's moral standing. 'I' not only commits the speaker to the content of the utterance, that is takes responsibility for it, but indexes a promise with local knowledge of the speaker's moral standing – for example trustworthy. Taking responsibility is something only a person can do. Only a person can use the word 'I'.

4.3 Reservation

Strawson has presented impressive arguments in favor the role of criteria of identity for persons based on the uniqueness of the spatio-temporal trajectory of a particular human body in determining whether this is the same or a different person.

However these criteria can be brought into question if psychic continuity, for example authenticity of memories, is called into question.

Even in ascribing material attributes to oneself 'I' is indexical. These are the attributes of the speaker. We, the listeners, can know which person these attributes belong to, only if we are present on the occasion of utterance or stand in some equivalent relation to this speaker.

4.4 The Overall Shape of the Analysis

The ontological ground of human life, as revealed in the discourses apropos of living that life, requires human beings in general to be considered both under the category of 'highest animal' and, as individuals, under the category of 'person'.

The mereological fallacy occurs in highest animal discourses only in an oblique way. Highest animals have parts, but persons, the recipients of psychological attributions, do not. Yet persons are embodied, that is reside at sites which do have parts. The distinguishing of predicates apropos of a person and only a human being qua person, depends on a generalised version of Hume's is-ought fallacy, rather than a simple mereological fallacy.

The embodiment of persons enables the human being to have access to a kit of tools for performing the tasks that the local culture requires, including mental tasks such as computation (the brain as the means by which the task is performed) and material but normatively constrained tasks such as gardening (the hand as the means by which the task is performed).

The use of indexicals in the conversations of everyday life displays the way that people take on and refuse responsibility, which with rights and duties, are the core moral concepts for living as a social being.

References

Bennett Max; Hacker, Peter (2003): *Philosophical Foundations of Neuroscience*. Oxford: Blackwell.
Cook, John (2010): "Locating Wittgenstein". In: *Philosophy* 85, 273–289.
Descartes, René (1641): *Meditations on First Philosophy*. Paris: Soly.
Hacker, Peter (2013): "Before the Mereological Fallacy: A Rejoinder to Rom Harré". In: *Philosophy* 88 141–148.
Hume, David (1972): *A Treatise of Human Nature*. London: Collins.

Moyal-Sharrock, Danièle (2004): *Understanding Wittgenstein's On Certainty*. New York: Palgrave-Macmillan.
Strawson, Peter (1954): "A Reply to Mr. Sellars". In: *Philosophical Review* 63, 216–231.
Wittgenstein, Ludwig (1922): *Tractatus Logico-Philosophicus*. London: Kegan Paul. [T]
Wittgenstein, Ludwig (1953): *Philosophical Investigations*. Oxford: Blackwell. [PI]
Wittgenstein, Ludwig (1973): *On Certainty*. Oxford: Blackwell. [OC]

Ingolf Max
Wittgensteins Philosophieren zwischen *Kodex* und *Strategie*: Logik, Schach und Farbausdrücke

Abstract: From an analytical point of view each interpreter of Wittgenstein's philosophizing in its totality should make her language of analysis as precise as possible. The proposal is to use a pair of concepts – c*odex* and *strategy* – which is relatively neutral with respect to Wittgenstein's writings and offers room for a variety of sophisticated uses. C*odex* can tentatively characterized as a totality of rules which characterize a concept, a system, a language, a formal game completely. *Strategy* can be explicated as intentionally performing actions which can be understood as following rules without claiming to make the aim (if there is any) as well as the underlying rules explicit and without presupposing the existence of an underlying codex. With respect to logic as *calculus* (pure codex, general form), *chess* (codex-based strategy) and *color expressions* (no designated codex at hand) we can identify different but interrelated stages in Wittgenstein's philosophizing.

Keywords: Wittgenstein, codex, strategy, chess, color expressions

1 Kodex und Strategie als Begriffe einer Analysesprache zur Interpretation des Gesamtwerks von Wittgenstein

Üblicherweise wird Wittgensteins Philosophieren in verschiedene Phasen eingeteilt: häufig einfach in die *frühe* Philosophie, die bis zur Fertigstellung der *Logisch-philosophischen Abhandlung* 1918 (1922 veröffentlicht als *Tractatus logico-philosophicus*) reicht und die *spätere* Philosophie, in deren Zentrum die erstmals 1953 veröffentlichen *Philosophischen Untersuchungen* stehen. Eine Datierung des Beginns des *späteren* Philosophierens auf 1928/29 erscheint äußerst problematisch, da dann z. B. die intensiven Debatten mit Ramsey seit 1923 genauso ausgeblendet bleiben, wie Wittgensteins Interesse an der Architektur im Zusammenhang mit dem Bau des Hauses für seine Schwester Hermine ab 1926, welches nur höchst bedingt als unabhängig von seinem Philosophieren verstanden werden kann. Wittgensteins eigene Auskunft im Vorwort der Philosophischen Untersuchungen von 1945 „Seit ich nämlich vor 16 Jahren mich wieder mit Philosophie zu beschäftigen anfing ..." bezieht sich offenbar auf intensives, fortgesetztes philosophisches Arbeiten unter höchster Anspannung gemäß seinen eigenen hohen Maßstäben. Indem er kurz darauf auf seine „schwere[n] Irrtümer" verweist, die er mit Ramsey während „der zwei letzten Jahre seines Lebens in zahllosen Gesprächen erörtert habe", wären wir zumindest bei Anfang 1928, da Ramsey am 19. Januar 1930 starb.

Eine andere Einteilung schiebt eine mittlere Phase dazwischen, die mit den *Some Remarks on Logical Form* von 1929 immerhin noch Wittgensteins zweite Veröffentlichung umfasst und mit der recht häufigen Verwendung der Begriffe *Phänomen* und *phänomenologisch* in Verbindung gebracht wird. Diese Phase ist so spannend, weil sie den Übergang von der allgemeinen (logischen) Satzform zur Vielfalt der (grammatischen) Formen als „ein kompliziertes Netz von Ähnlichkeiten, die einander übergreifen und kreuzen" (PU §66) markiert.

Wittgenstein selbst hat zwar sein eigenes Frühwerk in einigen Punkten äußerst heftig kritisiert, insbesondere den logischen Atomismus im *Tractatus*, es selbst aber nicht komplett verworfen, sondern als kontrastierendes Gegenstück zu seinem Spätwerk verstanden:

> Vor zwei Jahren aber hatte ich Veranlassung, mein erstes Buch (die ‚Logisch-Philosophische Abhandlung') wieder zu lesen und seine Gedanken zu erklären. Da schien es mir plötzlich, daß ich jene alten Gedanken und die neuen zusammen veröffentlichen sollte: daß diese nur durch den Gegensatz und auf dem Hintergrund meiner älteren Denkweise ihre rechte Beleuchtung erhalten könnten. (PU §232)

Mit der schönen Metapher „ihre rechte Beleuchtung" verweist Wittgenstein auf die Zusammengehörigkeit, letztlich die Familienähnlichkeit jener alten und neuen Gedanken.

Jeder Interpret, der versucht, das Philosophieren Wittgensteins in seiner Gesamtheit in den Blick zu nehmen, steht – in einem sprachanalytischen Programm agierend – vor der Aufgabe eine eigenständige Interpretationssprache zur Verfügung zu stellen. Diese *Analysesprache* muss hinreichend flexibel sein, um eine textadäquate Darstellung des Gesamtwerks zu erlauben.

Nachstehend wird skizziert, wie das Paar bestehend aus den aufeinander beziehbaren und von Wittgenstein eher nicht gebrauchten Begriffen *Kodex* und *Strategie* so bestimmt werden kann, dass es durch flexible Verwendung in der angestrebten Analysesprache optimale Interpretationsleistungen ermöglicht.

Ein äußerst provisorischer Versuch der Explikation von Kodex könnte lauten: *Kodex* ist die Gesamtheit all derjenigen Regeln, die einen Begriff, ein System, eine Sprache bzw. ein formales Spiel *vollständig* bestimmen. Relativ zu einem *Kodex* sind alle Charakterisierungen *intern*, d.h., es wird keinerlei externer Kontext benötigt um zu klären, welche Charakterisierung vorliegt. Der späte Wittgenstein spricht in solchen Fällen auch von „wesentlichen Regeln" (PU §562, §564). Ein Kodex kann selbst eine äußerst komplexe interne Struktur aufweisen, wobei solche Teilstrukturen eigene Kodizes bilden können, die auf unterschiedliche Weise untereinander in Beziehung stehen.

Ein paradigmatischer Fall liegt z. B. in der Bestimmung des Kodex eines logischen Systems durch die Angabe seiner axiomatischen Basis vor. Die axiomatische Basis umfasst neben der Angabe einer Formeldefinition (Teilkodex) die vollständige Auflistung aller speziellen Sätze (Axiome) und aller speziellen Grundregeln (z. B. Schluss- und Strukturregeln des Beweisens). Dies macht den Begriff *Theorem* zu einem wohldefinierten *internen* Begriff. Im Bereich einer empirischen Theorie wie z. B. der Syntaxtheorie des Deutschen erfolgt die Festlegung auf einen Kodex z. B. durch die Angabe eines Lexikons und aller für die jeweilige Theorie charakteristischen Grammatikregeln. Damit ließe sich z. B. der Begriff *Sprachkompetenz intern* charakterisieren.

Hier wird allerdings unterstellt, dass es immer nur eine Lesart von „allen Regeln" etc. gibt, ein System somit durch *seinen* Kodex eindeutig bestimmt ist. Wenn wir nun jedoch auf ein bestimmtes Spiel – z. B. das Schachspiel – schauen, dann ergibt sich die Schwierigkeit, dass wir einen homogen strukturierten Kodex für alle Aspekte des Spiels nicht ausmachen können bzw. der Gesamtkodex sogar verschiedene miteinander verwandte Spiele zulässt. Eine Schachpartie mit Zeitbegrenzung kann wegen Zeitüberschreitung verloren gehen, was bei einer Partie ohne eine solche Begrenzung nicht vorkommen kann. Somit sind die wesentlichen Regeln, die den Ausgang dieser Spieltypen bestimmen, verschieden und damit sind es auch ihre Kodizes.

Eine weitere Schwierigkeit ergibt sich daraus, dass ein Kodex recht verschiedene Bezüge haben kann. Ein Kodex kann eine *formale Theorie* (einen Kalkül) charakterisieren. Er kann aber ebenso Bestandteil einer *empirischen Theorie* sein, die den mit Blick auf den Kodex externen Begriff der *Anwendung* kennt (z. B. eine linguistische Syntaxtheorie). Durch die Angabe eines Kodex sind zudem eine ganze Reihe von Spielen, desweiteren Gesetzestexte, Handbücher, politische Rituale etc. charakterisierbar. Die *philosophische* Schwierigkeit entsteht aber erst dann, wenn sich *Kodex* bzw. *Strategie* nicht auf etwas Partielles, sondern auf die Gesamtheit als Gesamtheit beziehen soll. Wittgenstein variiert in verschiedenen Phasen seines Schaffens seine Sprechweise, wobei jede die Form „bestimmter Artikel + Singularkonstruktion" aufweist: „die Welt", „die Gesamtheit der Tatsachen", „die Wirklichkeit", „die Sprache" etc. (im *Tractatus*), „*the* ultimate analysis of the phenomena in question" (RLF §171) bzw. „das 'Sprachspiel'" (PU §7). Die konkrete – und damit nicht philosophische – Angabe eines Kodex ist nach Wittgenstein immer partiell. DIE Gesamtheit lässt sich daher nicht durch eine solche Angabe erfassen. DER Kodex (DIE Logik) *zeigt sich*.

Den potentiellen Partner von Kodex nennen wir *Strategie*. *Strategie* kann probeweise expliziert werden als intentionales Handeln, welches wir – in unserer Kultur und Praxis – als Regelfolgen auffassen unabhängig davon, ob wir eine Absicht (ein Handlungsziel, einen Handlungsplan) bzw. die jeweiligen Regeln explizieren können und zunächst unabhängig davon, ob es einen zu Grunde liegenden Kodex gibt oder nicht. Als einen typischen Strategie-Begriff mit Blick auf Spiele können wir bei Wittgenstein den Begriff *Witz* (eines Spiels) ausmachen (PU §62, §111, §142, §363, §564). Insbesondere wäre z. B. PU §564 im Spannungsfeld von Kodex und Strategie zu interpretieren: „Ich bin also geneigt, auch im Spiel zwischen wesentlichen und unwesentlichen Regeln zu unterscheiden. Das Spiel, möchte man sagen, hat nicht nur Regeln, sondern auch einen *Witz*." Mit Blick auf Schach*partien* lassen sich leicht Fälle angeben, in denen wir den Witz vermissen würden: Die Annahme eines Remis-Angebots nach einem Zug, womit die Partie Kodex-korrekt mit Unentschieden endet, obwohl „nicht richtig" gespielt wurde. Oder: Das Hin- und Herschieben von Schachfiguren als Kodex-korrekte Zugausführungen, jedoch ohne erkennbare Absicht auf ein Ziel hin.

2 FIDE-Gesetze des Schachs: Interne Kodex-Strukturiertheit und Vernetzung mit Aspekten der Strategie

Wittgenstein hat auf höchst originelle Weise spätestens ab 1930 Analogien zum Schach*spiel*, zum Schach*spielen* (Partien), zu Schach*figuren* und ihrer Verwendungsvielfalt, zur Geometrie des Schachbretts etc. benutzt, um bestimmte Aspekte seines Philosophierens einer ganz spezifischen Beleuchtung auszusetzen. Die Reichhaltigkeit der Aspekte und vor allem die vielen Verwandtschaften mit anderen Tätigkeitsformen – vor allem *Sprachspielen* – ist äußerst bemerkenswert. Schach verfügt über einen klaren *Kodex*-Bezug und ist zudem ein paradigmatisches Beispiel für ein *Strategie*-Spiel. Darüber hinaus ist es aber auch fest in *unserer Kultur* verankert.

Am Beispiel eines streng durchgearbeiteten Regelwerks – den FIDE-Gesetzen des Schachs[1] – wird gezeigt,

---

1 https://www.fide.com/fide/handbook.html?id=171&view=article, bzw. http://srk.schachbund.

- dass die FIDE-Gesetze bestimmte Teilmengen von Regeln bereitstellen, die tatsächlich in ihrer jeweiligen Gesamtheit als Kodizes in dem Sinne verstanden werden können, dass sie Begriffe wie *korrekter Zug* und *korrekte Stellung* vollständig definieren;
- dass die FIDE-Gesetze mehrere solcher Teilmengen beinhalten und in diesem Sinne intern strukturiert sind;
- dass Kodex-„Erweiterung" nicht einfach additiv geschieht;
- dass die FIDE-Gesetze zielbezogene und in diesem Sinne *strategische* Regeln enthalten sowie
- dass die FIDE-Gesetze genutzt werden können, um mit ihnen durchaus verwandte Tätigkeiten von dem durch sie definierten FIDE-Schach abzugrenzen, zugleich aber mehr oder weniger deutliche Verwandtschaften aufzuzeigen.

Naiv gesprochen ist Schach ein Spiel, bei dem gewisse Figuren auf einem Brett nach gewissen Regeln bewegt werden. Doch damit würden bereits Spielformen wie Computerschach, Blindschach, Fernschach usw. nicht mehr darunter fallen. Schach könnte ein Spiel sein, bei dem es um Gewinnen geht, wobei das Gewinnen im Mattsetzen des Gegners besteht. Doch der Gewinn kann auch dadurch erfolgen, dass der Gegner aufgibt oder – soweit man Schachuhren als Teil des Schachkodex zulässt – der Gegner die für eine bestimmte Anzahl von Zügen zur Verfügung stehende Bedenkzeit überschreitet und die Stellung nicht theoretisch remis (unentschieden) ist. Und auch der Gewinn muss nicht eintreten, da bestimmte Stellungen, Stellungswiederholungen, Zugfolgen bzw. Verabredungen zum Remis führen. Das (Schach-)Brett hat eine bestimmte Geometrie (und Farbgebung). Doch diese macht es nicht zu einem *Schach*-Koordinatensystem, denn worin läge der Unterschied zum *Dame*brett?

Einfache Wesensbestimmungen für *Schach* sind nicht zu sehen. Das macht es auch *philosophisch* interessant. Eine Alternative könnte darin bestehen, einen – möglicherweise intern strukturierten – Kodex zu erstellen, der eben genau *das* Spiel definiert. Die Frage ist nun, ob die *Laws of Chess* einen solchen Kodex darstellen. Die FIDE-*Gesetze* gehen in der jeweils geltenden Fassung auf den Beschluss eines Kongresses der FIDE (Fédération Internationale des Échec) zurück. Der letzte Beschluss wurde auf dem 84. Kongress in Tallinn (Estland) gefasst. Es gilt ausschließlich die englischsprachige Fassung.

Die Makrostruktur der Regeln umfasst eine Einführung, ein Vorwort, die Basisregeln des Spiels (Artikel 1 bis 5), die Wettkampfregeln (Artikel 6 bis 12),

---

de/files/dsb/ srk/downloads/LawsOfChess2014.pdf, wo die Änderungen zur vorherigen Fassung angezeigt werden. (Beides zuletzt aufgerufen am 28.01.2016.)

diverse Anhänge und ein Glossar. Die Anhänge regeln verwandte Spieltypen mit einem modifizierten Kodex (Schnellschach, Blitzschach, Chess 960), die algebraische Notation zur Aufzeichnung von Schachpartien, die Spielweise für blinde und sehbehinderte Spieler, Spielunterbrechungen und besondere Bedingungen für die Endphase einer Partie unter Zeitbegrenzung. Wir gehen vor allem auf die Basis- und ein wenig auf die Wettkampfregeln ein.

Die FIDE-Gesetze beziehen sich ausschließlich auf das „over-the-board play". Eine Schach*partie* folgt nur dann den FIDE-Gesetzen, wenn *tatsächlich Züge ausgeführt* werden (Artikel 4: The act of moving the pieces). Dies trifft z. B. auf Computerschach nicht zu.

Ein Aspekt, den die FIDE-Gesetze liefern sollten, ist eine regelbezogene Definition dafür, was ein *korrekter* Zug (*legal* move) ist. Dies geschieht explizit in Artikel 3.10a unter Verweis auf die Unterartikel 3.1–3.9. Es wird behauptet, dass *die Gesamtheit* dieser Artikel und damit ein fest umrissener Ausschnitt von Regeln *den Kodex für den Begriff korrekter Zug* darstellt. Dies ist jedoch nicht ganz zutreffend, da Teile von Artikel 2 ebenfalls zu diesem Kodex gehören. Die Artikel 3.1–3.9 bestimmen, welche allgemeinen Beschränkungen bei der Ausführung von Zügen bestehen, was es bedeutet, eine gegnerische Figur zu schlagen, ein Figur bzw. ein Feld anzugreifen (3.1), wie die einzelnen Figuren ziehen können, wenn die relevanten Einschränkungen dies zulassen (3.2: Läufer, 3.3: Turm, 3.4: Dame, 3.5: Verbot für diese drei Figuren über andere Figuren zu „springen", 3.6: Springer, 3.7: Bauer einschließlich „en passant"-Schlagen und Umwandlung, 3.8: König einschließlich Rochade) und was ein Schachgebot für Zugeinschränkungen nach sich zieht (3.9). Diese Regeln setzen bereits die Geometrie des Brettes und seine Position relativ zu den beiden Spielern voraus[2] (2.1), ebenso die Benennungen der Figuren, jedoch nicht deren Anzahl (2.2) und Definitionen von „Linie" („file"), „Reihe" („rank") und „Diagonale" (2.4.) Auf jeden Fall nicht benötigt wird Artikel 2.3, in dem die Ausgangsstellung der Figuren festgelegt wird. Artikel 3.10a. korrigierend können wir sagen, dass die Artikel 2.1, 2.2 (teilweise), 2.4 und 3.1 bis 3.9 den Kodex für den Begriff *korrekter Zug* darstellen. Weder dieser Teilkodex noch der FIDE-Gesamtkodex geben Auskunft darüber, in welcher konkreten Stellung der Zug erfolgt. Der Gesamtkodex begrenzt den logischen Raum, in dem alle möglichen FIDE-Schach*partien* liegen müssen. Es ergibt sich eine Familienähn-

---

[2] Interessanterweise wird in keinem Artikel eine Bezeichnungsweise für die einzelnen Felder des Brettes (z. B. „d4") eingeführt. Dies erfolgt erst im Anhang C. Algebraic notation und gehört somit zu den *unwesentlichen* Regeln des Schachs.

lichkeit zwischen verschieden Arten von Spielen, die darin übereinstimmen, dass *korrekte Züge* ausgeführt werden, selbst wenn nicht FIDE-Schach gespielt wird.[3]

In 3.10c wird der Begriff *unkorrekte Stellung* dadurch definiert, dass diese nicht auf dem Wege einer Folge korrekter Züge erreicht werden kann. Es findet sich keinerlei Angabe darüber, ob es einen ganz bestimmten Teilkodex der FIDE-Gesetze gibt, der dafür ausreicht. Wie viel Regelbezug wir benötigen, um eine konkrete Stellung als *unkorrekt* zu charakterisieren, hängt vom Einzelfall ab. In einigen Fällen können wir dies einfach „sehen" und brauchen uns nicht um die Zugfolge ihres Zustandekommens zu kümmern (z. B. ein weißer Bauer auf der ersten Reihe, 2 weiße Könige auf dem Brett u. ä.). In anderen Fällen ist dies schon etwas schwieriger: Wir könnten z. B. die weißen Bauern so auf dem Brett postieren, dass sie um dorthin zu gelangen mehr schwarze Figuren schlagen müssten, als verfügbar sind.[4] Ein extremer Fall würde dann vorliegen, wenn wir tatsächlich bis zur *Ausgangsstellung* zurückgehen müssten, um diese Frage zu entscheiden, wobei sogar relevant sein kann, wer in der zu beurteilenden Position am Zug ist.[5] Im Unterschied zum Teilkodex für den Begriff *korrekter* Zug, muss also die Regel für die Ausgangsstellung (2.3) zu diesem Teilkodex gehören. Außerdem führen unkorrekte *Züge* nicht unbedingt zu unkorrekten *Stellungen*.

Der für unser Gesamtanliegen spannendste Artikel ist jedoch gleich der erste. Er ist in mehrfacher Hinsicht nicht homogen in Bezug auf einen strengen Kodex-Begriff: Es gelingt wohl nicht den Unterartikel 1.2 ausschließlich als Kodex-Formulierung aufzufassen: „The objective of each player is to place the opponent's king 'under attack' in such a way that the opponent has no legal move. The player who achieves this goal is said to have 'checkmated' the opponent's king and to have won the game." Die Formulierungen „the objective of", „achieves this goal" als auch „to have checkmated" sind klar zielbezogen und damit s*trategischer* Natur. Zugleich finden sich jedoch mehrere Kodex-Bezüge: „under attack",

---

[3] Dazu gehören z. B. (1) die Analyse von Schachpartien, die schon deshalb keine FIDE-Partie darstellt, weil Züge zurückgenommen werden können; (2) Schachaufgaben verschiedenster Art (Matt/Hilfsmatt/Selbstmatt in *n* Zügen, Retroaufgaben, Studien), die kein FIDE-Schach darstellen, weil es keine Ausgangsstellung gemäß 2.3 gibt etc. Vgl. hierzu auch Wittgensteins Bemerkung zur Schachpartie zwischen Adelheid und dem Bischof (Goethe: Götz von Berlichingen mit der eisernen Hand, Zweiter Akt, Bamberg. Ein Saal) in PU 365.
[4] Eine Aufstellung der 8 weißen Bauern auf den Feldern a2, a3, a4, a5, a6, a7, h2, h3 würde bedeuten, dass 16 schwarze Figuren geschlagen worden sein müssten. Es sind aber nur 15 verfügbar. Auch jede Stellung mit den weißen Bauern auf den Feldern a2, a3, b2 ist *unkorrekt*.
[5] Es könnte leicht sein, dass komponierte Stellungen für Schachaufgaben (z. B. Selbstmatt in n Zügen) *unkorrekt* sind und allein schon aus diesem Grund ein anderer Schachtyp vorliegt. Ein Beispiel für eine Mattaufgabe, die keine FIDE-Schachaufgabe ist: https://de.wikipedia.org/wiki/Ott%C3%B3_Titusz_Bl%C3%A1thy, zuletzt aufgerufen am 28.01.2016.

„player", „opponent", „legal move", „checkmate" und „win", die durch Kodex-Regeln festgelegt werden. Es wird hier nicht nur die Vernetzung strategischer und Kodex-bezogener Regelaspekte deutlich, sondern auch eine spezifische Verflochtenheit von Teilkodizes: „(under) attack" wird erst in 3.1 explizit geregelt. „legal move" – wie oben ausgeführt – erst mit Blick auf den Teilkodex {2.1, 2.2, 2.4, 3.1–3.9}.

Die *Basis*regeln des Schachs (1.1–5.2) bestimmen, dass jede Schachpartie, die nach diesen Regeln gespielt wird, mit einer fixierten Ausgangsstellung beginnt und durch Ausführung einer endlichen Anzahl korrekter Züge zu einer Endstellung (rein stellungsbezogen oder durch Handlungen wie Aufgabe der Partie bzw. Annahme eines Remis-Angebots) gelangt. Nicht geregelt ist die Beendigung einer beliebigen Partie in endlicher Zeit. Dies ist u. a. die Aufgabe der *Wettkampf*regeln (Artikel 6 bis 12). Diese können jedoch nicht einfach als Ergänzungen betrachtet werden, da sie die Kodex-Bestimmungen der Basisregeln in verschiedener Weise modifizieren. Die Überschreitung einer vorgegebenen Bedenkzeit für eine bestimmte Anzahl von Zügen bedeutet das Ende der Partie. Man kann jetzt – selbst bei großer Überlegenheit – „nach Zeit verlieren" (6.9). Neu ist zudem, dass der *Schiedsrichter* im Fall, dass ein Spieler in derselben Partie aufeinanderfolgend zwei *unkorrekte* Züge ausführt, die Partie für diesen Spieler als verloren erklärt, falls die vorliegende Stellung nicht theoretisch remis ist.

3 Mögliche Beziehungen zwischen Kodex und Strategie

Es stellt sich nun die Frage nach den möglichen *Beziehungen zwischen Kodex und Strategie*. Sehr grob lassen sich folgende drei Fälle unterscheiden:

(1) Eine Untersuchung beschränkt sich allein auf den *Kodex*. Dies kann geschehen durch die Ausblendung strategischer Aspekte oder durch die Akzeptanz eines reduktionistischen Programms, welches besagt, dass „strategische" Aspekte in jedem relevanten Falle mittels eines erweiterten Kodex erfasst werden können. In diesem Sinne wäre z. B. die logische Analyse eine universelle Methode um zu einem Kodex zu gelangen.

(2) *Strategie* ist in dem Sinne gänzlich unabhängig von *Kodex*, dass sich aus dem Kodex allein keinerlei Auskunft über die zu realisierende bzw. realisierte Strategie gewinnen lässt. Zugleich setzt die Strategie jedoch den Kodex dahingehend absolut voraus, dass jeder *strategische* (gute bzw. schlechte) Zug ein *korrekter* Zug im Sinne des Kodex sein muss. Der Schach-Kodex bietet sich als ein paradigmatischer Fall an: Jeder relativ zu einer Partiestellung *gute* Zug muss auf

jeden Fall ein *korrekter* Zug sein. Anderseits lassen sich aus dem Kodex überhaupt keine speziellen Strategien ableiten. Der Kodex des Schach*spiels* bestimmt nur den Möglichkeitsraum aller in seinem Rahmen spielbaren Schach*partien*. Dieser Kodex fixiert auch ein definitives Ende einer jeden Schachpartie, gibt allerdings weder Auskünfte über den konkreten Partieverlauf noch über den Ausgang der Partie.

(3) Es könnte Fälle geben, in denen wir für bestimmte Tätigkeiten über keinen zu Grunde liegenden Kodex verfügen und dennoch davon ausgehen, dass diese Tätigkeiten bestimmten *strategischen* Regeln folgen. Wir können sogar versuchen, diese Regeln explizit zu machen, stellen dann aber fest, dass diese Regeln Kodex-Regeln bestenfalls in mancher Hinsicht ähneln, vielleicht aber auch ein ganz anderer Typ zu sein scheinen. Sitten, Gebräuche, Gewohnheiten sind in diesem Sinne Regeln der *Strategie*. Es fällt sofort auf, dass die Geltung solcher Regeln von ganz bestimmten Kontextbedingungen abhängt, dass sie Ausnahmen zulassen, dass sie historisch bzw. kulturell bedingt sein können. Das Sprichwort „Springer am Rand bringt Kummer und Schand" verkörperte in den Zeiten einer bestimmten Schacheröffnungspraxis möglicherweise einen guten Ratschlag. Später hat sich diese Praxis durch das Aufkommen neuer Eröffnungen so verändert, dass zur Aufrechterhaltung des Stellungsgleichgewichts nach einer bestimmten Anzahl von Zügen der Springer an den Rand gezogen werden *muss*.

Wittgensteins *Bemerkungen über die Farben* dienen im Rahmen eines Philosophieprogramms u. a. der Formulierung von *Strategie*-Regeln, die unsere Verwendung von Farbausdrücken in den Blick nehmen. Diese können recht systematisch vorgetragen werden, ohne dass sie zu einem *Kodex* werden. Wittgenstein bevorzugt für ein System von Strategie-Regeln den Begriff *Lehre* wie z.B. in „Harmonielehre der Farben" (BF I §74; III §91). Mit Blick auf „Goethes Lehre von der Entstehung der Spektralfarben", die er nicht als eine Theorie (Kodex) ansieht, spricht er davon, dass sie „eher ein vages Denkschema nach Art derer [ist], die man in James's Psychologie findet" (BF I §70; III §125). Die „Harmonielehre" von Schönberg wäre auch als ein Kodex der Harmonie missverstanden, da sie eher das Rüstzeug für die eigene Kreativität beim Komponieren vermitteln soll.

4 Kodex und Strategie in Wittgensteins Philosophieren

Das nun folgende Bild besitzt einige Attraktivität: Wittgenstein durchläuft die obigen drei Fälle in der angegebenen Reihenfolge im Verlaufe seines Philosophierens. Wir werden einige Argumente für die Plausibilität dieses Bildes anführen, zugleich aber betonen, dass es sich hier vorerst nur um eine äußerst grobe Skizze handelt.

(1) Wittgenstein gibt in T 6 „die allgemeine Form der Wahrheitsfunktion" bzw. „die allgemeine Satzform" an, ehe abschließend klar wird, dass sich diese Form nur zeigen, sie aber nicht ausgesprochen werden kann („schweigen" in T 7). T 1.12 – „Denn, die Gesamtheit der Tatsachen bestimmt, was der Fall ist und auch, was alles nicht der Fall ist" – zeigt bereits die gesamte Logik, die damit gänzlich *intern* ist. Es gibt zwar spezifische Räume (das Räumliche, das Farbige, vgl. T 2.171, den Farbenraum, den Raum der Tonhöhen etc., vgl. T 2.0131), aber jeder Raum muss auch ein logischer sein (T 2.182). Mit Bezug auf Farben muss Wittgenstein dann annehmen, dass es eine logische Struktur der Farbe gibt. Zudem geht Wittgenstein davon aus, dass die Situation in der „zwei Farben zugleich an einem Ort des Gesichtsfeldes sind, [...] unmöglich [ist], und zwar logisch unmöglich, denn es ist durch die logische Struktur der Farbe ausgeschlossen." (T 6.3751) Es gibt nur eine Möglichkeit logische Unmöglichkeit auszudrücken: durch eine *Kontradiktion*. Der Begriff *Kontradiktion* gehört zum „logischen Symbolismus" (T 4.4611) und damit zum *Kodex*. Ebenfalls zum *Kodex* gehört die Aussage, „dass das logische Produkt zweier Elementarsätze weder eine Tautologie noch eine Kontradiktion sein kann." (T 6.3751). Wittgenstein behauptet zudem: „Die Aussage, dass ein Punkt des Gesichtsfeldes zu gleicher Zeit zwei verschiedene Farben hat, ist eine Kontradiktion." (T 6.3751) Dies bedeutet, dass die komplexe Aussage „Dieser Fleck des Gesichtsfeldes ist rot *und* dieser (derselbe) Fleck des Gesichtsfeldes ist blau." eine logische Form haben muss, die sich als Kontradiktion erweist. Die zusammengesetzte Aussage wird damit zu einer, die vollständig durch den Kodex bestimmt ist. Die Konsequenz ist allerdings, dass zumindest eine der beiden Aussagen wie „Dieser Fleck des Gesichtsfeldes ist rot." bzw. „Dieser Fleck des Gesichtsfeldes ist blau" nicht die Form eines Elementarsatzes hat. An diesem Punkt setzt u. a. Ramseys Kritik in seiner Rezension des *Tractatus* an (Ramsey 1923).

(2) Bereits im *Tractatus* unterscheidet Wittgenstein sorgfältig zwischen den Redeweisen *Kontradiktion* und *Widerspruch*, was leider sowohl in der Übersetzung von Odgen (& Ramsey) als auch der von Pears und McGuinness gänzlich vernachlässigt wird, indem in beiden ausschließlich *inconsistency* verwendet wird. Aus unserer Sicht ist klar, dass allein der Begriff *Kontradiktion* zum Kodex gehört, wohingegen der Begriff *Widerspruch* in Zusammenhängen auftaucht, in denen noch nicht klar ist, ob die den Widerspruch darstellende Aussage tatsächlich die logische Form einer Kontradiktion hat. Der Unterschied ist, dass sich z. B. die Elementarsätze „p" und „~p" *widersprechen*, wenn gezeigt werden kann, dass „p . ~p" eine *Kontradiktion* ist. Im Falle der Sätze „Dieser Fleck des Gesichtsfeldes ist rot." und „Dieser Fleck des Gesichtsfeldes ist blau." benötigen wir die logischen Formen dieser Sätze – hier angedeutet, aber nicht angegeben mittels „A" und „B".

Der Nachweis, dass die komplexe Aussage „Dieser Fleck des Gesichtsfeldes ist rot und dieser (derselbe) Fleck des Gesichtsfeldes ist blau." widersprüchlich mit Bezug auf den Kodex ist, kann nur dadurch erfolgen, dass gezeigt wird, dass „A . B" eine Kontradiktion ist. Wittgenstein verwendet außerdem den Begriff Widerspruch mehrfach zusammen mit „kann ... nicht"-Konstruktionen. Hierbei handelt es sich nicht um eine möglicherweise kontradiktorische und daher sinn*lose* Redeweise von logischer Möglichkeit, sondern um die Zurückweisung von *Außerlogischem*, die Feststellung, dass das Verlassen des Kodex zu *unsinniger* Redeweise führt. Zum Beispiel:

> Etwas 'der Logik widersprechendes' in der Sprache darstellen, kann man ebensowenig, wie in der Geometrie eine den Gesetzen des Raumes widersprechende Figur durch ihre Koordinaten darstellen; oder die Koordinaten eines Punktes angeben, welcher nicht existiert. (T 3.032)

Hier – wie auch an einigen anderen Stellen – lässt sich „widersprechendes" nicht durch „kontradiktorisches" ersetzen. Letzteres wäre durch den Kodex geregelt, ersteres nicht.

Wittgenstein sieht sich ab 1929 gezwungen anzuerkennen, dass Sätze wie „Dieser Fleck des Gesichtsfeldes ist rot." und „Dieser Fleck des Gesichtsfeldes ist blau." in logischer Hinsicht elementar sein sollten. Dann ist aber die Kodex-Teilaussage aus T 6.3751 „Es ist klar, dass das logische Produkt zweier Elementarsätze weder eine Tautologie noch eine Kontradiktion sein kann." nicht zu halten. Wittgenstein versucht zunächst seine Konzeption der Wahrheitsfunktionen aufrecht zu erhalten und allein die logische Form der „Elementarsätze" aufzugeben, da er glaubt hier einen Handlungsspielraum zu haben, der das Grundkonzept einer Logik als *Kodex* aller Sprache und Welt nicht tangiert (vgl. Max 2013). In seinem Aufsatz *Some Remarks of Logical Form* (1929) manifestiert sich sein Ringen um eine Alternative. Wittgenstein spürt, dass er den Begriff *Kontradiktion* verliert. Stattdessen formuliert er „some sort of contradiction", „excludes any other" (RLF §167), „The mutual exclusion of unanalyzable statements of degree" (RLF §168), „I here deliberately say 'exclude' and not 'contradict', for there is a difference between these two notions, and atomic propositions, although they cannot contradict, may exclude one another." (RLF §168) und „the exclusion as opposed to a contradiction" (RLF §170).

In einem nächsten Schritt, in dem er immer häufiger auch auf Schach-Analogien zurückgreift – z.B. dokumentiert in *Wittgenstein und der Wiener Kreis* (WWK) ab 19. Juni 1930 –, bezieht Wittgenstein zunehmend Aspekte der *Strategie* ein, allerdings zunächst immer noch auf einen Kodex (das Schach*spiel*) bezogen, der häufig mit „Kalkül" angesprochen wird. Allerdings kann der Kodex z. B. in dem

Fall, dass sich die Anwendungen verschiedener Regeln einander ausschließen, durch die Hinzufügung einer neuen Regel modifiziert werden. Ein Kodex hat damit Kodex-*Alternativen*.

(3) Um die Grammatik der Farbausdrücke nun analog zu Spielfiguren im Schach betrachten zu können, müssten wir einen Kodex bzw. alternative Kodizes für das Spiel mit Farbausdrücken angeben können. Es würden sich dafür verschiedene Möglichkeiten anbieten. Wir könnten die Farben physikalisch über ihre Wellenlängen charakterisieren und sodann in eine Ordnung bringen. Doch diese Anordnung geschähe in Wittgensteins Terminologie über eine außerlogische, *externe* Relation. Wir suchen nach *internen* Relationen zwischen Farbausdrücken. Doch um diese zeigen zu können, müssten wir die logische Form der Farbtermini und auch „the ultimate connection of the terms" (RLF §162) bereits zur Verfügung haben. Die Verwendungen von Farbausdrücken stehen nach Wittgenstein zwar in internen Beziehungen zueinander. Diese können aber nach dem Aufgeben des logischen Atomismus nicht in Form eines Kodex angegeben werden.

> Ein Sprachspiel: Darüber berichten, ob ein bestimmter Körper heller oder dunkler als ein andrer sei. – Aber nun gibt es ein verwandtes: Über das Verhältnis der Helligkeiten bestimmter Farbtöne aussagen ... – Die Form der Sätze in beiden Sprachspielen ist die gleiche: „X ist heller als Y". Aber im ersten ist es eine externe Relation und der Satz zeitlich, im zweiten ist es eine interne Relation und der Satz zeitlos. (BF I §1)

Wir erfahren zunächst, dass die Bestimmung der Relationen „heller–als" bzw. „dunkler–als" als externe bzw. interne Relationen von dem Sprachspiel abhängen, in dem sie verwendet werden. Eine absolute Bestimmung wie im *Tractatus* scheidet daher aus. Aber vielleicht können wir die Verwendungen als interne Relationen betrachten und darauf eine Kodex-Eigenschaft gründen, die darin besteht, die Farbausdrücke auf eine bestimmte fixe Weise anzuordnen. Doch diese Hoffnung zerstört Wittgenstein bereits mit der unmittelbaren Fortsetzung: „In einem Bild, in welchem ein Stück weißes Papier seine Helligkeit vom blauen Himmel kriegt, ist dieser heller als das weiße Papier. Und doch ist, in einem andern Sinne, Blau die dunklere, Weiß die hellere Farbe (Goethe). Auf der Palette ist das Weiß die hellste Farbe." (BF I §1) Wir haben hier nun drei verschiedene Bestimmungen von „Weiß": (a) Weiß ist dunkler als Blau im Kontext von Papier–Himmel, (b) Weiß ist heller als Blau und (c) mit Bezug auf die Palette können wir sogar die absolute Position von Weiß (hellste Farbe) angeben. Es entscheiden immer *Sprachspiele* (vgl. BF I §6). Es gibt keine feststehende Position von Weiß im Farbraum und vor allem auch keine ausgezeichnete Position des Farbwortes „Weiß" im Raum der Grammatik, an die der Philosoph mittels einer Wesensbestimmung von Weiß andocken könnte. Alles in allem ist die sich abzeichnende Aussichtslosigkeit, die Grammatik der Farbbegriffe in der Form eines Kodex bzw.

beruhend auf einem solchen angeben zu können u. a. verantwortlich dafür, dass Wittgenstein sich nach einer alternativen Form umsieht, die er schließlich formuliert als „ein kompliziertes Netz von Ähnlichkeiten, die einander übergreifen und kreuzen. Ähnlichkeiten im Großen und Kleinen" (PU §66) und weiter:

> Ich kann diese Ähnlichkeiten nicht besser charakterisieren als durch das Wort „Familienähnlichkeiten"; denn so übergreifen und kreuzen sich die verschiedenen Ähnlichkeiten, die zwischen den Gliedern einer Familie bestehen: Wuchs, Gesichtszüge, Augenfarbe, Gang, Temperament, etc. etc. – Und ich werde sagen: die „Spiele" bilden eine Familie. (PU §67)

Selbst mit Bezug auf die Mathematik können wir uns Situationen überlegen, in denen Rechnungshandlungen ausgeführt werden, ohne einen zugrunde liegenden Kodex zur Verfügung zu haben: „Man kann sich denken, daß Leute eine angewandte Mathematik haben ohne eine reine Mathematik." (BGM IV §15) Wenn wir reine Mathematik als eine Form eines Kodex auffassen und angewandte Mathematik als eine bestimmte Form von Strategie, dann haben wir hiermit einen speziellen Fall von Strategie OHNE Kodex.

> Sie können z. B. – nehmen wir an – die Bahn berechnen, welche gewisse sich bewegende Körper beschreiben und deren Ort zu einer gegebenen Zeit vorhersagen. Dazu benützen sie ein Koordinatensystem, die Gleichungen von Kurven (*eine Form der Beschreibung wirklicher Bewegung*) und die Technik des Rechnens im Dezimalsystem. Die Idee eines Satzes der reinen Mathematik kann ihnen ganz fremd sein. / Diese Leute haben also Regeln, denen gemäß sie die betreffenden Zeichen (insbesondere z. B. Zahlzeichen) transformieren zum Zweck der Voraussage des Eintreffens gewisser Ereignisse. (BGM IV §15)

Wiederum wäre ein Satz der reinen Mathematik ein zum Kodex gehörender Satz. Die Regeln zur Voraussage können als bestimmte *strategische* Regeln aufgefasst werden.

5 Zusammenfassung und Ausblick

Die FIDE-Gesetze des Schachs charakterisieren die Rahmenbedingungen für *alle* FIDE-Schachpartien. Sie stellen in ihrer Gesamtheit keinen reinen Kodex dar, weil bereits Artikel 1.2 mit der Angabe des Ziels von Zugfolgen aus der Ausgangsstellung heraus, eine auf die *Strategie* bezogene Festsetzung enthält (*Witz* des Spiels). Dies macht den Text einerseits eher zu einem Gesetzbuch, keinesfalls aber zu einem reinen Kalkül. Im Unterschied zu anderen (juristischen) Gesetzbüchern enthält das FIDE-„Gesetzbuch" jedoch kalkülartige und miteinander vernetzte

Teilkodizes, die verwendet werden können, um bestimmte Behauptungen über Schachstellungen, Zugfolgen etc. zu *beweisen*.[6]

Das sprachphilosophische Problem besteht nun z. B. darin, der *Gesamtbedeutung* der Phrase „eine Partie Schach spielen" auf die Spur zu kommen: „Wo ist die Verbindung gemacht zwischen dem Sinn der Worte ‚Spielen wir eine Partie Schach!' und allen Regeln des Spiels? – Nun, im Regelverzeichnis des Spiels, im Schachunterricht, in der täglichen Praxis des Spielens." (PU §197) Hierbei ist zwar der Bezug auf ein Regelverzeichnis wie die FIDE-Gesetze und damit *auch* der Bezug auf Kodizes eine wichtige Komponente, aber diese „einseitige Diät" als eine „Hauptursache philosophischer Krankheiten" (PU §593) berücksichtig nicht die Vielzahl weiterer Regelabhängigkeiten, für die gar kein Kodex vorliegt und auch nicht die Fälle, in denen die strategischen Komponenten bei weitem überwiegen (Schachunterricht, tägliche Praxis des Spielens).

Mit Blick auf die Logik bzw. Grammatik der Farbausdrücke hat Wittgenstein zunächst mittels der logischen Formbestimmung (Kontradiktion) einen Kodex unterstellt (T) und später versucht, über eine Neubestimmung der logischen Form der Elementarsätze die Annahme eines reinen Kodex aufrechtzuerhalten. Als dies nicht gelang, hat er zunehmend strategische Aspekte in Bezug auf Handlungen relativ zu einem Kodex einbezogen, um schließlich vor allem Fälle zu betrachten, in denen es aus philosophischer Perspektive unsinnig wäre, einen speziellen Kodex vorauszusetzen bzw. seine Formulierung anzustreben. Der Wechsel in der Sprechweise von „Logik" zu „Grammatik" spiegelt diese Entwicklung eines sich ändernden Verständnisses der vielfältigen Strategiebezogenheit von Handlungen wider.

Die flexiblen Anwendungsmöglichkeiten des Begriffspaares Kodex–Strategie können als Teil einer umfangreicheren Analysesprache genutzt werden, um das Philosophieren Wittgensteins in seiner Genese und Vielfalt zu interpretieren. Zugleich wurde hier für die Attraktivität eines möglichen Interpretationsbildes plädiert. Letzteres bleibt natürlich ohne weitere Untersuchungen, in denen sich die angestrebte Analysesprache zu bewähren hat, hypothetisch.

Literaturverzeichnis

Max, Ingolf (2013): „Giving up logical atomism? Some remarks on Wittgenstein's *Some remarks on logical form* (1929)". In: *Argumentos. Revista de Filosofia* 5 (10), 9 – 25.

---

[6] Es kann z. B. bewiesen werden, dass jede Stellung mit einer bestimmten fixen Figurenanordnung *unkorrekt* ist. Es können sich Stellungen mit berechenbaren Wegen zum Matt ergeben. Es gab früher eine Partiepraxis mit Ansagen der Form „Ich setzte Dich in n Zügen matt!".

Ramsey, Frank Plumpton (1923): „Critical Notice of L. Wittgenstein's Tractatus".
In: *Mind* 32 (128), 465–478.
Wittgenstein, Ludwig (1922): *Tractatus Logico-philosophicus*. Translated by C. K. Odgen. With an Introduction by Bertrand Russell. London: Routledge & Kegan Paul.
Wittgenstein, Ludwig (1961): *Tractatus Logico-philosophicus*. Translated by David Pears and Brian McGuinness. London: Routledge. [T]
Wittgenstein, Ludwig (1929): *Some Remarks on Logical Form*. In: *Proceedings of the Aristotelian Society, Supplementary Volume 9, Knowledge, Experience and Realism*, 162–171. [RLF]
Wittgenstein, Ludwig (1984a): *Tractatus logico-philosophicus*, Tagebücher 1914–1916, Philosophische Untersuchungen. Werkausgabe Band 1. Frankfurt am Main: Suhrkamp. [T/PU].
Wittgenstein, Ludwig (1984b): *Bemerkungen über die Grundlagen der Mathematik*. Werkausgabe Band 6. Frankfurt am Main: Suhrkamp. [BGM]
Wittgenstein, Ludwig (1984c): *Wittgenstein und der Wiener Kreis*. Werkausgabe Band 3. Frankfurt am Main: Suhrkamp. [WWK]
Wittgenstein, Ludwig (1984d): *Bemerkungen über die Farben, Über Gewissheit, Zettel, vermischte Bemerkungen. Werkausgabe Band 8*. Herausgegeben von Elizabeth Anscombe und Georg Henrik von Wright. Frankfurt am Main: Suhrkamp. [BF]

Jonathan Rée
Wittgenstein, Kierkegaard and the Significance of Silence

Abstract: When Bertrand Russell and Dora Black passed through Innsbruck in August 1922, they invited Wittgenstein to join them to celebrate the imminent publication of the *Tractatus*. The meeting was a disaster, one of the reasons being that Wittgenstein spoke admiringly of Kierkegaard, while Russell dismissed him as a mystic. Russell obviously spoke from ignorance; but what about Wittgenstein? What did he know of Kierkegaard? In this talk I will suggest that he read some passages that appeared in German translation in the Innsbruck-based review *Der Brenner* from 1914 onwards, including some striking eulogies to silence ('Only someone who knows how to remain essentially silent can speak essentially.') Wittgenstein had once hoped that *Der Brenner* would publish the *Tractatus*, and I intend to explore the possibility that his references to silence at the end of that work were meant to echo Kierkegaard's.

Keywords: Wittgenstein, Kierkegaard, silence

The division between realists and relativists sometimes looks like a matter of style or even personality rather than argument or doctrine. Realists are the kinds of philosophers who think of themselves as in the right: working at the cutting of edge of contemporary research and moving towards some demonstrable truth. Relativists on the other hand are the type who find it hard to make up their minds: they suspect that anyone who disagrees with them is probably right, and their uncertainties multiply as time goes by, leaving them with no alternative but to laugh at themselves or lapse into silence. We could perhaps call the two camps the literalists and the ironists, and we might agree that Aristotle, Aquinas, Descartes, Hegel, Russell and Carnap belong with the literalists, while the ironists would include Socrates, Montaigne, Hume and William James. There are others whom it would be harder to classify however: and Wittgenstein is undoubtedly one of them.

Wittgenstein knew a lot about being clever: when he first came to Cambridge in 1911 he thought of Russell as supremely clever, and wanted to prove that he was just as good – a ask in which he succeeded, at least according to Russell; but back in Cambridge thirty five years later, in 1946, he saw Russell differently: "most disagreeable […] glib and superficial, though, as always, *astonishingly quick*" (Wittgenstein to Moore, 3 December 1946, in McGuinness 2008, 405).

DOI 10.1515/9783110524055-032

It is tempting to say that Wittgenstein started off sharp and clever but got kinder and softer as he grew older: that in the *Tractatus* he tried to lay down the law, insisting on the correctness of his account of propositional form, whereas in his later work – in his classes in Cambridge and in the *Investigations* and other *opera posthuma* – he let a thousand flowers bloom. This version of events seems to be backed up by something Wittgenstein said towards the end of his life: someone reproached him for saying, back in the early 1930s, that there was "no such subject as theology," and he responded by saying: "that is just the sort of stupid remark I would have made in those days" (Drury 1984b, 98).

Wittgenstein was perhaps too ready to accuse himself of stupidity, and as far as I know there is no evidence of him ever saying that there is *no such subject as theology*. But the remark might remind us of something that Wittgenstein was often said to have said: that there is *no such subject as philosophy*. Frank Ramsey, for example, who was one of the first to try to sum up his significance, described Wittgenstein in 1925 as "the greatest living philosopher," and said that his great achievement was to show that there is "no such subject as philosophy" (Ramsey 1931, 287 ff).

Ramsey is, as it happens, just as important as Russell for understanding Wittgenstein's attitude to being in the right. In October 1923, the 20-year old Ramsey came to Puchberg for a couple of weeks to discuss the *Tractatus* with Wittgenstein, and a certain intellectual intimacy grew up between them. But Wittgenstein always found Ramsey hard to like: he was "a very swift & deft critic," with a ruthless intelligence that inspired "a certain awe," but his criticisms were bad criticisms because, as Wittgenstein put it, they "didn't help along but held back." Ramsey suffered, he said, from an incapacity for "genuine enthusiasm, or genuine reverence, which is the same." He was a clever young man, but he had "an ugly mind," or – as Wittgenstein remarked shortly after Ramsey's death in 1930 at the age of 26 – a "bourgeois thinker." Real philosophical work was really "work on oneself," but it required "courage," whereas Ramsey preferred to play a "clever game." (Wittgenstein's diary, 27 April 1930, in Klagge/Nordmann 2003, 14 ff and Wittgenstein 1998, 24 ff)

Of course Ramsey objected to Wittgenstein as much as Wittgenstein objected to him, and what he most disliked about the *Tractatus* was the stuff about mysticism, and what can be shown but not said, and must therefore be passed over in silence. He could quote the concluding sentence with approval – *wovon man nicht sprechen kann, darüber muss man schweigen* – but wanted to leave it at that. "The chief proposition of philosophy is that philosophy is nonsense," he said, and "we must take seriously that it is nonsense, and not pretend, as Wittgenstein does, that it is important nonsense!" (Ramsey 1931, 263)

In a way Ramsey had a point: the *Tractatus* was not the kind of hard-hitting modernist manifesto that he or Russell, or for that matter Schlick and the members of the Vienna Circle, would have liked it to be. In fact it seems to me that the anti-dogmatic themes of peace and reconciliation that became conspicuous in Wittgenstein's later work were already present in the *Tractatus*, particularly in the distinction between what can be said and what can only be shown. But I do not have the courage to enter the battleground where titans clash over the doctrinal unity of Wittgenstein's work; I propose instead to explore the question through the apparently marginal issue of Wittgenstein's attitude to Søren Kierkegaard.

Amongst Wittgenstein's philosophical interlocutors, the first to find out about his interest in Kierkegaard seems to have been Russell, who – after a long interruption caused by the war – met Wittgenstein in The Hague in 1919. The meeting confirmed Russell in his conviction that Wittgenstein suffered from certain 'weaknesses' of character and that they were becoming more pronounced as time went by. He suspected that his experiences at the front, along with his unaccountable interest in Tolstoy and Dostoevsky, were turning him into "a complete mystic," and worst of all, from Russell's point of view, he spoke admiringly of Kierkegaard. Russell himself had no direct knowledge of Kierkegaard's writings – none had been translated into English at the time – but he must have heard enough about his advocacy of 'paradox' and 'irony' and his satires on 'scientific' thinking to be sure they were worthless, and he was sorry to find that such 'foibles', as he called them, had taken hold of the young man he had once seen as his natural successor in scientific philosophy and mathematical logic. (see Russell to Ottoline Morrell, 20 December 1919, in McGuiness 2008, 112n).

In August 1922 Russell arranged to meet Wittgenstein again, in Innsbruck, to celebrate the forthcoming publication of the *Tractatus:* an interesting occasion for them both, since Wittgenstein had despaired of ever seeing his work in print, and without Russell's selfless efforts it might not have appeared at all.[1] Russell was accompanied by his future wife Dora Black, and she remembered that Wittgenstein was distinctly unhappy at the time – 'in an agony of wounded pride'. He managed to insult Russell by telling him, 'with great earnestness', that it was 'better to be good than clever', and he then cut short the visit and returned to Vienna (Russell 1975, 160 and Russell 1969, 101).

---

[1] Russell went to some pains to arrange for the publication of Wittgenstein's essay, first as "Logisch-philosophische Abhandlung", in the *Annalen der Naturphilosophie*, edited by Wilhelm Ostwald, then as *Tractatus Logico-Philosophicus*, with English translation by C.K. Ogden.

Wittgenstein's interest in Kierkegaard was not a passing whim. When he returned to Cambridge in 1929 he marked the event by reading a paper to the atheistical 'Heretics Society'. His argument was that the subject-matter of ethics lay beyond the reach of verbal description – not because it was insignificant or merely 'subjective', but because it was, as he was inclined to put it, 'supernatural'. He admitted that any attempt to explain this quality was liable to lead to some sort of 'nonsense', involving improper use of words like 'safety' or 'existence'. But he suggested that we should embrace such nonsense rather than try to repudiate it: our intimations of ethical absolutes inevitably set us 'running against the walls of our cage', as he put it, or 'against the boundaries of language'. Anyone who wanted to subject these intimations to 'correct logical analysis', he said, or purge them of 'paradox', must have failed to understand their significance. 'These nonsensical expressions were not nonsensical because I had not yet found the correct expressions', he added: "their nonsensicality was their very essence". Devotees of scientific objectivity would be impatient with such indulgence towards nonsense, Wittgenstein said – but "I would not for my life ridicule it" (LE 224ff).[2]

Wittgenstein did not mention Kierkegaard by name, but the echoes are unmistakable, and over the coming years he repeatedly advised his students to read Kierkegaard, describing him as "by far the most profound thinker of the last century," and also "a saint." (see Lee 1999, and Drury 1984a, 87). On one occasion he gave them a sketch of Kierkegaard's approach to morality, with which he clearly sympathized: he explained that, for Kierkegaard, we have to make a choice between alternative ways of living, some based on sensual pleasure, others on ethical renunciation, and still others on religious rejoicing; but these different 'categories of life-style,' as Wittgenstein called them (later translators called them stages – I prefer Wittgenstein's 'categories'), differ so much as to be 'incommensurable', and it follows that if we take our choices seriously we will realize that they issue from unfathomable anguish rather than calm reason or dispassionate observation. If we think we have understood, as Kierkegaard would have said, we show that we have not done anything of the kind. "Mind you I don't believe what Kierkegaard believed", Wittgenstein said, "but of this I am certain, that we are not here in order to have a good time" (Drury 1984a, 87f).

Wittgenstein turned to Kierkegaard for inspiration about the nature of religion as well as ethics: the great thing about Kierkegaard, he said, was that he

---

[2] Shortly after delivering the lecture, Wittgenstein told Friedrich Waismann that "Kierkegaard too saw that there is this running up against something (*dieses Anrennen*) and he referred to it in a fairly similar way (as running up against paradox)" adding that "this running up against the limits of language is *ethics*" (WVC, 68).

never tried to make Christianity 'easy and cozy', and always preferred the raw difficulties of the Bible to the bland reassurances of theology; he had also suggested that no one could 'be' a Christian: the most you could hope for was to 'become' one. 'Just remember what the Old Testament meant to a man like Kierkegaard', as Wittgenstein remarked to a friend. 'I am not a religious man', he added, but 'I cannot help seeing every problem from a religious point of view." (see CV 36; Drury 1984b, 170 and Drury 1984a, 79)

By the 1930s Wittgenstein was good enough at Danish to read Kierkegaard in the original, but his students were not, and when English translations began to appear towards the end of the 1930s, he found them disappointing. They 'completely failed to reproduce the elegance of the Danish', he said, and on top of that they presented Kierkegaard as a Christian propagandist – either a herald of modern Protestantism (as his American advocates tended to think) or a prophet of Catholic revival (which was how he was usually seen in Britain) (Drury 1984a, 88). They lost the laughter of the original – the irony and the literary inventiveness. His writings were becoming 'fashionable', as one observer put it, through being subordinated to a 'personal history' involving a difficult childhood, a crippled body, and an unsatisfactory love affair. The pathos of 'the melancholy Dane' and 'Kierkegaard the cripple' proved attractive to a sentimental public, and provided mainstream philosophers with a pretext for turning their backs: he became the 'unhappy Danish genius' and who suffered from 'sexual disability', and – as the reviewer in *Mind* put it – 'sound philosophy ... is not likely to arise from such unhealthy foundations'.[3]

That leaves the question of what made Kierkegaard precious to Wittgenstein. There is no direct evidence, so far as I know, but there are a couple of clues. The first is that when Russell fretted about Wittgenstein succumbing the influence of Kierkegaard in 1919 and 1922, he was also alarmed by his references to Gotthold Lessing. This suggests that Wittgenstein was referring to an essay in which Kierkegaard commended Lessing for preferring the actuality of a "singular and restless striving after truth" to the prospect of "complete comprehension".[4] If Russell had followed up the reference, he would perhaps have realized that what Witt-

---

3 For the pathos, see *The Journals of Søren Kierkegaard* (Kierkegaard 1938), translated (largely from Haecker's German edition of 1923) by the English Roman Catholic Alexander Dru (close friend to Haecker, who converted to Catholicism in 1921); the stereotype of the 'melancholy Dane' – 'in whom Hamlet was mastered by Christ' – goes back to (Forsyth 1910, ix); see also (Martin 1950), and (Haecker 1948); for 'fashionable', see (Williams 1939, 213); for official disapproval, see reviews by (Laird 1946, 179), (Thomson 1948, 258), and (Paton 1948, 523).
4 Lessing's remarks about striving after truth (see Lessing 1993) were cited by Kierkegaard in "Something about Lessing" (see Kierkegaard 2009, 53 ff).

genstein admired in Kierkegaard was not quite what he had feared. Wittgenstein's Kierkegaard did not offer irrationalist short cuts to transcendent truth, but warnings against over-intellectualizing things: he sought to bring us back to what he called 'existence', or the sphere where we encounter dilemmas about how to live our individual lives, and realize, if we are honest, that no amount of reasoning will ever resolve them – that before we have a moral sense, we need to have a sense of humor.

The second clue is that the German translations in which Wittgenstein encountered Kierkegaard were not the ones that were published in many volumes at the turn of the century, but those that appeared just before the war in *Der Brenner*, a fortnightly avant-garde magazine based at Innsbruck. The editor of *Der Brenner* was an enterprising aristocrat called Ludwig von Ficker, whom Wittgenstein visited in July 1914, presenting him with a large sum of money – 100,000 crowns – to support his journal and his writers. In March of that year *Der Brenner* had announced a program of introducing its readers to unknown aspects of Kierkegaard, and it began in May with a translation of philosophical humoresque called *Johannes Climacus*, or *De omnibus dubitandum est*, which satirised the solemn pretentions of university philosophy. In July – just before Wittgenstein's meeting with von Ficker – it moved on to another essay, or rather a selection from it, to which it gave the title *Kritik der Gegenwart*. Kierkegaard appeared here as vehement critic of the 'the present age' – the age of 'the now-time' (*Nutiden*), or 'the age of publicity', were we are tormented by 'journalists' and overawed by 'the phantom of *the public*'. The 'public' had become the measure of all things: 'nothing ever happens, but there is instant publicity about it', he said, and the old-fashioned virtue of keeping silent was being swept away in a flood of idle talk, gossip, and empty chatter.

What is empty chatter? (*snakken* in Danish, *Schwätzen* in the German translation). It is the result of doing away with the passionate distinction between speaking and keeping silent. Only someone who knows how to remain essentially silent can speak essentially – or act essentially. (*Nur der, der wesentlich schweigen kann, kann wesentlich reden.*) Silence (*Verschwiegenheit*) is inwardness, but empty chatter interrupts essential speaking. ... Those who can speak essentially, because they know how to keep silent, will not speak about a profuse variety of things ... they will know the time to speak, and the time to keep silent.

Kierkegaard had written his polemic in 1846, but readers of *Der Brenner* in 1914 scarcely needed to be prompted to apply it to the terrible garrulousness of their own time: the epigrammatic satirist Karl Kraus, who was a hero to Wittgenstein at the time, took up Kierkegaard's praise of silence, and it is reasonable to assume that it impressed Wittgenstein too.⁵

Six years later, after his service in the Austrian army and incarceration in a prisoner of war camp in Austria, Wittgenstein had completed the manuscript that would become the *Tractatus*, and in 1920 he offered it to von Ficker with the assurance that it was "strictly philosophical and at the same time literary, without a trace of waffle" ("streng philosophisch und zugleich literarisch, es wird aber doch nicht darin geschwefelt"), and thus entirely in keeping with the modern artistic spirit of *Der Brenner*. It could be published under the stylish but enigmatic title *Der Satz*, it would not take up more than sixty pages, and it was suited to publication in parts over several issues, before being reissued as an independent pamphlet – just as Brenner was now doing with some of its Kierkegaard translations (Kierkegaard 1922). "The book's point is an ethical one" he explained.

Many people are just *waffling* about ethics at the moment, but I believe that I have sorted it all out in my book, by keeping silent about it. (*Was viele heute schwefeln, habe ich in meinem Buch festgelegt, indem ich darüber schweige.*)

Wittgenstein was annoyed when von Ficker hesitated, but when he realized the financial difficulties facing *Der Brenner* he accepted defeat, despairing of ever finding a publisher (see Wittgenstein to Russell, 12 June 1919 in McGuinness 2008, 92f and Wittgenstein to von Ficker, in Wittgenstein 1969, 32ff).⁶

I can't help thinking that the reception of Wittgenstein would have been very different if his masterpiece had appeared first not as *Logisch-philosophische Abhandlung* in 1921, or as *Tractatus Logico-Philosophicus* in 1922, but as *Der Satz* in 1920 – first as a serial in *Der Brenner* then as a Brenner-pamphlet – in other words, in the same format as Kierkegaard's reflections on *Schwätzen*, on *der*,

---

5 Extracts of (Kierkegaard 1846) were chosen and translated by Theodor Haecker as "Kritik der Gegenwart" and were published as (Kierkegaard 1914).The English version given here largely follows that of (Dru 1940) which is itself based on Haecker's translation and follows his selections; Karl Kraus would always praise *Der Brenner* for introducing Kierkegaard's polemic against 'the Press' to German readers, see for instance (Kraus 1916).

6 In the letter to von Ficker Wittgenstein writes: "Es wird nämlich das Ethische durch mein Buch gleichsam von Innen her begrenzt; und ich bin überzeugt, daß es, *streng*, *nur* so zu begrenzen ist. Kurz, ich glaube: Alles das, was *viele* heute *schwefeln*, habe ich in meinem Buch festgelegt, indem ich darüber schweige." (Note the play on *schwefeln*, to waffle, and *schweigen*, to keep silent.) See also (von Wright 1971). Cut from the indented quote: "I once meant to include in the preface a sentence which [...] may perhaps provide you with a key to the work. I was going to say that my work is composed of two parts: what is presented here, and then everything that I have *not* written. And it is precisely this second part that is the important one. The ethical is delimited through my book, from the inside as it were, and I am convinced that it cannot be *rigorously* delimited in *any* other way."

der wesentlich schweigen kann, and on *Verschwiegenheit.* Who knows? *Wovon man nicht sprechen kann, darüber muss man lächeln.*

References

Dru, Alexander (1940): *The Present Age.* London, Oxford University Press.
Drury, Maurice O'Connor (1984a): "Some Notes on Conversations with Wittgenstein". In: Rhees, Rush (ed.): *Recollections of Wittgenstein.* Oxford, Oxford University Press, 76–96.
Drury, Maurice O'Connor (1984b): "Conversations with Wittgenstein". In: Rhees, Rush (ed.): *Recollections of Wittgenstein.* Oxford, Oxford University Press, 97–171.
Forsyth, Peter Taylor (1910): *The Work of Christ.* London: Hodder and Stoughton.
Haecker, Theodor (1948): *Kierkegaard the Cripple.* Translated by Alexander Dru. London: Harvill Press.
Kierkegaard, Søren (1846): *En literair Anmeldelse.* Kjøbenhavn: C.A. Reitzel.
Kierkegaard, Søren (1914): "Kritik der Gegenwart". In: *Der Brenner. Halbmonatsschrift für Kunst und Kultur* 4 (19), 815–849.
Kierkegaard, Søren (1922): *Kritik der Gegenwart.* Translated with an afterword by Theodor Haecker. Innsbruck: Brenner Verlag.
Kierkegaard, Søren (1938): *The Journals of Søren Kierkegaard.* Translated by Alexander Dru. London: Oxford University Press.
Kierkegaard, Søren (2009): *Concluding Unscientific Postscript to the Philosophical Crumbs.* Edited and translated by Alastair Hannay. Cambridge: Cambridge University Press.
Klagge, James; Nordmann, Alfred (eds.) (2003): *Ludwig Wittgenstein: Public and Private Occasions.* Lanham: Rowman and Littlefield, 14–17.
Kraus, Karl (1916): "Kierkegaard und die Journalisten". In: *Die Fackel.* April 1916, 19–21.
Laird, John (1946): "Book Review of *Either/Or*". In: *Mind* 55, 179.
Lee, Desmond (1999): "Wittgenstein 1929–31". In: Flowers, F.A.; Ground, Ian (eds.): *Portraits of Wittgenstein.* London: Bloomsbury, 476–485.
Lessing, Gotthold Ephraim (1993): *Werke 1774–1778. Volume 9: Werke und Briefe.* Edited by Wilfried Barner. Frankfurt am Main: Deutscher Klassiker Verlag.
Martin, Harold Victor (1950): *Kierkegaard, The Melancholy Dane.* London: Epworth Press.
McGuinness, Brian (ed.) (2008): *Wittgenstein in Cambridge: Letters and Documents 1911–1951.* Oxford: Blackwell.
Paton, Herbert James (1948): "Book Review of *Le Vrai Visage de Kierkegaard*". In: *Mind* 57, 522.
Ramsey, Frank Plumpton (1931): *The Foundations of Mathematics and other Logical Essays.* Edited by R.B. Braithwaite. London: Kegan Paul.
Russell, Bertrand (1969): *Autobiography.* London: George Allen and Unwin.
Russell, Dora (1975): *The Tamarisk Tree.* London: Elek/Pemberton.
Thomson, Arthur (1948): "Review". In: *Mind* 57, 258.
von Wright, Georg Henrik (1971): "Historical introduction". In: Wittgenstein, Ludwig: *Prototractatus.* Edited by Brian McGuinness, Tauno Nyburg, and Georg Henrik von Wright, with a translation by David Pears and Brian McGuinness, an historical introduction by Georg Henrik von Wright, 7–25.

Williams, Charles (1939): *The Descent of the Dove*. London: Longmans.
Wittgenstein, Ludwig (1967): *Wittgenstein und der Wiener Kreis*, edited by Brian McGuinness. Oxford: Blackwell. [WVC]
Wittgenstein, Ludwig (1969): *Briefe an Ludwig von Ficker*. Edited by Georg Henrik von Wright. Salzburg: Müller.
Wittgenstein, Ludwig (1998): *Culture and Value*. Edited by Georg Henrik von Wright, translated by Peter Winch. Oxford: Basil Blackwell. [CV]
Wittgenstein, Ludwig (2014): *Lecture on Ethics*. Edited by Eduardo Zamuner, Ermelinda Valentina Di Lascio and D.K. Levy. Oxford: Wiley Blackwell. [LE]

Anja Weiberg
Zweifeln *können* und zweifeln *wollen*: Über Gewissheit § 217 – 231

Abstract: In the paragraphs 217–231 several issues are raised that are relevant to Wittgenstein's reflections in *On Certainty*, for example the differentiations between "error" and "mental disturbance" and between "knowledge" and "absence of doubt", the significance of memory in relation to knowledge claims, and the interweaving of different certainties on the one hand and of speaking and acting on the other hand. The variety of subjects in these paragraphs is bound together by the question posed in OC 221: "Can I be in doubt at *will?*" Some remarks suggest that we *cannot have* some doubts, whereas other passages imply that we *just don't have* these doubts. With recourse to Wittgenstein's distinction between factual and conceptual investigations I try to clarify these ostensibly conflicting remarks.

Keywords: Doubt, knowledge, craziness, certainty, conceptual investigation

1 Einleitung

In *Über Gewissheit* ist immer wieder die Rede davon, dass man etwas nicht könne oder dass es zumindest fraglich sei, ob man es könne: Manche Dinge scheint man nicht „sinnvoll bezweifeln" zu können (ÜG §2), bezüglich mancher Behauptungen glaubt man, sich nicht irren zu können (z. B. ÜG §15); manches kann man sich vorstellen, manches andere dagegen nicht (z. B. ÜG §106), für manche Überzeugungen kann man Gründe nennen, für andere nicht (z. B. ÜG §111), usw., usw.

Wittgensteinlesern sagt man damit natürlich nichts Neues, und diese Rede von „können" oder „nicht können" kommt darüber hinaus so häufig vor, dass sie kaum übersehen werden kann. Allerdings stellt sich die Frage, welchen Status diese Aussagen im Rahmen der Wittgensteinschen Argumentation haben, was er mit ihnen verdeutlichen will – und je nach Interpretation können sich hierauf verschiedene Antworten ergeben (diese werden im letzten Teil des Aufsatzes vorgestellt). Zur näheren Untersuchung dieses Status habe ich beispielhaft die Paragraphen 217–231 ausgewählt, in denen besonders häufig und mit großer Emphase ausgesagt wird, man *könne* gewisse Zweifel nicht haben bzw. man *könne* gewisse Annahmen nicht in Betracht ziehen.

Diese Häufigkeit ergibt sich daraus, dass in einem großen Teil dieser Paragraphen Reaktionen beschrieben werden auf den Versuch, einzelne unserer Gewissheiten zu erschüttern. In §217 wird hierzu das Beispiel gewählt, dass jemand die Zuverlässigkeit unserer Rechnungen anzweifelt, ab §218 geht es dann vor allem um jenes Beispiel, dass jemand unsere Überzeugung, nie in der Stratosphäre gewesen zu sein, in Zweifel zu ziehen versucht, und in §231 schließlich werden wir mit jemandem konfrontiert, der Zweifel an der Existenz der Erde vor 100 Jahren bekundet.

Ich werde nun zunächst in den folgenden beiden Abschnitten die Beispiele und Wittgensteins Erläuterungen dazu etwas näher betrachten, danach die Frage aus §221 aufgreifen, ob es in unserer Macht steht, an allem zu zweifeln, woran wir zweifeln wollen, und in den letzten beiden Teilen zu zeigen versuchen, dass die Rede vom „nicht können" viel von ihrer Dramatik verliert, wenn man sie als Element einer begrifflichen Untersuchung versteht.

2 Zwei Versuche der Erschütterung von Gewissheiten

2.1 Zuverlässigkeit beziehungsweise Unsicherheit unserer Rechnungen

In §217, in dem Wittgenstein die Unterscheidung zwischen der Klassifizierung einer Aussage als Irrtum oder aber als Geistesstörung behandelt, wird ein Beispiel herangezogen, dem Wittgenstein sich zuletzt in §212 gewidmet hatte, nämlich der Überzeugung, „z. B. eine Rechnung unter gewissen Umständen als genügend kontrolliert" anzusehen (ÜG §212). Zu den „gewissen Umständen" gehört beispielsweise, dass wir das Rechnen erlernt haben, dass wir weder betrunken noch übermüdet sind und dass es sich um eine nicht übermäßig komplizierte Rechnung handelt, deren Ergebnis wir zwei- oder dreimal kontrolliert haben. In Fällen wie diesen werden die meisten von uns die Kontrolle als ausreichend und das Ergebnis entsprechend als hinreichend geprüft und zuverlässig ansehen. Wittgenstein weist in diesem Paragraphen allerdings selbst darauf hin, dass man allfällige Rechtfertigungen dieses Vorgehens durchaus in Frage stellen kann, etwa durch den Hinweis, dass Erfahrung uns auch täuschen kann. Seines Erachtens ist hier eine jener Stellen erreicht, an denen es gilt, die Suche nach Rechtfertigungen zu beenden und sich stattdessen auf die (grammatische) Feststellung zu beschränken, „daß wir *so* rechnen" (ÜG §212), was schlicht bedeutet, dass wir[1] bestimmte Handlungsweisen „rechnen" nennen.

---

1 Hier stellt sich natürlich die Frage, wer „wir" sind. Im Fall des Rechnens würden die meisten von

Nun begegnen wir in § 217 aber jemandem, der weder die üblichen Rechtfertigungen akzeptiert noch an Wittgensteins Verfahren interessiert ist, sich auf die Beschreibung unserer Praktiken des Rechnens zu beschränken. Dieser Mensch stellt unsere Sicherheit beim Rechnen *grundsätzlich* in Frage, indem er die Ansicht äußert, dass wir uns eben nie ganz sicher sein könnten, dass es immer möglich sei, dass wir uns verrechnet haben, dass derjenige, der die Möglichkeit von Fehlern ausschließen wolle, sich allenfalls anmaßend verhalte usw.

Wittgenstein hält hier fest, dass wir diesen Menschen vermutlich für verrückt halten würden. Fraglich erscheint es ihm hingegen, ob wir im Fall dieser Ansicht von einem Irrtum sprechen würden: „Aber können wir sagen, er sei im Irrtum? Reagiert er nicht einfach anders: wir verlassen uns darauf, er nicht; wir sind sicher, er nicht." (ÜG § 217)

Von einem Irrtum würden wir etwa dann sprechen, wenn sich die Rechenresultate eines Menschen gelegentlich von den unseren unterscheiden, abgesehen davon aber sein Umgang mit den Resultaten der gleiche wäre. Dieser Mensch hingegen unterscheidet sich von uns gerade dadurch, dass er einen anderen Umgang mit den gleichen Rechnungsresultaten hat: „wir verlassen uns darauf, er nicht; wir sind sicher, er nicht." Obwohl dieser Mensch also die gleichen Rechentechniken verwendet wie wir, teilt er über weite Strecken unsere Praxis des Rechnens nicht, denn diese Praxis beinhaltet nicht nur die Techniken des Rechnens selbst, sondern ebenso die Überzeugung von der Zuverlässigkeit unserer Rechnungen und daher auch die zweifelsfreie Anwendung der Rechenergebnisse in verschiedensten Kontexten. Im Fall solcher Abweichungen würden wir entsprechend nicht von einem Irrtum sprechen, sondern von einer gewissen Verrücktheit.

In Bezug auf die Thematik dieses Aufsatzes lässt sich festhalten, dass die Frage des „Könnens" sich in diesem Paragraphen auf die Frage bezieht, wie wir das Sprechen und Handeln dieses Menschen begrifflich klassifizieren und in der Folge mit ihm umgehen würden.

---

uns wahrscheinlich nicht „wir Österreicher" oder „wir Europäer" zur Antwort geben, sondern an ein weit umfassenderes „wir" denken, allerdings eventuell in Betracht ziehen, dass es einige wenige Völker geben mag, die unsere Rechenpraxis nicht teilen. Beim Beispiel des Aufenthalts in der Stratosphäre hingegen hätte die Antwort zu Wittgensteins Zeit eventuell „alle wissenschaftlich entwickelten Kulturen" gelautet. Was schließlich das Beispiel der Existenz der Erde vor 100 Jahren betrifft, könnten einige sogar versucht sein, das „wir" mittels „alle vernünftigen Menschen" zu umschreiben. Da bereits diese drei Beispiele zeigen, dass es kein einheitliches „wir" zu geben scheint, auf das man sich im Rahmen aller Gewissheiten einigen kann, verzichte ich darauf, einen Versuch der näheren Bestimmung zu geben.

2.2 Aufenthalt in der Stratosphäre

Ab § 218 wird vermehrt die Unterscheidung von Wissen und Zweifellosigkeit thematisiert, und in diesem Kontext wird auch das nächste Beispiel präsentiert: „Kann ich für einen Augenblick glauben, ich sei je in der Stratosphäre gewesen? Nein. So weiß ich das Gegenteil, – wie Moore?" (ÜG §218).[2] An einen potentiellen Aufenthalt in der Stratosphäre könne man, so Wittgenstein, nicht einmal „für einen Augenblick glauben". Damit ist aber die eigene Überzeugung natürlich noch in keiner Weise als Wissen (im Sinne einer gerechtfertigten wahren Überzeugung) ausgewiesen, denn es wurden bisher ja keinerlei Gründe genannt. In der Aussage von § 218 wird entsprechend nicht mehr und nicht weniger als Zweifellosigkeit artikuliert, indem festgehalten wird, dass eine Hinterfragung der Überzeugung in keiner Weise in Betracht zu ziehen ist.

Unter den Vorzeichen dieser Unterscheidungen werden wir in der Folge noch etwas ausführlicher in die Perspektive jenes Menschen versetzt, der mit einem Angriff auf eine seiner Grundüberzeugungen konfrontiert wird. Zunächst wird auf die Vernünftigkeit rekurriert: So heißt es in §219, dass an dieser Überzeugung „für mich, als vernünftigen Menschen, kein Zweifel […] bestehen (kann)" (ÜG §219). Wer eine solche Möglichkeit auch nur kurz in Betracht zieht, ist nicht etwa als besonders kreativ, visionär oder fortschrittlich in seiner Denkweise anzusehen, sondern bezeugt durch den Zweifel an dieser Unmöglichkeit gerade seine Irrationalität bzw. Verrücktheit. „Der vernünftige Mensch hat gewisse Zweifel nicht." (ÜG § 220) Die jeweilige Klassifizierung einer Aussage als Wissen, Irrtum oder Verrücktheit steht also nicht zuletzt in engem Zusammenhang mit unserem Begriff der Vernünftigkeit, wobei Wittgenstein entgegen der vor allem in der Philosophie üblichen Betonung des *Hinterfragens* im Zusammenhang mit dem Begriff der Vernunft bzw. des Vernunftgebrauchs hier darauf verweist, dass der *Ausschluss bestimmter Zweifel* eine ebenso relevante Facette der Bedeutung von „Vernünftigkeit" bzw. „Vernunftgebrauch" ausmacht.

Wenn wir solche Aussagen wie die in den § 218 – 220 genannten in einem Gespräch mit einer Person äußern, die Zweifel an unseren diesbezüglichen Überzeugungen hat, wird sie sich allerdings damit voraussichtlich nicht zufriedengeben und weiter nachhaken. Denn wie gesagt artikulieren alle bisherigen Äußerungen ja nur Zurückweisung und benennen keinerlei Gründe für diese Ablehnung. Vor diesem Hintergrund muss man sich eventuell fragen, woher diese

---

[2] Hierbei handelt es sich um eine Abwandlung des Mooreschen Satzes „Seit seiner Geburt ist [mein Körper] mit der Oberfläche der Erde in Berührung oder doch nicht weit von ihr entfernt gewesen." (Moore 1969, 114).

Sicherheit kommt und ob die brüske Zurückweisung nicht allenfalls Ähnlichkeiten zu jenem Verhalten hat, das man sonst nur Verrückten zuschreibt: „Könnte ich nicht eben verrückt sein und das nicht bezweifeln, was ich unbedingt bezweifeln sollte." (ÜG §223) Damit wird aber plötzlich die Frage virulent, ob die so dezidierte und vehemente Ablehnung einer Zweifelsmöglichkeit nicht schlicht Resultat einer kurz- oder längerfristigen geistigen Umnachtung ist.

Unter solch bedrohlichen Vorzeichen bietet es sich an, die Bekundung der Zweifelsunmöglichkeit gegen einen Wissensanspruch einzutauschen in dem Sinn, dass man versucht, eine Begründung für die postulierte Unmöglichkeit eines Zweifels zu nennen: „„Ich *weiß*, daß es nie geschehen ist, denn wäre es geschehen, so hätte ich es unmöglich vergessen können.'" (ÜG §224) Dieser Begründungsversuch stellt einen ganz offensichtlich recht verzweifelten Versuch dar: Denn wenn jemand sagt, dass er etwas unmöglich bezweifeln kann, dann meint er (in diesem Fall) etwas ganz anderes als die Unmöglichkeit des Vergessens von bestimmten Ereignissen; er meint die Unmöglichkeit des Ereignisses selbst. Ein Satz wie dieser („ich hätte es nicht vergessen können") kann entsprechend in keiner Weise einen Beweis für den ersten Satz („ich war nie in der Stratosphäre") darstellen, er vergrößert die Sicherheit bezüglich der Wahrheit des ersten Satzes in keiner Weise.

Entsprechend leicht fällt der Einwand gegen diese versuchte Begründung: „Aber angenommen, es wäre geschehen, so hättest du's eben doch vergessen. Und wie weißt du, daß du's unmöglich hättest vergessen können? Nicht bloß aus früherer Erfahrung?" (ÜG §224) Das Rekurrieren auf frühere Erfahrungen mag zwar eine gewisse Sicherheit vermitteln, kann aber nicht begründen, dass mich mein Gedächtnis in diesem konkreten Fall nicht vielleicht doch täuscht.[3]

---

3 Es mag an dieser Stelle etwas überraschen, dass Wittgenstein mit einem so schwachen Argument aufwartet („ich hätte es nicht vergessen können") und nicht auf bestimmte physikalische Sätze verweist. Dies hatte er allerdings in § 108 bereits getan: „„Aber gibt es denn da keine objektive Wahrheit? Ist es nicht wahr, oder aber falsch, daß jemand auf dem Mond war?' Wenn wir in unserm System denken, so ist es gewiß, daß kein Mensch je auf dem Mond war. Nicht nur ist uns so etwas nie im Ernst von vernünftigen Leuten berichtet worden, sondern unser ganzes System der Physik verbietet uns, es zu glauben. Denn dies verlangt Antworten auf die Fragen: ‚Wie hat er die Schwerkraft überwunden?', ‚Wie konnte er ohne Atmosphäre leben?' und tausend andere, die nicht zu beantworten wären. Wie aber, wenn uns statt allen diesen Antworten entgegnet würde: ‚Wir wissen nicht, *wie* man auf den Mond kommt, aber die dorthin kommen, erkennen sofort, daß sie dort sind; und auch du kannst ja nicht alles erklären.' Von Einem, der dies sagte, würden wir uns geistig sehr entfernt fühlen." (ÜG § 108) Somit könnte man die Bemerkungen in § 224 gewissermaßen als Fortführung dieses Gesprächs lesen. Die auf den wissenschaftlichen Überzeugungen des eigenen Bezugssystems beruhenden Argumente wurden bereits vorgebracht, vom Gesprächspartner aber als irrelevant abgetan. Und wenn ich ein solches Gespräch dennoch

In diesen Paragraphen ist es wohl vor allem die Emphase der Rede von der Unmöglichkeit und einem „nicht können", die Wittgenstein zum einen besonders herausstreichen, zum anderen aber auch in ihrer mangelnden Überzeugungskraft für Andersdenkende deutlich machen möchte.

3 Wittgensteins Erläuterungen zu diesen Reaktionen

Wittgenstein beschreibt in den §217 bis 231 nicht nur unsere wahrscheinlichen Reaktionen im Fall des Angriffs auf eine unsere Gewissheiten, sondern erläutert diese auch. Hierbei werden vor allem drei zentrale Aspekte der Überlegungen in *Über Gewissheit* angesprochen:

3.1 Ein „Nest von Sätzen"

In §225 weist er darauf hin, dass bei diesen Beispielen nicht nur eine einzelne Überzeugung angegriffen wird (wie es etwa der Fall wäre, wenn man über das Datum eines bestimmten geschichtlichen Ereignisses streitet; vgl. ÜG §66). Vielmehr ist ein Satz wie „ich war nie in der Stratosphäre" (zu Wittgensteins Zeit) mit einem „Nest von Sätzen" (ÜG §225) verknüpft, mit vielen anderen – durchaus verschiedenartigen – Sätzen, von deren Wahrheit man ebenso zweifelsfrei überzeugt ist: „Kein vernünftiger Mensch hat je so etwas behauptet", „Menschen können die Schwerkraft nicht überwinden", „Menschen vergessen einschneidende Erlebnisse nicht" usw.

3.2 Sätze des Weltbilds

In §231 macht Wittgenstein anhand des dritten Beispiels deutlich, dass es im Fall mancher Überzeugungen nicht nur darum geht, dass von dem Zweifel an einer bestimmten Überzeugung auch verschiedene andere Überzeugungen betroffen wären, sondern dass durch manche Zweifel darüber hinaus unsere Untersuchungsmethoden fragwürdig oder gar hinfällig werden: „Wenn einer bezweifelte, ob die Erde vor 100 Jahren existiert hat, so verstünde ich das darum nicht, weil ich

---

weiterführe, dann erscheint es nicht mehr weiter verwunderlich, dass ich solche Aussagen tätige wie jene, dass ich einen Aufenthalt in der Stratosphäre keinesfalls vergessen haben könnte.

nicht wüßte, was dieser noch als Evidenz gelten ließe, und was nicht." (ÜG §231) Wenn angezweifelt wird, ob die Erde vor 100 Jahren existiert hat, werden dadurch nicht nur zugleich verschiedenste biologische, psychologische, geologische, physikalische und geschichtliche Fakten zur Illusion erklärt, sondern auch die mit den jeweiligen Wissenschaftsdisziplinen verknüpften Forschungsmethoden (da diese die Existenz der Erde seit langer Zeit voraussetzen). Wir haben es also mit dem Zweifel an einem Satz zu tun, der als „Grundsatz des Forschens und Handelns" (ÜG §87) verwendet und daher nicht selbst zum Gegenstand der Forschung wird (vgl. ÜG §88), vielmehr Teil eines Weltbilds ist (vgl. etwa ÜG §94f).

3.3 Verwobenheit von Sprache und Handeln

In §229 macht Wittgenstein auf den für ihn so wichtigen Aspekt der Verwobenheit von Sprache und Handeln aufmerksam: „Unsre Rede erhält durch unsre übrigen Handlungen ihren Sinn." (ÜG §229) In Bezug auf unsere Beispiele bedeutet das folgendes: Es ist eine Sache, darüber *nachzudenken*, ob unser Rechensystem wirklich so zuverlässig ist, wie wir glauben; ob wir nicht z. B. gelegentlich von Außerirdischen zu fremden Planeten entführt werden und danach unser Gedächtnis gelöscht wird; ob diese Außerirdischen uns nicht vielleicht sogar nur vorgaukeln, dass wir auf einem Planeten namens Erde leben usw. Eine ganz andere Sache aber ist es – zumindest aus unserer Perspektive –, solche Überlegungen mit unserem täglichen Handeln zu verknüpfen. Hierbei wird wohlgemerkt nicht behauptet, dass eine solche Verknüpfung per se unmöglich wäre; es wird schlicht festgehalten, dass manche Sätze keine Verankerung in unserem Sprachhandeln *haben*. Und daher stellt sich die Frage nach ihrem Sinn. Bei Sätzen wie z. B. „Vielleicht vergessen wir ja alle bestimmte einschneidende Erlebnisse, daher könnte das für unmöglich Gehaltene eventuell doch möglich sein" (vgl. ÜG §228) oder „vielleicht hat die Erde vor 100 Jahren nicht existiert" stellen unsere Sprachspiele keine Regeln des Gebrauchs zur Verfügung; wir wissen nicht, was wir mit derartigen Annahmen oder Zweifeln *anfangen* sollen, wie wir sie mit anderen Annahmen und Handlungen verknüpfen können. Und solange wir das nicht wissen oder können, fehlt diesen Annahmen bzw. Zweifeln auch der Sinn.

4 Eine seltsame Frage

In §221 stellt Wittgenstein recht unvermittelt die Frage: „Kann ich zweifeln, woran ich zweifeln *will?*" (ÜG §221) Diese Frage kann einem recht seltsam erscheinen – und zwar je nach Perspektive auf je verschiedene Art und Weise seltsam:

1. Die erste Perspektive ist die jener Menschen, die Wittgensteins Spätphilosophie nicht kennen oder nicht mögen. Werden diese mit der Überlegung konfrontiert, dass es eventuell nicht völlig in ihrer Macht stehe, woran sie zweifeln, könnten sie beispielsweise folgendermaßen reagieren: Es mag nicht in meiner Macht stehen, alles zu *wissen*, was ich wissen will (weil ich etwa nicht die Zeit habe, mir in verschiedensten Bereichen Kenntnisse zu erwerben); vielleicht steht es auch nicht in meiner Macht, alles zu *glauben*, was ich glauben will (so könnte ich mir z. B. wünschen, an die Existenz Gottes zu glauben und es dennoch nicht zustande bringen), aber wieso sollte es nicht in meiner Macht stehen zu *zweifeln*, woran ich zweifeln will? Wo sollte hier die Grenze zwischen „wollen" und „können" angesiedelt sein und wodurch wird sie gezogen? Darüber hinaus würden sie vielleicht noch darauf hinweisen, dass es doch gerade ein besonderes Kennzeichen des Menschen sei, aufgrund seiner Vernunft an allem zweifeln zu können.

Hierauf könnte man mit Wittgenstein eine ganze Menge antworten. Ich greife nur zwei dieser Antworten heraus, die im Zusammenhang mit der hier behandelten Paragraphenreihe relevant sind:

Zunächst kann man entgegnen, dass das, was als sinnvoller Zweifel gilt, durch die Regeln des jeweiligen Sprachspiels festgelegt ist und es daher auch nicht völlig meiner subjektiven Willkür unterliegt, woran ich zweifle („zweifle" in dem Sinn, dass ich nicht nur – ohne Zusammenhang mit meinem Leben – etwas sage, sondern sich dieser Zweifel auch in meinem Sprachhandeln manifestiert).

Des Weiteren könnte man mit Wittgenstein darauf aufmerksam machen, dass unsere Verwendung der Begriffe der Vernunft bzw. der Vernünftigkeit ja bei weitem nicht nur mit dem Hinterfragen bzw. Überprüfen von Sachverhalten verknüpft ist. In §219 lesen wir: „Es kann für mich, als vernünftigen Menschen, kein Zweifel darüber bestehen. – Das ist es eben. – "Wie bereits angedeutet, wird damit deutlich, dass unsere Verwendung des Vernunftbegriffs nicht nur auf die Tätigkeit des Bezweifelns abzielt, sondern der Ausschluss bestimmter Zweifel eine ebenso relevante Facette der Bedeutung von „Vernünftigkeit" bzw. „Vernunftgebrauch" ausmacht.

2. Die zweite Perspektive ist jene der Wittgensteinianer (einer alles andere als homogenen Gruppe): Zumindest in manchen Lesarten von *Über Gewissheit* mag die in §221 aufgeworfene Frage ebenfalls seltsam erscheinen. Während es Lesern der ersten Kategorie aber überraschend erscheinen mag, dass sie nicht eindeutig mit „ja" beantwortet wird („natürlich kann ich zweifeln, woran ich zweifeln will"), wird sie von einem Teil der Leser der zweiten Kategorie eher als unnötige, bestenfalls rein rhetorische Frage aufgefasst werden. Dies gilt vor allem für Interpretationen, in denen das Augenmerk besonders auf Wittgensteins Bemerkungen über das Weltbild bzw. Bezugssystem gelegt wird. Man denke etwa an Bemer-

kungen, in denen davon die Rede ist, dass manche Sätze kollektiv „dem Zweifel entzogen" sind (ÜG §87), zu jenem „harten Gestein" gehören, „das keiner [...] Änderung unterliegt" (ÜG §99) und „solchermaßen in allen meinen *Fragen und Antworten* verankert (sind), daß ich nicht an sie rühren kann" (ÜG §103). In solchen Interpretationen wird tendenziell die weltbildabhängige Unmöglichkeit bestimmter Zweifel als ausgemacht angesehen. Meines Erachtens geht eine solche Lesart allerdings damit einher, Wittgensteins Kennzeichnung seiner eigenen Untersuchungen als begriffliche Untersuchungen nicht ernst genug zu nehmen, worauf ich nun im letzten Teil dieses Beitrags noch näher eingehen werde.

5 Begriffliche Untersuchungen

Dass Wittgenstein begriffliche Untersuchungen durchführt, wird niemand bezweifeln, weist er doch schließlich in seinen späteren Schriften selbst oft genug darauf hin; auch in *Über Gewissheit* gibt es zumindest einige Bemerkungen, die daran erinnern, wenn Wittgenstein etwa darauf aufmerksam macht, dass er „eine logische, nicht eine psychologische (Bemerkung)" mache (ÜG §447), wenn er von der „Grammatik" bestimmter Ausdrücke schreibt (z. B. ÜG §313) oder sich die Frage stellt: „Was soll der Logiker hier sagen?" (ÜG §68)[4]

Weniger sicher erscheint mir, ob diese Einigkeit auch hinsichtlich der Fragen besteht, welche Art von Untersuchung hier genau gemeint ist und (vor allem) welche Art von Ergebnissen sie liefern soll. Gerade die Rede vom „nicht können" stellt in diesem Zusammenhang ein geeignetes Beispiel dar, um Wittgensteins Art der Untersuchungen etwas näher zu betrachten.

Wie schon gesagt verführen besonders die Aussagen über das Weltbild bzw. Bezugssystem dazu, die Bemerkungen, dass man etwas nicht bezweifeln oder nicht in Betracht ziehen könne, als Behauptungen über eine tatsächliche Unmöglichkeit zu verstehen. Entsprechend müsste man dann aber davon ausgehen, dass Wittgenstein uns hier vorrangig mitteilen will, er könne (in Übereinstimmung mit den anderen Mitgliedern seiner Gesellschaft bzw. sogar allen „vernünftigen" Menschen) weder an der Zuverlässigkeit unserer Rechnungen zweifeln noch daran, nie in der Stratosphäre gewesen zu sein, außergewöhnliche Erlebnisse zu vergessen, geschweige denn, dass er die Existenz der Erde vor 100 Jahren in Zweifel ziehen könne. Wäre dem so, dann wäre der Unterschied der Vorgehensweise zwischen Moore und Wittgenstein allerdings nicht allzu groß: Wo der eine Aussagen auflistet, die er zu wissen behauptet (vgl. Moore 1969 114–116), listet der

---

4 „Und zur Logik gehört alles, was ein Sprachspiel beschreibt." (ÜG § 56)

andere unhinterfragte Gewissheiten auf. Darüber hinaus gäbe es eine große Einigkeit zwischen den beiden 1. im Gestus der Bekundung ihrer Sicherheit und 2. bezüglich der Behauptung der Unbezweifelbarkeit der jeweiligen Aussagen, auch wenn Wittgenstein im Unterschied zu Moore die Weltbild- und Sprachspielabhängigkeit herausstreicht.

In dieser Lesart würde man also die Rede von einem „nicht können" bei Wittgenstein als die Behauptung einer *faktischen* Unmöglichkeit bestimmter Zweifel lesen. Wer das tut, übersieht aber meines Erachtens u. a. jene Stellen, die auf die Methode der begrifflichen Untersuchung hinweisen. Stellen wie jene z. B., an denen Wittgenstein deutlich macht, dass wir bei manchen Aussagen und Verhaltensweisen unsicher wären, ob wir diese noch „ein Zweifeln nennen sollten" (ÜG § 255). Nun ist es aber etwas völlig anderes zu sagen, dass man bestimmte Zweifel nicht *haben könne*, als zu sagen, dass wir im Fall von bestimmten Äußerungen und Handlungen nicht mehr wissen, ob wir diese noch ein Zweifeln *nennen* sollen. Ersteres hat den emphatischen Charakter der Behauptung einer faktischen Notwendigkeit bzw. Unmöglichkeit; Zweiteres stellt eine Erläuterung unserer Verwendung des Begriffs des Zweifels und damit einen weit weniger dramatischen Verweis auf Regeln des Sprachspiels dar, die manche Zweifelsbekundungen als sinnvoll erscheinen lassen, andere aber nicht.

Liest man die Paragraphen 217 bis 231 vor dem Hintergrund dieser Überlegungen nochmals durch, kann man festhalten, dass hier anhand einer Reihe von Beispielen verschiedene Begriffe hinsichtlich ihrer Verwendung untersucht werden, nämlich jene des Irrtums, der Verrücktheit, des Zweifels, des Wissens und der Vernünftigkeit. Und Aussagen wie „ich kann hieran nicht zweifeln", „kein vernünftiger Mensch kann daran zweifeln" oder „ich kann diese Annahme keiner ernsthaften Betrachtung würdigen" fungieren entsprechend als Beschreibung eines Verhaltens im Fall der versuchten Erschütterung einer Gewissheit, die uns dabei behilflich sein sollen, die Verwendung dieser Begriffe besser zu verstehen. Wenn ich beispielsweise im Fall desjenigen, der die Zuverlässigkeit unserer Rechnungen anzweifelt, meine, nicht sagen zu können, er sei im Irrtum, dann zeigt mir das etwas über den Gebrauch des Begriffs des Irrtums.[5] Wenn ich hinsichtlich allfälliger Reisen in die Stratosphäre sage, dass ich eine solche Möglichkeit auf keinen Fall in Betracht ziehen kann, dann beschreibt dies die Verwendung dessen, was als „sinnvoller Zweifel" bzw. „vernünftiger Zweifel" bezeichnet wird. Und wenn ich schließlich in diesem Zusammenhang vom „ver-

---

5 In ÜG § 71 beispielsweise wird das Charakteristikum der begrifflichen Untersuchung deutlicher: „Wenn mein Freund sich eines Tages einbildete, seit langem da und da gelebt zu haben, etc. etc., so würde ich das keinen Irrtum nennen, sondern eine, vielleicht vorübergehende, Geistesstörung."

nünftigen Menschen" spreche, dann wird hierdurch die Verwendung der Begriffe der Vernunft, der Vernünftigkeit bzw. des Vernunftgebrauchs erläutert.

Nach dieser Lesart sind also Aussagen wie „Es kann für mich, als vernünftigen Menschen kein Zweifel darüber bestehen" (ÜG § 219) oder „Ich kann, daß ich nie in der Stratosphäre war, unmöglich bezweifeln" (ÜG § 222), die so apodiktisch klingen, nicht als *sachliche Behauptungen*, sondern als *grammatische Bemerkungen* zu verstehen. Eine logische Unmöglichkeit ist keine sachliche Unmöglichkeit, und eine logische Unmöglichkeit in Wittgensteins Verständnis besagt nicht mehr und nicht weniger, als dass unsere Sprachspiele uns im Fall von manchen Zweifelsäußerungen nicht mit Regeln des Gebrauchs versehen.

Wer dagegen eine faktische Unmöglichkeit behaupten wollen würde, müsste sich entweder auf (postulierte) Tatsachen in der Welt berufen (wie z. B. auf Ergebnisse wissenschaftlicher Studien über das Alter der Erde) oder auf bestimmte mentale Zustände (seien es bestimmte Denkgesetze oder ein subjektives Sicherheitsgefühl). Letzterem widmet sich Wittgenstein in § 230, in dem er im Zusammenhang mit der „Aussage ‚ich *weiß* ...'" festhält: „Denn uns handelt sich's nicht um Vorgänge oder Zustände des Geistes." Hieraus kann man ableiten, dass die Untersuchung der Begriffe des Wissens, des Zweifelns o. ä. bei Wittgenstein nicht auf mentale Zustände oder Vorgänge abzielt, sondern auf unser Sprachhandeln im Rahmen von Sprachspielen. Daher gilt es auch nicht, sich „nach innen" zu wenden, um herauszufinden, ob man etwas weiß oder ob man etwas bezweifeln kann oder nicht, sondern es gilt die Regeln der Sprachspiele und unser Handeln zu betrachten, die aufzeigen, wann und unter welchen Bedingungen etwas als legitimer Wissensanspruch akzeptiert wird, wann ein Zweifel ausgeschlossen wird usw. In diesen Sprachspielen wird auch entschieden, ob etwas klassifiziert wird als „kein Wissen, sondern falsch" oder „kein Wissen, sondern unsinnig", wobei es hier nicht das *eine* Kriterium gibt, sondern sprachspielabhängig verschiedene.

Ob sich jemand nun auf Tatsachen in der Außenwelt oder auf mentale Zustände beruft – in beiden Fällen würde es sich um sachliche Untersuchungen handeln. Wittgenstein aber nimmt begriffliche Untersuchungen vor, und diese können (und sollen) nicht zu Aussagen über faktische Notwendigkeit oder Unmöglichkeit führen, sondern nur beschreiben. Wenn Wittgenstein also die Frage stellt, ob ich tatsächlich an allem zweifeln *kann*, an dem ich zweifeln *will*, dann wird hiermit nicht etwa die Frage nach einem tatsächlichen Können bzw. Wollen gestellt, sondern die Frage danach, was innerhalb bestimmter Sprachspiele als sinnvoller Zweifel gilt und was nicht; danach, was wir noch „zweifeln" nennen würden und was nicht.

Mit diesen Überlegungen soll wohlgemerkt nicht der Eindruck erweckt werden, es sei nach Wittgenstein ein leichtes, Dinge aller Art zu bezweifeln, da es sich ja ohnehin nur um eine Frage der Sprache handle (man ändere einfach die

Sprache, und schon wird bisher Unmögliches möglich). Dem steht zunächst vor allem sein Verweis auf die Verwobenheit von Sprache und Handeln entgegen. Darüber hinaus hält er auch explizit fest, dass die Regeln des Sprachspiels nicht unserer subjektiven Willkür unterliegen: Nachdem er in §316 erneut den Zweifel an der Existenz der Erde vor 100 Jahren thematisiert hatte, lesen wir in §317: „Dieser Zweifel gehört nicht zu den Zweifeln unser[e]s Spiels. (Nicht aber, als ob wir uns dieses Spiel aussuchten!)" Wittgenstein scheint also vorrangig betonen zu wollen, dass seine Untersuchungen gerade nicht darauf abzielen, äußere tatsachenbezogene und / oder innere Gegebenheiten zu entdecken, die einen Zweifel verunmöglichen. Vielmehr gilt seine Aufmerksamkeit den Sprachspielen, die die sinnvolle oder unsinnige Verwendung des Begriffs des Zweifels festlegen. Wenn man in diesem Zusammenhang des Weiteren Wittgensteins Hinweis berücksichtigt, dass Sprachspiele im Laufe der Zeit Veränderungen unterliegen (vgl. ÜG §256), dann ist der Emphase der faktischen Unmöglichkeit und Unausweichlichkeit jedenfalls der Boden entzogen.

Die Erinnerung an diese methodische Unterscheidung scheint mir vor allem deshalb wichtig zu sein, da sie so schwer konsequent umzusetzen ist; meines Erachtens liegt hierin sogar die größte Schwierigkeit der späteren Wittgensteinschen Philosophie: ständig auf der Hut zu sein, nicht doch wieder eine Vermischung von sachlicher und begrifflicher Untersuchung vorzunehmen. Dass diese Schwierigkeit nicht nur für die Interpreten, sondern durchaus auch für Wittgenstein selbst besteht, zeigt sich u. a. in einer Bemerkung aus den *Zetteln:*

> Statt „man kann nicht", sage: „es gibt in diesem Spiel nicht". Statt „man kann im Damespiel nicht rochieren" – „es gibt im Damespiel kein Rochieren"; statt „ich kann meine Empfindung nicht vorzeigen" – „es gibt in der Verwendung des Worts ‚Empfindung' kein Vorzeigen dessen, was man hat"; statt „man kann nicht alle Kardinalzahlen aufzählen" – „es gibt hier kein Aufzählen aller Glieder". (Z 134)

Diese Bemerkung kann man als Ermahnung Wittgensteins an sich selbst lesen, von dem methodischen Weg der Beschreibung von Sprachspielen nicht abzuweichen.

Da in den unredigierten Bemerkungen von *Über Gewissheit* aber bei weitem nicht so oft darauf hingewiesen wird, dass diese als begriffliche Bemerkungen zu lesen sind, wie dies etwa in den *Philosophischen Untersuchungen* geschieht, kann es relativ leicht geschehen, bei der Lektüre die entsprechenden Hinweise zu überlesen bzw. nicht ernst genug zu nehmen und in der Folge beispielsweise davon auszugehen, dass Wittgenstein zur Zeit der Abfassung von *Über Gewissheit* eine in mancher Hinsicht substantiell andere Philosophie vertrete als zur Zeit des Verfassens der *Philosophischen Untersuchungen*. Meines Erachtens hingegen besteht Wittgensteins Anliegen nach wie vor (ausschließlich) in begrifflichen Untersuchungen – der Unterschied liegt lediglich darin, dass sich seine Aufmerksamkeit nun auf andere, bisher nicht vorrangig behandelte Begriffe und damit verwobene Handlungsweisen konzentriert, wie die Begriffe des Wissens und des Irrtums, des Zweifels und der Zweifellosigkeit, der Vernünftigkeit und der Verrücktheit sowie andere damit verwandte Begriffe.

Danksagung: Danke an Karoline Paier, Katharina Sodoma und die weiteren Mitglieder des Wittgenstein-Lesekreises für Anregungen und kritische Anmerkungen.

Literaturverzeichnis

Moore, George Edward (1969): „Eine Verteidigung des Common Sense". In: Moore, George Edward: *Eine Verteidigung des Common Sense. Fünf Aufsätze aus den Jahren 1903–1941.* Mit einer Einleitung von Harald Delius. Aus dem Englischen von Eberhard Bubser. Frankfurt am Main: Suhrkamp, 113–151.

Wittgenstein, Ludwig (1984): *Bemerkungen über die Farben, Über Gewissheit, Zettel, vermischte Bemerkungen. Werkausgabe Band 8.* Herausgegeben von Elizabeth Anscombe und Georg Henrik von Wright. Frankfurt am Main: Suhrkamp. [ÜG/Z]

Nick Zangwill
Rules and Privacy: Remarks on *Philosophical Investigations* § 202

Abstract: Negative conclusions about private language are widely supposed to derive from Ludwig Wittgenstein's discussion of rule-following and the impossibility of following a rule privately. I argue that this is incorrect as an interpretation as well as being implausible on independent grounds.

Keywords: Wittgenstein, rule following, private language

> § 202. And hence also "obeying a rule" is a practice. And to *think* one is obeying a rule is not to obey a rule. Hence it is not possible to obey a rule "privately": otherwise thinking one was obeying a rule would bethe same thing as obeying it.

1 Language and Rules

In the *Philosophical Investigations* § 202, Wittgenstein clearly says that it is not possible to follow a *rule* privately. Does this not commit him to thinking, as the standard interpretation has it, that private language is impossible? (Saul Kripke thought so in Kripke 1982) Many commentators say that the 'real private language argument' occurs in section § 202, not later. So it is all over for private language in § 202. But this is only so given the assumption of a strong connection between language and rules. This we should examine.

Does language always involve rules? What does Wittgenstein think is the connection between language and rules? My view is that neither is obvious. If language *does* always involve rules, it quickly yields an anti-private language view, as follows:
1. It must be possible to follow rules.
2. We cannot follow rules privately.
3. Language is constituted by rules.
4. We cannot privately follow the rules that constitute a private language.
5. So language cannot be private.

But a premise here is that we understand language by following rules. And this is not obvious.

Of course in some minimal sense Noam Chomsky has shown that there are grammatical rules that we all follow in understanding language (Chomsky 1966).

But these general grammatical rules falls far short of what words mean (for example that 'dog' means dogs). So the necessity for Chomskyan grammatical rules that are common between very different languages does not mean that following such grammatical rules could constitute understanding the meanings of words.

2 Rules, Public and Private

What is a rule? What does Wittgenstein means by a "rule", or by "Regel" in German? A rule, at its most basic, is at least a two-term conditional relation. The antecedent is a fact, the consequent is either a prescription, or an act with a deontic property (Boghossian 2012): it says "If X then do Y"; or "If X then you ought to do Y". Or the consequent could be a negative prescription or negative deontic fact.

What is 'privacy'? The issues over private *languages*, private mental *states* and private *rules* seem all to be distinct. I shall return to make various distinctions in the next section, but for now I want to characterize a minimal sense of 'privacy' as characterizing mental phenomena that have no observable ('outer') causes or effects by which another person may know them.

How then does Wittgenstein get to his negative conclusion in §202 about the impossibility of following a rule privately?

Let us put *language* to one side for a while and just focus on rules: why should we agree with Wittgenstein that *rules* cannot be obeyed privately. In particular, why can there not be *private rules?* Wittgenstein might be right in §202 that *public* rules, interpersonal ones, cannot be obeyed *privately*. But if there are private rules then surely *those* rules *can* be obeyed privately.

Now in many cases—of the sort Wittgenstein discusses in the earlier part of the *Philosophical Investigations*—one person follows *another person's* acts or marks on paper or one person is following some previously established social regularity (PI §28, §48, §143, §145, §149, §156, §162 and §172). And it seems to be on the basis of these examples that Wittgenstein concludes that one cannot follow a rule privately, in §202. But why should all rules be of that public interpersonal kind? Wittgenstein seems to work with a one-sided diet of examples! If I have counted right, only one example is not interpersonal: one might follow the rule of copying one's own previous marks (PI §175). And even in that case, the marks one has to copy are physical perceivable marks, and the marks made after copying are also physical perceivable marks.

The more radical question is: why cannot some rules just concern what happens in our minds, where there is no behavioural manifestation of following the rule? For example, suppose someone makes a rule: think of an elephant if you think of a kangaroo. That is different from the rule: think of sheep whenever you think of an octopus. Or, what about the rule: if you think of a number, divide it by 2? These are private rules, it seems. Surely I can obey such rules privately, and no one can know that I have obeyed the rule, unless I tell them. It is a private rule, and such a rule is to be obeyed privately. Contra §202, thinking I have followed such a rule is not at all the same thing as actually following the rule. These are distinct despite the lack of public, interpersonal check. Thus what many see as a central claim of the whole *Philosophical Investigations* seems plain implausible.

This point can be strengthened. The examples of private rules that I have just given are of trivial rules. But many private rules, at least if rules are norms, are not trivial rules (like the rule to think of an elephant if you think of a kangaroo). Consider reasoning—practical or theoretical. It is not implausible that reasoning just is conducting our minds in accordance with private rules, rules that say what is rational. Some philosophers are attracted to the idea of the normativity of the mental. Such an idea says that there are rational norms binding us in virtue of the propositional attitudes that we have. (See for example Zangwill 2005, 2010.) And in reasoning we respect these norms. Furthermore, many people think that understanding logical constants is constituted by following the introduction and elimination rules that characterize the constants (Wittgenstein 2001, section 2; Gentzen 1935; Strawson 1952, 56; Kneale 1956; Hacking 1979). But the norms of rationality or logic are private rules, which we typically follow privately. Obeying such a rule is a private mental act of forming beliefs or intentions. These rules are not interpersonal rules, and they can be, and often they are, obeyed privately. I suppose they could in principle be obeyed with some outer behavioural manifestation such that another person could know the mental act expected by perceiving the outer behavior of the person following the rules. Perhaps some people's eyebrow twitches when they perform modus ponens and their nose twitches when they perform disjunctive syllogism. But in many cases, most cases, there is no outer perceivable manifestation of the rule-following that constitutes rationality or logical reasoning.

Since there is reasoning, there had better be such private rules—not just possibly but actually. And we had better actually follow them at least for much of the time.

The idea of such rules has a good philosophical pedigree. Consider what Descartes called 'Rules for the direction of the mind'? And following Descartes, Kant also commits us to rules of theoretical and practical rationality. They are central to his *Critique of Pure Reason*. For both these thinkers, without private rules and private rule-following, there would be no knowledge and no reasoning and no logic.

It seems clear that these are private rules that can be obeyed privately. This just looks like an oversight on Wittgenstein's part—a large over-sight. What *can* Wittgenstein have been thinking?! Granted—it is not possible to obey a *public* rule privately! But there is nothing inherently public about rules. What Wittgenstein says seems not just implausible as a generalization, but deeply wrong when we consider private rules that are not odd or frivolous, but the rules of rationality or logic that are central to our being who and what we are.

Someone might reply—contrary to Descartes and Kant—that there are *norms* of rationality, but not rules. However, even if the norms of rationality are not rules, surely we can upgrade them into rules, as Descartes did, and as do many decision theorists and Baysean epistemologists. Then these norms can become private rules, even though the principles themselves are merely norms for most of us. Having upgraded, it is possible to obey these rules privately. I can just reason well or badly, according to the internalized rules, without making a public song and dance about it. Of course, when I come to act on such reasoning, in the sense of making bodily movements not merely mental acts, then others can come to a justified view about my reasoning processes. But we might or might not make bodily movements as a result of reasoning. That is, having recognized the norms, we may articulate them in rules, which are private rules, followed privately. Why not?

3 'Rules' and 'Privacy'

Or is there a stronger sense of 'privacy' in which rules of rationality or logic are not 'private' in that stronger sense? Let us look more closely at what 'privacy' might mean in the context of rule-following.

'Privacy' can be characterized metaphysically, in terms of the nature of something, or epistemologically, in terms of what we can know about it. I prefer a metaphysical characterization that has epistemological consequences. Something is not metaphysically 'private' if and only if it has physical causes or effects and (here comes the epistemology) it is knowable by observing those causes and effects. If a thing is private, another person cannot know or understand the thing since the only way it can we know is by observing its causes and effects. This unknowability may be taken in a weak sense, where we add the rider "unless the person tells them". Or this may be taken in a strong sense in which another person cannot know and understand the thing and there is no possible way for the first person to communicate it to a second person. Thus, there are weak and strong senses of 'privacy'.

A *sensation* or *feeling* may clearly be private in a weak sense (see PI §272). We may not tell another person what our sensations or feelings are, for example. But it may also be *impossible* for someone to know what experience is being had if they have never had a similar experience. That is a stronger kind of privacy. Such privacy is relative to observers. For example, perhaps it is impossible for those who have given birth to explain what it is like to those who have not given birth. So both weak and strong senses of privacy apply to some sensations and other feeling states. Many sensations and feelings, of course, are not weakly or strongly private; but many others are weakly or strongly private.

In the case of private *language*, there is a strong epistemological notion of privacy in play according to which another person cannot, in principle, understand a private language. However, in the case of private language too, the modal definition cannot be fundamental. It must hold in virtue of the nature of the states in question. It is not possible to know the language *because* it is about private states. The emphasis placed on possibility in discussions of private language is puzzling. Possibilities are usually not interesting in philosophy apart from what they tell us about actuality. But this has not been heeded in discussions of private language, where the possibility takes centre stage. We need to ask: in virtue of what would it not be possible for another to understand a private language? I propose, we answer: in virtue of a) being about a felt state with no standard observable causes, behavioural effects or manifestation; b) there is no actual language for those states is in place; and c) the introduced meanings are fixed to the felt state introspectively. These are *why* it is not possible for another to grasp the meaning.

What is the analogue of privacy for mental states and private language for rule-following? Perhaps this: rule-following that is private has no causes, or behavioural effects or manifestation by which another person can know whether or not the rule has been followed. What would be the weak/strong distinction here? A strong sense of 'privacy' would be that another person could not in principle know whether or not the rule has been followed, and the rule cannot even be explained to others. Moreover, it would be in virtue of what it is to follow a private rule that another person cannot know in principle whether the rule has been followed or even understand it?

Let us now recall the distinction between private and public rules? The idea of following a *public* rule inwardly, and independent of observable manifestations does disappear, since the rule dictates observable actions. What on earth could be a private act of following a public rule? So public rules cannot even be weakly private.

But what of private rules? When we follow either trivial private rules or rules of reasoning or logic, obedience is a mental act that may or may not have a public observable manifestation. So private rule-following is not impossible, unlike public rule-following. Private rules may be weakly private. Private rules may be followed privately and no one else may know. But what of the strong sense of privacy, where it is impossible to know if the rule has been followed, and we cannot even explain the rule to others? Surely we can know whether others have reasoned well and logically, and we can explain the rules of rationality and logic to others. So in that sense, these rules are not strongly private. The idea that such rules are unintelligible to anyone else is unintelligible. So private rules are weakly but not strongly private.

4 Public Rules

Is there any reason to think that a strong and not a weak notion of 'privacy' is in question in §202 (unlike PI §258)? In the last section, we found it hard to believe that a strong sense of privacy is in question when Wittgenstein denies that we cannot obey a rule privately. So suppose that Wittgenstein is saying that we cannot follow a rule, any rule, privately, in a *weak* sense. But as we also saw, that seems like an implausible claim since it runs up against the existence of trivial mental rules and rules of reasoning and logic.

The only hypothesis I can think of is that by "rules", or "Regeln", Wittgenstein just *means* public rules. (I put aside the completely implausible hypothesis that Wittgenstein is some kind of behaviourist.) This hypothesis would explain why at §202 Wittgenstein suddenly makes what otherwise seems to be a complete non-sequitur, to conclude that one cannot obey rules privately, on the basis of considering only examples of public rules and no private rules. *Of course*, there must be observable behavioral manifestations of following public rules. Consider obeying an order, a public order, such as 'Right turn!'. It cannot be obeyed inwardly. A soldier on parade cannot obey the order to turn right inwardly or privately, just in his mind by mentally turning right. He must actually turn right. Otherwise there would be no distinction between actually mentally turning right and seeming to oneself that one is turning right. That seems to be what Wittgenstein is thinking. If this is right, rules just are by definition public rules, for Wittgenstein.

But this is strange. Consider orders. I can also obey the order: think of a number between one and ten. That order must be obeyed privately. What goes for orders goes for rules. There are public rules and private rules, just as there are public and private orders. And following and obedience should be public in one case and private in the other.

We can argue as follows. If something can be ordered, it can be made into a rule. I can be ordered to think thoughts or imagine things with no behavioural expression. Therefore there can be private rules. A real example: people in religious orders are ordered not to think lustful thoughts. Such rules are private rules, and obedience to them is private. Obedience is inner obedience. God sees: no one else does.

But if 'rules', for Wittgenstein, are by definition public rules, as on my hypothesis, then it would mean that not all norms correspond to rules. A rule is more than an ought. And while all rules are normative, in a very general sense, not all norms are rules. Hence, it could be, given what rules are, that rules are necessarily public rules, and following a rule depends on a public practice or custom, which is publically observable, as Wittgenstein says at §202. That makes some sense of the fact that we can raise the puzzling issue of whether a public rule could be obeyed only once or whether there must be a wider social practice with regular obedience (PI §199 and §200). Such a practice or institutional theory of *public* rules seems plausible. But if so, what about *norms* of reasoning? It may be suggested that there are norms of reasoning but no rules of reasoning, in this sense. If so, Wittgenstein's argument has less reach than it has been taken to have. If we give Wittgenstein a special limited public sense of 'rule', which he needs for §202 to be remotely plausible, then the implications of what he says are far less than have been supposed. In particular, there are no negative implications for private language, or private mental states. (Certainly there is no basis for attributing any critique of 'Cartesianism'.)

I distinguished public and private rules. Perhaps rules of rationality are not really rules but norms. Still, it seems that there are private rules, such as think of this if you think of that, or rules of rational reasoning. Even if Wittgenstein has in mind public rules, these private rules seem possible and Wittgenstein seems wrong. But if Wittgenstein accepts private rules of rationality, but just does not call them 'rules,' then what he says remains interesting, but it does not have as its concern deep matters of what it is to think or to reason.

5 Private Languages

Let us return to language, which is where we came in. Would Wittgenstein classify apparent 'rules' for private languages as 'rules' in the sense he is interested in (PI §258)? I am not sure. Wittgenstein is interested in how the connection between words and private mental states is to be set up. Whether this counts as a rule is less interesting. Rule or not, can it be done? 'Yes', I say. And I say that Wittgenstein also says 'Yes', although I shall not argue this here. (See Zangwill 2011, and in preparation.)

On the general issue of the connection between rules and language, we should probably see Wittgenstein as denying a general connection between the two. Language does not depend on rules and many rules do not concern language. (Chomskyan grammatical rules would not have concerned him.)

Language generally does not depend on rules for Wittgenstein. Mauro Englemann has pointed out that this was one of Piero Sraffa's important contributions to the *Philosophical Investigations* (Englemann 2011, 2013). Nevertheless, when a new language is introduced, self-consciously, as opposed to culturally evolving, it needs to be set up by means of an explicit rule. A private language is such an introduced language (see PI §258). So corresponding to a private language, there are rules, since the introduced language is set up by rules concerning inner ostensive definition. These rules may be private rules, not quite in the sense in which there are rules of rationality, but in the sense of linking a sensation type with the deployment of a linguistic physical type (a word). Where both antecedent and consequent of the rule are public, a rule is public. Where both antecedent and consequent are private, the rule is private. Where one is public and the other is private, I shall say that the rule is a 'hybrid' rule. Where one of the two items connected in the rule is a symbol—a sound or mark—which is to be deployed in some way given a mental state that one has, it is a hybrid rule, since it connects something private with something public—the perceivable symbol. By contrast, purely private rules connect two private items. Private language rules are hybrid rules. Most linguistic rules are public since the word (as physical token) is one public thing and the reality that corresponds to that public thing is another public thing, property or fact. There is no reason to think that there cannot be hybrid rules when one of the items in the rule is public and the other is private. Such a rule might be: if you see a red post box, then think of a sheep. Or consider the children's party song: "If you're happy and you know it clap your hands". The first is a public-private rule and the second is a private-public rule. What of private language? This seems to fall into the same category as: "If you're happy and you know it clap your hands". It is the hybrid rule: if, after associating an outer symbol "S" with an inner sensation type, you introspectively reidentify another instantiation of that inner sensation type, then utter the same word "S". No problem!

In my view, Wittgenstein nowhere commits himself against the possibility of such stipulated rules for private language. The question of private *rules* is a different one, and he does deny their possibility in §202. But, as we saw, he means something special by a 'rule'. And once rules and language are disconnected, there are no implications for private language from what he says about private rules. What the inner ostension achieves is not a rule in Wittgenstein's public sense—instead it is a mini intra-personal institution or linguistic habit, which can be stable enough, given a reliable memory, to set up meaningful private language, one in which a terms refers to private mental states or events. But this language is useless in the sense that it cannot be used for interpersonal communication. (Wittgenstein distinguishes use from meaning at PI §43.) The introduced private language is useless but it is not meaningless.

Acknowledgements: Thanks for written comments from Mauro Engelmann and conversations with Dawn Wilson.

References

Boghossian, Paul (2012): "What is Inference?". In: *Philosophical Studies* 169 (1), 1–18
Chomsky, Noam (1966): *Cartesian Linguistics: A Chapter in the History of Rationalist Thought*. New York: Harper & Row.
Englemann, Mauro Luiz (2011): "Wittgenstein's 'Most Fruitful Idea' and Sraffa". In: *Philosophical Investigations* 26, 155–178.
Englemann, Mauro Luiz (2013): *Wittgenstein's Philosophical Development: Phenomenology, Grammar, Method, and the Anthropological View*, London: Palgrave.
Gentzen, Gerhard (1935): "Untersuchungen über das logische Schliessen". In: *Mathematische Zeitschrift* 39: 176–210, 405–431.
Hacking, Ian (1979): "What is Logic?". In: *Journal of Philosophy* LXXVI, 285–319.
Kneale, William (1956): "The Province of Logic.". In: Lewis, H.D. (ed.): *Contemporary British Philosophy*, London: Allen and Unwin, 237–261.
Kripke, Saul (1982): *Wittgenstein on Rules and Private Language*. Cambridge, Mass: Harvard University Press.
Strawson, Peter (1952): *Introduction to Logical Theory*. London: Methuen.
Wittgenstein, Ludwig (2008): *Philosophical Investigations*. Oxford: Blackwell. [PI]
Wittgenstein, Ludwig (2001): *Wittgenstein's Lectures Cambridge 1932–35. From the Notes of Alice Ambrose and Margaret Macdonald*. Edited by Alice Ambrose. Blackwell: Oxford.
Zangwill, Nick (2005): "The Normativity of the Mental". In: *Philosophical Explorations* 8, 1–20.
Zangwill, Nick (2010): "Normativity and the Metaphysics of Mind", In: *Australasian Journal of Philosophy* 88 (1), 21–39.
Zangwill, Nick (2011): "Music, Essential Metaphor and Private Language", In: *American Philosophical Quarterly* 48 (1), 1–16.
Zangwill, Nick (in preparation): "Wittgenstein on Private Language".

Index of names

Abrams, M. H.   175
Ackoff, R.   96
Adamowsky, N.   53, 55
Al-Farabi   359
Alberti, L. B.   167f., 170–172, 175, 177, 180
Alexander of Aphrodisias   359, 363
Al-Kindi   359, 363
Alrøe, H. F.   96
Andreas of Neufchateau   358, 363
Angier, N.   88
Anscombe, E.   205, 313, 324–326, 388
Aristotle / Aristoteles   4, 7, 15, 130, 132, 136f., 143, 145–148, 274, 317ff., 324f., 358f., 362f., 425
Ashby, R.   74
Austin, W. J.   154

Baecker, D.   46f., 53
Baier, A.   339–345, 347, 349
Baker, G.   389
Barad, K.   153, 162
Barkin, J. S.   263
Barnes, B.   386, 394
Bateson, G.   45–48, 74
Beck, U.   138, 145f.
Beer, S.   85
Bellarmine, R.   120, 209–211
Benedict XVI   301, 312
Bennett, M.   399
Berger, P.   74, 256, 263
Bergmann, G.   131
Berkeley, G.   3, 13f., 130, 215
Bernstein, R.   187f.
Biermann, F.   158
Bird, A.   215, 224
Black, D.   425, 427
Blumer, N. 74
Boghossian, P.   31, 119, 122, 203f., 207–214, 221, 269, 272, 301, 309, 450
Bolz, N.   52
Bourdieu, P.   105
Brentano, F.   129, 133–136
Brink, D.   334
Brockman, J.   98

Budd, M.   389
Butler, J.   280
Büttner, F.   172

Campbell, K.   274
Carnap, R.   79, 242f., 273f., 425
Carpendale, J.   227
Cerbone, D. R.   390
Chakrabarty, D.   154
Chisholm, R.   280
Chomsky, N.   449
Chrudzimski, A.   133
Cicero   262
Collingwood, R.   198
Conway, G. D.   230
Cook, J.   402
Copp, D.   371
Crotty, M.   264
Crutzen, P.   153
Cyzman, M.   17f., 65

Daiber, J.   266
Damásio, A.   12
Darwall, S.   369, 371
David, M.   117
Davidson, D.   61f., 189f., 272, 360
Dellwing, M.   19
Descartes, R.   129–133, 244f., 399, 425, 451f.
Dilman, I.   215, 220
Dilthey, W.   108
Dipert, R. R.   266
Dretske, F.   269, 276
Dru, A.   429, 431
Drury, M.   426, 428f.
Duckworth, D.   194, 198
Dumouchel, P.   255
Dürer, A.   169, 173, 179–181
Durkheim, E.   382
Dux, G.   356

Edwards, L. E.   154–156
Elder-Vaas, D.   263
Engel, M. S.   21f.

Engel, P. 118
Englemann, M. L. 456
Enoch, D. 371

Falk, G. 74
Falkinger, N. 361
Felsch, P. 73 f.
Fish, S. 20
Fitzgerald, K. 255, 265
Flusser, V. 51 f.
Fode, K. 95
Forsyth, P. T. 429
Foucault, M. 17, 20, 103 f., 109–111, 114
Fox Keller, E. 138 f.
Freeland, C. A. 7
Friedman, M. 390
Fuchs, P. 160

Gadamer, H. G. 112
Gadenne, V. 31, 37, 97
Gatens, M. 7
Gehlen, A. 261
Gell-Mann, M. 161
Gentzen, G. 451
Georges, K. E. 261
Gerbner, G. 55
Gergen, K. 36–38, 74, 255
Giddens, A. 6
Gilbert, M. 261, 266, 374
Glanville, R. 73 f., 76, 78–80, 85, 93
Goethe, J. W. 251, 415, 417, 420
Goffman, E. 45–49
Goldman, A. 123, 127
Goodman, N. 32, 195, 198, 213
Green, B. 159
Grimm, J. & W. 45
Gross, L. 55
Grossmann, R. 131, 133
Gyatso, L. 198

Haag, G. 95
Habermas, J. 48, 336
Hacker, P. 389, 397, 399–401
Hacking, I. 104, 221, 256, 273, 451
Haecker, T. 429, 431
Hahn, S. 360
Hammond, J. 319

Handel, W. H. 48
Haraway, D. 154
Hardin, R. 342
Harman, G. 307, 328
Harper, W. 319
Hartmann, M. 340, 343
Hasebrink, U. 50
Havelock, E. 10 f.
Hawley, K. 342
Heidegger, M. 107, 137, 143 f., 146–148
Hertzberg, L. 340 f.
Hobbes, T. 262
Houkes, W. 266
Huemer, M. 121
Huizinga, J. 47
Hume, D. 14, 207, 244, 303, 353–355, 359, 402, 406, 425
Husserl, E. 110, 138
Hutcheson, F. 318

Ingham, G. 293

James, W. 274 f., 417, 425
Johnson, E. 155
Johnston, P. 389
Jolie, A. 137, 145
Johnson, M. 3

Kaati, G. 141
Kant, I. 5, 7, 35, 68, 104, 107, 110, 129, 133, 143, 194, 217, 226, 241, 247, 272 f., 275, 359, 451 f.
Karger, E. 277
Kauffman, L. H. 92
Kendel, E. R. 87
Kermani, N. 74
Kierkegaard, S. 425, 427–431
Klagge, J. 426
Klemke, E. D. 381
Kluge, F. 168
Kneale, W. 451
Konersmann, R. 158
Koppe, F. 360
Kraus, K. 430 f.
Krausz, M. 187, 190, 327, 334
Kripke, S. 449
Krippendorf, K. 53

Kroes, P. 266
Kügler, P. 65, 269
Kuhn, T. 68, 192, 215–220, 222–226, 230

Lagerspetz, O. 340f.
Laird, J. 429
Lakoff, G. 3
Latour, B. 7, 18
Lauer, R. H. 48
Lee, D. 428
Lem, S. 3, 9–11, 14
Lemke, T. 142–144
Lessing, G. E. 429
Lewis, C. 227
Lewis, D. 125, 271
Lewis, S. L. 156
Liessmann, K. P. 56
Lochhead, J. 160
Luckmann, T. 74, 256, 263
Luhmann, N. 74, 153, 160, 341
Lüscher, K. 170
Luscombe, D. E. 358
Lux, V. 142
Lynch, M. 118
Lyons, D. 332

Mackie, J. L. 328
Madell, G. 280
Mäkela, P. 347
Malcolm, N. 217
Marconi, D. 62f.
Margolis, J. 187, 189
Martin, H. V. 429
Maturana, H. 20, 73, 85
Mazouz, N. 360
McAndrews, J. 156
McClintock, B. 139f.
McFarlane, J. 117
McGinn, C. 389
McGuinness, B. 418, 425, 431
McLeod, C. 339
Mead, G. H. 233, 236–239
Mead, M. 77
Merricks, T. 283
Merrill, G. 271
Merten, K. 50, 53
Miebach, B. 48

Miller, D. 33
Mitterer, J. 6, 17–21, 23–27, 46, 53f., 59, 63f., 67, 70–72, 162, 183, 201, 233–235, 239, 252
Moore, A. 154
Moore, G. E. 205, 225, 241–243, 250, 353f., 425, 438, 443f.
Moore, J. W. 154
Moyal-Sharrock, D. 215, 217, 219, 226f., 230, 402, 404
Müller, A. 75–78
Müller, K. H. 98
Müller, U. 95
Musgrave, A. 40

Nagel, T. 216, 243–246, 250, 335f.
Neges, K. 18, 66, 71
Neuberger, O. 47
Nickles, T. 224
Nida-Rümelin, M. 199, 279f., 285, 287f., 290f.
Noe, E. 96
Nordmann, A. 426
Nozick, R. 285
Nüsslein-Vollhard, C. 139f.

Ockham, W. 274–277, 353, 358f.
Olson, D. R. 10
Ong, W. J. 11
Ontrup, R. 50

Pałubicka, A. 6
Parfit, D. 280, 283, 335f.
Park, A. 137
Pask, G. 74, 78, 85, 93, 95
Pasnau, R. 275
Paton, H. J. 429
Patton, M. Q. 263, 265
Paus-Haase, I. 50
Perelman, C. 17, 21
Perler, D. 269, 276
Peter Aureol / Petrus Aureoli 277
Pfaller, R. 56
Piaget, J. 73, 75, 78–80, 92
Pias, C. 79
Pickering, N. 255

Plato 3, 10–12, 14, 60, 241, 248–250, 270
Popper, K. 193, 225
Preston, B. 231, 266
Psillos, S. 394
Putnam, H. 32, 112, 126, 131, 134, 195, 217, 225, 269–273

Quine, W. V. O. 97, 269, 272, 275

Ramsey, F. P. 409f., 418, 426f.
Rawls, J. 353, 359, 371
Read, R. 224f.
Redpath, T. 381f., 390
Reicher, M. 266
Reid, T. 280
Rhees, R. 382, 390
Rodler, H. 172f.
Rodriguez-Pereyra, G. 274
Romanyshyn, R. D. 255, 264
Römpp, G. 47
Rorty, R. 4, 17, 19, 27, 59–63, 65–70, 105, 272f., 362
Rose, N. 138, 143
Rosenthal, R. 95
Roth, G. 31, 41f.
Rovane, C. 332f.
Roy, K. 194
Ruddiman, W. F. 154, 156
Russell, B. 79, 104, 402, 404, 425–427, 429, 431

Said, E. 104
Scanlon, T. 124, 306, 371
Schaber, P. 330, 365
Schicha, C. 50
Schleiermacher, F. 108
Schmidt, S. J. 18, 49, 52, 73
Schmücker, R. 266
Scholl, A. 160
Schönbach, K. 48
Schopenhauer, A. 21
Schott, R. M. 7
Schütz, A. 74
Scott, B. 74, 85, 93
Scotus, J. 275, 357f.

Searle, J. 34, 103, 109, 111–114, 134, 195, 266
Sharrock, W. 224f.
Sider, T. 270f., 275, 285
Skagestad, P. 198
Smith, A. 295
Smith, B. D. 154
Smith, P. 9
Sohst, W. 161
Southwood, N. 371
Sprague, J. 255
Stapp, H. P. 159
Steffen, W. 153, 156
Steinert, H. 74
Stemmer, P. 365, 371–373
Stern, D. 32, 390
Strawson, P. 207, 261, 404f., 451
Sturgeon, N. L. 331f.
Swinburne, R. 280
Sycara, K. 25

Thales 356
Thompson, M. 361
Thomson, A. 429
Tomasello, M. 236
Topitsch, E. 356
Twardowski, K. 133

Umpleby, S. 75, 85, 96

van Fraassen, B. 40, 61
van Inwagen, P. 257, 262
Varela, F. 73, 85
Velleman, D. 117, 312
Vermaas, P. E. 266
Vogel, S. 255
von Foerster, H. 73f., 76–79, 83, 85, 89–92, 95, 97, 158
von Glasersfeld, E. 4, 18, 26, 33, 73–76, 78f., 83, 85, 159, 184
von Savigny, C. 261
von Wright, H. 431

Waismann, F. 383, 388f., 428
Wallace, R. J. 366
Waters, C. 154–156
Weber, S. 64, 110

Weisman, A. 157
Welsch, W. 171
Wendel, H. J. 31
Westerbarkey, J. 54
Whalen, B. J. 255, 264
Whitehead, A. N. 18, 76, 161
Wiggins, D. 225, 313–317, 319–326
Willems, H. 47–49
Williams, B. 205, 313–317, 320, 326, 330
Williams, C. 429
Williams, M. 207

Willmann, U. 141
Wong, D. 205, 328
Wray, L. 293
Wright, C. 336

Young, M. 228

Zalasiewicz, J. 153
Zangwill, N. 449, 451, 456
Zeilinger, A. 159
Zybertowicz, A. 3, 5–8

Index of subjects

absolutism   119f., 187f., 190f., 193–195, 199–201, 230, 301f., 312, 381, 392–394
action   3f., 7–14, 137, 148, 158, 162, 205, 213, 217, 229, 233, 265, 293f., 335, 387f., 392, 409, 453
"Angelina-effect"   137f., 142
anthropocene   153–159, 161f.
argument from immersion   117, 122f.

brain-fundamentalism   241

chartalism   293, 295
colour-expressions / Farbausdrücke   409, 417, 420, 422
conceptual scheme   188–190, 215, 218f., 223, 263, 269, 271–275, 280
consciousness   110, 159, 161f., 198f., 244–248, 250f., 279, 291
constructivism   73, 76, 97f., 107, 109, 160f., 167, 221, 241, 251, 255f., 263, 272f., 327, 365
– radical constructivism / radikaler Konstruktivismus   17, 20, 31, 33, 73–76, 78–80, 83–86, 89, 92, 95–98, 159f, 184, 256
– social constructivism / Sozialkonstruktivismus   37f., 74, 103f., 106–109, 111, 113f.
cultural theory   3, 9
cybernetics   73, 75–80, 85, 90, 95

determinism   137–140, 142–144
discourse analysis   103, 109
dualism   18, 23, 61, 64, 162, 279f., 291

edifying philosophy   59, 68f
endo-mode   83, 93–98
epistemology   4, 6, 8, 75, 78, 97, 128, 133, 153f., 158, 452
– epistemic constructions   255f., 263–266
exo-mode   83, 89, 95f., 98

fallacy   256, 262, 330, 353, 399, 401, 406
– mereological fallacy   397–401, 406
naturalistic fallacy   353

fallibilism / Fallibilismus   31, 33, 104
fiction   14, 255f., 261f., 265
freedom   144, 293, 296–298

hermeneutics   103, 107f., 110, 218

idealism   65, 106–108, 114, 129, 133, 215f., 219, 241f., 248f., 251, 273, 326, 388
incommensurability   196, 215–218, 224
irony   59, 66, 71, 145, 427, 429
is/ought distinction / Sein-Sollen-Dichotomie   353

justice   294, 313, 316–322, 325, 335

metallism   293, 295
metaphysics   68, 130, 241, 270, 332
– metaphysical truth   327, 331, 335
mind body problem   241
money   9, 112f., 293–298, 430

nominalism   221, 269, 273f., 277
transcendental nominalism   269, 273–275
non-dualism / Non-Dualismus   17–20, 23–28, 45, 59, 65, 70, 153, 233, 235, 237, 252
normativity   117, 301, 308, 451
norms / Normen   124, 172, 188, 211, 265, 329f., 333f., 363, 365–371, 375f., 385, 401f., 451f., 455

ontology / Ontologie   8, 13, 103, 106, 109, 111–113, 132, 136, 155, 161f., 175, 183f., 192, 241, 249, 251f., 255f., 260, 265f., 269, 272f., 275, 277, 283f., 287, 400
– social ontology / Sozialontologie   103, 111f, 255, 267

person   34–36, 39f., 50, 69, 71, 90f., 94, 119, 142f., 197, 205, 227f., 241, 245–247, 261f., 280, 284f., 287–289, 296–298, 305–307, 314, 317, 321, 331, 334,

340f., 345–348, 350, 361, 368f., 385f., 389f., 397–406, 438, 450–453
– grammar of personhood   397
– metaphysics of human persons   241
picture-theory / Bildtheorie   167f., 174, 177
private language   403, 449f., 453, 455–457
probabilism   137f., 143–145

rationality   26, 68f., 187, 196, 200, 211, 301, 311f., 323–325, 402, 451f., 454–456
realism   3, 31, 83, 89, 97, 103f., 107, 129, 133, 135, 153, 160, 162, 167, 188, 195, 197, 199–201, 221, 223, 227, 241–243, 247, 255f., 279–281, 283, 285, 287–291, 313
– epistemological realism   129, 131–135
– idealistic realism 241, 251f.
– metaphysical / ontological realism 109, 111f., 131, 193, 243, 251f., 263, 269–271, 273-275
– moral realism   302f, 307-312, 320, 335, 365f., 368, 372, 375f.
relativism   117, 119, 121, 126–128, 187–195, 199–201, 203–209, 213–216, 219, 223f., 226f., 269, 271, 301f., 304, 306–311, 326f., 330, 332, 334, 336, 381, 392–394
– absolutist relativism   301, 305f.
– moral relativism   301f., 304–307, 327–337
– thoroughgoing relativism   227, 301, 305, 307
representation   5f., 60f., 69, 71, 105, 108, 129, 131f., 134, 158, 195, 243, 251, 261, 264, 293f., 296
rhetoric   17–24, 28, 67
rule following   381, 391, 449

self-refutation argument   187
slavery   313f., 316–326
sociology of knowledge   263, 381, 393

Tractatus   167–174, 176, 178f., 182–184, 221, 382, 402, 409–411, 418, 420, 425–427, 431
trust / Vertrauen   124, 145, 206–208, 211, 289, 339–350

values / Werte   20f., 32, 35, 104, 117f., 187–189, 201, 270, 294, 305, 308, 328–330, 333–335, 339, 348, 383
instrinsic values / intrinsische Werte   344–346, 348

www.ingramcontent.com/pod-product-compliance
Lightning Source LLC
Chambersburg PA
CBHW022102290426
44112CB00008B/523